Modern China and International Economic Law

This book series offers an essential forum for Chinese economic law scholars, as well as international scholars interested in China's practice in the context of international economic law. It is thus the aim of this book series to publish essential monographs/compilations in the field of international economic law that focus on China, or on uniquely Chinese characteristics. This book series above all focuses on research that closely relates current practices with past history, and future policies with current circumstances, pursuing a philosophy of understanding legal practices by combining the past and present. Accordingly, top scholars in China and beyond its borders will be invited to contribute to this project from their respective areas of focus, which can cover broad topics related to international law in the current context of China's peaceful rise, such as China's economic policy with various countries, its participation in the WTO legal system and bilateral investment treaty practices, etc.; as well as more specific topics such as China's domestic legislation regarding foreign business, its unique "one country, two systems" policy and its implications on external economic interactions between different "systems" within China.

More information about this series at https://link.springer.com/bookseries/13773

Xiuli Han

Legal Protection and Sustainability of Chinese Investments in Africa

Under the Concept of International Investment Rule of Law

Springer

Xiuli Han
School of Law
Xiamen University
Xiamen, China

ISSN 2364-8317 ISSN 2364-8325 (electronic)
Modern China and International Economic Law
ISBN 978-981-19-1881-0 ISBN 978-981-19-1882-7 (eBook)
https://doi.org/10.1007/978-981-19-1882-7

This Springer imprint is published by the registered company Springer Nature Singapore Pte Ltd.
The registered company address is: 152 Beach Road, #21-01/04 Gateway East, Singapore 189721, Singapore

Acknowledgments

This research would not have been finished without assistance, inspiration and moral encouragement from Prof. André Thomashausen. He is especially familiar with Africa and China-Africa relations. It is commendable that he can always give convincing reasoning and analysis on African development issues. When I was a visiting scholar at University of South Africa (UNISA) from 2015 to 2016, Prof. André Thomashausen was the Chair of Department of Public, Constitutional and International law, as well as the manager of Centre for Foreign and Comparative Law at the UNISA. I am fortunate to have him acting as my supervisor and colleague. Therefore, first and foremost, I appreciate Prof. André Thomashausen for his support to my research and for his enlightenment to my wisdom. Without his repeated emphasis, I would not have realized how important China is to the sustainable development of Africa and how this research can contribute to China-Africa relations.

I especially want to thank Mrs. Sonia Thomashausen, Prof. André Thomashausen' wife, for her looking after me and giving me great help when I was in South Africa. I appreciate meeting her in my life. I would like to remember every conversation between us about China, Africa and the meaning of life.

I would like to thank the then Chair of Department of Public, Constitutional and International law at College of Law UNISA, Dr. Douglas Mailula for his assistance to me so many times in dealing with various procedural issues. I want to thank the Acting Manager of the Verloren van Themaat Centre for Public Law Studies at College of Law UNISA, Dr. Babatunde Fagbayibo, who is an expert in African Union (AU) research. As a good friend, he discussed the AU issue with me and helped me to find African scholars whose research fields are relevant to mine. I want to thank the head of Graduate Studies, Research and Innovation at College of Law UNISA, Prof. Amos Saurombe. When I was a visiting scholar at UNISA, he helped me a lot and treated me as a good friend.

I owe a profound debt to Prof. Paul Stephan at the Virginia University Law School and his wife Dr. Pamela Clark. From the autumn of 2019 to the spring of 2020, when I was a visiting scholar there, they gave me much intellectual and material assistance. I must thank Ms. Xinh Luu, who is a lecturer and librarian for international and foreign law at the University of Virginia School of Law. Her friendship and help are always with me.

I am indebted to Prof. Huaqun Zeng, who has been my mentor from the time when he supervised my Ph.D. thesis to the present. As the President of Chinese Society of International Economic Law, he has always insisted on analyzing issues in the field of international economic law through the perspective of developing countries. His methodology influences me to do research for the sustainable development of China as well as African countries.

Heartfelt thanks are due to Prof. An Chen for his recommending this book as one of Modern China and International Economic law, the Springer Series. As the former President of Chinese Society of International Economic Law, Prof. An Chen is a highly renowned international lawyer in the world and a great pioneer of Chinese international economic law. I am deeply grateful for his encouragements and teachings.

I sincerely thank the anonymous experts who reviewed my writing plan. Ms. Lei Wang, Mrs. Padmavathi Jagadeishkumar, and Mr. Saravanan Murugan, the team members from the Springer are all cordially appreciated for their time and help.

Much gratitude is extended to my students as well as friends. Alphabetically, they are Akosua Serwaah, Alekseeva Iuliia, Aye Nge Nge Soe, Hui Lin, Isaias Teklia Berhe, Jianjian Mo, Jiayin Chen, Joseph Amoah, Misha Rehman, Patricia Nattabi, Peirong Zou, Perry Ackon, Qianli Yang, Ting Rong, Weifeng Wang, Yanhua Li and Yumeng Zhai. I benefited from their help in proofreading and commenting on this research. Certainly, all opinions and errors belong to the author.

Finally, I need to thank my husband, Prof. Bo Gao for his patience, company and assistance, which are indispensable to this research. I want to thank my son Sibo Gao for giving me motivation and courage to move forward together.

This research is supported by the Fundamental Research Funds for the Central Universities (Project Number: 20720191063).

Contents

About the Author

Xiuli Han, a Professor from Xiamen University Law School and Deputy Director of the Africa Research Center (ARC) from the Belt and Road Research Institute of Xiamen University (BRRI) in Fujian Province of China, specializes in international Economic law, especially international investment law and WTO law. She is interested in African research and has done field work in South Africa, Zambia, Kenya, Mauritius, and Mozambique. She has been a visiting scholar at New York University, Max Planck Institute for Comparative Public Law and International Law, Stellenbosch University, University of South Africa, and Virginia University. She was the Winner of the Education Ministry's New Century Excellent Talents Supporting Plan in 2011. Her two Chinese representative monographs are *the Principle of Proportionality in WTO and Environmental Protection Involving Chinese Overseas Investment: From the Perspective of International Investment Law*. She has also translated several English monographs into Chinese. She has membership in the International Law Association, Council of Chinese Society of International Law, and Council of Chinese Society of International Economic Law.

Abbreviations

ADR	Alternative Dispute Resolution
AfCFTA	Agreement Establishing the African Continental Free Trade Area
AU	African Union
B&R	The Belt and Road
B-BBEE	Broad-Based Black Economic Empowerment Act
BEE	Black Economic Empowerment
BIT	Bilateral Investment Treaty
BLEU	Belgium-Luxembourg Economic Union
BRI	The Belt and Road Initiative
BRICS	Brazil, Russia, India, China, South Africa
CEMAC	Central African Economic and Monetary Community
CEN-SAD	Community of Sahel–Saharan States
CFIA	Cooperation and Facilitation Investment Agreement
CFTA	Continental Free Trade Area
COMESA	Common Market for Eastern and Southern Africa
CRCICA	Cairo Regional Centre for International Commercial Arbitration
D.R. Congo	Democratic Republic of Congo
DPRK	Democratic People's Republic of Korea
DTI	Department of Trade and Industry, Republic of South Africa
EAC	East African Community
ECCAS	Economic Community of Central African States
ECJ	European Court of Justice
ECOWAS	Economic Community of West African States
ECOWAS Supplementary Act	Economic Community of West African States Supplementary Act on Common Investment Rules for the Community

ECT	Energy Charter Treaty
EPA	Economic Partnership Agreement
EU	European Union
FDI	Foreign Direct Investment
FET	Fair and Equitable Treatment
FOCAC	Forum on China Africa Cooperation
FPS	Full Protection and Security
FTA	Free Trade Agreement
GATT	General Agreement on Tariffs and Trade
ICC	International Chamber of Commerce
ICJ	International Court of Justice
ICJ Statute	Statute of the International Court of Justice
ICSID	International Centre for Settlement of Investment Disputes
ICSID Convention	Convention on the Settlement of Investment Disputes between States and Nations of Other States
IFDI	Inbound Foreign Direct Investment
IGAD	Intergovernmental Authority on Development
IIAs	International Investment Agreements
ILC	International Law Commission
IPFSD	Investment Policy Framework for Sustainable Development
ISDS	Investor-State Dispute Settlement
MAI	Multilateral Agreement on Investment
MFN	Most Favored Nation
MIGA	Multilateral Investment Guarantee Agency
MPRDA	Mineral and Petroleum Resources Development Act
NAFTA	North American Free Trade Agreement
OAU	Organization of African Unity
OECD	Organization for Economic Co-operation and Development
OFDI	Outbound Foreign Direct Investment
OPIC	Overseas Private Investment Corporation
PAIC	Pan-African Investment Code
PCA	Permanent Court of Arbitration
PCIJ	Permanent Court of International Justice
PIDA	Program for Infrastructural Development in Africa
PRI	Political Risk Insurance
REC	Regional Economic Community
SADC	Southern African Development Community
SADC FIP	Southern African Development Community Protocol on Finance and Investment

SADC Model BIT	Southern African Development Community Model Bilateral Investment Treaty
SCC	Stockholm Chamber of Commerce
Taiwan	Taiwan Province of China[1]
TFTA	Tripartite Free Trade Area
TIFA	Trade and Investment Framework Agreement
TRIMs	Trade-Related Investment Measures Agreement
TRIPS	Agreement on Trade-Related Aspects of Intellectual Property Rights
UMA	Arab Maghreb Union
UN	United Nations
UNCITRAL	United Nations Commission on International Trade Law
UNCTAD	United Nations Conference on Trade and Development
WTO	World Trade Organization

[1] Several African countries have signed BITs with Taiwan, but it should be emphasized that Taiwan is only a province of China.

Chapter 1
Introduction

Chinese investments in Africa have been expanding, and at the same time, Chinese investors need to face the reality of coexisting challenges and responsibility during the lifetime of their investment in Africa. As far as reality is concerned, Chinese investments in Africa have been soaring both on flows and stocks in the context of pursuing China–Africa friendship and sharing sustainable development, owing to a number of factors that include the formal announcement of China's "going abroad" policy,[1] the convening of the Forum on China–Africa Cooperation in 2000,[2] the implementation of the Belt and Road Initiative (BRI) starting in 2013, and the gradual incorporation of China–Africa cooperation into the BRI.[3] However, increasing Chinese investments in Africa are facing various challenges and risks, and at the same time, some legal obligations and social responsibilities may be practically ignored by some Chinese investors and their investment enterprises or projects to different degrees. Due to the challenges faced by Chinese investments in Africa, including regulatory and other kinds of challenges, corresponding protection is called upon. The obligation, responsibility, and performance of Chinese investors and their investments in Africa need to be emphasized to maintain the healthy development of China–Africa investment cooperation. Therefore, it is necessary to carry out a comprehensive examination of the expansions, challenges, and obligations of China's investments and investors in Africa.

---

[1] "Going abroad" Strategy is put forward at the fifth Plenum of the 15th Communist Party of China (CPC) Central Committee held in October 2000 in Beijing. In the "CPC Central Committee's Proposal for Formulating the 10th Five-Year Program for China's Economic and Social Development", the Strategy was adopted at this Plenum on October 11, 2000.

[2] About FOCAC, available at <http://www.focac.org/eng/ltjj_3/ltjz/>.

[3] The process of China–Africa cooperation being incorporated into the BRI can be divided into three stages, and they are: from 2013 to 2015, China–Africa cooperation was tentatively included in the BRI; from 2015 to 2018, China–Africa cooperation was officially included in the framework of the BRI; and from 2018 to 2021, China–Africa joint construction of the BRI and connecting main development strategies between China and Africa.

X. Han, *Legal Protection and Sustainability of Chinese Investments in Africa*,
Modern China and International Economic Law,
https://doi.org/10.1007/978-981-19-1882-7_1

1.1 Research Background

1.1.1 Expansion of Chinese Investments in Africa

Chinese overall outbound investment is a big backdrop for Chinese investments in Africa. Chinese outbound investment has been growing rapidly since China implemented its "going abroad" strategy until the flow rose to third in the world for the first time in 2012, second only to the US and Japan. Until 2017 and 2018, the Chinese outbound investment flow was still the third-largest in the world and became the second-largest in 2019.[4] After 2016, Chinese OFDI dropped below the record level. On the one hand, the Chinese government took the initiative to strengthen censorship toward the authenticity and legality of OFDI, which contributed to Chinese investors' return to rationality.[5] On the other hand, because of the prevalence of investment protectionism and the increase in investment barriers in European and American countries through taking harsh and stringent national security reviews on Chinese investment, it can be found that Chinese overseas investment in Europe and the US has dropped significantly. Chinese investment in countries that commit to BRI cooperation is expanding as a result. However, the Chinese overseas investment flow overall decreased in 2019. In 2020, China's overseas investment flow was lower than that in 2019 because of COVID-19.

In this context, the rapid growth and expansion of Chinese investments in Africa are remarkable. In recent years, China's investments have become one of the main sources of investment in Africa. Chinese investment in Africa is shown in Table 1.1 and Fig. 1.1.

Looking back in history, Chinese investments in Africa started to be active toward the end of the 1990s as a result of the rapid development and marketization of the Chinese economy. From 2003 to 2014, China's outward foreign direct investment (FDI) in African countries increased steadily. It is especially worth mentioning that China's OFDI flow to Africa dramatically increased during and after the 2008 American financial crisis due to acquiring 20% shares in the Standard Bank of South Africa by the Industrial and Commercial Bank of China (ICBC). The launch of the Belt and Road Initiative (BRI) in 2013 and its follow-up promotion and implementation greatly contributed to the growth of Chinese investments in Africa.

---

[4] UNCTAD. World Investment Report 2019: Special Economic Zones (United Nations 2019); Ministry of Commerce of People's Republic of China, National Bureau of Statistics of People's Republic of China, State Administration of Foreign Exchange, 2019 Statistical Bulletin of China's Outward Foreign Direct Investment (China Commerce and Trade Press, 2020) 4.

[5] See Ministry of Commerce of People's Republic of China, National Bureau of Statistics of People's Republic of China, State Administration of Foreign Exchange, 2017 Statistical Bulletin of China's Outward Foreign Direct Investment (China Statistics Press, 2018) 3,14, 20.

Table 1.1 FDI flows and stocks from China to Africa 2003–2020 (Unit: US$100 million)

Year	2003	2004	2005	2006	2007	2008	2009	2010	2011
Flows	0.75	3.17	3.92	5.20	15.74	54.91	14.39	21.12	31.73
Stocks	4.91	9.00	15.95	25.57	44.62	78.04	93.32	130.42	162.44
Year	2012	2013	2014	2015	2016	2017	2018	2019	2020
Flows	25.17	33.71	32.02	29.78	23.99	41.05	53.89	27.04	29.60
Stocks	217.30	261.86	323.50	346.94	398.77	432.97	461.04	443.90	473.50

Data Sources: The data from 2003 to 2010 are based on the Ministry of Commerce of People's Republic of China, National Bureau of Statistics of People's Republic of China, State Administration of Foreign Exchange, 2011 Statistical Bulletin of China's Outward Foreign Direct Investment (China Statistics Press 2012) 31, 36; The data from 2011 to 2019 are based on the Ministry of Commerce of People's Republic of China, National Bureau of Statistics of People's Republic of China, State Administration of Foreign Exchange, Statistical Bulletin of China's Foreign Direct Investment 2019 (China Commerce and Trade Press 2020)50, 56; UNCTAD, World Investment Report 2021: Investing in Sustainable Recovery (United Nations 2021) 249, 253

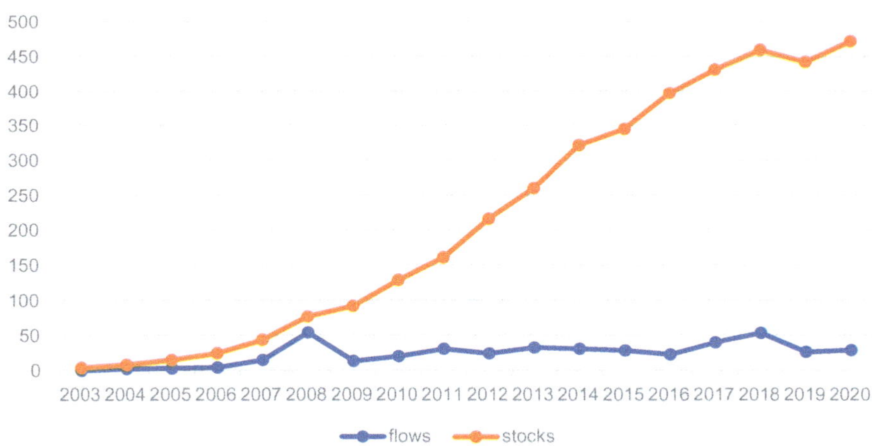

Fig. 1.1 Chinese FDI flows and stocks from China to Africa 2003–2020. (Unit: US$100 million)

China ranked third in terms of OFDI in the world in 2012, as mentioned above, and maintained this status until 2017.[6] In 2017, the Chinese OFDI flow to Africa, which was the fastest-growing target market for Chinese investors on the five continents, reached 4.1 billion US dollars, an increase of 70.8% over the same period last year. At the end of 2017, the Chinese FDI stock in Africa reached $ 43.3 billion and

[6] See UNCTAD, World Investment Report 2015: Reforming International Investment Governance, (United Nations 2015) 41; Ministry of Commerce of People's Republic of China, National Bureau of Statistics of People's Republic of China, State Administration of Foreign Exchange, 2017 Statistical Bulletin of China's Outward Foreign Direct Investment (China Statistics Press, 2018) 4.

Table 1.2 Comparison of Chinese FDI flows to Africa and total outflow 2003–2020 (Unit: US$100 million)

	2003	2004	2005	2006	2007	2008	2009	2010	2011
Africa	0.75	3.17	3.92	5.20	176.34	54.91	14.39	21.12	31.73
Total	28.55	54.98	122.61	176.34	265.06	559.07	565.29	688.11	746.54
	2012	2013	2014	2015	2016	2017	2018	2019	2020
Africa	25.17	33.71	32.02	29.78	23.99	41.05	53.89	27.04	29.60
Total	878.04	1078.44	1231.20	1456.67	1961.49	1582.88	1430.37	1369.08	1329.40

Data Sources: The data from 2003 to 2010 are based on the Ministry of Commerce of People's Republic of China, National Bureau of Statistics of People's Republic of China, State Administration of Foreign Exchange, 2011 Statistical Bulletin of China's Outward Foreign Direct Investment (China Statistics Press, 2012) 31, 36; The data from 2011 to 2019 are based on the Ministry of Commerce of People's Republic of China, National Bureau of Statistics of People's Republic of China, State Administration of Foreign Exchange, Statistical Bulletin of China's Foreign Direct Investment 2019 (Commerce and Trade Press, 2020) 50, 56; UNCTAD, World Investment Report 2021: Investing in Sustainable Recovery (United Nations 2021) 249, 253

ranked fifth among investor economies,[7] against the background of the continuous negative growth of global OFDI flows to Africa and Chinese global OFDI flows declining 19.3% on a year-on-year basis in 2017. In 2018, Chinese total OFDI flows decreased by 9.6% year-on-year, but the OFDI flows to Africa increased by 31.5% year-on-year;[8] comparatively, in 2019, Chinese investments to Africa were $2.71 billion and decreased sharply by 49.9% year-on-year.[9] In 2020, China's investment flow to Africa was against the trend of China's overseas investment and increased by US $2.96 billion, so that the investment stock in Africa reached US $47.35 billion. Overall, the scale of China's investment in Africa has been on a significant upward trend (Table 1.2; Fig. 1.2).

In addition to the attraction of other factors, such as rich natural resources, a high economic growth rate, and a huge consumer market, Chinese investment engagement also stimulates other countries, including India, Brazil, Russia, European countries, and the US, to invest or reinvest in Africa and make Africa a place of investment

[7] See UNCTAD. World Investment Report 2019: Special Economic Zones (United Nations 2019) 34; See also Ministry of Commerce of People's Republic of China, National Bureau of Statistics of People's Republic of China, State Administration of Foreign Exchange, 2017 Statistical Bulletin of China's Outward Foreign Direct Investment (China Statistics Press, 2018) 3, 4,14, 20.

[8] See Ministry of Commerce of People's Republic of China, National Bureau of Statistics, 2018 Statistical Bulletin of China's Outward Foreign Direct Investment (China Statistics Press, 2019) 7, 15.

[9] See Ministry of Commerce of People's Republic of China, National Bureau of Statistics, 2019 Statistical Bulletin of China's Outward Foreign Direct Investment (China Statistics Press, 2020) 16.

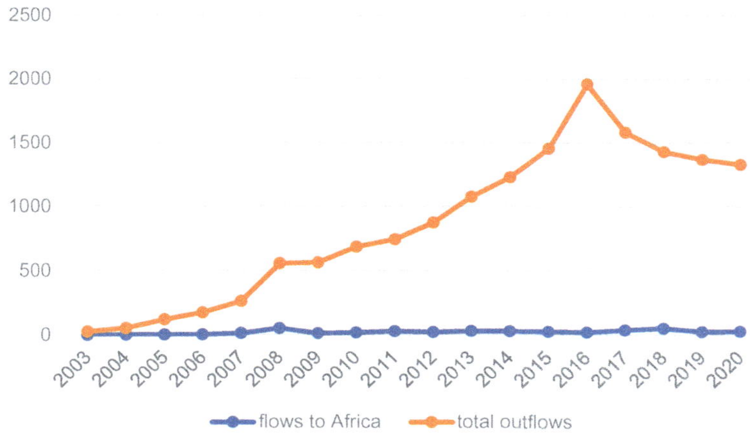

Fig. 1.2 Comparison of Chinese FDI flows to Africa and total outflows 2003–2020. (Unit: US$100 million)

competition.[10] On the whole, the IFDI into Africa increased to US$ 50.6 billion in 2018, a 22% increase over the previous year, but the IFDI into Africa decreased to US$45.5 billion in 2019, an 11% decrease over the previous year.[11]

Chinese investment mainly comes from Chinese enterprises. Chinese enterprises are expanding their footprints in Africa and now have invested in 52 countries (Swaziland and Somalia are exceptions) on the continent, although Chinese investments are mainly located in South Africa, Congo, Zambia, Nigeria, Angola, Ethiopia, Algeria, Zimbabwe, Ghana, Kenya, Tanzania, Sudan, and Mauritius.[12] In regard to the number of companies, there were over 3,800 Chinese companies in Africa as of December 2019.[13]

Although investments in mineral resources occupy a predominant proportion of China's OFDI in African countries, the industrial distribution of China's OFDI in African countries is diversifying. Chinese investments in Africa cover natural resource exploration, finance, infrastructure, electric power generation, textile and

[10] Although the Trump administration does not place much emphasis on Africa, President Joe Biden's virtual remarks on the occasion of the 34th African Union Summit expressed his hope to "rebuild partnerships around the world and re-engage with international institutions like the African Union".

[11] UNCTAD, World Investment Report 2020: International Production Beyond the Pandemic (United Nations 2020) 238.

[12] See Ministry of Commerce of People's Republic of China, National Bureau of Statistics of People's Republic of China, State Administration of Foreign Exchange, 2019 Statistical Bulletin of China's Outward Foreign Direct Investment (China Statistics Press, 2020) 22.

[13] See Ministry of Commerce of People's Republic of China, National Bureau of Statistics of People's Republic of China, State Administration of Foreign Exchange, 2019 Statistical Bulletin of China's Outward Foreign Direct Investment (China Statistics Press, 2020) 45.

Table 1.3 Comparison of Chinese FDI stock in Africa and total stock 2003–2020 (Unit: US$100 million)

	2003	2004	2005	2006	2007	2008	2009	2010	2011
Africa	4.91	9.00	15.95	25.57	44.62	78.04	93.32	130.42	162.44
Total	332.22	447.77	572.06	750.26	1179.11	1839.71	2457.55	3172.11	4247.81
	2012	2013	2014	2015	2016	2017	2018	2019	2020
Africa	217.30	261.86	323.50	346.94	398.77	432.97	461.04	443.90	473.50
Total	5319.41	6604.78	8826.42	10,978.65	13,573.90	18,090.37	19,822.66	21,988.81	23,518.00

Data Sources: The data from 2003 to 2010 are based on the Ministry of Commerce of People's Republic of China, National Bureau of Statistics of People's Republic of China, State Administration of Foreign Exchange, 2011 Statistical Bulletin of China's Outward Foreign Direct Investment (China Statistics Press 2012) 31, 36; The data from 2011 to 2019 are based on the Ministry of Commerce of People's Republic of China, National Bureau of Statistics of People's Republic of China, State Administration of Foreign Exchange, Statistical Bulletin of China's Foreign Direct Investment 2019 (Commerce and Trade Press 2020)50, 56; UNCTAD, World Investment Report 2021: Investing in Sustainable Recovery (United Nations 2021) 249, 253

household effects, and so on.[14] In addition, among various Chinese investors, the percentage of state-owned enterprises (SOEs) has been decreasing although investments of SOEs still take the dominant position, and a large number of private enterprises are investing in Africa.[15]

Despite impressive growth, the amount of Chinese investment in Africa is still small compared to its total overseas investment, accounting for only 2% (Table 1.3; Fig. 1.3).[16]

Furthermore, Chinese total investment in Africa is still behind that in the major developed countries. According to the ranking of investment stock, French investment had been ranked first in Africa until 2017, and the Netherlands remained the second-largest source of foreign investment in Africa. The investment flow from the US and UK has declined in recent years due to divestment and the repatriation of investment profits,[17] but the stock has remained third and fourth. Chinese investment stock ranked behind these countries and ranked fifth in 2017.[18] In 2018,

[14] See Ministry of Commerce of People's Republic of China, National Bureau of Statistics of People's Republic of China, State Administration of Foreign Exchange, 2019 Statistical Bulletin of China's Outward Foreign Direct Investment (China Statistics Press, 2020) 28.

[15] See Ministry of Commerce of People's Republic of China, National Bureau of Statistics of People's Republic of China, State Administration of Foreign Exchange, 2019 Statistical Bulletin of China's Outward Foreign Direct Investment (China Statistics Press, 2020) 41.

[16] Ministry of Commerce of People's Republic of China, National Bureau of Statistics of People's Republic of China, State Administration of Foreign Exchange, 2019 Statistical Bulletin of China's Outward Foreign Direct Investment (China Statistics Press, 2020) 22.

[17] A comparison between Chinese FDI and US FDI has been done by Johns Hopkins. Since at least by 2014, US FDI flow to Africa has been lower than Chinese FDI flow to Africa. See Johns Hopkins, School of Advanced International Studies, Data: Chinese Investment in Africa, available at <http://www.saisari.org/chinese-investment-in-africa>.

[18] See UNCTAD, World Investment Report 2019: Special Economic Zones, (United Nations 2019) 34, 38–39.

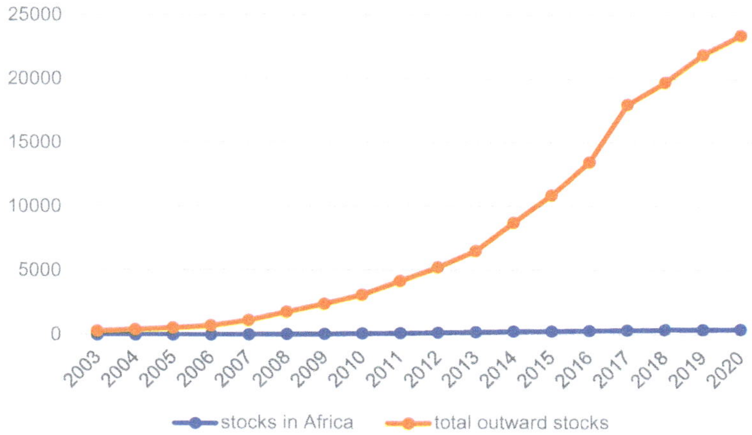

Fig. 1.3 Comparison of Chinese FDI stocks in Africa and total stocks 2003–2020. (Unit: US$100 million)

China remained the fifth-largest investor economy by FDI stocks in Africa, after the Netherlands, France, the United Kingdom, and the US.[19] On the whole, it can be said that although Chinese investment growth in Africa is rapid and as a "newcomer", great achievements have been made, developed countries still play the leading role in investment volume in Africa.

The sustainable development of Africa demands the engagement and contribution of Chinese investments. The FDI contribution index shows that foreign affiliates in developing countries have relatively high contributions to the host country's economy, especially Africa, in terms of value added, employment and wage generation, tax revenues, export generation, and capital formation.[20] In fact, China's rapid economic development has also benefited from the policy to attract foreign investment, and according to Xiaoping Deng, the "chief designer" of China's reform and opening-up policy, it is impossible for any country to develop and isolate itself from the world, and it is impossible not to strengthen international intercourse and not to introduce the advanced experience, advanced science and technology, and funds of more developed countries. President Xi Jinping, the creator of BRI and the founder of the idea of a Community of a Shared Future for Mankind, has repeatedly stressed that China's open door will not be closed but will only open up greater and China's policy of utilizing foreign capital will not change, the protection of the legitimate rights and interests of foreign-invested enterprises will not change, and the provision of better service for foreign enterprises to invest in China will not change. For a new round of economic development, China is adopting new policies to push the

[19] See UNCTAD, World Investment Report 2020: International Production Beyond the Pandemic. (United Nations 2020) 28.

[20] See UNCTAD, World Investment Report 2012: Towards a New Generation of Investment Policies (United Nations 2012) 1.

liberalization, promotion, facilitation, and protection of foreign investment, which is fully reflected in the newly adopted foreign investment law.[21]

However, the deficit of investment has always been a constraint on African development. From 2009 to 2011, Africa, the region with the highest number of LDCs continued to experience a decline in FDI.[22] Although the FDI inflow into Africa increased by 14.6% in 2012, there was only a 4% increase in 2013 and an even 0.1% decrease in 2014.[23] From 2015 to 2017, the FDI inflows to Africa declined from $57 billion to 53 billion and then $42 billion.[24] Compared with 2018, "the slump in FDI flows to Africa in 2019, by 10% to $45 billion", and FDI inflows to the region in 2020 are expected to fall sharply by 25 to 40% as a result of the COVID-19 pandemic.[25]

Therefore, the increase in Chinese FDI in Africa is critical to Africa's economic and social development, especially when some other Western countries' enterprises continued to reduce investments in Africa due to external factors such as financial crises, regional conflicts, falling commodity prices, and negative political will. The BRI was put forward by China in 2013, and one of its objectives was to promote the common sustainable development of China and other countries involved in the BRI through investment cooperation. The BRI initially covered only part of one African country, Egypt along the Belt and Road (B&R),[26] and then embraced some countries in North Africa and East Africa. During the 2018 FOCAC, China signed

---

[21] Foreign Investment Law of the People's Republic of China, Order No. 26 of the President of the People's Republic of China, issued on March 15, 2019, and came into force on January 1, 2020. This law is the first foreign investment law in China, and in the past, China only has foreign-funded enterprise laws. The policy orientation of this new law is to increase facilitation, promotion, protection, and liberalization of foreign investment. China also introduced detailed implementing regulation for this law; see Regulation for Implementing the Foreign Investment Law of the People's Republic of China, Order No. 723 of the State Council of the People's Republic of China, issued on December 26, 2019, and came into force on January 1, 2020.

[22] UNCTAD, World Investment Report 2012: Towards a New Generation of Investment Policies (United Nations 2012) 3–4.

[23] See UNCTAD, World Investment Report 2014: Investing in the SDCs: An Action Plan (United Nations 2014) xiv; See UNCTAD, World Investment Report 2015: Reforming International Investment Governance (United Nations 2015) 32.

[24] See UNCTAD, World Investment Report 2018: investment and new industrial policies (United Nations 2018) 184.

[25] See UNCTAD. World Investment Report 2020: International Production Beyond the Pandemic (United Nations 2020) x, 11.

[26] The original 65 countries along the "Belt and Road" that are covered by "Belt and Road" initiative include the following: One country in East Asia (Mongolia); 10 ASEAN countries (Singapore, Malaysia, Indonesia, Myanmar, Thailand, Laos, Cambodia, Vietnam, Brunei, and the Philippines); 18 countries in West Asia (Iran, Iraq, Turkey, Syria, Jordan, Lebanon, Israel, Palestine, Saudi Arabia, Yemen, Oman, UAE, Qatar, Kuwait, Bahrain, Greece, Cyprus, and Egypt's Sinai Peninsula); 8 countries in South Asia (India, Pakistan, Bangladesh, Afghanistan, Sri Lanka, Maldives, Nepal, and Bhutan); 5 countries in Central Asia (Kazakhstan, Uzbekistan, Turkmenistan, Tajikistan, and Kyrgyzstan); 7 countries of Commonwealth of Independent States (Russia, Ukraine, Belarus, Georgia, Azerbaijan, Armenia, and Moldova); 16 countries in Central and Eastern Europe (Poland, Lithuania, Estonia, Latvia, Czech Republic, Slovakia, Hungary, Slovenia, Croatia, Bosnia and Herzegovina, Montenegro, Serbia, Albania, Romania, Bulgaria, and Macedonia); See Xinhua Silk Road, available at <https://www.imsilkroad.com/news/p/76186.html>.

the Memorandum of Understanding with 28 African countries together to build the BRI jointly, and up to April 18, 2019, China had signed cooperation instruments with 38 African countries, and by the end of January 2021, China had signed BRI cooperation instruments with 46 African countries altogether.[27]

At the current stage, China and African countries have been working together to effectively link the BRI with the African Union's "2063 Agenda", the United Nations' "Transforming our World: The 2030 Agenda for Sustainable Development", and other development strategies of African countries. It can be expected that China–Africa cooperation and Chinese investments in Africa can be promoted further. On the whole, Chinese investment engagement is positively correlated with Africa's economic and social development although, with a critical attitude, the positive aspects of Chinese investment in Africa have always been ignored. Following the growth of foreign investment in the 1970s, the decline of the 1980s and 1990s, and the recovery in the late 1990s in Africa, Africa's rapid economic and social development in the twenty-first century is positively correlated with the rapid growth of Chinese investment in Africa after China launched FOCAC in 2000.[28]

1.1.2 Challenges Faced by Chinese Investments in Africa

There are 55 countries in Africa,[29] each with its own uniqueness. Especially between black African countries located in sub-Saharan Africa and Arabian African countries located in North Africa, there are very different political, economic, and cultural patterns. That is why the World Bank's approach on regional classification treats sub-Saharan Africa as one region, North Africa and the Middle East together as another region,[30] and the International Centre for Settlement of Investment Disputes (ICSID) also separates sub-Saharan Africa from North Africa when it does case statistics.[31] Some Chinese always treat Africa as a whole; however, Africa is not a country but a continent. Africa is a collection of 55 countries with completely different histories, languages, and religions, and its people are as divergent as those in North America and in Southeast Asia.[32]

---

[27] As of February 17, 2021, Belt and Road Portal Yidaiyilu. A list of countries that have signed the cooperation with China, available at <https://www.yidaiyilu.gov.cn/xwzx/roll/77298.htm>.

[28] André Thomashausen, China in Africa. available at <https://unisouthafr.academia.edu/AndreThomashausen>.

[29] According to the official website of AU, the AU has 55 Member States, "The AU is make up of 55 Member States which represent all the countries on the African continent"; see Member States, AU, available at <https://au.int/en/member_states/countryprofiles2>.

[30] Browse Our Locations, September 17, 2019, available at <https://www.worldbank.org/en/where-we--work>.

[31] The ICSID Caseload–Statistics, September 17, 2019, available at <https://icsid.worldbank.org/en/Pages/resources/ICSID-Caseload-Statistics.aspx>.

[32] See Dambisa Moyo, Dead Aid: Why Aid Is Not Working and How There Is a Better Way for Africa (Farrar, Straus and Giroux, 2009).

China and Africa have kept friendly political relations since the last century due to their similar colonial history and shared developing country identity, which provides a favorable climate for Chinese investments in Africa. However, this does not mean that there are no difficulties and obstacles in China–Africa investment cooperation and that there are no risks in Chinese investment. The challenges come from heated competition among investors from different countries, the weak and improper implementation of law or instability of law in some host African states, and the drawbacks of some Chinese investors themselves. Challenges and risks that Chinese investments have to face are emerging, even more than that with investments from other countries. In fact, Chinese investors have held the perception that Africa is a high-risk place.

The risks are different from the known or established obstacles or barriers to investment, which have already existed, such as underdeveloped markets, shortages of skilled workers, poorly developed infrastructure, and low efficiency of host state governance.[33] Risks may refer to expropriation, breach of contract, social violence, unrest and even civil wars, commercial risks, or market risk, for example, the fluctuation and uncertainties of commodity market and price.

However, in this research, the commercial risks that investors may avoid through their own due diligence are not included. Commercial risks need commercial judgment, and investors must undertake this kind of risk. The risks in this research are similar to what has been discussed by guarantee agencies such as Multilateral Investment Guarantee Agency (MIGA), although the risks will be dealt with in different ways in addition to insurance. As mentioned above, these risks may cover expropriation, currency inconvertibility and transfer restriction, war, terrorism and civil disturbance, breach of contract and non-honoring of financial obligations, and so on.[34]

Here are just three typical aspects of showcasing resistance and risk encountered by Chinese investments in Africa.

1.1.2.1 Neo-Colonialism Propaganda

In international law, propaganda means "[the] systematic dissemination of doctrine, rumor, or selected information to promote or injure a particular doctrine, view, or cause" and "[t]he ideas or information so disseminated".[35]

---

[33] Some performance requirements, that is, "measures that relate to entry and establishment, like bans on foreign investment in certain sectors, screening, and approval requirements; measures that deal with ownership and control, like compulsory joint ventures, transfer of technology, or managerial know-how; and finally, operational measures, like performance requirements, operational permits or licenses, or local content restrictions can become impediments to international investments". See Michael V. Gestrin, A Stocktaking of Investment-Related Barriers in Africa 3 (OECD-Africa Round-table), available at <http://www.oecd.org/daf/inv/investmentfordevelopment/21040978.pdf>.

[34] Get coverage, Applying for MIGA's Investment Guarantees, available at <https://www.miga.org/a-pply>.

[35] See Bryan A. Garner, Black's Law Dictionary (7th edition, Thomson Reuters, 1999) 1232.

With the convening of the Forum on China–Africa Cooperation in 2000 and deepening economic and trade relations between China and Africa, Chinese economic engagement in Africa has attracted greater attention, Africa has become another "battlefield" for the US to suppress China, and China has been "branded" or "characterized" with "neo-colonialism" from time to time. It is unforgettable that the former US secretary of state, Hillary Clinton, provoked discord in 2011 to warn Africans of Chinese " neo-colonialism".[36]

With the introduction and in-depth implementation of the BRI, some Western media and politicians have become more worried about China, as is manifested in trying to vilify and distort the BRI, propagating the presumption of the so-called "China's Marshall Plan" and "Chinese neo-colonialism", and describing China–Africa economic cooperation as "neo-colonialism". For example, on December 30, 2014, CNBC criticized Chinese investment in Africa for creating the colonialism problem.[37] The English version of the New York Times put forward a similar question on May 1, 2017, when reporting Chinese investment in Africa, that is, "is China the world's new colonial power?" and "is China presenting a new model of development to the world, or is the BRI itself a new type of colonialism?"[38] Even more alarming is "China in Africa: neo-colonialism?" was the subject of a hearing before a subcommittee of the US Senate in 2018.[39] Furthermore, the New African Strategy of the US Trump Administration used the phrase "predatory" practice when blaming China,[40] but in essence, it is only another expression of "neo-colonialism". It can be seen that criticism from some Western countries on Chinese "neo-colonialism" has become heated since the BRI was proposed in 2013.

Under the propaganda of Chinese "neo-colonialism", even exceptional officials from African countries echo this argument,[41] and the writings of some scholars

---

36 See Clinton Warns Africa Against "China's Neocolonialism", China Times, June 11, 2011.

37 See Mark Esposito, Terence Tse and Merit Al-Sayed, Recolonizing Africa: A modern Chinese story? CNBC, December 30, 2014, available at <https://www.cnbc.com/2014/12/30/recolonizing-africa-a-modern-chinese-story.html> .

38 See James A. Millward, Is China a Colonial Power? The New York Times, available at <https://www.msn.com/en-ph/news/opinion/is-china-a-colonial-power/ar-AAwLkFz>.

39 See China in Africa: The New Colonialism? Hearing before the Subcommittee on Africa, Global Health, Global Human Rights and International Organizations of the Committee on Foreign Affairs, House of Representatives, One Hundred Fifteenth Congress, Second Session, Washington: U.S. Go-vt. Print. Off., March 7, 2018. available at <https://www.govinfo.gov/content/pkg/CHRG-115 hhrg2-8876/pdf/CHRG-115hhrg28876.pdf>.

40 See Remarks by National Security Advisor Ambassador John R. Bolton on the Trump Administration's New Africa Strategy, delivered on December 13, 2018, Heritage Foundation, Washington, D.C. available at <https://www.whitehouse.gov/briefings-statements/remarks-national-sec urity-advisor-ambassador-john-r-bolton-trump-administrations-new-africa-strategy/>.

41 For example, on March 14, 2013, Hua Chunying, a spokesman of Foreign Ministry of China, presided over a regular press conference, she said, "We have taken note of the remarks made by the President of the Nigerian Central Bank. These remarks do not accord with the facts, and China expresses its concern and dissatisfaction with this". available at <http://www.china-un.org/chn/fyrth/t102132-4.htm>.

portray China as a greedy resource grabber who came to Africa without bringing economic growth opportunities to Africa.[42]

The fallacy that China's economic engagement in Africa is " neo-colonialism" will not only affect the reputation of China but also cast a shadow over China–Africa political relations; it will also bring obstacles to trade and investment relations between China and Africa and thus ultimately affect the development of Africa and China. At present, "Chinese investments in Africa are becoming the target of hostile propaganda and are suffering attacks"[43]; therefore, it is of theoretical and practical significance to examine the nature of Chinese economic engagement, which includes investment in Africa, and it is also a topic that cannot be circumvented when studying the economic cooperation between China and Africa, which covers the topic "legal protection and sustainability of Chinese investments in Africa". However, there are a few academic studies on this theoretical issue from the perspective of international law.[44]

The term "neo-colonialism" is used primarily to describe situations in which the former colonies are politically independent but their economies are still under the control and exploitation of the former suzerains. China became a semi-feudal and semi-colonial country and suffered from aggression, oppression, and exploitation by imperialist powers after the Opium War in 1840. The People's Republic of China founded in 1949 has united with a vast number of developing countries, especially African countries, to resist colonialism in all forms resolutely since the founding of the People's Republic of China. Obviously, the accusation of "neo-colonialism" against Chinese economic engagement in Africa has no historical and realistic basis.

---

42 See for example, Elizabeth Manero, China's Investment in Africa: The New Colonialism? (2017) Harvard Political Review, February 3, 2017; Markus Weimer and Alex Vines, 'China's Angolan Oil Deals 2003–11', in Marcus Power and Ana Cristina Alves eds, China & Angola, A Marriage of Convenience? Pambazuka Press, 2012, 85–102; A. J. Bergesen, The New Surgical Colonialism: China, Africa and Oil. Paper presented at the annual meeting of the American Sociological Association, Boston, July 31, 2008, available at <http://citation.allacademic.com/meta/p237190_index.html>; H. Jauch, Chinese Investments in Africa: Twenty-First Century Colonialism? (2011) 20(2) New Labor Forum, 48–55; K. Sharife, China's New Colonialism, in Foreign Policy, 2009, available at <http://www.foreignpolicy.com/articles/2009/09/25/chinas_new_colonialism>; Patrick Loch OtienoH. Jauch, Chinese Investments Lumumba, Africa in the age of China influence and global geo dynamics, <https://lasentinel.net/tag/africa-in-the-age-of-chinas-global-influence-and-global-geodynamics>.

43 Excerpt from a letter sent by André Thomashausen, the University of South Africa on September 28, 2018.

44 Existing domestic research in China mainly focuses on political or economic perspective, for example, Liu Ailan, Wang Zhixuan & Huang Meibo, Neocolonialism in China's Aid to Africa? Empirical Evidence from Trade Effects of China and EU Aid to Africa, Journal of International Trade, No. 3, 2018; Hanzhi Ma & Enfu Cheng, China–Africa Economic and Trade Relation is Not "Neocolonialism", in Contemporary World; Wen Zhou & Fang Zhao, Is China-Africa cooperation under China's "Belt and Road" initiative "neocolonialism"? (2017) 1 Studies on Marxism. Another study from the legal perspective focuses on trade and investment areas between China and Africa and demonstrates that China–Africa economic relation is based on mutual benefit, and both sides have benefited from this relationship, so that the nature of Chinese investment and trade in Africa is not neo-colonialism. See Ying Chen, China's Investment and Trade in Africa: Neo-Colonialism or Mutual Benefit (2016)24 Cardozo International & Comparative Law Review 511–529.

Nevertheless, this will bring systemic risks to Chinese investment in Africa because the anti-neo-colonialism sentiment of the African host state and the African people is also an important part of the local investment climate.

So-called "neo-colonialism" propaganda will irritate African sentiment that was hurt in the past in view that anti-colonialism is still a popular slogan and voice in Africa.[45] This propaganda and these exaggerated criticisms as backdrops must have negative effects on China's FDI in Africa because they might incite flames of discontent from local Africans and even some investment disputes under the circumstances that some interest frictions and conflicts between Chinese investors and African host states have already unavoidably existed. Just since concern and sensitivity to Chinese investment and facts will eventually prevail over fiction, how Chinese investors perform responsibly will affect the protection and sustainability of Chinese investments.[46]

Chinese OFDI into Africa has inevitably touched some countries' acquired (existing) interests and is naturally suffering from hostility to some degree. In other words, the Chinese gradually increasing engagement in Africa arouses concern and anxiety from some Western countries, and this anxiety could also be transmitted to some African countries from time to time. Moreover, the features of Chinese investments make "China in Africa" an easy target and arouse more concern. These salient features include the following:

First, it seems that Chinese investments are much more governmental policy oriented or pushed more than investments from other capitalist countries, and the amount of Chinese investments is regarded as "aggressive". For example, FDI stock was committed from US$32.4 billion in 2014 to US$100 billion by 2020 under the *Johannesburg Plan of Action* of the 2015 Summit. China's aid to Africa, as may promote Chinese investments incidentally, has also led to concerns about the debt overburden of Africa, which is even distorted as creating a debt trap for Africa to achieve the objective of neo-colonialism.

State-owned enterprises (SOEs) are the main investors in Chinese overseas investment, and the orientation of national policy has attracted special attention. It is submitted that "much of the FDI is generated through alternative ways of financing as well as by the state-owned enterprises",[47] and the Export–Import Bank (EXIM

[45] The author of this research is very impressed that the first academic conference held by UNISA is 3rd Annual Spring Law Conference: Decolonising the Mind, Knowledge and System in Africa: South Africa Coming of Age, from September 29 to October 2, 2015. The author's presentation for this conference is "China's Footprint of Colonization and Decolonization: From Dismantling Unequal Treaties to Exploring New International Economic Order from the perspective of international economic law".

[46] In most cases, the sustainability only refers to the sustainability of the host state in international investment law, See, e.g., De Mestral, Armand LC. Improving international investment agreements. Routledge, 2013, part IV. But in the present research, the word "sustainability" also refers to the sustainability of investment.

[47] Sanne Van Der Lugt et al., Assessing China's Role in Foreign Direct Investment in Southern Africa, 2011, 18, available at <http://www.ccs.org.za/wpcontent/uploads/2011/03/Final-report-CCS-Mar-ch-2011-CCS.pdf>.

Bank) has played an important role in implementing the national policy of "going abroad", "China–Africa Cooperation", and BRI.

The main part of Chinese investments in Africa is still operated by SOEs, which can easily lead to a false connection with some Western countries' practice of establishing or utilizing colonial companies in the colonies to achieve their colonialist expansion and domination.[48] However, it should be noted that Chinese SOEs have already existed since the founding of the PRC, and they are the characteristics of the Chinese socialist market economy but are not specifically set up for overseas trade or investment like the situation mentioned above. In addition, they operate as independent legal persons and do not perform government functions; therefore, China has no longer insisted that Chinese SOEs must enjoy judicial immunity in a foreign court. In fact, private enterprises in some countries are also supported by their governments, which has been the case in the past and is still the case. Therefore, whether the investor is a SOE or a private enterprise cannot determine whether it is a government tool or whether it will cause unfair competition. Nevertheless, under some Western discourses, China's state-owned enterprises and even the economic system are always subject to unreasonable criticism.

Second, China's foreign aid and investment projects in Africa are very prominent and sometimes sensitive. "Large Chinese infrastructure projects like the building of dams, hospitals, government offices, stadiums, and streets throughout Africa are at the forefront of public attention".[49] These projects are beneficial for Africans, but the purpose of building them is often deliberately misinterpreted.

Third, there are incidental problems with inexperienced Chinese investments in Africa. Some Chinese investments inevitably have a negative impact on the natural environment, such as hydropower dams and large-scale mining. Industry investments satisfying African countries' needs may also bring industrial pollution to some degree. Environment and human rights related to Chinese investments in African host states are of particular concern.[50]

---

[48] Doreen Lustig, Veiled Power: International Law and the Private Corporation (Oxford University Press, 2020)19, 22. According to the study of this book, historically, there is inextricably linked relations between large private companies in Africa and their home countries, the western colonists, relying on the support of their home countries. Therefore, we can conclude that there is a close relationship between the companies and their home countries. The relationship does not depend on whether it is private or state-owned.

[49] Ian Taylor, The International Relation of Sub-Saharan Africa (Continuum, 2010) 71. For example, Most African knows Kenya's Thika Superhighway and African Union's headquarters building in Addis Ababa, Ethiopia, are aided by China.

[50] Catherine Elkemann & Oliver C. Ruppel, Chinese Foreign Direct Investment into Africa in the Context of BRICS and Sino-African Bilateral Investment Treaties (2015)13(4) Richmond Journal of Global Law & Business 593–621.

1.1.2.2 Regulatory Measure

Overall, an legal framework, including national law and international law, may bring regulatory risks to investors. The most fundamental investment law, that is, the Constitution, can even be arbitrarily enacted or amended by the head of the State in rare circumstances. This will bring systematic risks to Chinese investments. Taking Zimbabwean land measures as an example, the international community widely recognizes that expropriation as an exceptional measure is only permissible subject to requirements including compensation; however, the Zimbabwe Constitutional Amendment Act of 2005 permits its government to confiscate or expropriate private farms without any compensation and forbids its courts to give awards to any such foreign investor's claim.[51] Thus, "no compensation would be payable for the land itself, and no court could review the acquisition".[52]

Another example is that the South African government may deprive the property of South Africans and foreign investors by "custodianship" for the "disadvantaged" according to the decision of the South African Constitutional Court, and compensation will not be available under this circumstance. In the case of Agri South Africa (Agri SA) v. Minister for Minerals and Energy, Judge Mogoeng found that Sebenza, which used to own the coal-mining right in issue, had suffered a "compulsory deprivation" of its right under the Mineral and Petroleum Resources Development Act, and "the custodianship" of this resource was now "vested in the state on behalf of the people of SA"; however, the state had not acquired ownership of the mining right and just wanted to make "broader and equitable access to mineral resources could be realized". Therefore, no expropriation had occurred, and correspondingly, no compensation was payable.[53] It seems reasonable that foreign investors, due to the market cycle, may keep the mineral unexploited during the depression of the market. But the situation is that if the mineral is regarded as unused (and unconverted), the mining right "ceased to exist" under the Mineral and Petroleum Resources Development Act.

The 2013 Promotion and Protection of Investment Bill further stipulates that the following act does not amount to act of expropriation: any measure which results in the deprivation of property but where the State does not acquire ownership of such property provided that there is no permanent destruction of the economic value of the investment; or the investor's ability to manage, use, or control his or her investment in a meaningful way is not unduly impeded.[54] Although this stipulation was deleted

---

[51] Zimbabwe Constitutional Amendment Act (No 17), 2005, Sect. 2.2.

[52] Krista Nadakavukaren Schefer, International Investment law: Text, Cases and Materials (2nd edition, Edwar Elgar Pub, 2013) 181.

[53] See Agri South Africa v. Minister for Minerals and Energy, Constitutional Court of South Africa, Case No. CCT 51/12, Date of Judgment, April 18, 2013.

[54] See article 8.2.d, The Promotion and Protection of Investment Bill, 2013 (2013)581(1) the Government Gazette 14No 36995, November 1, 2013.

from the 2015 Protection of Investment Act,[55] it is possible to be incorporated into the proposed Expropriation Act.[56]

Resistance to the international investment agreement and the award can also lead to looming risks to FDI.

For the purpose of implementing domestic policy and avoiding the constraint of international investment law, at the international or regional level, South Africa, Botswana, Namibia, and Zimbabwe are trying to stay away from the international investment rule of law, including terminating BITs and denying the decision of SADC Tribunal. Botswana and Namibia reconsidered their approaches to BITs in 2013 and 2014 by halting future BIT negotiations.[57] The concrete content of their measures will be introduced in Chapter 4. Coincidentally, Namibia, which previously had actively negotiated BITs, selects a negative attitude toward BITs and believes that "there is no correlation between investment flows and the prevalence of BITs" and "is currently reviewing its investment act". In fact, Namibia plans to rely on the investment act instead of BIT in the future.[58]

Although the legal and regulatory framework is uncertain and unfriendly to FDI in exceptional African countries, most African countries have a complete legal system. However, the loose enforcement of the law will expose foreign investment to real risks. The law on paper alone may not be the best predictor of stability and predictability; therefore, improving the implementation of laws is as important as making laws. It is generally accepted that some African countries have built an impressive arsenal of laws as colonies out of Western countries, and the legal system is one of the most important legacies inherited by them, but the implementation lags behind substantially. A common discrepancy exists between the activism of legislation and the neglect of corresponding implementation and enforcement.

In practice, Chinese investments have met all kinds of risks or uncertainties during their operation in Africa. Some cases can exemplify possible expropriations or nationalizations that have happened to Chinese investors. After the mining right to the "Obangue" oil field of Addax Petroleum, a subsidiary of Sinopec was revoked by the Gabonese government as a measure by the Gabonese government to implement the nationalization of the oil industry, and the dispute was filed with the International

[55] See Protection of Investment Act, 2015, Act No. 22 of 2015, Government Gazette, Republic of South Africa, Vol. 606 Cape Town, December 15, 2015, available at <https://www.gov.za/sites/defa-ult/files/gcis_document/201512/39514act22of2015protectionofinvestmentact.pdf>. This Act came into operation on June 13, 2018, available at <https://www.gov.za/sites/default/files/gcis_document/-201807/41766gen395.pdf>.

[56] Expropriation Bill B 23–2020, October 15, 2020, available at <https://www.gov.za/sites/default/fi-les/gcis_document/202010/expropriation-bill-b23-2020.pdf>; Expropriation Bill: Explanatory summary, October 9, 2020, available at <https://www.gov.za/sites/default/files/gcis_document/202010/43-798gon1082.pdf>.

[57] See UNCTAD, World Investment Report 2015: Reforming International Investment Governance (United Nations 2015) 108, 110; See also UNCTAD, World Investment Report 2018 (United Nations 2018) 119.

[58] See Malan Lindeque, The Statement of Namibia, World Investment Forum 2014: Investing in Sustainable Development, IIA Conference, October 16, 2014.

Court of Arbitration of International Chamber of Commerce.[59] Addax blamed Gabon for not renewing its license[60]; however, the government asserted that Addax failed to pay custom duties and respect other laws.[61] The claim of Addax was denied by the tribunal.[62] Although Addax signed a new agreement with the Gabonese government to drill for oil in the onshore Tsiengui, Obangue, and Autour fields to end a long-running disagreement with Gabon,[63] it proves that expropriation or nationalization risks do exist to Chinese investors. In addition, the Gabonese government canceled the China Machinery Engineering Corporation's right to the "Bélinga" iron ore mine in 2012.[64] In 2014, the exploration license CNPC (China National Petroleum Corporation) was revoked by the Chadic government due to an environmental accident, and CNPC was claimed to pay US$ 1.2 billion. Finally, CNPC and Chad reached a settlement agreement through which CNPC was free of claims filed with the international arbitral tribunal and national court by Chad, and in turn, Chad gained a share of CNPC.[65] It seems that nationalization or expropriation occasionally happens in sectors of natural resources in Africa, and unfortunately, Chinese investments concentrate in the mining sector and construction sector.[66] Expropriation is one of the most salient issues in light of nationalization, and various land reform initiatives are taking place in some African countries.

It was also reported that Zhongfu International Investments' project of over US$ 60 million in the free trade zone in Nigeria has been terminated unlawfully by the Ogun State government.[67]

---

[59] See, e.g., Alyx Barker, Gabon Faces ICC Claim from Chinese Oil Producer, Global Arbitration Review, March 19, 2013, available at <https://www.globalarbitrationreview.com/news/article/31421/>.

[60] Emma Farge, China's Addax Locks in $ 1 Billion Dispute with Gabon-Sources, available at <http://www.reuters.com/article/2013/06/05/gabon-china-idUSL5N0E93DB201306>.

[61] Daniel Flynn, Africa Investment, China Brings Goods and Roads, Now Africa Wants Jobs, REUTERS (July 21, 2013) available at <http://www.reuters.com/article/2013/07/21/africa-china-idUSL6N-0FI3TE20130721>.

[62] See the Economic and Commercial Counselor's Office of the Embassy of the People's Republic of China in the Republic of Cameroon, Recollecting Gross Economic Events in Africa, January 20, 2014, available at <http://cm.mofcom.gov.cn/article/ztdy/201401/20140100466867.shtml>.

[63] See Energy Asia, CHINA: Sinopec's Addax Petroleum signs new oil drilling agreement to end long-running dispute with Gabon, January 22, 2014, available at <http://energyasia.com/blog/china--sinopecs-addax-petroleum-signs-new-oil-drilling-agreement-end-long-running-dispute-gabon/>.

[64] The Africa Report, Asian companies naive to African challenges, February 7, 2013, available at <www.theafricareport.com/News-Analysis/asian-companies-naive-to-african-challenges.html>.

[65] Economic and Commercial Counselor's Office of the Embassy of the People's Republic of China in the Republic of Chad, Chad and CNPC Signed Settlement Agreement, November 3, 2014, available at <http://tchad.mofcom.gov.cn/article/ybxx/201411/20141100782963.shtml>.

[66] See Ministry of Commerce of People's Republic of China, National Bureau of Statistics of People's Republic of China, State Administration of Foreign Exchange, 2013 Statistical Bulletin of China's Outward Foreign Direct Investment (China Statistics Press, 2014)14.

[67] See Centre for Chinese Studies, Stellenbosch, South Africa, Chinese company petitions to take Nigeria's Ogun State Government to Court, The Weekly China Briefing, September 9, 2016.

In another example, a Chinese mining company has invested US$10 million in Cameroon. The investor received mining licenses by performing legal procedures and paying extra costs demanded. However, a conflicting property right appeared in the same mining area. Finally, the Chinese investor lost its investments and had to leave Cameroon regretfully.[68]

In yet another example, Tanzania imposed new conditions on the Bagamoyo port development project, and it can only be continued if Chinese investors agree to these new conditions; otherwise, they have to retreat from the project. In fact, after the transition of the administration, the new Tanzanian government terminated the project once.[69] Therefore, the transition of the Tanzanian government and the demanding change of the existing contract undoubtedly increased the investment costs and risks of Chinese investors.

Finally, the most recent case is that the Kenyan government canceled the coal-fired power project invested by Chinese investors because of the resistance of local communities and environmental activists.[70]

1.1.2.3 Social Unrest

In addition, the political and social situations are not stable in some African countries, with serious ethnic conflicts, occasional wars, and frequent civil disturbances. Over the last 40 years, nearly 20 African countries (or approximately 40% of Sub-Saharan Africa) have experienced at least one period of civil war.[71] During the "revolution" of the Arab spring between 2010 and 2011, the African countries in Arab North Africa were highly unstable and strife-torn.[72] In 2019, the peace index of the Democratic Republic of the Congo, Libya, Central Africa, Somalia, and South Sudan ranked as the worst; the peaceful environment in Burkina Faso, Zimbabwe, Togo, Sierra Leone, and Namibia worsened; and overall, public security in some African countries was poor.[73] Chinese investments in these countries had been inevitably affected owing to war or similar events. In Libya's uprising in 2011, more than 50 Chinese investment

---

[68] Ma Qianru's field interview in Cameron, March 31, 2017. Ma Qianru works as a Legal Affairs Coordinator at Global Environment Institute (GEI) in Beijing.

[69] Tanzania gives Chinese firm conditions for Bagamoyo port, October 21, 2019, available at <https://www.theeastafrican.co.ke/business/Tanzania-gives-chinese-firm-conditions-for-agamoyo-port-/2560-5318790-10s5do7/index.html>.

[70] Shi Yi, Kenyan Coal Project Shows Why Chinese Investors Need To Take Environmental Risks Seriously, March 9, 2021, available at <https://chinadialogue.net/en/energy/lamu-kenyan-coal-project-chinese-investors-take-environmental-risks-seriously/>.

[71] See Ibrahim Elbadawi & Nicholas Sambanis, Why Are There So Many Civil Wars in Africa? (2000)9(3) Journal of African Economies 244.

[72] All 54 African countries can be divided into two parts: countries of Sub-Saharan Africa, generally encompassing countries lying south of the Sahara Desert, and countries of Arab North Africa.

[73] Institute for Economics & Peace. Global Peace Index 2019: Measuring Peace in a Complex World, Sydney, June 2019, available at <http://visionofhumanity.org/reports>.

projects were damaged.[74] Under these circumstances, it is pressing to protect Chinese investments in these areas.

Social insecurity and tensions are prevalent in some African countries, and consequently, the personal safety of Chinese investors and staff in Africa is often threatened. For instance, petroleum exploration staff of the China National Offshore Oil Corporation (CNOOC) in Sudan were kidnapped by the local tribe as an anti-government armed force.[75] Furthermore, the risks faced by Chinese investments still include emerging terrorism, strike led under the union, systemic corruption,[76] issuance of work permits, remittance of profits, sovereign bankruptcy,[77] and so on.

1.1.3 Responsibility Extended to Chinese Investors

Corporate social responsibility, in addition to legal responsibility, has been increasingly emphasized by the international community and especially the host state. Some African countries have upgraded corporate social responsibility as mandatory performance requirement. Although Chinese investments are conducive to promoting the economic, trade, and employment growth of Africa, corporate social responsibility seems to be increasingly prominent and even attracts more attention.[78] Although most Chinese enterprises in Africa have actively fulfilled their social responsibilities and have gained appreciation from African governments and the local people, some Chinese investments indeed have some irregular conduct for subjective and objective reasons according to public media reports. Here are some cases.

Corruption reports concerning Chinese investors sometimes appear in the media. The Shulin Su case shows corrupt behavior by Chinese investors in exceptional circumstances. It was reported that former Sinopec leader Shulin Su, with the help of middleman Xu Jinghua, was involved in a number of corrupt practices in the

---

[74] Guochao Qi, The Impact of Libyan War to Chinese Investment, December 1, 2011, available at <http://www.bjqx.org.cn/qxweb/n45602c776.aspx>.

[75] Qing Wang, Sudan Tragedy Shocked the World; Who killed Chinese Oil Workers? November 2, 2008, available at <http:/news.enorth.com.cn/system/2008/11/02/003753127.shtml>.

[76] Although corruption exists in both developed countries and developing countries, and it is difficult to eradicate in any society, the situation in Africa is more serious. Corruption is prevalent in most African countries. Transparency International, a non-governmental organization (NGO) that has spearheaded the fight against corruption, together with Social Accountability International, has statistics of corruption in African countries. For details, see Transparency International, Business Principles for Countering Bribery, available at <http://www.transparency.org/globalpriorities/private-sector/business-principles>.

[77] For example, in 2016, Mozambique was declared in "default" by the IMF and basically nobody could get payments as they had no foreign currency. See Dalia Saris, Mozambique on course for default, Global Risk Insights, June 8, 2016, available at <http://globalriskinsights.com/2016/06/mozambique-course-default/>.

[78] See Hongmin Zhang, ed., Annual Report on Development in Africa, No.16 (2013–2014), New Trend of the Great Power's Africa Policy and the International Environment for Developing China-Africa Relations (Social Sciences Academic Press, China, 2014) 66.

process of obtaining an Angolan oil block.[79] Although they were punished by Chinese criminal law, their misconduct had a bad effect on Chinese investors' reputations. Another example is that in 2019, Chi Ping Patrick Ho, a Hong Kong Chinese, was sentenced to 3 years in prison by the New York District South Court for bribing African government officials on behalf of a Chinese energy corporation.[80]

In the claim of labor abuse, it has been said that certain Chinese-funded enterprises have poor treatment of workers, for instance, in terms of using forced labor or providing poor working conditions. It was reported that in Zambia's Ke Blue Mining Co., Ltd. (Collum Coal Mining Industries Ltd), labor disputes have been in existence since the initiation of the company, and the operating license has been revoked for labor abuse.[81] On September 6, 2018, a Chinese citizen was deported from Kenya for labor abuse.[82] Such behaviors will affect the overall image of Chinese investors and investments. Currently, every country has strict labor laws; in case of violations of the relevant laws and even touching the bottom line of racial discrimination, the delinquent will be subject to corresponding sanctions.

Environmental pollution and environmental damage caused by the production and exploitation of Chinese enterprises in Africa are labeled "environmental neo-colonialism". Although environmental pollution and destruction during economic activities have nothing to do with neo-colonialism, the unavoidable environmental problems accompanying Chinese investments in Africa have been attracting concern.

Worst of all, it may bring a bad reputation to Chinese investments and provoke sentiments of Chinese investment. These investments will encounter obstacles sooner or later if Chinese investors do not take the social responsibility problems seriously. Therefore, not only how to promote and protect China's overseas investment but also how to regulate China's overseas investment must be studied.

In short, Chinese investors should abide by the laws, regulations, administrative guidelines, and policies of the African host state and should undertake social responsibility seriously. For the continued success of the economic expansion of China in Africa, it will be very necessary for the Chinese government to help control and reduce

---

[79] See Markus Weimer and Alex Vines, 'China's Angolan Oil Deals 2003–11', in Marcus Power & Ana Cristina Alves(eds), China and Angola: A Marriage of Convenience? (Pambazuka Press, 2012) 85–104; Dana Sanchez, China-Angola Middleman Arrested on Corruption Charges, October 16, 2015, available at <http://afkinsider.com/104982/china-angola-middleman-arrested-on-corruption-charges/>.

[80] See Department of Justice, US Attorney's Office, Southern District New York, Patrick Ho, Former Head of Organization Backed by Chinese Energy Conglomerate, Sentenced to 3 Years in Prison for International Bribery and Money Laundering Offenses, available at <https://www.justice.gov/usao-sdny/pr/patrick-ho-former-head-organization-backed-chinese-energy-conglomerate-sentenced-3>.

[81] The License of Collum Coal Mining Company of Chinese Invested in Zambia was revoked to calm down the sentiments of anti-China, February 22, 2013, available at <http://finance.sina.com.cn/world/qtdq/20130222/113614617915.shtml>.

[82] See Kwadwo Baffoe Donkor, Chinese manager stabs Ghanaian worker for idling, General News, September 7, 2018, available at <https://www.google.com/amp/s/www.graphic.com.gh/news/general-news/chinese-manager-stabs-ghanaian-worker-for-idling.amp.html>.

the irregular activities of exceptional Chinese individuals and private companies in Africa. The Chinese government is expected to do more than some other Western governments because of the exceptional national condition and social system.

It is clear from the foregoing that if Chinese investors plan to have long-term sustainable development in Africa, they must know how to deal with the risks and challenges and how to advance the reputation of Chinese investors and investments to make themselves sustainable. Thus, the protection and sustainability of Chinese investments in Africa under the concept of international investment rule of law are a meaningful and challenging research topic.

It is necessary to introduce the research background of this research to reflect the practical significance of this research.

In summary, the general research background is that with the implementation of a "going abroad" strategy focusing on investing abroad in 2000, the convening of the Forum on China–Africa Cooperation in 2000, the introduction of the "Belt and Road" initiative in 2013, and the corresponding deepening of economic relations between China and Africa, Chinese economic engagement focusing on investment in Africa has attracted greater concern from politicians, media, and scholars.

The benefit that Chinese investment has brought to Africa's development is realistic and has been praised and welcomed by African countries. Obviously, Chinese investment in Africa has also changed the situation that some developed countries ignored investing in Africa and has led investors from these countries to compete to invest in Africa, which is good for African development if African countries can make good use of them.

However, there are some misunderstandings and derogatory remarks about Chinese investment, and a few isolated cases of violating the law or neglecting social responsibility by Chinese investors have been extremely magnified, and sometimes even made a baseless statement or a groundless accusation. Chinese investment is described as ambitious, aggressive, destroying resources and the environment, plundering land, minerals, and building military bases in Africa. However, the contribution of Chinese investment to Africa and the good performance of Chinese investors in fulfilling social responsibility are rarely reported, and various risks and protection issues faced by Chinese investment in Africa are often ignored.

Thus, in the context of the various risks, including the risks of neo-colonialism public opinion, it is necessary to consider how to protect Chinese investment and how to regulate and sanction Chinese investors and their investments in the event of deliberate or negligent violations of the domestic laws of the host state, Chinese domestic law, or international law so that Chinese investment itself can achieve sustainable development in Africa and thereby promote sustainable development of Africa.

1.2 Literature Review

The start of this research presents a review of the scholarship published on international rule of law. Only through canvassing the existing scholarship, can the value orientation of this work be understood. This research in focus will discuss the following literature related to the topic to find the significance of this writing.

1.2.1 Literature Review on International Rule of Law

As far as the history and the concept of rule of law and other academic research on rule of law are concerned, there is an immense literature because the rule of law is an enduring and a long-standing topic in the history of human civilization[83] Comparatively, scholars have produced relatively few studies on the international rule of law. Nevertheless, the literature on international rule of law is becoming overwhelmingly rich. The scholarship on international rule of law will be summarized in the following aspects.

1.2.1.1 Introduction of the Concept of International Rule of Law

With the establishment of international institutions after World War II, the concept of the international rule of law was proposed. Although American scholars clearly put forward the concept of international rule of law in the 1960s, Chinese scholars did not carry out extensive research on the international rule of law until the beginning of the twenty-first century, and this kind of research is still in the ascendant.

Even though the international social order was restructured by devising a series of international legal systems after World War II, the corresponding concept of international rule of law did not appear at the same time. Rhyne (1959) put forward the "rule

---

[83] See, e.g., Stephen Everson, Aristotle: The Politics (Cambridge University Press, 1988), Chapters 10,11,15 and 16; A.V. Dicey, Introduction to the Study of the Law of the Constitution (Liberty Fund, 1885), Chap. 4; Ronald Dworkin, 'Political Judges and the Rule of Law', in Ronald Dworkin (ed.), A Matter of Principle (Harvard University Press, 1985), Chap. 1; Fallon, 'The Rule of Law as a Concept in Constitutional Discourse' (Jan. 1997) 97(1) Columbia Law Review 1; J. Finnis, 'Natural Law and Natural Rights' (Autumn 1980) The University of Toronto Law Journal 441–447; Lon L. Fuller, The Morality of Law (Yale University Press, 1964), Chapter 2; Friedrich A. Hayek, The Road to Serfdom (University of Chicago Press, 1944) 72; Friedrich A. Hayek, The Constitution of Liberty (University of Chicago Press, 1960); Joseph Raz, 'The Rule of Law and its Virtue', in Joseph Raz (ed.), The Authority of Law: Essays on Law and Morality (Oxford University Press, 1979)210; J. Rawls, A Theory of Justice (Belknap Press of Harvard University Press, 1971)55–60, 235–241; and B. Tamanaha, On the Rule of Law: History, Politics, Theory (Cambridge University Press, 2004); Tom Bingham, The Rule of Law (Penguin Press, 2010).

of law among nations" by defining it as the regulation of interstate interaction, international contracts, and personal relations through legal concepts, standards, systems, and procedures.[84]

The phrase "international rule of law" was utilized for the first time by Arthur Larson. Larson (1961) outlined all kinds of research projects to explore and develop the research on international rule of law, and Earl D. Osborn, the then President of the Institute for International Order, then also pointed out that the international rule of law "refers to a world in which resort to law in the settlement of disputes and the conduct of international affairs is as habitual as it is on the domestic scene" in the preface.[85] Bishop (1961) also used the concept of "international rule of law" and refuted the viewpoint of other scholars that there was no international rule of law at all by stressing that the issue was nothing more than how to make the international rule of law more effective. In general, he believed that the concept of international rule of law means the reliance on law rather than arbitrary powers in international relations, the legal settlement of disputes, instead of force, and that the law could and should serve as a tool for the promotion of social purposes such as the preservation of human freedom and dignity.[86] Bishop's understanding of the rule of law at the international level laid the foundation for subsequent academic research. Incidentally, Bodenheimer (1962) mentioned the "World Rule of Law Centre", which used the concept of the "world rule of law" to describe the rule of law in international affairs.[87] The director of the Centre was precisely Professor Arthur Larson.

The international rule of law that was envisaged by Charles Rhyne, Arthur Larson, and the subsequent American scholars was nothing more than the rule of law led by the US, which attempted to assimilate the communist states' position to that of the rest of the world. The introduction of the ideal of the rule of law and their emphasis on international law are historically progressive beyond the doubt and in line with the needs of the US to maintain the postwar world order and the needs of the world's realities at that time.

However, after 1961, the concept of international rule of law had only been referred to once in a while and the foreign scholars roughly started from the 1990s because the United Nations General Assembly began to include the rule of law on its agenda in 1992 and Chinese scholars since 2000s have gained keen interest on the research bearing on international rule of law, similar to the foreign scholars engaged in international rule of law research.

Because Chinese scholars are interested in this topic, the background is the work pursued by the UN on international rule of law. From the beginning of the 2000s, the UN General Assembly began to emphasize the issue of international rule of law. The UN General Assembly resolutions regarded the rule of law as a value and

---

[84] Charles Rhyne, Opening Statement before Boston Conference on World Peace through Law, March 27, 1959, A.B.A. Special Committee on World Peace through Law, The Rule of Law among Nations: Digest of Proceedings of Regional Conferences of Lawyers 47 (1959).

[85] Arthur Larson, The International Rule of Law (The Institute for International Order, 1961) 3.

[86] William W. Bishop, 'The International Rule of Law' (1960–1961) 59 Mich. L. Rev. 553–574.

[87] Bodenheimer, Edgar, 'Reflections on the Rule of Law' (1962) 8(1) Utah L. Rev.

fundamental principle and called upon states to implement rule of law in general at the national level and the international level.[88] The UN General Assembly listed the "rule of law at the national and international levels" on the subject under discussion of the Sixth Committee in 2006.[89] Henceforth, the UN General Assembly has consistently discussed the issue of international rule of law year after year.[90] Under this circumstance, the international rule of law has become an important academic issue attracting scholars to carry out research both at home and abroad.

1.2.1.2 Existence and Implication of the International Rule of Law

Regarding the existence of international rule of law, there is a disagreement among the existing literature. Scholars who affirm the international rule of law have elaborated their views from the perspectives of morality, instrumentality, and analogy. These scholars especially define the international rule of law from a functional perspective. The meaning of international rule of law is that the dynamics of international relations should be governed by international law rather than dictated by arbitrary power. The law instead of power should be obeyed in international relations. Restricted power here refers to not only the power of the state but also the power of international organizations including international judicial institutions that can guarantee the constraint on power to a certain extent. Some scholars have further clarified that the purpose of restricting power is to protect the rights of the private.

In contrast, some international law scholars who think the international rule of law is just a slogan or propaganda doubt the existence of international rule of law, not to mention scholars in other fields. For example, Anderson (2016) considers that international law has always been a tool of hegemony and self-interest, not truly international, nor real law.[91] However, in addition to the aforementioned, Bishop (1961) affirmed the existence of the international rule of law. Nardin (2004) further criticized realists who opposed international law because they did not understand the place of international law in the global order and the inherent morality of the idea of international rule of law, which differentiates law as a constraint on power from the law as an instrument of power, and confirmed that the Kantian theory of international law can help to recover that moral element.[92]

On the existence and realization of the international rule of law, Brownlie (1998) believed that international law played an important role and was effective only if

---

88 The United Nations, Resolution adopted by the General Assembly on September 16, 2005, A/RES/60/1 2005, para. 134.

89 The United Nations, Resolution adopted by the General Assembly on December 4, 2006, UN Doc. A/RES/61/392006.

90 United Nations and the Rule of Law, 'Key Documents', https://www.un.org/ruleoflaw/key-documents/.

91 Perry Anderson, International Law: Is it International? Is it Law? October 25, 2016, Lecture at Beijing University Law School. 2016.

92 Terry Nardin, 'Theorising the International Rule of Law' (Jul. 2008) 34(3) Review of International Studies 385–401.

a state's government officials took international law into account in their decision-making.[93] Pizhao (2009) advocated that the international rule of law is "the governance of international law", and the construction of the international rule of law will be a gradual process to build a more orderly, more efficient, and fairer international society.[94] After examining the compliance dimension and analogy between the rule of law at the national and international levels, Hurd (2016), from the perspective of the instrument, emphasized that the international rule of law is the political resource of a country and the instrument that can make its foreign policy legitimate.[95]

Beaulac (2007)[96]and Beaulac (2009)[97]canvass the international legal system and finally confirm the existence of international rule of law although the international rule of law was flawed, by strictly following three essential elements of rule of law identified by A. V. Dicey, that is, to be ruled by law, to be equal before the law, and to be submitted to the jurisdiction of ordinary courts.

Chesterman (2008) emphasized that the rule of law at the international level should be understood as applying the rules and principles of law in international relations rather than using arbitrary powers or adopting similar approaches. In other words, the governing approach of international relations should be the rule of law, and power should be bound by the law.[98] Examining the international rule of law from a functional point of view, Lautenbach (2013) considered, in general, that both the national rule of law and the international rule of law requested the power of the government to be restricted by law to ensure that they were not abused.[99]

Regarding the role played by independent judicial institutions in the international rule of law, Higgins (2007) emphasized the role of the International Court of Justice (ICJ) in promoting and protecting international rule of law through meticulously applying international law in an impartial manner to disputes before it.[100] Sampford (2016) emphasized that no state can surmount and override (international) law and that all states should recognize and comply with international law, including decisions

---

93 Ian Brownlie, The Rule of Law in International Affairs: International Law at the Fiftieth Anniversary of the United Nations (The Hague: Martinus Nijhoff Publishers, 1998) 17.

94 Pizhao Che, 'What Kind of International Rule of Law We Can Expect' (2009) 49(4) Jilin University Journal Social Science Edition 5–13.

95 Ian Hurd, 'What is the International Rule of Law?' in Javier Solana & Angel Saz-Carranza (eds.), The Global Context: How Politics, Investment and Institutions Impact European Businesses (ESADE, 2015) 148–157.

96 Stéphane Beaulac, An inquiry into the international rule of law. EUI Max Weber Programme Series Working Paper, 2007, 2007/14.

97 Stephane Beaulac, 'The Rule of Law in International Law Today' in Gianluigi Palombella & Neil Walker (eds.), Relocating the Rule of Law (Oxford: Hart Publishing, 2009) 197–223.

98 Simon Chesterman, 'An International Rule of Law?' (2008) 56(2) The American Journal of Comparative Law 331–362.

99 Geranne Lautenbach, The Concept of the Rule of Law and the European Court of Human Rights (Oxford University Press, 2013).

100 Rosalyn Higgins, The ICJ and the Rule of Law, speech held at the United Nations University, April 11, 2007.

from independent judicial bodies.[101] Furthermore, De Baere et al. (2016) argued that despite the important role played by international courts and tribunals in the implementation of the international rule of law, they are certainly not a panacea for addressing the challenges facing the international community.[102] Nollkaemper (2011) argued that domestic courts can also become a key component of the protection of the international rule of law after expounding his understanding of the "four elements" of international rule of law.[103] In contrast, Kumm (2003) held reservations to the role of the national court to promote international rule of law.[104]

On the requirement for international organizations including judicial institutions to abide by the rule of law, in view of the many wrongful acts committed by international organizations, including the United Nations, and the failure to hold international organizations accountable, Alvarez (2016) recommended that international organizations should also respect the rule of law at the international level and stressed it is important for international organizations to be subject to the binding international rule of law in order to realize the essence of the international rule of law.[105] In fact, the European Court of Justice (ECJ)'s challenge to the United Nations Security Council's arbitrary intervention in human rights was also mentioned in the discussions on the international rule of law in De Sena and Vitucci (2009).[106] Chesterman (2009) briefly addressed the content of the rule of law at the international level and then discussed the challenge to this idea posed by the United Nations Security Council, thus expressing the ideal that international organizations have to act within the powers conferred by law.[107]

It needs to be emphasized that Sandholtz (2019) pointed out that modern rule of law and postwar constitutionalism are both anchored in "rights-based limitations on state authority", and "rule-of-law norms and principles, at both domestic and international levels, are designed to protect the freedom and dignity of the person", thus criticizing resurgent authoritarian practices diminishing international rule of

[101] Charles Sampford, '"Thin Theories" of the Domestic and International Rule of Law' in Vesselin Popovski(ed.), International Rule of Law and Professional Ethics (Routledge, 2016) 57–83.

[102] De Baere, Geert, et al., 'International Courts as Keepers of the Rule of Law: Achievements, Challenges and Opportunities' (2016) 48(3) New York University Journal of International Law and Politics 715.

[103] André Nollkaemper, National Courts and the International Rule of Law (Oxford University Press, 2011) 3–5, 6, 10.

[104] Mattias Kumm, 'International Law in National Courts: The International Rule of Law and the Limits of the Internationalist Model' (2003) 44 Va. J. Int'l L.19.

[105] Jose E. Alvarez, International Organisations and the Rule of Law, IILJ Working Paper 2016/4.

[106] Pasquale De Sena & Maria Chiara Vitucci, 'The European Courts and the Security Council: Between Dédoublement Fonctionnel and Balancing of Values' (2009) 20(1) European Journal of International Law 193–228.

[107] Chesterman, Simon, 'I'll Take Manhattan': The International Rule of Law and the United Nations Security Council (2009) 1 Hague Journal on the Rule of Law 67–73.

law.[108] De Baere (2016) also emphasized that the real purpose of international rule of law is to protect the well-being of human individuals, instead of sovereign states.[109]

1.2.1.3 Classification of International Rule of Law

The existing literature divides the international rule of law into formal international rule of law (thin rule of law) and substantive international rule of law (thick rule of law). For the former, scholars have convergent views, but there are differences in the ideals and values pursued within substantive international rule of law.

The traditional theory of the (national) rule of law divides the rule of law into formal rule of law and the substantive rule of law, also known as the "thin" formal rule of law and the "thick" substantive rule of law.[110] The dichotomy of formal rule of law and substantive rule of law is also conducive to the understanding of international rule of law and has been transplanted into the theory of international rule of law by scholars.

Bishop (1961) proposed that the international rule of law combined the formal rule of law with the substantive rule of law and thought the former is a tool for the realization of the latter.[111] Sampford (2016) recommended that elements such as the clarity, consistency, predictability, effectiveness, and stability of the law be adopted in the international rule of law.[112] On the substantive rule of law, Chesterman (2008) argues that the substantive international rule of law can be understood as containing a series of ideas, such as the protection of human rights, specific forms of an orderly government, or specific economic arrangements for free-market capitalism.[113] He (2010) proposed improving the international rule of law from two aspects: the formal rule of law and the substantive rule of law.[114] He (2014) further emphasized the function of "Sound Law and Good Governance" of the international rule of law.[115] Jovanović (2015) attempted to incorporate "responsibility to protect doctrine" into

---

108 Wayne Sandholtz, 'Resurgent Authoritarianism and the International Rule of Law, KFG Working Paper Series, No. 38', September 2019, available at <https://core.ac.uk/download/pdf/232003878.pdf>.

109 De Baere, Geert, et al., 'International Courts as Keepers of the Rule of Law: Achievements, Challenges and Opportunities' (2016) 48(3) New York University Journal of International Law and Politics 715–794, 793.

110 Brian Z. Tamanaha, On the Rule of Law: History, Politics, Theory (Cambridge University Press, 2004) 91.

111 William W. Bishop, 'The International Rule of Law' (1961) 59 (4) Mich. L. Rev. 553–574.

112 Charles Sampford, "'Thin Theories' of the Domestic and International Rule of Law", in Vesselin Popovski ed., International Rule of Law and Professional Ethics (Routledge, 2016) 57–83.

113 Simon Chesterman, 'An International Rule of Law?' (2008) 56(2) The American Journal of Comparative Law 342–343.

114 Zhipeng He, 'The Perfection of Global Institutions and International Rule of Law' (2010) 50(5) Jilin University Journal Social Science Edition 132–160.

115 Zhipeng He, 'Why Sound Law and Good Governance Are Equally Important: The Criteria of International Rule of Law Revisited' (2014) 44(3) Journal of Zhejiang University (Humanities and Social Sciences) 131–149.

the value system pursued by the international rule of law to ultimately protect the human rights of individuals.[116]

Some Chinese scholars have also attempted to introduce ideas to reshape the theory of international rule of law. According to Xie (2018), Zhang (2018), Luo (2018), Ma (2020), and Li (2020), the international rule of law is the path to realize "a Community with a Shared Future for Mankind";[117] in turn, the idea of "a Community with a Shared Future for Mankind" can innovate the values of international rule of law. Some studies have been devoted to China's thoughts on the international rule of law. For example, Huang (2017) illustrated Xi Jinping's thoughts on the international rule of law,[118] and He (2018) discussed the history and reality of Chinese international rule of law thought in the new era.[119]

1.2.1.4 Relationship Between the Rule of Law at the International Level and the National Level

Regarding the difference and connection between the international rule of law and the national rule of law, although scholars have slightly different views, most of them recognize that an analogy can be made between them to a certain degree,[120] and the difference, mutual influence, or interaction between them are also well recognized.

Higgins (2007) noticed the difficulties in rigidly transposing the national rule of law model to the international context in view that the international rule of law is

---

[116] Miodrag A. Jovanović, 'Responsibility to Protect and the International Rule of Law' (Dec. 2015) 14(4) Chinese Journal of International Law 757–776.

[117] Haixia Xie, 'The Establishment of a Community of Shared Future for Mankind and the Developments of International Law' (2018) 33(01) Legal Forum 23–33; Hui Zhang, 'Building a Community with a Shared Future for Mankind: China's View of International System in the New Era' (2018) 2(01) International Law Review of Wuhan University 20–34; Huanxin Luo, 'Innovation of Common Community of Human Destiny in International Law: A Comparative Analysis of "Obligations Erga Omnes" (2018) 2 Chinese Review of International Law 3–20; Zhongfa Ma, 'On the Innovation of the International Rule of Law in Constructing a Community of Shared Future for Mankind' (2019) 6 Journal of Xiamen University (Arts& Social Sciences) 21–31; Shouping Li, 'The Idea of a Community with a Shared Future for Mankind Leads the Reform of the International Rule of Law: Logical Justification and Realistic Path' (2020) 37(1) Studies in Law and Business, 44–56.

[118] Jin Huang, Xi Jinping's Global Governance and International Rule of Law, 2017 (5) China Legal Science 5–22.

[119] Zhipeng He, 'Chinese Thought on International Rule of Law in the New Era' (2018) 39(2) The Journal of International Studies 38–54.

[120] As the exception, some scholars believe that the two cannot be compared, for example, Ian Hurd argued that the international rule of law cannot be derived from the domestic rule of law. The functions of the two are not the same. The domestic rule of law plays a governance role, while the existence of the international rule of law only aims to justify the actions of the state. See Ian Hurd, 'The International Rule of Law and the Domestic Analogy' (Nov. 2015) 4(3) Global Constitutionalism 365, 395.

still in progress.[121] Watts (1993) distinguished international rule of law from municipal rule of law, emphasized the international relevance of the rule of law, identified specific requirements for the international rule of law, and expressed an anticipation to the international rule of law in the future international community.[122] Although the structure of international society is different from that of domestic society, which limits the complete analogy between the international rule of law and the national rule of law, Brownlie (1998) argued that the standards in domestic law, as paradigms or ideas, have penetrated to a large extent into the field of international law.[123] Nollkaemper (2009) emphasized in detail the insufficiency of the bifurcation of rule of law, pointing out the interaction and interface between the international rule of law and the domestic rule of law, and put forward the concept of "internationalized rule of law", which means "the rule of law as it applies to the overlapping sphere of domestic and international law".[124] Zhao (2014) explored international and domestic rule of law from the perspective of global governance and emphasized the interaction between the national rule of law and the international rule of law.[125]

Opinions on the Current Situation and Future of the International Rule of Law

In recent years, international rule of law has become a much hotter topic than before, and different international law issues have been inserted and addressed under the topic of international rule law. Krieger et al. (2019), in effect, attempts to answer the question of the "rise or decline" of the international rule of law not only in history but also in times of anti-globalism and populism, and the rise or decline of international rule of law as examined by scholars in various fields,[126] in fact, shows concern about the international rule of law and insistence on it.

Some scholars have noticed the erosion faced by international rule of law. Sandholtz (2019) pointed out that authoritarian practices damage the international rule of law.[127] Hughes (2017) stressed the significance of insisting on the Charming Besty doctrine for the US so as not to sacrifice its national interest in the long run by

[121] Rosalyn Higgins, The ICJ and the Rule of Law, speech held at the United Nations University, April 11, 2007.

[122] Arthur Watts, 'The International Rule of Law' (1993) 36 German Yearbook of International Law 15.

[123] Ian Brownlie, The Rule of Law in International Affairs: International Law at the Fiftieth Anniversary of the United Nations (The Hague: Martinus Nijhoff Publishers, 1998) 213.

[124] André Nollkaemper, 'The Internationalized Rule of Law' (2009) 1(1) Hague Journal on the Rule of Law 74–78.

[125] Jun Zhao, 'International and Domestic Rule of Law from the Perspective of Global Governance' (2014) 10 Social Sciences in China 79–99.

[126] Heike Krieger, Georg Nolte & Andreas Zimmermann, The International Rule of Law: Rise or Decline? (Oxford University Press 2019).

[127] Wayne Sandholtz, 'Resurgent Authoritarianism and the International Rule of Law, KFG Working Paper Series, No. 38', September 2019, available at <https://core.ac.uk/download/pdf/232003878.pdf>.

violating international law for short-term policy goals.[128] Galea (2016) and Moran (2017) noticed US President Donald Trump's derogating international rule of law and argued that the realization of the international rule of law requires a country to maximize its international rule of law obligations at home.[129] In response to some retrogressions in the international rule of law, Crawford (2018) expressed his distress but also his faith in the international rule of law, arguing that the behaviors of some countries with the nature of nativism and unilateralism would not prevent progress in the international rule of law and stressing the need to take action to defend the communitarian values of international law.[130] In fact, Crawford (2003) put forward four basic values of the international rule of law and called upon international lawyers to make efforts to realize the international rule of law as their fundamental goal.[131] Isanga (2020) argues "it is in the national interest of the United States to adopt a radically different approach: stay engaged and try to improve International Law from within".[132] Zhao (2020), who was an ex-WTO Appellate Body Member, expressed her disappointment at the setback of WTO rule of law, concerns about challenges to the international rule of law, and expectations for upholding the international rule of law in international relations.[133]

In summary, around the 1960s and since the twenty-first century, whether booming or in crisis, international rule of law has become a hot topic in the academic circle of international law. Many famous lawyers in the international law field have expounded on this issue, and rich scholarship will certainly promote the development of international rule of law both in theory and in practice. However, almost all literature ignores the issue of safeguarding sovereign power and imposing private person obligations, which make the international rule of law confine itself to the constraints of power too much.

In contrast, in addition to this flaw, much of the Chinese domestic literature does not define the international rule of law in a specific and explicit way but directly uses it as a vague, abstract, and known concept that is absolutely good to be utilized for

---

[128] Justin Hughes, An "America First" Presidency, International Rule of Law and the Charming Betsy Doctrine, Loyola Law School, Los Angeles Legal Studies Research Paper, 2017.2017–16. According to Charming Besty doctrine, national statutes should be interpreted in such a way that the interpretation does not conflict with international laws. So Justin Hughes' intention is to suggest that American domestic law should conform to international law and practice international rule of law.

[129] Ion Galea, A New Perspective on the Relation between International Law and Domestic Law Based on the Rule of Law. (2016) Analele Universitatii Din Bucuresti: Seria Drept 72; Moran, Clare Frances, 'Crystallising the International Rule of Law: Trump's Accidental Contribution to International Law' (Nov. 2017) 56(3) Washburn Law Journal 491.

[130] James Crawford, 'The Current Political Discourse Concerning International Law' (Jan. 2018) 81(1) The Modern Law Review 1–22.

[131] James Crawford, 'International Law and the Rule of Law' (2003) 24(1) Adelaide Law Review 3–12.

[132] Joseph M. Isanga, 'The U.S. Withdraws: Impact on the U.S. and International Rule of Law' (Winter 2020) 32(2) Florida Journal of International Law 215–270.

[133] Hong Zhao, 'International Law at a Crossroad—The International Rule of Law: An Ideal and the Reality' (2020) 10(1) Journal of WTO and China 3–10.

global governance. Many scholars even use the phrase "international rule of law" with the same meaning as "international law" instead of the original meaning of "international rule of law". Moreover, without digging deep into the essence of the international rule of law, some Chinese scholars prefer to carry out a particularly grand discourse, which led to the writer expounding with certainty, but the reader is not very much clear about what the writer said. At the same time, the existing research in China also lacks a complete survey of the deep history of the international rule of law.

As an idea of public international law, the international rule of law reflects the ideal and expectation of international law scholars for the future of international society. These research achievements focus on understanding international rule of law from different perspectives and provide a theoretical basis for this research, but the rich scholarship also reflects the shortcomings of the understanding of international rule of law. On the one hand, they emphasize one-sidedly the constraint on the exercise of public power without mentioning the need to preserve the public power of the state as an embodiment of sovereignty. On the other hand, they unilaterally focus on the human rights of the private person without emphasizing their obligations. In other words, in the current literature on the international rule of law, two major aspects of the structure of international rule of law are missing.

1.2.2 Literature Review on International Investment Rule of Law

The development of international rule of law research has naturally covered or extended to the field of international investment law. In effect, as early as the 1960s, Larson (1961) listed "international investment" as one of the projects on the international rule of law, and the idea of making an investment code was put forward. Regarding the content of the code, the guiding ideology is as follows: Only a code on international investment that can balance the interests and rights between investors and the host states, respect the sovereignty of the host state, and consider the interests in the social and economic and human needs of the people of the host state can be accepted by both sides, even though in theory or in practice, the host states may protect themselves through their national law and regulations.[134] Nevertheless, on the whole, in the past days before the twenty-first century, the legal protection of private international investment is a key topic both in practice and in theory; therefore, this ideal conception of the rule of law for international investment is far from being realized. After the protection of investors goes to the extreme, balancing rights and interests and reforming international investment arbitration have become comparatively new topics that have attracted the attention of many scholars. Schill (2011) performed a detailed literature review on international investment law from 2004

[134] Arthur Larson, Design for Research on International Rule of Law (World Rule of Law Center, Duke University School of Law, 1961) 93–94.

to 2011 and appraised that "[f]ew international legal fields have seen an increase in literature over the past decade as steep as international investment law".[135]

1.2.2.1 Divergent Opinions on International Investment Law as a Public Law

Among all kinds of scholarship on international investment law, if they are understood from the perspective of international rule of law, in the final analysis, the main exploration is to find the boundary to control the power of the host state, and thus, the strive to settle the legitimacy crisis of international investment rule of law truly stands out.

As representative works advocating international investment law as public law, Schill (2010a, b; 2012a, b) stressed that rule of law is a concept of public law, and its objective is to subject public power to legal control, primarily formal rule of law; the public law nature of international investment law is similar to domestic administrative and constitutional law and argues to conceptualize and understand international investment law by taking a comparative public law approach that has already accepted in more mature systems of law and dispute resolution.[136] This public law approach also complements that mature legal regimes "have developed not only in limiting the exercise of state powers but also in empowering the state by illustrating its regulatory space".[137] The early work of Schill (2006) pointed out that the FET was an embodiment of rule of law, [138] and Schill (2015) further considered that both substantive standards and arbitration under investment treaties could play a role in rule of law and emphasized that the rule of law should be the benchmark of international investment law.[139]

---

[135] Stephan W. Schill, 'W (h) ither Fragmentation? On the Literature and Sociology of International Investment Law' (2011) 22(3) European Journal of International Law 875–908.

[136] See Stephan W. Schill, 'The Public Law Challenge: Killing or Rethinking International Investment Law?' No. 58 Columbia FDI Perspectives (Jan. 2012) in Columbia FDI Perspectives (Vale Columbia Centre on Substainable International Investment, Columbia University, 2012); Stephan W. Schill, 'General Principles of law and International Investment Law' in International Investment Law (Brill Nijhoff, 2012) 163–164; Stephan W. Schill, 'International Investment Law and Comparative Public Law–An Introduction' in S. W. Schill (ed.), International Investment Law and Comparative Public Law (Oxford University Press, 2010) 3–37.

[137] Stephan W. Schill, 'Fair and Equitable Treatment, the Rule of Law, and Comparative Public Law', in Stephan W. Schill (ed.), International Investment Law and Comparative Public Law (Oxford University Press, 2010) 151.

[138] Stephan W. Schill, Fair and Equitable Treatment Under Investment Treaties as an Embodiment of the Rule of Law (2006) 5 Transnational Dispute Management (TDM) 35.

[139] Stephan W. Schill, 'International Investment Law and the Rule of Law', in Jeffrey Lowell, J Chiristopher & Jan van Zyl Smit (eds.), Rule of Law Symposium 2014: The Importance of the Rule of Law in Promoting Development (Academy Publishing, 2015) 81–102.

In contrast, as radical revolutionism, Schneiderman (2008) attempted to totally repudiate investor-state arbitration and considered it a threat to domestic constitutional values and processes and the sovereignty of the host state,[140] although it also examines international investment law from the perspective of public law. Out of defending national sovereignty and strengthening the international investment rule of law, Van Harten (2007) recommended a permanent international investment court to replace investor-state arbitration.[141] Later, however, a return to domestic law and domestic courts for investor-state disputes were advocated by Van Harten (2007) rather than a permanent international investment court.[142] Van Harten (2010) suspects the role of the rule of law played by investor-state investment arbitration because judicial independence and fairness are problematic.[143] Stoll (2018) advocated that international investment law should be viewed and improved from the perspective of rule of law.[144] However, Sattorova (2018) questioned whether, to what extent, and how investment treaty norms can induce governments into compliance with the rule of law and good governance standards.[145]

1.2.2.2 The Effect of Rule of Law on the Investment Arbitration

There are other divergences among scholarships. Wälde (2007) considered that investment arbitration restricts the host country's behavior toward foreign investors and their investments, thus promoting good governance by the host state, which is a kind of rule of law.[146] Ortino (2013) submitted that the "judicial review" even provides a "more useful, holistic methodology to balance the protection of foreign investment and the sovereign right to regulate in the public interest".[147] Ernst-Ulrich (2009) regarded that judicial administration of justice through reasoned interpretation, application, and clarification of legal principles and rules is among the oldest

140 David Schneiderman, Constitutionalizing Economic Globalization: Investment Rules and Democracy's Promise (Cambridge University Press, 2008) 223.

141 Gus Van Harten, Investment Treaty Arbitration and Public Law (Oxford University Press,, 2007) 45, 180–184.

142 Gus Van Harten, Schneiderman, David, Sornarajah, M. 'Public Statement on the International Investment Regime' (August 31, 2010), Pulic Statement, available at <https://www.bilaterals.org/IMG/pdf/Public_Statement.pdf>.

143 Gus Van Harten, 'Investment Treaty Arbitration, Procedural Fairness, and the Rule of Law', in Stephan W. Schill (ed.), International Investment Law and Comparative Public Law (Oxford University Press, 2010).

144 Peter-Tobias Stoll, 'International Investment Law and the Rule of Law' (2018) 9 No.1 Goettingen Journal of International Law 267–292.

145 Mavluda Sattorova, The Impact of Investment Treaty Law on Host States: Enabling Good Governance (Oxford: Hart Publishing, 2018).

146 Thomas W. Wälde, Investment Arbitration as a Discipline of Good Governance, in Thomas W. Wälde (ed.), NAFTA, Investment Law and Arbitration (Transnational Publishers, 2004) 475–493.

147 Federico Ortino, 'The Investment Treaty System as Judicial Review' (2012) 24(3) American Review of International Arbitration (Dec. 2013) 437–468.

paradigms of constitutional justice, but whether investor-state arbitration can ensure constitutional justice is a concern.[148]

Out of concerns about the rule of law in the field of international investment law, the International Law Association set up a Committee on the "Rule of Law and International Investment Law" in April 2015.[149] On August 9, 2016, the Committee organized by Professor August Reinisch discussed the codification and implementation of investment laws to raise the level of the rule of law at both the national and international levels, emphasizing the implication of the rule of law to host countries and the rule of law elements of investment standards and the contribution of investment arbitration to the rule of law. These discussions aimed to promote the international rule of law in the field of international investment. Obviously, the Committee especially stressed the investment protection standards as the rule of law.[150]

Facing the backlash to international investment law, Ranjan (2016) positively argued that ongoing national contestation of international investment law and new treaty practice would promote the formal elements of international rule of law, and greater deference to host states in exercising their public power triggered by national contestation would not weaken international rule of law.[151] Rajput (2019) specifically expressed confidence in the international investment rule of law in India after examining changes in India's foreign investment policy, and it concluded that although there "may appear to be a decline of the international rule of law, a nuanced approach shows that it is rather a rise" because India has not renounced the international rule of law but rather stands for "a more rule-based investment protection" in place of "prior sketchy treaty provisions".[152] Zivkovic (2018), however, took a dialectical view of the opportunities and challenges facing the rule of law in international investment.[153]

---

148 Ernst-Ulrich Petersmann, 'International Rule of Law and Constitutional Justice in International Investment Law and Arbitration' (Summer 2009) 16(2) Indiana Journal of Global Legal Studies513.

149 International Law Association, Committee, Rule of Law and International Investment Law, available at <http://www.ila-hq.org/index.php/committees>.

150 Committee on the Rule of Law and International Investment Law, 77 Int'l L. Ass'n Rep. Conf. 331 (2016) 2016; 'ILA Committee on "Rule of Law and International Investment Law" Workshop: Investment Protection Standards and the Rule of Law Vienna, December 3, 2018, 9:00 – 18:10', available at <https://juridicum.univie.ac.at/fileadmin/user_upload/f_rechtswissenschaft/downloads/Investment_Protection_Standards_and_the_Rule_of_Law__03_12_2018.pdf>.

151 Prabhash Ranjan, 'National Contestation of International Investment Law and International Rule of Law' in M Kanetake & André Nollkaemper (eds.), Rule of Law at National and International Levels: Contestations and Deference (Hart Publishing, 2016)115–142.

152 Aniruddha Rajput, 'Protection of Foreign Investment in India and International Rule of Law: Rise or Decline?', in Heike Krieger, Georg Nolte & Andreas Zimmermann (eds.), The International Rule of Law: Rise or Decline? (Oxford University Press, 2019).

153 Velimir Zivkovic, 'International Rule of Law Through International Investment Law - Strengths, Challenges and Opportunities' (Jun. 2018), in KFG Working Paper Series, No. 16 (Berlin Potsdam Research Group: The International Rule of Law – Rise or Decline? 2018.

1.2.2.3 The Investor Obligation and Investor Responsibility

It is very rare for Chinese scholars to study this topic systematically from the perspective of law, but some foreign scholars have already discussed this issue in detail. Shao (2015) highlighted that under international law, transnational corporations may be the subject of crime.[154] Li (2019) pointed out that the addition of relevant provisions on investor obligations in investment treaties is a new exploration to balance the relationship between the host state and investors and is also one of the future directions for the reform of international investment law.[155] Miles (2013) illustrated the need to introduce corporate social responsibility to reform, reshape, and transform international investment law by criticizing the history of international investment law that has been influenced and shaped by imperialist countries from its inception to the present.[156] Sattorova (2019) also argued that the reform of IIAs "should begin to more directly incorporate investor responsibility".[157] In view of the asymmetry of traditional international investment law, Jarrett (2019) believed that in investor-state arbitration, the investor as a victim was in violation of the law would affect the apportionment of liability or reduce the responsibility of the host state as a respondent, and it also used the municipal law defensive method as a reference to classify the investor misconduct, such as mismanagement, investment reprisals, and postestablishment illegality, and further argued that such instances of misconduct provide the host state with a defense to any breach of investment treaty obligations.[158] Ryngaert (2018) explored a wide range of corporate accountability tools and hopes to promote "lasting, human rights-friendly changes in overseas corporate activities".[159]

In fact, responsible investment has started to be a hot topic for scholars in recent years, such as the "Responsible Investment Project" of Harvard University and the study team of the International Law Association led by Ida Levine to study social responsibility. In 2019, a series of seminar papers titled "Investor Responsibility: The Next Frontier in International Investment Law" were published in "AJIL Unbound", and these papers explored why and how the existing international investment law system, which aims to correct the wrongdoings of investors but not that by investors, needs to introduce the new paradigm of "investor responsibility", which also shows

---

[154] Shaping Shao, 'The Impact of International Rule of Law on the Responsibilities of Transnational Corporations' (2015) 68(05) Wuhan University Journal (Philosophy & Social Sciences) 84–90.

[155] Bin Li, 'On the Investor' s Obligation Clause under Investment Treaty' (2019) 3 Journal of International Economic Law 15–28.

[156] Kate Miles, The Origins of International Investment Law: Empire, Environment and the Safeguarding of Capital (Cambridge University Press, 2013).

[157] Mavluda Sattorova 'Investor Responsibilities from a Host State Perspective: Qualitative Data and Proposals for Treaty Reform' (2019) 113 AJIL Unbound 22–27.

[158] Martin Jarrett, Contributory Fault and Investor Misconduct in Investment Arbitration (Cambridge University Press, 2019).

[159] Cedric Ryngaert, 'Accountability of Multinational Corporations for Human Rights Abuses' (2018) 14(2) Utrecht Law Review 1–5.

that this issue is or possibly is one of the frontier issues of international investment law,[160] although it may not be a new issue.[161]

In summary, the "international investment rule of law" has become a hot issue that has attracted some scholars' attention in recent years. On the one hand, scholars may want to find more theoretical implications from the practice of international investment law; on the other hand, the challenges faced by international investment law may be the reasons why the concept of international rule of law is introduced to the field of international investment law.

The literature and their exploration from the perspective of international rule of law on international investment law would certainly be able to promote the development of international investment rule of law in theory and in practice. However, most scholarship ignores illustrating investor obligation or investor responsibility under the rule of law, or although investor obligation or investor responsibility is increasingly highlighted, the existing literature does not discuss these issues under the idea of the rule of law but only emphasizes that traditional and imbalanced international investment law one-sidedly protects the interests of investors, and investor obligation is usually treated as a separate issue outside of the international investment rule of law. In addition, the topic of excessive restriction on the power of the host state, and thus more policy space should be granted to the host state, is also not dealt with thoroughly.

1.2.3 Literature Review on African and China–Africa Investment Rule of Law

1.2.3.1 The Significance of African Regionalism IIAs for International Investment Governance

The significance of African regionalism in international investment governance is focused on and explored in this aspect. Schill (2017) pointed out that the rising regionalism in Africa has broken the domination of European-style IIA practice in Africa, the Pan-African Investment Code (PAIC), which is drafted by Africans and embodies African features, such as the pronounced example of integrating direct investor obligation into the Code.[162] Furthermore, Denters and Gazzini (2017) thought, from the point of view of international investment law, regional economic integration in Africa represented the evolution of international investment law and showed the rising of

---

[160] James Gathii, & Sergio Puig, 'Introduction to the Symposium on Investor Responsibility: The Next Frontier in International Investment Law' (Jan. 2019) 113 AJIL Unbound1-3.

[161] Shaw, Jackson Kern, 'Investor Responsibility as Familiar Frontier' (Jan. 2019) 113 AJIL Unbound 28–32.

[162] Stephan W. Schill, 'Editorial: The New (African) Regionalism in International Investment Law' (2017) 18(3) The Journal of World Investment & Trade 367–369.

regional investment treaties hinting at the "progressive abandonment of the traditional bilateral approach".[163] Mbengue (2016, 2017) put forward the proposition of the "Africanization" of international investment law on the basis of the PAIC, the first African model investment treaty, and concluded that the PAIC was unique and had been drafted from the perspective of developing and least-developed countries with a view to promote sustainable development, as is embodied in the reformulated and innovative provisions, and especially the introduction of direct obligations for investors.[164] In Adeleke (2018), the role of regional economic integration in Africa was emphasized because the collective interests of African countries could not be achieved by BITs which aim at the national interest.[165] Páez (2017), however, facing conflicting and interacting IIAs in Africa, questioned the necessity of a "Continental Investment Agreement".[166]

1.2.3.2 The Nature of the African BIT and China–Africa BIT

The so-called nature of African BITs and China–Africa BITs mainly refers to whether they are South–South BITs or the same as South–North BITs in terms of provisions in these BITs.

De Brabandere (2017) confirmed that there were no significantly different FET and "full protection and security" (FPS) clauses in IIAs just because one side of the contracting parties are African states, but the specific circumstances in the contracting African states did affect the interpretation of these provisions.[167]

Several articles have focused on the nature of China–Africa BITs. Kidane (2013) submitted that China claims a "South" identity, but its pursuits bear all the hallmarks of the "North", rendering China's position in China–Africa BITs ambiguous.[168]

---

163 Erik Denters & Gazzini, Tarcisio, 'The Role of African Regional Organizations in the Promotion and Protection of Foreign Investment' (2017) 18(3) The Journal of World Investment & Trade 449–492.

164 Makane Mbengue, 'The Quest for a Pan-African Investment Code to Promote Sustainable Development' (June 2016) 5(5) Bridges Africal ICTSD; Makane Moïse Mbengue & Stefanie Schacherer, 'The 'Africanization' of International Investment Law: The Pan-African Investment Code and the Reform of the International Investment Regime' (2018) 18(3) The Journal of World Investment & Trade 414–448.

165 Fola Adeleke, International Investment Law and Policy in Africa: Exploring a Human Rights Based Approach to Investment Regulation and Dispute Settlement (Routledge, 2017).

166 Laura Páez, 'Bilateral Investment Treaties and Regional Investment Regulation in Africa: Towards a Continental Investment Area?' (2017) 18(3) The Journal of World Investment & Trade 379–413.

167 Eric De Brabandere, 'Fair and Equitable Treatment and (Full) Protection and Security in African Investment Treaties Between Generality and Contextual Specificity' (2017) 18(3) The Journal of World Investment & Trade 530–555.

168 See Won Kidane, 'Reflections on China-Africa BITs, China-Africa Investment Treaties and Dispute Settlement: A Piece of the Multipolar Puzzle' (2013) 107 Proceedings of the ASIL Annual Meeting 225–227.

Kidane (2016) further commented on China–Africa BITs as "a simple, benign, and convenient replication of existing text".[169]

In the same vein, Ofodile (2013) further recommended that because the "South–South BITs do not appear to offer a different legal framework for FDI" from South–North BITs, "Countries in Africa must approach every BIT negotiation with caution" when the other contracting party is China.[170]

1.2.3.3 The Role of African BIT and China–Africa BIT

Regarding the role of African BITs in attracting foreign investments, Johnson (2009) confirmed that although BITs represent the most efficient means to attract FDI, they appear to have failed in Sub-Saharan Africa because they do not conform to the national conditions of these countries.[171]

Seatzu and Vargiu (2015) appraised African approaches and contributions to international investment law by Africanizing BITs.[172] Furthermore, AfSIL (2016) put forward 15 principles for reference when African states enact investment legislation or negotiate investment agreements, and it especially emphasizes the sustainable development of the African host state and the obligations of investors.[173]

Regarding the role of China–Africa BITs, Gen (2010) affirmed the role of China–Africa BITs in attracting investment but considered these BITs insufficient to protect China's outward investment in Africa.[174] For further assessment of China–Africa BITs, Kidane and Zhu (2014) argued that "[t]he existing China–Africa BITs have significant shortcomings, indeed, they are all outdated" and that the "China–African investment regime must be backed by a robust dispute settlement mechanism".[175] Chen (2013) considered that China–Africa BITs are not an important part of China's BITs, and recent approaches in China's BITs will not have a significant impact on

169 Won Kidane, 'China's Bilateral Investment Treaties with African States in Comparative Context' (2016) 49 Cornell International Law Journal 141–177.

170 See Uche Ewelukwa Ofodile, 'Africa-China Bilateral Investment Treaties: A Critique'(2013) 35(1) Michigan Journal of International Law 207.

171 Johnson, Alec R, 'Rethinking Bilateral Investment Treaties in Sub-Saharan Africa' (2010) 59(4) Emory Law Journal 966.

172 Francesco Seatzu & Paolo Vargiu, 'Africanizing Bilateral Investment Treaties ('BITs'): Some Case Studies and Future Prospects of a Pro-active African Approach to International Investment' (2015) 30 Connecticut Journal of International Law 143.

173 AfSIL, African Society of International. '2016 AfSIL Principles on International Investment for Sustainable Development in Africa' available at <https://www.justiceinternationale-chaire.ulaval.ca/sites/cdiph.ulaval.ca/files/2016_afsil_principles_on_international_investment_for_sustainable_development_in_africa.pdf>.

174 Liu Gen, Research about Bilateral Investment Treaty Between China and Africa, Xiangtan University, P. R. China, Master Dissertation, 2010.

175 Kidane Won & Weidong Zhu, 'China-Africa Investment Treaties: Old Rules, New Challenges' (2014) 37(4) Fordham International Law Journal 1085–1086.

future China–Africa BITs.[176] In contrast, African scholars expressed concern about the main provisions in China–Africa BITs, such as national treatment, FET, and ISDS; advocated special and differential treatment; and emphasized the host state's regulatory power to the environment and human rights and investors' obligations.[177]

1.2.3.4 The Shift of the South African Investment Policy from BIT to Domestic Law

Regarding the shift of South African investment policy from BIT to domestic law, academic discussions are largely concentrated in the period before and after South Africa started to terminate its BITs and enacted its investment law.

Jeffery (2014) admonished that according to the decision of the South African Constitutional Court and the relevant provisions of the Promotion and Protection of Investment Bill, the South African government may deprive the property of the South African or foreigner by "custodianship" for the disadvantaged instead of "ownership", and deprivation and expropriation are distinct without compensation, and in addition, the weak investment protection and potential conflict among the survival provisions of BITs between South Africa and EU countries, SADC Protocol, and the proposed Bill indicates the protectionist investment policy's side effect to the investments from EU and US.[178] Greve (2015) and Jeffrey (2015) criticized South Africa for being partial and unwise for only retaining its agreements with China and other emerging countries in view of the huge gap between their investment stock and inflow in South Africa and suggested that the proposed Bill should be revised according to South Africa–China BIT.[179] Kleyn (2013) pinpointed that "the Bill does not provide the same standard of protection for foreign investors as provided under South Africa's various BITs. The Bill includes provisions that are no longer in line with international best practice".[180]

In contrast, Mossallam (2015) supported the shift of South African investment policy because the purpose of the existing BITs is to guarantee the ability of governments to enact legislation and regulatory measures aimed at promoting public policy

---

176 Huiping Chen, 'Recent Approaches in China's BITs and Impact on African Countries, China-Africa Investment Treaties and Dispute Settlement: A Piece of the Multipolar Puzzle' in Proceedings of the One Hundred Seventh Annual Meeting of the American Society of International Law (April 3–6, 2013) 228–230.

177 See Oliver C. Ruppel & Frida Shifotoka 'Foreign Direct Investment Protection in Africa—Contemporary Legal Aspects Between BITS and BRICS' (2016) 12(1) African Yearbook of International Law 50–52.

178 See Anthea Jeffery, Bill Goes Far Beyond Bilateral Trade, Business Day, February 25, 2014.

179 See Natalie Greve, 'Changes to investment Bill a 'self-inflicted' economic blow' (October 27, 2015) Think Tank Warns, available at <http://www.engineeringnews.co.za/print-version/changes-to-investment-bill-a-self-inflicted-economic-blow-thinktank-warns-2015-10-27>.

180 Madelein Kleyn, 'Promotion and Protection of Investment Bill, 2013—A Review'. 49 Les Nouvelles, 138.

objectives and put forward specific suggestions on the implementation.[181] Masamba (2014) also suggested that a country should protect foreign investments through its general domestic legal system, which should reflect the international standard of protecting foreign investment.[182] Coleman and Williams (2008) argued that the Piero Foresti v. South Africa reflected the apparent conflict between South Africa's BITs and the Mineral and Petroleum Resources Development Act 28 of 2002 (MPRDA), and the case should be settled by the contracting parties of the BITs between South Africa and Italian and Benelux, instead of an investment tribunal.[183]

In summary, the existing scholarship on international rule of law can provide useful analytical tools, but the weakness is that private obligations and responsibilities have not been emphasized by the theory of the international rule of law, which is also an important reason that leads to the imbalance of the international investment rule of law. In recent years, with the increase in attracting foreign investment in Africa and the development of international investment law both internally and externally in Africa, international investment law in Africa has attracted the attention of scholars, but a canvass on IIAs and investment measures on issues related to African countries is still unavailable. The implications of the regional economic integration approach to the protection and sustainability of foreign investment have not been addressed. Most fundamentally, there are a few studies on the international investment legal framework in Africa and the protection and sustainability of Chinese investment in Africa from the international rule of law perspective.

Through a literature review, this introduction examines in detail the academic literature on the international rule of law, the international investment rule of law, the investment rule of law in Africa, and the investment rule of law between China and Africa.

With regard to the literature on the international rule of law, although it cannot be compared with the richness of that on the national rule of law, the available research results are still abundant. The existing literature shows that American scholars embarked on an ambitious research project covering all aspects of international affairs in the late 1950s and early 1960s after Eisenhower (1959) proposed that the rule of law in international affairs should be adhered to just as in national affairs. The research at this time mainly established the existence of the international

---

[181] Mossallam, Mohammad, 'GEG Working Paper 2015/97 Process Matters: South Africa's Experience Exiting Its BITs' (Jan. 2015) The Global Economic Governance Programme, University of Oxford, available at <https://www.geg.ox.ac.uk/sites/geg.bsg.ox.ac.uk/files/GEG%20WP_97%20Process%20matters%20-%20South%20Africas%20experience%20exiting%20its%20BITs%20Mohammad%20Mossallam.pdf >.

[182] See Magalie Masamba, 'Africa and Bilateral Investment Treaties: To 'BIT' or Not?', July 16, 2014, available at <https://www.polity.org.za/article/africa-and-bilateral-investment-treaties-to-bit-or-not-2014-07-23>.

[183] See Matthew Coleman & Kevin Williams, 'South Africa's Bilateral Investment Treaties, Black Economic Empowerment and Mining: A Fragmented Meeting?' (Jan. 2008) 9 (1) Business Law International 59.

rule of law and how to make the international rule of law more effective. However, it goes without saying that the international rule of law here refers to the international rule of law under the leadership of the US. However, research in the name of international rule of law only began to revive in the 1990s. Until now, although some scholars believe that the international rule of law is only a slogan and international relations are still mainly dominated by power, most of the academic literature recognizes the existence of the international rule of law, even if it is a flawed existence. At present, international rule of law has become a hot topic, many prominent international law scholars have touched on this topic, and scholars in various fields of international law are examining the rise or decline of international rule of law.

Regarding the international rule of law, the central view is that the international rule of law is a tool that functionally constrains the power of government to protect human rights, and the international rule of law also limits the power of international organizations, including international judicial bodies, although they simultaneously promote and guarantee the rule of law at the international level. Some existing academic studies also imitate the national rule of law, classifying the international rule of law as the "thin" formal rule of law and the "thick" substantive rule of law and then describing the content or elements of the two forms of rule of law. Some Chinese scholars introduce "Community with a Shared Future for Mankind" as a "thick" substantive international rule of law and argue that to achieve "Community with a Shared Future for Mankind", international rule of law is necessary. Under the premise of recognizing the differences between the domestic community and international society, scholars also emphasize the interaction between the national rule of law and the international rule of law.

There is also a flaw in the existing literature, namely they emphasize one-sidedly the limitation on the exercise of public power without mentioning the aspect of preserving the public power of the state, and on the other hand, they only focus on protecting private human rights without emphasizing their obligations.

With regard to the international investment rule of law, it is an integral part of the international rule of law research project launched by American scholars in the late 1950s and early 1960s. The project put forward the expectation of developing a balanced international investment rule of law that "respects the sovereignty of the host state and considers the interests in the social and economic and human needs of the people of the host state". In past years, the rule of law function of international investment law has received attention from academic circles; however, the development of the international investment rule of law has deviated from this idea.

The rich academic literature of the twenty-first century has two opposite discussions: one is that international investment law, especially international investment arbitration, plays the rule of law function of public law by controlling the host state's regulatory power, and the other is that the international investment rule of law should be denied in view of the legitimacy crisis of international investment arbitration. However, the dialectical view adopted in this research is, on one hand, to recognize the problems of the existing international investment rule of law and, on the other hand, to advocate the international investment rule of law and reform it, which includes two aspects: Strengthening the protection of the host state's legitimate regulatory power and imposing investor obligation or investor responsibility. In recent years, investor responsibility has become a new academic frontier, and relevant research aims to establish the position and responsibility of investors within the existing and future international investment rule of law.

The international investment rule of law in Africa is an integral part of the international investment rule of law, including the effectiveness of African BITs in attracting foreign investment to Africa, the effectiveness and distinctive features of the African regional integration investment agreements, the possibility of regional investment agreements replacing the BIT, and whether an African country, as the IIAs contracting party, receive a special and differential treatment. In addition, there are some studies on cases involving African countries in international investment arbitration, and the conclusion reveals a negative attitude toward international investment arbitration. Regarding the shift of South Africa's BIT policy, most relevant research does not think it is the best choice.

Regarding the China–Africa BIT, there is an academic view that considers that there is no substantial difference between the China–Africa BIT and other BITs and reminds African countries to be careful when signing a BIT with China. However, most viewpoints are that China–Africa BITs, which have ineffective and outdated defects, can only play a limited role in protecting Chinese overseas investment.

Through canvassing the literature, the author believes that both the ideas of international rule of law and the international investment rule of law affect the development of international investment law. However, the theme of this research is not directly studied in the existing academic literature, and this writing will absorb and make use of existing academic achievements and is hoped to be an effort to promote the development of international rule of law and the international investment rule of law from the Chinese perspective.

Specific research combining theory with practice should be carried out. The most distinctive research method for this research is that to complete the writing of it, the present author in person went to related enterprises and institutions in South Africa, Zambia, Mauritius, Mozambique, and Kenya to conduct surveys and interviews and acquired the perceptual understanding of risk, protection, and investor responsibility faced by Chinese investment in Africa. This research method strengthens "problem awareness" and makes the writing more targeted to the problem. In addition, the research attaches importance to dialectical research methods. For example, when facing investment arbitration and public law, Gus Van Harten and Stephan W. Schill's viewpoints are diametrically opposed to each other. The former emphasizes that the public power of the host state should be preserved, while the latter emphasizes constraints according to the principle of public law. However, the international investment rule of law adopted by this research considers both constraint and protection of the public power of the host state.

In summary, based on the above review, it is hoped that the academic ideas and academic views in this research can be slightly innovative and have a realistic guiding role in guiding Chinese investment in Africa and China–Africa investment cooperation.

Chapter 2
Revisiting the International Rule of Law in an Era of Resistance

The adverse effects of globalization, liberalization, and the rise and fall of national power have led some states toward the other extreme of globalization and liberalization. A significant manifestation is their opposition to the international rule of law, such as impeding or withdrawing from international institutions and international treaties and further replacing the international rule of law with their own national rule of law to the extent of excessively and extraterritorially applying their national rule of law. These problems are evident in many fields of international law, such as international climate change law, international investment law, and WTO law.[1] This cannot help but make one reconsider the international rule of law to confirm and predict its practical necessity and future direction.

In fact, some authoritative scholars have traced the evolution of the rule of law from ancient to modern times in all major legal traditions to explain the rule of international law.[2] It is generally believed that the expression or phrase "rule of law" was popularized by Albert Venn Dicey in his work "Introduction to the Study of the Law of the Constitution".[3] Dicey's understanding of the rule of law stressed that the conduct and authority of a government should be bound by the law to restrain the

---

[1] For example, the Trump Administration of the United States denounced the Paris Agreement, obstructed the operation of the WTO Appellate Body, and withdrew from the World Health Organization, and the United States imposed a series of sanctions on China in accordance with its domestic law.

[2] See Vesselin Popovski, "From Domestic to International Rule of Law: A Long and Unfinished Journey", in Vesselin Popovski (ed.), International Rule of Law and Professional Ethics (Ashgate, 2014) 5–18; Simon Chesterman, "'Unqualified Human Good' or a Bit of 'Ruling-Class Chatter', The Rule of Law at the National and International Level", in Vesselin Popovski (ed.), International Rule of Law and Professional Ethics (Ashgate, 2014) 19–48.

[3] See Albert Venn Dicey, Introduction to the Study of the Law of the Constitution (1st edition, Macmillan, 1885).

X. Han, *Legal Protection and Sustainability of Chinese Investments in Africa*,
Modern China and International Economic Law,
https://doi.org/10.1007/978-981-19-1882-7_2

abuse of power and protect citizens' freedom by law.[4] In addition to indicating the functional similarity between the international rule of law and the national rule of law, however, this research will not touch upon national rule of law but elaborate on the international rule of law in theory, including the ideal and reality, defects in its past, and the right direction in its future. Primarily, the present research attempts to clarify the abstract idea and concrete elements of the international rule of law from the perspective of functionalism.

Whether the international rule of law is opposed or supported, it is the core concept in contemporary international law but with no unified or well-recognized understanding. The international rule of law may be defined in very diverse ways because different people understand it from different perspectives. As an "umbrella notion", the international rule of law, as well as rule of law, has many facets. For example, in addition to function, the international rule of law is considered to cover both formal and substantive elements or requirements.[5] This research attempts to show a whole picture of the international rule of law from the perspective of functionalism based on the existing scholarship and the present author's deliberation.

2.1 International Rule of Law from Ideal to Reality

First and foremost, the international rule of law is a lexicon that indicates an abstract ideal, notion, or concept. Although there are doubts about its real existence in the current world, just as somebody thinks there only exists power politics, without any international rule of law in an international arena where "the fittest survives", nobody denies that it is a legal or political ideal of humankind in the contemporary era and is the expectation of an ideal international community.

As far back as 1959, the then President D. Eisenhower of the US put forward the notion that "the time has come for mankind to make the rule of law in international affairs as normal as it is now in domestic affairs".[6] In the same year, former American Bar Association President, Charles Rhyne, referred to the "rule of law among nations" as "regulation of mutual intercourse of nations, and international contracts

---

[4] See Ted Honderich (ed.), The Oxford Companion to Philosophy (Oxford University Press, 1995) 780–781; Dicey Albert Venn, Introduction to the Study of the Law of the Constitution (8th edition, Macmillan, 1915) 198.

[5] See Machiko Kanetake, The Interfaces Between the National and International Rule of Law: A Framework Paper, Amsterdam Center for International Law Research Paper 07 (2014), ACIL 2014–27, p.8.

[6] Dwight D. Eisenhower, "Remarks Upon Receiving an Honorary Degree of Doctor of Laws at Delhi University" (December 11, 1959), available at <http://www.eisenhowermemorial.org/speeches/1959>.

and relations of individuals, by legal concepts, standards, institutions and procedures".[7] Although both Eisenhower and Rhyne understood the international rule of law as a notion covering a wide range, these so-called rule of law, legal concepts, standards, institutions, and procedures, which were deeply imprinted with the brand of the US, the invention of the ideal of the "international rule of law" or "rule of law among nations" itself is a tremendous historical progress. As an objective or consequential state of affairs, Earl D. Osborn, the President of the Institute for International Order of the US, pointed out that "the 'international rule of law' refers to a world in which resort to law in the settlement of disputes and the conduct of international affairs is habitual as it is on the domestic scene".[8] In contrast, Simon Chesterman proposed a core definition of the international rule of law—"being seen as a means rather than an end, as serving a function rather than defining a status",[9] yet he did not deny the international rule of law as a political ideal.

One reason to challenge the international rule of law is that it is inappropriate to analogize the international rule of law with the national rule of law. However, the horizontal structure instead of the vertical hierarchy of international society cannot deny the existence of international rule of law. As Terry Nardin writes, "what is important is whether the subjects of the law acknowledge the law's authority and not the existence of a central authority".[10] Simon Chesterman argues that the international rule of law should be understood "as a means rather than an end" from a functionalist instead of a formal perspective.[11] He reiterates that the international rule of law should be regarded as a means to realize all kinds of substantive objectives, and a rigidly formal analogy to national rule of law is not advisable.

William W. Bishop has long denied the argument that "there is no international rule of law" by contending that the issue is how to "bring about a more effective rule of law internationally".[12] Some modern scholarship endorses the idea that "the rule of law should become a fundamental governance value within the international community as it is within sovereign states".[13] From a political perspective, states always

[7] Charles Rhyne, Opening Statement before Boston Conference on World Peace through Law, March 27, 1959, A.B.A. Special Committee on World Peace through Law, The Rule of Law among Nations: Digest of Proceedings of Regional Conferences of Lawyers 47 (1959).

[8] See Arthur Larson, The International Rule of Law (The Institute for International Order, 1961).

[9] Simon Chesterman, "An International Rule of Law?" (2008) 56(2) American Journal of Comparative Law 331–361, at 360.

[10] Terry Nardin, "Theorising the International Rule of Law" (2008) 34(3) Review of International Studies 385–401.

[11] See Simon Chesterman, "An International Rule of Law?" (2008) 56(2) American Journal of Comparative Law 331–361.

[12] See William W. Bishop, "The International Rule of Law" (1960–1961) 59 Michigan Law Review 553.

[13] Charles Sampford, "Professions without Border: Global Ethics and the International Rule of Law", in Vesselin Popovski (ed.), International Rule of Law and Professional Ethics (Ashgate, 2014) 129–147, at 146; Vesselin Popovski, "From Domestic to International Rule of Law: A Long and Unfinished Journey", in Vesselin Popovski (ed.), International Rule of Law and Professional Ethics (Ashgate, 2014) 5–18.

"invoke international law to explain and justify their policy"[14] since international law provides instruments "for foreign policy and international affairs".[15] "International law rhetoric pervades international relations" to rationalize the behavior of the subject in international affairs.[16] The international rule of law is commonly seen as "a framework of mutual interests, cemented by state consent, which displaces power politics and coercion".[17] The "relations between States and other subjects of international law" should apply "rule of law principles.[18] Vesselin Popovski argues that the international rule of law should be "a process of recognition of the ascendancy of law above power internationally, a result of gradual acceptance of the rule of law in more countries in the world, and application of the rule of law principles by international institutions, by international courts, etc.". To say the least, "the international rule of law has a strong practical orientation and value—*what it delivers*, rather than *how we define it*, is more fundamental".[19] All things considered, the international rule of law, as an ideal, means international society should be governed by law instead of power, and international rule of law should be the value orientation of international society.

Currently, no state expressly opposes that the international rule of law should be an ideal for mankind. UN Charter, as the "constitution" of international society, declares the essence of international rule of law, although the wording of "international rule of law" is not used explicitly in most circumstances. At the UN World Summit 2005, the UN General Assembly recognized rule of law, both at domestic and international levels, as one of the universal and indivisible core values and principles of the UN.[20] Therefore, member states recognized the need for international rule of law and reconfirmed their commitment to international rule of law.[21] In 2006,

[14] See Lan Hurd, "What is the International Rule of Law?", in Javier Solana and Angel Saz-Carranza (eds.), The Global Context: How Politics, Investment and Institutions Impact European Business (Esadegeo-Center for Global Economy and Geopolitics, 2015), Charter 8, at 149.

[15] Lan Hurd, "What is the International Rule of Law?", in Javier Solana and Angel Saz-Carranza (eds.), The Global Context: How Politics, Investment and Institutions Impact European Business (ESADEgeo-Center for Global Economy and Geopolitics, 2015), Charter 8, at 155.

[16] See Jack L. Goldsmith and Eric A. Posner, The Limits of International Law (Oxford University Press, 2005) 171.

[17] Andrew Guzman, How International Law Works: A Rational-Choice Theory (Oxford University Press, 2008).

[18] See Simon Chesterman, "'Unqualified Human Good' or a Bit of 'Ruling-Class Chatter', The Rule of Law at the National and International Level", in Vesselin Popovski (ed.), International Rule of Law and Professional Ethics (Ashgate, 2014) 19–48.

[19] Vesselin Popovski, "From Domestic to International Rule of Law: A Long and Unfinished Journey", in Vesselin Popovski (ed.), International Rule of Law and Professional Ethics (Ashgate, 2014) 5–18.

[20] UN: 2005 World Summit Outcome, UN Doc. A/RES/60/1 (October 24, 2005), para.119, available at <https://www.un.org/en/development/desa/population/migration/generalassembly/docs/globalcompact/A_RES_60_1.pdf>.

[21] UN: 2005 World Summit Outcome, UN Doc. A/RES/60/1 (October 24, 2005), para.134, available at <https://www.un.org/en/development/desa/population/migration/generalassembly/docs/globalcompact/A_RES_60_1.pdf>.

the UN General Assembly included the issue of "rule of law at the national and international levels" on the agenda of the Sixth Committee for the first time. Since then, every year, the UN General Assembly has discussed the issue of international rule of law. The UN repeatedly reaffirms that the rule of law is the footstone to dealing with equal relations among nations.[22] This is proof that there is such a thing as the international rule of law, although it is not so normative and institutional in most fields of international society.

The implication of the faith in international rule of law lies in taking it as guidance for international actors. Therefore, the overarching and innate notion of international rule of law makes all the difference because it predicts that international actors seek international law to regulate their international intercourse, both usual conduct and dispute settlement, by complying with international law instead of evading international law painstakingly or escaping from international law obligation on the ground of internal politics and policies. Moreover, when any international dispute happens, international rule of law requires settling it through legal avenues instead of reckless solutions through the use of force. The dispute settlement system is essential to showcase international rule of law. In reality, the solution through political avenues involves legal factors; in other words, it needs to take the authority of law as a prerequisite or means.

The current international community is sometimes in anarchy. The overall international law is not uniform but fragmented.[23] In addition, the level of rule of law is differential in different fields. Beyond any doubt, however, the international community is marching toward the rule of law to a greater extent.

In contemporary international society, the reality is increasingly institutionalized, and international law is also increasingly playing its role. From UN sanctions to the UN climate deal,[24] from the WTO dispute settlement mechanism to the international investment arbitration system, the importance of international rule of law is shown although the resistance of hegemony to it occurs from time to time. Thus, the rule of law is an objective development trend of international society. "These phenomena

---

22 World Leaders Adopt Declaration Reaffirming Rule of Law as Foundation for Building Equitable State Relations, Just Societies, Sixty-seventh General Assembly, Plenary, 3rd, 4th & 5th Meetings, September 24, 2012, GA/11290, available at <http://www.un.org/press/en/2012/ga11290.doc.htm>.

23 See Wellens, Karel C, "Diversity in Secondary Rules and the Unity of International Law: Some Reflections on Current Trends" (1994) 25 Netherlands Yearbook of International Law 3–37; Oriol Casanovas y La Rosa, Unity and Pluralism in Public International Law (Martinus Nijhoff Publishers, 2001) 272.

24 For example, when the UN Security Council instigates sanctions targeting specific individuals and entities, it will make great efforts to follow close to the rule of law; see Jeremy Matam Farrall, United Nations Sanctions and the Rule of Law (Cambridge University Press, 2007); see Ang Sun, "Due Process of United Nations Security Council Sanctions Regimes Focusing on the Reform of 1267 Sanctions Regime" (2015) 6 Chinese Review of International Law 3–17; on December 12, 2015, at the UN Climate Change Conference held in Paris, 195 countries adopted the first universal climate agreement after two weeks' heated discussion. It is said a "legal binding" deal. See United national conference on climate change, COP21/CMP 11, available at <http://www.cop21.gouv.fr/en/>.

rest on and reinforce the idea that international affairs should be governed by the rule of law".[25]

The President of the International Court of Justice (ICJ), H.E. Judge Hisashi Owada, has observed that "it must be emphasized that the importance of the rule of law in the contemporary international community is growing rapidly, against the backdrop of the deepening process of globalization."[26] "International law is of value because it conduces to the safety and prosperity of individuals by promoting a peaceful world order",[27] and "[p]rospects for a peaceful world depend heavily on the acceptance of a genuine international legal system".[28] Good governance and the rule of law at the national and international levels are essential for sustainable development and the eradication of poverty and hunger.[29] The international rule of law is not a panacea to the governance of the international community but a primary prescription to maintain peace and order in an anarchical international society. The international rule of law is desirable because "human rights, international stability, and perhaps even the progress of civilization itself are to be dependent on international rule of law".[30]

The trend of rule of law in international society embraces the ideal of international rule of law. The cardinal symbol of this trend is that treaties and international institutions, especially international courts and tribunals founded on the treaties, become the overriding means of governance in international society.

Treaty, as a positive law that equals legislation in the domestic legal system, lays down rules binding to the countries in question. Significantly, a treaty replaces customary international law or incorporates or compiles the latter into a treaty by clearly defined rules, which are the qualitative requirements of the international rule of law. Treaty provides normative frameworks for international affairs. Many international treaties dealing with all kinds of subject matters represent the development of the international rule of law.

International institutions are also one of the essential elements of the development of international rule of law. The growth of international institutions has promoted international rule of law to a great extent. International organizations as international

[25] See Lan Hurd, "What is the International Rule of Law?", in Javier Solana and Angel Saz-Carranza (eds.), The Global Context: How Politics, Investment and Institutions Impact European Business (Esadegeo-Center for Global Economy and Geopolitics, 2016), Charter 8, at 149.

[26] International Court of Justice, Press Release, The International Court of Justice has a central role to play in the promotion of the rule of law, the President of the Court affirms before the United Nations General Assembly, No. 2010/35, October 29, 2015.

[27] Nehal Bhuta, "Are Sovereigns Entitled to the Benefit of the International Rule of Law? An Introduction" (2011) 22(2) The European Journal of International Law 313–314, at 313.

[28] Arthur Larson, The International Rule of Law (The Institute for International Order, 1961) 19.

[29] See UN: 2005 World Summit Outcome, UN Doc. A/RES/60/1 (October 24, 2005), para.11, available at <https://www.un.org/en/development/desa/population/migration/generalassembly/docs/globalcompact/A_RES_60_1.pdf>.

[30] Lan Hurd, "What is the International Rule of Law?", in Javier Solana and Angel Saz-Carranza (eds.), The Global Context: How Politics, Investment and Institutions Impact European Business (ESADEgeo-Center for Global Economy and Geopolitics, 2016), Charter 8, at 150.

lawmakers[31] promote the international rule of law for "international organizations have internalized the rule of law in their own procedures".[32] The UN Security Council has preferred the rule of law as a form of conflict resolution to maintain peace; international human rights organizations have advocated the rule of law as the foundation of a rights-respecting state; international development organizations deem rule of law the premise of economic development.

It is worth mentioning that the proliferation of international courts and tribunals gives tremendous impetus to the progress of international rule of law.[33] These international courts and tribunals become peaceful arbitral or judicial avenues to settle all kinds of disputes. The decisions made by international courts and tribunals are one of the secondary sources of international law, and arbitral or judicial interpretation is an international judicial law-making process.[34] Many international courts and tribunals adopt common approaches to questions of procedure and remedies, leading to the emergence of a common law of international adjudication.[35] On the other hand, "the extent to which a nation will accept the compulsory jurisdiction of an international tribunal and thereafter comply with its decisions will be closely related to its concept of sovereignty".[36] Many states accept the compulsory jurisdiction of international courts and tribunals, as manifests the growing consciousness among the states of the importance of the rule of law in the international community. Conversely, the evolution of the rule of law is embodied in greater acceptance of the compulsory jurisdiction of international courts and tribunals.

Taking the ICJ as an example, dating back to 1958, Sir Hersch Lauterpacht observed that although "it would be an exaggeration to assert that the Court has proved to be a significant instrument for maintaining international peace", it had "made a tangible contribution to the development and clarification of the rules and principles of international law".[37] Although there are disagreements among scholars about whether the ICJ should judicially make law, there is consensus on its influence

---

[31] See José E. Alvarez, International Organizations as Law-Makers (Oxford University Press, 2005).

[32] Simon Chesterman, "An International Rule of Law?" (2008) 56(2) American Journal of Comparative Law 331–361, at 332.

[33] Here is just a list of some courts and tribunals, for example: International Court of Justice (ICJ) (prior Permanent Court of International Justice (PCIJ)), International Criminal Tribunal for the Former Yugoslavia (ICTY), International Criminal Tribunal for Rwanda (ICTR), Special Court for Sierra Leone and the Extraordinary Chambers in the Courts of Cambodia, International Criminal Court (ICC). In addition, some regional courts are very effective. Among others, European Court of Justice (prior Court of Justice of the European Communities has been commended as "a real step forward toward the international rule of law"; see William W. Bishop, "The International Rule of Law" (1961) 59 Michigan Law Review 553, 560 is the leader of regional rule of law.

[34] See Ingo Venzke, How Interpretation Makes International Law: On Semantic Change and Normative Twists (Oxford University Press, 2012).

[35] See Chester Brown, A Common Law of International Adjudication (Oxford University Press, 2007).

[36] Arthur Larson, The International Rule of Law (The Institute for International Order, 1961) 28.

[37] Hersch Lauterpacht, The Development of International Law by the International Court (Stevens & Sons, 1958) 4 and 5.

and contribution to international law development.[38] The ICJ has played a crucial role in developing international rule of law, including the law of treaties, the law of claims, the law of spatial regimes, the law of United Nations, the law of armed conflict, and the law of community concerns.[39] The President of the ICJ, H.E. Judge Hisashi Owada, stressed in particular that "[w]hile every part of the Organization has a role to play in the promotion of the rule of law, the Court, as the principal judicial organ of the United Nations, is expected to play a central role in this area".[40] The ICJ is a part of international rule of law and plays a vital function in it.[41]

"In an era of globalization, there is a need for complex new forms of governance that stretch across traditional state boundaries," and "the international order has become ever more rule-bound with increasingly interconnected and interdependent rules."[42] It is undeniable that international society is stepping toward international rule of law firmly, as is also demonstrated by international economic law. The development of international rule of law is unbalanced. The most advanced part is the area of international economic law. Many countries have partially ceded sovereignty and accepted restraints on exercising their own economic powers to benefit from a rule-bound international economic order,[43] including WTO, ICSID, European Union, and many regional economic organizations. Considering WTO as an example, from WTO's achievements in three major functions, negotiating trade issues, supervising existing trade agreements, and settling trade disputes,[44] one can find the progress made by WTO with regards to law-making, law-enforcing, law-abiding, which is a development from "power-oriented" to "rule-oriented".[45] The WTO represents international rule of law on the multilateral trading system as a global public good, especially its dispute settlement system. The WTO has played an important role

[38] See Christian J Tams and James Sloan, The Development of International Law by the International Court of Justice (Oxford University Press, 2013) 3–5.

[39] See Christian J Tams and James Sloan, The Development of International Law by the International Court of Justice (Oxford University Press, 2013).

[40] International Court of Justice, Press Release, The International Court of Justice has a central role to play in the promotion of the rule of law, the President of the Court affirms before the United Nations General Assembly, No. 2010/35, October 29, 2015.

[41] International Court of Justice, Press Release, The International Court of Justice has a central role to play in the promotion of the rule of law, the President of the Court affirms before the United Nations General Assembly, No. 2010/35, October 29, 2015.

[42] Katharina Pistor, "Advancing the Rule of Law: Report on the International Rule of Law Symposium Convened by the American Bar Association November 9–10, 2005" (2007) 25 Berkeley Journal of International Law 7, at 11.

[43] See Katharina Pistor, "Advancing the Rule of Law: Report on the International Rule of Law Symposium Convened by the American Bar Association November 9–10, 2005" (2007) 25 Berkeley Journal of International Law 7, at 11.

[44] See William J. Davey, "The WTO and Rules-Based Dispute Settlement: Historical Evolution, Operational Success and Future Challenges" (2014) 17(3) Journal of International Economic Law 679.

[45] See John H. Jackson, "The Crumbling Institutions of the Liberal Trade System" (1978) 12 Journal of World Trade Law 93, at 99; John H. Jackson, The Jurisprudence of GATT and the WTO: Insights on Treaty Law and Economic Relations (Cambridge University Press, 2000) 6–10.

in safeguarding international rule of law related to international trade, although the Appellate Body went out of action on December 10, 2019, for a well-known reason.

Being confined to the purpose and theme of this research, the present author will not indulge in a lengthy examination of the practice of international rule of law in all areas of international law, although the international rule of law has already materialized in various fields of international law. As a whole, suffice it to say that nobody can deny that international rule of law illuminates the international community's development direction, and no one should repudiate that the international rule of law is the only way to achieve permanent peace in the world.[46] "[T]he importance of the international rule of law is routinely affirmed by governments, international organizations, scholars, and activists".[47]

It is imperative for some states to treat international rule of law seriously. As the chief designer, the US founded the framework of international rule of law after World War II. Therefore, traditionally, the US is the most prominent defender of the international rule of law. However, a historic regression occurred during the Trump administration following his denouncement and impediment of the international rule of law. However, the leading international law scholar in the US criticized this behavior of going against the trend of the times. For example, it is believed that "[i]t might be better for the stability of US foreign relations if presidential withdrawal authority were subject to greater constraints".[48]

In fact, two hundred years ago, the US represented the tradition of deference to international law. In Murray v. Schooner Charming Betsy,[49] Chief Justice John Marshall stated that "an act of Congress ought never to be construed to violate the law of nations if any other possible construction remains." From then on, the Charming Betsy canon or presumption has influenced the US's attitude and standing to international law. According to this doctrine, federal statutes should be interpreted in harmony with international law; in other words, US law should be consistent with international law or at least not inconsistent with international law.

The international rule of law that the US Trump administration understood is different from that of China because the former emphasized that U.S. interests were a priority. China adheres to the international rule of law based on the purposes and

---

46 In addressing a perpetual peace between states, Kant Immanuel did not use the phrase of "international rule of law", but he indeed mentioned that "peace between neighboring States-which can only be furnished under conditions that are regulated by Law". See Immanuel Kant, Perpetual Peace: A Philosophical Sketch (1795), available at <http://fs2.american.edu/dfagel/www/Class%20Readings/Kant/Immanuel%20Kant,%20_Perpetual%20Peace_.pdf>.

47 Lan Hurd, "What is the International Rule of Law?", in Javier Solana and Angel Saz-Carranza (eds.), The Global Context: How Politics, Investment and Institutions Impact European Business (ESADEgeo-Center for Global Economy and Geopolitics, 2016), Charter 8, at 149.

48 Curtis A Bradley, "Exiting Congressional-Executive Agreements" (2018) 67 Duke Law Journal 1615–1645; Justin Hughes, An "America First" Presidency, International Rule of Law and the Charming Betsy Doctrine. Loyola Law School, Los Angeles Legal Studies Research Paper, 2017–16.

49 See Murray v. Schooner Charming Betsy, 6 U.S. 64, 2 L.Ed.208 (1804), available at <https://supreme.justia.com/cases/federal/us/6/64/>.

principles of the Charter of the United Nations and increasingly emphasizes the international rule of law.[50] It can be said that China is a leading advocate of international rule of law in today's world. China's leaders emphasize the international rule of law on various occasions.[51] Both China's performance in the United Nations and the WTO show that China abides by the international rule of law in the international political and economic fields.[52] Moreover, China is making its individual contribution to the development and improvement of the international rule of law. For example, China has put forward the concept of a "Community with a Shared Future for Mankind" intending to conceptualize the development of international rule of law. China also attempts to develop the BRI within the framework of the international rule of law. Both the Community with a Shared Future for Mankind and the BRI have received United Nations' support. In the context of global governance reform, China is striving to promote the construction of the international rule of law and advocates that the international rule of law should play an important role in global governance in a just, reasonable, and effective way. From the Five Principles of Peaceful Coexistence[53] to win–win cooperation under the idea of a Community with a Shared Future for Mankind, both are the pillars of China's concept on international rule of law and public products provided by China to the international community.

Regarding the impact of China and other BRICS countries on international rule of law, it is considered that the activities of "BRICS countries and other rising powers represent qualitative as well as quantitative progress".[54] However, some scholars mistakenly believe that BRICS countries such as China simply uphold traditional norms of national sovereignty and non-intervention, thus having not promoted the development of international law, and it is the conservatism of rising countries that

[50] See Yi Wang, China: A Staunch Defender and Builder of the International Rule of Law (Oxford University Press, 2014); Jielong Duan, "Statement on the Rule of Law at the National and International Levels" (2007) 6(1) Chinese Journal of International Law 185–188; Jovanović, Miodrag A., "Responsibility to Protect and the International Rule of Law" (2015) 14(4) Chinese Journal of International Law 757–776.

[51] See Zhenmin Liu, "Following the Five Principles of Peaceful Coexistence and Jointly Building a Community of Common Destiny" (2014) 13(3) Chinese Journal of International Law 477–480; Zhenmin Liu, "Laying the Foundations of Peace and Stability for an Asian Community of Shared Destiny" (2014) 49 Chinese International Studies 17–26; Jiaxuan Tang, "Work Together for Peace, Prosperity and a Beautiful Future" (2014) 49 China International Studies 5–16; Yi Wang, "Peaceful Development and the Chinese Dream of National Rejuvenation" (2014) 44 China International Studies 18–44.

[52] See Burnay, Matthieu, Chinese Perspectives on the International Rule of Law: Law and Politics in the One-Party State (Edward Elgar Publishing, 2018).

[53] The Five Principles include: mutual respect for territorial integrity and sovereignty; mutual non-aggression; non-intervention in each other's internal affairs; equality and mutual benefit; peaceful coexistence. They are guiding principle put forward by Prime Minister Zhou Enlai in 1953 and utilized by China to deal with the foreign relations between China and other states.

[54] Aniruddha Rajput, "The BRICS as 'Rising Powers' and the Development of International Law", in Heike Krieger, Georg Nolte, and Andreas Zimmermann, The International Rule of Law: Rise or Decline? (Oxford University Press, 2019) 105–124, at 124.

makes it increasingly difficult to adopt new international law.[55] The present author disagrees with this argument because the ongoing efforts and contributions made by rising countries, especially China, to the development of international law are not ignorable. China has experienced distrusting the international rule of law to accept it and transforming unreasonable parts of the existing international rule of law.

Simply put, international rule of law is not imaginary but has changed from idea to reality in real international relations. The real problem is the scope and degree of the role of international rule of law, and different states have more or less different understandings of international rule of law. The worst thing is that when the international rule of law is insufficient to protect its interests and hegemony, some powerful states will not hesitate to sacrifice the international rule of law, even arbitrarily withdraw from the constraints of various international treaties and international organizations, and resort to unilateral use of power to deal with international relations. This practice at the expense of reputation undoubtedly shows that the international rule of law cannot progress smoothly, but the necessity and reality of the international rule of law in international relations cannot be eliminated. In contrast, it can only prove that the international rule of law is inadequate and predicts the future of international society moving toward the international rule of law. Most countries will obey the international rule of law out of a custom or a desire for peace and order. The international rule of law has a substantial protective effect on the economic development of all countries, and these countries would not hope the international rule of law to be destroyed entirely.

2.2 International Rule of Law as a Tool to Constrain Power

International rule of law affects states and international organizations by restricting their powers from the external. According to the origin of rule of law in different families of law, the original intention was to constrain the powers of the ruler, including the King and the State.[56] International scholarship on the international rule of law is diverse, but at the very heart of it, or the fundamental point in common, is considering international rule of law as a constraint on power. It is well established that

---

[55] See Simon Chesterman, "International Law and Its Others: Comment on Aniruddha Rajput", in Heike Krieger, Georg Nolte, and Andreas Zimmermann, The International Rule of Law: Rise or Decline? (Oxford University Press, 2019).

[56] In history, although other states also have the tradition of rule of law, and different traditions understand and emphasize different sides of rule of law, modern ideal on rule of law mostly comes from the Western countries. It can be said that the rule of law in English is achieved by the head of the King. According to British constitutional scholar AV Dicey, the rule of law refers to the "supremacy of the law". As a whole, the "instrumental limitations on the exercise of State authority" is essence of rule of law idea. See Dicey Albert Venn, Lectures Introductory to the Study of the Law of the Constitution (1st edition, Macmillan London, 1885) 171; generally, the notions of rule of law from the Germany and France which "focused on the nature of State, particularly on the role of constitutionalism" are more abstract and more difficult to grasp. See UN, "What is the Rule of Law", available at <http://www.unrol.org/article.aspx?n=What%20is%20the%20rule%20of%20law?>.

the international rule of law means controlling the arbitrary exercise of power or authority. The underlying intent of international rule of law is to tame power. The international rule of law means regulating the exercise of authority by states, international organizations, and other subjects of international law through international law.[57] Therefore, at the international level, power mainly refers to the power of the state and the power of international institutions. In the Declaration of the High-level Meeting of the General Assembly on the Rule of Law at the National and International Levels adopted in September 2012,[58] the General Assembly recognized that "the rule of law applies to all States equally, *and to international organizations, including the United Nations and its principal organs*".[59]

Jeremy Waldron's opinion that states are not the ultimate subjects of international law conflicts with traditional international law theory and is open to discussion, but his analogy analysis makes sense: government agencies and officials are subordinate to the law of the land, specifically, constitutional law and administrative law, as is similar to the subordination of sovereigns to international law at the international level. In other words, officials and municipal agencies are analogous to international institutions and nation-states in international law.[60] The exercise of power must be in good faith, fairly, reasonably, and without exceeding the limits of such power. This understanding is instructive to this research.

2.2.1 Attributes of International Rule of Law as a Tool to Constrain Power

Both national and international rules of law play a role in restrictions on public powers. "[T]he exercise of public powers should be based upon authority conferred by law and must be controlled by law", and conversely, "the rule of law requires that public powers cannot set or change the law at will".[61] If the public powers

[57] See Machiko Kanetake, "The Interfaces between the National and International Rule of Law: A Framework Paper", in Machiko Kanetake and André Nollkaemper (eds.), The Rule of Law at the National and International Levels: Contestations and Deference (Hart Publishing, 2015); Amsterdam Center for International Law No. 2014–27, Amsterdam Law School Research Paper No. 2014–44, footnote 5.

[58] See UN General Assembly Resolution adopted on September 24, 2012, "Declaration of the High-level Meeting of the General Assembly on the Rule of Law at the National and International Levels" UN Doc. A/RES/67/1, November 30, 2012, available at <https://www.un.org/ruleoflaw/files/37839_A-RES-67-1.pdf>.

[59] UN General Assembly Resolution adopted on September 24, 2012, "Declaration of the High-level Meeting of the General Assembly on the Rule of Law at the National and International Levels" UN Doc. A/RES/67/1, November 30, 2012, para. 2, available at <https://www.un.org/ruleoflaw/files/37839_A-RES-67-1.pdf>.

[60] See Jeremy Waldron, "Are Sovereigns Entitled to the Benefit of the International Rule of Law" (2011) 22(2) European Journal of International Law 315–343, at 329.

[61] See André Nollkaemper, National Courts and the International Rule of Law (Oxford University Press, 2011) 3–5.

contravene their legal obligation, the rule of law requires that public powers are accountable based on law.

The classical theory of rule of law divides rule of law into formal rule of law and substantive rule of law.[62] The corresponding theory is called "thin" formalistic rule of law theory and "thick" substantive rule of law theory. The former "emphasizes the formally instrumental limitations on the exercise of state power" and formal features of the law. The latter "incorporates substantive notions of justice, fairness and human right",[63] and the substantive rule of law comprises a set of elements, such as "protection of human rights", "specific forms of organized government", or "particular economic arrangements such as free-market capitalism".[64]

Although different social structures at the international and domestic levels will not allow us to equate international rule of law to national rule of law, the analogy or application of the classification of formal rule of law and substantive rule of law is still helpful to understand and clarify international rule of law. Combining formal rule of law and substantive rule of law can better play the role of controlling power.

For international rule of law, Charles Sampford suggested adopting qualities from the "thin" theory, such as clarity, predictability, consistency, effectiveness, and stability[65]; at the same time, no State should be above the law, thus States should recognize and comply with international law, including the decisions of independent judicial institutions.[66] It is acknowledged that the invention and the purpose of Western scholarship on rule of law are to push the development of these values or aspects in the name of the rule of law. Primarily, it seems that the substantive rule of law is open-ended, and many important and well-recognized values can be input into it. The elements that form part of the rule of law are open to debate and become more controversial in the field of international rule of law. However, at least some fundamental elements should be part of international rule of law.

International rule of law also requires normative law, which is necessary to regulate power. In other words, the prerequisite of norm compliance is that the law possesses normativity. The international rule of law can provide predictability and enhance the freedom of individual actors. "The rule of law secures fixed points of reference by stabilizing social relationships and providing them with predictability. In this way,

---

[62] See Dicey Albert Venn, Lectures Introductory to the Study of the Law of the Constitution (1st edition, Macmillan London, 1885); Paul Craig, "Formal and Substantive Conceptions of the Rule of Law: An Analytical Framework in Public law" (1997) Public Law 467; Brian Z. Tamanaha, On the Rule of Law: History, Politics, Theory (Cambridge University Press, 2004) 91, Chaps. 7–9.

[63] Simon Chesterman, "'Unqualified Human Good' or a Bit of 'Ruling-Class Chatter', The Rule of Law at the National and International Level", in Vesselin Popovski (ed.), International Rule of Law and Professional Ethics (Ashgate, 2014) 19–48.

[64] Simon Chesterman, "An International Rule of Law?" (2008) 56(2) American Journal of Comparative Law 331–361, at 342–343.

[65] See Charles Sampford, "'Thin Theories' of the Domestic and International Rule of Law", in Vesselin Popovski (ed.), International Rule of Law and Professional Ethics (Ashgate, 2014) 49–76.

[66] See Charles Sampford, "Professions without Border: Global Ethics and the International Rule of Law", in Vesselin Popovski (ed.), International Rule of Law and Professional Ethics (Ashgate, 2014) 129–147.

the international rule of law protects and enhances the freedom of various actors, creating a predictable environment in which actors can make meaningful choices."[67]

In the present author's opinion, international rule of law requires rules to be laid down clearly in advance. The importance of legal normativity, certainty, determinacy, and predictability is not less important to international rule of law than to national rule of law. Whether states and international institutions exercising regulatory power or private institutions who are protected, all expect to clearly know the boundary of their power and the scope of their obligations, as well as what protections they can rely on. Whether it is due to the coerciveness of international law, trust in international law, the habit of observing norms, the awareness of being a good actor, or for broader and long-term self-interest, international law, including unfavorable awards, has largely complied with.

It is of the realization that the nature of international law as public law only determines if there is no unambiguous provision to delegate some authorities, the State as the major subject of international law cannot exercise these powers; thus, the normative requirements on international law are not so stringent.[68] This argument is open to discussion. The formal international rule of law requests international law itself to strengthen normativity. International society pays more attention to concluding treaties to clarify vague customary international law. If the treaty per se is increasingly normative, both can be regarded as the process of advancing international rule of law with a complete system and proper form. In particular, "the emergence of a normative regime that touches individuals directly" demands normativity.[69]

The aspirations of justice and fairness associated with the rule of law are widely shared, although the concept of the rule of law is difficult to define and understood differently due to its broad and indefinite meaning. This idea should be incorporated into international rule of law as the requirements for both substantive and procedure law.

Finally, in the present author's opinion, international law can also be "good law" or "bad law", "legitimate law", or "illegitimate law". The latter can be challenged, amended, or abolished. Only the "good law" should be complied with. The basic benchmark of international rule of law must be "good international law" to realize "good global governance" through international organizations and institutions. "Good law" means "good values" should be contained or embodied in the law, as is the substantive requirement of international rule of law. At the international level, the justice and protection of individual rights at the national level can evolve into protecting human rights, peace, and promotion of development. Within the UN, the values of human rights, economic development, peace, and security are carried

[67] Matthias Kumm, "International Law in National Courts: The International Rule of Law and the Limits of the Internationalist Model" (2003) 44(19) Virginia Journal of International Law 25–26.

[68] See Jeremy Waldron, "Are Sovereigns Entitled to the Benefit of the International Rule of Law" (2011) 22(2) European Journal of International Law 315–343.

[69] See Simon Chesterman, "An International Rule of Law?" (2008) 56(2) American Journal of Comparative Law 331–361, at 355–356; Simon Chesterman, "'Unqualified Human Good' or some 'Ruling-Class Chatter', The Rule of Law at the National and International Level", in Vesselin Popovski (ed.), International Rule of Law and Professional Ethics (Ashgate, 2014) 19–48.

out by different organs, such as the UDHR, UNDP, UN Security Council, and ICJ. Concretely, in the international investment rule of law, corresponding values should include the protection of property rights of investors, promotion of sustainable development of the host state, and maintenance of peace through peaceful settlement of investment.

William W. Bishop's understandings of the international rule of law have laid a foundation for subsequent scholarship. He believes the concept of international rule of law "includes reliance on law as opposed to arbitrary power in international relations, the substitution of settlement by law for settlement by force; and the realization that law can and should be used as an instrumentality for the cooperative international furtherance of social aims, in such fashion as to preserve and promote the values of freedom and human dignity for individuals."[70] In effect, this definition combines formal rule of law and substantive rule of law and takes the former as a tool to realize the latter. Therefore, most discourses on this topic have not separated themselves from this basic understanding. The international rule of law requires good values.

This kind of external restriction from the international rule of law is favorable to a certain extent for a state. Take the development of South Africa and China as an example. In South Africa, "GDP per capita declined 22% from 2011 to 2018", and "[t]he decline correlates with a marked increase in economic regulation and maladministration".[71] In contrast, after China's reform and opening up in 1978, especially after China acceded WTO, it has been integrating the international rule of law, forcing the introduction and improvement of the national rule of law to be consistent with the international rule of law to enhance governance practices under pressures. China's foreign investment law has strengthened the restrictions on state power,[72] which to some extent reflects the requirements of the international investment rule of law.

2.2.2 *Constraint on State Power*

From the perspective of public law, it is argued that "the rule of law should be understood as a concept with at least two core elements: the control of power and law, and these elements are included in any view on the rule of law".[73] The two elements

---

[70] William W. Bishop, "The International Rule of Law" (1960–1961) 59 Michigan Law Review 553, at 553.

[71] André Thomashausen, China in Africa, available at <www.legesmundi.com>.

[72] Foreign Investment Law of the People's Republic of China, Order No. 26 of the President of the People's Republic of China, laws, issued on March 15, 2019, entered into force on January 1, 2020. For example, in article 1, it provides that "regulating the administration of foreign investment", and in article 4, it provides that "The state applies the administrative system of pre-establishment national treatment plus negative list to foreign investment".

[73] See Geranne Lautenbach, The Concept of the Rule of Law and the European Court of Human Rights (Oxford University Press, 2013) 19.

are related by legality, which means controlling governmental powers by law.[74] When we talk about international rule of law, nobody mentions the rule of law at the same time. In other words, the international rule of law cannot be understood without analogy with national rule of law even though complete copy or transplantation is unfeasible due to the different social structures, such as without a common superior legislature or a compulsory jurisdiction. "The two rest on unique historical and political foundations and consequently they operate very differently in practice", however, "the two have some features in common", for example, the choice of an actor will be made in light fixed rules in a rule-of-law system, both international rule of law and national rule of law.[75]

Therefore, an analogy approach with the domestic rule of law is reasonable to some extent, and some shared fundamental elements and values can be imported into the international level without barriers. The only difference is for international rule of law; the control of governmental power is from the external at the international level instead of the internal of a state at the national level. External law mainly refers to international law, including treaty, customary international law, and the "general principle of law recognized by civilized nations".[76] In summary, putting power behind the law instead of before the law is the key meaning of rule of law, both at the domestic and international levels. The state is the principal subject of international law and, accordingly, the main object constrained by international rule of law. Vesselin Popovski concludes that "the rule of law places the law above the executive and makes it a supreme governor".[77] For the international rule of law, legislative power, executive power, and judicial power of a state, all may be controlled.

From the perspective of State, that the authority is constrained means a State must comply with international law, as is based on *pacta sunt servanda* principle. "The conventional account of the international rule of law defines it in terms of the obligation on states to comply with their legal commitments".[78] Broadly speaking, the States comply with "their international legal obligations" or "their legal commitments" may stem from "a legal, political, and moral imperative".[79] Therefore,

---

[74] See Geranne Lautenbach, The Concept of the Rule of Law and the European Court of Human Rights (Oxford University Press, 2013) 1, 20.

[75] See Lan Hurd, "What is the International Rule of Law?", in Javier Solana and Angel Saz-Carranza (eds.), The Global Context: How Politics, Investment and Institutions Impact European Business (Esadegeo-Center for Global Economy and Geopolitics, 2016), Charter 8, at 152.

[76] For the sources of international law, see Statute of International Court of Justice, article38, 59 Stat. 1060 (1945), available at <https://www.icj-cij.org/en/statute>.

[77] Vesselin Popovski, "From Domestic to International Rule of Law: A Long and Unfinished Journey", in Vesselin Popovski (ed.), International Rule of Law and Professional Ethics (Ashgate, 2014) 5–18.

[78] Lan Hurd, "What is the International Rule of Law?", in Javier Solana and Angel Saz-Carranza (eds.), How Politics, Investment and Institutions Impact European Businesses (Esadegeo-Center for Global Economy and Geopolitics, 2016), Chap. 8, at 150.

[79] Lan Hurd, "What is the International Rule of Law?", in Javier Solana and Angel Saz-Carranza (eds.), The Global Context: How Politics, Investment and Institutions Impact European Business (Esadegeo-Center for Global Economy And Geopolitics, 2016) Charter 8, at 149; Guzman points out that "countries that decide against developing a strong reputation for compliance with international

States' compliance with commitments made by themselves is the basic aspect of international rule of law.

The UN Charter preamble expresses determination "to establish conditions under which justice and respect for the obligations arising from treaties and other sources of international law can be maintained".[80] This sentence stresses the notion of international rule of law is to abide by all kinds of obligations originating from different sources of international law. Therefore, the strengthening of international rule of law requires national implementation and compliance with international law.[81] The UN "requires participation and effective national implementation of international law's main bodies at the national and international levels. The UN rule of law activities aim to find better ways to support member States to achieve compliance with international obligations, ensure the domestic implementation of international norms and standards, and, most critically, strengthen the institutions, policies, processes and conditions that ensure an effective and just national and international order".[82] In discussing the rule of law in the international legal order, it is submitted that "the rule of law requires compliance by the state with its obligations in international law as in national law".[83] The international rule of law requires that actions conform to international law in international or transnational relations between States or between a State and a foreigner. This connotes that a state's standard or model of conduct should conform to international law. Thus, international law should be reasonably well observed. Ian Brownlie also considers this a vital element of international rule of law.[84] The UN identifies international rule of law "as an international legal standard that is set for domestic legal systems".[85]

Thus, it can be deduced that domestic legal systems should be consistent with international legal standards as a means of compliance. In the present author's opinion, compliance is indeed a benchmark to measure or assess the level of international rule of law because the rule of law should not only be the "law in the books" but also be the "law in action".[86] International rule of law is mainly disregarded because public international law cannot be complied with on many occasions. Simon Chesterman

obligations choose short-term benefits over long-term gains", Guzman Andrew T, "A compliance based theory of international law" (2002) 90 California Law Review 1823–1887, at 1850.

80 UN Charter, preamble, para.3, available at <https://www.un.org/en/about-us/un-charter/preamble>.

81 See Report of the Secretary-General, "Delivering Justice: Programme of Action to Strengthen the Rule of Law at the National and International Levels", UN Doc. A/66/749, March 16, 2012, available at <https://www.un.org/ruleoflaw/files/SGreport%20eng%20A_66_749.pdf>.

82 Rule of law at the national and international levels, available at <http://www.unrol.org/article.aspx?article_id=25>.

83 Tom Bingham, The Rule of Law (Allen Lane, 2010) 110.

84 See Ian Brownlie, The Rule of Law in International Affairs: International Law at the Fiftieth Anniversary of the United Nations (Martinus Nijhoff Publishers, 1998) 79.

85 Geranne Lautenbach, The Concept of the Rule of Law and the European Court of Human Rights (Oxford University Press, 2013) 7.

86 See Simon Chesterman, "An International Rule of Law?" (2008) 56(2) American Journal of Comparative Law 331–361, at 345.

proposed that one of the possible meanings for the international rule of law can be the "privilege of international law over national law".[87] Furthermore, compliance can promote the realization of international rule of law.

"The UN is currently developing a common approach to strengthening the rule of law at the international level, which involves respect for the Charter of the United Nations and international law, and is premised on shared fundamental principles and values long supported by member States".[88] States expressly embraced the objective of an international rule of law at the 2005 World Summit and in subsequent United Nations General Assembly Resolutions.[89] At present, the measures adopted by the UN to promote international rule of law to govern state-to-state relations are very primary to "distill common divisors". These fundamental principles and values, for the most part, are international rules involving international peace, safety, fundamental human rights, and freedom.

On the other hand, the difference between international rule of law and national rule of law lies in external and internal constraints. One typical case is that these human rights "treaties set limits on the manner in which governmental power may be exercised, and independent legal procedures have been set, and they provide a form of external control".[90] Therefore, the enhancement of national rule of law is conducive to making international rule of law come true. The so-called international rule of law should include the extension of national rule of law at the international level. Simply put, a prerequisite and foundation for complying with international rule of law are to improve national rule of law. Therefore, the UN devotes itself to assisting some countries in advancing their national rule of law. As far as the level of rule of law is concerned, there exists a gap between developed and developing countries. "In the former, the rule of law has become almost standardized, with specific institutional features, including an independent judiciary, an independent and fairly autonomous private bar, and a set of formal rules that are announced in advance and enforced impartially. In the latter countries, the precise institutional form of the rule of law is still in the making."[91] Therefore, the UN provides a postconflict state with the

---

[87] Simon Chesterman, "An International Rule of Law?" (2008) 56(2) American Journal of Comparative Law 331–361, at 355.

[88] Rule of law at the national and international levels (Agenda item 82), resolution 68/116, General Assembly of the United Nations Legal-Sixth Committee, available at <http://www.un.org/en/ga/sixth/69/rule_of_law.shtml>; also available at <http://www.unrol.org/article.aspx?article_id=25>.

[89] See 2005 World Summit Outcome, UNGA Res 60/1 (October 24, 2005) UN Doc A/RES/60/1 [134], available at <https://www.un.org/en/development/desa/population/migration/generalassembly/docs/globalcompact/A_RES_60_1.pdf>; UNGA Res 63/128 (January 15, 2009) UN Doc A/RES/63/128, available at <https://www.un.org/ruleoflaw/files/A-RES-63-128.pdf> ; UNSC Presidential Statement (June 22, 2006) S/PRST/2006/28, available at <https://www.securitycouncilreport.org/atf/cf/%7B65BFCF9B-6D27-4E9C-8CD3-CF6E4FF96FF9%7D/IJ%20SPRST%202,006%2028.pdf>.

[90] Geranne Lautenbach, The Concept of the Rule of Law and the European Court of Human Rights (Oxford University Press, 2013) 2.

[91] See Katharina Pistor, "Advancing the Rule of Law: Report on the International Rule of Law Symposium Convened by the American Bar Association November 9–10, 2005" (2007) 25 Berkeley Journal of International Law 7.

assistance of drafting a rule of law-based constitution, and its main strategy is to encourage and assist states in incorporating international standards.[92] In addition, in some cases, national courts also contribute to the maintenance of international rule of law by providing judicial control over the exercises of public powers that may conflict with international law.

The further issue arising from compliance is with regard to the relation between international law and national law. Should national law have some room? From a national law perspective, Vesselin Popovski infers and considers that the international rule of law cannot be understood as "the supremacy of obligations from international law above those from domestic law, enshrined in modern constitutions".[93] This argument has some reasonable grounds and is founded on the overall supremacy of the constitution within the national legal system.

Concerning the relation between international law and national law, many countries' constitutions expressly stipulate the supremacy of the constitution.[94] Generally, the hierarchy is the constitution, legislative treaty, and national law.[95] Certainly, with regard to those countries that stipulate national law prevails over international law, this kind of stipulation may only produce legal effects within their national legal system and at the international level, the supremacy of national law may trigger international responsibility. Nevertheless, the vigilance against international law and the intention of keeping power in hand is clear. It can also be inferred that the constraint of international rule of law on national power has its limits.

A state may evade or withdraw from international rule of law out of national policy consideration. National courts may also not defer to international rule of law out of respect for the constitution and the executive's discretionary power.[96] It is

---

[92] See Laura Grenfell, "The UN and 'Rule-Of-Law Constitutions'" (2012) Working Paper no 1.6, Centre for International Governance and Justice, Canberra, 1–25, at 1.

[93] Vesselin Popovski, "From Domestic to International Rule of Law: A Long and Unfinished Journey", in Vesselin Popovski (ed.), International Rule of Law and Professional Ethics (Ashgate, 2014) 5–18, at 11.

[94] For example, South African Constitution stipulates the Supremacy of Constitution, that is, "This Constitution is the supreme law of the Republic; law or conduct inconsistent with it is invalid, and the obligations imposed by it must be fulfilled." See Constitution of the Republic of South Africa, No. 108 of 1996, article 2, available at <https://www.gov.za/documents/constitution/constitution-republic-south-africa-1996-1>.

[95] For example, besides the Supremacy of Constitution, South African Constitution stipulates that unless an international agreement is a technical, administrative, or executive nature, an international agreement binds the Republic only after it has been approved by resolution in both the National Assembly and the National Council of Provinces. Thus, the status of this kind of treaty is equal to an Act of Parliament. In addition, the customary international law only is law in the republic when it is consistent with the Constitution or an Act of Parliament. Therefore, its status is inferior. See Constitution of the Republic of South Africa, No. 108 of 1996, articles 231, 232, available at <https://www.gov.za/documents/constitution/constitution-republic-south-africa-1996-1>.

[96] See Machiko Kanetake, "The Interfaces between the National and International Rule of Law: A Framework Paper", in Kanetake, Machiko and André Nollkaemper (eds.), The Rule of Law at the National and International Levels: Contestations and Deference (Hart Publishing, 2015); Amsterdam Center for International Law No. 2014–27, Amsterdam Law School Research Paper No. 2014–44.

on record that international courts and tribunals have never decided if a constitution violates international law. In the present author's opinion, this does not presume a one-sided international law constitutionalist view is inappropriate, or domestic courts simply as enforcement tools for the international rule of law may be problematic, as it tends to leave the politics behind the international rule of law unchecked.[97] However, it connotes that international treaties and awards should seriously consider public policy and room for states' public policy.

History and reality make clear that a young nation cherishes sovereignty to a higher degree.

> It is true, of course, that there seems to be a sort of law of nature which decrees that the younger a nation is the more nationalistic it is. However, the newer nations of the world are developing and changing rapidly, and the extent to which they change in the direction of accepting the limitations that international rule of law places upon unrestrained sovereignty will depend to a considerable extent on the degree to which they are convinced that this principle is one of their own making and not something imposed from outside.[98]

In the same way, a state may either refuse international intercourse entirely or accept international rule of law to constrain its power by exercising sovereignty out of its own free will. The prime role of international rule of law is to constrain government power and requires power to be exercised within the law. Without a doubt, this constraint is still limited.

2.2.3 *Restraint of International Institutions' Power*

International rule of law can be a limitation of national rule of law to a greater or lesser extent. The national-level shortcomings can sometimes be overcome by supra-national institutions or state–state organizations, including regional or international levels. Although it is member States to create an international organization, the international organization can play the role of administrating its member States and affecting privates through its norms and proceedings.[99] The inherent implication of international rule of law is that international organizations' power must also be controlled. At the international level, "appropriate rules of international law apply to the *Organization* as they do to States".[100]

---

[97] About the concern that international rule of law may disregard national politics. See, e.g., Mattias Kumm, "International Law in National Courts: The International Rule of Law and the Limits of the Internationalist Model" (2003) 44 Virginia Journal of International Law 19.

[98] Larson, Arthur, The International Rule of Law (The Institute for International Order, 1961) 28.

[99] See Sabino Cassese, "Administrative Law without the State? The Challenge of Global Regulation" (2005) 37 New York University Journal of International Law and Politics 663.

[100] "What is the rule of law?", available at <http://www.unrol.org/article.aspx?n=What%20is%20the%20rule%20of%20law?>.

International organizations possess international personality, which is often included explicitly in the text of a treaty or constitutive instrument.[101] They have their political and judicial organs. This implies that the UN Security Council, as the political organ of the UN and that the ICJ, as the judicial organ of the UN, is subject to international rule of law. Nothing contained in the UN Charter shall authorize the UN to intervene in matters which are essentially within the domestic jurisdiction of any state except the application of enforcement measures under its Chapter VII and UN Security Council decisions are also constrained by norms of *ius cogens*.[102] The ICJ is considered a form of international public authority[103]; therefore, it should also be regulated.

In addition, for disputes within the UN, the UN Administrative Tribunal was established by the UN General Assembly Resolution 351A (IV) of November 24, 1949. It is an independent organ competent to hear and pass judgment upon applications alleging non-observance of contracts or terms of employment by staff members of the UN Secretariat. The President of the ICJ, H.E. Judge Hisashi Owada, has stated that "the rule of law now pervades every aspect of the activities of the United Nations, from the sustenance of peace and security to the protection of human rights, from the fight against poverty to the protection of the global environment, including the case of climate change".[104] This implies that when exercising authority, the UN complies with rule of law and their power is regulated.

Within some regional organizations of economic integration, the control of power is stricter than that of the UN. For example, "The court of European Economic Community, in addition to its jurisdiction of disputes between member States, has jurisdiction of appeals by individuals or companies against decision of organs of the community on certain grounds".[105] In the same vein, the Court of Justice of the European Union, as the European Economic Community court's successor, plays a judicial review to the EU's executive organ.

"International institutions", as a concept in a broader sense, include formal international organizations, as well as international courts,[106] although, in effect, not all international courts and tribunals have international personality.

---

[101] The UN's legal personality was established by the International Court of Justice (ICJ) in Reparation for Injuries Suffered in the Service of the United Nations (Advisory Opinion) ([1949] ICJ Rep 173).

[102] See Charter of the United Nations, signed on June 26, 1945, came into force on October 24, 1945, articles 1.7, 103.

[103] See Armin von Bogdandy and Ingo Venzke, "Beyond Dispute: International Judicial Institutions as Law-makers" (2011) 12(5) German Law Journal 979, 981.

[104] International Court of Justice, Press Release, The International Court of Justice has a central role to play in the promotion of the rule of law, the President of the Court affirms before the United Nations General Assembly, No. 2010/35, October 29, 2015.

[105] Larson, Arthur, The International Rule of Law (The Institute for International Order, 1961) 55.

[106] See Machiko Kanetake, "The Interfaces between the National and International Rule of Law: A Framework Paper", Amsterdam Center for International Law No. 2014–27, Amsterdam Law School Research Paper No. 2014–44, fn21. According to Machiko Kanetake, the difference between international organization and international institution lies in whether international personality is possessed.

In any case, by an extension of the above logic, other international courts and tribunals, with international personality or not, their authorities, should be controlled similarly. International institutions need to be more constrained by rules and procedures in exercising their delegated authority. The rule of law within these international institutions has received more attention than in the past.

Under the ICJ Statute, "the court shall be composed of a body of independent judges, elected regardless of their nationality from among persons of high moral character, who possess the qualifications required in their respective countries for appointment to the highest judicial office or are juris consults of recognized competence in international law in order to guarantee the independence and equity.[107] Additionally, the persons to be elected should "individually possess the qualifications required but also that in the body as a whole, the representation of the main forms of civilization and the principal legal systems of the world should be assured".[108]

From the outside, the international institution itself is bounded by all kinds of international actors. For example, a state may decide not to enforce the decision of an international court or tribunal on the ground of injustice because judgment compliance depends on the independence and fairness of the decision. An NGO can unexpectedly affect the conduct of an international institution.

William W. Bishop stressed the significant aspect that international rule of law is the situation of one or more governments as parties to the dispute, including "a dispute between an individual (or corporation) and a foreign government, or between the governments of two or more nations".[109] In fact, the further theoretical issue is the need for an independent dispute settlement body to solve the dispute impartially, as is the requirement of the international rule of law. However, William W. Bishop did not explore this issue anymore.

Jeremy Waldron develops an analogy between government authorities under municipal law and sovereign states under international law. He argues that individual national sovereigns must fulfill governmental functions in the international law

---

As for international institutions, a still broader definition is "sets of rules that stipulate the ways in which states should cooperate and compete with each other"; see John J. Mearsheimer, "The False Promise of International Institutions" (1994–1995) 19(3) International Security 5–49. For the purpose of this research, this broad definition is not adopted. In the present author's opinion, the "institution" is a word with broad meaning; it may mean an organization, a system, or a custom. As for international institutional law, see Henry G. Schermers and Niels Blokker, International Institutional Law (4th edition, Martinus Nijhoff, 2003); Jan Klabbers, An Introduction to International Institutional Law (Cambridge University Press, 2002); Nigel D. White, The Law of International Organizations (2nd edition, Manchester University Press, 2005); René-Jean Dupuy ed., Handbook on International Organizations (Springer, 1988).

[107] Statute of the International Court of Justice, article 2, available at <http://www.icj-cij.org/documents/?p1=4&p2=2>.

[108] Statute of the International Court of Justice, article 9, available at <http://www.icj-cij.org/documents/?p1=4&p2=2>.

[109] William W. Bishop, "The International Rule of Law" (1960–1961) 59 Michigan Law Review 553, 554.

regime because there is no world government.[110] As a result of this inexact analogy, at the international level, the power of sovereignty should also be restricted. This inference can also be applied to international institutions if they perform governmental functions.

The global administrative law school of thought led by Benedict Kingsbury argues that "global governance" is performed in all kinds of forms by regulatory regimes such as intergovernmental regulatory bodies and informal intergovernmental regulatory networks and is a kind of administrative action in nature. Therefore, such activity itself should be regulated by administrative law-type principles, rules, and mechanisms, particularly those relating to participation, transparency, accountability, and review, to ensure the legality and legitimacy of "global governance".[111] Therefore, all international institutions must abide by transparency, participation, review, and the rule of law when making regulatory decisions.[112] Although the theory of global administrative law does not use the phrase "international rule of law" and puts too extensive governing subjects under global administrative law, it shows that the powers of international institutions themselves should be restricted. The requirements of the rule of law itself, such as participation, transparency, and clarity, are being strengthened. It is put forward that transparency can bring impartiality and objectivity, in turn, legitimacy.

Armin von Bogdandy and his school of thought construct their theoretical system through other categories or concepts, such as "international public authority" and "Publicness of Public International Law", and "the constitutionalization of international law",[113] but he also argues that the exercise of public authority at the international level through all kinds of institutions or instruments, including general instruments and instruments concerning individuals and individual states, should be

---

[110] See Jeremy Waldron, "Are Sovereigns Entitled to the Benefit of the International Rule of Law" (2011) 22(2) European Journal of International Law 315–343, 316.

[111] See Nico Krisch and Benedict Kingsbury, Introduction: Global Governance and Global Administrative Law in the International Legal Order, (2006)17(1) European Journal of International Law 1–13; Benedict Kingsbury, What, How and Who Should Public International Law Regulate? New Problems of Global Administrative Governance in the Lecture Series of the United Nations Audiovisual Library of International Law. All documents are available at <www.iilj.org/GAL/default.asp>.

[112] See Benedict Kingsbury, Nico Krisch and Richard B. Stewart, "The Emergence of Global Administrative Law" (2005) 68 Law and Contemporary Problems 15.

[113] See Armin von Bogdandy and Ingo Venzke, "In Whose Name? An Investigation of International Courts' Public Authority and Its Democratic Justification" (2012) 23(1) European Journal of International Law 7–41; Armin von Bogdandy and Ingo Venzke, In whose name? A Public Law Theory of International Adjudication (Oxford University Press, 2014); Armin von Bogdandy, "Developing the Publicness of Public International Law: Towards a Legal Framework for Global Governance Activities", in Armin von Bogdandy, etc. (eds.), The Exercise of Public Authority by International Institutions: Advancing International Institutional Law (Springer Science and Business Media, 2010); Armin von Bogdandy, "General Principles of International Public Authority: Sketching a Research Field", in Armin von Bogdandy, etc. (eds.), The Exercise of Public Authority by International Institutions: Advancing International Institutional Law (Springer Science and Business Media, 2010).

controlled. The reason "that any kind of governance activity by international institutions, be it administrative or intergovernmental, should be considered as an exercise of international public authority" and be controlled because it may determine "individuals, private associations, enterprises, states, or other public institutions",[114] It is necessary "to find out how, and by whom, they are controlled, and to develop legal standards for ensuring that they satisfy contemporary expectations for legitimacy".[115]

Although the above schools of thought address the same global governance phenomena, the latter is more comprehensive because it explores the issue from a public law perspective and utilizes "constitutionalist, administrative and institutionalist thinking to focus on the phenomenon of public authority."[116] At the national law, the rule of law is a fundamental principle of administrative law and constitutional law; thus, it seems not to be enough to only consider global governance as an administrative law action.

International rule of law and accountability should be established to exercise authority by states and international institutions. Both Chesterman and William Bishop emphasize that international rule of law can be understood as the application of rule of law principles instead of arbitrary power to international relations; in a similar manner, power should be bounded by law.

In short, international rule of law should not be a rhetorical device but an important tool to restrain sovereign power and the power of international institutions. The international authority exercised by international institutions should be regulated.[117]

2.3 International Rule of Law as a Tool to Protect Private Rights

On the premise that both states and international institutions are the object controlled by international rule of law, Jeremy Waldron argues that individuals instead of states

---

114 See Armin von Bogdandy, "Developing the Publicness of Public International Law: Towards a Legal Framework for Global Governance Activities", in Armin von Bogdandy, etc. (eds.), The Exercise of Public Authority by International Institutions: Advancing International Institutional Law (Springer Science & Business Media, 2010) 5.

115 Armin von Bogdandy, "Developing the Publicness of Public International Law: Towards a Legal Framework for Global Governance Activities", in Armin von Bogdandy, etc. (eds.), The Exercise of Public Authority by International Institutions: Advancing International Institutional Law (Springer Science & Business Media, 2010) 4.

116 Armin von Bogdandy, "Developing the Publicness of Public International Law: Towards a Legal Framework for Global Governance Activities", in Armin von Bogdandy, etc. (eds.), The Exercise of Public Authority by International Institutions: Advancing International Institutional Law (Springer Science & Business Media, 2010) 26.

117 See Machiko Kanetake, "The Interfaces between the National and International Rule of Law: A Framework Paper", in Machiko Kanetake and André Nollkaemper (eds.), The Rule of Law at the National and International Levels: Contestations and Deference (Hart Publishing, 2015); Amsterdam Center for International Law No. 2014–27, Amsterdam Law School Research Paper No. 2014–44, 6.

are entitled to benefit from the international rule of law.[118] Indeed, the other side of controlling power is to protect private rights, or the ultimate purpose of controlling power is to protect private rights. The presumption of no obligation on a private person is widely accepted because the private person is not regarded as the subject of international law.

However, the subsequent issue is, is there any obligation to those privates who are entitled to the benefit of the international rule of law? Nobody discusses this issue under the framework of traditional international rule of law, although the following understandings of national rule of law imply this point: "all persons and authorities within the state, whether public or private, should be bound by and entitled to the benefit of laws publicly made, taking effect (generally) in the future and publicly administered in the courts"[119]; "the minimum requirement of rule of law is that all actors, including both private individuals and the State, behave in accordance with the law".[120] Although they refer to the national rule of law, they should also connotate international rule of law.

In international investment law, it is reminded that for the private sector, "the notion of the rule of law is limited to security for investment, property rights, and contract enforcement. However, ...civil society and multinational organizations have broader concerns."[121] Therefore, private investors and other entities have different concerns. They stress the implications of the rule of law that they understand respectively, which is a reminder that the overall picture of international rule of law should be examined.

On the one hand, the private person is the beneficiary of international rule of law through the constraint to power, that is, the private person enjoys the legal right to be protected; in the same vein, the private person must perform certain legal obligations for his or her rights to be protected. For example, the embedded obligation in the legal right is that this right must be legitimate and legal. Likewise, the private person should carry out other legal obligations.

The rationale behind this opinion is that the relation between legal rights and legal obligations is a dialectical relation with the unity of opposites, and legal rights and legal obligations are mutually dependent instead of isolated existence and development. The legal rights reflect the value objectives of law directly, and the legal obligation guarantees the realization of value objectives and legal rights. The legal rights are the end, and the legal obligations are the means.[122] In other words, they

---

[118] See Jeremy Waldron, "Are Sovereigns Entitled to the Benefit of the International Rule of Law" (2011) 22(2) European Journal of International Law 315–343, 325–326.

[119] Tom Bingham, The Rule of Law (Allen Lane, 2010) 8.

[120] See Renáta Uitz, "The Rule of Law in Post-Communist Constitutional Jurisprudence", in Gianiluca Palombella and Neil Walker (eds.), Relocating the Rule of Law (Hart Publishing, 2009) 82.

[121] Katharina Pistor, "Advancing the Rule of Law: Report on the International Rule of Law Symposium Convened by the American Bar Association November 9–10, 2005" (2007) 25 Berkeley Journal of International Law 7, 35.

[122] See Wenxian Zhang, Jurisprudence (4th edition, Higher Education Press, 2012), Chap. 8, Right and Obligation.

are the two sides of a coin, and one cannot have one without the other. Just as Karl Marx said, "there is no any right without the corresponding obligation, and there is no any obligation without the accompanying right".[123] Consequently, nobody can only enjoy right without performing obligation. The private person has rights only in thus far as they are a correlative of obligation. It can also be said that the legal right is an end and the legal obligation is a means.

The legal right that is stipulated or recognized by law and defended or safeguarded by law is inviolable since the legal right must be exercised under the law and cannot be exercised by hook or crook. In turn, legal obligations set under the law, both action and omission are inherently and legally mandatory. A violation of legal obligation means legal liability. Furthermore, legal rights cannot be enjoyed without any limitation, whereas legal obligations cannot be assumed with any boundary.[124]

While national administrative law and constitutional law impose restrictions on governmental power, they stipulate that a private person must carry out corresponding obligations. The performance of a legal obligation is the prerequisite of enjoying legal rights. This is a general principle of modern administrative and constitutional law.

Generally, the concerned person has an administrative obligation to abide by administrative regulations, rules, administrative directives, or decisions as well as any other normative document issued by the administrative organ. The concerned person must assist the administrative organ in the performance of their official business and should therefore accept administrative supervision or comply with legal procedures. Failure to do so may otherwise result in the concerned person's request not being satisfied, even if some corresponding liability has to be assumed.

In most modern constitutions, similarly, citizens are required to perform certain obligations. Initially, the written constitution did not specify citizen obligation or duty. Starting from the constitutions during the French Revolution, the citizen obligation was juxtaposed into constitutional text.[125] German Weimar Constitution 1919 defined citizen obligations in detail.[126] Placing constitutional rights and obligations side by side is the outcome of social development and practical trial and error. Practice shows that it is difficult for the right without accompanying obligation to keep enduring. Accordingly, after World War II, numerous states imputed special chapters focusing on balancing citizens' rights and obligations in their constitutions. For example, the obligation or duty of citizens of the People's Republic of China is as follows: working; receiving an education; practicing family planning; safeguarding the unity of the country; abiding by the constitution and the law; safeguarding the security, honor, and interests of the motherland; defending the motherland and

---

[123] Central Compilation and Translation Bureau on Marx, Engels, Lenin and Stalin's Classic, Complete Works of Karl Marx and Frederick Engels, Vol. 16 (People's Publishing House, 1956) 16, available at <http://cpc.people.com.cn/GB/64184/180145/180182/10879028.html>.

[124] See Renbo Wang, and Liaoyuan Cheng, On the Rule of Law (Shandong Renmin Press, 1992) 174–175.

[125] See French Constitution of 1791, 1793, 1795.

[126] See Weimar Constitution 1919, Basic rights and obligations of the Germans, available at <http://www.zum.de/psm/weimar/weimar_vve.php#Basic rightsandobligationsoftheGermans>.

resisting aggression; paying taxes in accordance with the law.[127] In the same vein, the South African Constitution stipulates that "all citizens are equally subject to the duties and responsibilities of citizenship".[128]

On the legal obligation of a private person, a paucity of literature on rule of law and international rule of law mentions it. As an exception, Jeremy Waldron mentions the obligation of a citizen. Quoting Waldron at length:

> But the ROL applies to the individual, too. What does the ROL require of the ordinary citizen? Well, it requires that she obey the laws that apply to her. She should be alert to changes in the law; she should arrange for her legal advisors to keep her informed of her legal obligations; she should refrain from taking the law into her own hands; and she should not act in any way that impedes, harms, or undermines the operation of the legal system, its institutions, and its procedures.
>
> She must obey the law where it does exist, but she has no particular obligation where it does not. It is not up to individual citizens or businessmen to do the lawmakers' job for them. For example, they have no duty to extend the scope of the law's constraint (in accordance with common sense, morality, the spirit of the law, social purposes, or anything else) if the sources of law do not disclose an unambiguous enactment to that effect.[129]

However, the mention of the citizen obligation by Jeremy Waldron aims to demonstrate that "for the citizen, absence of regulation represents an opportunity for individual freedom, but the absence of regulation represents a very different case for the state".[130] This difference between public power and private right is unrelated to the present research.

Therefore, the "clean hands" (*mains propres*) doctrine explains that the rights of private persons may be affected if they have some illegal behavior in the context of international rule of law. The "clean hands" doctrine comes from maxims such as "*ex dolo malo non oritur actio*", "*ex iniuria non oritur isu*", and "he who comes to equity for relief must come with clean hands".[131] Moreover, "clean hands" doctrine based on good faith is applied in many national systems of law and may be considered a general principle of law. The effect of this doctrine is basically to prevent at some stage in the proceedings an action being brought where such action arises from or is involved with the willful wrongdoing of the complainant.[132]

In reference to the applicability of this doctrine to inter-state disputes, Sir Gerald Fitzmaurice maintained that "he who comes to equity for relief must come with clean hands". Thus, "a State which is guilty of illegal conduct may be deprived of

---

[127] See Constitution of the People's Republic of China, adopted on December 4, 1982, articles 10, 46, 49, 52–56, available at <http://english.www.gov.cn/archive/laws_regulations/2014/08/23/content_281474982987458.htm>.

[128] Constitution of the Republic of South Africa, No. 108, 1996, article 3.2.b, available at <https://www.gov.za/documents/constitution/constitution-republic-south-africa-1996-1>.

[129] Jeremy Waldron, "Are Sovereigns Entitled to the Benefit of the International Rule of Law" (2011) 22(2) European Journal of International Law 315–343, 337–338.

[130] Jeremy Waldron, "Are Sovereigns Entitled to the Benefit of the International Rule of Law" (2011) 22(2) European Journal of International Law 315–343, 339.

[131] Chittharanjan F. Amerasinghe, Diplomatic Protection (Oxford University Press, 2008) 212.

[132] See Chittharanjan F. Amerasinghe, Diplomatic Protection (Oxford University Press, 2008) 212.

the necessary *locus standi in judicio* for complaining of corresponding illegalities on the part of other States, especially if these were consequential on or were embarked upon to counter its illegality, in short, were provoked by it."[133] According to Dr Jenks's observation, both majority opinion and dissenting opinion share the view that the clean hands as a general principle of law were applicable in *Netherlands v. Belgium* (Meuse Water Case).[134] On the whole, "a number of States have maintained the vitality and applicability of the principle of clean hands in inter-State disputes; and the ICJ has not rejected the principle though it has generally failed to apply it."[135]

In any event as applied to state–private relations, clean hands could also be called upon to the State's defense no matter whether it may be lesser or more effective. Sometimes in view that corporate social responsibility has been incorporated into some national company laws,[136] international investment agreements and some corporate social responsibility initiatives themselves also take into account relevant laws and regulations and repeatedly mention the "law and regulation"; thus, legal obligations and social responsibility are mixed with each other.[137] The present research also argues that "soft law", which contains a normative element leading to compliance expectations by a private person who has already committed to complying with it (express commitments) can also constitute a part of international rule of law.[138] In fact, in most cases, corporate social responsibility initiatives can be regarded as

[133] See Gerald Fitzmaurice, "The General Principles of International Law, considered from the Standpoint of the Rule of Law" (1957) 92(2) Collected Courses of the Hague Academy of International Law 1–227, 119.

[134] See C Wilfred Jenks, The Prospects of International Adjudication (Stevens & Sons, 1964) 326, footnote 30.

[135] Stephen M Schwebel, "Clean hands, principle", Max Planck Encyclopedia of Public International Law, Max Planck Institute for Comparative Public Law and International Law (Heidelberg and Oxford University Press, 2010), article last updated in March 2013, also available at <http//www.mpepil.com>.

[136] The responsibility can be considered as a variant form of obligation.

[137] See China Chamber of Commerce of Metals, Minerals and Chemicals Importers and Exporters (CCCMC), Guidelines for Social Responsibility in Outbound Mining Investments, Launch of Guidelines on October 24, 2014, article 1.1. "Ensure compliance with all applicable laws and regulations. Companies must ensure that their investments and operations are in line with applicable Chinese and host country laws and regulations and with industry minimum standards. Compliance with all applicable laws and regulations is a basic requirement of corporate social responsibility. It is, however, encouraged to exceed requirements of laws and regulations." These guidelines will be very useful to Chinese outbound mining investment in Africa because the nature of Chamber is semi-official and its budget comes from national appropriation. To some extent, the Chamber is exercising the function of Chinese government. Therefore, the guidelines could be enforced very well.

[138] See Christine M. Chinkin, "The Challenge of Soft Law: Development and Change in International Law" (1989) 38(4) International and Comparative Law Quarterly 850–866.

such soft law, which is less than strict law but more than moral or political commitments.[139] "The realm of 'soft law' begins once legal arrangements are weakened",[140] and at present, the legal conceptualization of corporate social responsibility is still not enough. Although it is controversial whether private law is the subject of international law, it is indisputable that "the ascent of individuals as subjects of international law has reduced reliance on interstate litigation for the protection of national abroad".[141] In addition, an investor can be the right subject and by implication an obligatory subject.

In reality, just as investors' rights are deemed human rights, it is well recognized that property rights are not an absolute right, considering that public interests are its boundary while legality is an inherent restriction.

Succinctly, it is wrong to think that the international rule of law does not involve or affect individuals, but States, just as it is wrong to believe that there is no international rule of law without an overarching world government.

Chapter Summary

The international rule of law should at least be a state of "ought to be", which has moral correctness and attraction to most countries. The modern States mostly adopt the rule of law model and realize their legitimacy in a sense by legality. In other words, legitimacy is promoted on the basis of the rule of law. Furthermore, the rule of law should come from the domestic level and the international level. This is also the argument in this research and why international rule of law is advocated in this research.

There are different dimensions to understanding the international rule of law. The prominent understanding is to make an analogy between international rule of law and national rule of law and emphasize international rule of law as the control of power since international rule of law is the rule of the Constitution. However, this research does not share the so-called international constitution's view in the current international community. Suppose the term international constitution is used, it only means by analogy or metaphor such as the United Nations Convention on the Law of the Sea is a constitution for the ocean. Still another example, Heike Krieger, etc. goes forward by taking a particular perspective of international rule of law and defines the "international rule of law" as "the more recent and 'thicker' understanding of international law",[142] that is, it emphasizes the value of the international law perspective. In effect, it does not examine the international rule of law from the functional or formal perspective.

---

[139] About a comprehensive understanding on international soft law, see Daniel Thürer, "Soft Law", Max Planck Encyclopedia of Public International Law, article last updated in March 2009.

[140] Kenneth Abbott and Duncan Snidal, "Hard and Soft Law in International Governance" (2000) 54(3) International Organization 421–456.

[141] Natalie Klein, "Dispute Settlement Options for the Protection of Nationals Abroad", in Natalie Klein (ed.), Litigating International Law Disputes: Weighing the Options (Cambridge University Press, 2014) 436–459, 437.

[142] See Heike Krieger and Georg Nolte, The International Rule of Law—Rise or Decline? Points of Departure (November 9, 2016). KFG Working Paper Series, No. 1, October 2016.

Although the international rule of law can be understood from many dimensions, this research is mainly carried out from the perspective of functionism. It emphasizes the obligation of the private person even if the subject status of the private person in international law is controversial in addition to the constraint on power.

Chapter 3
Conceptualizing International Investment Rule of Law

From the perspective of historical origin, no one can deny that the international investment rule of law is a tool for capital-exporting countries to protect the interests of their overseas investors and investments. The original BITs one-sidedly constrained the host state's regulatory power and protected investors' interests of the capital-exporting countries and therefore is the international investment rule of law that the capital-exporting country imposed on the importing country. The international investment rule of law has not emphasized investor obligations and the regulatory power of the host state from the beginning. Going further, it is worth noting that emphasis on investor protection has its historical gene, behind which is "unresolved power dynamics". In other words, there is an imbalance of power between the capital-exporting state and the capital importing state.[1] Even so, protecting the interests of investors by law rather than gunboats is historic progress.

With the development of the international investment rule of law, its content and form are constantly being improved and have even been widely used among developing countries. Nevertheless, it is not neutral and objective to think that the international investment rule of law is completely fair and reasonable. For example, from its inception, the ICSID has registered and adjudicated many cases, but at the same time, it has been criticized for many reasons. It has been submitted that the ICSID should promote conciliation, enhance transparency, and prepare an appellate mechanism or permanent investment tribunal to meet challenges.[2] However, it is not advisable to adopt a completely critical and negative attitude toward the international investment rule of law. It is rather wise to strive to perfect the existing international investment rule of law and make it serve the common goal of sustainable development of the human being. Therefore, it is necessary to reorient, reconceptualize, and transform the international investment rule of law. The way to shift and reshape the

---

[1] See Kate Miles, the Origin of International Investment Law: Empire, Environment and the Safeguarding of Capital (Cambridge University Press, 2013) 386–387.

[2] Antonio R. Parra, The History of ICSID (2th edition, Oxford University Press, 2017) 289–293.

X. Han, *Legal Protection and Sustainability of Chinese Investments in Africa*,
Modern China and International Economic Law,
https://doi.org/10.1007/978-981-19-1882-7_3

international investment rule of law is to integrate provisions on policy space for the host state and investor responsibility.[3]

There are many discussions on the role of international investment law in the rule of law. From the perspective of economics, some scholars have also argued that International Investment Agreements (IIAs) have a similar function, that is, from the host state's side, to discipline policy of the host state that will impose international externalities on the foreign investors, and from the investor's side, to curtail inefficient risks associated with foreign investments.[4] The problem is that it only analyses the regulatory function of IIAs from only these two different perspectives, without noticing that IIAs should also play a binding role on foreign investors.

Although numerous writings on international investment law have touched upon or elaborated on every aspect of it, this research attempts to review history, canvass reality, and predict the future of international investment law according to the elements and descriptive logic of the international rule of law adopted in this research. In other words, the theory of international rule of law will be integrated into the analysis of international investment law. The purpose of this research is to demonstrate whether the historical development process and the way forward of international investment law are and should be international rule of law.

3.1 International Investment Rule Inheriting from International Rule of Law

3.1.1 Tracing the Ideal and Origin of International Investment Rule of Law

As an ideal for building the international investment rule of law, the effort to negotiate a multilateral treaty from international organizations to NGOs and even private

[3] See Kate Miles, the Origin of International Investment Law: Empire, Environment and the Safeguarding of Capital (Cambridge University Press, 2013) 388–389.

[4] See Alan O. Sykes, 'The Economic Structure of International Investment Agreements with Implications for Treaty Interpretation and Design' (2009) 113(3) American Journal of International Law 482–534.

sectors has never ceased since 1928.[5] Although none of these efforts to set out multilateral substantive rules of foreign investment protection have made the multilateral approach a reality, their ideal pursuing international investment rule of law cannot be ignored. The effect of this ideal on the development of international investment law, in reality, cannot be disregarded. For example, much of the Harvard Draft Convention reflected customary international law, and various provisions were later included in the International Law Commission's Articles on State Responsibility, which is a part of the sources of international investment law. In reality, many ideas or clauses in these documents have been absorbed by subsequent BITs or FTAs.[6]

Although from the historical perspective there are different opinions on the origin of international investment law, some scholarly works even go back to ancient Greek and Roman law times.[7] Some scholars consider that it can be traced back to the massive friendship, commerce, and navigation treaties (FCNs) from the 1700s to 1960s that mainly focused on trade with no express reference to investment,[8] although "by the end of nineteenth century, FCN treaties began to include substantive standards which guarantee against expropriations without due process and full compensation in some cases, currency transfer restrictions, and treatment of investment were also

[5] These efforts include: At the League of Nations in 1928 and the Havana Conference of 1948, the proposals on a multilateral treaty; The Draft Statutes of The Arbitral Tribunal for Foreign Investment and The Foreign Investment Court Published By The International Law Association (ILA) in 1948; The International Convention For The Mutual Protection of Private Property Rights in Foreign Countries Proposed The Germany-Based Society to Advance The Protection of Foreign Investments in 1957. See the Abas-Shawcross Draft Convention on Investment Abroad in 1959, available at <https://www.international-arbitration-attorney.com/wp-content/uploads/137-volume-5.pdf>; The Harvard Draft Convention on The International Responsibility of States for Injuries to Aliens in 1961, the Draft Convention on the Protection of Foreign Property: Text with Notes and Comments Issued by the Organization for Economic Cooperation and Development (OECD) in 1962, and the Reissued Version with Minor Amendments in 1967, available at <http://www.oecd.org/investment/internationalinvestmentagreements/39286571.pdf>; the Multilateral Agreement on Investment (MAI) Proposed by OECD in 1998, available at <https://www.oecd.org/daf/mai/pdf/ng/ng987r1e.pdf>. See Chester Brown, 'Resolving International Investment Disputes', in Natalie Klein (ed.), Litigating International Law Disputes: Weighing the Options (Cambridge University Press, 2014) 406–407.

[6] For example, in "the Abas-Shawcross Draft Convention on Investments Abroad in 1959" and "the Draft Convention on the Protection of Foreign Property: Text with Notes and Comments issued by the Organization for Economic Cooperation and Development (OECD) in 1962", the idea of investor-state arbitration subject to certain conditions has been put forward. See article 7 of the Abas-Shawcross Draft Convention and article 7 of the Draft Convention of OECD.

[7] See Krista Nadakavukaren Schefer, International Investment Law: Text, Cases and Materials (Edward Elgar Pub Press, 2013) 4.

[8] See Chester Brown, 'Resolving International Investment Disputes', in Natalie Klein (ed.), Litigating International Law Disputes: Weighing the Options (Cambridge University Press, 2014) 401–435; See also Trinh Hai Yen, The Interpretation of Investment Treaties, in Jeswald W. Salacuse (ed.), The Law of Investment Treaties (2nd edition, Oxford University Press, 2015) 156–157.

covered".[9] As far as dispute settlement is concerned, only state-to-state arbitration or settlement by the International Court of Justice (ICJ) is authorized.[10]

Some scholars also reviewed in detail that during the late 1800s and early 1900s, "many mixed claims commissions largely concerned the treatment by states of foreign nationals and their property",[11] and later as diplomatic protections, the Permanent Court of International Justice (PCIJ) and the ICJ heard some famous cases brought by way of diplomatic protection, such as the Factory at Chorzów case,[12] the Barcelona Traction case,[13] and the Elettronica Sicula case.[14]

However, the real international investment law with modern meaning just started from modern BITs which include substantive standards and procedure clauses, that is, the 1959 Germany–Pakistan BIT[15] and especially the 1968 Netherland-Indonesia BIT which are the first BIT to include an investor-state arbitration clause[16] and are the first tribunal established on the basis of an ICSID dispute settlement provision contained in an investment treaty,[17] became important landmarks of international investment rule of law. In other words, the present article argues that modern international investment law originates from the first Germany–Pakistan BIT of 1959,

[9] See Andreas Paulus, Treaties of Friendship, Commerce and Navigation, last updated in March 2011, Max Planck Encyclopedia of Public International Law [MPEPIL]; See also Trinh Hai Yen, the Interpretation of Investment Treaties, in Jeswald W. Salacuse (ed.), the Law of Investment Treaties (2nd edition, Oxford University Press, 2015) 157–158.

[10] Trinh Hai Yen, the Interpretation of Investment Treaties, in Jeswald W. Salacuse (ed.), the Law of Investment Treaties (2nd edition, Oxford University Press, 2015) 157, 159.

[11] See Makane Moïse Mbengue, African Perspective on Inter-State Litigation, in Natalie Klein (ed.), Litigating International Law Disputes: Weighing the Options (Cambridge University Press, 2014) 401–435; Kate Parlett, Diplomatic Protection and the International Court Of Justice, in C. Tams & J. Sloan (eds.), The Development of International Law by the International Court of Justice (Oxford University Press, 2013) 87–106; Kate Parlett, The Individual in the International Legal System: Continuity and Change in International Law (Cambridge University Press, 2011) 122–175.

[12] Certain German Interests on Polish Upper Silesia (German v. Polish) (Merits), PCIJ Case No. 7, dated May 25, 1926; Factory at Chorzów (German v. Polish) (Merits), PCIJ Case No. 17 dated September 13, 1928.

[13] Barcelona Traction, Light and Power Company Ltd. (Belgium v. Spain), ICJ Case No. 3 dated February 5, 1970.

[14] Elettronica Sicula SpA (United States of America v. Italy), ICJ case No. 76 dated March 2, 1987.

[15] Treaty between the Federal Republic of Germany and Pakistan for the Promotion and Protection of Investments, available at <http://investmentpolicyhub.unctad.org/Download/TreatyFile/1387>.

[16] Netherlands and Indonesia Agreement on Economic Cooperation (with Protocol and Exchanges of Dated), available at <http://investmentpolicyhub.unctad.org/Download/TreatyFile/3329>. This treaty has been terminated by Indonesia. The original text is that: "The Contracting Party in the territory of which a national of the other Contracting Party makes or intends to make an investment, shall assent to any demand on the part of such national and any such national shall comply with any request of the former Contracting Party, to submit, for conciliation or arbitration, to the Centre established by the Convention of Washington of March 18, 1965, 1 any dispute that may arise in connection with the investment."

[17] Asian Agricultural Products Ltd. (AAPL) v. Republic of Sri Lanka, ICSID Case No. ARB/87/3, dated June 27, 1990. Before this case, the instrument that was invoked in all cases before the ICSID was the contract, instead of a treaty.

which includes wide substantive clauses to protect foreign investment and signifies the advent of BITs across the world.[18]

The final draft of the ICSID Convention was accepted by the Executive Council of the Bank in 1965, and in the next year, the ICSID was established. Following the 1968 Netherland-Indonesia BIT, investor-state arbitration as a tool of depoliticization between states was incorporated into BITs, especially after the 1990s. The ICSID is regarded by Shihata, who was the ICSID Secretary General from 1983 to 2000 as an outcome of depoliticizing investor-state disputes, and he described it as "a forum for conflict resolution in a framework which carefully balances the interests and requirements of all the parties involved, and attempts in particular to 'depoliticize' the settlement of investment disputes".[19]

It is suggested that similar substantive and procedural clauses in these BITs and FTAs have contributed to the "multilateralization of international investment law".[20] Modern mega-FTAs such as the Comprehensive and Progressive Agreement for Trans-Pacific Partnership (CPTTP), Agreement Establishing the African Continental Free Trade Area (AfCFTA), and Regional Comprehensive Economic Partnership (RCEP) can further overcome the shortcomings of the fragmentation of international investment law and realize the depoliticization of international investment rule of law.

3.1.2 Analyzing the Depoliticization of International Investment Rule of Law

The present author in particular considers the development of international investment law as a process of depoliticization of the rule of law. The "postmodern international adjudication procedures go as far as incorporating diplomacy into adjudicatory processes".[21] Indeed, on investor-state dispute settlement, almost all BITs prioritize consultation or negotiation over arbitration. In addition, the UNCTAD suggests that

---

[18] Treaty between the Federal Republic of Germany and Pakistan for the Promotion and Protection of Investments, available at <http://investmentpolicyhub.unctad.org/Download/TreatyFile/1387>, articles 11.1, 11.2. The original text: "(1) In the event of disputes as to the Interpretation or application of the present Treaty, the Parties shall enter into consultation for the Purpose of finding a solution in a spirit of friendship. (2) If no such solution is Forthcoming, the dispute shall be submitted (a) to the International Court of Justice if both Parties so agree or (b) if they do not so agree to an arbitration tribunal upon the request of either Party."

[19] Ibrahim F. I. Shihata, 'Towards a Greater Depoliticization of Investment Disputes: The Role of ICSID and MIGA' (1986) 1 (1) Foreign Investment Law Journal 1–25.

[20] Stephan W. Schill, the Multilateralization of International Investment Law (Cambridge University Press, 2009) 70–71.

[21] Makane Moïse Mbengue, 'African Perspective on Inter-State Litigation', in Natalle Klein (ed.), Litigating International Law Disputes: Weighing the Options (Cambridge University Press, 2014) 177.

alternative dispute resolution (ADR) should avoid the frequent elevation of investor-state disputes into arbitration or limit the excessive use of arbitration.[22] However, in any case, it does not mean that investor-state arbitration should be replaced with diplomatic or political methods between states.

In contrast, investor-state investment arbitration has been the typical method of settling disputes instead of interstate investment arbitration, although almost all BITs or other international investment treaties juxtapose the article of "settlement of dispute between contracting parties" and the article of "settlement of disputes between investors and one Contracting Party".[23]

However, the inter-state investment arbitration under BITs or other international investment treaties has rarely been used to the extent that it has become a "stand-alone clause". The reason behind this may be to avoid the politicization of investor-state disputes. To date, only two cases have occurred under inter-state investment arbitration clauses. However, inter-state investment arbitration always gives way to investor-state investment arbitration. For example, in the case of Empresas Lucchetti SA and Lucchetti Peru SA v. Peru, the respondent requested that the proceedings be suspended "in view of the fact that 'Claimants' Request for Arbitration [was] … the subject of a concurrent state to state dispute between the Republic of Peru and the Republic of Chile".[24] However, the tribunal discontinued the inter-state claim instead of suspending the investor-state proceeding.[25] In the same vein, during Chevron Corporation and Texaco Petroleum Company v. Ecuador, the tribunal interpreted article II.7 of the Ecuador-United States BIT (1993).[26] However, Ecuador was not satisfied with the interpretation and commenced another inter-state dispute settlement proceeding against the US based on the interpretation and application of this article. Finally, this inter-state claim was rejected on jurisdictional grounds.[27]

Regarding diplomatic protection, its utilization has decreased after the emergence of investor-state investment arbitration to obviate depoliticization. In particular, "[n]o Contracting State shall give diplomatic protection, or bring an international claim, in respect of a dispute which one of its nationals and another Contracting State shall have consented to submit or shall have submitted to arbitration under this Convention unless such other Contracting State shall have failed to abide by and comply with

---

[22] UNCTAD, Investor-State Disputes: Prevention and Alternatives to Arbitration, UNCTAD Series on International Investment Policies for Development U.N. Doc. UNCTADDIAEIA20-0911 (2010).

[23] E.g., Agreement between the Government of the People's Republic of China and the Government of the United Republic of Tanzania Concerning the Promotion and Reciprocal Promotion of Investments, signed on March 24, 2013, came into force on April 17, 2014, articles 12, 13.

[24] Empresas Lucchetti SA and Lucchetti Peru SA v. Peru (Award), ICSID Case No. ARB/03/4, dated February 7, 2005, para. 7.

[25] Empresas Lucchetti SA and Lucchetti Peru SA v. Peru (Award), ICSID Case No. ARB/03/4, dated February 7, 2005, para. 9.

[26] Chevron Corporation and Texaco Petroleum Company v. Ecuador (Interim Award), UNCITRAL, PCA Case No. 34877, dated December 1, 2008.

[27] L. Peterson, United States Defeats Ecuador's State-to-State Arbitration: Will Out-come Dissuade Argentine Copycat Case? Available at <www.Iareporter.com/articles/201209033>.

the award rendered in such dispute".[28] Therefore, although diplomatic protection is traditionally considered as discretion of a state, the state cannot exercise this right if the investor has filed its claims with the ICSID convention arbitral tribunal.

For BITs, there are 2895 BITs in existence according to the World Investment Report 2020, and most states are still continuing to negotiate BITs, although the trend is descending; in addition, other treaties with investment provisions (TIPs) are increasing in a more rapid manner, with the number reaching 389.[29] The two basic parts of these treaties are substantive obligations of the state parties and provisions that set forth dispute settlement procedures. The former set boundaries for states' actions, and the latter define the authority of arbitral tribunals such as jurisdiction *ratione personae*, jurisdiction *ratione materiae*, and jurisdiction *ratione temporis*.[30]

Comparatively, the Convention on the Settlement of Investment Disputes between States and Nationals of Other States (ICSID Convention) and the Multilateral Investment Guarantee Agency Convention (MIGA Convention) have achieved great success. As of March 24, 2021, the number of contracting states to the ICSID Convention was 155,[31] while 825 arbitration and 13 conciliation cases were settled by the ICSID to facilitate the resolution of international investment disputes,[32] and the MIGA Convention was ratified by 182 members.[33] In addition, MIGA has guaranteed projects to help foreign investors in developing countries by providing all kinds of political risk insurance (PRI), such as currency inconvertibility and transfer restriction, expropriation, war, terrorism, civil disturbance, breach of contract, non-honoring of financial obligations, and other additional services.[34]

On the whole, the international investment rule of law is a more developed part of the international rule of law. International investment law, whether substantive rules or dispute settlement procedures, deals with the state's relationships with individuals who are subject to the exercise of public authority by the state. In the relationship between investors and the state, the rule of law means limiting arbitrary governmental actions from the external to protect private rights and interests.

However, on the one hand, political settlement or diplomatic channel cannot provide definitive solutions to the disputes in question, in particular, the legal rights and wrongs of the disputing parties cannot be clarified. On the other hand,

---

[28] Convention on the Settlement of Investment Disputes between States and Nationals of Other States, ICSID/15/Rev., January 1, 2003, article 27.1.

[29] UNCTAD, World Investment Report 2020: International Production Beyond the Pandemic, United Nations, 2020, p. 106.

[30] See Chester Brown, 'Resolving International Investment Disputes', in Natalie Klein (ed.), Litigating International Law Disputes: Weighing the Options (Cambridge University Press, 2014) 401–435.

[31] Database of ICSID Member States, available at <https://icsid.worldbank.org/about/member-states/database-of-member-states>.

[32] ICSID Cases, available at <https://icsid.worldbank.org/cases/case-database>.

[33] MIGA, About Member Countries, available at <https://www.miga.org/member-countries>.

[34] MIGA Investment Guarantees, Overview, available at <https://www.miga.org/investment-guarantees>; MIGA Projects, Overview, available at <https://www.miga.org/projects>.

politicization is not the overall development direction of international investment law.

In fact, the investor-state investment arbitration itself is the outcome of depoliticization to avoid going against the bilateral relationship between the two states. Until now, investor-state investment arbitration has been the typical dispute settlement method.

Substantive treatment standards aim to regulate "the action or omission of the host state that has allegedly had an adverse effect on the investment"; therefore, the action or omission "must be attributable to the government of the host state in accordance with the international law of the state responsibility".[35]

From a historical point of view, at the international level, for the protection of foreign investments, the first stage is diplomatic protection, that is, the home state of the investor exercised its discretionary power to decide whether diplomatic protection should be adopted to present its own claim against the host State in its own name under customary international law or treaties. The second stage is investor-state dispute settlement, that is, investor files arbitration and claims against the host state directly in its own name under the treaty, the contract, or the domestic law of the host state. From diplomatic protection to investor-state arbitration, this is actually a depoliticization process.[36] The trend of investment dispute settlement from diplomatic protection to international adjudication shows the development of the international investment rule of law. Law, superseding political and military arbitrary use or threat of power plays a key role. In view that diplomatic protection is often accompanied by force or coercion from the home state, the international investment regime is also considered a "reaction to the process of decolonization".[37]

Diplomatic protection should be the last remedy because it may affect the relation between two countries. In addition, beyond doubt, the purpose of diplomatic protection is to ensure the host state's respect for the rules of international law[38] or implementation of international legal responsibility.[39] The means of diplomatic protection include "diplomatic action or other means of peaceful settlement".[40] This

[35] James Crawford, The International Law Commission's Articles on State Responsibility: Introduction, Text and Commentaries (Cambridge University Press, 2002) 91–123.

[36] In eighteenth century, Vattel first elaborated diplomatic protection, he said "whoever ill-treats a citizen indirectly injures the State, which must protect that citizen". Although his proposition is regarded as a "fiction" (Vattelian fiction), but it became basis to the practice of diplomatic protection. See Kate Parlett, the Individual in the International Legal System: Continuity and Change in International Law (Cambridge University Press, 2011) 87–106.

[37] José E. Alvarez, The Public International Law Regime Governing International Investment (Cambridge University Press, 2011) 94.

[38] See Mavrommatis Palestine Concessions (Greece v. Gr. Brit.), PCIJ case No. 2, dated August 30, 1924.

[39] U.N.ILC, 58th Sess., article 1. U.N. Doc. A/61/10 (2006). Int'l Law Comm'r, Draft Articles on Diplomatic Protection, on the work of its Fifty-eighth Session, U.N. Doc. A/61/10, article 1 (2006).

[40] U.N.ILC, 58th Sess., article 1. U.N. Doc. A/61/10 (2006). Int'l Law Comm'r, Draft Articles on Diplomatic Protection, on the work of its Fifty-eighth Session, U.N. Doc. A/61/10, article 1 (2006).

is especially the case when the home state adopts peaceful international judicial proceedings with the host state.

International investment law purports to regulate host states' authority exercised against foreign investors. Consistent with the traditional domestic rule of law, which requires the restraint of state power and the protection of individual rights, the principles of international investment law are similar to those of domestic constitutional and administrative law.[41]

3.1.3 Clarifying the Advanced Nature of the International Investment Rule of Law

The international investment law is a specific and developed area in international law as a whole, while the rules of international investment law are an integral part of the general rules of international law. Dispute settlement in international investment law should be considered an integral part of the dispute settlement mechanism of international law. The enforcement of international investment awards is an aspect of compliance with international law. Moreover, international investment law is obviously a more developed part of international law, and the advancement of international investment law can also be seen in the quantities of international investment treaties and investor-state arbitration cases.

From international investment laws and policies, it is clear that not only the US and the EU but also China have all led the direction of the international investment rule of law. For example, the 2012 US Model BIT retains investor-state dispute settlement clauses and provides extremely detailed rules for the investor-state arbitration procedure with a length of 12 pages.[42] For another example, The Lisbon Treaty, which entered into force on December 1, 2010, unifies foreign investment policies with the EU's terms of reference, thus introducing a unified foreign investment policy at the EU level. At present, the conclusion of investment agreements between the EU as a whole and third countries has ushered in the process of establishing permanent bilateral and multilateral investment courts. This practice undoubtedly shows that the permanent international investment court may make judicialization of the settlement of international investment disputes a reality. Judicialization is actually the further development of the international investment rule of law.[43] The judicialization

[41] About the relevant demonstration, see Steven W. Schill, 'General Principles of Law and International Investment Law', in Tarcisio Gazzini (ed.), International Investment Law: The Sources of Rights and Obligations (Brill Nijhoff, 2012) 133–181.

[42] US Department of State, 2012 US Model Bilateral Investment Treaty, available at <http://www.ustr.gov/sites/default/files/BIT%20text%20for%20ACIEP%20Meeting.pdf>.

[43] About the international judicialization, see Cesare P. R. Romano, The Shadow Zones of International Judicialization (the Oxford University Press, 2013) 90; Benedict Kingsbury, 'International Courts: Uneven Judicialization in Global Order', in James Crawford (ed.), The Cambridge Companion to International Law (Cambridge University Press, 2012) 203.

of investment protection may become one of the greatest achievements of the international investment rule of law in recent decades. The China-EU Comprehensive Investment Agreement (CAI), which was completed periodically on December 30, 2020, also declares that state-of-the-art provisions related to investment protection and investment dispute settlement will be developed within two years.[44]

International investment law has made sufficient progress in the process of internationalization of the rule of law. The history of international investment law is a process, from only how to protect foreign investment to how to protect both foreign investment and the public interests of the host state. The historical development of international investment law is also a process to strengthen the rule of law. International investment agreements are concluded and considered to govern the conduct of the host state's regulation and that of the investor, especially in the future. In the investment dispute between an investor and the host state, the investor can sue the host state in an international arbitral tribunal. Furthermore, international investment law can be applied in the dispute settlement process, and arbitral awards can be implemented by the host state. Although it is sometimes difficult to judge whether a state has complied with public international law in practice, it is easier to decide whether a state has complied with international investment law because international investment law is more normative. Additionally, it is clear whether a loser state has made monetary compensation decided by the arbitral award.

The international investment rule of law has a crucial and direct part in building peace in view of the fact that foreign investment is no longer allowed to be protected by force; instead, it is protected by the international investment rule of law. In addition, the economic development of host states, especially developing countries, may in turn promote peace.

> The connection between the protection of acquired rights, including international investment, and the forwarding of world peace is plain. In the long range, this connection lies mostly in the prospect that orderly economic development of the newly developing countries will, by raising the standard of living, of education, of health and the like, lead eventually to greater stability and responsibility, and diminish the pressure for drastic and violent upheavals stemming from gross disparities in economic position.[45]

A steady increase in BITs is not ignorable, and other IIAs and even mega-regional agreements cannot substitute BITs completely. Among many countries, the condition is not mature to conclude FTAs. This is the current case between China and the US, as well as between China and the EU. Therefore, there is first of all the need for them to negotiate and conclude BITs.

International investment law is one of the most developed fields within international law. Its subjects are no longer merely states in their mutual relations but private investors, including natural persons and legal persons. In addition, international investment treaties and arbitral tribunals can affect the functioning of the national legislative, executive and judicial branches.

---

[44] The European Commission, the EU – China Comprehensive Agreement on Investment (CAI), available at <https://trade.ec.europa.eu/doclib/press/index.cfm?id=2237>.

[45] Arthur Larson, The International Rule of Law (The Institute for International Order, 1961) 32.

The significance of the international investment rule of law is to enable the host state to attract sustainable investment and thus to promote its own sustainable development. There are completely opposite views on whether BITs can promote foreign capital inflows. This research believes that in general, BITs and foreign capital inflows are positively related and that the active role of the international investment rule of law cannot be denied. However, because BITs are only one element of the host state's investment climate, it is not surprising that in a specific country, the increase in foreign capital inflows does not happen due to its BITs or that a specific country has attracted considerable foreign capital inflows without any BIT. For example, Brazil attracts a great amount of foreign capital inflows without any BIT, but this does not completely mean that a BIT is useless. On the one hand, "although Brazil received substantial amounts of FDI even in the absence of BITs, had they enacted any BIT, the inflow in the period would have been greater",[46] in addition to its advantages on the investment climate. On the other hand, Brazilian outbound investment also needs protection and restriction from BITs. Furthermore, whether an investment is sustainable or whether an investment can promote the sustainable development of the host state depends on the screening and regulation of the host state on the basis of its domestic laws.

3.2 International Investment Rule of Law Constraining and Protecting the Regulatory Power of the Host State

3.2.1 Examining Substantive and Procedural Rule of Law

The essence and center of international investment law is traditionally the protection of foreign investors and thus the corresponding constraint on the regulatory power of the host state. Even though investment facilitation and promotion have become high profiles in recent years, protection and constraint are key points of the international investment rule of law, and investment facilitation and promotion provisions cannot replace protection and restriction provisions.[47] Therefore, in the opinion of the present author, the "Investment Cooperation and Facilitation Agreement" (CFIA) initiated by Brazil based on Brazil's Model CFIA 2015[48] cannot play a comprehensive role in the international investment rule of law.

Because the actions of the government affect investments and such governmental actions often are not, or even cannot be foreseen at the time the investor made its

[46] Paulo Cavallo, Brazil, BITs and FDI: A Synthetic Control Approach (2019) 20 (1) the Journal of World Investment & Trade 68–97.

[47] Rukia Baruti, 'Investment Facilitation in Regional Economic Integration in Africa: The Cases of COMESA, EAC and SADC' (2017) 18 (3) the Journal of World Investment & Trade 493–529.

[48] 2015 Brazil Model CFIA, article 14.

decision to invest,[49] the central issue of the international investment rule of law is how to make the host state implement "good governance", thus protecting foreign investment.

Restrictions on the power of the host state are reflected in most of the substantive rules and procedural provisions of IIAs. Measures of the host state should not be outside the scope of its legitimate right to regulate and should not constitute an abuse of regulatory discretion. The investor should only be governed by law instead of unbridled arbitrary power. In the practice of international investment arbitration, the principle of proportionality has become an important analytical method to constrain the power of the host state. For example, it may be utilized when applying FET to determine the proportionality of state measures to the alleged policy objective.[50]

Here, the government may include legislative, executive and judicial branches. It is not difficult to understand for the former two branches to be subject to international dispute bodies, but it should also be mentioned that the judicial acts of a state may also become the subject of international investment claims subject to certain conditions if a wrongful judicial act causes state responsibility such as where "the state is responsible for a breach attributable to the state, the investment tribunal has jurisdiction over the particular dispute, and the damage that the investor has suffered is a result of the particular breach".[51]

Although the rule of law in international investment law is undergoing challenges and changes, it has never been abandoned. The Investor-State Dispute Settlement (ISDS) changes under the United States–Mexico–Canada Agreement (USMCA) cannot prove that the importance of the international investment rule of law is diminished or that there is a fundamental "de-internationalization" of the international investment rule of law. The scope of arbitrable issues and procedures for the application of ISDS is limited to accommodate the need to protect the host state's regulatory power. According to the USMCA, although investors from the US may still utilize arbitration to settle investment disputes, not only is there a strict limit on the scope of the dispute submitted for arbitration but also stringent local remedies and time limits are imposed on investors. In particular, the USMCA drops disputes arising from investment establishment, indirect expropriation, and FET from arbitration.[52]

Economic and trade agreements, including investment chapters and investment protection agreements signed by the EU in recent years, have shifted to adopt a combination of bilateral investment arbitral tribunals and permanent appeal mechanisms to resolve investor-state disputes and pursue the "establishment of a multilateral

---

[49] See Krista Nadakavukaren Schefer, International Investment Law: Text, Cases and Materials (Edward Elgar Pub, 2013) 3.

[50] UNCTAD, Review of ISDS Decisions in 2018: Selected IIA Reform Issues, IIA Issues Note: International Investment Agreements, 2019, Issue 4, p. 13.

[51] Berk Demirkol, Judicial Acts and Investment Treaty Arbitration (Cambridge International Trade and Economic Law) (Cambridge University Press, 2018) 108.

[52] United States–Mexico–Canada Agreement, Annex 14-D, 14-E, November 30, 2018, available at <https://ustr.gov/trade-agreements/free-trade-agreements/united-states-mexico-canada-agreement/agreement-between>.

investment tribunal and appellate mechanism" in the future.[53] The establishment of a permanent tribunal reflects the path taken by the EU to reform the international investment rule of law and is in fact taking a step closer to the international investment rule of law.

Argentina is deeply involved in international investment arbitration as a respondent and has lost most cases. However, Argentina has not terminated any BIT or its ICSID Convention membership. On the one hand, Argentina commits to perform arbitral awards and is fulfilling some awards through settlement by issuing national bonds and discounts.[54] On the other hand, Argentina has resorted to concluding new BITs with some innovations since 2016. To avoid repeating the same mistakes, the two newest BITs tried to define the "investment" narrowly, protect the regulatory power of the host state to a greater extent, and exclude third-party funding that may help to bring about litigation. The 2018 Argentina–United Arab Emirates BIT and 2018 Argentina–Japan BIT are two pieces of evidence.[55]

It is observed that the international investment rule of law in India is on the rise with "a more rule based investment protection" in place of "prior sketchy treaty provisions".[56] The India 2015 Model BIT is a more balanced model BIT,[57] and after it, the first BIT was signed between India and Belarus on the basis of this Model BIT.[58]

Withdrawal from the international investment rule of law is only the practice of a small number of countries. Latin American countries such as Bolivia, Venezuela, Ecuador and others have successively withdrawn from the ICSID Convention and gradually terminated their BITs. Due to its special national circumstances, South Africa has gradually terminated BITs and provided domestic remedies for investment dispute settlement under its domestic laws.[59] Russia ended its temporary application of the Energy Charter treaty (ECT) because of the Yukos v. Russia case.[60] However, the withdrawal from the international investment rule of law and domestic social

---

53 EU-Viet Nam Investment Protection Agreement, signed on June 30, 2019, article 3.38, 3.39, 3.41; Multilateral Dispute Settlement Mechanism of EU-Singapore Investment Protection Agreement, signed on October 15, 2018, article 3.9, 3.10, 3.12; EU-Canada Comprehensive Economic and Trade Agreement, October 30, 2016, article 8.28, 8.29.

54 Luis Alberto Erize, 'Argentina', in Stephen Jagusch QC and Epaminontas Triantailou (eds.), Investment Treaty Arbitration 2018 (Law Business Research, 2018) 11.

55 Agreement for the Reciprocal Promotion and Protection of Investments Between the Argentine Republic and the United Arab Emirates, Arg.–U.A.E., April 16, 2018, articles 1, 10, 24; Agreement Between the Argentine Republic and Japan for the Promotion and Protection of Investment, Arg.–Japan, notes 2–3, December 1, 2018.

56 See Aniruddha Rajput, Protection of Foreign Investment in India and International Rule of Law: Rise or Decline? (2017) 10 SSRN Electronic Journal 3.

57 2015 India Model BIT, December 28, 2015.

58 Belarus–India BIT, signed on September 24, 2018.

59 Mmiselo Freedom Qumba, South Africa's Move Away from International Investor-State Dispute: A Breakthrough or Bad Omen for Investment in the Developing World? (2019) 52(1) De Jure Law Journal 358.

60 About the case, see Yukos Universal Limited (Isle of Man) v. The Russian Federation, UNCITRAL, PCA Case No. 2005-04/AA227, available at <https://www.italaw.com/cases/1175>.

security problems have also reduced the attraction of these countries for foreign investment in recent years.

The main substantive rules on treatment in IIAs include national treatment, most-favored nation (MFN) treatment, FET, FPS, non-expropriation of the investment unless satisfying certain conditions, and observance of undertaking (e.g., umbrella clause). These specific requirements are constraints on the regulatory power of the host state.

The national treatment and MFN clauses can be classified by a joint name: "non-discrimination treatment", which means that the host state must treat foreign investors "no less favorable" than the treatment that it accords to its local investors or investors from another state (third state) in like circumstances. The potent power of an MFN clause in IIAs lies in its ability to produce a "ratchet effect" by which the obligations assumed by the host states can become greater than what is actually agreed upon in a particular IIA.[61]

The case law about FET clauses shows that the host state cannot act in a way with the following features:

> [T]he minimum standard of fair and equitable treatment is infringed by conduct attributable to the State and harmful to the claimant if the conduct is arbitrary, grossly unfair, unjust, or idiosyncratic, is discriminatory and expose the claimant to sectional or racial prejudice, or involves a lack of due process leading to an outcome which offends judicial propriety-as might be the case with a manifest failure of natural justice in judicial proceedings or a complete lack of transparency and candour in an administrative process.[62]

In addition, the host state cannot conduct itself in a way that is inconsistent with the investor's legitimate expectations.[63] The FPS clause requires the host state to provide physical protection for the investor's property to protect it from actual damage caused by state officials or by the actions of others where the state has failed to exercise due diligence.[64]

Under the "expropriation of the investment satisfying certain conditions" clause, legal expropriation, both direct and indirect,[65] generally needs to satisfy the following requirements: the measure must be for a public purpose; must be non-discriminatory;

---

[61] C. Mclachlan, L. Shore & M. Weiniger, International Investment Arbitration (2nd Edition, Oxford University Press, 2017) 254.

[62] Waste Management, Inc. v. Mexico, ICSID Case No. ARB (AF)/00/3, dated April 30, 2004, para. 98.

[63] Saluka Investment BV v. Czech Republic, UNCITRAL, Partial Award, PCA Case No. IIC 210, dated March 17, 2006, paras. 300–308; see also Joseph Charles Lemire v. Ukraine, ICSID Arbitral Tribunal, Case No. ARB/06/18, dated January 14, 2010, para. 284.

[64] See, e.g., Asian Agricultural Products Ltd. v. Sri Lanka, ICSID Case No. ARB/87/3, dated January 27, 1990, paras. 78–86; Wena hotels Ltd. v. Egypt, ICSID Case No. ARB/98/4, dated December 8, 2000, paras. 84–95; Saluka Investments BV v. Czech Republic, ICSID Case No. ARB/01/12, Partial Award, July 14, 2006, para. 408; Siemens AG v. Argentina, ICSID Case No. ARB/02/8, dated February 6, 2007, para. 303.

[65] "The direct expropriation refers to the host state adopts a measure which transfers title of an investor's property to the host state; The indirect expropriation basically means the measure does not deprive the investor of title to its property, but it nonetheless has the effect of substantially depriving the investor of its ability to exercise rights over its investment."

and must be accompanied by the payment of prompt, adequate, and effective compensation and due process. If only one of these requirements cannot be satisfied, the action constitutes illegal expropriation.

The significance of the observance of undertaking (umbrella clause) is to elevate the host state's undertaking, especially contractual commitment, into an international law obligation.[66] The general formulation is something like "Each Contracting Party shall observe any other obligation it may have entered into with regard to investments of investors of the other Contracting Party".[67]

There are an increasing number of exceptions to national treatment and MFN treatment. Therefore, foreign investors can be treated differently from national investors or third-party state investors only if there is a justification for the different treatments.[68]

According to the case law, if the regulatory measure is for a public purpose within the police powers of the host state, it can be non-compensable.[69] In other words, the exercise of the right to regulate is not limited and thus must have its boundaries.[70] In fact, it is difficult to distinguish compensable expropriation from non-compensable regulation through adjudication. Therefore, an increasing number of IIAs provides explicit requirements for non-compensable regulation and attempt to preserve space for the governance of the host state.

It is submitted that the international investment arbitration may hold a government accountable to the law, in addition, "in the face of uncertainty, international investment arbitration should encompass serious and engaged review of domestic legal issues".[71] The procedural clause of investor-state disputes constrains the regulatory power of the host state by compulsory jurisdiction of the arbitral tribunal. Regarding the joint role of the procedural and substantive rules on the host state, the UNCTAD has stated indirectly that investors:

> Having means at their disposal to ensure the host country's compliance with the obligations under BITs increases the level of certainty regarding the business environment in which

[66] The relevant cases, for example, Noble Ventures, Inc. v. Romania, ICSID Case No. ARB/01/11, Award dated October 12, 2005, paras. 51, 61; SGS Société Général de Surveillance SA v. Philippines, ICSID, Case No. ARB/02/6, Decision on Jurisdiction, dated January 24, 2004, paras. 113–129; Bureau Veritas, Inspection, Valuation, Assessment and Control, Bivac B.V. v. The Republic of Paraguay, ICSID Case No. ARB/07/9, Decision of the Tribunal on Objections to Jurisdiction, dated May 29, 2009, paras. 159–161.

[67] See for example, Agreement Between the Government of the People's Republic of China and the Government of the Republic of South Africa concerning the Reciprocal Promotion and Protection of Investments, China–South Africa, December 30, 1997, article 10.2.

[68] About the exception of national treatment, see Saluka Investment BV v. Czech Republic, UNCITRAL, Partial Award, dated March 17, 2006, para. 313.

[69] See, e.g., Methanex Corporation v. United States, UNCETRAL, Final Award, dated August 3, 2005, Part IV, para. 7; Fireman's Fund Insurance Company v. Mexico, ICSID Case No. ARB (AF)/02/1, Award dated July 17, 2006, para. 176(j).

[70] ADC Affiliate Limited and ADC & ADMC Management Limited v. The Republic of Hungary, ICSID Case No. ARB/03/16, Award dated October 2, 2006, para. 423.

[71] Paul B. Stephan, International Investment Law and Municipal Law: Substitutes or Complements? (2014) 9 (4) Capital Markets Law Journal 354–372.

investors operate in the host country. In addition, this mechanism ensures that the dispute is decided on legal grounds, thus separating legal from political considerations.[72]

3.2.2 Exploring Formal and Substantive Rule of Law

The formal rule of law refers to the normativity of the international investment rule of law. In the past, BITs were relatively short and ambiguous instruments, especially Europe-style BITs.[73] Currently, the BITs and investment chapters in other IIAs are becoming lengthier. At the same time, the normativity of these BITs and IIAs has increased. For example, clarifying the MFN clause in IIAs can only be applied to the substantive standard of protection instead of procedural rights such as investor-state arbitration provision. In the past, the ambiguity of this kind of clause led to contradictory interpretations by tribunals, although on some occasions, the reason is that different IIAs use different wording.

The substantive rule of law means the value orientation of the international investment rule of law. International investment law is criticized for only focusing on investment protection but not showing grave concern over the environment, labor, human rights, and other social values. In addition, these inadequacies are considered to have deep roots in investment treaty negotiation, investment treaty structure, and the rule of law deficits of the international investment arbitration system.[74]

The recent developments of international investment law are addressing the challenges from these aspects. This is reflected not only in the expansion of the regulatory space of the host state in international investment treaties with more respect to other values but also in the transformation of investment arbitration practice. Under the circumstances of resisting and backlashing the partial international investment law, the awards supporting the host state's regulatory power among international investment arbitration practices have also been increasing. For example, in the case where Philip Morris Asia Limited challenged Australian plain packing law under the Australia–Hong Kong BIT, the arbitral tribunal denied jurisdiction and accordingly protected the public health value.[75] In Philip Morris v. Uruguay, when facing a conflict between the host state's regulatory power to maintain public health and the investor's investment interests, the arbitral tribunal supported Uruguay and decided that the claimants must pay the arbitration cost to the respondent.[76]

---

[72] UNCTAD, Bilateral Investment Treaties 1995–2006: Trends in Investment Rulemaking (United Nations, 2007) 100.

[73] For example, the Germany–Pakistan BIT which was written in German and English is 12 pages (including exchange of note); the United Kingdom–Egypt BIT (1975) is eight pages long.

[74] F. Garcia, L. Ciko, A. Gaurav & K. Hough, 'Reforming the International Investment Regime: Lessons from International Trade Law' (2015) 18 (4) Journal of International Economic Law. 869, 871–873.

[75] Philip Morris Asia Limited v. The Commonwealth of Australia, UNCITRAL, PCA Case No. 2012-12, see more available at <http://www.italaw.com/cases/851>.

[76] Philip Morris Brands Sàrl, Philip Morris Products S.A. and Abal Hermanos S.A. v. Oriental Republic of Uruguay, ICSID Case No. ARB/10/7, Award dated July 8, 2016, paras. 287–307, 590.

The research by Mavluda Sattorova reveals that many government officials do not even know about IIAs, let alone attach importance to IIAs, so the investment treaty law cannot enable good governance.[77] However, international investment law can promote the rule of law in the host country and positively influence and change the legislation of the host country. Take China as an example. In Ekran v. China, the Malaysian investor Ekran Berhad claimed that rights under a 70-year lease over 900 ha of land in the Chinese province of Hainan held by the investor's local subsidiary were unjustly revoked by the local government.[78] Similarly, in *Ansung Housing v. China*, the Korean investor claimed the provincial government's alleged actions in relation to its investment in the construction of a golf and country club and luxury condominiums in Sheyang-Xian, Jiangsu province, was against the commitment it received.[79] It is against this background where the administrative actions of local governments have given rise to international investment arbitration that China's newly enacted Foreign Investment Law stipulates that "the local people's governments at all levels and their relevant departments shall fulfil their policy commitments legally made to foreign investors and foreign-funded enterprises and various contracts legally concluded", and "[w]here any policy commitment or provision of a contract needs to be changed in the national or public interest, such change shall be made according to the statutory powers and procedures, and foreign investors and foreign-funded enterprises shall be compensated according to the law for their losses so incurred."[80]

Many "new-generation" IIAs are sustainable development oriented and noteworthy among the recently adopted BIT models, such as 2020 Italy Model BIT, 2019 Morocco Model BIT, 2019 Belgium–Luxembourg Economic Union Model BIT, 2019 Netherlands Model BIT, 2016 Czech Republic Model BIT, and 2015 India Model BIT,[81] which is of course conducive to the protection of the host state's regulatory power.

---

[77] Mavluda Sattorova, 'the Impact of Investment Treaty Law on Host States: Enabling Good Governance?' (2018) 29 European Journal of International Law 109–111.

[78] Ekran Berhad v. People's Republic of China, ICSID Case No. ARB/11/15, discontinuance, dated May 16, 2013. This dispute was finally settled.

[79] Ansung Housing Co., Ltd. v. People's Republic of China, ICSID Case No. ARB/14/25, Award dated March 9, 2017. In this case, the arbitral tribunal did not exercise jurisdiction because of the lapse of three-year prescription.

[80] Foreign Investment Law of the People's Republic of China, National People's Congress, article 25, 26.

[81] All these Model BITs are available at <https://investmentpolicy.unctad.org/international-investment-agreements/model-agreements>.

3.3 International Investment Rule of Law Binding the Arbitral Tribunal

In international investment arbitration, the arbitral tribunal can of course constrain the regulatory power of the host state by applying substantive and procedural rules. However, the power of the arbitral tribunal itself is also constrained.

Simon Chesterman considers that the international rule of law has two functions: one is to set standards for the international legal system, and the other is to set standards for the national legal system.[82] According to José E. Alvarez, concerning the international investment regime, global administrative law means that "rules that seek to make host state adhere to the 'rule of law' need themselves to adhere to the rule of law".[83] Therefore, if they are regarded as lacking legitimacy due to their deviation from the rule of law, their destiny is to be discarded or reformed to a degree.

Many of the investment arbitral awards have touched upon the boundary between two conflicting values: the public interest of the host state and the private interest of the investor. However, some scholars and practitioners have expressed criticisms and discontents to investment tribunals, such as against the arbitral awards' inconsistency, neglect of public interests and public welfare of the host state, and indulgence to irresponsible investors.[84] At the same time, the revival of the Calvo doctrine occurred in some countries.[85] One arbitral tribunal notes that "[i]ts decisions are increasingly seen as failing to respond to pressing social needs, and its institutional processes criticized for failing basic rule of law criteria such as coherence, predictability, neutrality, and accountability."[86]

Another note is, "[a]s ISDS increasingly involves regulatory challenges against states with highly developed rule of law systems, it becomes increasingly important to strengthen traditional democratic and rule of law desiderata such as participation,

---

82 Simon Chesterman, 'I'll Take Manhattan: The International Rule of Law and the United Nations Security Council' (2009) 1 (1) Hague Journal on the Rule of Law 68–69.

83 José E. Alvarez, the Public International Law Regime Governing International Investment (Cambridge University Press, 2011) 444.

84 Susan D. Franck, 'The Legitimacy Crisis in Investment Treaty Arbitration: Privatizing Public International Law through Inconsistent Decisions' (2005) 73 Fordham Law Review 1537–1538; Michael Walbel, Asha Kaushal, Kwo-Hwa Chung & Claire Balchin, The Backlash Against Investment Arbitration: Perceptions and Reality (Kluwer Law International, 2010) viii, 108; Howard Mann, The Right of States to Regulate and International Investment Law: A Comment, in UNCTAD, the Development Dimension of FDL Policy and Rule-Making Perspectives, UNCTAD/ITE/IIA/2003/4, 211–223, at. 212; Todd Weiler, 'Balancing Human Rights and Investor Protection: A New Approach for a Different Legal Order' (2004) 27 Boston College International & Comparative Law Review 2.

85 For instance, Bolivia, Ecuador and Venezuela have withdrawn from the ICSID Convention. South Africa has decided to terminate all its BITs gradually and enacted Protection of Investment Act in 2015, which does not include investor-state arbitration clause.

86 Frank J. Garcia, Lindita Ciko, Apurv Gaurav & Kirrin Hough, 'Reforming the International Investment Regime: Lessons from International Trade Law' (2015) 18 (4) Journal of International Economic Law 862.

transparency and inclusiveness in investment dispute resolution."[87] Thus, a neutral, independent dispute settlement mechanism is being explored.

With the ICSID as a typical case,[88] the restriction on international institutions can be embodied in every aspect to make the powers conferred on them exercised in good faith, reasonably, equitably and within the limits of such power. For example, the constituent instrument of ICSID provides for the jurisdiction of ICSID in article 25 of ICSID Convention, including subject matter jurisdiction, personal jurisdiction, consent to jurisdiction and reservation to jurisdiction,[89] and if the arbitral tribunal "has manifestly exceeded its powers", either party may request annulment of the award.[90] The ad hoc annulment committee only has limited authorization to set aside entirely or partly the arbitral award on the basis of five procedural grounds listed in article 52 of the ICSID Convention.[91] Therefore, the ad hoc annulment committees have seldom annulled the arbitral award to avoid exceeding their authority. Nevertheless, in recent years, the annulment committee mechanism, which is actually the internal supervisory mechanism of the ICSID, has been increasingly resorted to by disputing parties.[92]

The constituent instrument of the ICSID also requires that "the Panel of Conciliators and the Panel of Arbitrators shall each consist of qualified persons"[93] and the arbitrators shall be of high moral character and recognized competence.[94] In addition, the procedure of "replacement and disqualification of conciliators and arbitrators" is provided for in the ICSID Convention.[95] The transparency and participation in arbitration proceedings can guarantee fair decisions. Thus, the 2006 amendments of the ICSID arbitration rules mandated the ICSID to publish excerpts of the legal reasoning of awards even in the absence of such consent, and the amendments of

---

[87] Joost Pauwelyn, The Rule of Law Without the Rule of Lawyers? Why Investment Arbitrators are from Mars, Trade Panelists Are from Venus, July 29, 2015, at 4, available at <https://papers.ssrn.com/sol3/papers.cfm?abstract_id=2549050>.

[88] "The Centre shall have full international legal personality. The legal capacity of the Centre shall include the capacity: (a) to contract; (b) to acquire and dispose of movable and immovable property; (c) to institute legal proceedings". See Convention on the Settlement of Investment Disputes between States and Nationals of Other States, ICSID/15/Rev., January 1, 2003, article 18.

[89] Convention on the Settlement of Investment Disputes between States and Nationals of Other States, ICSID/15/Rev., January 1, 2003, article 25.

[90] Convention on the Settlement of Investment Disputes between States and Nationals of Other States, ICSID/15/Rev., January 1, 2003, article 52.b.

[91] Convention on the Settlement of Investment Disputes between States and Nationals of Other States, ICSID/15/Rev., January 1, 2003, article 52.

[92] As of February 26, 2020, 136 of ICSID's 493 concluded arbitration cases have undergone the annulment proceedings, available at <https://icsid.worldbank.org/en/Pages/cases/AdvancedSearch.aspx>.

[93] Convention on the Settlement of Investment Disputes between States and Nationals of Other States, ICSID/15/Rev., January 1, 2003, article 12.

[94] Convention on the Settlement of Investment Disputes between States and Nationals of Other States, ICSID/15/Rev., January 1, 2003, article 14.1.

[95] Convention on the Settlement of Investment Disputes between States and Nationals of Other States, ICSID/15/Rev., January 1, 2003, articles 57, 58.

the rules confirmed the authority of the arbitral tribunals to accept and consider *amicus curiae* briefs and to allow third parties to attend or observe hearings if neither disputing party objects.[96]

The ongoing ICSID Arbitration Rules amendment process was announced in October 2016 to kick off in next year by ICSID's Administrative Council.[97] The amendments are also in the process to remedy some of the concerns regarding investor-state investment arbitration and to increase the ICSID's level of international investment rule of law from all sides including limiting its own power on the basis of years of experience.[98] It is believed that not only the amendment itself is an improvement in the international investment rule of law but also that the amended ICSID Rules and Regulations can further promote the development of the rule of international investment law.

In fact, both the United Nations Convention on Transparency in Treaty-based Investor-State Arbitration (Mauritius Convention on Transparency) which came into force on October 18, 2017 and the "UNCITRAL Working Group III: Investor-State Dispute Settlement Reform",[99] are aimed at strengthening constraint on the arbitration institutions themselves, thereby improving international investment rule of law.

In national rule of law, fair trials by a competent, independent and impartial judiciary is an objective criterion to measure the rule of law and this reflects the Anglo-American tradition which especially stresses the judicial independence and judicial process.[100] It should be the same at the international level.

3.4 International Investment Rule of Law with Emerging Investor Obligation or Responsibility

According to the concept of the rule of law, although the abuse of power needs to be constrained by law and the exercise of discretionary power should be limited where necessary to protect private rights, there should still be a balance between private

---

[96] The latest amendments of the ICSID Rules adopted by the Administrative Council of the Centre came into effect on April 10, 2006, see Rules of Procedure for Arbitration Proceedings (Arbitration Rules), Rule 32, Rule 37, available at <https://icsid.worldbank.org/-ICSID/StaticFiles/basicdoc/CRR_English-final.pdf>.

[97] ICSID News Release, 50th Annual Meeting of ICSID's Administrative Council, available at <https://icsid.worldbank.org/en/Pages/News.aspx?CID=196>.

[98] ICSID Rules and Regulations Amendment Process, available at <https://icsid.worldbank.org/en/amendments>.

[99] United Nations Commission on International Trade Law, Working Group III: Investor-State Dispute Settlement Reform, available at <https://uncitral.un.org/en/working_groups/3/investor-state>.

[100] U.N. What is the Rule of Law, available at <http://www.unrol.org/article.aspx?n=What%20is%20the%20rule%20of%20law?>.

rights and public rights. The excessive constraint on public power will affect the realization of public order or public welfare.

Under the traditional concept of the international investment rule of law, however, the host state only assumes obligations, while investors only enjoy rights, which is extremely unreasonable. The responsibility for an investment involving human rights, labor rights, environmental protection, and anti-corruption has always existed in the form of soft law such as the United Nations Code of Conduct for Transnational Corporations (draft) of 1986, the International Labor Organization's Tripartite Declaration of Principles Concerning Multinational Enterprises and Social Policy of 1977, and Social Accountability International SA8000 for the fulfilment of social responsibility by transnational corporations.

Due to political and economic realities, these legal instruments of the UN General Assembly have not been accepted by developed countries and the obligations of investors have not been emphasized. However, according to the UNCTAD Investment Policy Framework for Sustainable Development (IPFSD) of 2015, six types of investor obligations or responsibility clauses are suggested in international investment agreements to promote compliance by investors with domestic or international norms at the entry and operation state.[101]

The International Institute for Sustainable Development (IISD), as an independent think tank, developed a model IIA with similar provisions. The IISD Model IIA includes entire sections on Corporate Social Responsibility (Article 16), Investor Liability (Article 17), and the effects of the investor misconduct on the dispute settlement process (Article 18).[102]

Since many BITs are concluded based on a model BIT, the provisions in the model BITs can explain the shift in investor responsibility. Some recent model BITs have made specific reference to investor obligation or responsibility. These include 2015 India Model BIT, 2015 Norway Draft Model BIT, 2015 Brazil Model CFIA,[103] 2016 Czech Republic Model BIT,[104] 2019 Belgium–Luxembourg Economic Union Model BIT,[105] 2019 Netherlands Model BIT, 2019 Morocco Model BIT,[106] and 2020 Italy Model BIT.[107] Take three of them as examples.

The 2015 Indian Model BIT is improved after reflecting its experience as the respondent, and it provides the legal obligation of the investors as follows:

---

[101] UNCTAD, Investment Policy Framework for Sustainable Development, 2015, pp. 109–110.

[102] H. Mann, K. Moltke, L. Peterson & A. Cosbey, IISD Model International Agreement on Investment for Sustainable Development: Negotiators' Handbook, Second Edition, International Institute for Sustainable Development, April 2005, available at <https://www.researchgate.net/publication/27514673-9IISD_Model_International_Agreement_on_Investment_for_Sustainable_Development>.

[103] 2015 Brazil Model CFIA, article 14.

[104] 2016 Czech Republic Model BIT, December 28, 2016.

[105] 2019 Belgium–Luxembourg Economic Union Model BIT, March 28, 2019, article 18.

[106] 2019 Morocco Model BIT, June 1, 2019, articles 18–20.

[107] 2020 Italy Model BIT, article X.

(i) Investors and their investments *shall* comply with all laws, regulations, administrative guidelines and policies of a Party concerning the establishment, acquisition, management, operation and disposition of investments.

(ii) Investors and their investments *shall not*, either prior to or after the establishment of an investment, offer, promise, or give any undue pecuniary advantage, gratification or gift whatsoever, whether directly or indirectly, to a public servant or official of a Party as an inducement or reward for doing or forbearing to do any official act or obtain or maintain other improper advantage nor shall be complicit in inciting, aiding, abetting, or conspiring to commit such acts.

(iii) Investors and their investments *shall* comply with the provisions of law of the Parties concerning taxation, including timely payment of their tax liabilities.

(iv) An investor *shall* provide such information as the Parties may require concerning the investment in question and the corporate history and practices of the investor, for purposes of decision making in relation to that investment or solely for statistical purposes.[108]

It also provides extra corporate social responsibility as non-mandatory obligations as follows:

Investors and their enterprises operating within its territory of each Party shall *endeavour to voluntarily* incorporate internationally recognized standards of corporate social responsibility in their practices and internal policies, such as statements of principle that have been endorsed or are supported by the Parties. These principles may address issues such as labour, the environment, human rights, community relations and anti-corruption.[109]

These two types of provisions indicate that investor obligations can be divided into legal obligations and extralegal obligations. Although the latter cannot be enforced through investor-state arbitration, the "good faith" requirement in the definition of "investment" means that investments violating investors' social responsibility should not be fully protected by the treaty.[110]

The 2015 Norway Draft Model BIT improves corporate social responsibility clauses as follows:

The Kingdom of Norway and the ..., *Emphasising* the importance of corporate social responsibility ...[111]

3. The Joint Committee shall: ... viii. where relevant, discuss issues related to corporate social responsibility, the preservation of the environment, public health and safety, the goal of sustainable development, anticorruption, employment and human rights, and ...[112]

The Parties agree to encourage investors to conduct their investment activities in compliance with the OECD Guidelines for Multinational Enterprises, the UN Guiding Principles on Business and Human Rights and to participate in the United Nations Global Compact.[113]

---

[108] 2015 Indian Model BIT, article 11.

[109] 2015 Indian Model BIT, article 12.

[110] 2015 Indian Model BIT, article 1.4.

[111] 2015 Norway Draft Model BIT, pmbl, available at <http://investmentpolicyhub.unctad.org/Download/TreatyFile/3350>.

[112] 2015 Norway Draft Model BIT, pmbl, article 23, available at <http://investmentpolicyhub.unctad.org/Download/TreatyFile/3350>.

[113] 2015 Norway Draft Model BIT, article 31, available at <http://investmentpolicyhub.unctad.org/Download/TreatyFile/3350>. The Bold is added by 2015 Norway Draft Model BIT on the

To focus on the 2019 Netherlands Model BIT, it provides the direct obligations of the investors such that:

> Investors and their investments shall comply with domestic laws and regulations of the host state, including laws and regulations on human rights, environmental protection and labor laws …
>
> Investors shall be liable in accordance with the rules concerning jurisdiction of their home state for the acts or decisions made in relation to the investment where such acts or decisions lead to significant damage, personal injuries or loss of life in the host state.[114]

In the practice of concluding IIAs, there is a tendency for investors' obligation to evolve into hard law, and there are many examples to demonstrate it. The Mauritius–Egypt BIT expressively provides that the Agreement shall not apply to investments made with capital or assets of illegal origin.[115] Both article 12 of the 2016 Argentina–Qatar BIT and article 24 of the 2016 Morocco–Nigeria BIT adopt the form of direct investor obligations. The IIAs concluded by the EU are requested to incorporate the OECD Code of Conduct for Transnational Corporations. This is because it is not enough to characterize social responsibility as a moral obligation or a soft law obligation, and it is not possible to punish all kinds of serious human rights and labour rights violations, excessive exploitation of natural resources, serious pollution of the environment and ugly acts of corruption. One of the EU's claims in the ongoing China–Europe BIT negotiation is the introduction of investor obligations related to corporate social responsibility.[116]

There are still many soft laws on investor obligations in the international community, which cannot truly play a role in constraining investors, but to some degree, international investment arbitral tribunals can play a role in the area of more responsible investments by making adverse awards to investors. To this end, international investment arbitral tribunals have increasingly relevant practices, and illegal "investments" will not be qualified to obtain protection from international investment arbitrations. The investor's conduct that "constitutes an abuse of right (or abuse of process)" is not admissible and will be sanctioned by the arbitral tribunal. In Philip Morris v. Australia under Australia–Hong Kong BIT, due to corporate nationality planning

basis of 2007 Draft Model BIT, available at <http://investmentpolicyhub.unctad.org/Download/TreatyFile/2873>. In fact, these three instruments mentioned here are the most prominent codes of conduct developed by international organizations. They set forth labor standards, Environmental protection, bribery of foreign government officials and human rights. These Guide-lines aim to form a baseline for the ethical business conduct of MNEs instead of binding Obligations. In addition, the International Labour organization (ILO) promulgated the ILO Tripartite Declaration of Principles Concerning Multinational Enterprises; there is CERES Principles in the area of environmental protection; the Global Sullivan Principles of Corporate Social Responsibility developed by a coalition of US companies under the leadership of the Reverend Leon Sullivan.

114 2019 Netherlands Model BIT, March 22, 2019, articles 7.1, 7.4.

115 Agreement Between the Government of the Republic of Mauritius and the Government of the Arab Republic of Egypt on the Reciprocal Promotion and Protection of Investments, Mauritius–Egypt BIT, article 3.3.d, June 25, 2014. This will provide the basis for international investment arbitral tribunal.

116 European Commission, 'Impact Assessment Report on the EU-China Investment Relations, Commission Staff Working Document', SWD (2013) 185 final, 20–21 (May 23, 2013).

and investment dispute having already existed before the "investment", the tribunal decided that "[t]he claims raised in this arbitration are inadmissible" and rejected the jurisdiction over this dispute.[117] Furthermore, the tribunal ordered the claimant to reimburse the respondent costs caused by the arbitration and corresponding interest, if any.[118]

It is well recognized that a company's activities cannot be disassociated from the practice of citizenship actions, and therefore, in addition to purely economic objectives, a company should assume corporate social responsibility. In a narrow sense, corporate social responsibility, as an increasingly topical concept, means companies voluntarily incorporate environmental and social issues in their businesses and interaction with the government, clients, employees, investors, etc.[119] However, in a broad sense, corporate social responsibility and legal norms are inseparable or corporate social responsibility includes voluntary and mandatory responsibility.[120] Corporate social responsibility was mainly a concept of social science and political science but is gradually transforming into a legal concept.

In short, imposing obligations on foreign investors has become a new dimension in the development of the international investment rule of law. In the future, direct obligations on investors may become a trend. Investors have to bear obligations to the government, as well as other social entities in the host state. For example, for the former, investors shall not bribe government officials of the host state; for the latter, investors shall not violate the legitimate rights of other social entities. In any case, the provisions involving investor obligations will bring continuous pressure to investors because even if they cannot be enforced by law, they will certainly play a role in influencing and changing investor behavior. In other words, a rational investor will avoid violating the law.

What needs to be added is that in principle, "corporations do not have international legal personality"[121]; however, the issue of whether a corporation has an international legal personality does not affect its obligations under treaties in its specific investment relations with the host state, nor does it affect its obligations in specific arbitrations or litigations. In the investment treaty relationship between states, now that the state can grant investors various rights, it can of course impose various obligations on them

---

[117] Philip Morris Asia Limited v. The Commonwealth of Australia, UNCITRAL, PCA Case No. 2012-12, Award on Jurisdiction and Admissibility dated December 17, 2015, paras. 585, 588 and VII.

[118] Philip Morris Asia Limited v. The Commonwealth of Australia, UNCITRAL, PCA Case No. 2012-12, Final Award Regarding Costs dated March 8, 2017, paras. 105, 108.

[119] Amália Quintão & Regina Santos, 'Chinese Corporate Practice in Angola-Myths and Facts', in Marcus Power & Ana Cristina Alves (eds.), China and Angola: A Marriage of Convenience (Pambazuka Press, 2012) 150.

[120] Jennifer A. Zerk, Multinationals and Corporate Social Responsibility: Limitation and Opportunities in International Law (Cambridge University Press, 2006) 32–36; Ramon Mullierat, Corporate Social Responsibility: The Corporate Governance of the 21st Century (2nd edition, Kluwer Law International, 2005) 3.

[121] James R. Crawford, Brownlie's Principles of Public International Law (9th Edition, Oxford University Press, 2019) 112.

by providing investors' obligations and responsibilities, which ultimately depend on the will of the state instead of the investors' wishes. In short, the issue of the subject status of an investor in international law should not be a theoretical obstacle to incorporating investor obligations into the structure of the international investment rule of law.

3.5 The Future of International Investment Rule of Law

The limitation of international investment rule of law involves both formal rule of law and substantive rule of law. The provisions of previous IIAs, particularly European-style treaties, were too simplistic, thus leading to the vague and broad meaning of the articles, which would leave arbitral tribunals with too much discretion. In practice, there are many problems arising; for example, there is controversy about what subprinciples the FET contains,[122] whether the MFN clause may apply to the rules of procedure and how to define the unclear boundary between expropriation and the regulatory measure of non-expropriation. International investment arbitration mechanisms lack transparency and an appeal mechanism for arbitral awards. In the substantive rule of law, excessive protection of investors' rights undermines other values in the host state and may cause a chilling effect on the regulatory power of the host country.

The future of the international investment rule of law is to have more normativity. For investment dispute settlement, two typical approaches may be parallel in the future: improved investor-state arbitration and permanent international investment court. It was submitted very early that "one possible device that should have further consideration is a system of international courts of claims in which individuals and companies could obtain a speedy settlement of their claims both against other non-states and against governments".[123]

For the substantive international investment rule of law, the general description is not enough, that is, to balance the protection of foreign investors and the regulatory power of the host state, or in other words, the balance of rights and obligations between foreign investors and the host state. The values of sustainable development, environmental protection and public health should be protected, and the legal obligations of investors should be stressed. Not only the "North–South divide" but also the "Private–Public debate" should be addressed.[124]

---

[122] Katarína Chovancová, The Fair and Equitable Treatment and Its Current Status in International Investment Law' (2019) 61 Yearbook on International Arbitration 171, 178–179; Kendra Leite, 'The Fair and Equitable Treatment Standard: A Search for a Better Balance in International Investment Agreements' (2016) 32 (1) American University International Law Review 363.

[123] See Arthur Larson, The International Rule of Law (New York: The Institute for International Order, 1961) 55.

[124] Wenhua Shan, 'From "North–South Divide" to "Private–Public Debate": Revival of the Calvo Doctrine and the Changing Landscape in International Investment Law' (2007) 27 (3) Northwestern Journal of International Law & Business 631.

In the future, international investment rules should include more specific language that emphasizes the fact that investment promotion and protection should not undermine other important values such as human rights, environmental concerns, and labor concerns and that investments should always promote sustainable development. It would be recommended to impose direct legal obligations on the investors themselves, such as a requirement to comply with the laws of the host state when establishing and operating an investment (e.g., environmental cleanup).[125]

Finally, with regard to the reservation of the host state's legitimate regulatory rights in the structure of international investment rule of law, apart from the fact that sovereignty is a fundamental principle of international law and regulatory power is a concrete manifestation of sovereignty. The reason for this lies in that environment, public health, and other collective human rights can only be protected through the exercise of regulatory power. In fact, these rights should also be protected by the host state under international legal instruments such as the Universal Declaration of Human Rights, the Charter of the United Nations, and the United Nations International Covenant on Economic, Social and Cultural Rights. Collective human rights such as the environment, public health, and labor rights, and the protection of these rights should also be protected by the host country under international legal documents such as the Universal Declaration of Human Rights, the Charter of the United Nations, and the United Nations International Covenant on Economic, Social, and Cultural Rights. The increase of "exception clauses" for public welfare purposes such as the protection of national security, human, animal and plant life, cultural diversity, and environment in the international investment treaties, and the emphasis on the host state's regulatory power in the preamble and text of the international investment treaties, are aiming to maintain the space for the host state to safeguard collective human rights and public policies to reduce and avoid the chilling effect that may be caused by excessive protection of investors.

Chapter Summary

The traditional international investment rule of law is in line with the international rule of law or forms an integral part of international rule of law and is influenced by the international rule of law, emphasizing only the constraint on national sovereignty and without emphasis on private obligations, which has created a crisis in the current international investment rule of law.

The international investment rule of law is the most representative international rule of law or the relatively developed part of the international rule of law. The practice of international investment rule of law reflects the rationality of protecting the regulatory power of the host state and imposing obligations on investors. Through a large number of international investment agreements, a large number of international investment arbitration jurisprudences and the ongoing reforms in the international investment rule of law, the trend of international investment rule of law embodies

[125] Div. On Inv. & Enter., United Nations Conference on Trade & Development, Investment Policy Framework for Sustainable Development 39 (n.d.), available at <http://unctad.org/en/Publications Library/webdiaepcb2012d6_en.pdf>.

the constraints on the power of the host state and the power of the investment arbitral tribunal. After legitimacy has been challenged, attention to the legitimate regulatory space of the host state and investor responsibilities as well as the impartiality and independence of the arbitral tribunal are increasing. A powerful and efficient ISDS tribunal should not be what the host state fears, the host state only worries about an arbitrary ISDS tribunal.

This research adheres to the international investment rule of law and believes that the international investment rule of law can promote the rule of law in the host country and promote good governance and thus the economic development and well-being of the host country. Making a general survey of the countries that have withdrawn from the international investment rule of law, it can be said that withdrawal has not improved their investment governance or broader social governance.

Compliance with the international investment rule of law may be used as an "anti-driving mechanism" by some countries to promote the proper national rule of law within the countries. In Zimbabwe, the rights of investors cannot be protected immediately by the international investment rule of law because after the Mike Campbell SADC Tribunal made an award in favor of the investor,[126] the High Court of Zimbabwe refused to enforce the award under the pretext that the award was contrary to the national public policy,[127] and Zimbabwe has not implemented other awards made by ICSID tribunals since. However, later, Zimbabwe amended its constitution and other relevant laws to improve its governance. As emphasized by the United Nations, the consequence of controlling the exercise of power at the international level is that state power is constrained, and domestic constitutional and legal impediments to international third-party adjudication are moved.[128]

Of course, the international investment rule of law is also not a perfect international rule of law. It also needs to cope with challenges and continuously adjust to serve the sustainable development of various actors in international investment relations. Fortunately, in today's world, major countries have not abandoned the international investment rule of law but have made efforts to meet the challenges faced by the international investment rule of law through reform.

---

[126] Mike Campbell (Pvt) Ltd. and Others v. Republic of Zimbabwe, SADC(T) Case No. 2/2007, Southern African Development Community Tribunal, judgment, dated November 28, 2008.

[127] Gramara (Pvt) Ltd. and Colin Bailie Cloete v. Government of the Republic of Zimbabwe, Case No. HH 169-2009, HC 33/09, X-ref. HC 5483/09, High Court of Zimbabwe, Opposed Application dated January 26, 2010.

[128] U.N. Secretary-General, The Rule of Law at the National and International Levels: Comments and Information Received from Governments, para. 19, U.N. Doc. A/62/121 (2007).

Chapter 4
African Host State Measures in Arbitral Awards: Implication for International Investment Rule of Law

From a functional point of view, it is generally believed that the international rule of law plays a role in limiting state power and protecting private rights at the international level.[1] The international rule of law in the field of international investment (hereinafter referred to as "international investment rule of law") is actually the concrete manifestation and a relatively developed part of the international rule of law, as can be demonstrated by a large number of investor-state arbitral awards. In fact, the role of the international investment rule of law is reflected not only in specific legal provisions in international investment agreements (IIAs) but also in the interpretation and application of relevant treaty provisions by arbitration tribunals in arbitration awards. In essence, the international investment rule of law means regulating the measures of the host state, but there are few studies on the measures specifically.[2] It is even rarer for scholarship to bring the obligations of investors related to the measures of the host state into the framework of international investment rule of law.

As for the implication that African countries are heavily involved in investment arbitration administered by the ICSID and other fora because of the challenged measures, from the perspective of international investment rule of law, it can be said that these African countries have undoubtedly made important contributions

[1] See several representing writings on this topics: André Nollkaemper, National Courts and the International Rule of Law (Oxford University Press, 2011) 3–5; Vesselin Popovski, 'From Domestic to International Rule of Law: A Long and Unfinished Journey' in Vesselin Popovski (ed.), International Rule of Law and Professional Ethics (Ashgate, 2014) 5–18; William W. Bishop, 'The International Rule of Law' (1960–1961) 59 Mich. L. Rev. 553; Geranne Lautenbach, The Concept of the Rule of Law and the European Court of Human Rights (Oxford University Press, 2013) 19.

[2] See, e.g., Gus Van Harten, Sovereign Choices and Sovereign Constraints: Judicial Restraint in Investment Treaty Arbitration (Oxford University Press, 2013), Chapters 3 and 4. By examining the degree of deference of the arbitral tribunals to the executive and legislative measures of the host state, the book implies more judicial restraint in investment treaty arbitration should be adopted for promoting the development of investor-state arbitration mechanism. However, the book is not intended to define and classify the measures. Kenneth J. Vandevelde, U.S. International Investment Agreements (Oxford University Press, 2009) 191–196.

X. Han, *Legal Protection and Sustainability of Chinese Investments in Africa*,
Modern China and International Economic Law,
https://doi.org/10.1007/978-981-19-1882-7_4

to international investment jurisprudence[3] because the relevant rule of law is clarified, confirmed and developed through the arbitral jurisprudence. However, from the perspective of African countries themselves, they need to learn from the experience of a large number of cases because "African countries are likely to be involved in the ISDS system for a very long time".[4] Many African countries have indeed been involved in ICSID and non-ICSID cases, and the trend is rising.[5] These arbitral jurisprudences also constitute a warning to foreign investors.

The measures of African countries reflected in investor-state arbitral awards are in constant change since new measures and cases increasingly come into the field. This research will perform a thorough examination of these measures as of the day of writing by using the international investment rule of law as an analytical tool. Investor-state disputes involving African countries are mostly dealt with by the ICSID, although the Permanent Court of Arbitration (PCA), International Chamber of Commerce (ICC) and other ad hoc tribunals also address some cases. The scope of this research is to examine measures in cases that are administered by the ICSID as well as other international investor-state arbitration institutions, but in any case, it will not touch upon the cases before national courts or tribunals, and these cases that their arbitral awards are not made public and the relevant case information could not be accessed for they are discontinued or settled outside arbitral tribunal proceedings. Therefore, the present analysis will mainly be based on awards on jurisdiction and/or merits in the public domain or publicly known.

4.1 Definition and Classification of Measures and an Overview of Challenged African Host State Measures

Often, investment disputes are caused by "measures" of the host state; therefore, defining measures is a preliminary question in investment arbitration. The determination of a measure has been dealt with by some arbitral tribunals until now,[6] but

[3] Olabisi D. Akinkugbe, 'Reverse Contributors? African State Parties, ICSID and the Development of International Investment Law' (2019) 34(2) ICSID Review-Foreign Investment Law Journal 434–454.

[4] Uché Ewelukwa Ofodile, 'African States, Investor–State Arbitration and the ICSID Dispute Resolution System: Continuities, Changes and Challenges' (2019) 34(2) ICSID Review-Foreign Investment Law Journal 296–364.

[5] The statistics of cases involving African countries as respondents thus far is made and can been found in the Annexes 2–5 of this research.

[6] See, e.g., Ethyl Corporation v. The Government of Canada, UNCITRAL, Award on Jurisdiction dated June 24, 1998, para. 85; Loewen Group, Inc., and Raymond L. Loewen v. United States, ICSID Case No. ARB(AF)/98/3, Decision on Hearing of Respondent's Objection to Competence and Jurisdiction dated January 5, 2001, para. 70; Canfor Corporation v. United States, UNCITRAL, Decision on Preliminary Question dated June 6, 2006, paras. 149, 258; United Parcel Service of

controversy still exists. Most IIAs in the past are silent on the definition, classification, and identification of "measures"; nevertheless, the definition of a "measure" has been increasingly appearing in IIAs in recent years.

4.1.1 Defining the Host State Measures

Although a "measure" provided in IIAs could have been called an "investment measure", only in exceptional circumstances is the term "investment" used in conjunction with the term "measures", for example, "trade-related investment measures".[7] Another case is that the World Trade Organization (WTO), Organization for Economic Co-operation and Development (OECD) and United Nations Conference on Trade and Development (UNCTAD) have publicly reported "investment measures" taken by G20 members since 2009. The 2016 report, 2019 report and 2021 report jointly prepared by the OECD and UNCTAD, for instance, state that specific investment measures consist of any action that either imposes or removes restrictions on international capital movements such as investment security review measures or other investment access measures or imposes or removes differential treatment of foreign or non-resident investors compared to the treatment of domestic investors in similar situations.[8] On the whole, "investment measures" in these reports only refer to national policy measures at the macro level, including restrictive or regulatory measures, and measures aimed at liberalization, promotion or facilitation of investment. Moreover, it is certain that investment measures are not limited to investment access measures and discriminatory treatment measures. In contrast, investment measures here are much narrower than those in investment agreements and in the practice of investment arbitration. Therefore, this research does not use the phrase "investment measures" or "investment measure".

However, it should be noted that although the consequences of investment loss caused by measures can be protected by the tribunal, in the past, personal injury to investors is generally not subject to the jurisdiction of the arbitration tribunal, as has been illustrated in the *Biloune v. Ghana* case. In this case, although Mr. Biloune argues his arrest and detention for thirteen days of him and his eventual deportation to Togo,

America, Inc. (UPS) v. Government of Canada, ICSID Case No. UNCT/02/1, Award on Jurisdiction dated November 22, 2002, para. 172.

[7] See Agreement on Trade-Related Investment Measures (the TRIMs Agreement), article 2 and Annex. "Investment measures" in this Agreement refer to those investment approval conditions that distort or restrict trade, for example, local content requirements and trade-balancing requirement.

[8] See, e.g., OECD & UNCTAD, 'Sixteenth Report on G20 Investment Measures' (November 10, 2016), available at <https://unctad.org/system/files/official-document/unctad_oecd2016d16_en.pdf>; 'Twenty-first UNCTAD-OECD Report on G20 Investment Measures' (June 24, 2019), available at <https://investmentpolicy.unctad.org/publications/1205/twenty-first-unctad-oecd-report-on-g20-invest-ment-measures>; 'Twenty-fifth Report on G20 Investment Measures' (June 28, 2021), available at <https://unctad.org/webflyer/unctad-oecd-report-g20-investment-measures-25th-report>.

the tribunal noted that its jurisdiction under the agreement between the investor and the host state was limited to disputes relating to an investment.[9] Therefore, the tribunal held that it was not competent to deal with human rights violation of the foreign investor, but only to the extent that such a violation affects the foreign investment and thus becomes an investment dispute, and concluded that "the Government of Ghana, by its acts and omissions culminating with Mr. Biloune's deportation, constructively expropriated MDCL's assets, and Mr. Biloune's interest therein".[10] In the same vein, the tribunal in Bernhard von Pezold and others v. Zimbabwe refused to extend its jurisdiction to include human rights violation.[11] In fact, arbitral cases based on a similar reason still appear. For example, in Hope Services v. Cameroon, claims arose out of the alleged illegal arrest and imprisonment of the founder of the claimant company on fraud charges, followed by the government's attempt to acquire the online fundraising platform from the claimant.[12]

Recently, an increasing number of BIT models have contained "measure" clauses, and the IIAs concluded on the basis of these models correspondingly include "measure" clauses. Therefore, this research adopts the method of examining the main model BITs to understand the measure.

On the form of a measure, the 2012 US Model BIT stipulates that the treaty applies measures adopted and maintained by a Party relating to investors and covered investments, and the measure "includes any law, regulation, procedure, requirement, or practice", the same as the definition in the 2004 US Model BIT,[13] although the previous model BITs of the US before 2004 did not define it. 2004 Canada Model BIT has totally same definition as the 2004 US Model BIT,[14] but 2021 Canada Model BIT has a slight change in the wording without any further explanation and provides that the measure "includes a law, regulation, procedure, requirement or practice".[15] 2019 Morocco Model BIT has a clause that is more like a definition, "measures

---

[9] Biloune and Marine Drive Complex Ltd. v. Ghana Investment Centre and the Government of Ghana, UNCITRAL, Award on Jurisdiction and Liability dated October 27, 1989, para. 61.

[10] Biloune and Marine Drive Complex Ltd. v. Ghana Investment Centre and the Government of Ghana, UNCITRAL, Award on Jurisdiction and Liability dated October 27, 1989, 85.

[11] Bernhard von Pezold and others v. Republic of Zimbabwe, ICSID Case No. ARB/10/15, Procedural Order No. 2 dated June 26, 2012, paras. 57–60.

[12] Hope Services LLC v. Republic of Cameroon, ICSID Case No. ARB/20/2, Procedural Order No. 2 dated October 19, 2020.

[13] 2012 US Model BIT, adopted in 2012, Section A, Article 1, 2.1: Definitions; 2004 US Model BIT, adopted in 2004, Section A, Article 1, 2.1: Definitions. The only two BITs after 2004 US Model BIT are United States–Rwanda BIT (signed on February 19, 2008 and came into force on January 1, 2012) and United States–Uruguay BIT (signed on November 4, 2005 and came into force on October 31, 2006), and they follow the provision of the measure in 2004 US Model BIT.

[14] 2004 Canada Model BIT, Agreement Between Canada and … for the Promotion and Protection of Investment (2004 Model FIPA), Article 1: Definitions.

[15] 2021 Canada Model BIT, Agreement Between Canada and … for the Promotion and Protection of Investment (2021 Model FIPA), Article 1: Definitions.

include any laws, regulations or administrative decisions that are directly related to and affect the investment in the territory of that party".[16]

The 2019 Belgium–Luxembourg Economic Union Model BIT provides a more detailed and wide list, that is, the measure "shall mean *inter alia* a law, regulation, rule, procedure, decision, administrative action, requirement, practice or any form of treatment".[17] Without the phrase of "any form of treatment" under the 2015 Indian Model BIT, it was provided that a measure "includes a law, regulation, rule, procedure, decision, administrative action, requirement or practice", further the "law" in 2015 India Model BIT is clarified as:

> (i) the Constitution, legislation, subordinate/delegated legislation, laws & bylaws, rules & regulations, ordinance, notifications, policies, guidelines, procedures, administrative measures/executive actions at all levels of government, as amended, interpreted or modified from time to time; (ii) decisions, judgments, orders and decrees by Courts, regulatory authorities, judicial and administrative institutions having the force of law within the territory of a Party.[18]

Thus, the scope of measures in the form of law under the 2015 Indian Model BIT is rather extensive.

On the institutions taking measures, some treaties also give a detailed list; for example, the 2019 Belgium–Luxembourg Economic Union Model BIT defines them as follows:

> (a) central, regional or local governments and authorities; and
>
> (b) non-governmental bodies in the exercise of powers delegated by central, regional or local governments or authorities; and
>
> (c) only for the purposes of Chapter II [Investment promotion and protection] and Chapter IV [Investor-to-state dispute settlement], any entity which is in fact acting on the instructions of or under the direction or the control of a Contracting Party in carrying out its conduct.[19]

In contrast, any measure taken by a local government is excluded from the 2015 Indian Model BIT.[20] As a result, the measure is limited to those adopted by the central government. The terms of the 2012 US Model BIT and 2004 Model BIT also make it clear that a measure may be adopted by "a state enterprise or other person when it exercises any regulatory, administrative, or other governmental authority delegated to it by that party".[21]

---

[16] Morocco Model BIT, adopted on June 1, 2019, Article 3.6. The original text is "Mesures comprend toute législation, réglementation ou décision administrative prise par une Partie directement liée à un investissement dans le territoire de cette Partie et ayant des répercussions sur ledit investissement".

[17] 2019 Belgium–Luxembourg Economic Union Model BIT, adopted on March 28, 2019, article 2.12.

[18] 2015 India Model BIT, adopted on December 28, 2015, articles 1.8, 1.6.

[19] 2019 Belgium–Luxembourg Economic Union Model BIT, adopted on March 28, 2019, article 2.12.

[20] 2015 India Model BIT, adopted on December 28, 2015, article 2.4(i).

[21] 2012 US Model BIT, article 2.2(a); 2004 US Model BIT, article 2.2(a).

Occasionally, there are provisions on the measure in domestic law. Among national laws, for example, the Protection of Investment Act, 2015, South Africa stipulates that a measure "refers to binding governmental action directly affecting an investor or its investment, and includes laws, regulations and administrative action", and the government means "the government of the Republic of South Africa".[22] Comparatively, in the Promotion and Protection of Investment Bill, 2015, which became the Protection of Investment Act, 2015 after being examined, amended and approved by the Parliament and announced by the President, "measure" only refers to "administrative measure". The original text in this Bill reads that "an administrative action by a person or body duly authorized thereto, acting within the scope of authority granted by the Constitution or a law of general application".[23] Thus, it can be found that the scope of measures is expanded in the Protection of Investment Act, 2015, South Africa.

In summary, measures are increasingly provided in international investment agreements or domestic investment laws. There are differences in the enumeration of measures in different treaties. The measures can be embodied in various forms, but they are, mostly, a measure that expresses the exercise of a host state's regulatory power. In the broad sense, the scope of the measure covers legislative, executive, judicial, central, regional, and local. For this reason, it is often referred to as "regulatory measures" or "governmental measures". Of course, in IIAs, the specific definition of measures depends on the agreements of the contracting parties; in contrast, in domestic law, the scope of measures depends on the will of the state itself. Only covered measures under an IIA or other instruments are subject to relevant legal obligations. A measure means any act (including omission, i.e., failure to act) attributable to a host state that may be challenged in investor-state dispute settlement proceedings except for it is provided as an exception. It should be emphasized that the measure needs be attributable to the respondent state or the respondent state has sufficient involvement with the measure, and only such measures may be challenged in investor-state arbitration. Certainly, the measure may be taken by the government itself or any entity or body authorized by the host state.[24] The measures of the host state do not have to be adopted by the state itself. In some cases in which the arbitral tribunal exercised jurisdiction, the defendants were state-owned enterprises. These cases explain that state-owned enterprises can be defendants, but whether the host

[22] 2015 Protection of Investment Act, Act No. 22 of 2015, Government Gazette, Republic of South Africa, Vol. 606 Cape Town, December 15, 2015, No. 39514, available at <https://www.thedti.gov.za/business_regulation/acts/Investment_Act_22of2015.pdf>.

[23] Minister of Trade and Industry, Promotion and Protection of Investment Bill, 2015, B18-2015, July 28, 2015, article 1, available at <https://www.gov.za/sites/default/files/gcis_document/201508/150728bill28jul2015.pdf>.

[24] A person's acts or omissions on behalf of a state can also attributed to a host state only if it is demonstrated. See Jams Crawford, The International Law Commission's Articles on States Responsibility: Introduction, Text and Commentaries (Cambridge University Press, 2002) 82.

state is ultimately liable also depends on whether the measures can be attributed to the state.[25]

4.1.2 Classifying the Host State Measures

(i) Act or omission

Corresponding to the positive and negative obligations of the host state under the IIAs or other instruments, the measure can be divided into act or omission. It is possible that an act or omission of the host state, even in times of war, can be alleged to have an adverse effect on the investment, and both act and omission could be interpreted as measures. For example, in several cases in which Libya was the respondent, claims arose out of the government's alleged actions and omissions during the civil war, which resulted in the destruction of the claimants' investments, and this type of measure may be taken as a breach of FPS obligation under IIAs.[26] Another typical example is the omission by the Egyptian Government during the Arab Spring, where "claims arising out of the alleged Government's failure to protect a gas pipeline in which the claimants had invested from attacks that took place".[27]

Typically, obligations under IIAs prohibit a particular action of the host state; thus, the measure in question would represent an act on the part of the host state. However, in the less frequent situation, failing to meet the positive obligation would also lead to a measure to be challenged.

(ii) Measures in different sectors and industries

The measures can be classified differently according to measures in different sectors and industries, for example, measures in water supply, sewerage, waste management and remediation activities, electric power and other energy, mining and quarrying, agriculture, forestry and fishing, construction, finance, information and communication, tourism, service and trade, transportation, tobacco, tax, etc. This classification is conducive to understanding from which economic sectors investment disputes are prone to arising, as well as reminding investors and host states to be cautious about their investments and pay due diligence to regulatory methods in these sectors. This classification may also carry other meanings; for example, a contract for undertaking a project in the construction field can constitute an investment.[28]

---

[25] See, e.g., Consortium R.F.C.C. v. Kingdom of Morocco, ICSID Case No. ARB/00/6, Award dated December 22, 2003; Helnan International Hotels A/S v. Arab Republic of Egypt, ICSID Case No. ARB/05/19, Award dated July 3, 2008; Jan de Nul N.V. and Dredging International N.V. v. Arab Republic of Egypt, ICSID Case No. ARB/04/13, Award dated November 6, 2008.

[26] Cengiz İnşaat Sanayi ve Ticaret A.S. v. Libya, ICC Case No. 21537/ZF/AYZ, Award dated November 7, 2018; D.S. Construction FZCO v. Libya, PCA Case No. 2017-21, pending.

[27] Yosef Maiman, Merhav (MNF), Merhav-Ampal Group, Merhav-Ampal Energy Holdings v. Arab Republic of Egypt, PCA Case No. 2012–26, Partial Award dated December 28, 2017.

[28] See, e.g., Holiday Inns S.A. and others v. Morocco, ICSID Case No. ARB/72/1, Decision on Jurisdiction dated May 12, 1974; Consortium R.F.C.C. v. Kingdom of Morocco, ICSID Case

(iii) Measures from different branches and levels of governments

Classification can also be conducted according to the source of power adopting measures, that is, legislative measures, executive measures, and judicial measures from corresponding host state bodies. Although most of the measures come from executive or legislative branches, the measure may also originate from the judicial branch of the host state.[29] For instance, in De Sutter and others v. Madagascar (I), the host state lost arbitration because its local court was subject to intervention from its Attorney-General.[30] In OTH v. Algeria, the claims arose out of a series of alleged judicial measures against the claimant, including a court judgment against the investor through imposing a fine of approximately US $1.3 billion and a criminal sentence against a member of the investor's senior executive team.[31] In Puma Energy v. Benin, the claims arose out of the decision of an appeals court in Benin and Benin's alleged failure to comply with an emergency order issued under the Stockholm Chamber of Commerce (SCC) Rules to prevent enforcement of the court decision.[32]

Furthermore, as introduced above, measures can be divided into local government measures and central government measures. However, no matter what kind of measures are taken, the central government should assume state responsibility at the international level only if the local government measures are not explicitly excluded in the applicable instruments.

(iv) Measures challenged according to different instruments

The measures can also be classified by category of instrument(s) invoked to seek protection, that is, a BIT, a FTA, other IIAs, investment law or investment contract. Contrary to the general idea, among ICSID cases involving an African State Party, less than half are based on the State's consent to arbitration or conciliation provided in BITs negotiated by these African States, and the majority are based on investment law or investment contracts.[33] In the early days of ICSID arbitration, the investors mainly challenged the measures on the basis of the contract. For example, the measure challenged in *Holiday Inns v. Morocco* is whether the Moroccan government violated its obligation to provide loans and incentives under "basic agreement" between the

---

No. ARB/00/6, Award dated December 22, 2003; Impresa Pizzarotti & C. S.p.A. v. Kingdom of Morocco, ICSID Case No. ARB/19/14, pending, 2019.

[29] See Gus Van Harten, Sovereign Choices and Sovereign Constraints: Judicial Restraint in Investment Treaty Arbitration (Oxford University Press, 2013) 52.

[30] Kristof De Sutter, Peter De Sutter, DS 2 S.A. and Polo Garments Majunga S.A.R.L. v. Republic of Madagascar (I), ICC, 2013.

[31] Orascom Telecom Holding S.A.E v. People's Democratic Republic of Algeria, PCA Case No. 2012–20, Settled on April 18, 2014. This case was eventually settled.

[32] Puma Energy Holdings (Luxembourg) SARL v. the Republic of Benin, SCC Case No. SCC EA 2017/092, Award dated June 8, 2017.

[33] The ICSID Caseload-Statistics Special Focus-Africa (May 2017), 11.

disputing parties, i.e., whether the respondent paid the contract price to the claimant in relation to a public procurement contract for the construction of a highway.[34]

(v) Measures in different specific forms

According to the manifestations of measures taken by the host states, a specific measure may be taken in various forms, such as "revoking a license", "revoking a project contract", "interfering with the normal operation and management of an enterprise invested by the investor", "enacting a decree on nationalization or adopting an expropriation measure",[35] "sealing up, seizuring, and freezing investor's property", and "confiscating investor's assets".

In cases involving African countries as respondents, measures of "revoking a license" are very common. For example, in Winshear v. Tanzania, claims arose out of the government's cancellation of retention licenses for mineral rights and the transfer of related mining rights to the government, including those held by the claimant's local subsidiary for the gold project,[36] and in Qatar Airways v. Egypt, claims were partly due to the government's alleged revocation of the claimant's licenses to operate.[37]

Although it is difficult to find a unified classification standard, another classification of measures is also adopted, such as classifying measures into ordinary regulatory measures, extraordinary crisis measures, transition measures, tax measures, culturally sensitive measures, and financially disproportionate measures.[38]

Different classifications may contribute to a deeper understanding of measures from different perspectives. The above different types of measures will be divided into two broad categories in the ensuing paragraphs: conforming measures and non-conforming measures. On this basis, the reasons for the legal or illegal reasons of a measure will be analyzed in detail to help the investor and the host state understand the binding effect of international investment law on non-conforming measures, which can also be referred to as the function of international investment rule of law.

Most of the measures of the host state are means through which the host state exercises its regulatory power and are specific governance or control taken by the host state against foreign investors. From its very nature, the sovereignty of the State

---

[34] Holiday Inns S.A. and others v. Morocco, ICSID Case No. ARB/72/1, Decision on Jurisdiction dated July 23, 2001; See also Pierre Lalive, 'The First "World Bank" Arbitration (Holiday Inns v. Morocco): Some Legal Problems' (1980) 51(1) BYBIL 123–62.

[35] It is generally considered that nationalization is "general" and expropriation is "specific". Nationalization measures are always taken in the form of nationalization decrees and in a large-scale confiscation of an investors' property in a certain industry or field, and the State or State institutions possesses and utilizes these assets.

[36] Winshear Gold Corp. v. United Republic of Tanzania, ICSID Case No. ARB/20/25, pending, 2020.

[37] The Qatar Airways Group Q.C.S.C. v. Arab Republic of Egypt, pending, 2020.

[38] Fola Adeleke, International Investment Law and Policy in Africa: Exploring a Human Rights Based Approach to Investment Regulation and Dispute Settlement (Routledge, 2017) 63–72; Maupin, Julie A., 'Recurring Problems in Investor-State Disputes & How South Africa Might Respond to Them', available at <https://www.saiia.org.za/wp-content/uploads/2015/03/CALS-Wits-Presentation_Maupin_10-Mar-2015.pdf>.

is the fundamental attribute of a statehood, and it entitles a State an inherent and exclusive power to deal with its domestic and foreign affairs. However, as a way of exercising sovereignty, a state may restrict its own regulatory power through unilateral commitment, contracts, domestic law, or international law. Under these circumstances, the specific measures that a state adopts should meet the corresponding voluntary restrictions. If whether a measure satisfies such voluntary restrictions is subject to international investment arbitration to determine its legality, it means that the host state's measure will be constrained by the international investment rule of law.[39]

Under international investment rule of law, the most common constraints encompass obligations from national treatment, most favored national treatment, FET, exemption from arbitrary, unreasonable and/or discriminatory measures, FPS, and expropriation only satisfying requirements. Each of these obligations has specific requirements for a host state's measure, and they reflect fundamental requirements under the international investment rule of law.

4.1.3 Examining African State Measures in Investor-State Arbitration

African countries have long embraced the investor-state arbitration system, although some scepticism and objections have also appeared.[40] African countries have been involved in some famous and far-reaching cases because of measures adopted. For example, the Salini test or Salini criteria that establish the characteristics of a protected investment originated from Salini v. Morocco.[41] The Salini test or Salini criteria have been cited and accepted by most tribunals and are also incorporated into many IIAs with the development of investment definitions by listing assets and features of an investment.

In fact, the very first case accepted by the ICSID was one with an African State as the respondent, namely, Holiday Inns S.A. and others v. Morocco mentioned above.[42] Of the first 20 cases registered by the ICSID, 14 involved African countries

---

[39] See, e.g., M. Merafhe Söhne AG v. Central African Republic, ICSID Case No. ARB/07/10, Award dated May 12, 2011; RSM Production Corporation v. Central African Republic, ICSID Case No. ARB/07/2, Award dated July 11, 2011.

[40] See Uché Ewelukwa Ofodile, 'African States, Investor–State Arbitration and the ICSID Dispute Resolution System: Continuities, Changes and Challenges' (2019) 34(2) ICSID Review-Foreign Investment Law Journal 304.

[41] The Salini criteria includes (1) contribution of asset; (2) a certain duration of performance of the contract (generally over 2 years); (3) an assumption of risk; and (4) contribution to the host state's economic development. See Salini Costruttori S.p.A. and Italstrade S.p.A. v. Kingdom of Morocco, ICSID Case No. ARB/00/4, Decision on Jurisdiction dated July 23, 2001, para. 52.

[42] Holiday Inns S.A. and others v. Morocco, ICSID Case No ARB/72/1, Decision on Jurisdiction May 12, 1974.

as parties.[43] As of May 31, 2017, the ICSID had registered 613 cases under the ICSID Convention and Additional Facility Rules, and 135 of these cases involved an African State Party as the respondent.[44] As of April 2019, 106 cases were known to have African countries as the respondents.[45] There were 9 new cases registered with ICSID in 2020 alone, in which African states acted as respondents.[46] As of July 12, 2021, of the 862 cases registered under the ICSID Convention and Additional Facility Rules, African countries accounted for 180 cases.[47]

Among the new cases rapidly increasing in recent years, Egypt, Algeria, Libya, D.R. Congo, Gambia, Morocco, Rwanda, Tanzania, Guinea, Cameroon, Senegal, and Zimbabwe suffered the most cases. There are reasons why cases are concentrated in these countries. For Egypt, Libya, Tunisia, Algeria, and Morocco, most cases have been directly or indirectly related to the measures under the circumstances of civil unrest since 2010 and 2011.[48] In other words, the acts or omissions of governments in these countries during civil unrest are the main reason for investment controversies.

In addition, it cannot be denied that there is certain correlation between concluding many IIAs and encountering many arbitral cases as a respondent state because the IIA is the basis of bringing an arbitration case in many cases. Of course, this correlation is not absolute. For example, because of irregular investment measures, instead of the high number of treaties concluded is the fundamental reason for the largest number of cases involving Egypt. As a typical counterexample, there are 36 IIAs in force in Mauritius up to now, but as of August 8, 2021, the registered cases involving Mauritius as the respondent are only 3 according to the UNCTAD's statistics.[49] Indeed, the investment climate in Mauritius is very friendly, and the measures are relatively standard. Thus, many foreign investors have taken Mauritius as the first stop toward Africa.[50] Nevertheless, as of March 21, 2021, China has concluded 134

---

[43] See ICSID, Concluded Cases with Details, as of February 15, 2021, available at <https://icsid.worldbank.org/en/Pages/cases/ConcludedCases.aspx?status=c>.

[44] The ICSID Caseload-Statistics Special Focus-Africa (May 2017) 7.

[45] Africa, United Nations Economic Commission, 'Assessing Regional Integration in Africa ARIA IX: Next Steps for the African Continental Free Trade Area 2019', 175–176.

[46] These cases are 1 (Algeria), 1 (Egypt), 1 (Benin), 1 (Cameroon), 1 (Nigeria), 1 (South Sudan), 2 (Tanzania), 1 (Zambia). See the ICSID Caseload-Statistics, Issue 2021-1, 24.

[47] See ICSID, Concluded Cases with Details, as of March 15, 2021, available at <https://icsid.worldbank.org/en/Pages/cases/ConcludedCases.aspx?status=c>.

[48] Just as Egypt said in its "necessity" defense in a case, "the situation in Egypt was horrendous. It reached historic levels of violence and was out of control due to riots and clashes across the country. Police could not bring the situation under control", see Unión Fenosa Gas, S.A. v. Egypt, ICSID Case No. ARB/14/4, Award dated August 31, 2018, para. 8.10.

[49] Mauritius, IIAs, available at <https://investmentpolicy.unctad.org/international-investment-agreements/countries/134/Mauritius>; Mauritius, Cases as Respondent State, available at <https://investment-policy.unctad.org/investment-dispute-settlement/country/134/mauritius/respondent>.

[50] Ingé Lamprecht, 'Four things SA can learn from Mauritius' (September 1, 2015), Moneyweb Today, available at <http://today.moneyweb.co.za/article?id=506755&acid=BsX0kdu%2BXj0eZeuwhd4cWQ%3D%3D&adid=WgZYmOBdjTEeZeuwhd4cWQ%3D%3D&date=2015-0901#.VeU3XouIpjq>.

BITs, of which 113 have taken effect, but China has only been the respondent in 4 cases.[51]

Regarding African countries in international investment arbitration, the risks and costs of arbitration between African states and private persons have been noticed, and African states have been warned about the serious dangers of investment arbitration.[52]

4.2 Dichotomy of Measures of African Host states as Respondents

It should be noted that an investor cannot file an abstract general measure claim in investor-the host state arbitration but only a claim against the specific application of an abstract general measure. In other words, an investor may only bring a case against the specific application of a particular policy, law, rule, or norm adopted by a host state; the "as applied" claim, instead of the "as such" claim, can be initiated against the host state.[53] The measure that specifically targeted the claimant may be reviewed by the arbitral tribunal.

In any case, however, the challenged measures may be divided into two broad categories according to the applicable law or legal basis by the complaint: conforming measures and non-conforming measures. For investors, their right of action is limited to the losses caused by the non-conforming measures, and generally, only monetary compensation can be obtained. In other words, the non-conforming measures themselves cannot be claimed to be amended. The following dichotomy analysis is conducted on the available arbitral awards thus far that African countries act as respondents.

[51] China's BITs, available at <http://tfs.mofcom.gov.cn/aarticle/Nocategory/201111/20111107819474.html>, and <https://investmentpolicy.unctad.org/international-investment-agreements/countries/42/china>; China, Cases as Respondent State, available at <https://investmentpolicy.unctad.org/investment-dispute-settlement/country/42/china/respondent>.

[52] See OHADA, 'Serious Dangers of Arbitration for the States/www.ohada.com makes its recommendations: States Must not Underestimate the Risks of Arbitration' (December 25, 2014), available at <http://www.ohada.com/actualite/2413/serious-dangers-of-arbitration-for-the-states-www-ohada-com-makes-its-recommendations.html>.

[53] See, e.g., in Philip Morris v. Australia, the challenged measures are the enactment and enforcement by the Government of the Tobacco Plain Packaging Act 2011 and its alleged effect on investments in Australia owned or controlled by the claimant. See Philip Morris Asia Limited v. The Commonwealth of Australia, PCA Case No. 2012–12, Award on Jurisdiction and Admissibility dated 17 December 2015.

4.2.1 Conforming Measures Supported by Arbitral Tribunals

The operation and management of foreign investment in the host state should be protected by law, including local law and relevant international law. However, it is also undeniable that the government of the host state, as the executor and undertaker of state power, has the power to intervene reasonably in the operation and management of investment enterprises in accordance with its local law for reasonable reasons to protect specific public interests, such as ensuring the stability of the local economy and social order. Therefore, although the host state's measures interfere with or cause damage to foreign investment, under certain circumstances, they are regulatory behaviors consistent with relevant international investment law. In other words, in some cases, the regulatory power of the African host states has been maintained to a certain extent by tribunals.

In Helnan v. Egypt, the investor claimed that the rights under a contract for the management and the operation of a hotel were damaged due to the malmanagement behavior of the host state. For the challenged measure, however, the tribunal considered the decision of the Egyptian Ministry of Tourism to downgrade the hotel's classification from five stars to be normal regulatory behavior, and it was not the direct cause of the claimant's eviction from the contract. Finally, all claims of BIT breaches alleged by claimants were denied by the tribunal, and the arbitral award was also maintained by the subsequent ad hoc committee during the annulment proceeding.[54] If there is no causal link between the loss suffered by foreign investment and the regulatory measures taken by the host state, correspondingly, the host state has no liability to the investor.

In Champion Trading and Ameritrade v. Egypt, the investor claimed that Egyptian officials offered compensation in an obviously discriminatory way in regard to compensation. The tribunal pointed out that the principle of national treatment under article II (2)(a) of the Egypt–US BIT (1986) only prohibits a state from taking measures to cause differential treatment under the "like situations", but in this case, the investor and other enterprises receiving compensation are not in the "like situations", and the investor has nothing to do with the compensations. Therefore, the tribunal identified that the challenged measure is legal because the Egyptian government did not discriminate the investor in compensation and the principle of national treatment was not violated.[55] It is thus clear that the national treatment obligations are limited to granting national treatment under similar or similar circumstances. National treatment is concrete rather than abstract since national treatment obligations are limited to granting national treatment under similar circumstances.

In S.P.P. (Middle East) Limited v. Egypt, the investor reached a "Heads of Agreement" with the Egyptian General Organization for Tourism and Hotels, a public sector enterprise under the control of the Minister of Tourism, and then started up

[54] Helnan International Hotels A/S v. Arab Republic of Egypt, ICSID Case No. ARB/05/19, Award dated July 3, 2008 and Decision of the ad hoc Committee dated June 14, 2010.

[55] Champion Trading Company and Ameritrade International, Inc. v. Arab Republic of Egypt, ICSID Case No. ARB/02/9, Award dated October 27, 2006, para. 134.

the development and operation of the Pyramids Oasis project. The government later cancelled the project, claiming that the project might cause harm to an undiscovered world cultural heritage. The tribunal noted that the cancellation of the project made it difficult for investors to raise additional funds from the international market and to obtain more investment projects, violating the rights of investors as shareholders. The government of Egypt was therefore liable. However, at the same time, the tribunal recognized the legitimacy of the government's cancellation of tourism projects to protect cultural heritage, and this consideration mitigated the liability of the host state.[56] Due to the duality of measures taken by the host state, during the proceedings of annulment, settlement was agreed upon by the parties.[57]

In Ahmonseto v. Egypt, the claims arose out of the modification by a bank allegedly controlled by Egypt of its credit policy toward the claimants, certain customs duties and taxes assessed against the claimants, and four separate criminal proceedings initiated against them. The tribunal held that these actions taken against the claimants were to a large extent beyond the scope of BIT, as they were within the competence reserved by Egypt, but the tribunal still had the power to decide whether the state acted arbitrarily in taking measures of detention. The tribunal pointed out that whether detention constitutes a measure of serious violation of the rights of detainees and thus constitutes a violation of BIT should depend on whether it constitutes excessive impairment of investment. Finally, all claims were dismissed at the merits stage.[58] The key point of this case is that the relevant international investment law protects investment free from damage only within its scope, and the jurisdiction of criminal cases against investors still belongs to the host state's courts. Furthermore, this case also shows that if the host state's measure, which affects the investment, is not excessive or in compliance with the principle of proportionality, the relevant international investment obligation is not violated.

The above conforming measures are reflected in some cases of African countries as respondents. It is shown that if a measure is maintained by tribunals, the host state does not have to assume liability to investors. The cases are as follows: there is no causal relationship between the measures and the losses of investors; the investors are not in "like situations", and therefore, the measures do not violate national treatment. The regulatory measures implemented to the investor in accordance with the laws of the host state conform to the principle of proportionality; in other words, they do not cause excessive damage to investment, and therefore, the host state does not need to assume liability for its measures.

---

56 Southern Pacific Properties (Middle East) Limited v. Arab Republic of Egypt, ICSID Case No. ARB/84/3, Award dated May 20, 1992.

57 Southern Pacific Properties (Middle East) Limited v. Arab Republic of Egypt (ICSID Case No. ARB/84/3), Decision dated March 9, 1993.

58 Ahmonseto, Inc. and others v. Arab Republic of Egypt, ICSID Case No. ARB/02/15, Award dated June 18, 2007, paras. 264, 266, 268.

4.2.2 Non-conforming Measures Denied by Arbitral Tribunals

There are far more non-conforming measures that can be found than conforming measures in African countries as respondents. In many cases, an investor in a dispute would argue that the measures adopted by a host state have violated a few obligations, and consequently, a few alleged breaches may be found by the tribunal. Taking Olin v. Libya as an example, breaches of host state obligations were found by the tribunal to cover FET or the minimum standard of treatment, including denial of justice, arbitrary, unreasonable and discriminatory measures, national treatment, and direct expropriation.[59] Taking Wena Hotels v Egypt as another example, the investment consisted of rights under two long-term hotel lease and development agreements concluded with a company wholly owned by the Egyptian Government. Claims arose out of the alleged breach of agreements to develop and manage two hotels in Luxor and Cairo, Egypt, as well as an alleged campaign of continual harassment to the investor by the Government of Egypt. The investor invoked the ICSID dispute settlement mechanism under the 1975 Egypt-UK BIT. The tribunal found IIA breaches of indirect expropriation, FET or minimum standard of treatment, and FPS. The award dictated that Wena Hotels be compensated for a total of US $8 million, with interest amounting to US $11.4 million.[60]

For the sake of clarity, the non-conforming measures will be described separately in the following in accordance with the main breach of obligations.

4.2.2.1 Measures Related to Nationalization or Expropriation

Measures of Nationalization

Nationalization or expropriation accounts for half of the non-conforming measures. In the 1960s and 1970s, newly independent African countries set off three large-scale waves of nationalization to develop their economies and control their national sovereignty, but this has rarely happened since then. Nationalization was once considered an act of sovereignty, so in the absence of commitments in the domestic law of the host state or relevant international treaties, investors could not normally ask the host state for compensation for the damage caused by nationalization. However, if the host state has made a commitment not to nationalize the investment, the situation is another matter.

In AGIP S.p.A. v. Congo, the issue concerned is the nationalization of an oil distribution company in which the investor held shareholdings. The tribunal noted that the Government of People's Republic of the Congo had committed itself in the 1974 Agreement not to nationalize the company; thus, the subsequent Decree

[59] Olin Holdings Limited v. State of Libya, ICC Case No. 20355/MCP, Award dated May 25, 2018.

[60] Wena Hotels Ltd. v. Arab Republic of Egypt, ICSID Case No. ARB/98/4, Award dated 8 December 2000.

No. 6/75, which nationalized the company, was still a breach of the agreement, and the host state was liable for compensation, although it was not inconsistent with international law.[61] Obviously, the award the tribunal decided in favor of the investor was based on the specific commitment made by the host state to the investor.

In Indorama v. Egypt, the claims arose out of the alleged Egyptian government's renationalization of Indorama's Shebin al-Kom textile factory in Menoufia Province, and the investor claimed that shareholding in the factory was nationalized by the host state. According to Article 5 of the 1975 Egypt-United Kingdom BIT, "[i]nvestments of nationals or companies of either Contracting Party shall not be nationalized, expropriated or subject to measures having effect equivalent to nationalization …". In view of this commitment, finally, the host state and the investor reached a settlement, and the investor was awarded $54 million through settlement.[62]

Expropriation Correlated with Indigenization

In general, indigenization is different from nationalization because it is the private subject within the host state who benefits directly from indigenization measures instead of the government of the host state. Indigenization requires that domestic shareholders achieve a certain shareholding in the enterprise, and the main purpose of the measure is to transfer the ownership of foreign shareholdings to the hands of domestic shareholders. Indigenization may also be that the land in the hands of foreigners is transferred to the hands of the natives. African countries have gained momentum in adopting investment policy of indigenization, and since 2000, under the influence of "resource nationalism", nearly 20 African States have adopted legislation of indigenization. For example, the "[t]he Mining Act (2016) restricts foreign participation in the mining sector and reserves the acquisition of mineral rights to Kenyan companies".[63]

Indigenization measures may sometimes trigger expropriation cases. Among others, South Africa and Zimbabwe are two typical examples.

In the Piero Foresti v. South Africa case, the measure is the enactment of the Mineral and Petroleum Resources Development Act No 28 of 2002 in South Africa and continuing implementation of it. According to the law, the investor has to transfer private ownership of mineral resources to "historically disadvantaged South Africans", accompanied by a licensing system through which the previous owners could apply for so-called "new order rights", and at least 26% of the ownership stake

[61] AGIP S.p.A. v. People's Republic of the Congo, ICSID Case No. ARB/77/1, Award dated November 30, 1979.

[62] Indorama International Finance Limited v. Arab Republic of Egypt, ICSID Case No. ARB/11/32, Award dated 2 December 2011.

[63] See '2020 Investment Climate Statements: Kenya', available at <https://www.state.gov/reports/2020-investment-climate-statements/kenya/>.

in the applying enterprise must be held by black South Africans.[64] Eight investors claimed that the measures terminating their mining rights and forcing them to deinvest constituted expropriation. "The case was discontinued, and eventually settled in a compromise by the host state for the company was not required to fully meet the ownership stake requirements (5% instead of 26%)".[65] The reason for settlement is the government's "fears of copycat action by other mining companies if the investors prevailed".[66] This case is the only case in which South Africa was challenged before the ICSID (AF)Tribunal, which has played a decisive role in South Africa's withdrawal from international investment rule of law because South Africa was aware that the legislation and policy it is pursuing is contrary to the provisions of the BIT concluded between South Africa and European countries.

In Bernhard von Pezold and others v. Zimbabwe,[67] claims arose out of the indigenization without compensation of three estates owned by the claimants, including forestry and agricultural businesses in the context of Zimbabwe's 2000 land reform programme. The government was accused of uncompensated and discriminatory expropriation and not redistributing the land after acquiring land ownership, so it was also not for a public purpose. For the defense of crisis, the investor argued that the government's crisis was only a matter of regulatory measures, which did not exist before its regulatory measure. In addition, it was argued that there was racial discrimination while taking the regulatory measure and that racial discrimination violated the peremptory norms. The government's actions were decided as illegal direct expropriation and other breaches by the tribunal to protect investors' interests. This case is just one of the cases in Zimbabwe aroused by land reform, but all cases were decided in favor of the investor.[68] In addition to the indigenization on the land, Zimbabwe enacted the Indigenization and Economic Empowerment Act in 2007 to

---

[64] Piero Foresti, Laura de Carli and others v Republic of South Africa, ICSID Case No ARB(AF)/07/1, Award dated August 4, 2010, para. 56; Mineral and Petroleum Resources Development Act No 28 of 2002, October 10, 2002, South Africa.

[65] Engela C. Schlemmer, 'An Overview of South Africa's Bilateral Investment Treaties and Investment Policy' (2016) 311 ICSID Review-Foreign Investment Law Journal 186.

[66] Africa, United Nations Economic Commission, Assessing Regional Integration in Africa ARIA IX: Next Steps for the African Continental Free Trade Area 2019.

[67] Bernhard von Pezold and others v. Republic of Zimbabwe, ICSID Case No. ARB/10/15, Award dated July 28, 2015.

[68] Border Timbers Limited, Timber Products International (Private) Limited and Hangani Development Co. (Private) Limited v. Republic of Zimbabwe, ICSID Case No. ARB/10/25, Award dated July 28, 2015. In this case, claims arose out of the Government's compulsory acquisition of claimants' farms and forestry plantations following Zimbabwe's land reform, the alleged expropriation of foreign exchange from claimants' bank accounts and the State's alleged failure to prevent invasions to the forestry plantations by illegal squatters; Bernardus Henricus Funnekotter and others v. Republic of Zimbabwe, ICSID Case No. ARB/05/6, Award dated April 22, 2009. In this case, claims arose out of the enactment of a Land Acquisition Act and other measures authorizing the Government to acquire compulsorily any rural land when the acquisition was deemed necessary for agricultural settlement purposes under which the claimants' properties were allegedly expropriated without compensation, including the presence of war veterans and settlers that forced the claimants to vacate their farms; Mike Campbell (Pvt) Limited v. The Republic of Zimbabwe, Southern African Development Community Tribunal, SADC(T) Case No. 2/2007, December 11, 2007.

impose a cap on the shareholdings of foreign investors in all kinds of enterprises and required foreign investors to transfer 51% of their shareholdings to local natural or legal persons.

Expropriation Lack of Due Process

In Middle East Cement v. Egypt, the main reason for indirect expropriation is the lack of due process. The license granted the claimant the right to import and store bulk cement on a depot ship, but Decree No. 195 prohibits such import for Gray Portland Cement, which is as alleged by the investor, a "de facto revocation of the License". The tribunal decided that the decree amounted to indirect expropriation of the claimant's investment, and the reason for the Egyptian government's liability is not because of the cancellation of the license but because of the lack of due process in the cancellation of the license. Furthermore, after examining the relevant domestic law of Egypt, the tribunal found the auction procedure of the ship to have also not been "under due process of law", and especially that the notification procedure was not sufficient and led to the auction price of the ship not reflecting the market price. This was considered a serious procedural defect and was inconsistent with the provision of the "due process of law" in Article 4(a) of the Egypt–Greece BIT (1993).[69]

In Olin v. Libya, the claims arose out of the alleged expropriation of the claimant's dairy and juice factory in Tripoli. The tribunal decided that the respondent failed to comply with the due process when expropriating the investment because the Libyan Investment Law prohibited expropriation without law or judicial decisions. However, the tribunal also determined that the lack of due process in the Libyan national courts did not amount to denial of justice just because the "[c]laimant did not satisfy the burden and relatively high threshold of proving a denial of justice under international law."[70]

Expropriation Related to Personal Coercion

Different legal consequences will go to the host state when the host state deports foreign investors for different reasons: If the host state takes deportation regulatory measures because the foreign investor violates the laws of the host state, the host state may take such measures. However, if the host state deports the foreign investor for the purpose of encroaching on the interests of the investor, it will be considered illegal. In S.A.R.L. Benvenuti & Bonfant v. Congo, the Congolese government failed to meet its obligations under the agreement between the disputing parties. In addition, the investors claimed that the Congolese government had attempted to bring criminal charges against Mr. Bonfant, which caused him to leave the host

---

[69] Middle East Cement Shipping and Handling Co. v. Arab Republic of Egypt, ICSID Case No. ARB/99/6, Award dated April 12, 2002, paras. 103, 178, 139, 143, 147.

[70] Olin Holdings Limited v. State of Libya, ICC Case No. 20355/MCP, Award dated May 25, 2018.

state at the warning of diplomats. The Arbitral Tribunal held, in combination with other acts of the respondent, that such acts constituted a deprivation of the investor's shareholdings.[71]

In Antoine Goetz and others v. Burundi, the investors claimed that the government of Burundi had taken various measures against its four companies, AFFIMET, ABC, CCA and CCA Maintenance, in the host state, forcing them to stop operations, including customs blockade of AFFIMET materials, suspension of the export duty and tax exemption for AFFIMET. The tribunal confirmed the existence of indirect expropriation and ordered the host state to compensate the investors for their losses.[72]

Expropriation Associated with Breach of an Investment Contract

One of the ways for foreign investors to invest in the host state is to sign a concession agreement with the host state and obtain a project investment license. The concession agreement refers to the agreement between the investor and the host state through which investors obtain certain rights that exclusively belong to the host state and invest in the construction of public utilities, exploitation of natural resources and other special economic activities under certain procedures and conditions.

In Letco v. Liberia, the tribunal found that the Concession Agreement, which was validly entered into and binding, was improperly revoked by the Government of the Republic of Liberia before the date fixed for its expiration, and this conduct constitutes a breach of the Concession Agreement and therefore entitles Letco to the corresponding award of damages to be paid by Liberia as a result of the expropriation.[73]

In AHS Niger and Menzies Middle East and Africa S.A. v. Niger, under the Investment Agreement between AHS Niger and Niger and Investment Code of Niger which encompass consent to ICSID arbitration, the claimants argued that Niger's termination of the Investment Agreement and withdrawal of the license approval constituted a violation of the Investment Agreement, the Investment Code and international law. The tribunal found that the respondent's violation constituted expropriation and ordered the respondent to compensate the claimants for their loss of profit and loss of seized property.[74]

In APCL v. Gambia, the investor claimed its investment of the alleged US $64 million in the exploration of oil in the licensed areas was lost due to the alleged wrongful termination by the Government of licenses for exploration of two offshore oil blocks and constituted expropriation. The tribunal ordered to discontinue the

---

[71] S.A.R.L. Benvenuti & Bonfant v. People's Republic of the Congo, ICSID Case No. ARB/77/2, Award dated August 18, 1980.

[72] Antoine Goetz and others v. Republic of Burundi, ICSID Case No. ARB/01/2, Award dated June 21, 2012.

[73] Liberian Eastern Timber Corporation v. Republic of Liberia, ICSID Case No. ARB/83/2, Award dated March 31, 1986, paras. 87, 115.

[74] AHS Niger and Menzies Middle East and Africa S.A. v. Republic of Niger, ICSID Case No. ARB/11/11, Award dated July 15, 2013, paras. 121–131.

proceeding pursuant to ICSID Arbitration Rule 43.1 dated June 7, 2018, and the case was also finally settled.[75]

In Goetz v. Burundi (I), the investors argued that the Burundi government had deprived them of a certificate of free zone conferring tax and customs exemptions through issuing a ministerial decision, which constitutes indirect expropriation. The tribunal concluded that the measure was adopted in the public interest and was not discriminatory and followed the procedure prescribed by Burundian national law. Therefore, indirect expropriation was found only because there was no compensation. In other words, legal indirect expropriation needs to meet four requirements at the same time. Therefore, the tribunal recommended that Burundi either terminate the contested measure or pay compensation. Finally, the Award was made based on the parties' settlement agreement, which provided for reimbursement of taxes and custom duties and reinstatement of the certificate of free zone.[76]

DP World v. Djibouti is relevant here, and a presidential decree was issued to unilaterally terminate the concession agreement given to DP World to operate container terminal in the Port of Doraleh in 2018. The London Court of Arbitration found the Djibouti government's measures illegal and decided that the measure had resulted in expropriation of property of the DP World. The High Court of England and Wales also decided in favor of the claimant who sought US $1 billion in compensation.[77]

In fact, in all cases of settlement, both sides have their own considerations and have made some concessions to each other, which also means that the regulatory measures of the host state are illegal to some extent.

If any of the requirements of expropriation cannot be met, the expropriation is illegal. In Olin v. Libya, an order of land expropriation was passed, but title to land resorted back to the Claimant five years later, and while eviction notices were served, the factory was never dismantled; therefore, the issue was whether expropriation can be found where decision to expropriate was made but the investment was not actually taken from the Claimant. The tribunal decided that the measures, even if temporary, can have an effect equivalent to expropriation if their length and impact on the investment are sufficiently important.[78] Finally, the tribunal decided that due to lack of compensation, the respondent also failed to comply with conditions for lawful expropriation under the BIT.[79]

Some disputes are settled, and there is no award available, but according to the case, investors will mostly claim compensation for expropriation. In Mærsk v. Algeria, the wholly owned subsidiary of the oil production A.P. Moller-Mærsk Group

---

[75] APCL Gambia B.V. v. Republic of The Gambia, ICSID Case No. ARB/17/40, Settled on June 7, 2018.

[76] Goetz v. Burundi (I) Antoine Goetz and others v. Republic of Burundi (I), ICSID Case No. ARB/95/3, Award (Embodying the Parties' Settlement Agreement) dated February 10, 1999, paras. 124, 126–128, 129.

[77] See 'DP World wins latest Doraleh court case' (January 14, 2020), available at <https://www.portstrategy.com/news101/world/africa/dp-world-wins-latest-doraleh-court-case>.

[78] Olin Holdings Limited v. State of Libya, ICC Case No. 20355/MCP, Award dated May 25, 2018.

[79] Olin Holdings Limited v. State of Libya, ICC Case No. 20355/MCP, Award dated May 25, 2018.

held rights in several Algerian blocks under certain production sharing contracts concluded with Algeria's national oil company for the exploration and production of liquid hydrocarbons. Claims arose out of the government's imposition of a windfall tax collected by the Algerian national oil company, Sonatrach S.P.A. The investor alleged that the Algerian national oil company contravened the terms of a production sharing contract previously concluded between the investor and the national oil company. The final award was US $920 million through settlement.[80]

Additionally, due to taxation, Total E&P v. Uganda relates to the shareholding in four oil and gas blocks in the Lake Albert Rift basin in Uganda, and the claims arose out of an allegedly unlawful tax levied by the Ugandan government because a tax relief term is included in its product sharing agreement for exploration block 2 with the Ugandan government. The dispute was settled without an award.[81] It is speculated that the government may have made some concessions in the settlement.

4.2.2.2 Measures Breaching National Treatment and FET

Different arbitral tribunals make awards according to different FET clauses using different treatment languages in different treaties, and the interpretation of FET is very uncertain. Sometimes, it means customary international law minimum standard, and sometimes it means an independent self-contained treaty standard.

Article 2 of the Tanzania–UK BIT (1994) does not define the meaning of FET, and the tribunal in Biwater v. Tanzania interpreted it as the customary international law minimum standard, and found that the measures alleged by the claimant include the termination of infrastructure project agreements and subsequently "a series of events that allegedly led to the deportation of the investor's senior management, as well as the seizure of its assets and takeover of its business", violated the FET clause of the BIT for their arbitrariness, unreasonableness, and discrimination.[82]

In Olin v. Libya, regarding whether the respondent breached the obligation to accord national treatment, the tribunal found a breach because factories operating in the same business sector and located nearby are appropriate comparators, but two comparable Libyan-owned factories were exempted from the expropriation order.[83]

Regarding whether the respondent frustrated the claimant's legitimate expectation that Libya would not act in violation of its Investment Law and thereby breached its FET obligation, the tribunal decided that it was reasonable and legitimate for the claimant to expect that Libya would not act in breach of its newly enacted Investment

[80] Mærsk Olie, Algeriet A/S v. People's Democratic Republic of Algeria, ICSID Case No. ARB/09/14, Settled on September 30, 2013.

[81] Total E&P Uganda BV v. Republic of Uganda, ICSID Case No. ARB/15/11, Settled on August 3, 2018; 'Uganda's unending oil tax disputes: will URA survive another Total Disaster' (March 10, 2019), available at <http://www.ugandaoil.co/2015/04/10/ugandas-unending-oil-tax-disputes-will-ura-survive-another-total-disaster/>.

[82] Biwater Gauff (Tanzania) Limited v. United Republic of Tanzania, ICSID Case No. ARB/05/22, Award dated July 24, 2008, para. 592.

[83] Olin Holdings Limited v. State of Libya, ICC Case No. 20355/MCP, Award dated May 25, 2018.

Law.[84] In addition, the respondent breached the FET obligation by maintaining the claimant in a situation of heightened uncertainty; that is, while their factory was not physically destroyed, the claimant was prevented from operating its plant under normal business conditions. FET provision entails respect for investors' ability to operate their investment with a minimum level of certainty and to implement basic business decisions in an unfettered manner.[85]

In Unión Fenosa Gas, S.A. v. Egypt, as to whether the disputed measure that the Egyptian SOE suspended gas supplies to the claimant's liquefied nature gas plant was in contravention of the gas purchase agreement, thus, the respondent's revocation of tax-free status of SEGAS (claimant's majority-owned plant operator) constituted an FET breach, the Tribunal decided that the respondent frustrated the investor's legitimate expectations because of the Egyptian Ministry of Petroleum's undertaking in regard to the investment, thus violated the FET standard in the BIT.[86]

4.2.2.3 Measures Contravening FPS

In AMT v. Zaire, a typical case involving FPS, the investment was majority shareholding in a company engaged in the production and sale of automotive and dry cell batteries and in the importation and resale of consumer goods and foodstuffs. Claims arose out of two alleged episodes of looting in which soldiers of the Zairian armed forces destroyed, damaged, or took away certain property, finished goods, raw materials and other objects of value belonging to the local subsidiary of the investor. IIA breaches were found, especially including breach of the FPS clause, or similar losses sustained due to insurrection, war, or similar events.[87]

The civil war in Libya led to a series of cases in which investors felt that their investment interests were not effectively protected during the war. In most of these cases, the investors claimed that the government failed to protect their investments since the start of the civil war in 2011, including acts or omissions of the government or that may be attributed to the government.[88] In these cases, the investors targeted Libya's omission during the war, not the losses caused by the war itself.[89] There are other cases involving Libya due to regulatory measures or breach of contract from

[84] Olin Holdings Limited v. State of Libya, ICC Case No. 20355/MCP, Award dated May 25, 2018.

[85] Olin Holdings Limited v. State of Libya, ICC Case No. 20355/MCP, Award dated May 25, 2018.

[86] Unión Fenosa Gas, S.A. v. Egypt, ICSID Case No. ARB/14/4, Award dated August 31, 2018.

[87] American Manufacturing & Trading, Inc. v. Republic of Zaire, ICSID Case No. ARB/93/1, Award dated February 21, 1997.

[88] Some of these cases are pending, see, e.g., Trasta Energy v. Libya, UNCITRAL, pending, 2019; Simplex Projects Ltd. v. Libya, pending, 2018; D.S. Construction FZCO v. Libya, UNCITRAL, PCA Case No. 2017-21, pending, 2016; Tekfen, TML, Tekfen-TML joint venture v. Libya, ICC, pending, 2015; Way2B ACE v. Libya, ICC, pending, 2015.

[89] See M. Sornarajah, The international law on foreign investment (fifth edition, Cambridge University Press, 2021) 261.

the government side, but almost all ended in the government's defeat if the outcome was available.[90]

4.2.2.4 Measures Violating the Principle of Proportionality

In Unión Fenosa Gas, S.A. v. Egypt, The Tribunal held that the claimant had an investment in Egypt and claims were treaty claims in nature, although the respondent argued that an agreement for supply of gas was purely a commercial transaction, and the claimant's shares in SEGAS were pledged to a bank. The respondent further defended Egypt's conduct coincidence in time with events during Arab Spring by necessity under customary international law. However, the tribunal did not support this defense because the respondent's conduct was not the only way to safeguard its essential interests, and the investment was affected disproportionally. The tribunal ordered the respondent to pay approximately US $2 billion in compensation to the claimant for the measure, violating the principle of proportionality.[91]

4.2.2.5 Measures Involving Arbitrary, Unreasonable and Discriminatory Measures

In Al-Kharafi v. Libya and others, claims arose out of the issuance of a decision by the Libyan Minister of Industry, Economy and Trade by virtue of which a license previously granted to the claimant for the establishment of a touristic investment project in Tripoli, Libya, was annulled. The tribunal decided in favor of the investor because of arbitrary, unreasonable, and discriminatory measures by the host state. This case represents at least one of the highest amounts awarded in Africa, and the amount is US $935 million.[92]

Judging from the cases decided, the number of non-conforming measures far exceeds the number of conforming measures. On the one hand, this shows that the regulatory risks of investing in Africa are relatively high. On the other hand, it can also be understood that through investment arbitration, the non-conforming regulatory measures of the African host state can be controlled so that investors

---

[90] See, e.g., Cengiz v. Libya, ICC Case No. 21537/ZF/AYZ, Award dated November 7, 2018.

[91] Unión Fenosa Gas, S.A. v. Egypt, ICSID Case No. ARB/14/4, Award dated August 31, 2018, para. 13.8.

[92] Mohamed Abdulmohsen Al-Kharafi & Sons Co. v. Libya and others, CRCICA (Cairo Regional Center for International Commercial Arbitration), ad hoc arbitration, Final Arbitral Award dated March 22, 2013; Fola Adeleke, International Investment Law and Policy in Africa: Exploring a Human Rights Based Approach to Investment Regulation and Dispute Settlement (Routledge, 2017). This case is also very controversial, and the arbitrator nominated by Libya even refused to sign on the award, and the moral damages and prospected profit loss awarded to the investor were also criticized as excessive, because damages were awarded for the loss of a 90-year revenue stream from a resort project that had never been constructed. The case also highlights problems with the existing international investment rule of law.

obtain protection to a certain extent. The investigation of ICSID cases involving African countries as respondents shows that arbitral tribunals have not given special preferential treatment or special consideration to the respondents because they are African developing countries and least developed countries.[93]

As a type of international rule of law, international investment arbitration on investment measures is instrumental in promoting the national rule of law because the losing host state may modify its measures. As a typical example, Zimbabwe amended its constitution to replace the 2005 Constitution with the 2013 Constitution after losing a series of international arbitrations on land expropriation. According to the 2005 Constitution, there is no compensation for the expropriated land except for improvements on the land, and investors cannot have access to their domestic courts for this expropriation. That is, "no compensation shall be payable for land referred to in paragraph (a) except for any improvements effected on such land before it was acquired", and "a person having any right or interest in the land—(a) shall not apply to a court to challenge the acquisition of the land by the State, and no court shall entertain any such challenge".[94]

In addition to attaching substantive and procedure conditions to deprivation,[95] the current 2013 Constitution stipulates that those different types of persons are entitled to different "compensation for acquisition of previously acquired agricultural land". Specifically, these persons can be divided into three categories: indigenous Zimbabweans, persons whose home state has an agreement with Zimbabwe to protect the investment, and persons who are not the above two kinds of persons.[96] Thus, the indigenous Zimbabweans can have compensation for the land as well as the improvements, and it should also be stressed that compensation under the BITs and other IIAs concluded by Zimbabwe, these remedies are available to foreign investors that their home states are party to those agreements. In addition, Zimbabwe enacted the New Mines and Minerals Act Amendment in 2013. In particular, Zimbabwe enacted the Investment and Development Agency Act in 2020, and the new law granted foreign investors non-discrimination treatment, FET, guarantees against expropriation, and procedural rights to utilizing ISDS provided in international investment treaties and trade agreements.[97]

It should be added that in some cases, the issue of the legality of the measures taken by the host state has not been addressed due to the refusal of the arbitral tribunal to exercise competence or jurisdiction.

---

[93] See Uché Ewelukwa Ofodile, 'African States, Investor–State Arbitration and the ICSID Dispute Resolution System: Continuities, Changes and Challenges' (2019) 34(2) ICSID Review-Foreign Investment Law Journal 297, 327, 363.

[94] Zimbabwe Constitutional Amendment Act (No 17), 2005, Sections 2.2.b and 2.3.a.

[95] Constitution of Zimbabwe Amendment (No 20) Act, 2013, Sections 71.3 and 71.3.c.

[96] Constitution of Zimbabwe Amendment (No 20) Act, 2013, article 295.

[97] LexAfrica, 'Boon for investors as Zimbabwe enacts new investment promotion law' (February 25, 2020), available at <https://www.lexafrica.com/2020/02/boon-for-investors-as-zimbabwe-enacts-new-investment-promotion-law/>.

In Capital Financial Holdings v. Cameroon, the investment is majority shareholding in Commercial Bank of Cameroon, and the claimant argued unlawful expropriation of its investment by the Government in 2009 when its bank was placed under State control since the Government exercised executive powers instead of the bank's CEO and board of directors. However, the tribunal declined the jurisdiction by finding that it had neither "*ratione personae*" nor "*ratione materiae*" jurisdiction over the case and decided in favor of the host state by ordering the claimant to reimburse the respondent for US $242,098 ICSID arbitration costs.[98] The ad hoc Annulment Committee deferred to the arbitral award during the ICSID annulment proceedings and decided that the claimant assumed all costs during the ICSID annulment proceeding.[99]

It should be added that to illustrate that most of the measures challenged by investors in these cases may be illegal, it can be understood through the following figures. As of May 31, 2017, "in the arbitrations involving an African State Party that have concluded, 42% were settled by the parties or discontinued before a final determination of the tribunal … the other 58% were resolved by a final award by the tribunal … 22% of the awards declined jurisdiction, a further 22% dismissed all claims, and 56% upheld the claims in part or in full".[100] The implication behind the statistics is for those settled cases, the government may think that its regulatory measure is inappropriate more or less and is willing to reach a compromise; of the decided cases, the winning case for investors is 56%, which may indicate that the measures taken by the host state is illegal in these cases. This ratio is much higher than the domestic administrative litigation success rate, indicating a stronger role of the rule of law in international investment. In contrast, among the decided cases roughly during the same period, the award upholding the claimants in part or in full in ICSID arbitration is approximately 46%.[101]

4.3 Relationship Between Non-conforming Measures of the African Host State and Investor Obligations

The basic implication of the international investment rule of law is to limit the power of the host state to protect the rights of investors. However, in cases involving investors' violation of their legal obligations, the host state's liability originating from its measures may be reduced and exempted, or the investor's loss may not be compensated.

---

[98] Capital Financial Holdings Luxembourg S.A. v. Republic of Cameroon, ICSID Case No. ARB/15/18, Award dated June 22, 2017, C. Dispositif.

[99] Capital Financial Holdings Luxembourg S.A. v. Republic of Cameroon, ICSID Case No. ARB/15/18, Decision on Annulment dated October 25, 2019.

[100] The ICSID Caseload-Statistics Special Focus-Africa (May 2017), 15.

[101] The ICSID Caseload-Statistics 2017-2 (Issue 2017-2), 15.

It is recognized by many arbitral tribunals that the legality requirements for an investment applied even when it is not explicitly mentioned in the IIAs,[102] let alone an explicit wording of "in accordance with host state law" is encompassed in the IIAs. In fact, legality is an implicit or explicit obligation on the investment because it is the inherent requirement of the principle of good faith.

Investor misconduct may happen at different phases of investment, including at the time of initiation of the investment, during the operation of the investment and in the dispute resolution process and arbitration proceedings. The most common investor misconduct encompasses bribing public officials of the host state, fraud, non-compliance with regulatory requirements, lack of due diligence, environmental damage, and human rights violations. These investor misconduct may affect the jurisdiction, admissibility or other merits issues in the arbitration process to different degrees.[103] Arbitration practice shows that investor misconduct may also lead to a counterclaim by host state,[104] although there is rare such precedent in investment arbitration involving African countries.

In the final analysis, foreign investors' enjoyment of their rights is contingent on investors' compliance with their obligations, and foreign investors must comply with national law and international law relating to investments and international public policy or transnational public policy. The most typical international public policy is the obligation not to be corrupt, and there are many investment disputes involving this problem that put investors at a disadvantage. No bribery is the minimum standard of conduct in international law and a well-established transnational public policy, and even if the law of the host state does not provide for it, bribery cannot meet the international minimum standard of conduct, which will impede the alleged rights of investors under contract (or treaty) from being protected.[105]

---

[102] See, e.g., in Álvarez y Marín Corporación and others v. Panama, the Claims arose out of decisions by the Panamanian National Authority of Lands Administration (ANATI), which allegedly contradicted prior authorizations and judicial decisions centering on whether the claimants' investment is located within the indigenous protected area of Ngäbe-Buglé, but the tribunal declined to exercise the jurisdiction due to the implied legal requirement on the investment. See Álvarezy Marín Corporación S.A., Estudios Tributarios AP S.A., Stichting Administratiekantoor Anbadi, Bartus van Noordenne and Cornelis Willem van Noordenne v. Republic of Panama, ICSID Case No. ARB/15/14, Award dated October 12, 2018.

[103] See Andrew Newcombe, 'Investor Misconduct: Jurisdiction, Admissibility or Merits?' in Chester Brown & Kate Miles (eds.), Evolution in Investment Treaty Law and Arbitration (Cambridge University Press, 2011) 190.

[104] Perenco Ecuador Limited v. Republic of Ecuador (Petroecuador), ICSID Case No. ARB/08/6, Interim Decision on the Environmental Counterclaim dated August 11, 2015. In this case, the investor was compensated for the losses caused by Ecuadorian measures, and Ecuador also obtained the investor's reparation for its environmental losses through a counterclaim pursuant to Rule 40 of the ICSID Rules of Procedure for Arbitration Proceedings.

[105] Guy Marcel Nono, 'Fighting Bribery and Corruption in Africa: From AU and OECD conventions to a general principle of international investment law, International Institute for Sustainable Development' (March 10, 2020), available at <https://www.iisd.org/itn/en/2020/03/10/fighting-bribery-and-corruption-in-africa-from-au-and-oecd-conventions-to-a-general-principle-of-international-investment-law-guy-marcel-nono/>.

In Rawat v. Mauritius, the disputed measures are a series of measures taken by the government of Mauritius, allegedly including the illegal appointment of special administrators who took control over two insurance and banking companies as well as related companies in which the claimant held interests and the subsequent transfer or sale of their assets to state-owned companies and third parties. The claimant, a dual Mauritian-French national, was found not to be eligible for BIT protection, and the tribunal refused the jurisdiction and ordered "Rawat to pay one-third of Mauritius' total fees and expenses for the jurisdictional objection phase". Thus, the case was decided not in favor of the investor. In fact, Mauritius also argued that its actions were justified because Rawat and his family members coordinated a *money laundering* scheme.[106] Presumably, it has a subtle influence on the arbitral tribunal's decision.

4.3.1 Mitigating Non-conforming Measures Resulting from Breach of Investor Obligations

In the landmark case of World Duty Free v. Kenya, the claimant alleged Kenya violated various contractual obligations and international law by illegally taking and destroying the claimant's property and claimed compensation in the ICSID Arbitral Tribunal because the contract provides the ICSID as the forum for dispute settlement. During the arbitral proceeding in December 2002, however, a document filed by the claimant revealed that the claimant previously bribed the former President of Kenya, Daniel Arap Moi, to conclude the 1989 Agreement. Under this circumstance, Kenya argued that the contract was void and unenforceable as a matter of public policy. The Arbitral Tribunal held the claimant had procured the 1989 Agreement through a bribe to the former Kenyan President and that, consequently, the claimant had no right to pursue or recover under any of its pleaded claims, all of which arose from that 1989 Agreement.[107] The Arbitral Tribunal also held that bribery is contrary to transnational public policy;[108] as a result, to protect the public, the Arbitral Tribunal held

> [i]n light of domestic laws and international conventions relating to corruption, and in light of the decisions taken in this matter by Courts and Arbitral Tribunals, this Tribunal is convinced that bribery is contrary to the international public policy of most, if not all, States or, to use another formula, to transnational public policy. Thus, claims based on contracts of corruption or on contracts obtained by corruption cannot be upheld by this arbitral tribunal.[109]

---

[106] Dawood Rawat v. Republic of Mauritius, PCA Case No. 2016-20, Award on Jurisdiction dated April 6, 2018, paras. 2, 58, 60.

[107] World Duty Free Co. Ltd. v. Republic of Kenya, ICSID Case No. ARB/00/7, Award dated October 4, 2006, para. 179, available at <https://www.italaw.com/cases/3280>.

[108] World Duty Free Co. Ltd. v. Republic of Kenya, ICSID Case No. ARB/00/7, Award dated October 4, 2006, paras. 141–157, available at <https://www.italaw.com/cases/3280>.

[109] World Duty Free Co. Ltd. v. Republic of Kenya, ICSID Case No. ARB/00/7, Award dated October 4, 2006, paras. 181, 157, available at <https://www.italaw.com/cases/3280>.

The arbitral tribunal took the "objective minimum standard of conduct" as the benchmark instead of the host state's standard.[110] The rationale behind this decision is that investors have obligations to comply with international law and domestic law in the host states in which they invest, and investors' misconduct in certain circumstances can affect investors' legal rights *vis-à-vis* host states.

In addition to the most common corruption, investors may also violate other legal obligations. In the case of Cortec Mining v. Kenya, the British investor has not acquired environmental impact assessment when it obtained a mining license for his investments consisting of a 21-year mining license for the extraction of rare earths at the Mrima Hill project in Kenya. The claim was, however, dismissed due to the absence of environmental impact assessment. The tribunal confirmed that environmental impact assessment was one of the requirements for legal investment under Kenyan law. Therefore, it was an unlawful investment because the investor did not perform his environmental impact assessment obligation stipulated by Kenyan law in advance and was not a protected investment. The protested investment must be made in accordance with Kenyan law, which is unnecessary to be expressed in "explicit" language in the United Kingdom–Kenya BIT. The tribunal also decided that "violation must be sufficiently serious so that denial of treaty protection is proportionate response"; in this case, without an environmental impact assessment, it is a serious violation.[111] Therefore, if the investor fails to meet the conditions attached to the license granted, the host state may revoke the license after it is issued.

In some cases, the host state's measure was maintained because the investor had violated the obligations under the arbitration proceedings, and thus, the arbitral tribunal refused jurisdiction and denied admissibility. In Orascom v. Algeria, the tribunal held that the investor's "pursuit of its claims" constituted an abuse of right under the circumstances.[112] Investment tribunals have sometimes found an abuse of right when an investment was restructured to benefit from a treaty's dispute settlement clause in situations where a dispute was foreseeable.

[110] World Duty Free Co. Ltd. v. Republic of Kenya, ICSID Case No. ARB/00/7, Award dated October 4, 2006, paras. 156, 172, available at <https://www.italaw.com/cases/3280>.

[111] Cortec Mining Kenya Limited, Cortec (Pty) Limited and Stirling Capital Limited v. Republic of Kenya, ICSID Case No. ARB/15/29, Award dated October 22, 2018. Cf: in South American Silver v. Bolivia, Claims arising out of the Government's decree that revoked mining concessions held by the claimant's subsidiary, following protests and social unrest within the indigenous populations in the mining area, the Respondent argued that the Claimant did not have "clean hands" and failed to comply with requirement of legality of investment, therefore, the Tribunal lacked jurisdiction. The Tribunal decided that legality requirement applies even when not mentioned in an IIA, but the alleged violations do not "go to the essence" of investment, therefore, denial of BIT protection would be disproportionate, finally, the direct expropriation was found. See South American Silver Limited v. The Plurinational State of Bolivia, PCA Case No. 2013-15, Award dated August 30, 2018.

[112] Orascom TMT Investments S.à r.l. v. People's Democratic Republic of Algeria, ICSID Case No. ARB/12/35, Award dated May 31, 2017, paras. 539, 540.

4.3.2 *Unaffecting Non-conforming Measures Due to Insufficient Evidence*

In Unión Fenosa Gas, S.A. v. Egypt, the investment at issue is majority shareholding (80%) in SEGAS, an Egyptian company that operated the Damietta liquefied nature gas plant in the port of Damietta. The respondent argued that the investment was illegal because the claimant committed acts of corruption when developing the project and concluding the gas purchase agreement. Nevertheless, the tribunal decided by the majority that the investment was legal and awarded in favor of the investor because of insufficient proof.[113] In this case, the Arbitral Tribunal did not give any discretion to Egypt's then chaotic situation or the investor's bribery potential and dictated Egypt to bear full reparation under customary international law. Therefore, it was debatable how the burden of proof for investor bribery should be apportioned,[114] but in any event, the key point is that Egypt succeeded in discharging its burden of proof to provide evidence of corruption for the investor to procure the investment. For example, if Egypt had ever prosecuted the investor for its criminal conduct regarding its investments, then the tribunal would not exercise jurisdiction to the case. In other words, investors have an obligation to make legal investments.

Similarly, in AHCA v. Congo, the defendant argued that there was no contract because the contract was obtained through the corrupt practices of the Mobutu regime in which the claimant was heavily involved; however, the defendant did not provide persuasive evidence so that the tribunal rejected the allegation of the defendant.[115]

The practice of investment arbitration where African countries are the respondents shows that even if there is no explicit legal requirement in the investment treaty, investors still have the obligation to ensure that their investment is legal. Illegality of investment is a jurisdictional impediment because it is presumed that the State's consent to arbitrate was limited to investments made in accordance with host state laws. In other words, illegal investment cannot be protected. In addition, illegal nationality planning for access to arbitration also becomes an obstacle to jurisdiction. Furthermore, illegal operation of the investment or misconduct to gain benefits during the arbitration will provide the state with a defense on the merits of the case, assessing damages, apportionment of the costs of the arbitration and parties' legal fees. Moreover, in Africa, in addition to legal obligations, investors should attach importance to social responsibility to obtain "social licenses". For example, in some investments involving the protection of the local historical and cultural heritage or

---

[113] Unión Fenosa Gas, S.A. v. Egypt, ICSID Case No. ARB/14/4, Award dated August 31, 2018, paras. 7.4, 7.20, 7.56, 7.57, 7.110.

[114] Dissenting Opinion of Mark Clodfelter in Unión Fenosa Gas, S.A. and Arab Republic of Egypt, ICSID Case No. ARB/14/4, Dissenting Opinion dated August 31, 2018.

[115] See African Holding Company of America, Inc. and Société Africaine de Construction au Congo SARL v. Democratic Republic of Congo, Sentence sur les déclinatoires de compétence et la recevabilité, Affaire CIRDI No ARB/05/21, le 29 juillet 2008, paras. 48, 49, 53.

environment, disputes may arise if the affected communities fail to agree with the establishment or operation of the investment.[116]

Chapter Summary

Through the investigation of the available cases and the known awards in which African States are respondents, it is shown that the various regulatory measures taken by African host states, such as the exercise of legislative, executive, and judicial power, are constrained by the international investment rule of law, and African countries have lost in many investor-state arbitrations because the regulatory measures do not conform to the international investment rule of law. Therefore, governments of African countries should identify the boundary between legal and illegal measures for the implementation of national policy to avoid losing the case in international investment arbitration. The specific basis of legality and illegality is, of course, the provisions of the IIAs, domestic law or contract, if any, applicable in the case. There are legal and illegal boundaries, such as whether the measures are discriminatory, excessive, or conforming to the principle of proportionality. African countries should keep a close eye on the legality of their regulatory measures and the preservation of their policy space in both treaties and domestic laws.

Therefore, in the future, foreign investors may face similar real regulatory risks in investing in Africa and need to envisage strategies to protect themselves,[117] especially in African countries, where many investor-state disputes have arisen. These regulatory measures may have various manifestations and may differ in specific cases, but investors invariably need to pay close attention to the risks of regulatory measures in some African countries to protect their own legitimate interests.

At the same time, the cases in which investors violate their legal obligations also show that in the international investment rule of law, at this stage, investors already need to assume certain responsibilities and duties to ensure that their investments are legal. For their own sustainable development, investors should also avoid misconduct. These misconducts include violations of environmental and social permits, fraud in

[116] Andrew Mizner, 'Win for Mauritius in World Heritage Development Dispute. African Law and Business' (March 18, 2020), available at <https://iclg.com/alb/10906-win-for-mauritius-in-world-heritage-development-dispute>; Thomas Gosling and others v. Republic of Mauritius, ICSID Case No. ARB/16/32, Award dated February 18, 2020.

[117] For example, the very first case against an African state by a mainland Chinese investor happened before the LCIA arbitral tribunal in 2021. In this case, the Chinese investor Beijing Everyway Traffic and Lighting Company Limited initiated an arbitration against Ghana under the China–Ghana BIT by claiming compensation from Ghana for cancellation of traffic management contract. Ghanaian government's chaotic management has also been criticized at home. See Damien Charlotin, 'Chinese Investor Doubles Down on ad hoc Treaty Arbitration Against Ghana by Filing Parallel LCIA Claim' (June 28, 2021), available at <https://www.iareporter.com/articles/chinese-investor-doubles-ad-hoc-treaty-arbitration-against-ghana-with-parallel-lcia-claim/>; 'IMANI Alert: The Accra Intelligent Traffic Management Project (AITMS); How to use Legal Plunder to Terminate an ongoing Project, in spite of glaring Court Judgement Debts', available at <https://imaniafrica.org/2020/11/23/imani-alert/>; 'Chinese company claims US $55 m from Ghana for cancellation of traffic management contract' (February 13, 2021), Business News of Saturday, available at <https://www.ghanaweb.com/GhanaHomePage/business/Chinese-company-claims-US-55m-from-Ghana-for-cancellation-of-traffic-management-contract-1179277>.

obtaining investment contracts, money laundering, bribery, and abuse of rights. The investors are reminded to pay close attention to the obligations of those claimants who lose the case.

In sum, it can be found that the international investment rule of law has played an important role in protecting the reasonable measures of the African host state on the one hand and constraining the unreasonable abuse of power of those African host states on the other. In addition, international investment rule of law has started to ensure that investor obligations clause relevant to measures become "the living law" in investment arbitration jurisprudence related to African countries, instead of the "dead clause" or "sleeping clause" in the treaties.

Chapter 5
African International Investment Rule of Law: A Survey of African IIAs

African countries have not only played an important role in the formation and development of the international investment rule of law but will also greatly affect the future direction of the international investment rule of law. The international investment rule of law in Africa that is embodied in international investment agreements (IIAs), especially regional integration agreements, has strong African characteristics. In recent years, the African international investment rule of law, as an important part of the international investment rule of law in the world, has attracted the attention of scholars. This is evident from the works of many scholars in recent years.[1] However, there are still very limited comprehensive studies on the African international investment rule of law. This research will examine the international investment rule of law in Africa at the bilateral, regional, and multilateral levels from the functional perspective of the rule of law. Finally, South Africa's practice will be addressed as a case study.

---

[1] For example, Yenkong Ngangjoh Hodu and Makane Mois Mbengue, African Perspectives in International Investment Law (Manchester University Press, 2020); Olabisi D Akinkugbe, 'Reverse Contributors? African State Parties, ICSID and the Development of International Investment Law' (2019) 34(2) ICSID Review-Foreign Investment Law Journal 434–454; Won Kidane, 'The Culture of Investment Arbitration: An African Perspective' (2019) 34(2) ICSID Review-Foreign Investment Law Journal 411–433; Mustaqeem De Gama, Hamed El-Kady, 'The Reform of the International Investment Regime: An African Perspective' (2019) 34(2) ICSID Review-Foreign Investment Law Journal 482–495; Gracious Avayiwoe, 'The Republic of Ghana and Bilateral Investment Treaties: A Burgeoning Expert?' (2020) 35(1–2) ICSID Review-Foreign Investment Law Journal 50–62; Antonio R Parra, 'The Participation of African States in the Making of the ICSID Convention' (2019) 34(2) ICSID Review-Foreign Investment Law Journal 270–277; Makane Mois Mbengue, "Somethin' ELSE': African Discourses on ICSID and on ISDS—An Introduction' (2019) 34(2) ICSID Review-Foreign Investment Law Journal 259–269.

X. Han, *Legal Protection and Sustainability of Chinese Investments in Africa*,
Modern China and International Economic Law,
https://doi.org/10.1007/978-981-19-1882-7_5

5.1 African State Practices in International Investment Rule of Law at Bilateral Level

African countries have a positive attitude toward concluding IIAs. It was reported in 2019 that "...[s]ince the 1960s, African countries have concluded 852 BITs, of which 515 are currently in force and 173 are intra-African" and that "African BITs represent approximately 28% of BITs worldwide".[2] North African countries are the most active countries in the contracting BIT, for example, Egypt boasts the biggest stock of signed BIT(100), followed by Morocco(68), Tunisia(55), and finally Algeria(46).[3] Since the mid-1990s, African BITs have increased rapidly. The nature of such BITs was pointed out profoundly: "this surge was mainly driven by the traditional trade and investment partners of the continent, reflecting the colonial linkage and heritage. They were primarily geared to protect and lock in vested investment interests of the developed-country partners already prevalent in the region, in particular for sectors such as the minerals and natural resource extraction industries".[4]

However, in terms of the number of annual treaties concluded, a decline has been seen since the beginning of the twenty-first century.[5] From the point of view of the present author, African countries have signed relatively more BITs globally, and the decline may be mainly due to two reasons. First, the global treaty stock is already huge, and the space for further concluding treaties is becoming narrow. Second, in recent years, the role of BITs in promoting foreign investment has come under question. The increase in the number of arbitral cases involving African countries has acted as a deterrent to African countries under circumstances challenging the legitimacy of international investment arbitration. Therefore, although African countries are actively reaching investment agreements on the regional and continental level, some African countries have chosen to take a wait-and-see attitude toward the conclusion and enforcement of BITs, renegotiating or even withdrawing from the mechanism altogether. For example, South Africa is terminating a number of its BITs gradually, while Kenya has been reviewing its BITs.[6] It was pointed out with concern that "[t]he

[2] United Nations Economic Commission for Africa, African Union, Assessing Regional Integration in Africa ARIA IX: Next Steps for the African Continental Free Trade Area 2019, 174, available at <https://archive.uneca.org/sites/default/files/PublicationFiles/aria9_report_en_4sept_fin.pdf>.

[3] See United Nations Economic Commission for Africa, African Union, Assessing Regional Integration in Africa ARIA IX: Next Steps for the African Continental Free Trade Area 2019, 175.

[4] United Nations Economic Commission for Africa, Investment Policy and Bilateral Investment Treaty in Africa: Implication for Regional Integration, Addis Ababa, Ethiopia:2016, 3, 18, available at <https://archive.uneca.org/sites/default/files/PublicationFiles/eng_investment_landscaping_study.pdf>.

[5] See United Nations Economic Commission for Africa, African Union, Assessing Regional Integration in Africa ARIA IX: Next Steps for the African Continental Free Trade Area 2019, 174.

[6] See Engela C. Schlemmer, 'An Overview of South Africa's Bilateral Investment Treaties and Investment Policy' (2016) 31(1) ICSID Review-Foreign Investment Law Journal 167–193; James Kariuki, 'Kenya told to review bilateral trade agreements' (September 16,

Majority of African BITs concluded between 1980 to 2012 are still in effect, with outdated and broad standards limit the right of African host countries to regulate investment in their territories", and those BITs "unduly expose African countries to investor-State dispute settlement(ISDS) with potentially costly consequences".[7]

The author believes that for African IIAs' complexity, there is a need to distinguish between African countries' internal and external BITs and, in the external BITs category, between BITs with developed countries and those with developing countries. In terms of the specific clauses, BITs with developed countries impose more stringent restrictions on the regulatory power of the host state. In addition, some new-generation African BITs include innovative provisions that allow for the promotion of sustainable development, environmental, and human rights considerations,[8] the power of host states to regulate and the obligation of the investor. While the BIT does play a role in advancing the international investment rule of law to a certain degree, the current BIT practice may be too demanding in African countries without considering their development level.

5.1.1 *BITs Between African States*

In the past, there was little investment between African countries, but some African countries still chose the BIT to express their desires to promote and protect intra-African investments. "The first BIT between two African countries was signed in 1982 by Egypt and Somalia".[9] In contrast, "[a]t that time, African countries had already signed 110 BITs with non-African counterparts".[10] In fact, "it was only in the late 1990s that BITs gained currency among African countries".[11] With the development of intra-African investment, intra-African BITs increased accordingly.

2014), available at <https://www.tralac.org/news/article/6244-kenya-told-to-review-bilateral-trade-agreements.html>.

[7] See United Nations Economic Commission for Africa, African Union, Assessing Regional Integration in Africa ARIA IX: Next Steps for the African Continental Free Trade Area 2019, 175.

[8] See Chrispas Nyombi, Tom Mortimer and Narissa Ramsundar, 'The Morocco-Nigeria BIT: Towards a New Generation of Intra-African BITs' (2018) 29(2) International Company and Commercial Law Review 69–80.

[9] Africa, United Nations Economic Commission, Investment Policy and Bilateral Investment Treaty in Africa: Implication for Regional Integration, Addis Ababa, Ethiopia: 2016, IX.

[10] Africa, United Nations Economic Commission, Investment Policy and Bilateral Investment Treaty in Africa: Implication for Regional Integration, Addis Ababa, Ethiopia: 2016, 20–21.

[11] See Africa, United Nations Economic Commission, Investment Policy and Bilateral Investment Treaty in Africa: Implication for Regional Integration, Addis Ababa, Ethiopia: 2016, 21.

In recent years, BITs between African countries have become more popular as intra-African investment flows have increased, and "African countries have concluded over 860 BITs, of which approximately 160 are intra-African treaties".[12]

After examining its specific terms, it can be found that the 2016 Morocco–Nigeria BIT is representative of the new generation of African BITs. The treaty shows the features of a new generation of BITs between African developing countries, "one of the most innovative and balanced BITs ever concluded".[13] Although it is submitted that the treaty "tilts towards the host state's regulatory powers".[14]

For the value orientation of the BIT, sustainable development is emphasized instead of protection of investors. In the preamble of Morocco–Nigeria BIT 2016, sustainable development, in line with UNCTAD's Reform Package for the International Investment Regime, is mentioned four times, in addition to the special need for developing countries to exercise regulatory rights as well as the balance of rights and obligations of investors on the whole.[15] Aside from the preamble, the substantive text also mentions sustainable development under Article 1.3, the definition of investment.

For investor protection and indirect restrictions on regulatory power of the host state, it is worth noting that the terms used are more rigorous, whether it is under the definitions of investors, investments, and "like circumstances" to determine national treatment, or the clarification to the scope and implication of FET, FPS, expropriation, the MFN, and compensation for damages and loss.[16]

This BIT stresses the role of the Joint Committee composed of representatives of both parties in settling investor-state disputes. If the Joint Committee cannot solve the dispute and after the exhaustion of local remedies by the claimant, the international arbitration mechanisms on investor-state investment dispute can be resorted to.[17]

For direct authorization of regulatory powers of the host state, the BIT emphasizes the right to regulate sustainable development as well as to achieve the host state's legitimate social and economic policy objective.[18] The BIT clarifies the environmental law and environmental regulatory power of the Party.[19] The BIT stresses the labor and human rights protection obligations on the Parties to align them with

---

[12] See El-Kady Hamed and De Gama Mustaqeem, 'The Reform of the International Investment Regime: An African Perspective' (2019) 34(2) ICSID Review-Foreign Investment Law Journal 482–495, 482.

[13] Tarcisio Gazzini, 'The 2016 Morocco–Nigeria BIT: An Important Contribution to the Reform of Investment Treaties', available at <https://www.iisd.org/itn/en/2017/09/26/the-2016-morocco-nigeria-bit-an-important-contribution-to-the-reform-of-investment-treaties-tarcisio-gazzini/>.

[14] Okechukwu Ejims, 'The 2016 Morocco–Nigeria Bilateral Investment Treaty: More Practical Reality in Providing a Balanced Investment Treaty?' (2019) 34(1) ICSID Review-Foreign Investment Law Journal 62–84, 84.

[15] See Morocco-Nigeria BIT, signed on 3 December 2016, preamble.

[16] See Morocco-Nigeria BIT, signed on December 3, 2016, articles 1, 6–9.

[17] See Morocco-Nigeria BIT, signed on December 3, 2016, articles 26, 27.

[18] See Morocco-Nigeria BIT, signed on December 3, 2016, article 23.

[19] See Morocco-Nigeria BIT, signed on December 3, 2016, article 13.

international standards and obligations under international treaties.[20] It is also worth noting that the inclusion of anti-corruption clauses imposes an anti-corruption obligation on the parties.[21] In addition, the flexibility increases in amending or terminating the BIT, and the "survival clause" is not included in the BIT.[22]

For the investor's obligations, the 2016 Morocco–Nigeria BIT places environmental and social impact assessment obligations on investors or the investment.[23] Furthermore, a violation of the corruption provision of the BIT by the investor or their investment constitutes a breach of the domestic law of the host state. Both contracting parties are liable to prosecution, conviction, and penalization of the investor.[24] Investors and investments shall continually fulfill postestablishment obligations related to labor, the environment and human rights and conform to high standards of corporate governance and practices.[25] The BIT also provides investors with civil liability under home state law if they cause significant damage, personal injuries, or loss of life in the host state.[26] In addition to the articulation of legal liability, the BIT suggests non-legally binding corporate social responsibility to investors.[27]

Therefore, the 2016 Morocco–Nigeria BIT reconceptualizes the traditional BIT, indicating that BITs between African countries are no longer BITs with simple provisions or copied BITs from developed countries. In other words, African countries are becoming BIT makers and innovators.

However, Morocco's later BIT contracting practices are not highly consistent in that they do not follow the concept and structure in the 2016 Morocco–Nigeria BIT. For instance, the Morocco–Serbia BIT,[28] Morocco–Rwanda BIT,[29] Morocco–Congo BIT,[30] and Guinea-Bissau–Morocco BIT,[31] still follow the model of the traditional BIT.

The 2016 Morocco–Nigeria BIT will not be the only revolutionary aspect of Africa's IIA future practice. It is said that "the Investment Protocol of the AfCFTA, scheduled to be negotiated as part of phase II of the African continental integration process, could potentially replace over 170 intra-African BITs".[32] If this becomes a reality, the international rule of law in the mutual investment among African countries will have a unified African feature and will be a balanced rule of law at a relatively low level.

---

[20] See Morocco-Nigeria BIT, signed on December 3, 2016, article 15.

[21] See Morocco-Nigeria BIT, signed on December 3, 2016, article 17.

[22] See Morocco-Nigeria BIT, signed on December 3, 2016, articles 30, 31, 34.

[23] See Morocco-Nigeria BIT, signed on December 3, 2016, article 13.

[24] See Morocco-Nigeria BIT, signed on December 3, 2016, article 17.

[25] See Morocco-Nigeria BIT, signed on December 3, 2016, articles 18, 19.

[26] See Morocco-Nigeria BIT, signed on December 3, 2016, article 20.

[27] See Morocco-Nigeria BIT, signed on December 3, 2016, article 24.

[28] See Morocco-Serbia BIT, signed on June 6, 2013.

[29] See Morocco-Rwanda BIT, signed on October 19, 2016.

[30] See Morocco- Congo BIT, signed on April 30, 2018.

[31] See Morocco-Guinea-Bissau BIT, signed on May 28, 2015.

[32] UNCTAD, Taking Stock of IIA Reform: Recent Developments, July 7, 2019.

5.1.2 BITs Between African and Non-African States

The BIT originated in Europe, and the first BIT in the world, the Germany–Pakistan BIT, was signed in 1959. In 1960, Chad and France signed the first BIT on the continent and established a traditional where African countries signed BITs with countries outside Africa, particularly their ex-colonists.[33] In addition, some African countries have BITs with the US, such as Cameroon, D.R. Congo, Congo, Egypt, Morocco, Mozambique, Rwanda, and Tunisia.[34]

In view of the asymmetric investment flow and bargaining power, the BITs between the developed states and the developing state mostly stress limiting the powers of developing host states and protecting the interests of investors from developed countries. The same is true for BITs between African states and developed states. South Africa has denounced its traditional BITs with European countries for this reason.

As far as procedural provisions are concerned, many BITs include ISDS to protect the interests of investors and bind the power of the host state through dispute resolution. Many BITs include an ICSID dispute settlement clause and refer to the United Nations Commission on International Trade Law (UNCITRAL) arbitration and the International Chamber of Commerce (ICC) arbitration for selection.

To date, there has been no fundamental change in BITs between African and Western countries. Since the twenty-first century, Canada has signed BITs with a range of African countries, including Guinea, Burkina Faso, Côte d'Ivoire, Mali, Senegal, Cameroon, Tanzania, and Benin.[35] These BITs are based on the 2012 Canadian Model BIT and reflect the "realpolitik".[36] Take the Tanzania–Canada BIT as an example. This BIT clearly embodies the characteristics of the North–South BIT.[37] Similarly, the US–Rwanda BIT, based on the 2004 US Model BIT, does not give special consideration to Rwanda's least developed country status; it even includes national treatment clauses for the pre-establishment phase.[38] Thus far, Rwanda's first and only case before ICSID was just filed by a US investor, and the applicable IIA is this Rwanda–US BIT.[39]

---

[33] See Africa, United Nations Economic Commission, Investment Policy and Bilateral Investment Treaty in Africa: Implication for Regional Integration, Addis Ababa, Ethiopia: 2016, IX, 21.

[34] See Bilateral Investment Treaties Currently in Force, available at <https://tcc.export.gov/Trade_Agreements/Bilateral_Investment_Treaties/index.asp>.

[35] See Canada, 'Bilateral Investment Treaties' (November 20, 2019), available at <https://investmentpolicy.unctad.org/international-investment-agreements/countries/35/canada>.

[36] See J. Anthony VanDuzer, 'Canadian Investment Treaties with African Countries: What Do They Tell Us About Investment Treaty Making in Africa?' (2017) 18(3) The Journal of World Investment and Trade 556–584.

[37] See Canada-Tanzania BIT, signed on May 17, 2013, entered into effect on December 9, 2013.

[38] See Rwanda-United States BIT, signed on February 19, 2008, entered into effect on January 1, 2012.

[39] See Bay View Group LLC and The Spalena Company LLC v. Republic of Rwanda, ICSID Case No. ARB/18/21, pending, 2018.

In the Kenya–Japan BIT, sustainable development is not mentioned in the preamble. The definition of investment is very broad, as shown by portfolio investment, sovereign debt, ordinary commercial transaction is not excluded, and even the "in accordance with host state laws" requirement is not contained. For the substantive treatment of investments, FET is maintained without an exhaustive or indicative list and expropriation without carving-out general regulatory measures. In fact, the regulatory power of the host state is not stressed very much. In addition, the BIT has a list of prohibited performance requirements. There is no obligation on the investor. For the procedure aspect, ISDS is included and applied to provisions in the BIT without any limitation or exclusion.[40] Therefore, it can be found that the Kenya–Japan BIT is a typical "high-level" BIT dominated by Japan and is favorable to investors one-sidedly. The most recent Japan–Morocco BIT does not show substantial improvement.[41]

For the BITs between African countries and Brazil, in fact, all African countries that signed BITs with Brazil adopted Brazil's model. The constitutional requirements impeded the ratification of 14 BITs signed by Brazil in the 1990s.[42] Thus, Brazil adopted the 2015 Model "Cooperation and Facilitation Investment Agreement" (CFIA) and initiated the introduction of investment agreements to facilitate and promote investment to replace the traditional protection approach. Brazil has thus far signed CFIAs with Morocco, Ethiopia, Angola, Malawi, and Mozambique.[43] These agreements are similar in clauses, are all based on the 2015 Brazil Model CFIA, and do not contain substantive protection clauses. They also omit ISDS procedural provisions that to some extent can restrict the power of the state and only include dispute prevention and state-state dispute settlement mechanisms. Thus, while such treaties have no full meaning of the international investment rule of law, they emphasize the traditionally neglected approach to investment, which perhaps facilitation and promotion need to be given attention in the future.

In summary, in the process of creating an international investment rule of law, "African states tend to be rule-takers in North–South relations, yet enjoy greater agency in negotiations of South-South BITs".[44] African countries are becoming rule

---

[40] See Kenya-Japan BIT, signed on August 28, 2016, entered into force on September 14, 2017.

[41] See 2020 Japan-Morocco BIT, signed on January 8, 2020.

[42] See UNCTAD, World Investment Report 2017: Investment and the Digital Economy, Chapter III.

[43] See IIAs by Economy, Brazil, available at <https://investmentpolicy.unctad.org/international-investment-agreements/countries/27/brazil>.

[44] See Wolfgang Alschner and Dmitriy Skougarevskiy, 'Rule-takers or rule-makers? A new look at African bilateral investment treaty practice' (2016) 4 Transnational Dispute Management, available at <https://ssrn.com/abstract=2791474>.

makers as well.[45] This is perhaps most evident in China–Africa BIT, which will be discussed in detail in Chap. 6.

5.1.2.1 Recent Developments in African BITs

Some African countries are currently reviewing or have recently revised their model BITs.[46] At the same time, some countries in Africa have actively signed BITs with other countries. The most salient case is the BITs signed between African countries and Canada, in total 9 BITs, as mentioned above. In addition, five countries signed CFIAs with Brazil: Malawi-Brazil CFIA (June 25, 2015), Angola-Brazil CFIA (April 1, 2015), Mozambique-Brazil CFIA (March 30, 2015), Ethiopia-Brazil CFIA (April 11, 2018), and Morocco-Brazil CFIA (June 13, 2019).[47] These CFIAs establish institutional frameworks and thematic agendas for investment cooperation and facilitation and mechanisms for risk mitigation and dispute prevention.

Additionally, the Côte d'Ivoire–Singapore BIT (August 27, 2014), the Burkina Faso–Singapore BIT (August 27, 2014), the Ethiopia–United Arab Emirates BIT (February 23, 2016), and the Mauritius–United Arab Emirates BIT (September 20, 2015) have already been signed. BITs between African countries are also emerging, such as the Mauritius–Zambia BIT, which was signed on July 14, 2015, the Angola–Mozambique BIT on November 9, 2015,[48] the Mauritius–Egypt BIT on June 25, 2014, and the Mauritius–Gabon BIT on July 18, 2013.[49]

South Africa does not follow the trend and decides not to renew the expiring BITs and to refrain from concluding new agreements.[50] It seems that the China–South Africa BIT and other BITs with African countries will not be continued when they expire and will face the same fate as the BITs between South Africa and EU member states that have been abrogated. After introducing the 2013 Promotion and Protection of Investment Draft Bill and the 2015 Promotion and Protection of Investment

[45] See Emmanuel T. Laryea and Oladapo O. Fabusuyi, 'Africanisation of international investment law for sustainable development: challenges' (2021) 20(1) Journal of International Trade Law and Policy 42–64; Wolfgang Alschner and Dmitriy Skougarevskiy, 'Rule-takers or rule-makers? A new look at African bilateral investment treaty practice' (2016) 4 Transnational Dispute Management, available at <https://ssrn.com/abstract=2791474>; Makane Mois Mbengue, 'Africa's voice in the formation, shaping and redesign of international investment law' (2019) 34(2) ICSID Review-Foreign Investment Law Journal 455–481, 456.

[46] For example, Botswana and Namibia are reconsidering their approaches to BITs. See UNCTAD, World Investment Report 2015: Reforming International Investment Governance (2015, United Nations) 108, 110. Morocco introduced the 2019 Morocco Model BIT.

[47] See UNCTAD, General Hub News, Brazil and Mozambique Signed CFIA (April 1, 2015), available at <http://investmentpolicyhub.unctad.org/News/Hub/Archive/287>.

[48] See Angola and Mozambique Sign Investment Promotion Agreement, available at <http://allafrica.com/stories/201511110181.html>.

[49] See UNCTAD, International Investment Agreements, Most Recent IIAs, available at <http://investmentpolicyhub.unctad.org/IIA/MostRecentTreaties#iiaInnerMenu>.

[50] See the Department of Trade and Industry Republic of South Africa, Policy Statement: The South African Government's Approach to Future International Investment Treaties (July 2010).

Bill,[51] South Africa enacted the 2015 Protection of Investment Act was enacted on December 15, 2015.[52] Obviously, it tries to regulate foreign investment in South Africa exclusively through national rule of law instead of international rule of law, that is, BITs and other IIAs.

It is clear from the above that African countries, with the exception of South Africa, do not oppose or reject ratifying or updating old BITs and have remarkably concluded new BITs.[53] Under these circumstances, China should make every effort to cause existing China–Africa BITs to come into effect or to be updated and negotiate new BITs with African countries.

It is also clear from state practices in Africa that African countries do not oppose investment protection, nor do they object to investor-state investment arbitration, according to their internal IIAs or BITs. In contrast, African states acknowledge the need for appropriate investment protection and ISDS, and this can be illustrated by the following.

First, the Southern African Development Community (SADC) Protocol on Finance and Investment (PFI) is an investment treaty in force among SADC members. It stipulates that those investments and investors shall enjoy FET in the territory of any State Party, and this treatment shall be no less favorable than that granted to investors of the third State, which means MFN treatment for investors within SADC. The Protocol encourages its members to accede to the ICSID convention and other multilateral agreements related to investments and provides that the "State Parties may conclude BITs with third States".[54] For ISDS, the investor or the State Party concerned in a dispute may refer the dispute either to the SADC Tribunal, an ICSID Convention arbitral tribunal, the ICSID Additional Facility arbitration, or an international arbitrator or ad hoc arbitral tribunal under UNCITRAL Arbitration Rules.[55] Although the SADC Tribunal has suspended jurisdiction to the investor-state dispute

---

[51] See Minister of Trade and Industry, Promotion and Protection of Investment, 2013, draft Bill, published in Government Gazette, Vol.581, No.36995, November 1, 2013, available at <http://www.gov.za/sites/www.gov.za/files/150728Bill_28Jul2015.pdf>; See Minister of Trade and Industry, Promotion and Protection of Investment, 2015, Bill, B18-2015, July 28, 2015, available at <http://www.gov.za/sites/www.gov.za/files/150728Bill_28Jul2015.pdf>.

[52] See 2015 Protection of Investment Act, Act No. 22 of 2015, Government Gazette, Republic of SouthAfrica, Vol. 606 Cape Town, No.39514, December 15, 2015, available at <https://www.thedti.gov.za/gazzettes/39514.pdf>.

[53] For example, Zimbabwe ratified its 1999 BIT with Iran on January 26, 2015. See Zimbabwe, Bilateral Investment Treaties (BITs), available at <http://investmentpolicyhub.unctad.org/IIA/Country> Bits/233#iiaInnerMenu.

[54] South African Development Community, SADC Protocol on Finance and Investment, Annex I (Co-operation on Investment), signed on August 18, 2006 and came into force on April 16, 2010, articles 6, 21, 26, available at <http://investmentpolicyhub.unctad.org/Download/TreatyFile/2730>.

[55] See South African Development Community, SADC Protocol on Finance and Investment, Annex I (Co-operation on Investment), article 28.

"after several judgements ruling against the Zimbabwean government", other international arbitrations are not yet canceled.[56] Certainly, nobody knows the future of the PFI after it is revised.

Second, from the Investment Agreement for the Common Market for Eastern and Southern Africa (COMESA) Common Investment Area of 2007, evidence of open and liberal practice of IIAs within Africa can also be seen. The agreement offers FET, national treatment, and MFN treatment to the investor and compensation for expropriation and losses in war or caused by requisition or destruction of the investment.[57] It encourages the member states to accede the ICSID Convention and other multilateral agreements related to investment and vests the host state with the right of the counterclaim.[58]

Third, the Mauritius–Egypt BIT is one of the latest BITs concluded between African countries.[59] Under this BIT, the judicial action in the host state is not a compulsory procedure before international arbitration is initiated because the text depicts that either party to the dispute "shall be entitled to" instead of "shall" initiates judicial action in the host state.[60] Subject to fork-in-the-road clause, the arbitral clause lists the Cairo Regional Centre for International Commercial Arbitration, the LCIA-MIAC Arbitration Centre in Mauritius, the ICSID and other arbitral tribunals for the disputing party to choose.[61] It should be mentioned that the limitation of actions is five years instead of three years, which is the more general standard in BITs.[62]

It is submitted that the new generation South-South BITs cannot be said to simply conform to a lower level of investment protection. The new-generation African BITs (Mauritius–Egypt BIT as a typical example) tend to balance the interests between investors and the host state. In contrast, the Mauritius–South Africa BIT (as a typical example of an older BIT) shows lopsided protection to foreign investors.[63] As a

---

56 See Southern African Development Community: Towards a Common future, SADC Tribunal, available at <http://www.sadc.int/about-sadc/sadc-institutions/tribun/>.

57 See Investment Agreement for the COMESA Common Investment Area, signed on May 23, 2007, articles 14, 17, 19, 20, available at <https://investmentpolicy.unctad.org/international-investment-agreements/treaty-files/3092/download>.

58 See Investment Agreement for the COMESA Common Investment Area, articles 6, 28.

59 See Agreement Between the Government of the Republic of Mauritius and the Government of the Arab Republic of Egypt on the Reciprocal Promotion and Protection of Investments, signed on June 25, 2014, available at <https://investmentpolicy.unctad.org/international-investment-agreements/treaty-files/3285/download>.

60 See Agreement Between the Government of the Republic of Mauritius and the Government of the Arab Republic of Egypt on the Reciprocal Promotion and Protection of Investments, article 10.3.

61 See Agreement Between the Government of the Republic of Mauritius and the Government of the Arab Republic of Egypt on the Reciprocal Promotion and Protection of Investments, article 10.4.

62 See Agreement between the Government of the Republic of Mauritius and The Government of the Arab Republic of Egypt on the Reciprocal Promotion and Protection of Investments, article 10.

63 See Agreement Between the Government of the Republic of Mauritius and the Government of the Republic of South Africa for the Promotion and Reciprocal Protection of Investments, signed

modern BIT, the Mauritius–Egypt BIT includes the essence and the newest development elements of BITs, such as sustainable development, environmental protection, and regulatory space. In addition, the drafting standard of the Mauritius–Egypt BIT is concise and delicate and more nuanced or detailed than the older generation African BITs.

Overall, African countries still support the international investment rule of law, and their principal concern is how to keep the balance between the interests of state and those of investors. For example, Egypt has a positive attitude toward IIAs, as it suggests "to see an IIA regime that protects investors effectively, but that also protects the state against frivolous and unfounded claims", and it emphasizes the sustainable development objective and the balance of investor rights and obligations.[64] Egypt has concluded over 70 BITs, and the newest treaties with investment provisions (TIPs) is the 2020 Egypt-United Kingdom Association Agreement.[65] Zambia also wants to "retain sufficient policy space to promote economic development, without undermining the effectiveness of IIA."[66] Nigeria objectively realizes that "IIAs definitely provide some comfort for investors in various sectors and that realization alongside other factors" but is also concerned about the state right to regulate in public interest and public policy.[67] Even though South Africa shifted its stance to BIT in 2010, it also declared "a new National Investment Act should incorporate, codify and interpret core international law concepts".[68] Indeed, the 2015 Protection of Investment Act mentions the concepts of "international law" or "customary international law".[69]

on February 17, 1998, available at <https://investmentpolicy.unctad.org/international-investment-agreements/treaty-files/1991/download>.

64 See Ms. W S Ibrahim, Vice Chairman, General Authority for Investment (GAFI), Egypt, World Investment Forum 2014: Investing in Sustainable Development, IIA Conference, October 16, 2014.

65 See Egypt BITs, as of April 14, 2021, available at <https://investmentpolicy.unctad.org/international-investment-agreements/countries/62/egypt>; Egypt TIPs, as of April 14, 2021, available at <https://investmentpolicy.unctad.org/international-investment-agreements/countries/62/egypt>.

66 See Mr. T Mulimbika, Director, Department of Industry Ministry of Commerce Trade and Industry (MCTI), Zambia, World Investment Forum 2014: Investing in Sustainable Development, IIA Conference, October 16, 2014.

67 See Mrs. P Okala, Legal Adviser, Investment Promotion Commission (NIPC), Nigeria, World Investment Forum 2014: Investing in Sustainable Development, IIA Conference, October 16, 2014.

68 The Department of Trade and Industry Republic of South Africa, Policy Statement: The South African Government's Approach to Future International Investment Treaties (July 2010).

69 See 2015 Protection of Investment Act, Act No.22 of 2015, Government Gazette, Republic of South Africa, Vol. 606 Cape Town, No. 39514, December 15, 2015, preamble, articles 3, 9, available at <https://www.thedti.gov.za/gazzettes/39514.pdf>.

5.2 African States' Reconceptualization of Investment Rule of Law at Regional Level

Africa's current regional investment agreements are more impressive than Africa's BITs in that they reflect the views of African countries on the international investment rule of law, express Africa's specific needs, and thus create a regional investment rule of law with African characteristics. "[R]egional integration initiatives in Africa have a long history whose origins can be traced back to the colonial period. Since the independence era (the late 1950s, early 1960s), there has been a proliferation of regional organisations on the continent". [70]

5.2.1 African Regional Investment Agreements Among African States

5.2.1.1 An Overview of the Agreements

The regional investment rule of law in Africa is mainly founded by eight regional economic communities (RECs) under the banner of the African Union (AU) or recognized by AU, although there are currently 14 regional economic communities coexisting in Africa. These eight building blocks include the Arab Maghreb Union (UMA), Common Market for Eastern and Southern Africa (COMESA), Community of Sahel–Saharan States (CEN-SAD), East African Community (EAC), Economic Community of Central African States (ECCAS), Economic Community of West African States (ECOWAS), Intergovernmental Authority on Development (IGAD), and Southern African Development Community (SADC).[71] The ultimate economic goal of the AU under its 2063 Agenda is to set up the African Continental Free Trade Area (CFTA)[72] by merging these 8 "building blocks" into a single economic bloc.[73]

Most of these subregional economic communities have their own legal instruments regarding the regulation of foreign investment, binding or non-binding to enhance

---

[70] See Rudahindwa, Jonathan Bashi, Regional Developmentalism Through International Law: Establishing an African Economic Community (Routledge, 2018) 25.

[71] See Regional Economic Communities (RECs), available at <https://au.int/en/organs/recs>. In addition, some other legal instruments, such as Common Convention on Investments in the States of the Customs and Economic Union of Central Africa (Central African Economic and Monetary Community (CEMAC) Investment), which was signed on December 14, 1965 and entered into effect on April 1, 1966; Community Investment Code of the Economic Community of the Great Lakes Countries (ECGLC Investment Code), which was signed on January 31, 1982 and came into effect on October 4, 1987; CEMAC Community Investment Charter of 1999; ECOWAS Protocol on Movement of Persons and Establishment; also deal with investment issues. However, since they are only indirectly related to investment, they will not be covered by this research.

[72] See African Union, 'CFTA-Continental Free Trade Area', available at <https://au.int/en/ti/cfta/about>.

[73] See Agreement Establishing the African Continental Free Trade Area, Preamble, article 5.b.

cooperation and coordination among members within the regional community in investment policy. For example, the EAC has an EAC Model Investment Code to serve as a template for its member states or the EAC itself to negotiate investment treaties[74] and a Protocol on the Establishment of the EAC Common Market with investment provisions.[75] The treaty establishing COMESA has a full chapter on investment promotion and protection, and the investment measures by the host state within the COMESA are also bound by the provisions concerning expropriation, compensation, FET, and the Treaty lists many rights for investors.[76]

Furthermore, COMESA adopted the COMESA Investment Agreement in 2007.[77] SADC has a 2012 SADC Model BIT as a BIT template, which offers different choices for each element of an investment treaty.[78] The SADC Protocol on Finance and Investment came into force in 2010 and was amended in 2016.[79] ECOWAS has the Supplementary Act on Common Investment Rules for the Community (The 2008 ECOWAS Supplementary Act).[80] The ECOWAS Energy Protocol has a substantive set of investment protection measures similar to that in a general BIT to discipline the power of the host state within the ECOWAS, such as FET, MFN treatment, expropriation and an investor-state dispute settlement mechanism.[81] Even though it has never come into effect, it shows the intention of the Member States of ECOWAS to put

[74] See EAC, East African Model Investment Code, drafted in 2002 and adopted in 2006. In 2015, the EAC adopted a new Model Investment Treaty, but it is not yet officially public.

[75] See East African Community, East African Protocol on the Establishment of the East African Community Common Market (2009 EAC Protocol), signed in November 2009, and entered into force on July 1, 2010, available at <https://d3n8a8pro7vhmx.cloudfront.net/eatradehub/pages/1358/attachments/original/1443771,779/EAC_Common_Market_Protocol.pdf?1,443,771,779> . The Protocol stipulates the protection of cross-border investment, the purpose of promoting investment within the East African Community, and the ultimate goal is to build an East African Common Investment Zone. Comparatively, the East African Community Establishment Treaty contains the parties agreeing to take measures to allow the free movement of persons and services, but it does not contain substantive investment protection clauses.

[76] See Treaty Establishing A Common Market for Eastern and Southern Africa (COMESA), signed on November 5, 1993, entered into force on December 8, 1994, Chapter 26.

[77] See The full name is Investment Agreement for the COMESA Common Investment Area, also see Peter Muchlinski, 'The COMESA common Investment Area: Substantive Standards and Procedural Problems in Dispute Settlement' (2010), SOAS School of Law Research Paper.

[78] See SADC Model Bilateral Investment Treaty Template (SADC Model BIT), article 4.2.

[79] See South African Development Community, SADC Protocol on Finance and Investment, signed on 18 See August 2006 and entered into force on April 16, 2010, available at <https://investmentpolicy.unctad.org/international-investment-agreements/treaty-files/2730/download>. Agreement Amending Annex 1 (Cooperation on Investment) of the SADC Protocol on Finance and Investment, adopted in August 2016, available at <https://www.tralac.org/resources/by-region/sadc.html#FIP>.

[80] See Supplementary Act A/SA.3/12/08 Adopting Community Rules on Investment and the Modalities for their Implementation with ECOWAS, signed on December 19, 2008, entered into force on January 19, 2009, available at <https://investmentpolicy.unctad.org/international-investment-agreements/treaty-files/3266/download>.

[81] See ECOWAS Energy Protocol A/P4/1/03, signed on January 31, 2003, Chapter III and Chapter V.

energy investment under the international investment rule of law. The Tripartite Free Trade Area (TFTA) Agreement was concluded in June 2015 by COMESA, EAC and SADC, and according to Article 45 of this Agreement, a Protocol on Cross-Border Investment will be adopted in the future. The most striking legal instrument, however, is PAIC, which was adopted by AU in 2016. Although it is not legally binding and does not become an Investment Protocol Annex of AfCFTA, it is submitted that it will lay the foundation for the investment protocol,[82] which is expected to come after the second-round negotiation of AfCFTA, which is a preliminary operationalization of Pan-Africanism on the Continent.[83]

At first glance, one can discern major problems with the regional IIA framework. For instance, the effectiveness of the treaties has yet to be determined, and the attitude toward the treaties is still wavering when the interests of the state itself are touched upon under the framework of regional investment agreements within African States. The Investment Agreement for the COMESA Common Investment Area (2007 COMESA investment Agreement), for example, has not yet entered into force. The SADC tribunal should have played a role in maintaining international investment rule of law through ISDS arbitration[84] but was suspended after Zimbabwe experienced adverse outcomes in the cases in which Zimbabwe was a respondent.[85] Fragmentation, lack of coordination and incoherence are obvious problems to be dealt with. On the other hand, under the circumstances of the prevalence of nationalism and the "return" of the host state, African countries are still adhering to the regionalization approach of investment rule of law and have developed the international investment rule of law within the region with African characteristics. They express their common aspirations that cannot be ignored, thus helping to improve the international investment rule of law and contributing to the development of the international investment rule of law.

---

[82] See United Nations, Economic Commission for Africa, Assessing Regional Integration in Africa ARIA IX: Next Steps for the African Continental Free Trade Area, 2019, xvi.

[83] See Rob Davies, The Politics of Trade in the Era of Hyper-globalisation: A Southern African Perspective (South Centre, 2019) 59–60.

[84] The SADC Tribunal had decided some cases, for example, Mike Campbell (PVT) Limited and Another v Republic of Zimbabwe (2/07) [2007] SADCT 1 (December 13, 2007); Mike Campbell (Pvt) Ltd. and Others v Republic of Zimbabwe (2/2007) [2008] SADCT 2 (November 28, 2008); Tembani v Republic of Zimbabwe (SADC (T) 07/2008) [2009] SADCT 3 (August 14, 2009); Fick and Another v Republic of Zimbabwe (SADC (T) 01/2010) [2010] SADCT 8 (July 16, 2010); Swissbourgh Diamond Mines (Pty) Ltd. and Others v Kingdom of Lesotho (SADC (T) 04/2009) [2010] SADCT 4 (June 11, 2010); Bach's Transport (Pty) Ltd. v Democratic Republic of Congo (SADC (T) 14/2008) [2010] SADCT 6 (June 11, 2010); United Republic of Tanzania v Cimexpan (Mauritius) Ltd. and Others (SADC (T) 01/2009) [2010] SADCT 5 (June 11, 2010); United Republic of Tanzania v Cimexpan (Mauritius) Ltd. and Others (SADC (T) 01/2009) [2010] SADCT 5 (June 11, 2010).

[85] See The SADC Tribunal has been suspended since 2010 due to Zimbabwe's resistance after it made several judgments against Zimbabwe. Among others, the landmark case is Mike Campbell (PVT) Ltd. and 78 others v. The Republic of Zimbabwe. See SADCCAT, available at <https://www.sadc.int/about-sadc/sadc-institutions/tribun/>.

Moreover, even if an investment agreement has never entered into force, it is not meaningless and may have implications for subsequent agreements. For example, the 2007 COMESA Investment Agreement is the first regional investment agreement in Africa that not only focuses on sustainable development but also emphasizes the need to formulate investor obligations.[86] Although it is still not approved by COMESA members, it has, to some extent, affected the paradigm of international investment rule of law under the PAIC. Therefore, the following discourse in this research will not care about whether the investment agreement has entered into force or not and will take a comprehensive analysis of various regional investment agreements.

5.2.1.2 Constraining the Power of the Host State to Protect Investors

The restriction on the host state's power and the protection given to the investor's rights are usually two sides of a coin. In IIAs, substantive and procedural restrictions on the power of the host country or protection of investment are mainly reflected in the MFN treatment clause, national treatment clause, FET clause, expropriation and compensation clause, transfer of funds clause, ISDS clause and other provisions. The following is a survey of the specific provisions in these legal instruments related to African regional integration to identify their changes and trends.

MFN Treatment

The 2007 COMESA investment Agreement provides MFN treatment with two traditional exceptions: regional integration agreements and taxation agreements.[87] The 2009 Protocol on the Establishment of the EAC simply specifies MFN treatment for investors of the other partner in just one sentence.[88] The 2008 ECOWAS Supplementary Act on Common Investment Rules for the Community provides MFN treatment to investors and their investments.[89] The 2006 SADC Protocol on Finance and Investment (2006 SADC PFI) also provides MFN treatment to investors and investments. In addition, it links MFN treatment to FET and requires that the FET "shall be no less favorable than that granted to investors of the third state".[90]

---

[86] See the Investment Agreement for the COMESA Common Investment Area, preamble, article 13.

[87] See Investment Agreement for the COMESA Common Investment Area, article 19.

[88] See EAC, Protocol on the Establishment of the East African Community Common Market, signed in November 2009 and entered into force in July 2010, article 29.2.b.

[89] See Supplementary Act A/SA.3/12/08 Adopting Community Rules on Investment and the Modalities for their Implementation with ECOWAS, article 6.

[90] See South African Development Community, SADC Protocol on Finance and Investment, article 6 of Annex 1.

However, the MFN treatment and FET clauses under the 2006 SADC PFI were deleted when Annex 1 was amended in 2016.[91] This deletion followed the recommendation of South Africa.[92] In fact, previously, the Drafting Committee of the 2012 SADC Model BIT Template recommended excluding an MFN provision through giving a detailed explanation.[93]

After the traditional MFN treatment clause, the extent of MFN treatment is mainly reflected in how to impose restrictions on "like circumstances" and whether to exclude pre-establishment and investor-state dispute settlement procedures from the scope of the MFN provisions.

First, on "like circumstances", the 2007 COMESA investment Agreement lists the considerations that are similar to factors of "like circumstances" considered in national treatment.[94] The wordings of "like circumstances" are not utilized and provided in the MFN clause of the 2009 Protocol on the Establishment of the EAC. The 2008 ECOWAS Supplementary Act on Common Investment Rules for the Community specifies the factors to be considered in determining "like circumstances" in the national treatment clause, not in the MFN clause.[95] The 2006 SADC PFI does not mention "like circumstances" in its MFN clause, the 2016 SADC PFI excludes the MFN clause, and correspondingly, there is no issue of "like circumstances". The PAIC uses the 2007 COMESA investment Agreement for reference and adds several considerations, including "the health of the populations", "the global commons", and "company size"; thus, the identification of "like circumstances" is provided as a more comprehensive standard beyond economic consideration, and the "like circumstances" are more strictly restricted.

The PAIC provides that "in like circumstances", each Member State shall accord to investors of another Member State and their investments MFN treatment.[96] Whether two investments are "in like circumstances" requires "an overall examination, on a case-by-case basis, of all the circumstances of an investment". The factors to be considered include the effects of an investment on third persons, and the local community; the local, regional or national environment, the health of the populations, the global commons; the sector that the investor is active in; the aims of the measure in question; the regulatory process generally applied in relation to this measure; company size; and other factors. In addition, the examination should not be limited

---

[91] See Agreement Amending Annex 1 (Cooperation on Investment) of the SADC Protocol on Finance and Investment.

[92] See Tinashe Kondo, 'A Comparison with Analysis of the SADC FIP before and after Its Amendment' (2017) 20 Potchefstroom Electronic Law Journal.

[93] See Southern African Development Community, South African Development, SADC Model Bilateral Investment Treaty Template with Commentary 2012, article 4.6, available at <http://www.iisd.org/itn/wp-content/uploads/2012/10/sadc-model-bit-template-final.pdf>.

[94] See Investment Agreement for the COMESA Common Investment Area, article17.

[95] See Supplementary Act A/SA.3/12/08 Adopting Community Rules on Investment and the Modalities for Their Implementation with ECOWAS, article 5.4.

[96] See African Union Commission, Economic Affairs Department, Draft Pan-African Investment Code, December 2016, articles 7.1, 7.2, available at <https://au.int/sites/default/files/documents/32844-doc-draft_pan-african_investment_code_december_2016_en.pdf>.

to or biased toward any one factor; therefore, it should be a comprehensive examination.[97] This provision will provide a comprehensive review criterion for the arbitral tribunal and is therefore not only helpful in determining that the claimant's investment is in a similar physical environment to that of another investor from a third state but also makes it more difficult for investors and their investments to obtain MFN treatment under the PAIC.

To determine a reasonable counterpart to compare and thereby determine whether the MFN treatment is awarded to the investors and their investments of the other member states, many treaties refer to "like circumstances" as the criteria of comparison, but the criteria of "like circumstances" are not provided or only provide in "the same sector" or "the existence of competitive relationship". On the basis of the 2007 COMESA investment agreement, however, the PAIC has gone beyond economic and environmental considerations, making "like circumstances" more difficult to satisfy.

Second, regarding the applicable extent of MFN treatment, neither the 2009 EAC Protocol nor the 2006 SADC PFI clarify the applicable extent of MFN treatment. In other words, whether MFN treatment is applicable to pre-establishment may cause controversy in specific disputes. The 2007 COMESA Investment Agreement includes establishment, acquisition and other aspects.[98] Comparatively, the PAIC, like the 2008 ECOWAS Supplementary Act, provides that it applies to the "management, conduct, operation, expansion, sale or other disposition of investment"[99]; thus, the pre-establishment stage is not included in the MFN treatment. In general, it can be concluded that MFN treatment explicitly applies only to measures in the postestablishment phase.

Finally, the 2006 SADC PFI, 2007 COMESA Investment Agreement and 2009 EAC Protocol are all silent on whether the MFN clause is applicable to dispute settlement procedures. The 2008 ECOWAS Supplementary Act limits MFN treatment to substantive provisions.[100] To further clarify the meaning of the MFN provision, in consistency with the 2008 ECOWAS Supplementary Act, the PAIC expressly excludes dispute settlement procedure from the scope of application of MFN treatment.[101] This approach follows the trend toward the evolution of international investment treaties, with the aim of protecting the outcome of negotiations on the provisions of dispute settlement procedures, enhancing the clarity of treaty application and preventing "treaty shopping" by states to limit the application of MFN treatment.

[97] See Draft Pan-African Investment Code, article 7.3.

[98] See Investment Agreement for the COMESA Common Investment Area, article 19.1.

[99] Draft Pan-African Investment Code, articles 7.1, 7.2.

[100] See Supplementary Act A/SA.3/12/08 Adopting Community Rules on Investment and the Modalities for their Implementation with ECOWAS, article 6.

[101] See Draft Pan-African Investment Code, article 7.4.

National Treatment

The provisions related to national treatment in African regional economic integration agreements vary. The 2009 EAC Protocol simply specifies NT for investors of the other partner in just one sentence, and there are no provisions on extent or exceptions to MFN treatment.[102] The 2007 COMESA investment agreement provides "with respect to the establishment, acquisition, expansion, management, operation and disposition of investments", each member state shall accord to a COMESA investor and their investments national treatment.[103] The 2008 ECOWAS Supplementary Act provides "management, conduct, operation, expansion and sale or other disposition of investments" as the applicable scope of national treatment. The 2008 ECOWAS Supplementary Act also provides whether national treatment should be determined on a case-by-case basis. National treatment shall be accorded only "in like circumstances", which include all kinds of factors that need to be considered, but a comprehensive approach is not mentioned.[104] In contrast, the 2016 SADC PFI provides national treatment and furnishes an indicative list of factors when considering "like circumstances", which are extremely similar to those listed in the MFN clause of the 2016 PAIC. However, the 2016 SADC PFI further stresses that "notwithstanding the provisions of paragraph 1,[105] State Parties may, in accordance with their respective domestic legislation grant preferential treatment to domestic investments and investors in order to achieve national development objectives."[106]

In contrast, the 2016 PAIC embodies a moderate way. The drafters of the 2016 PAIC did not blindly follow the practice of pre-establishment national treatment advocated by some developed countries but only awarded foreign investors postestablishment national treatment for the admission and establishment of foreign investment are still required to comply with the relevant provisions of domestic law in the host state. In terms of the criteria for determining the subject for comparison, by illustrating the factors needed to consider as far as possible, foreign investors from member states are treated the same as investors from the host state if they are in "like circumstances".[107] Thus, the scope of application of national treatment is narrowed down. In addition, the 2016 PAIC does not adopt a "*proviso*" to significantly weaken national treatment, as the 2016 SADC PFI does.

---

102 See EAC, Protocol on the Establishment of the East African Community Common Market, signed in November 2009 and entered into force in July 2010, article 29.2.b.

103 See Investment Agreement for the COMESA Common Investment Area, article 17.

104 See Supplementary Act A/SA.3/12/08 Adopting Community Rules on Investment and the Modalities for their Implementation with ECOWAS, article 5.

105 Here, paragraph 1 refers to "national treatment".

106 Agreement Amending Annex 1 (Cooperation on Investment) of the SADC Protocol on Finance and Investment, article 6.3.

107 See Draft Pan-African Investment Code, article 9.3.

Fair and Equitable Treatment

The 2008 ECOWAS Supplementary Act takes FET as a part of "minimum regional standards".[108] The FET in the 2007 COMESA Investment Agreement "includes the obligation not to deny justice in criminal, civil, or administrative adjudicatory proceedings in accordance with the principle of due process embodied in the principal legal systems of the world", which refers in fact to "the minimum standard of treatment", and further, the FET depends on the level of development of the host states.[109]

Through examining the fair and equitable clause in African investment agreements (including those within Africa, those between African countries and countries outside Africa), some scholars have pointed out that, on the one hand, there is no fundamental difference between African countries and Western countries on the understanding of FET; on the other hand, although a similar language is used, the FET clause of these intra-African investment agreements leaves room for African countries to take into account their level of development as the host states.[110] The 2007 COMESA investment agreement may reflect considerations of the level of development of African countries.

The traditional FET clause is simple and abstract, which has always led to divergent understanding of the meaning of the clause and conflicting arbitral awards during its application in specific cases. It's precisely because the meaning of the clause is too obscure, investors invoke the provision as the basis for their claims in many cases. Therefore, some states have started to question the legitimacy of the provision and to constrain this clause in terms of concepts, applicable circumstances and exceptions, while other states have taken a more aggressive approach by removing the fair and equitable clause directly from investment agreements once and for all.

Therefore, the 2009 EAC Protocol does not mention FET. FET was originally provided in the 2006 SADC PFI, and investments and investors enjoy FET, which is no less favorable than MFN treatment.[111] In view that this obscure and broad provision will lead to adverse interpretation for the host state, the 2016 SADC PFI excludes the FET. The 2016 PAIC also does not adopt this treatment.

Expropriation and Compensation

Expropriation is regarded as the most serious violation of the property rights of foreign investors by the host state and is the leading political risk faced by foreign

[108] See Supplementary Act A/SA.3/12/08 Adopting Community Rules on Investment and the Modalities for their Implementation with ECOWAS, article 7.

[109] See Investment Agreement for the COMESA Common Investment Area, article 14.

[110] See Eric De Brabandere, 'Fair and Equitable Treatment and (Full) Protection and Security in African Investment Treaties Between Generality and Contextual Specificity' (2017) 18(1) The Journal of World Investment and Trade 530–555.

[111] See South African Development Community, SADC Protocol on Finance and Investment, article 6.

investors. To a great extent, the provisions of international investment agreements on expropriation can reflect the level of protection of the host state for the interests of foreign investors. Generally, expropriation is not allowed, and where expropriation is considered to be legal, the taking of property must be made in the public interest, on a non-discriminatory basis, under the due process of law, and with some compensation.[112]

On the issue of expropriation, the 2006 SADC PFI and the 2016 SADC PFI stipulate that investment in signatory states is protected against uncompensated expropriation. The 2007 COMESA Investment Agreement, 2002 EAC Model Investment Code, and 2008 ECOWAS Supplementary Act have similar provisions.

The 2008 ECOWAS Supplementary Act requires compensating the investor in convertible currency based on market value without delay. The 2006 SADC PFI expropriation clause guarantees investors' compensation under the "Hull Formula", and it provides that investments nationalized or expropriated shall be "subject to the payment of prompt, adequate and effective compensation".[113] However, the 2016 SADC PFI denounces the "Hull Doctrine" and provides that nationalization or expropriation shall be done subject to "the payment of fair and adequate compensation", which "shall be assessed in relation to the fair market value of the expropriated investment immediately before the expropriation took place 'date of expropriation' and shall not reflect any change in value occurring because the intended expropriation had become known earlier. However, where appropriate, the assessment of fair and adequate compensation shall be based on an equitable balance between the public interest and interest of those affected, have regard to all relevant circumstances and take into account the indicative list of factors.[114] Therefore, a more balanced approach in determining compensation by considering equitable factors should be adopted.

To protect the interests of investors, under the 2016 SADC PFI, the "payment shall be made in a freely convertible currency",[115] a right before "a judicial or other independent authority" to challenge the expropriation or the valuation of the compensation shall be awarded.[116] However, the 2016 SADC PFI also gives more consideration to the host state, where payments are significantly burdensome on a host

---

[112] See Chin Leng Lim, Jean Ho and Martins Paparinskis, International Investment Law and Arbitration: Commentary, Awards and other Materials (Cambridge University Press, 2021) 338–346; UNCTAD, Expropriation: A Sequel (2012) United Nations 28, available at <https://unctad.org/system/files/offici-al-document/unctaddiaeia2011d7_en.pdf>; ADC Affiliate Limited and ADC and ADMC Management Limited v. Republic of Hungary, ICSID Case No. ARB/03/16, Award dated October 2, 2006.

[113] South African Development Community, SADC Protocol on Finance and Investment, article 5.

[114] See Agreement Amending Annex 1 (Cooperation on Investment) of the SADC Protocol on Finance and Investment, article 5.2.

[115] Agreement Amending Annex 1 (Cooperation on Investment) of the SADC Protocol on Finance and Investment, article 5.3.

[116] See Agreement Amending Annex 1 (Cooperation on Investment) of the SADC Protocol on Finance and Investment, article 5.8.

state; such a state may pay the amount due "yearly over a three-year period" or "the investor and the host state may agree on a suitable period and interest rate.[117]

With regard to the criteria for the amount of compensation for expropriation, the 2016 PAIC partly draws on the "Hull Doctrine" and provides that "adequate compensation" and compensation should be paid in freely convertible currency.[118] However, the requirements for the "prompt" are not high because it gives the host state a six-month period to compensate, and "single interest", instead of compound interest, will arise if the compensation has not yet been paid at expiration of the period.[119] With regard to the criterion of "adequate" compensation, the 2016 PAIC expressly excludes indirect and unavoidable losses or speculative and windfall profits.[120] Moreover, the application of fair market value is not absolute and should be governed by the principle of proportionality, i.e., considering the balance between the public interest of the host state and the interests of the affected investor. The 2016 PAIC therefore provides restrictive factors for the assessment of the amount of compensation by requiring factors such as the use of the property in question, the income generated, the profits that the investor has made by using the investment and the duration of the investment.[121]

Transfer of Funds

The 2007 COMESA Investment Agreement, 2008 ECOWAS Supplementary Act, and 2002 EAC Model Investment Code provide investors with the right to transfer all property. However, the 2006 SADC PFI uses wordings cautiously, and it provides that "State Parties shall encourage the free movement of capital", but "may regulate capital movements subject to their domestic laws and regulations, when necessitated by economic constraints"[122] To clarify what a genuine economic constraint is, the 2016 SADC PFI further introduces a non-exhaustive indicative list of what could qualify as economic constraints on the basis of maintaining the 2006 SADC PFI.[123]

The 2016 PAIC specifies transferable items in the form of summarization and enumeration, and Member States shall, subject to national laws, permit all transfers relating to an investment to be made freely and without delay.[124] However, Article 16 instead provides restrictions and exceptions to the transfer of funds. Exceptions

[117] See Agreement Amending Annex 1 (Cooperation on Investment) of the SADC Protocol on Finance and Investment, article 5.4.

[118] See Draft Pan-African Investment Code, articles 11.1.a, 12.4.

[119] See Draft Pan-African Investment Code, article 12.3.

[120] See Draft Pan-African Investment Code, article 12.1.

[121] See Draft Pan-African Investment Code, article 12.2.

[122] South African Development Community, SADC Protocol on Finance and Investment, articles 15.1, 15.2 of Annex 1.

[123] See Agreement Amending Annex 1 (Cooperation on Investment) of the SADC Protocol on Finance and Investment, article 13.

[124] See Draft Pan-African Investment Code, article 15.

to the transfer of funds are permitted under some conditions, and a Member State may prevent a transfer in a non-discriminatory manner and in accordance with its laws relating to some exceptional circumstances.[125]

Investor-State Dispute Settlement

For investor-state dispute settlement, the 2008 ECOWAS Supplementary Act provides that any dispute between an Investor and the host state, if not amicably settled through mutual discussions, may be submitted to arbitration by a national court or similar national agency. Where "there is disagreement as to the method of dispute settlement to be adopted, the dispute shall be referred to the ECOWAS Court of Justice",[126] ICSID or ad hoc UNCITRAL arbitration is not mentioned. The 2007 COMESA Investment Agreement provides the fora that a COMESA investor may choose, including the competent court of the host state, COMESA Court of Justice, ICSID Convention arbitration, ICSID Additional Facility arbitration or ad hoc UNCITRAL arbitration, or any other arbitration agreed upon by both parties. However, the choice of investors is limited by the fork-in-the-road requirement and three-year prescription.[127]

The 2002 EAC Model Investment Code provides that the certified investor can submit the dispute to ICSID for arbitration in case of a dispute with the host state.[128] In contrast, the 2012 SADC Model BIT advises treaty negotiators to not include any ISDS provisions, at most including ISDS provisions with obligation to exhaust local remedies.[129]

For the investor-state arbitration, the 2006 SADC PFI provides that "Disputes between an investor and a State Party concerning an obligation of the latter in relation to an admitted investment of the former, which have not been amicably settled, and after exhausting local remedies shall, after a period of six months from written notification of a claim, be submitted to international arbitration if either party to the dispute so wishes".[130] The investor and the host state may agree that the international arbitration be conducted through a SADC tribunal, ICSID tribunal or ad hoc UNCITRAL tribunal.[131] Here, "local remedies" refers to "access to the courts, judicial and

[125] See Draft Pan-African Investment Code, articles 16.3,16.4, 16.5.

[126] Supplementary Act A/SA.3/12/08 Adopting Community Rules on Investment and the Modalities for Their Implementation with ECOWAS, articles 33.6, 33.7.

[127] See Investment Agreement for the COMESA Common Investment Area, articles 28.1, 28.2.

[128] See EAC, East African Model Investment Code, drafted in 2002 and adopted in 2006, article 15.

[129] See Southern African Development Community, South African Development, SADC Model Bilateral Investment Treaty Template with Commentary 2012, at 55, available at <http://www.iisd.org/itn/wp-content/uploads/2012/10/sadc-model-bit-template-final.pdf>.

[130] South African Development Community, SADC Protocol on Finance and Investment, article 28.

[131] See South African Development Community, SADC Protocol on Finance and Investment, article 28.

administrative tribunals, and other authorities competent under the laws of the Host State".[132] However, under the 2016 SADC PFI, the international arbitration between the investor and the State is totally removed because it only provides "[a]ny dispute between State Parties to this Annex shall be resolved in the manner provided under the Protocol on the Tribunal".[133]

The investor-state dispute settlement mechanism is the most controversial issue in the 2016 PAIC drafting process, and the provision of this mechanism is the only one on which the drafters cannot reach consensus. This is because at the 2016 PAIC expert meeting, several states, led by South Africa, expressly opposed the provision of an investor-state dispute settlement mechanism included in the 2016 PAIC.[134] However, because most African states consider that the ISDS system is still necessary, the 2016 PAIC finally adopted the system. In the face of some states' doubts and criticisms on the ISDS arbitration mechanism, the 2016 PAIC made a compromise by stipulating that "Member States may, in line with their domestic policies, agree to utilize the Investor-State dispute settlement mechanism",[135] that is, allowing Member States to refuse the mechanism according to their own situations.

The 2016 PAIC attached certain restrictions to the ISDS arbitration mechanism, which are the outcome of rational reflection of the African states to the current ISDS arbitration mechanism. The 2016 PAIC provides that "[d]isputes arising between investors and Member States under the specific agreements that govern their relations shall be resolved under those agreement".[136] If the recommended consultations fail, "the dispute may be resolved through arbitration, subject to the applicable laws of the host State and/or the mutual agreement of the disputing parties, and subject to exhaustion of local remedies".[137] Furthermore, "the arbitration may be conducted at any established African public or African private alternative dispute resolution center".[138] At the same time, the 2016 PAIC also excluded procedural provisions from the applicable scope of MFN treatment.[139]

The 2016 PAIC places an emphasis on an African seat of arbitration to settle the dispute instead of ICSID, which means African countries are expecting to change the international investment rule of law and protect investors through local forums to settle investment disputes instead of relying on existing international arbitration mechanisms.

---

[132] See South African Development Community, SADC Protocol on Finance and Investment, article 27.

[133] Agreement Amending Annex 1 (Cooperation on Investment) of the SADC Protocol on Finance and Investment, article 26.

[134] See Makane Moïse Mbengue and Stefanie Schacherer, 'The "Africanization" of International Investment Law: The Pan-African Investment Code and the Reform of the International Investment Regime' (2017) 18(3) Journal of World Investment and Trade 414–448, 442.

[135] Draft Pan-African Investment Code, article 42.1.

[136] Draft Pan-African Investment Code, article 42.1.a.

[137] Draft Pan-African Investment Code, article 42.1.c.

[138] Draft Pan-African Investment Code, article 42.1.d.

[139] See Draft Pan-African Investment Code, article 7.4.

In summary, the trend of African regional integration investment agreements has imposed detailed and reasonable restrictions on investment protection rather than indiscriminately, vaguely and generally committing to protect investors and investments.

5.2.1.3 Keeping the Right to Regulate in the Hands of the Host State

When restricting the power of the host state to protect the interests of investors, African regional integration investment agreements also try to keep the regulatory power in the hands of the host state as much as possible mainly through the following ways.

First, regulatory power is emphasized in the preamble or specific clauses of the agreement.[140]

Both the 2012 SADC Model BIT and the 2016 PAIC stress the host state's right to regulate.[141] The 2016 PAIC pays more attention to balancing the rights and obligations between the host state and investors, promoting the sustainable development of the host state by foreign capital, and emphasizing the protection of the host state's public interests such as environment and human rights.

The 2006 SADC PFI provides for the right to regulate that "Nothing in this Annex shall be construed as preventing a State Party from exercising its right to regulate in the public interest and to adopt, maintain or enforce any measure that it considers appropriate to ensure that investment activity is undertaken in a manner sensitive to health, safety or environmental concerns".[142]

The 2016 SADC PFI stresses the "right of a State Party to regulate" for sustainable development and other legitimate social and economic objectives that originate from customary international law and other general principles of international law. The nature of this right is "a balance of the rights and obligations of investors and investments and Host States" and states that "[n]on-discriminatory measures taken by a State Party to comply with its international obligations under other treaties shall not constitute a breach of this Annex".[143]

Second, specific exceptions and general exceptions to increase regulatory flexibility are incorporated in the agreement to keep regulatory power.

---

[140] See Preamble can play many functions in international such as the interpretive function, the Supplementary Function, the Incorporative Function, see Makane Moïse Mbengue, Preamble, Encyclopedia entries, Max Planck Encyclopedias of International Law [MPIL], September 2006.

[141] See South African Community, Development. SADC Model Bilateral Investment Treaty Template with Commentary 2012, articles 20, 21, 25; Draft Pan-African Investment Code, article 43.

[142] South African Development Community, SADC Protocol on Finance and Investment, article 14.

[143] Agreement Amending Annex 1 (Cooperation on Investment) of the SADC Protocol on Finance and Investment, article 12.

Exceptions are mainly made based on the development needs of member states, which can ensure the flexibility of member states' policies and provide policy space for them to pursue development goals while protecting foreign investment.

Special exceptions apply only to specific obligations; for example, the 2006 SADC PFI provides that "State Parties may in accordance with their respective domestic legislation grant preferential treatment to qualifying investments and investors in order to achieve national development objectives",[144] as is an exception of its MFN clause.

The 2008 ECOWAS Supplementary Act lists customs unions, free trade areas, common market agreements, international taxation agreements, and other international arrangements as exceptions to MFN treatment.[145]The 2007 COMESA Investment Agreement has similar provisions. In addition to these exceptions, the 2016 PAIC provides that the host state may adopt regulatory measures for legitimate public welfare objectives, national security, public morals, and so on.[146]

Comparatively, the 2016 SADC PFI does not contain the MFN clause or the FET clause. However, the national treatment in the 2016 SADC PFI has been qualified to satisfy the development needs of the host state, and it provides that host states may grant "preferential treatment to domestic investments and investors in order to achieve national development objectives".[147] This is to ensure the regulatory power of the host state. South Africa and Zimbabwe, as members of SADC, with special national conditions, have "persons or categories of persons who have been disadvantaged by unfair discrimination".[148] To enforce their policy for redressing the injustices of the past, they, respectively adopted the Constitution of the Republic of South Africa, 1996, the Constitution of the Republic of Zimbabwe, 2005, Broad-Based Black Economic Empowerment Act (B-BBEE) of South Africa, the Mineral and Petroleum Resources Development Act of South Africa, the Indigenization and Economic Empowerment Act of Zimbabwe, and so on. However, the lessons experienced by South Africa[149] and Zimbabwe in international investment arbitration show that it is necessary to set exceptions for national treatment and exclude some measures from indirect expropriation to protect their regulatory power of implementing special policies.[150] The inclusion of the exception in the 2016 SADC PFI is consistent with

[144] South African Development Community, SADC Protocol on Finance and Investment, article 7.1.

[145] See Supplementary Act A/SA.3/12/08 Adopting Community Rules on Investment and the Modalities for their Implementation with ECOWAS, article 6.5.

[146] See Draft Pan-African Investment Code, article 8.

[147] Agreement Amending Annex 1 (Cooperation on Investment) of the SADC Protocol on Finance and Investment, article 6.3.

[148] South Africa-Zimbabwe BIT, signed on November 27, 2009, entered into force on September 15, 2010, article 3.4.c.

[149] See Piero Foresti, Laura de Carli and others v Republic of South Africa, ICSID Case No ARB(AF)/07/1, Award dated August 4, 2010.

[150] See Mike Campbell (Pvt) Limited v The Republic of Zimbabwe, Southern African Development Community Tribunal, Award dated December 13, 2007; Border Timbers Limited, Timber Products International (Private) Limited and Hangani Development Co. (Private) Limited v. Republic of

that in the 2015 South African Protection of Investment Act and the 2012 SADC Model BIT.[151]

In terms of conditions of applying national treatment, the 2016 PAIC allows exception to national treatment for enhancing "legitimate public welfare objectives" or achieving "national development objectives". On the one hand, the host state may grant preferential treatment to qualifying investments and investors; on the other hand, the host state reserves the right to deny national treatment to investors and investments subject to certain requirements.[152]

The 2007 COMESA Investment Agreement provides the "Sensitive and the Temporary Exclusion List" as the exception to national treatment. The 2007 COMESA Investment Agreement also excludes the lawful exercise of police power from indirect expropriation and provides:

> "Consistent with the right of States to regulate and the customary international law principles on police powers, *bona fide* regulatory measures taken by a Member State that are designed and applied to protect or enhance legitimate public welfare objectives, such as public health, safety and the environment, shall not constitute an indirect expropriation under this Article."[153]

The 2016 PAIC adopts the same exception approach to indirect expropriation.[154]

In addition, the 2016 SADC PFI also excludes some specific measures from indirect expropriation because it provides that "a measure of general application by a State Party that is designed and applied to protect or enhance legitimate public welfare objectives, such as public health, safety and the environment, shall not constitute an indirect expropriation"[155] Thus, some frivolous and litigious suits related to indirect expropriation can be excluded.The issuance, revocation, limitation, or creation of compulsory licenses to intellectual property rights that are "consistent with applicable international agreements on intellectual property" are also excluded.[156]

Different from traditional international investment rule of law, more general exceptions chapters that embody protection to the authority of the host state are inserted in the agreement. These exceptions apply to all the obligations in a treaty.

Zimbabwe, ICSID Case No. ARB/10/25, Award dated July 28, 2015; Bernhard von Pezold and others v. Republic of Zimbabwe, ICSID Case No. ARB/10/15, Award dated July 28, 2015; Bernardus Henricus Funnekotter and others v. Republic of Zimbabwe, ICSID Case No. ARB/05/6, Award dated April 22, 2009.

[151] See Protection of Investment Act, 2015, Act No.22 of 2015, Government Gazette, Republic of South Africa, Vol. 606 Cape Town, No. 39514, December 15, 2015, article 8, available at <https://www.thedti.gov.za/gazzettes/39514.pdf>, <https://www.thedti.gov.za/business_regulation/acts/Investment_Act_22of2015.pdf>; South African Development Community, SADC Model Bilateral Investment Treaty Template with Commentary 2012, article 4.

[152] See Draft Pan-African Investment Code, article 10.

[153] Investment Agreement for the COMESA Common Investment Area, article 20.8.

[154] See Draft Pan-African Investment Code, article 11.3.

[155] Agreement Amending Annex 1 (Cooperation on Investment) of the SADC Protocol on Finance and Investment, article 5.7.

[156] Agreement Amending Annex 1 (Cooperation on Investment) of the SADC Protocol on Finance and Investment, article 5.5.

For example, the general exceptions under COMESA CIAA are drafted on the basis of Articles XX and XXI of the GATT to further the specified policy objectives listed.[157]

COMESA CIAA also provides its non-application to taxation measures except the claim for tax measures constituting expropriation, and a member state can also take emergency safeguard measures or adopt measures to safeguard the balance of payments under certain circumstances.[158] The 2008 ECOWAS Supplementary Act provides a "general exceptions" chapter that includes "national security" and "general reservations and exceptions". According to the article on "national security", a host state needs not "furnish or allow access to any information" because "the disclosure of which it determines to be contrary to its essential security interest".[159] For "the fulfillment of its obligations under the United Nations Charter with respect to the maintenance or restoration of international peace or security, or the protection of its own essential security", the host state may apply "measures that it considers necessary". According to "general reservations and exceptions", the host state may apply "any law or other measures" that aim at promoting "the achievement of equality in its territory, or designed to protect or advance persons, or categories of persons, disadvantaged by long-term historic discrimination in its territory" subject to procedural fairness, and the host state may also take measures to "avoid or abate a balance of payments emergency".[160]

Third, the host state may impose performance requirements on the investor. Performance requirements are the requirements or measures imposed by the host state on foreign investors and their investments and are important domestic measures to guide and manage foreign investors and investments.[161] Some common performance requirements include foreign exchange balance requirements, trade balance requirements, local component requirements, technology transfer requirements, local employment, and training requirements. The purpose of creating jobs, increasing domestic added value, promoting exports, restricting imports, alleviating imbalances of foreign trade and foreign exchange, and promoting technology transfer and regional development can be achieved through performance requirements to some degree.[162] In terms of nature, the essence of the performance requirements is the regulation on foreign investment by the host state and the embodiment of a state's economic sovereignty.

---

[157] See Investment Agreement for the COMESA Common Investment Area, article 22.

[158] See Investment Agreement for the COMESA Common Investment Area, articles 23, 24, 25.

[159] Supplementary Act A/SA.3/12/08 Adopting Community Rules on Investment and the Modalities for their Implementation with ECOWAS, article 37.

[160] Supplementary Act A/SA.3/12/08 Adopting Community Rules on Investment and the Modalities for their Implementation with ECOWAS, article 38.

[161] See Suzy H. Nikièma, 'Performance requirements in investment treaties' (2014) 30 IISD Best Practices Series, available at <https://www.iisd.org/system/files/publications/best-practices-performance-requirements-investment-treaties-en.pdf>.

[162] See UNCTAD, Foreign Direct Investment and Performance Requirements: New Evidence from Selected Countries, United Nations, 2003, 21–32.

Since performance requirements hinder investment and increase the risk of investment, some developed countries have advocated a prohibition of performance requirements in international investment agreements.[163] Moreover, WTO members are required to comply with the provisions of prohibiting performance requirements in the TRIMs Agreement under the WTO framework. According to article 2 of the TRIMs Agreement, WTO members cannot impose the performance requirements of local content, trade balance and foreign exchange balance.[164]

However, since the prohibition of the performance requirement clause has played a role in weakening the host state's regulatory power, many new bilateral and regional investment agreements do not provide for a prohibition of the performance requirements, as indicates that these states do not want to give up the positive effects of performance requirements for their own national development.

The intention of African states to utilize the performance requirement to defend their right to regulate is very clearer. Allowing the less developed states to apply performance requirements to promote the realization of their own development goals is also conducive to guiding these states to clarify their regulatory space. This practice of allowing the host states to impose performance requirements reflects respect for the differences in economic development among the member states.

Although the 2012 SADC Model BIT does not specify that the member states may make performance requirements, its relevant provisions leave room for the establishment of the performance requirements.[165] The 2008 ECOWAS Supplementary Act provides that performance requirements may be imposed to promote the development benefits brought by investment in the host state.[166]

The 2016 PAIC clearly stipulates that member states may impose performance requirements through indicative provisions, although there is no direct and specific performance requirements clause; thus, the member states can flexibly formulate their own specific performance requirements according to their specific circumstances.[167] The host states could make various performance requirements to investors and could take regulatory measures for the sake of sustainable development goals, thus leaving more regulatory room for the host states.

It should be noted that encouraging investors to transfer technology itself does not belong to the performance requirements itself but only expresses an expectation on the investors. The 2016 PAIC supports and encourages technology transfer and has provisions from the perspectives of foreign investors and the host states.[168] The 2016

[163] See Andrew Newcombe, 'Performance Requirement Prohibitions in International Investment Law' (2020) ICSID Review-Foreign Investment Law Journal 1–5; Alexandre Genest, 'Examples of the Main Types of Performance Requirement Prohibitions and Related Treaty Provisions' in Alexandre Genest (ed.), Performance Requirement Prohibitions in International Investment Law (Brill Nijhoff, 2019) 231–238.

[164] See article 2 of TRIMs, "National Treatment and Quantitative Restrictions".

[165] See SADC Model Bilateral Investment Treaty Template with Commentary, 17, 40–41.

[166] Supplementary Act A/SA.3/12/08 Adopting Community Rules on Investment and the Modalities for Their Implementation with ECOWAS, article 24.

[167] See Draft Pan-African Investment Code, article 17.2.

[168] See Draft Pan-African Investment Code, article 29.

PAIC especially provides "Member States and investors should take all practicable steps to promote, facilitate, and finance, as appropriate, the transfer of, or access to, environmentally sound technologies and know-how" and "Investors are encouraged to provide adequate financial resources, including for the transfer of technology" to help host states cope with climate change.[169]

Fourth, the provisions of the host state's right to counterclaim are strengthened.

The 2016 PAIC inherits and develops the structure of the 2007 COMESA investment Agreement,[170] 2012 SADC Model BIT,[171] and 2008 ECOWAS Supplementary Act.[172] According to the 2016 PAIC, "Where an investor or its investment is alleged by a Member State party in a dispute settlement proceeding under this Code to have failed to comply with its obligations under this Code or other relevant rules and principles of domestic and international law…a Member State may initiate a counterclaim against the investor before any competent body dealing with a dispute under this Code for damages or other relief resulting from an alleged breach of the Code". The competent body hearing such a dispute shall consider "whether this breach, if proven, is materially relevant to the issues before it, and if so, what mitigating or off-setting effects this may have on the merits of a claim or on any damages awarded in the event of such award".[173]

For the conditions under which the host state may file counterclaims, on the one hand, the 2016 PAIC makes clear that the legal basis for determining that investors are in violation of the law is the 2016 PAIC, the relevant rules and principles in national and international law. On the other hand, the 2016 PAIC relaxes the requirement of the correlation between counterclaim and the dispute and only requires that counterclaim be "materially relevant" to the current ISDS arbitration. Comparatively, a counterclaim means "arising directly out of the subject matter of the dispute" under the ICSID Convention.[174]

The rules on counterclaim provide guarantees for the effective implementation of the investor obligation clause, while the investor obligation clause provides the substantive basis for the host state's counterclaim. They complement each other, supporting the exercise of the host state's regulatory power from the procedure and merits, respectively, and thus change the passive position of the host state in the dispute settlement procedure. The counterclaim system allows the host state to make a more powerful "counterattack" against the investor's claims; otherwise, the defense taken by the host state may only aim at the jurisdiction of the arbitral tribunal. In addition to providing a legal basis for its own regulatory conduct and offsetting some compensation or damages claims made by the investor, the counterclaim may also require the investor to perform certain obligations or be liable for reparation.

---

[169] See Draft Pan-African Investment Code, article 30.

[170] See Investment Agreement for the COMESA Common Investment Area, article 28.9.

[171] See SADC Model BIT, articles 19, 29.19.

[172] See Supplementary Act A/SA.3/12/08 Adopting Community Rules on Investment and the Modalities for Their Implementation with ECOWAS, article18.6.

[173] Draft Pan-African Investment Code, article 43.1.

[174] See ICSID Convention, article 46.

Finally, restrictions on regulatory powers are reduced, and some provisions are deleted to protect the power of the host state.

For example, the 2016 PAIC adopts a single "nature standard" for determining legal regulatory measures and provides that non-discriminatory measures of member states to protect or strengthen legitimate public welfare goals do not constitute indirect expropriation.[175] In contrast to the "effect and nature standard", the "nature standard" advocates that as long as the host state takes a non-discriminatory measure to protect its public interests, the measure cannot be considered indirect expropriation. In addition, the 2016 PAIC does not impose restrictions such as "the principle of proportionality" while strengthening police power. Therefore, this regulation clearly shows the firm stand of African states in safeguarding their regulatory power for public interests.

As indicated in the previous paragraphs, some agreements delete important provisions that protect investors and investment to refrain from unintended consequences of subverting the power of the host state.

For example, the 2006 SADC PFI did not provide national treatment, and the 2016 SADC PFI further removed the MFN clause, FET clause and ISDS clause.[176] The SADC Model BIT considers that both the traditional standards of MFN and FET could reasonably not be included in IIAs.[177]

5.2.1.4 Strengthening Investor Obligations or Responsibility

The 2009 EAC Protocol does not mention investor responsibility, and the 2006 SADC PFI provides that "foreign investors shall abide by the laws, regulations, administrative guidelines, and policies of the host state" as "corporate responsibility".[178] Similarly, the 2016 SADC PFI provides in a highly general manner that "[i]nvestor and their investments shall abide by the laws, regulations, administrative guidelines and policies of the Host State for the full life cycle of those investments".[179] The 2007 COMESA investment agreement, in general terms, confines investor obligations to compliance with domestic measures of the host country, "COMESA investors and their investments shall comply with all applicable domestic measures of the Member State in which their investment is made".[180]

---

[175] See Draft Pan-African Investment Code, article 11.3.

[176] See Agreement Amending Annex 1 (Cooperation on Investment) of the SADC Protocol on Finance and Investment; Amendments of Annex 1 to the SADC Finance and Investment Protocol: Are they in force yet? July 13, 2017.

[177] See South African Development Community, SADC Model Bilateral Investment Treaty Template with Commentary 2012, article 29 "Special Note".

[178] South African Development Community, SADC Protocol on Finance and Investment, article 10.

[179] See Agreement Amending Annex 1 (Cooperation on Investment) of the SADC Protocol on Finance and Investment, article 8 (investor responsibility).

[180] Investment Agreement for the COMESA Common Investment Area, article 13.

However, under the 2008 ECOWAS Supplementary Act, an unambiguous framework of investor obligations and details of the obligations are put forward. The obligations framework sets up general obligations, pre-establishment impact assessment, anti-corruption, postestablishment obligations, corporate governance and practices, corporate social responsibility, and investor liability. The vast majority of investor obligations are mandatory and come from the Supplementary Act and domestic law of the host state and home state. Due to the complexity of the specific obligation, the main obligations and their characteristics are summarized here.

First, the obligations cover a broad scope and comprehensive content stating that "investors and investments are subject to the laws and regulations of the host state" and its measures and jurisdiction. This is in addition to obligations contributing to development and providing information.[181]

Second, the specific contents of the obligation touch upon pre-establishment environmental and social impact assessment, which stresses the requirement of the home state, right to information of the local community, and precautionary principle.[182]

Third, the postestablishment obligations mainly address human rights by complying with "hygiene, security, health and social welfare rules" and "fundamental labor standards as stipulated in the ILO Declaration on Fundamental Principles and Rights of Work, 1998".[183]

Fourth, corporate governance and practice should emphasize transparency and accounting practices, especially the transparency of investment contracts or agreements; for this purpose, liaison processes between investors and the local community should be established.[184]

Fifth, corporate social responsibility includes legal obligations and obligations beyond law coming from "all applicable laws and regulations of the host Member State" and the obligations in the Supplementary Act, and investors should endeavour to apply and achieve the standards increased.[185]

Sixth, investor liability covers civil liability and criminal liability in the host state and the home state, especially for all kinds of corrupt conduct. For the ISDS under the Supplementary Act, if the investor breaches the anti-corruption obligation established by "a court of competent jurisdiction of the host state",[186] the investor will lose standing to initiate an ISDS process. Furthermore, if it is proven that the investor

[181] See Supplementary Act A/SA.3/12/08 Adopting Community Rules on Investment and the Modalities for their Implementation with ECOWAS, article 11.

[182] See Supplementary Act A/SA.3/12/08 Adopting Community Rules on Investment and the Modalities for their Implementation with ECOWAS, article 12.

[183] Supplementary Act A/SA.3/12/08 Adopting Community Rules on Investment and the Modalities for their Implementation with ECOWAS, article 14.

[184] See Supplementary Act A/SA.3/12/08 Adopting Community Rules on Investment and the Modalities for their Implementation with ECOWAS, article 15.

[185] See Supplementary Act A/SA.3/12/08 Adopting Community Rules on Investment and the Modalities for their Implementation with ECOWAS, article 16.

[186] Supplementary Act A/SA.3/12/08 Adopting Community Rules on Investment and the Modalities for their Implementation with ECOWAS, article 18.1.

has breached its obligations related to pre-establishment impact assessment, anti-corruption, postestablishment obligations, and corporate governance ad practices, the merits of a claim or any damages awarded by the ECOWAS tribunal will be affected. In addition, if an investor breaches obligation, the host state may initiate a counterclaim before an ECOWAS tribunal.[187]

Finally, some obligations are imposed on the home state to guarantee that investors comply with their obligations instead of condoning and contributing to crime. For example, "[h]ome States shall, when possible, provide all available information that might assist a dispute settlement tribunal under this Supplementary Act in determining whether there has been a breach of an anti-corruption obligation".[188]

Big differences from the 2008 ECOWAS Supplementary Act are developed, or it can be said that the understanding given to investor obligations varies in the two legal instruments. The 2016 PAIC gives much more considerable weight to investor obligations. The 2016 PAIC adopts a positive and radical model, which provides specific and detailed obligations of investors in one chapter. The obligation standards are either directly stipulated or internationally recognized standards are invoked in the provisions. These articles adopt the mode of direct obligation for investors, and the investors and their investment need to undertake the direct legal binding obligations under the treaty. The 2016 PAIC stipulates procedural clauses to guarantee the implementation of obligation clauses. If investors violate their treaty obligations, two consequences may appear. First, the respondent state can take the investor's breach of treaty obligations as a defense, and the adjudicator should review the relevance of the violation to the case and consider its possible offsetting effect on the investor's claim for damages.[189] Second, in the dispute settlement procedure, counterclaims can be filed by the respondent state on the grounds of violation of obligations by the investor.[190] There are six types of provisions that aim at corporate governance structure, social-political obligations, bribery, corporate social responsibility, obligations as to the use of natural resources, and business ethnics and human rights.[191]

First, for corporate governance, investments shall, in particular, meet standards for transparency and accounting practices, and investors shall "ensure the equitable treatment of all shareholders", "encourage active cooperation between corporations and stakeholders" and ensure timely and accurate disclosure of information related to material matters.[192]

---

[187] See Supplementary Act A/SA.3/12/08 Adopting Community Rules on Investment and the Modalities for their Implementation with ECOWAS, Chapter III, (Obligations and Duties of Investors and Investments).

[188] Supplementary Act A/SA.3/12/08 Adopting Community Rules on Investment and the Modalities for their Implementation with ECOWAS, article 30.2.

[189] See Draft Pan-African Investment Code, article 43,1.

[190] See Draft Pan-African Investment Code, article 43.2.

[191] See Draft Pan-African Investment Code, articles 19–24.

[192] See Draft Pan-African Investment Code, article 19.

Second, the sociopolitical obligation mainly refers to non-intervention in sovereignty, internal political affairs, intergovernmental relations, and "the appointment of persons to public office or finance political parties" in the host state, and "[i]nvestors shall refrain from exercising restrictive practices and from trying to achieve gains through unlawful means".[193]

Third, bribery, or participation in bribery in all ways to public officials, business associates or other people are not permitted.[194]

Fourth, corporate social responsibility requires investors to "abide by the laws, regulations, administrative guidelines and policies of the host state" and contribute to the sustainable development and progress of the host state.[195]

Fifth, the exploitation and utilization of natural resources shall not detriment the rights and interests of the host state and the local populations.[196]

Finally, investors should comply with business ethics and human rights principles.[197]

By and large, the parallel existence of the regional integration investment agreements in Africa, with the relationship of reference, development and inheritance, reflects the African continent's understanding of the international investment rule of law and the current choice. The development trend of these investment agreements in Africa is to restrict the protection of investors and attach importance to the policy space of host states, especially the obligations of investors. Because the 2016 PAIC, reflecting a continental consensus on the investment issue, was adopted by the African Union Commission in October 2017, and it is submitted as the baseline of the future investment protocol negotiation of AfCFTA, thus Africa has moved to the forefront of innovation of regional investment treaty-making. The 2016 PAIC emphasizes sustainable development, gives more regulatory space to the state, and imposes direct obligations on investors. The principle of non-intervention in internal affairs and natural resources in several international law instruments that have not been recognized by some Western states at the UN General Assembly is implemented through these agreements. Ironically, China has also always adhered to the principle of non-intervention in the internal affairs of African countries, but this has been criticized by some Western countries because they think the principle of non-intervention in the internal affairs of African countries would connive corruption in Africa.[198]

In summary, Africa's regional investment agreements have a process of gradual development, inheritance, adjustment, harmonization and innovation, and the 2016 PAIC, as the first continent-wide model investment treaty, is the African great achievement in the international investment rule of law. The 2016 PAIC is the crystallization of collective wisdom, including African experts, academia, governments,

---

[193] Draft Pan-African Investment Code, article 20.

[194] See Draft Pan-African Investment Code, article 21.

[195] See Draft Pan-African Investment Code, article 22.

[196] See Draft Pan-African Investment Code, article 23.

[197] See Draft Pan-African Investment Code, article 24.

[198] See Peterson Nnajiofor, 'Chinese and Western Investments in Africa: A Comparative Analysis' (2020) 10(3) International Critical Thought 473–482.

regional communities, and the AU. Therefore, it can represent a distinct African voice on international investment rule of law, especially on African value orientation of international investment rule of law. These views will profoundly affect the development of the rule of law in international investment.

5.2.2 *African Regional Investment Agreements with Foreign Parties*

In the context of the current decline of multilateralism, the rise of regionalism in Africa under the guidance of the Pan-Africanism ideology is prominent. At the same time, relations between some countries outside the continent and African regional integration organizations are strengthening. Either the US or the EU has not only the Trade and Investment Framework Agreement (TIFA) or Economic Partnership Agreement (EPA) with individual African countries,[199] but also such arrangement between them and African regional integration organizations, which will expand the scope of application for TIFA or EPA. By nature, although some are in effect and some have not yet entered into force, they are all treaties with investment provisions (TIPs).

TIFAs can "provide strategic frameworks and principles for dialogue on trade and investment issues between the US and the other parties to the TIFA".[200] There are some practices between African regional organizations and the US: COMESA-US TIFA was signed and entered into force on October 29, 2001;[201] EAC-US TIFA

[199] For example, US-Angola TIFA, US-Ghana TIFA, US-Liberia TIFA, US-Mauritius TIFA, US-Mozambique TIFA, US-Nigeria TIFA, US-Rwanda TIFA, US-South Africa TIFA, available at <https://ustr.gov/trade-agreements/trade-investment-framework-agreements>. In addition, at the time of Brexit, the United Kingdom also began to sign EPA with African countries, such as 2020 Kenya- United Kingdom EPA, 2020 Côte d'Ivoire-United Kingdom Stepping Stone EPA, 2019 SACU and Mozambique-United Kingdom EPA; The UK has also signed Association Agreements with some African countries, for example, 2020 Egypt-United Kingdom Association Agreement and 2019 Morocco-United Kingdom Association Agreement. See Investment Policy Hub, available at <https://investmentpolicy.unctad.org/international-investment-agreements>.

[200] Office of the United States Trade Representative, Trade and Investment Framework Agreements, available at <https://ustr.gov/trade-agreements/trade-investment-framework%20agreements#:~:text=Trade%20and%20Investment%20Framework%20Agreements%20%28TIFAs%29%20provide%20strategic,%20cooperation%20and%20enhancing%20opportunities%20for%20trade%20and%20investment>.

[201] See Agreement Between the Government of the United States of America and the Common Market for Eastern and Southern Africa Concerning the Development of Trade and Investment Relations, available at <https://ustr.gov/sites/default/files/uploads/agreements/tifa/asset_upload_file367_7725>.
pdf.

and SACU-US TIFA were signed and entered into force on July 16, 2008[202]; and ECOWAS–US TIFA was signed on August 5, 2014.[203]

These TIFAs are similar in content and emphasize the importance of investment to each other's economies and therefore require the creation of a stable and transparent environment for investment, which reflects the US's views and understanding of investment climate. The most effective setting is the establishment of the Trade and Investment Council for a structured dialogue on trade and investment issues, which meets at least once a year. The aim is to consult on trade- and investment-related issues that are of concern to bilateral parties, and the bilateral parties also commit to further negotiate and conclude agreements on issues of investment and other bilateral concerns, such as market access issues, labor, the environment, protection and enforcement of intellectual property rights.[204]

The TIFA between the US and the EAC was signed in 2008 and became operational in the same year.[205] Furthermore, the US negotiated an investment treaty with the EAC, and although there were controversial issues among the member states of the EAC on the specific provisions, such as the definition of investment, national treatment, MFN treatment and performance requirements, the EAC was working to review these controversial provisions.[206] Therefore, it is possible that an investment treaty could be concluded between the US and the EAC in the future.

The US African Growth and Opportunity Act (AGOA) (Title I, Trade and Development Act of 2000; P.L. 106–200) aims to remove barriers and other obstacles to trade between the US and sub-Saharan Africa and enhance trade preferences in favor of sub-Saharan Africa. At the 17th AGOA Forum in 2018, the US presented a plan to negotiate a model FTA with Saharan African countries and hoped it to promote integration of the African various regions and the continent.[207]

The aim of the EPAs is alleged by the EU to promote trade and thereby engender sustainable development and the alleviation of poverty in Africa.[208] The EU has

---

202 See Trade and Investment Framework Agreement between the United States and the East African Community (EAC), available at <https://investmentpolicy.unctad.org/international-investment-agreements/treaties/treaties-with-investment-provisions/3235/eac---us-tifa-2008->.

203 See Trade and Investment Framework Agreement Between the Government of the United States of America and the Economic Community of West African States, available at <https://ustr.gov/sites/default/files/files/agreements/tifa/U.S.%20Economic%20Community%20of%20West%20African%20States%20ECOWAS%20TIFA.pdf>.

204 See Office of the United States Trade Representative, Trade and Investment Framework Agreements, available at <https://ustr.gov/trade-agreements/trade-investment-framework-agreements>.

205 See Trade and Investment Framework Agreement between the United States and the East African Community (EAC), available at <https://investmentpolicy.unctad.org/international-investment-agreements/treaties/treaties-with-investment-provisions/3235/eac---us-tifa-2008->.

206 See Africa Economic Commission, Investment policy and Bilateral Investment Treaty in Africa: Implication for Regional Integration, 2016, 34.

207 See USTR, Statement of USTR Robert Lighthizer at the opening plenary of the 2018, July 11, 2018.

208 See European Commission, Economic partnerships, available at <https://ec.europa.eu/trade/policy/countries-and-regions/development/economic-partnerships/>.

been working on EPAs with African regional integration organizations, including ECOWAS, COMESA, SADC, etc. Sometimes, the EU has also sought to undertake subregional and individual negotiations to supplement the stagnation of EPA.[209] The EU has attempted to cover the foreign direct investment topic within the context of EPAs, which is controversial between the EU and Africa. In fact, the Cotonou Agreement has long provided that "[t]he Parties also agree to introduce, within the economic partnership agreements, and while respecting the respective competencies of the Community and its Member States, general principles on protection and promotion of investments, which will endorse the best results agreed in the competent international fora or bilaterally".[210]

The most recent practice is the signing of an EPA with SADC on June 10, 2016.[211] Although known as the "framework agreement", it has numerous clauses, in particular, it provides for the prospect of investment cooperation and the future conclusion of BITs. In the future, if non-party members of the investment agreement are to apply for accession, they will have to negotiate on a conditional basis to become a party member.[212]

Regional investment agreements beyond African states are mainly framework agreements designed to maintain the relationship between the former colonialists and their colonies and reflect the interests of European countries and the US. In terms of the significance of the international investment rule of law, although they are framework agreements, their effectiveness in protecting investor interests and restricting the power of the host state will be strong, and they will have a greater impact on the shaping of the specific international investment rule of law in the future.

5.3 African States' Involvement in Investment Rule of Law at Multilateral Level

The African international investment rule of law is first and foremost reflected in its active participation in the multilateral international investment rule of law. African

209 See European Commission, Economic partnerships, available at <https://ec.europa.eu/trade/policy/countries-and-regions/development/economic-partnerships/>; SADC-EU Economic Partnership Agreement Documents and Resources, available at <https://www.tralac.org/resources/by-region/sadc/sadc-eu-economic-partnership-agreement.html>.

210 Cotonou Agreement, signed on June 23, 2000, entered into force on April 1, 2003, article 78.3, available at <https://eur-lex.europa.eu/legal-content/EN/TXT/?uri=celex%3A22000A1215%2801%29>.

211 See EU-SADC Interim Agreement, signed on January 11, 2009, available at <https://investmentpolicy.unctad.org/international-investment-agreements/treaty-files/5811/download>; EU-SADC EPA Group Agreement, signed on June 10, 2016, available at <https://trade.ec.europa.eu/doclib/docs/2014/october/tradoc_152818.pdf>.

212 See Economic Partnership Agreement between the European Union and its Member States, of the one part, and the SADC EPA States, of the other part, article 74, available at <https://investmentpolicy.unctad.org/international-investment-agreements/treaty-files/5812/download>.

countries have played a positive role in formulation, finalizing and entering into effect of the ICSID Convention.[213] Currently, 46 out of 55 countries have ratified and acceded to the ICSID Convention. That is, among the 155 contracting parties to the ICSID Convention, 46 are African countries, and Ethiopia, Guinea-Bissau and Namibia have signed the Convention although have still not ratified it. In addition, 15 of the first 20 parties to the ICSID Convention are African States.[214] Only 1 in 55 African countries is not a member of the Multilateral Investment Guarantee Agency (MIGA). 42 out of 55 countries have joined the WTO, and 9 countries are in the process of acceding the WTO. African countries are also represented in the United Nations Commission on International Trade law (UNCITRAL) and other non-binding instruments related to investment.[215]

The African international investment rule of law is particularly reflected in the various IIA clauses that African countries have concluded, including bilateral BITs, regional integration investment agreements, and the 2016 PAIC throughout the African continent. The different types of BITs also reflect the will of African countries to different degrees. By comparison, the integration investment agreements in the African region, both subcontinental and continental levels, can better reflect the expectations of African countries to the international investment rule of law.

This chapter will examine the networks of international investment agreements that an Africa state is one party, through the lens of international investment rule of law. Finally, it will also supplement the attitude of some African countries to the international investment rule of law. The changes in the attitude to ISDS in the domestic laws of some African countries are also an integral part of this study of African international investment rule of law, as they also reflect their retreat from the international investment rule of law.

5.4 South Africa's Unique Stance on International Investment Rule of Law

The Bilateral Investment Treaty Policy Framework Review presented by the South African Department of Trade and Industry in June 2009 (the *Review*),[216] Policy Statement on Approach to Future International Investment Treaties by the South African

[213] See Antonio R Parra, 'The Participation of African States in the Making of the ICSID Convention' (2019) 34(2) ICSID Review-Foreign Investment Law Journal 270–277.

[214] See Database of ICSID Member States, available at <https://icsid.worldbank.org/about/member-states/database-of-member-states>.

[215] See Africa, United Nations Economic Commission, Investment Policy and Bilateral Investment Treaty in Africa: Implication for Regional Integration, Addis Ababa, Ethiopia: 2016, VIII-IX, XIII.

[216] See Bilateral Investment Treaty Policy Framework Review, Government Position Paper (Department of Trade and Industry, Republic of South Africa, June 2009), available at <http://www.thedti.gov.za/ads/bi-lateral_policy.pdf>.

Department of Trade and Industry in July 2010 (the *Policy Statement*),[217] together with a speech delivered by the Minister of Trade and Industry (Dr. Rob Davies) at the occasion of the South African Launch of the UNCTAD Investment Policy Framework for Sustainable Development on July 26, 2012 (the *Speech*), manifest the changes that South Africa envisages.[218]

The *Review* noted at the outset that the BITs after 1994 "were heavily stacked in favor of investors without the necessary safeguards to preserve flexibility in a number of critical policy areas" due to inexperience and lack of knowledge of the negotiators at that time.[219] The *Review* stressed that no mention of any exclusion to national treatment creates a real danger that international arbitral tribunals could find that regulatory state measures breach obligations under the national treatment clause. The *Review* noticed that some investors are using BITs to "challenge treatment of foreign investments in various sensitive areas". The *Review* criticized that "existing international investment agreements are based on a 50-year-old model that remains focusing on the interests of investors from *developed countries.* Major issues of concern for developing countries are not being addressed in the BIT negotiating processes," but "damaging binding investment rules with far-reaching consequences for sustainable development" are imposed.[220] It is clear that the conclusion of the *Review* is totally based on examining BITs with Western countries that violate the policy space of the developing host state.

In the *Policy Statement*, along with the stance of terminating old BITs and refraining from concluding new BITs, the South African government stated that it aims to "empower the domestic adjudication of investment disputes" because:

> "The South African judiciary has an international reputation for excellence and independence. We therefore propose that the domestic judiciary, which is well equipped, should deal with investment disputes, while a new National Investment Act should incorporate, codify and interpret core international law concepts that have been subject to conjecture and dispute in international investment arbitrations."[221]

R Davies' *Speech* is based on the *Review* and the *Policy Statement*. He summarized the following points. First, the first-generation South African BITs reflect the

---

[217] See Department of Trade and Industry, Republic of South Africa, Policy Statement: The South African Government's Approach to Future International Investment Treaties, p. 2, available at <www.jadafa.co.za/LinkClick.aspx?fileticket=9A6eXZstR10%3Dandtabid=432>.

[218] See Speech delivered by the Minister of Trade and Industry Dr Rob Davies at the South African launch of the United Nations Conference on Trade and Development (UNCTAD) Investment Policy Framework for sustainable development at the University of The Witwatersrand (July 26, 2012), available at <http://unctad.org/meetings/en/Miscellaneous%20Documents/South-Africa-Investment-statement_Rob_Davies.pdf>.

[219] See Department of Trade and Industry of the Republic of South Africa, Bilateral Investment Treaty Policy Framework Review: Executive Summary of Government Position Paper, June 2009, in Government Gazette Vol.529, No.32386, July 7, 2009, 5.

[220] Bilateral Investment Treaty Policy Framework Review, Government Position Paper (Department of Trade and Industry, Republic of South Africa, June 2009), 5, 37, 11.

[221] Department of Trade and Industry, Republic of South Africa, Policy Statement: The South African Government's Approach to Future International Investment Treaties, 2.

policy that the government should protect the benefits of foreign investors at the expense of the regulatory power of the government. Second, some investment benefits cannot be realized automatically, and the state must assume an important role in their realization. Third, the relationship between BITs and FDI is ambiguous, but BIT "imposes risks and limitations on the ability of the Government to pursue its Constitutional-based transformation agenda". Fourth, South Africa doubts and denies the existing international investment arbitration regime. Thus, fifth, to countries without BIT relations with South Africa, "South Africa should refrain from entering into BITs in future, except in cases of *compelling* economic and political circumstances". Sixth, to the countries with first-generation BIT relations with South Africa, South Africa should review them "with a view to termination, and possible renegotiation on the basis of a new Model BIT to be developed".[222] Seventh, two types of typical BIT provisions should be codified into domestic law, specifically, the protection of the investor and the legitimate exception for public policy considerations. Eighth, the investment regulation pursuit of South Africa is to "achieve an appropriate balance between the rights and obligations of investors" and "inclusive growth and sustainable development".

As a result of these fundamental shifts to its investment policy, the South African government adopted two kinds of measures at the international level and national level.

At the international level, South Africa is a party to 50 signed BITs, of which 12 are still in force. However, since 2010, no BIT has been signed, and since the beginning of October 2012, South Africa has canceled its 10 BITs with Belgium-Luxembourg, Spain, Germany, Switzerland, the Netherlands, Austria, Denmark, France, Italy, and the United Kingdom.[223] In fact, the country intends to phase out all BITs with EU countries. In addition, the South Africa-Argentina BIT has also been terminated. South Africa has signed BITs with Ethiopia, Sudan, Guinea, Madagascar, Congo, Tanzania, Gabon, Angola, D.R. Congo, Equatorial Guinea, Tunisia, Rwanda, Algeria, Uganda, Egypt, Ghana, Mozambique, Mali Kuwait, Israel, Qatar, Yemen, Libya, Turkey, Czech Republic, Chile, and Canada, but they have never entered into force.

At the national level, the Promotion and Protection of Investment Draft Bill (the *Draft Bill*) was published for comment on November 1, 2013. Considering it in light of the terminated BITs, the main changes include the following.[224] First, some investment treatments, such as FET and MFN treatment, are removed; thus, foreign investors can only demand equal rights with reference to national treatment. Second, regarding regulatory powers, the *Draft Bill* especially empowers the South African

[222] To develop a new-model BIT is the initial thought, but it seems to have not been on the agenda because the National Investment Act came into effect in 2016.

[223] See UNCTAD hub, South Africa, Bilateral Investment Treaties (BITs), available at <http://investmentpolicyhub.unctad.org/IIA/CountryBits/195#iiaInnerMenu>.

[224] See Minister of Trade and Industry, Promotion and Protection of Investment, 2013, draft Bill, published in Government Gazette, Vol.581, No.36995, November 1, 2013.

government to "take measures to…redress historical, social and economic inequalities", "promote and preserve cultural heritage and practices, indigenous knowledge and biological resources related thereto or national heritage", and "achieve the progressive realization of socioeconomic rights". Third, regarding expropriation and compensation, the *Draft Bill* generally stipulates that only "just and equitable" instead of "market value" compensation will be awarded to an investor in case of legal expropriation and lists four exceptions of legal expropriation without compensation. fourth, no recourse of investor-state international arbitration is afforded in the *Draft Bill*, and only mediation and other alternative domestic remedies can be available.

Comparatively, the revised Promotion and Protection of Investment Bill in 2015 (the *Bill*) has improved the legislative technique to a great degree,[225] and it is more elaborated and clear-cut. On November 17, 2015, South Africa's National Assembly approved the *Bill*.[226]

However, it retains the exclusion of national treatment of pre-establishment, clarification of "like circumstances", and emphasis of "redressing historical, social and economic inequalities and injustices" as well as necessary national security in the section on regulatory powers. The following aspects are different. First, in the preamble, "the need to take measures to protect or advance persons, or categories of persons, historically disadvantaged in the Republic due to discrimination" is added to show the priority and importance of this legislative objective. Second, in the definitions section, the *Bill* seeks to redefine the concept of "dispute" by no longer requiring that the "measure" make the investor incur loss or damage but supplementing that the "measure" shall only include "administrative action"; therefore, the disputable issues are still narrowly confined. Third, the *Bill* redefines the concept of "investment" by outlining characteristics instead of enumerating the types of assets constituting "investment"; nevertheless, the result is still one of considerable ambiguity. Fourth, the *Bill* adds seven exceptions to national treatment and especially excludes "any law or other measure, the purpose of which is to promote the achievement of equality in South Africa or designed to protect or advance persons, or categories of persons historically disadvantaged by unfair discrimination on the basis of race, gender or disability in the Republic". Fifth, the investment security afforded is that of a national treatment guarantee, subject to the available resources and capacity of South Africa. However, the *Draft Bill* has a provision similar to that of the China–South Africa BIT.[227] Sixth, the *Bill* dropped the controversial expropriation clause and only stipulates that the investor shall enjoy property rights in accordance with Sect. 25 of the

---

225 See Minister of Trade and Industry, Promotion and Protection of Investment, 2015, Bill, B18-2015, July 28, 2015.

226 See Paul Vecchiatto, 'SA MPs Back Foreign Investment Bill' (November 18, 2015), Bloomberg, available at <http://www.iol.co.za/business/news/sa-mps-back-foreign-investment-bill-1.1946986>.

227 See Agreement Between the Government of the People's Republic of China and the Government of the Republic of South Africa concerning the Reciprocal Promotion and Protection of Investments, available at <https://investmentpolicy.unctad.org/international-investment%20agreements/treaties/bit/971/china-south-africa-bit-1997->.

South African Constitution, which includes only direct expropriation and a different standard of compensation for direct expropriation. Seventh, the *bill* adds "protecting the environment and the conservation and sustainable use of natural resources" to the host state's regulatory powers and requires regulatory authorities to conform to other acts (relevant legislations) as well as the constitution. Eighth, the *Bill* states that state-state arbitration may be accepted by South Africa on a case-by-case basis. Ninth, a section on "transitional arrangement" is found in the *Bill*, but the relation between the *Bill* and the BITs is still ambiguous.

In effect, the new investment regulatory framework will not only be limited to the Promotion and Protection of Investment Act. It is predicted that some matched Bills will come into force one after the other. These Bills especially include Minerals and Petroleum Resource Development Act Amendment Bill No. 15 of 2013, Property Valuation Bill No. 54 of 2013, Private Security Industry Regulation Act Amendment Bill No. 27 of 2012, and Expropriation Bill No. 4 of 2015.[228]

Chapter Summary

African countries have actively integrated the international investment rule of law; thus, in recent years, the practice of concluding international investment agreements in African states has become very rich, and the "Africanization" of the international investment rule of law in Africa is striking.

African countries have increased their efforts to sign BITs within the continent to enjoy the advantages of a wider economic market.[229] African countries are also actively signing BITs with countries beyond the continent. "African signatories of BITs with the rest of the world surpass intra-African signatories".[230] The BITs signed by African countries can be divided into two categories: BITs with developed countries and BITs with developing countries. Due to the lack of negotiation power, the former mainly reflects the will of developed countries or mainly reflects the protection of investors' interests. Regarding the extent to which the international investment rule of law advocated by Africa can be achieved, some scholars believe that it depends on the relative political and economic strength between the contracting parties. Taking the investment treaty concluded between African countries and Canada as an example, it shows that African countries' claims are often not realized.[231]

While actively promoting BIT, African countries prefer regional approaches to develop legal frameworks for foreign investment from the member states of regional integration organizations. The biggest leap forward is the entry into force of the AfCFTA on May 30, 2019, and the 2016 PAIC adopted by the AU in 2016 is

228 All these Bills are available at <http://www.gov.za/>.

229 See Africa, United Nations Economic Commission, Investment Policy and Bilateral Investment Treaty in Africa: Implication for Regional Integration, Addis Ababa, Ethiopia: 2016, 16.

230 Africa, United Nations Economic Commission, Investment Policy and Bilateral Investment Treaty in Africa: Implication for Regional Integration, Addis Ababa, Ethiopia: 2016, 20.

231 See J. Anthony VanDuzer, 'Canadian Investment Treaties with African Countries: What Do They Tell Us About Investment Treaty Making in Africa?' (2017) 18(3) The Journal of World Investment and Trade 556–584.

expected to serve as a model basis for the second phase of consultations on the investment protocol[232] because it reflects the consensus within AU member states. Africa's regional integration investment agreements are based on Africa's regional integration. Regional integration can better address some of the obstacles to Africa's development, such as tariff and non-tariff barriers, existing restrictions on investments, free movement of people and capital, and high transaction costs. The benefits they bring to African countries will be more obvious if they can be fully implemented. The most important internal driving force of African integration is Pan-Africanism, which is deeply rooted in African blood, so its development trend is also irresistible.

In regional investment agreements, African countries are trying to strike a balance between protecting investors and constraining the regulatory power of the state. Their outstanding feature is to give the government sufficient policy space for sustainable development objectives, attempt to settle disputes through African dispute mechanisms, and emphasize investor responsibility.

These regional integration investment agreements have African characteristics, reflect the African consensus, and reflect that political economy plays a decisive role in the real lawmaking process. Although it cannot exercise leadership over the international investment rule of law, it can affect the direction of the change in the rule of international investment law. In addition, the US and European countries are also actively signing investment agreements with these African regional integration organizations.

In general, the rule of law in investment in Africa may be a reduction in the level of protection, manifested by various exceptions to protection treatment standards.[233] As a result, the expansion of the host state's regulatory power is also reflected in the exclusion or restriction of ISDS provisions.[234] This adjustment is reasonable to a certain degree because it corrects the excessive protection of investors in the past investment rule of law. However, it reveals that the proper limits in righting a wrong might also be exceeded. The African investment rule of law also imposes obligations and performance requirements directly on investors, which can help investors become responsible investors, but it can also make investors' obligations too heavy. Therefore, both of those may require attention in future development.

The purpose of this chapter is to show that from the perspective of African countries' participation and shaping of the international investment rule of law, African countries are not on the periphery. The international investment rule of law in Africa is burgeoning. While African countries are actively developing bilateral, regional

[232] See Makane Moïse Mbengue and Stefanie Schacherer, 'The 'Africanization' of International Investment Law: The Pan-African Investment Code and the Reform of the International Investment Regime' (2017) 18(3) The Journal of World Investment and Trade 414–448, 446.

[233] For an explanation of these exceptions, see Makane Moïse Mbengue and Stefanie Schacherer, 'The 'Africanization' of International Investment Law: The Pan-African Investment Code and the Reform of the International Investment Regime' (2017) 18(3) The Journal of World Investment and Trade 414–448, 426–432.

[234] See Makane Moïse Mbengue and Stefanie Schacherer, 'The 'Africanization' of International Investment Law: The Pan-African Investment Code and the Reform of the International Investment Regime' (2017) 18(3) The Journal of World Investment and Trade 414–448, 441–445.

and extra regional investment agreements, China should also actively adapt to this trend to develop the investment rule of law with African countries. From an economic perspective, African economic integration will promote the inflow of foreign investment to the region and the free flow within the region because there are various preferences and facilities in the region. At the same time, foreign investment should consider the possibility of using regional integration investment agreements. Chinese investors should also consider the possibility of applying African investment agreements if they come into force. For example, the 2007 COMESA Investment Agreement applies to the "legal entity duly constituted or otherwise organized under the applicable laws and regulations of a Member State" of COMESA, but owned or controlled by Chinese, only if it maintains substantial business activity in the Member State in which it is duly constituted or organized. Of course, Chinese investors should also be aware of their obligations under these investment agreements.

Chapter 6
International Investment Rule of Law Between China and Africa

The international investment rule of law between China and Africa is an integral part of the overall African investment rule of law, and of course, it is also an integral part of the Chinese investment rule of law. This part of the international investment rule of law plays an important role in maintaining the normal development of investment relations between China and Africa.

6.1 An Overall Assessment of China's Practices of IIAs

Looking back on the history of the Chinese Model BITs based on existing academic literature, we can find four generational Model BITs: the 1984 Chinese Model BIT, the 1989 Chinese Model BIT, the 1997 Chinese Model BIT,[1] and the 2010 Draft Chinese Model BIT.[2] Correspondingly, BITs concluded by China can be classified into four generations: the first-generation (1982–1989), the second-generation (1990–1997), the third-generation (1998–2009),[3] and the fourth-generation BITs that concluded on the basis of 2010 Draft Chinese Model BIT. Another classification of China's BITs may take the year of 1993 (China acceded "ICSID Convention"), the year of 1998 (China signed BIT with Barbados), the year of 2012 (China concluded

[1] About three Model versions, see Norah Gallagher and Wenhua Shan, Chinese Investment Treaties: Policies and Practice' (Oxford University Press, 2008) Appendices, 423–439. Here, 1984, 1989 and 1997 are only approximate time.

[2] For 2010 Draft Chinese Model BIT Version IV, see Xiantao Wen, Comments on the Draft of China's Model BIT (I) (2011) 18(4) Journal of International Economic Law (Chinese) 169; see also Xiantao Wen Comments on the Draft of China's Model BIT(II) (2012) 19(1) Journal of International Economic Law (Chinese) 132; see also Xiantao Wen, Comments on the Draft of China's Model BIT(III)' (2012) 19(2) Journal of International Economic Law (Chinese) (III) 57.

[3] See Norah Gallagherand and Wenhua Shan, Chinese Investment Treaties: Policies and Practice (Oxford University Press, 2009)35–43.

X. Han, *Legal Protection and Sustainability of Chinese Investments in Africa*,
Modern China and International Economic Law,
https://doi.org/10.1007/978-981-19-1882-7_6

BIT with Canada), and the year of 2020 (China concluded BIT with the EU) as the timeline of classifying the Chinese BITs.

This research, which adopts the former method to classify the China–Africa BITs for the current China–Africa BITs, can better reflect the characteristics of Chinese Model BITs (see Appendix 8). Overall, the investment protection in the first two generations of Chinese BITs is weak, and accordingly, the host state retains more regulatory power. Under the first-generation and second-generation China–Africa BITs, only the amount of compensation for expropriation is arbitrable. Moreover, such clauses have caused problems in the practice of arbitration because different arbitral tribunals have made two kinds of completely different interpretations of the "expropriation" provision. The second-generation BITs introduced national treatment provisions. Under third-generation BITs, investors enjoy more protection with higher treatment standards. The fourth-generation BITs further attempt to rebalance the rights and obligations between the host state and the investor. China's contracting practices of BITs are going forward venturesome even though some Chinese scholars admonish this,[4] and China also faces an increasing number of cases before the ICSID.[5]

In addition to its BITs, China has also concluded many free trade agreements (FTAs). Some Chinese FTAs have ambitious investment chapters, such as China–Korea FTA and China–Australia FTA.[6] It is scheduled that China and Korea will conduct a second-stage negotiation,[7] aiming to adopt the national treatment of pre-establishment and the negative list. The China–Australia FTA includes detailed ISDS provisions and provides the national treatment of pre-establishment, and the negative list will be negotiated in the future.[8] In other words, China–Korea FTA and China–Australia FTA may introduce the negative list and national treatment of pre-establishment in the future.

---

[4] See e.g., An Chen, 'Should the Four Great Safeguards in Sino-Foreign BITs Be Hastily Dismantled?' (2006) 7(6) The Journal of World Investment and Trade 899, 933; see also An Chen, 'Distinguishing Two kinds of Countries and Properly Granting Differential Reciprocity Treatment: Recomments on the Four Safeguards in Sino-Foreign BITs Not to Be Hastily and Completely Dismantled' (2007) 8(6) The Journal of World Investment and Trade 771, 795.

[5] China became the contracting state of the ICSID Convention on February 6, 1993, the only member to accept the ICSID Convention among the BRICS countries. See List of Contracting States and Other Signatories of the Convention (as of July 25, 2012), ICSID/3, available at <https://icsid.worldbank.org/ICSID/FrontServlet>. These ICSID cases are available at <https://icsid.worldbank.org/apps/ICSIDWEB/cases/Pages/AdvancedSearch.aspx?gE=s&rspndnt=People's%20Republic%20of%20China>.

[6] The detailed provisions of these FTAs can be found on the Service Network for China's Free Trade Area, available at <http://fta.mofcom.gov.cn/index.shtml>.

[7] Free Trade Agreement Between the Government of the People's Republic of China and the Government of the Republic of Korea (China-Korea FTA), signed on June 1, 2015, and come into force on December 20, 2015, Chapter 22 Final Provisions, Annex 22-A Guidelines for Subsequent Negotiations, A.3–4.

[8] Free Trade Agreement Between the Government of Australia and the Government of the People's Republic of China (Australia-China FTA), signed on June 17, 2015, and come into force on December 20, 2015, Chapter 9, Section B; article 9.9.3.c.

The transformation of the international investment rule of law becomes evident in the new development of international investment agreements and readjustment of arbitration practices. The common trend is to rebalance the rights and obligations between the host state and the investor through both substantive and procedural provisions. The transformation is inspired by reflections of states on neo-liberal economic theory and practice,[9] as well as the changes of attitude and stance to BITs and the ICSID Convention from countries such as Indonesia, India, South Africa, and especially some Latin American countries, which also remind other countries to review their BIT policies. In addition, the critiques of the international investment system by some scholars and NGOs play a very important role.[10]

At the international level, China's investment policy is to speed up the negotiation and conclusion of investment agreements with relevant countries and regions, including BITs, and at the same time, support the regionalization and multilateralization of international investment regulations. As of September 30, 2021, China has concluded 134 BITs, of which 113 are in force,[11] a number ranking China just after Germany.

China is determined to be a responsible world power and therefore will seriously abide by all international legal obligations out of its exercising sovereignty. The Chinese government does not consider the international investment rule of law to be totally detrimental to its economic development. In contrast, it is actively concluding BITs and other economic treaties to construct the international investment rule of law. Furthermore, China has attempted to promote the rule of law in multilateral international investment. China put investment high on the agenda during its G20 presidency in 2016 and supported the adoption of "Guiding Principles for Global Investment Policymaking" that, among other things, emphasized the importance of multilateralism.

The motivations and reasons for China's BIT development lie in that, on the one hand, international investment law is undergoing transformation, and modern international investment law has put more emphasis on interest balance between the host states and foreign investors; additionally, the value orientation of sustainable development is well established. On the other hand, the fundamental reason lies in the substantial change of China's realistic economic status, "hybrid identity" of

[9] See José E. Alvarez 'Why are We 'Re-Calibrating' Our Investment Treaties?' (2010) 4 World Arbitration and Mediation Review 144; See also Gillard Government Trade Policy Statement: Trading Our Way to More Jobs and Prosperity, Investor-State Dispute Resolution, available at <www.dfat.gov.au/publications/trade/trading-our-way-to-more-jobs-and-prosperity.html>, December 13, 2015.

[10] See, for example, Stephan W. Schill, The Public Law Challenge: Killing or Rethinking International Investment Law? Available at <www.vcc.columbia.edu/content/public-law-challenge-killing-or-rethinking-international-investment-law#_ftnref5>. December 14, 2015; See also Gus Van Harten, Public Statement on the International Investment Regime' (August 31, 2010), available at <www.osgoode.yorku.ca/public_statement>, November 5, 2015.

[11] See China's Bilateral Investment Treaty, available at tfs.mofcom.gov.cn/aarticle/Nocategory/201111/20111107819474.html, and available at <https://investmentpolicy.unctad.org/international-investment-agreements/countries/42/china>.

both capital importing and exporting country, as provides practical and intrinsic requirements for China's concluding modern BITs.[12]

The innovation and modernization of China's BITs are mainly reflected in its 2010 Model BIT. The 2010 Model BIT represents this transformation of Chinese investment policy. Taking its preamble as an example, it stresses values such as "reciprocal encouragement, promotion and protection of investments *on the basis of equality and mutual benefits*", "mutual respect economic sovereignty", promoting the "healthy and stable economy and sustainable development", and raising the "living standards of citizens".

For the substantive provisions for protecting the investment, the 2010 Draft Chinese Model BIT not only provides guidelines for national treatment, MFN treatment, and FET, and expropriation provisions but also attaches to them some limitations, especially regarding the following four aspects:

First, national treatment does not apply to establishments, acquisitions, or expansions of investments.

Second, dispute settlement procedures in other agreements cannot be invoked by the investor under MFN treatment provisions, thus excluding dispute settlement procedures from MFN treatment.

Third, FPS does not equal the need to offer more preferential treatment than that for nationals of the Contracting Party, and the violation of other provisions of the treaty and provisions of the other treaties does not mean the violation of FET.

Fourth, the article on expropriation becomes more meticulous. In addition to expropriation being treated as an exception, it must conform to four requirements: a) for public interest; b) under domestic legal procedure or relevant due process; c) without discrimination; and d) payment of compensation. Furthermore, under article 6.1, indirect expropriation must be decided on facts and case by case evaluations, and a series of factors must be considered according to the proportionality principle.

For the procedural provisions, the ISDS provision becomes lengthier and more restrictions are imposed on the rights of investors. The main differences and the new elements are as follows: a) the determination of the disputes that the investor can lodge before the domestic courts, the ICSID, and ad hoc tribunals established under UNCITRAL rules, or other arbitral agencies or ad hoc arbitral tribunals, in terms of articles 2–9 or 14; b) the immutability of the forum choice once it has been made; c) the rule that domestic administrative review procedures must be exhausted before an international arbitration may be invoked; d) the prescription of action of a right to invoke arbitration within three years; e) the prevalence of the law chosen by the parties as the applicable law; f) the rule that an arbitral award must be sound in monetary compensation and interest, if applicable, and/or restitution; g) the clarification what will constitute a final and enforceable arbitral award; and h) the burden of arbitral costs which the arbitral tribunal may determine.

One important change for the regulatory power of the host state is the incorporation of exception of indirect expropriation under article 6.3 of 2010 China's Model BIT:

---

[12] Xiuli Han, 'Transformation of International Investment Law in the Post-Crisis Era' (2012) 17(6) Journal of Xiamen University (Arts and Social Sciences) 21.

> Except in rare circumstances, for example, the measure adopted is excessively beyond necessary for maintaining legitimate public welfare, non-discriminatory regulatory actions by a Party that are designed and applied to protect legitimate public welfare objectives, such as public health, safety, and the environment, do not constitute indirect expropriations.

Thus, the policy space of the host state will be reserved and guaranteed. In addition, articles 4, 8, 11, and 13 of 2010 Chinese Model BIT provide for exceptions to MFN treatment and free transfer of funds. Some taxation measures are also excluded from the ISDS arbitration. Finally, the interpretation of treaty provisions between the parties at the request of the host state is binding on the ISDS arbitral tribunal. However, China's Model BIT 2010 does not make special provisions for investor responsibilities except for making an investment "in accordance with the laws and regulations" of the host state.

After the 2010 Draft Chinese Model BIT, China concluded the China–Uzbekistan BIT, China–Canada BIT, China–Japan–Korea Tripartite Investment Agreement, and China–Tanzania BIT.[13] The China–Tanzania BIT reflects the transformation of China's BIT practices. The China–Uzbekistan BIT is extraordinarily similar to the China–Tanzania BIT. On the other hand, the China–Canada BIT and the China–Japan–South Korea Tripartite Investment Agreement share marvelous similarities but develop higher protection standards and go further than 2010 Draft Chinese Model BIT.[14] They are a further important transformation of the Chinese BIT regime but still fall into fourth-generation BITs.

The negotiation of the China–US BIT was suspended, although it was said that negotiation was almost concluded. The negotiation of the China–EU BIT, which can be regarded as the fifth Chinese generation BIT, was concluded at the end of 2020 and is waiting for ratification from the EU side. The China–EU BIT is more ambitious, especially the negative list and national treatment of pre-establishment, so-called new issues in the twenty-first century, which means beyond the prohibited and restricted areas clearly outlined in the list, and all other sectors will free open to foreign investment. In addition, more sophisticated rules of investment protection should be included in the future.

In view of the latest developments in China's BIT, it is submitted that in addition to promoting and protecting foreign investments, the motives of China's BITs include the promotion of diplomatic relations, the preservation of regulatory policy space, and the development of international investment law at the international level.[15]

---

[13] China-Tanzania BIT was signed on March 24, 2013 and came into force on April 14, 2014, China-Uzbekistan BIT was signed on April 19, 2011 and came into force on September 1, 2011; China-Canada BIT was signed on September 9, 2012 and came into force on October 1, 2014; China-Japan-Korea tripartite investment agreement was signed on May 13, 2012 and came into force on May 17, 2014.

[14] See Agreement among the Government of Japan, the Government of the Republic of Korea and the Government of the People's Republic of China for the Promotion, Facilitation and Protection of Investment, available at <www.meti.go.jp/english/press/2012/0513_01.html>.

[15] Axel Berger, 'The Political Economy of Chinese Investment Treaties', in Ka Zeng (ed.), Handbook on The International Political Economy of China (Elgar, 2019) 151–168.

The state practice and policy of China on international investment protection is consistent with the international trend that focuses on the balance of rights and obligations and a modernist view of investment protection and liberalization. China adopts a proactive attitude toward international investment law by embracing international investment law and bringing its foreign investment law to conform to its BITs when some states react negatively to the BITs. Even within the BRICS, China's performance on BITs is unique.[16] Furthermore, China differentiates BITs with developed states from those with developing states.

To coincide with the development of China's international investment policy, China wants to make its national law in line with international investment rules by integrating its three foreign investment laws into one. The Foreign Investment Law of the People's Republic of China came into force on January 1, 2020. For investment liberalization, it adopts the regulatory mode of national treatment of pre-establishment and negative list. For investment protection, it includes provisions on FET, expropriation, requisition, state compensation, transfer, transparency, trade secrets protection, investment dispute settlement, and so on. It expressly provides detailed rules for addressing and coordinating complaints and attempts to avoid the investment dispute from deteriorating into an international arbitration case.

China intends to raise the level of rule of law on foreign investment to further attract foreign investment. In fact, the proposed foreign investment law reflects China's policy to expand and deepen the breadth and depth of reform and opening up and to promote China's economic development by "forcing mechanisms", which means perfecting national law to satisfy the standard of international law.

6.2 General Observations of IIAs Between China and African Countries

More recently, the investment status of African countries in relation to the world's major economies has gained renewed importance. Concluding new BITs with African countries seems to have become a race among the world's large economies. Canada–Africa BITs have been flourishing in the last several years.[17] The US only has 9 BITs in force with African countries as of February 15, 2021.[18] However, in addition to these BITs, the US has more other International Investment Agreements (IIAs), that is, Trade and Investment Framework Agreements (TIFAs), with African

[16] Brazil, the Russian Federation, India, China and South Africa comprise BRICS partnership. In December 2010, South Africa, at the invitation of China, became a member of the alliance. Among the BRICS members, China is the most active actor to the international investment law.

[17] This conclusion can be evidenced by the BITs concluded with Benin, Burkina Faso, Cameroon, Côte d'Ivoire, Guinea, Mali, Nigeria, Senegal, Tanzania, see Canada, Bilateral Investment Treaties (BITs), available at <http://investmentpolicyhub.unctad.org/IIA/CountryBits/35#iiaInnerMenu>.

[18] They are BITs with Cameroon, D.R. Congo, Congo, Egypt, Morocco, Mozambique, Rwanda, Senegal, Tunisia, See United States of America, Bilateral Investment Treaties(BITs), available at <http://investmentpolicyhub.unctad.org/IIA/CountryBits/223#iiaInnerMenu>.

countries and regions than any other major economic power.[19] The IIAs have laid down foundations for future negotiations on promoting and protecting US-Africa investment. Remarkably, the US has also resumed exploratory BIT discussions with several African countries, for example, Ghana, and at present, the US is negotiating a high-standard BIT with Mauritius.[20]

Regarding the European countries, they have always had many BITs with African countries due to their historically close economic relations. In addition, the EU and African countries are either implementing EPA with BIT-equivalent provisions or have concluded EPA negotiations, as complementary regimes to BITs,[21] although EPAs have also met obstacles.[22]

Comparatively, for a long time, the negotiation and research of BITs in China have mainly focused on the China–US BIT and the China–EU BIT. However, Chinese investments in Africa may face greater risks than investments from other countries. Although Chinese investments spread in 52 African countries, China only has 20 BITs in effect with African countries at present, and most of these have shortcomings, as they are early-generation BITs. 14 signed BITs have not come into force.[23] This situation does not adequately reflect the expansion of China's outward investment in Africa and the economic relationship (especially investment relationship) between China and African countries, which is becoming increasingly important.

This research will introduce the overall picture of China–Africa BITs and review the important clauses of China–Africa BITs briefly by selecting four examples from four generations of China–Africa BITs. Then, by correlating the transformation of international investment law and the recent development of African BITs, this research argues that the optimal BIT for balancing interests between investors and host states based on South-South cooperation can be explored.

There are in total 20 BITs in force between China and African countries, and they are the BITs with Ghana, Egypt, Morocco, Mauritius, Zimbabwe, Algeria, Gabon, Nigeria, Sudan, Cameroon, Cape Verde, South Africa, Ethiopia, Tunisia, Equatorial Guinea, Madagascar, Mali, Mozambique, Tanzania, and the Republic of the Congo. Among them, 1 BIT was concluded in the 1980s, 12 BITs in the 1990s, and 7 BITs in the 2000s. Correspondingly, only 10 BITs include the ICSID arbitral

---

[19] United States of America, Other Investment Agreements (Other IIAs), available at <http://investm-entpolicyhub.unctad.org/IIA/CountryOtherIias/223#iiaInnerMenu>. According to this website, the US has 13 TIFAs thus far.

[20] See Office of the United States Trade Representative, Ghana, available at <https://ustr.gov/countries-regions/africa/west-africa/ghana>; See Office of the United States Trade Representative, United States and Mauritius Launch Investment Treaty Talks, available at <https://ustr.gov/about-us/policy-offices/press-office/press-releases/2009/august/united-states-and-mauritius-launch-investment-treat>.

[21] Overview of EPA Negotiations, updated February 2016, available at <http://trade.ec.europa.eu/doclib/docs/2009/september/tradoc_144912.pdf>.

[22] EPAs Tumble as Three West African States Refuse to Sign, News Ghana, March 1, 2016.

[23] China's Bilateral Investment Treaty are available at tfs.mofcom.gov.cn/aarticle/Nocategory/201111/20111107819474.html, and available at <https://investmentpolicy.unctad.org/international-investment-agreements/countries/42/china>.

clause, and they are the BITs with Morocco, Gabon, Tunisia, Ethiopia, Equatorial Guinea, Madagascar, Mali, Tanzania, Cameroon and Congo. Furthermore, except for the BITs with Equatorial Guinea, Madagascar, Mali, Nigeria, Congo, and Tanzania, only disputes concerning the amount of compensation for expropriation may be submitted to an arbitral tribunal in the other 14 BITs in force.

The remaining 14 BITs have not yet entered into force due to various types of reasons submitted by China's counterparts. Most of the BITs that are not in force are earlier two-generation BITs that may no longer come into effect as they are obsolete. Other BITs awaiting entry into force are third-generation BITs that prefer investment protection. They cannot come into force easily in view of the challenges and crises faced by international investment law as well as doubts that have arisen in some African countries, albeit not in the Congo. China has not concluded any BITs with the remaining 20 African countries even though these include important investment destinations for Chinese investors, such as Angola. In contrast, some countries, such as Senegal and Rwanda, have BITs in force with the US but not with China.

Furthermore, a closer look at the specific provisions of BITs between China and African countries shows that using chronological classification is not always accurate for China–Africa BITs. For example, the China–South Africa BIT was concluded on December 30, 1997; however, it is obvious that it belongs to the third-generation BIT after comparing the provisions of the China–South Africa BIT with those of the 1997 Chinese Model BIT and China–Barbados BIT, which was concluded on July 20, 1998 and is believed to be the starting point of China's third-generation BIT by some scholars. In contrast, although the China–Ethiopia BIT and the China–Cape Verde BIT were concluded on May 11, 1998 and April 21, 1998, respectively, they are still part of the first-generation BITs according to their provisions. Of course, they are exceptions.

Different generations of BITs reflect their corresponding Model BITs and have different features. The first-generation BITs and the 1984 Chinese Model BIT place emphasis on the regulatory sovereignty of the host states. The second-generation BITs and the 1989 Chinese Model BIT give slightly more investment protection but have no significant changes from the first-generation BITs. The third-generation BITs and the 1997 Chinese Model BIT prefer to protect the benefits of investors. The fourth-generation BIT and 2010 Draft Chinese Model BIT attempt to balance the benefits between investors and host states.

Therefore, the present first-generation BITs in force include 8 BITs with Ghana, Egypt, Mauritius, Zimbabwe, Algeria, Sudan, Cape Verde, and Ethiopia; the second-generation BITs in force include 3 BITs with Morocco, Cameroon, and Gabon; the third-generation BITs in force cover 7 BITs with Nigeria, South Africa, Equatorial Guinea, Madagascar, Tunisia, Mali, and Congo; the only fourth-generation BITs in force is the China–Tanzania BIT.

On the whole, nearly half of the BITs between China and African countries have not come into force, and most of the BITs in force are first-generation and second-generation BITs with insufficient protection to investors. One of the most typical features of these treaties is that at most only the amount of compensation for expropriation may be submitted to an international arbitral tribunal. For other investment disputes, the host state reserves the right to give consent to international arbitration on a case-by-case basis, and the exhaustion of local remedies may be required. In addition, according to first-generation BITs, investors and their investment cannot even enjoy national treatment, which grants investors and their investment no less favorable treatment than that the host state's own investors, and their investment may enjoy in "like circumstances". Therefore, first-generation and second-generation BITs can only play a very limited role in protecting the benefits of Chinese investors. In fact, African investments in China have also become increasingly dynamic and could also benefit from promotion and protection through BITs.

Third-generation China–African BITs offer higher-level protection for investments. The investor enjoys substantive protection, such as national treatment, MFN treatment, and FET, and especially enjoys the procedural right to take investment disputes to international investment arbitration. However, it is necessary to update BITs, which can balance the interests of all parties involved between China and African states. The China–Tanzania BIT is a good example to show that integrating sustainable development considerations into the China–Africa BIT may make "host African states attain meaningful development while protecting investors".[24]

It is said that "China's 'One Belt One Road' (OBOR) also envisages the negotiation of FTAs with partners, although this is not strongly pushed in the Forum of China Africa Cooperation (FOCAC)".[25] However, there is no much development in this area over the years. Various instruments under FOCOCA and Memorandum of Understanding to build the BRI are not FTA in nature.

As of this writing, China–Mauritius FTA is the first and only FTA that China signed with an African country.[26] Mauritius is an African island nation located in the southwestern Indian Ocean and approximately 2200 km off the east coast of the continent. Mauritius, as one of the countries with better economic development in Africa, is a country with a superior natural environment and a peaceful, stable and healthy social and economic climate and is devoting itself to undertake efforts to serve as a gateway for investment in Africa.[27] Mauritius aims to develop into an African "Singapore" and identifies itself to become a developed country in the tertiary sector and is to develop tourism, information and communications and financial services as its economic pillar industries based on its traditional sugar and export processing industries. Under the guidance of this industrial policy, Mauritius' economy has developed rapidly and has been hailed as the "Miracle of Mauritius". According to the World Bank's 2019 Ease of Doing Business Index, Mauritius ranks first in Africa

---

[24] Sanford U. Mba,'Africa for the Chinese? Revisiting Sino-African Bilateral Investment Treaties', (2017)58(4) Hungarian Journal of Legal Studies 434–448.

[25] Rob Davies, The Politics of Trade in the Era of Hyperglobalisation: A Southern African Perspective (South Centre, 2019)73–74.

[26] See Free Trade Agreement Between the Government of the Republic of Mauritius and the Government of the People's Republic of China (China-Mauritius FTA), signed on October 17, 2019, came into force on January 1, 2021, available at <http://fta.mofcom.gov.cn/topic/enmaur%20itius.shtml>.

[27] 2020 Investment Climate Statements: Mauritius, available at <https://www.state.gov/reports/2020-investment-climate-statements/mauritius/>; Country (Region) Guidance to Foreign Investment Cooperation, Mauritius, 2019.

and 20th worldwide (out of 190 countries), and the ranking of the Mauritius Peace Index is also the best in Africa.[28]

As an important manifestation of high-level economic liberalization, Mauritius has concluded 48 BITs. Mauritius has been active in concluding IIAs with developing countries and, in particular, African countries to improve its international investment rule of law, thus promoting Mauritius as a safe, secure place to do business due to its favorable investment climate and helping enterprises use the country as a platform to further expand investment cooperation in Africa. At present, an increasing number of investors have taken Mauritius as their first stop to Africa, rather than South Africa.[29] It is possible for Mauritius to replace South Africa as the gateway for Chinese investors to invest in Africa.

The investment chapter in China–Mauritius FTA, compared with 1996 China–Mauritius BIT, makes great progress. In terms of scope of protection, level of protection and dispute settlement mechanism, it upgrades the 1996 China–Mauritius BIT. This chapter conforms to the policy of Mauritius to attract Chinese investments and represents the development of the investment rule of law between China and Mauritius. It is pointed out that the BITs signed between China and African countries and their role as an important and effective investment protection tool readily available to Chinese investors in Africa and vice versa.[30] However, after exploring the aim of China–Africa BITs to promote and protect foreign investment and so its tensions with the notion of South-South cooperation, it is still suggested that China has the willingness to accommodate African counterparts' proposals.[31]

6.3 Investment Rule of Law Under China–Africa IIAs

Almost all BITs between China and African countries are brief and succinct, and each of them has only 12–14 provisions, including the preamble, definitions, and provisions on the promotion and protection of investments, investment treatments, expropriation and compensation, compensation for losses, transfers, subrogation, settlement of disputes between contracting parties, settlement of disputes between

[28] Institute for Economics and Peace. Global Peace Index 2019: Measuring Peace in a Complex World, Sydney, June 2019. Available at <http://visionofhumanity.org/reports> (November 15, 2019).

[29] See Ingé Lamprecht, Four things SA can learn from Mauritius, September 1, 2015, Moneyweb Today, available at <http://today.moneyweb.co.za/article?id=506755&acid=BsX0kdu%2BXj0e Ze uwhd4cWQ%3D%3D&adid=WgZYmOBdjTEeZeuwhd4cWQ%3D%3D&date=2015-09-01#.VeU3XouIpjq>.

[30] Xiao Jin, A Chinese perspective: Africa-China Bilateral Investment Treaties, March 16, 2015, available at <https://www.kwm.com/en/uk/knowledge/insights/bilateral-investment-treaties-20150316>.

[31] Lorenzo Cotula, Xiaoxue Weng, Qianru Ma and Peng Ren, China-Africa Investment Treaties: Do They Work? (The International Institute for Environment and Development, 2016), available at <www.iied.org>.

investors and states, entry into force, application, duration, and termination. At most, 18 provisions are included in the China–Tanzania BIT, which introduces and draws on the new development of BITs. In contrast, the China–Mauritius FTA is intricate, lengthy and holds high standards.

For a more detailed and in-depth understanding of China–Africa BITs and FTAs, this research breaks down them into four generations. This section deals with the first-generation BITs (based on 1984 Chinese Model BIT), and they mainly include China–Ghana BIT, China–Egypt BIT, China–Zimbabwe BIT, China–Algeria BIT, China–Sudan BIT, China–Cape Verde BIT, China–Ethiopia BIT and China–Mauritius BIT; the second-generation BITs (based on 1989 Chinese Model BIT), and they mainly include Morocco BIT and China–Gabon BIT; the third-generation BITs (based on 1997 Chinese Model BIT), and they mainly include the fourth-generation BITs (based on 2010 Draft Chinese Model BIT), and they mainly include China–Madagascar BIT, China–South Africa BIT, China–Congo BIT, China–Tunisia BIT, China–Equatorial Guinea BIT, China–Mali BIT and China–Nigeria BIT; and finally China–Mauritius FTA is the only China–Africa FTA thus far. Among them, Mauritius and Madagascar are two island nations, and the BITs between China and them are slightly special.

Six types of key treaty provisions are selected to represent and expound the four generations of BITs between China and African countries. After surveying all BITs between China and Africa, it is determined that these selected provisions can best reflect the trend and limitation of BITs between China and African countries. Furthermore, this research basically takes on a textual analysis approach in view that there is no case between Chinese investors and African countries decided such far although it is reported that some Chinese investors are preparing to or have filed arbitration against Sudan, Ghana and Nigeria. In addition, except for the preamble, the structure of the sections under each specific subtitle will follow the order of the four selected BITs to make the narration clear.

6.3.1 Rule of Law Spirit in the Preamble

The preamble declares the value orientation, guides the concrete provisions of the treaty, and helps in interpreting the treaty. The preamble not only determines the substantive and procedural provisions of the BIT but can also guide the interpretation of the language in the BIT because "a treaty shall be interpreted in good faith in accordance with the ordinary meaning to be given to the terms of the treaty in their context and in the light of its object and purpose" and "the context for the purpose of the interpretation of a treaty shall comprise in addition to the text, including its preamble and annexes" under articles 31.1 and 31.2 of the Vienna Convention on the Law of Treaties. In fact, the object and purpose of a treaty can often be found and confirmed in the preamble. In recent years, an increasing number of cases involving disputes between host states and investors show that the "preamble tends to play a guiding role of interpreting rights and obligations covered in the international investment agreements".[32]

The languages used in the preambles of all four generations of BITs show that one point particularly remains consistent in the BITs: the "promotion and protection of investment", which is the major common feature of almost all BITs. Although the wording is slightly different,[33] in most first-generation, second-generation and third-generation BITs, for the purpose of developing economic cooperation and increasing prosperity in both states, promoting and protecting investment on the basis of *"the principles of mutual respect for sovereignty, equality and mutual benefit"* is emphasized, and these principles embody two of the Five Principles of Peaceful Coexistence under which China has dealt with its foreign relations until now. It is thus clear that China considers investment relationships with African countries as a kind of economic cooperation and the integral part of equal diplomatic relations between China and African countries.

All China–Africa BITs' preambles mention recognizing the principle of "equality and mutual benefit", with the exception of China–Madagascar BIT and China–Mauritius BIT for the former only mentions intensifying the investment relation between two countries and recognizing the BIT "will be conducive to transfers of operational capital and technology in both States",[34] and the latter only stresses "creat[ing] favorable conditions for investment" and "the encouragement and reciprocal protection" of such investments.[35]

Among second-generation and third-generation BITs, in addition to increasing prosperity through intensifying investment cooperation "on the basis of equality and mutual benefits", "investor's duty to respect the host state's sovereignty and laws" is added in China-Nigeria BIT,[36] and recognizing the right of any Contracting Party to enact laws relating to admission and establishment of investments in its territory is emphasized in China-Mali BIT.[37]

---

[32] See, e.g., Aguas Del Tunari, S.A. v Republic of Bolivia, ICSID Case No. ARB/02/3, Decision on Respondent's Objections to Jurisdiction, para. 241.

[33] See e.g. China-Ghana BIT, signed on October 12, 1989, entered into force on November 22, 1990. Preamble; China-Egypt BIT, signed on April 21, 1994, entered into force on April 1, 1996. Preamble; China-Zimbabwe BIT, signed on May 21, 1996, entered into force on March 1, 1998. Preamble; China-Algeria BIT, signed on October 17, 1996, entered into force on January 28, 2003. Preamble; China-Sudan BIT, signed on May 30, 1997, entered into force on July 1, 1998. Preamble; China-Cape Verde, signed on April 21, 1998, entered into force on October 1, 2001. Preamble; China-Ethiopia BIT, signed on May 11, 1998, entered into force on May 1, 2000. Preamble; China-Gabon BIT, signed on May 9, 1997, entered into force on February 16, 2009. Preamble; China-South Africa BIT, signed on December 30, 1997, entered into force on April 1, 1998. Preamble; China-Congo BIT, signed on March 20, 2000, entered into force on July 1, 2015. Preamble; China-Tunisia BIT, signed on June 21, 2004, entered into force on July 1, 2006. Preamble; China-Equatorial Guinea BIT, singed on October 20, 2005, entered into force on November 15, 2006. Preamble.

[34] China-Madagascar BIT, signed on November 21, 2005, entered into force on July 1, 2007. Preamble.

[35] China- Mauritius BIT, signed on May 4, 1996, enter into force on June 8, 1997. Preamble.

[36] China-Nigeria BIT, signed on August 21, 2001, entered into force on February 18, 2010. Preamble.

[37] China-Mali BIT, signed on February 12, 2009, entered into force on July 16, 2019. Preamble.

Although the idea of environmental protection and sustainable development has become popular due to the Rio Declaration on Environment and Development and UN Agenda 21 adopted by the United Nations Conference on Environment and Development in 1992, the preambles of most China–Africa BITs do not reflect this reality.

The China–Tanzania BIT, as the only fourth-generation China–Africa BIT, becomes more comprehensive and inclusive, and it continues to emphasize "equality and mutual benefit" and "economic sovereignty". However, the modern part of the China–Tanzania BIT preamble is "encouraging investors to respect corporate social responsibilities" and "promoting healthy, stable and sustainable economic development and to improve the standard of living of nationals".[38] Admittedly, these points reflect the efforts of protecting the host state and its people, supporting the inclusion of corporate social responsibility, and thus promoting the balance of interests between the investors and the host state.

In the preamble of the China–Mauritius FTA, establishing "transparent and predictable rules governing the trade and investment between the Parties" is imported, and this FTA, on the one hand, stresses economic partnership and liberalization of bilateral investment to produce mutual benefits; on the other hand, "the rights of their governments to regulate in order to meet national policy objectives, and to preserve their flexibility to safeguard the public welfare" are upheld.[39]

In sum, it is clear from the preambles that China considers investment relations with Africa as a kind of economic cooperation based on equality and mutual benefit and mutual respect for sovereignty and an embodiment of friendly international relations. The right to regulate, sustainable development objectives and other non-economic values, such as human rights, labor, health, CSR, poverty reduction, environment, such as plant or animal life, biodiversity and climate change, were not included in the first three generations of China–Africa BIT preambles. However, the modern fourth-generation of China–Africa BITs and China–Mauritius FTA reflect the most recent developments of international investment law.

6.3.2 Constraining the Power of the Host State for Protecting Investors

6.3.2.1 First-Generation China–Africa BITs

Under the provisions in the China–Ghana BIT, the first China–Africa BIT, it can be found that it was concluded on the basis of the 1984 Chinese Model BIT. The term "investments" means every kind of asset, and the treatments that shall be awarded to the investments made "in accordance with the laws and regulations" of the host state are "equitable treatment" and "MFN treatment", and further the equitable treatment

[38] China-Tanzania BIT, signed on March 24, 2013, entered into force on April 17, 2014, preamble.

[39] China-Mauritius FTA, preamble.

shall only not be less favorable than MFN treatment. Finally, preferential treatment shall be applicable when the laws and regulations of the host state award investments more favorable treatment than that of the BIT.[40] Thus, the host state enjoys the sovereignty to grant better treatments to investments. In terms of treatment, most first-generation BITs have similar provisions, and all later first-generation BITs further specify "equitable treatment" as "FET".[41] Most first-generation BITs also provide that "[if] the treatment to be accorded by one Contracting Party in accordance with its laws and regulations to investments or activities associated with such investments of investors of the other Contracting Party are more favorable than the treatment provided for in this agreement, the more favorable treatment shall be applicable",[42] but this provision is not mentioned with one exception.[43]

The China–Ghana BIT makes an affirmative statement as to expropriation or nationalization and provides that "Either Contracting State may, for the national security and public interest, expropriate, nationalize or take similar measures..." Such actions are only subject to these requirements: (a) under the domestic legal procedure; (b) without discrimination; (c) payment of compensation. In addition, the investor may request the host state to review the expropriation or nationalization measures.[44] However, all other first-generation BITs adopt a negative expression, that is, "neither Contracting Party shall expropriate, nationalize or take similar measure" against investments unless the corresponding conditions are met.[45]

The first-generation BITs provide MFN treatment to investors of one contracting state who suffer losses with respect to their investments in the territory of the other contracting state owing to war or other similar events on the condition that whether "the host state takes relevant measures".[46]

According to first-generation BITs, the host state may guarantee the repatriation of investment and returns of investors subject to its laws and regulations.[47]

Under the China-Ghana BIT, only the dispute concerning the amount of compensation for expropriation may be submitted to an international ad hoc arbitral tribunal by the investor, and the ICSID Convention arbitration, which is not mentioned for

---

[40] See China-Ghana BIT, articles 1, 3, 12.

[41] China-Egypt BIT, articles 3.1, 3.2,3.4; China-Zimbabwe BIT, article 3.1, 3.2; China-Algeria BIT, article 3.1, 3.2; China-Sudan BIT, articles 3.1, 3.2; China-Cape Verde, articles 3.1, 3.2; China-Ethiopia BIT, articles 3.1, 3.2.

[42] China-Egypt BIT, article 3.4; China-Algeria BIT, article 10; China-Sudan BIT, article 10; China-Cape Verde, article 10; China-Ethiopia BIT, article 10.

[43] China-Zimbabwe BIT, signed on May 21, 1996, entered into force on March 1, 1998.

[44] See China-Ghana BIT, article 4.

[45] China-Egypt BIT, article 4; China-Zimbabwe BIT, article 4; China-Algeria BIT, article 4; China-Sudan BIT, article 4; China-Cape Verde, article 4; China-Ethiopia BIT, article 4.

[46] China-Ghana BIT, article 4; China-Egypt BIT, article 5; China-Zimbabwe BIT, article 5; China-Algeria BIT, article 5; China-Sudan BIT, article 5; China-Cape Verde, article 5, China-Ethiopia BIT, article 5.

[47] China-Ghana BIT, article 5; China-Egypt BIT, article 6; China-Zimbabwe BIT, article 6; China-Algeria BIT, article 6; China-Sudan BIT, article 6; China-Cape Verde, article 6, China-Ethiopia BIT, article 5.

China, was not yet a Contracting State of the ICSID Convention at that time. It is thus obvious that this BIT reserves sovereignty for the host state free from the jurisdiction of international investment arbitral tribunal proceedings, except for disputes concerning the amount of compensation for expropriation. Although the investor may request the competent court of the host state to review the expropriation, neither the exhaustion of local remedy nor fork-in-the-road are required when the investor chooses international investment arbitration. The substantive law that shall be applied is the law of the host state, including its rules on the conflict of laws, the provisions of the BIT and the generally recognized principles of international law accepted by both contracting states.[48] The China–Egypt BIT grants either disputing party to initiate the review procedure related to any investment dispute before the competent court of the host state, and introduces the fork-in-the-road clause for the dispute involving the amount of compensation for expropriation.[49] Furthermore, the China–Ethiopia BIT provides that if both parties approve the ICSID Convention, the investor can also invoke ICSID arbitration.[50]

The first-generation of China–Africa BITs are extremely simple, and the level of rule of law was not well developed. For example, the level of investment treatment is relatively low; for instance, no national treatment is offered to the investor; therefore, national treatment cannot be guaranteed to the investments. For the compensation for loss during war conditions or similar situations, it should be said that this is not demanding on the host state because it depends on whether the host state takes relevant measures, and only MFN treatment, which is a relative treatment, is required.

Moreover, the arbitral tribunal can only arbitrate the amount of compensation for expropriation. In the arbitration practice related to Chinese investors' claims against the host country, one of the tricky problems is the application of such provision. It is possible for the arbitral tribunal to adopt a narrow interpretation of such provision and only agree to arbitrate "the amount of the compensation for expropriation", instead of including the liability of expropriation, thereby refusing to exercise jurisdiction and preventing investors' interests from being protected. In the Beijing Shougang and others v. Mongolia, the tribunal considered that under the China–Mongolia BIT, only the dispute involving the amount of compensation for expropriation can be awarded and therefore declined the claim of the claimants.[51] On November 25, 2019, the US District Court Southern District of New York denied the Chinese companies' petition

[48] See China-Ghana BIT, articles 4.3, 10.

[49] China-Egypt BIT, article 9; China-Zimbabwe BIT, article 9; China-Algeria BIT, article 9; China-Sudan BIT, article 9; China-Cape Verde, article 9.

[50] China-Ethiopia BIT article 9.3. Ethiopia signed the ICSID Convention on September 21, 1965, but so far Ethiopia has not ratified this Convention. In contrast, the ICSID Convention entered into force for China on February 6, 1993, see Database of ICSID Member States, available at <https://icsid.worldbank.org/about/member-states/database-of-member-states>.

[51] Beijing Shougang Mining Investment Company Ltd., China Heilongjiang International Economic and Technical Cooperative Corp., and Qinhuangdaoshi Qinlong International Industrial Co. Ltd. v. Mongolia (PCA Case No. 2010–20), Award dated June 30, 2017.

to vacate the award and confirm arbitration.[52] In Ping An v. Belgium, the claimant attempted to avoid an unfavorable clause in an old BLEU (Belgium-Luxembourg Economic Union)—China BIT (1984), that is, only "a dispute which arises from an amount of compensation for expropriation, nationalization or other similar measures" can be settled through arbitration to invoke BLEU-China BIT (2005) to assume the jurisdiction. However, the tribunal decided that the dispute happened before the new BIT came into force and therefore declined the jurisdiction.[53] In fact, the arbitral tribunal's decisions are inconsistent with regard to the premise of the amount of compensation, that is, whether there is jurisdiction over the issue of liability for expropriation by the host state, as evidenced by five cases involving Chinese investors (including those cases related to investors from Hong Kong and Macau) suing foreign governments in recent years.[54]

The China–Mauritius BIT is an exception on the point that it provides "If the legislation of either Contracting Party or international obligations existing at present or established hereafter between the Contracting Parties in addition to this Agreement, result in a position entitling investments by nationals and/or companies of the other Contracting Party to treatment more favorable than is provided for by this Agreement, such position shall not be affected by this Agreement. In addition to those specified in this agreement, each Contracting Party shall observe any commitment made by it in accordance with its laws to nationals and/or companies of the other Contracting Party as regards their investments".[55] This means that "[n]on-derogation clause (in case of IIA's conflict with other norms, more favorable rules apply to investors" and "umbrella clause" are available.

6.3.2.2 Second-Generation China–Africa BITs

The second-generation BITs provide that the investment in every kind of asset or capital contribution invested directly or indirectly by investors in accordance with the host state's laws and regulations shall enjoy "fair and equitable treatment and protection" as well as "adequate and full protection". In addition, FET should not be less than *national treatment* and MFN treatment. The second-generation BITs also provide that those investments should be free from "unjustified or discriminatory measures" from the other side.[56]

The China–Gabon BIT takes a negative stance to expropriation or nationalization, which is shown by the expression that "Neither Contracting Party shall take any

---

[52] Beijing Shougang Mining Investment Company, Ltd. V. Mongolia (1:17-cv-07436-ER), Opinion and Order of the United States District Court for the Southern District of New York, paras. 27–28.

[53] Ping An Life Insurance Company of China, Limited and Ping An Insurance (Group) Company of China, Limited v. Kingdom of Belgium (ICSID Case No. ARB/12/29), Award dated April 30, 2015.

[54] For these five cases, see UNCTAD Hub, Investment Dispute Settlement, China, available at <https://investmentpolicy.unctad.org/investment-dispute-settlement/country/42/china/investor>.

[55] China-Mauritius BIT, article 4.2.

[56] See China-Gabon BIT, articles 1.1, 1.3, 2.2, 3.1; China-Morocco BIT, articles 1.1, 1.3, 2.2, 3.1.

measures of expropriation, nationalization or any dispossession having the effect equivalent to nationalization or expropriation…". The expropriation or nationalization, as a kind of exception, must be subject to four conditions: (a) for the public interests; (b) under the domestic legal procedure; (c) without discrimination; and (d) against compensation.[57] The China–Morocco BIT also provides that nationalization or expropriation measures, which could be taken by the authorities of the host state against investments, must fulfil these four conditions.[58]

Similarly, according to China's second-generation BIT, MFN treatment shall be accorded to investors who suffer losses owing to war or other similar events in the territory of the host state, in regard to restitution, indemnification, compensation, or other settlement, if any.[59]

For the free transfers of investments and all kinds of profits, the host state shall guarantee MFN treatment to investors subject to foreign exchange laws and regulations.[60]

If any dispute between the investor and the host state cannot be settled through negotiations within six months under the China–Gabon BIT, the investor may choose and submit the dispute to (a) the competent court of the host state or (b) the ICSID. Since China and Gabon are members of the ICSID Convention, it is not unexpected that the China–Gabon BIT would include an ICSID Convention arbitration clause. However, even so, the contracting parties agreed that only the dispute with respect to the amount of compensation in the case of expropriation can be submitted to the tribunal, and other disputes submitted to the arbitral proceedings shall be under additional mutual consent of both contracting parties.[61]

Thus, relatively speaking, the treatment and protection of investments have no fundamental change compared with first-generation BITs because only the amount of compensation for expropriation can be submitted to arbitral procedures with "non-withdrawal consent". However, it is possible for the investor to enjoy a higher level of protection and more rights than in the first-generation China–Africa BIT because the national treatment clause is introduced. Therefore, the progress made by second-generation BITs is subtle, the terms in the treaties are more detailed, and the protection to investors and their investments is slightly strengthened.

6.3.2.3 Third-Generation China–Africa BITs

Among the third-generation BITs, the China–Madagascar BIT is a special case, and the China–South Africa BIT also has a feature. Therefore, in the following paragraphs, third-generation BITs will be discussed based on these two BITs.

[57] See China-Gabon BIT, article 4.1.

[58] See China-Morocco BIT, article 4.1.

[59] See China-Gabon BIT, article 5; China-Morocco BIT, article 5.

[60] See China-Gabon BIT, article 6; China-Morocco BIT, article 6.

[61] See China-Gabon BIT, article 10; China-Morocco BIT, article 10.

The China–Madagascar BIT places more emphasis on the protection of investment that was made in accordance with the laws and regulations of the host state than the first two generations of BITs. Concerning the treatment of investment: first, FET is stressed as an international law principle, and it shall not be impeded in law or in fact, and the legal or de facto obstacles to the FET are illustrated further[62]; second, MFN treatment or national treatment is offered and held depending on whichever treatment is more favorable[63]; third, preferential treatment according to domestic law of either Contracting Party or *international obligations* existing at present or established in the future should be applied.[64] The BIT also states that investments shall enjoy full and *comprehensive* protection and security.[65]

The China–Madagascar BIT not only takes a negative stance toward expropriation or nationalization but also provides that expropriation must meet more rigorous requirements such as "(a) adopting measures for the public interests under *good* legal framework; (b) without discrimination and *not contrary to the commitments* of the Contracting Parties; (c) against *fair* compensation when adopting measures".[66] Therefore, the requirements on expropriation are quite special. Finally, investors who suffer losses owing to war or other similar activities in the territory of the host state shall be accorded MFN treatment, and national treatment as well as regards restitution, indemnification, compensation, or other settlement.[67]

For the transfer, the China–Madagascar BIT guarantees the free transfer of all payments related to an investment in principle and also gives a non-exhaustive list of free transfers.

Under the China–Madagascar BIT, there is no fork-in-the-road clause; thus, the investor can choose arbitral or judicial procedures within the territory of the host state or ICSID to settle *any investment dispute* if the dispute cannot be settled through negotiations within six months. Therefore, the investor is awarded options among different forums to settle *any investment dispute.* Although the host state involved in the dispute may require the investor concerned to complete the domestic administrative review procedures specified by the laws and regulations of that host state before the submission to international arbitration, it cannot impede the investor to file the case with ICSID.[68]

The China–South Africa BIT provides all kinds of treatment and protection. First, investments and activities associated with investments of investors of either Contracting Party shall be accorded "fair and equitable treatment"; therefore, "unreasonable or discriminatory measures" shall not be imposed on investments of investors.

---

62 See China-Madagascar BIT, articles 3.1, 3.2.

63 See China-Madagascar BIT, article 4.1.

64 See China-Madagascar BIT, article 9.

65 See China-Madagascar BIT, article 5.1.

66 See China-Madagascar BIT, article 5.

67 See China-Madagascar BIT, article 6.

68 See China- Madagascar BIT, article 10.

More concretely, in the China–South Africa BIT, "fair and equitable treatment" means without "unreasonable or discriminatory measures".[69]

On the other hand, although the FET is an absolute treatment standard, FET shall not be less favorable than MFN treatment, that is, the treatment and protection offered by FET shall not be less favorable than that accorded to investments and activities associated with such investments of investors of a third state. Consequently, the FET is limited and changed into a relative treatment.[70]

Second, national treatment is provided to the investments of the investors, that is, "*without prejudice to its laws and regulations*, each Contracting Party shall accord to investments and activities associated with such investments by the investors of the other Contracting Party treatment no less favorable than that accorded to the investments and associated activities by its own investors".[71]

Third, "If the treatment to be accorded by one Contracting Party in accordance with its laws and regulations to investments or activities associated with such investments of investors of the other Contracting Party is more favorable than the treatment provided for in this Agreement, the more favorable treatment shall be applicable".[72] That is, preferential treatment also shall be applicable to the investment and activities associated with such investments by an investor of the other Contracting Party when the laws and regulations of the host state award the preferential treatment to that of the other Contracting Party. This kind of provision is a preferential treatment provision, which means that domestic laws and regulations can award more favorable treatment to the investment than that in the China–South Africa BIT.

Fourth, the free transfer of payments clause is guaranteed subject to the exhaustive list.[73]

Last, the host state shall observe other obligations that it has committed to the investors of the other Contracting Party as to their investment.[74] This "Umbrella Clause" means that contract obligations of the host state with the investor are also incorporated into the treaty. In other words, this provision aims to put the non-treaty commitment from the host state under BIT protection and upgrade the host state's behavior violating the contract or domestic law obligation into behavior violating BIT obligation. This kind of "Umbrella Clause" is objected by some scholars who suggest that the "Umbrella Clause" should be excluded when China concludes BITs with other countries.[75]

---

[69] See China-South Africa BIT, article 3.1.

[70] See China-South Africa BIT, article 3.2.

[71] China-South Africa BIT, article 3.3.

[72] China-South Africa BIT, article 10.1.

[73] China-South Africa BIT, article 6.

[74] China-South Africa BIT 10.2.

[75] See CL Xu, 'Disputes over Applicable Scope of Umbrella Clause and Our Countermeasure' (2008) 4Journal of the East China University of Political Science and Law 49 at59; J. Wong, 'Umbrella Clauses in Bilateral Investment Treaties: Of Breaches of Contract, Treaty Violations, and the Divide between Developing and Developed Countries in Foreign Investment Disputes' (2006) 14/1 George Mason Law Review 137 at 176–9.

Under the China–South Africa BIT, the principle is not to expropriate investment by investors of the other Contracting Party, and expropriation is an exception. The requirements of legal expropriation are as follows: (a) for public purposes; (b) under domestic legal procedure; (c) non-discrimination; (d) payment of compensation. Such compensation shall be at least equal to the *market value* of the investment expropriated, shall include interest at a normal commercial rate until the date of payment, shall be made without delay, and be effectively realizable. For expropriation, judicial reviews can be accessed by investors from domestic courts and other independent and impartial forums of the host state under domestic laws and regulations.[76]

Investors of one Contracting Party, who suffer losses with respect to their investments in the territory of the other Contracting Party owing to war or other similar events shall enjoy MFN treatment. In addition, without derogating from the MFN treatment, investors of one Contracting Party who suffer losses in the territory of the other Contracting Party resulting from "(a) Requisitioning of their property by the forces or authorities of the latter Contracting Party, or (b) Destruction of their property by the forces or authorities of the latter Contracting Party, which was not caused action or was not required by the necessity of the situation, shall be accorded restitution or adequate compensation".[77]

Under the China–South Africa BIT, six-month negotiation as the amicable settlement approach is emphasized first. If it does not work, either Party to the dispute shall be entitled to submit the dispute to an international arbitral tribunal provided that the Contracting Party involved in the dispute may require the investor to initiate administrative review procedures in accordance with its laws and regulations and provided that the investor has not submitted the dispute to a domestic court of that Contracting Party. This means administrative review may be the prerequisite for international investment arbitration under the request of the host state, and if the domestic court of the host state were chosen, international arbitration would not be available. This is a fork-in-the-road clause that provides the investor one choice between domestic court and international arbitration. In addition, *either party* to the dispute shall be entitled to submit the dispute to an international arbitral tribunal. Therefore, the host state and the investor acquire the same litigation standing.[78]

Finally, since South Africa is not a contracting party of the ICSID Convention,[79] either disputing party can only choose the ad hoc arbitral tribunal under Article 9 of the China–South Africa BIT. This kind of arbitration is weak in many aspects compared with ICSID Convention arbitration.

Although the wording is more or less different, other third-generation BITs, mainly including the China–Congo BIT, China–Tunisia BIT, China–Equatorial Guinea BIT, China–Mali BIT, and China–Nigeria BIT, all offer similar treatments and

[76] China-South Africa, article 4.

[77] China-South Africa, article 5, and China-Congo BIT article 5.2 has a similar provision.

[78] China-South Africa BIT, article 9.

[79] List of Contracting States and Other Signatories of the Convention (as of July 25, 2012), ICSID/3, available at <https://icsid.worldbank.org/ICSID/FrontServlet>.

protections as the China–South Africa BIT except for the national treatment exception clause considering the special national conditions of South Africa. In addition to the "umbrella clause", all other third-generation BITs further provide that if the legislation of the host state or its international obligations existing at the present or established thereafter result in a position entitling investments by investors of the home state to a treatment more favorable than is provided for by the said BIT, such position shall not be affected by the said BIT.[80] The China–Tunisia BIT is special in that it clearly stipulates that MFN is suitable for any treatment, so it is also applicable to procedural issues, although it is extremely possible for the MFN provisions interpreted by tribunals to be applicable to procedural issues because there is no explicit exclusion of procedural issues from the MFN clause in other third-generation BITs.

For ISDS, only the ad hoc arbitration mechanism provided under the China–Nigeria BIT and ICSID is not included.[81]

For the first three generations of China–Africa BITs, some modes of investment that now seem controversial, such as portfolio investment, sovereign debt, and ordinary commercial transactions, are not excluded from the asset-based investment definition, instead of asset plus characteristic-based investment definition. For investors, there is no exclusion of dual nationals, and there is no requirement of substantial business activity on the investor, nor do they define ownership and control of legal entities, nor is the denial of benefits clause included. There is no national treatment clause included in first-generation BITs, and while second- and third-generation BITs introduce national treatment, they make no reference to "like/similar circumstances" to judge national treatment and MFN treatment. The MFN clause applies to the post establishment of the investment, but there are no procedural issue exceptions from MFN obligation. FET is not defined and does not mention prohibition on unreasonable, arbitrary, or discriminatory measures explicitly.

6.3.2.4 Fourth-Generation China–Africa BITs

The China–Tanzania BIT points out that each Contracting Party shall protect the investments of the other Contracting Party "in accordance with its laws and regulations". The investors and their investments shall enjoy national treatment, MFN treatment, and FET. However, unlike the previous BITs between China and other African countries, the applicable scope of these treatments is clarified and limited. National treatment only applies to the operation, management, maintenance, use, enjoyment, and sale or disposition of investments. Aside from these aspects, the MFN treatment also applies to the establishment, acquisition, and expansion of investments, which in fact is the provision of admission of the investment and reflects a degree of liberalization of investment, but not so ambitious to include national treatment of admission of

---

[80] See China-Congo BIT, article 10; China-Tunisia BIT, article 10; China-Equatorial Guinea BIT article 10; China-Mali BIT 10.

[81] China-Nigeria BIT, article 9.

the investment. The FET is qualified and clarified to include three aspects: fair judicial proceedings, no obvious discriminatory or arbitrary measures, and FPS, which require that the host state take reasonable and necessary police measures.[82]

Some exceptions, such as limitations, are also being attached to the three treatments. For national treatment, the host state can grant "incentives or preferences to its nationals for the purpose of developing and stimulating local entrepreneurship provided that such measures shall not significantly affect the investments and activities of the investors". For the MFN treatment, in addition to the traditional exception of regional economic integration organization and taxation arrangement, it also excludes dispute settlement provisions to prevent the MFN treatment clause from being abused. For FET, it is stressed that a breach of another article of the China–Tanzania BIT or an article of another agreement does not constitute a breach of FET; therefore, FET is no longer an "Empire Clause" in the China–Tanzania BIT.[83]

The expropriation clause in the China–Tanzania BIT indicates specific factors to consider when deciding whether a measure constitutes expropriation to avoid the abuse of discretion by arbitral tribunals. These factors include economic effects, the extent of discrimination, the extent of interference with reasonable expectation, the character and purpose of a measure or a series of measures, and proportionality. Aside from legal expropriation and illegal expropriation, the expropriation clause also clarifies the boundary of expropriation and non-expropriation and clearly defines the measures for maintaining reasonable public welfare, for example, protecting public health, safety, and the environment, provided that these active measures are non-discriminatory and proportionate and constitute legitimate regulatory measures instead of expropriation.

Article 10.2 of this BIT echoes and complements the above non-expropriation clause and provides that "nothing in the Agreement shall be construed to prevent a Contracting Party from adopting or maintaining environmental measures necessary to protect human, animal or plant life or health", "provided that such measures are not applied in an arbitrary or unjustifiable manner, or do not constitute a disguised restriction on international investment".

For the compensation for damages and losses owing to an armed conflict or other similar events in the territory of the host state, the investors and their investments shall enjoy national treatment or MFN treatment, whichever is more favorable to the investor concerned. However, in view of the fact that these two treatment standards are relative treatment standards, it is not necessary for investors to receive compensation. However, for losses suffered in the territory of the host state resulting from the requisition or destruction of an investment by the host state's armed forces or authorities, which were not due to combat action or required by the necessity of the

[82] See China-Tanzania BIT, articles 3, 4 and 5.

[83] See China-Tanzania BIT, articles 3, 4 and 5; A German scholar likened FET standard in the international investment law to the bona fide principle in the civil code. See R. Dolzer, 'Fair and Equitable Treatment: A Key Standard in Investment Treaties' (2005) 39 The International Lawyer 91.

situation, restitution or reasonable compensation is a legal obligation of the host state. As a new provision, it also reflects new concerns for the need to protect investors.

In short, it can be seen that the requirements on expropriation or the limitation on the power of the host state are increasingly demanding from the first-generation China–Africa BITs to the third-generation China–Africa BITs. In addition, they only differentiate legal expropriation and illegal expropriation. However, fourth-generation BIT further clarifies and subdivides the regulatory action of the host state into legal expropriation, illegal expropriation, and legitimate exercising regulatory power, thus keeping more necessary regulatory space for the host state and establishing clear limitations on expropriation. For the losses owing to war or other similar activities in the host state, the former two generations of BITs only provide MFN treatment, but the third-generation BITs offers investor MFN treatment or national treatment. The fourth-generation BIT further agrees that the investor can enjoy more favorable treatment to the investment between MFN treatment and national treatment. More importantly, the requisition or destruction of an investment by the host state authorities shall be indemnified under the fourth-generation BITs.

For any legal dispute between an investor and the host state, if the dispute cannot be settled through negotiation and conciliation within six months, a domestic judicial approach and an international institutional arbitration or ad hoc arbitration can be chosen by the investor, although domestic administrative reconsideration may be requested by the host state before the arbitration. However, these legal approaches only apply to Articles 2–9 or 14.2 of the BIT.

Article 10 (health, safety, and environmental measures) and Article 11 (denial of benefits, which generally means that the "substantive business operations" criterion is not satisfied or that "investors from states with no diplomatic relations or under economic/trade restrictions" leads to the host state discretionary or mandatory denial of benefits under the IIAs to the "investor") are excluded from the domestic judicial forum and international arbitration procedure. The exclusion of Article 10 also makes certain omission of the host state on health, safety, and environment under the Article 10.1 loses justifiability or arbitrability, and in turn, the dispute arising from Article 10.1 can only be settled through consultation between the two states. If the home state considers that the host state has offered an encouragement measure under Article 10.1, it may only request consultation with the host state.

In addition, both the fork-in-the-road clause (once the investor chooses the domestic judicial channel or international arbitration procedure, the choice shall be deemed final) and the prescribed period for arbitration (three years) play a role in restricting access to international arbitration. The specific compensation form decided by an arbitral award and the finality of an arbitral award are also defined, and only the final arbitral award in force is legally binding and can thus be enforced. Finally, the arbitral tribunal can determine that one disputing party shall bear a higher proportion of the costs than the other to punish the disputing party who commenced a frivolous or unreasonable arbitration.

6.3.2.5 The China–Mauritius FTA

For investment protection, the investment chapter of the China–Mauritius FTA delimits investment as an investment "in accordance with the laws and regulations" of the host state and defines investment by listing assets and characteristics of an investment.[84] The investment chapter of the China–Mauritius FTA offers legal guarantees for investors and their investments. The national treatment grants postestablishment national treatment[85] and MFN treatment, which grants postestablishment MFN treatment but excludes treatment coming from international investment agreements "in force or signed prior to the date of entry into force of this Agreement" and "dispute resolution mechanisms or procedures". In addition, the "like circumstances" under both treatment clauses are clarified.[86] The minimum standard of treatment includes FET and FPS and thus confines these two treatments to customary international law, the minimum standard of treatment of aliens, and further makes the implication of the minimum standard of treatment with great certainty.[87] Measures relating to losses caused by "armed conflict, a state of national emergency, or civil strife" shall be adopted or maintained without discrimination, and restitution or compensation shall be provided if necessary for investment losses.[88]

The expropriation clause includes direct and indirect expropriation and compensation, and the compensation shall "be equivalent to the fair market value of the expropriated investment". For greater certainty, "compulsory licenses granted in relation to intellectual property rights" under or consistent with the TRIPS Agreement do not belong to expropriation, and "a mere fact that a subsidy or grant" has been changed or not issued, no matter whether there is loss in place or not, "does not constitute an expropriation".[89] As far as the free transfer of payments clause, on the one hand, the covered investment shall be awarded great freedom to transfer abroad, on the other hand, the host state maintains its ability to administer its capital account and "may prevent a transfer through the equitable, non-discriminatory, and good faith application of its laws and regulations relating to" under specific circumstances.[90]

According to the China–Mauritius BIT, only "a dispute involving the amount of compensation" related to expropriation between an investor and the host state has the chance to be settled through ad hoc arbitration.[91] The China–Mauritius FTA details

[84] China-Mauritius FTA, Section A, Chapter 8, article 8.1.

[85] China-Mauritius FTA, Section A, Chapter 8, article 8.3.

[86] China-Mauritius FTA, Section A, Chapter 8, article 8.4 and footnote 10.

[87] China-Mauritius FTA, Section A, Chapter 8, article 8.5.

[88] China-Mauritius FTA, Section A, Chapter 8, article 8.6.

[89] China-Mauritius FTA, Section A, Chapter 8, article 8.7.

[90] China-Mauritius FTA, Section A, Chapter 8, article 8.8.

[91] China-Mauritius BIT, article 13.3. The original text is "If a dispute involving the amount of compensation resulting from any measure referred to in paragraph (1) of Article 6 cannot be settled within six months after resort to negotiation as specified in paragraph (1) of this Article by the national and/or company concerned, it may be submitted to an international arbitral tribunal established by both parties. The provisions of this paragraph shall not apply if the national and/or company concerned has resorted to the procedure specified in paragraph (2) of this article".

every aspect of ISDS by a section, including consultations, submission of a claim to arbitration, consent of each party to the arbitration, conditions, and limitations on the consent of each party, constitution of the tribunal, conduct of the arbitration, governing law, awards, expert reports, domestic remedies, and service of documents.

Under the FTA, investor enjoys broad rights; for instance, there is no requirement of exhaustion of local remedies, the investor may initiate an arbitration under an "investment agreement", and the investor may also choose arbitration among ICSID arbitration, ICSID Additional Facility arbitration, UNCITRAL arbitration and other institutional or ad hoc arbitration. At the same time, the investor's right to claim is also restricted to some extent, such as loss or damage suffered by investor due to the breach of the host state, three-year limitation, 24 months "cooling off Period", and the arbitration under the FTA is limited to breach of specific articles in the FTA.

There are also some restrictions on the tribunal: Punitive damages by a tribunal are not allowed; a tribunal shall follow "a joint decision of the Parties declaring their interpretation of a provision of this Agreement", and the award shall be publicly available unless opposed by the respondent.[92]

6.3.3 Keeping the Right to Regulate

All first-generation BITs make exceptions to the MFN treatment clause by providing that preferential treatment based on a customs union, a free trade zone, an economic union, an agreement relating to avoidance of double taxation or for facilitating frontier trade are excluded.[93] Thus, in these three respects, the host country may refuse to grant MFN treatment to foreign investments.

Under the second-generation BITs, exception to the MFN treatment is extended to include preferential treatment provided by other forms of area economic organizations or similar international agreement, or any other taxation agreements.[94]

All third-generation BITs keep the traditional exception to the MFN clause except the China–Nigeria BIT, which does not mention any agreement for facilitating frontier trade.[95] Under some third-generation BITs, the regulatory power of the host state is further expanded in addition to the traditional exception to the MFN clause. As for exception to expropriation under the China–Madagascar BIT, the measures taken for reasons of security, public order, health, ethical and environmental protection, and other reasons shall not be regarded as obstacles to the FET.[96] "The transfer

---

[92] China-Mauritius FTA, Section B, articles 8.22–8.33.

[93] China-Ghana BIT, Article 3.3; China-Egypt BIT, article 3.3; China-Zimbabwe BIT, article 3.3; China-Algeria BIT, article 3.3; China-Sudan BIT, article 3.3; China-Cape Verde, article 3.3; China-Ethiopia BIT, article 3.3; China-Mauritius BIT, article 5.

[94] China-Gabon BIT, article 3.2; China- Morocco BIT, article 3.2.

[95] See, e.g., China-Congo BIT article 3.4, China-Tunisia BIT article 3.3, China-Equatorial Guinea BIT article 3.4, China-Mali BIT article 3.4, and China-Nigeria BIT 3.4.

[96] See China-Madagascar BIT, article 3.2.

shall be subject to laws and regulations of the Contracting Parties, and fulfill the procedure and obligation requirements by the laws and regulations provided in these laws and regulations".[97] In addition, "[i]f there are special difficulties for international payment balance, the Contracting Parties may conduct temporary on the free transfers be in accordance with the standards and requirements provided in the International Monetary Fund Agreement, and shall be subject to fair, non-discriminatory, good faith standards".[98]

Under the China–South Africa BIT, preferential treatment and privilege granted by economic integration arrangement, tax arrangement, border trade arrangement and development assistance become the common exception of the FET, MFN treatment and national treatment, not only limited to the MFN treatment.[99]

The national treatment imposes restrictions by stating "*without prejudice to its laws and regulations,*

specifically, any domestic legislation relating wholly or mainly to taxation and "*special treatments and measures aiming at eliminating the consequences of past racial discrimination in South African are excluded from the national treatment.*"[100]

In contrast, the BITs between South Africa and other developed countries do not include the latter exception of national treatment,[101] which is considered the major cause for the South African government to terminate its BITs with European states. The first case against South Africa by foreign investors before the arbitral tribunal of the ICSID Additional Facility involved such measures.[102] It should be affirmed that the special treatment standards and measures aiming to eliminate racial discrimination in South African history correspond well with South Africa's national situations and provide justification for South Africa to take such measures.

Fourth, the free transfer of payments is guaranteed under the exhaustive list "subject to its laws and regulations, guarantee to the investors of the other Contracting Party the transfer of their investments and returns".[103]

The preamble of the China–Mali BIT expressly recognizes that each party has the right to enact laws on admission and establish investment in its territory.[104] The China–Mauritius BIT provides that "[t]he provisions of this Agreement shall not in

---

[97] China-Madagascar BIT, article 1.

[98] China-Madagascar BIT, article 7.4.

[99] China-South Africa BIT 3.4.

[100] China-South Africa BIT 3.3.

[101] See UNCTAD, South Africa, Bilateral Investment Treaties (BITs), available at <http://investmentpolicyhub.unctad.org/IIA/CountryBits/195#iiaInnerMenu>.

[102] See Piero Foresti, Laura de Carli and others v Republic of South Africa (ICSID Case No. ARB (AF)/07/1), award, August 4, 2010, at 14–17, available at <https://icsid.worldbank.org/ICSID/FrontServlet>. This case relates to Mineral and Petroleum Resources Development Act, No 28 of 2002. This law is part of South Africa's efforts to increase participation by historically disadvantaged South Africans in the mining industry, in other words, it is a measure to implement Black Economic Empowerment (BEE) Programme, which seeks to mandate black participation in commercial enterprises.

[103] China-South Africa BIT, article 6.

[104] China-Mali BIT, signed on February 12, 2009, entered into force on July 16, 2019.

any way limit the right of either Contracting Party to apply prohibitions or restrictions of any kind or take any other action which is directed to the protection or its essential security interests, or to the protection of public health or the prevention of diseases and pests in animals or plants or the protection of its environment".[105]

In other China–Africa BITs, essential security exceptions and general public policy exceptions are not included, and prudential financial measures are not carved out.

The China–Mauritius FTA lists a series of performance requirements that cannot be applied by the parties during the whole investment life because these investment measures can restrict or distort investment, such as requirements on exports, imports, local content, technology transfer, and so on.[106] However, at the same time, many exceptions are excluded from the forbidden performance requirements. In addition, the nationality of the member of "senior management and board of directors" shall not be imposed on restrictions except "a minimum number of persons resident" in the host state.[107] To measures of general application, detailed transparency requirements are made.[108] Thus, these provisions focus on the protection of the interests of investors; at the same time, they also attach certain exceptions so that the balance of interests between the investor and the host state is feasible to achieve.

To carry out thoroughly "the rights of their governments to regulate in order to meet national policy objectives and to preserve their flexibility to safeguard public welfare" provided in the preamble, the China–Mauritius FTA uses specific articles to stress separate exceptions, such as non-conforming measures, special formalities and information requirements, non-derogation, denial of benefits, essential security interests, prudential measures, taxation and other exceptions, which are provided in the investment section of the FTA.[109]

6.3.4 Investor Obligations

Most China–Africa BITs do not impose specific obligations on investors. However, all China–Africa BITs provide that the investment means assets invested "in accordance with the laws and regulations" of the host state.

All China–Africa BITs in their Article 1 provide that investments are all kinds of assets invested by investors of either Contracting Party in the territory of the other Contracting Party in accordance with the laws and regulations of the other

---

[105] China-Mauritius BIT, article 11(Prohibitions and Restrictions).

[106] China-Mauritius FTA, article 8.9.

[107] China-Mauritius FTA, article 8.10.

[108] China-Mauritius FTA, article 8.11.

[109] China-Mauritius FTA, Articles 8.12, 8.13, 8.14, 8.16, 8.17,8.18,8.19,8.20.

Contracting Party, and the assets are listed with an exhaustive list,[110] or non-exhaustive list.[111] The China–Mauritius BIT further clarifies that "[f]or the avoidance of any doubt, it is declared that all investments shall, subject to this Agreement, be governed by the laws in force in the territory of the Contracting Party in which such investments are made"[112] The China–Nigeria BIT mentions in its preamble that "…recognizing investor's duty to respect the host country's sovereignty and laws". Such provisions impose a legal obligation on the investment, which is consistent with the domestic laws and regulations of the host state.

In fact, even if there is no explicit manifestation, the practice of investment arbitral tribunals shows that protected investments must be legal and in good faith; therefore, to be precise, under China–Africa BITs, investors have the obligation to make their investments legal.

In addition, the China–Madagascar BIT provides that "[t]he transfer shall be subject to laws and regulations of the Contracting Parties, and fulfill the procedure and obligation requirements by the laws and regulations provided in these laws and regulations".[113]

No investor obligations, such as anti-corruption, transparency, or corporate social responsibility, are mentioned in the first three generations of China–Africa BITs. However, in the preamble of the China–Tanzania BIT, "Encouraging investors to respect corporate social responsibilities" is mentioned.

Chapter Summary

Of the 34 signed BITs between China and African countries thus far, only 20 BITs are in force, and most of these are early generation BITs. Since Chinese investors have invested in almost all 55 states in Africa, this *status quo* of China–Africa BITs demonstrates the inadequacy of the international investment rule of law between China and Africa and thus the inadequacy of investor protection. This may bring about unfavorable effects for China-Africa investment relations, as such relations should rely on the rule of law between China and Africa to guard against all kinds of investment uncertainties and risks. More effective and equitable BITs between China and African countries are needed in support of the development of China-Africa win–win cooperation and to respond to the transformation of international investment law. The optimal China–Africa BIT can balance the regulatory space of the host states and the interests of foreign investors on the basis of the South-South Cooperation and Partnership and conform to the real needs of China and African countries and the modern trends of international investment law. This prospect of China–Africa BITs should be thoroughly explored, as it carries a significant meaning for the future development of China-Africa investment relations.

---

[110] For example, China-Ghana BIT, signed on October 12, 1989, entered into force on November 22, 1990, article 1.

[111] For example, China- Tanzania BIT, signed on March 24, 2013, entered into force on April 17, 2014, article 1.

[112] China-Mauritius BIT, article 10.

[113] China-Madagascar BIT, article 7.1.

On the whole, China-Africa investment treaties increasingly carry meanings of the rule of law over politically friendly foreign relations. According to the survey of the three generations of China–Africa BITs, from the first-generation to the third-generation, there is a shift away from unfavorable protection to more protection to investments. Comparatively, the fourth-generation China–Africa BITs, taking the China–Tanzania BIT as an example, may show the future direction of China–Africa BITs toward the international investment rule of law. The China–Tanzania BIT adds provisions such as Article 10 (health, safety, and environmental measures), Article 11 (denial of benefits), Article 16 (consultations), and Article 17 (interpretation). It further clarifies and refines many other provisions. In particular, in terms of protecting the host state's regulatory power, the public interests and especially the essential security interest of the host state are protected, and some important values, such as health, safety, environment and sustainable development, are given due consideration. It is especially important to note that a failure of the host state to act with respect to health, safety and environmental measures cannot be taken by the investor to arbitration. The China–Tanzania BIT also refers to corporate social responsibility in its preamble.

It is evident that investment protection and treatment standards are intensified gradually from first-generation BITs and second-generation BITs to third-generation BITs. However, the China–Tanzania BIT, as a representative fourth-generation BIT, tries to reduce the rights of investors and reinforce the regulatory power of the host state, thus achieving a balance of conflicting interests. The general trend of these BITs is that the rights and obligations are definded more clearly; thus, the "thin" form or normativity of the rule of law is enhanced to constrain the discretion of the arbitral tribunals when interpreting the BITs.

In terms of the scope of protection, the level of protection, and the dispute settlement mechanism, the China–Mauritius FTA upgrades the 1996 China–Mauritius BIT, but this FTA does not one-sidedly pursue the rule of law with a high degree of investment protection. This FTA is embodied in a more specific and detailed international investment rule of law and reflects the international investment rule of law requirements on non-discrimination and transparency.

On the one hand, this FTA provides stronger legal protection for Chinese enterprises to invest in Mauritius and promotes Mauritius' position as the first stop for Chinese investors to extend investment cooperation in Africa. On the other hand, investors in Africa or other countries may also try to use this FTA's favorable terms to invest in China. It should also be added that Mauritius is not a typical African country according to its location and other aspects, and thus, the China–Mauritius FTA is a special case as a China–Africa FTA.

The Protection of Investment Act, which was adopted by South Africa in 2015,[114] and commenced in 2018,[115] narrowed investor protection. For the substantive clauses,

[114] Protection of Investment Act, 2015, Act No. 22 of 2015, Government Gazette, Republic of South Africa, Vol. 606 Cape Town, December 15, 2015, No. 39514, available at <https://www.thedti.gov.za/gazzettes/39514.pdf>, and <https://www.thedti.gov.za/business_regulation/acts/Investment_Act_22of2015.pdf>.

[115] Protection of Investment Act: Commencement, Government Gazette 41,766, July 13, 2018, available at <https://www.gov.za/sites/default/files/gcis_document/201807/41766gen395.pdf>.

the Act replaces FET with "fair administrative treatment", thus making FET limited to only "processes and denial of administrative and judicial justice"; national and MFN are reduced because of the added exceptions. For the procedure, the ISDS, which is considered the most powerful means to protect investors, is not covered, and only mediation and domestic litigation are available to investors. State-state arbitration is only available subject to the government's consent. On the right to regulate, the Act includes redressing social-economic inequalities and injustices, constitutional rights, economic development, and environmental protection.[116] As this Act equally applies to South African and foreign investments, its relationship with China–South Africa BIT is also worth considering.

The development of the history of BITs should be a process that needs elaboration, clarity and improvement, and China–Africa BITs, as a product of the stage, still have space to be innovated in the future. The purpose of this chapter is to show that the rule of law in international investment between China and Africa is being improved in BIT and FTA practice. To adapt to the development trend of the rule of law in international investment and to protect China's investment in Africa and to impose responsibilities on Chinese investors, the rule of law on international investment between China and Africa must be further improved. In these investment agreements, this research emphasizes that the China–South Africa BIT should be retained and updated and that the China–Tanzania BIT and China–Mauritius FTA are of guiding significance for the future of China and Africa. The China-Tanzania BIT and Canada–Tanzania BIT clearly reflect the difference between the South-South BIT and North–South BIT. The China–Kenya BIT and Japan–Kenya BIT can also demonstrate this difference. Therefore, China–Africa IIAs need to adhere to the South-South model.

---

[116] Protection of Investment Act, 2015, Act No. 22 of 2015, Government Gazette, Republic of South Africa, Vol. 606 Cape Town, December 15, 2015, No. 39514, available at <https://www.thedti.gov.za/gazzettes/39514.pdf>, and <https://www.thedti.gov.za/business_regulation/acts/Investment_Act_22of2015.pdf>.

Chapter 7
Constructing the China–Africa Investment Rule of Law in the Future

The current international investment rule of law between China and Africa shows that it still has some imperfections, which means that it cannot better meet the practical needs of developing China–Africa investment relations. Therefore, it is necessary to put forward improvement suggestions based on the existing problems.

7.1 Chinese Innovative Economic Engagement Against Neo-colonialism in Africa

As far as China's economic presence involving investment in Africa is concerned, in recent years, some Western countries have attached the label of neo-colonialism to China, accusing it of plundering resources in Africa, abusing labor, destroying traditional industries, pushing African economies into a debt crisis, and damaging the ecological environment in Africa, and so on.[1] Reality shows that China is by no means a neo-colonialist in Africa, although these problems during investment are inevitable. In contrast, Chinese economic existence in Africa, which embodies a new development model of China–Africa win–win cooperation, is an innovative practice of anti-colonial international law. Chinese investments have contributed to the sustainable development of Africa.

[1] See Jian Junbo & Dontata Frasheri, 'Neo-colonialism or De-colonialism? China's Economic Engagement in Africa and the Implications for World Order' (2014)8(7) African Journal of Political Science and International Relations.185–201; See Howard W. French, China's Second Continent: How a Million Migrants Are Building a New Empire in Africa (Vintage Books, 2015); Brahma Chellaney, 'China Ensnares Vulnerable States in a Debt Trap' (2018)20 Nikkei Asian Review.

X. Han, *Legal Protection and Sustainability of Chinese Investments in Africa*,
Modern China and International Economic Law,
https://doi.org/10.1007/978-981-19-1882-7_7

7.1.1 *International Rule of Law Related to Anti-colonialism and Anti-neo-colonialism*

Colonialism and neo-colonialism are important concepts in the development of modern international law and contemporary international law, although they are not a single legal concept.[2] Therefore, the development of international anti-colonialism and anti-neo-colonialism law needs to be explored based on the analysis of these two concepts.

7.1.1.1 Colonialism and the Colonization of Africa

Colonialism can be defined in both broad and narrow senses. In the broad sense, between two or more unequal groups of power, one more (politically/economically) powerful group controls and rules the other group and makes efforts to impose its cultural order on the other weaker group. In a narrow sense, it refers exclusively to Europe's political, economic, and cultural imperial expansion into Latin America, Africa, Asia, and the Pacific. Based on the broad definition of colonialism, the concepts of so-called domestic colonialism, welfare colonialism, and so on arose.[3]

According to the interpretation of an authoritative dictionary, colonialism is "the principle or practice in which a powerful country rules a weaker one and establishes its own trade and culture there".[4] Colonialism is a "policy of acquiring colonies and keeping them dependent".[5] Thus, in general, colonialism is a policy or practice of conquest and domination by powerful states using various means of aggression to transform backward countries into their colonies, semi-colonial or dependent states. Typical colonialism refers to European colonialism, which is often based on conquest by force. It needs to be emphasized that colonialism is the practice and policy of a foreign state and that the policy of capitalist powers to conquer, rule, oppress, enslave, extract, and exploit weak countries or regions is colonialism. On the other hand, the presence of one state's private subject in another state cannot generally be called

[2] In African scholarship, decolonization has become a sort of hot topic, especially in South Africa. See Sundhya Pahuja, Decolonising international law: Development, Economic Growth and the Politics of Universality (Cambridge University Press, 2011).

[3] See James Midgleym & David Piachaud, eds., Colonialism and welfare: Social policy and the British imperial legacy (Edward Elgar Publishing, 2011); Gurminder K. Bhambra and John Holmwood, 'Colonialism, postcolonialism and the liberal welfare state' (2018)23(5) New Political Economy 574–587.

[4] See Pearson Education Group, Longman Dictionary of Contemporary English (English-English English-Chinese) (5th edition, Foreign Language Teaching and Research Press, 2004) 1312.

[5] See A S Hornby, Oxford Advanced Learner's English-Chinese Dictionary, editor and translator, Beida Li (4th edition, Oxford University Press (China) Ltd.,1994) 266.

colonialism unless it is a tool for a country to pursue its policies, such as the British East India Company and the British South African Company.[6]

Referring specifically to the process of colonization in Africa, from the late nineteenth century to the beginning of the twentieth century, some Western countries used force to divide Africa into their respective colonies and to secure gains through unequal treaties. Among them, the 1885 Congo Conference marked the official beginning of the partition of Africa. The conference, led by the German Empire's General Act of the Berlin Conference Regarding Africa, signed by some Western countries, is an important treaty in the process of colonization in Africa. The Treaty provided guarantees of free trade in the Congo River basin and the Niger River Basin and the principle of effective possession of land by the European States in Africa and to submit statements to other countries.[7] Moreover, the different manifestations of the colonies, such as "protectorate", "sphere of influence", and "leased land", were achieved through the conclusion of unequal treaties between some Western countries and African colonies and the conclusion of treaties between these Western countries.[8] Similarly, consular jurisdictions were established in African countries, seriously interfering with the right of African countries to judicial independence.[9] Under the colonial system of international law, some Westerners enjoyed privileged status in Africa, while colonial territories and colonial peoples were essentially the objects of international law.[10] In African colonies, the colonists threatened with force plundered Africa's natural resources and made Africa a market for commodity sales and industrial raw materials. Raw materials were supplied, and the colonists even traded Africans for more than 400 years as slaves.[11] By the time of the abolition of the slave trade in the twentieth century, the colonists had sold an estimated 100

[6] See Peter Slinn, 'Commercial Concessions and Politics During the Colonial Period: The Role of the British South Africa Company in Northern Rhodesia 1890–1964' (1971) 70(281) African Affairs 365.

[7] General Act of the Berlin Conference Regarding Africa, signed in Berlin on February 26, 1885, available at <https://loveman.sdsu.edu/docs/1885GeneralActBerlinConference.pdf>.

[8] For example, on November 4, 1911, Germany and France signed the Treaty on the Land of Equatorial African Land between Germany and France in Berlin. Similar practice is that the West defeated China through a series of wars such as the Opium War and then transformed China into a colonial and semi-colonial country with a series of unequal treaties.

[9] About Consular jurisdiction in Egypt and African countries, see Gengsheng Zhou, International Law (Part One) (Wuhan University Press, 2009) 251, 252, 258, and footnote ① on p. 252; Gengsheng Zhou, Outline of International Law (China Founder Press, 2004) 77–78; Western countries also exercised consular jurisdiction in China against China's national sovereignty through unequal treaties under the pretext of China's "harsh criminal law", "bad prison conditions", "judicial is not separated from administration", "discrimination against aliens, and the law does not grant equal treatment to aliens" and so on.

[10] See U. O. Umozurike, 'International Law and Colonialism in Africa: A Critique' (1971)3 Zam. LJ.95 96, 123.

[11] See Shengzu Wang (ed), History of International Relations (Part one) (Wuhan University Press, 1983) 127.

million people in Africa as slaves, and France built the Suez Canal in Egypt, a project that took the lives of more than 20,000 Egyptian workers.[12]

7.1.1.2 The Similar Nature of Neo-colonialism and Colonialism

Neo-colonialism, by contrast, is "the economic and political influence which a powerful country uses to control another country"[13] or "use of economic or political pressure by powerful countries to obtain or keep influence over other countries, especially former colonies".[14] In view of the definition of neo-colonialism, which contains the term "influence", some scholars use the word "influence" when referring to Chinese engagement in Africa instead of using the term "neo-colonialism", with the implication that they mean the same thing.[15] It has also been submitted as a notion frequently referred to currently that neo-colonialism "encompasses any form of alien economic, political, or cultural *domination* in present international relations that resembles classic colonialism".[16]

From a historical point of view, it can be argued that neo-colonialism was a means for the indirect domination of the former colonies by some Western developed countries after the dissolution of the old colonial system and the success of the decolonization movement. In this way, the old colonialism, which had been under the naked direct rule of the conquest by force, continued and developed in the new postcolonial period. Compared with colonialism, the external manifestations of neo-colonialism have changed, the means are diverse, and the form of presentation is no longer naked but more hidden. Neo-colonialism involves political, economic, religious, ideological, and cultural aspects.

On the economic front, the neo-colonialist instruments of some Western countries used in developing countries included controlling world markets and commodity prices, exploiting, and controlling former colonies through colonial investment, the provision of usury and conditional assistance, and monopolizing trade in services such as shipping and insurance, among others. In other respects, neo-colonialism has used marketing films, preaching, propaganda activities, intelligence activities, assassination operations, the establishment of military bases, the provision of arms, and

[12] See Shengzu Wang (ed), History of International Relations (Part one) (Wuhan University Press, 1983) 125.

[13] Pearson Education Group, Longman Dictionary of Contemporary English (5th edition, Foreign Language Teaching and Research Press, 2004) 1312.

[14] A S Hornby, Oxford Advanced Learner's English-Chinese Dictionary, editor and translator, Beida Li (4th edition, Oxford University Press (China) Ltd., 1994) 986.

[15] See 'China Lecture: Kenyan Law Professor Lumumba Deported from Zambia', September 30, 2018, available at <https://www.modernghana.com/news/886502/china-lecture-kenyan-law-professor-lumumba-deported-from-za.html>.

[16] Susan Demeske, 'Trade Liberalization: De Facto Neocolonialism in West Africa' (1997) 86 the Georgetown Law Journal 157.

armed intervention to impose dominance.[17] Moreover, some of the economic arrangements between the EU and the former colonies were also seen as colonialism under modern camouflage,[18] namely, neo-colonialism. Indeed, South Africa is phasing out bilateral investment treaties with some Western countries because of awareness of "the reflection of colonial relations with BITs between traditional trade and investment partners" and "the violation of South Africa's sovereignty by BITs concluded based on inequality".[19]

The vicissitudes of the times and the manifestations of neo-colonialism had kept pace with the times, but the nature of neo-colonialism had not changed. Kwame Nkrumah, Ghana's first president, had earlier used the term neo-colonialism, and in his view, the essence of neo-colonialism was that the State controlled by neo-colonialist was theoretically independent and had the appearance of a sovereign state, but in practice, its economic system and political policies were governed by external forces.[20] After losing direct political control, imperialist powers shifted to using neo-colonialism to maintain and expand their economic control in order to achieve political coercion.[21]

The definition and implementation mechanism of old and new colonialism reflected that although they behaved differently in the external form, they were essentially consistent in their impact, that is, the plundering, exploitation, and control of colonies or former colonies by some Western countries on the basis of sovereign inequality. The colonists always believed in their superiority and therefore legitimacy and effectiveness their religion, civilization, government, law and culture.[22]

The definition of colonialism and neo-colonialism was crucial and affected the recognition of the existence of neo-colonialism, for which there were differences among scholars. For example, some scholars have understood colonialism as actual possession, so colonialism is considered to be only a short-lived phenomenon and no longer exists, but some scholars argue that colonialism still exists today and constitutes an integral part of international law, except that it does not use neo-colonialist

---

[17] See Jack Woddis, 'An introduction to neo-colonialism: The New Imperialism in Asia, Africa & Latin America' (London: International Publishers, 1967) 45–52; 85–103; Kwame Nkrumah, Neo-Colonialism: The Last Stage of Imperialism, Chinese version, translated by Beijing Compilation & Translation (World Affairs Press, 1966) 246, 248–258.

[18] See Danielle Robertson, 'EU-ACP Economic Partnership Agreements: Modern Colonialism Disguised in Violation of the WTO' (2017)50 The Vanderbilt Journal of Transnational Law 463.

[19] United Nations, Economic Commission for Africa, Investment Policies and Bilateral Investment Treaties in Africa: Implications for Regional Integration (2016)3, 17; South Africa, Bilateral Investment Treaties (BITs), available at <http://investmentpolicyhub.unctad.org/IIA/CountryBits/195#iia InnerMenu>.

[20] See Kwame Nkrumah, Neo-Colonialism: The Last Stage of Imperialism, Chinese version, translated by Beijing Compilation & Translation (World Affairs Press, 1966) 1.

[21] See Kwame Nkrumah, Neo-Colonialism: The Last Stage of Imperialism, Chinese version, translated by Beijing Compilation & Translation (World Affairs Press, 1966) 33.

[22] See Robert J. Miller, 'The International Law of Colonialism: A Comparative Analysis' (2011)15 Lewis & Clark Law Review 847.

language.[23] In particular, the blurring of the understanding of neo-colonialism had also led to the generalization and misuse of the term neo-colonialism, as is the case with the so-called "neo-colonialism" of Africa by China. It was also not possible to judge whether neo-colonialism was a formality; for example, some would argue that having substantial direct investment in the host country constituted neo-colonialism, but Nkrumah had long pointed out that anti-neo-colonialism was not the exclusion of foreign capital per se but opposed the impoverishment of foreign capital, which should be used to develop rather than exploit host countries.[24]

To illustrate the attribution of colonialism and neo-colonialism, in addition to mastering the definition and nature of neo-colonialism, it was important to distinguish the context in which colonialism existed from that of neo-colonialism. Referring back to history, colonialism and neo-colonialism had, respectively, followed Western European Imperialism and the rise of US hegemony after World War II. The history of colonialism and neo-colonialism was in fact the history of Western expansion and corresponding maintenance of a dominant position in inter-State relations, while colonialism and neo-colonialism had also undergone an evolutionary process of illegality in international law. Oddly enough, however, there were few entries in the legal dictionary for the two frequently used terms, such as colonialism and neo-colonialism,[25] which also indicated the need to study the issue from a legal point of view.

In summary, from the perspective of international law research, neo-colonialism defined in this research refers to the post-World War II era and the decolonization movement thereafter. The practice and policy of some Western countries, especially the former colonial powers, on the basis of sovereign inequality, utilized various economic or political means and exercised economic or political influence to plunder, exploit, and control weak countries, particularly the former colonies, to achieve their own interests at the expense of the interests of the weak. Neo-colonialism is not only immoral and reprehensible, but also contrary to contemporary international law.

7.1.1.3 Development of Anti-colonialism International Law

Colonialism has been an important issue in international law, and the development of colonialism has been aided by international law. Colonialism had been formed and consolidated in the name of modern traditional/customary international law, especially with the creation of unequal treaties, which had been dominated by some

---

[23] See James Thuo Gathii, 'Neoliberalism, Colonialism and International Governance: Decentering the International Law of Governmental Legitimacy' (2000)98(6) Michigan Law Review 1996, 2019 and footnote 57.

[24] See Kwame Nkrumah, Neo-Colonialism: The Last Stage of Imperialism, Chinese version, translated by Beijing Compilation & Translation (World Affairs Press, 1966) 1–2.

[25] There are no these two entries in: Bryan A. Garner, Black's Law Dictionary (9th edition, Thomson Reuters, 2009); Susan Ellis Wild, Webster's New World Law Dictionary (Wiley Publishing, Inc., 2006); Daniel Oran, Oran's Dictionary of the Law (3rd edition, West Legal Studies, 2000); Leslie Basil Curzon, The Longman Dictionary of Law (6th edition, Law Press, 2002).

Western countries and had further had an important impact on the development of international law.

Under the old system of colonialism, colonialism was manifested in the political, economic, social, cultural, and legal control and exploitation of colonies by the imperial sovereign State, the loss of sovereignty, and the lack of autonomy and discrimination against colonized peoples, often based on the military conquest of the colonies by the imperial sovereign State and fixed in the form of so-called "treaties".

The Treaty of the League of Nations, signed in 1919, established the system of appointment to classify the colonies of the defeated countries in World War I[26] and decide whether to allow colonies to be independent, depending on whether they had reached a certain level of autonomy. However, its guiding philosophy was that "independence is not the best way to improve the well-being of the Colonies", which led to only Egypt gaining independence in 1922 among African countries before 1945.[27] Therefore, the Covenant of the League of Nations did not truly characterize or solve the problem of the illegality of colonialism; for many colonies, the only difference was that their old colonial masters were replaced by new ones, as was the case for most former German territories.

After the war, due to the active participation of socialist countries and the vast number of developing countries, modern international law based on the Charter of the United Nations gained transformative development. According to the modern principles of international law generally accepted by all countries, because colonialism is based on the conquest of force and the establishment of unequal treaties, its emergence and existence should be regarded as lacking legitimacy and legality. After the founding of the United Nations in 1945, the issue of decolonization had become an important agenda for successive UN-general conferences, and after more than 30 years of efforts, the colonial system had finally collapsed.[28] Southwest Africa, now Namibia, became independent in 1990, and all African countries have become politically independent states.

Many resolutions adopted by the United Nations General Assembly, especially the *Declaration on the Granting of independence to Colonial countries and peoples*, proclaimed by resolution 1514 (XV) of the General Assembly on December 14, 1960, declared the illegality of colonialism. One of the main objectives of the declaration was "a speedy and unconditional end to colonialism in all its forms and manifestations", and at the United Nations General Assembly, through which it had even declared the continuation of colonialism in all its forms and manifestations as a criminal act and constituted a violation of the *Charter of the United Nations* and the *Declaration on the Granting of independence to Colonial countries and peoples* and

[26] See Tieya Wang, Introduction to International Law (Peking University Press, 1998) 291; Shengzu Wang (ed.), History of International Relations (Part one) (Wuhan University Press, 1983) 329.

[27] See Shengzu Wang (ed.), History of International Relations (Part one) (Wuhan University Press, 1983) 365.

[28] See Zewei Yang, History of Macro International Law (Wuhan University Press, 2001) 303.

the principles of international law.[29] In short, these instruments of international law negate the legality and legitimacy of colonialism.

It is worth mentioning that, outside the United Nations system, the *Declaration on the Promotion of World Peace and Cooperation* agreed at the 1955 Conference (Asian–African Conference)/Bandung Conference, advocated the principles of anti-colonialism, anti-imperialism, and peaceful coexistence and gave a strong impetus to the independence movement in Africa.[30]

7.1.1.4 Development of International Law Against Neo-colonialism

Although the postwar decolonization movement had been a great success, traces of colonial rule in some Western countries persisted, and new forms of colonialism had proliferated. Nkrumah once pointed out that neo-colonialism was a stage of historical development that replaced colonialism as the main instrument of imperialism and was "the last, perhaps the most dangerous, stage of imperialism".[31] After the War, although the vast number of colonial and semi-colonial countries had gained political independence, as a condition for political independence, they were often forced to sign unequal treaties at the time of independence, for the colonists to retain vested interests or to obtain new preferential treatment.[32] Thus, as emerging developing countries, their economic, social, cultural, legal, and other sovereignty remained under the control of the former colonists, some Western developed countries, for a considerable period. As a result of the indirect influence of colonialism on the political, social, economic, and cultural life of former colonial societies, colonialism still has a profound impact on Africa, a colonial heritage that was neo-colonialism.[33] Africa's "neo-colonialism is the continuation of the ongoing Western control and domination".[34]

After a long process of decolonization, the influence of the former colonial powers on their former colonies remained, albeit through the adoption of new institutions,

---

[29] See Robert Jennings & Arthur Watts, Oppenheim's International Law, translated by Wang Tieya, (Encyclopedia of China Publishing House, 1995) Part I, 180.

[30] See Zewei Yang, History of Macro International Law (Wuhan University Press, 2001) 296–297.

[31] See Kwame Nkrumah, Neo-Colonialism: The Last Stage of Imperialism, Chinese version, translated by Beijing Compilation & Translation (World Affairs Press, 1966) 1.

[32] See Joy Asongazoh Alemazung & Hochschule Bremen, 'Post-Colonial Colonialism: An Analysis of International Factors and Actors Marring African Socio-Economic and Political Development' (2010) 3(10) The Journal of Pan African Studies 62, 63.

[33] See Joy Asongazoh Alemazung & Hochschule Bremen, 'Post-Colonial Colonialism: An Analysis of International Factors and Actors Marring African Socio-Economic and Political Development' (2010)3(10) The Journal of Pan African Studies 63.

[34] See Joy Asongazoh Alemazung & Hochschule Bremen, 'Post-Colonial Colonialism: An Analysis of International Factors and Actors Marring African Socio-Economic and Political Development' (2010)3(10) The Journal of Pan African Studies 65.

new structures, and new relations.[35] To promote neo-colonialism, postwar imperialist countries ostensibly recognized the independent rights of the peoples of the former colonies and affiliates of Africa while in fact using various deceptive means to exercise control and infiltration from all sides in the face of African countries that had gained political independence. Their colonial approach evolved into strengthening national capital exports, where transnational corporations had become an important tool for the pursuit of neo-colonialism, opening the road to private capital expansion in the name of aid and using a monopoly on modern science and technology to control and plunder developing countries. In particular, it needs to be emphasized that some Western transnational corporations even directly or indirectly interfered in the sovereign affairs of developing countries, and at the end of the twentieth century, some oil multinationals, as new global actors, were "able and often acted as neo-colonialists".[36]

In this context, the former colonies, after gaining the status of independent States, placed particular emphasis on the principle of permanent sovereignty over natural resources, emphasized the establishment of a New International Economic Order, the right to regulate transnational corporations, and the right to nationalization and expropriation of the property of foreigners on a *pro bono* basis, with appropriate compensation at best.[37] These actually emphasize the fight against neo-colonialism. To date, countries such as Zimbabwe and South Africa still, in the name of eliminating the remaining colonial influence, have adopted regulatory measures for the free expropriation of land without law by amending their respective Constitutions and terminating BITs with Western countries.[38]

Neo-colonialism, which is contrary to the fundamental principles of sovereign equality and independent international law, is illegal and not legitimate in nature, is not only indirectly reflected in the aforementioned documents of international law, but is more directly reflected in a series of international law documents establishing the New International Economic Order after the war. Below are some examples. *The Declaration on the Establishment of a New International Economic Order* states, "… The remaining vestiges of alien and colonial domination, foreign occupation, racial discrimination, apartheid and neo-colonialism in all its forms continue to be among the greatest obstacle to the full emancipation and progress of the developing

[35] See Josalee S. Deinla, 'International Law and Wars of National Liberation against Neo-Colonialism' (2014)88 Philippine Law Journal 1, 28.

[36] See Robert P. Barnidge, Jr., 'Neocolonialism and International Law, with Specific Reference to Customary Counterterrorism Obligation and the Principle of Self-Defense' (2009)49(1) Indian Journal of International Law 21, 31.

[37] See United Nations General Assembly, Programme of Action on the Establishment of a New International Economic Order, A/RES/S-6/3202(S-VI), May 1, 1974; United Nations General Assembly, Declaration on the Establishment of a New International Economic Order, A/RES/S-6/3201, May 1, 1974; United Nations General Assembly, Charter of Economic Rights and Duties of States, A/RES/3281(XXIX), December 14, 1974.

[38] Government clarifies misunderstanding on land expropriation target, July 6, 2018, available at <https://www.gov.za/speeches/government-clarifies-misunderstanding-land-expropriation-target-6-jul-2018-0000>.

countries and all the peoples involved", and it is, therefore, necessary to strengthen assistance to developing countries, peoples, and regions that had been oppressed by neo-colonialism in all forms.[39]

The Programme of Action on the Establishment of a New International Economic Order emphasizes that every effort should be made "to put an end to all forms of foreign occupation, racial discrimination, apartheid, colonialism, neo-colonialism and alien domination and exploitation through the exercise of permanent sovereignty over natural resources".[40]

The Charter of Economic Rights and Duties of States provides:

> It is the right and duty of all States, individually and collectively, to eliminate colonialism, apartheid, racial discrimination, neo-colonialism, and all forms of foreign aggression, occupation, and domination, and the economic and social consequences thereof, as a prerequisite for development. States which practise such coercive policies are economically responsible to the countries, territories, and peoples affected for the restitution and full compensation for the exploitation and depletion of, and damages to, the natural and all other resources of those countries, territories, and peoples. It is the duty of all states to extend assistance to them.[41]

In conclusion, the resolutions adopted by the General Assembly emphasize the economic sovereignty of newly independent States, affirming the inalienable right of dependent peoples to independence, self-determination, and the enjoyment of their natural resources and regulatory oversight over all their economic affairs, including domestic foreign investment. The principles and spirit of the fight against neo-colonialism also included the right to participation in decision-making in international economic affairs, especially on matters that had an impact on the African states. While there were differences between developed and developing countries in the characterization of those General Assembly resolutions, in any event, the role, effectiveness, and significance of those resolutions in international law could not be completely denied.[42]

Since the postwar period, the principle of self-determination of people corresponding to decolonization has been recognized as a fundamental principle of international law, and the principle of self-determination of people was based on the principle of sovereignty and covered political, economic, and cultural aspects, which, on the other hand, confirmed the binding nature of the anti-colonial provisions of the

---

[39] United Nations General Assembly, Declaration on the Establishment of a New International Economic Order, A/RES/S-6/3201, May 1, 1974, 1; 4(i), available at <http://www.un-documents.net/s6r3201.htm>.

[40] United Nations General Assembly, Programme of Action on the Establishment of a New International Economic Order, A/RES/S-6/3202(S-VI), May 1, 1974, I.1(a), available at <http://www.un-documents.net/s6r3202.htm>.

[41] United Nations General Assembly, Charter of Economic Rights and Duties of States, A/RES/3281(XXIX), December 14, 1974, article 16.1, available at <https://www.aaas.org/sites/default/files/SRHRL/PDF/IHRDArticle15/Charter_of_Economic_Rights_and_Duties_of_States_Eng.pdf>.

[42] See Malcolm N. Shaw, International law (7th edition, Cambridge University Press, 2014) 81–82.

General Assembly document.[43] Neo-colonialism, contrary to the fundamental principles of international law established in the Charter of the United Nations, including respect for the sovereignty and territorial integrity of States, sovereign equality, and non-intervention in internal affairs, is undoubtedly not legitimate.

7.1.2 China's Fundamental Principles of International Law in Handling China–Africa Relations

To understand the argument that Chinese economic engagement in Africa is anti-neo-colonialism, we must start from China's practice at the international level; that is, China has always adhered to the basic principles of dealing with international relations. Under the leadership of the Communist Party of China (CPC), since the establishment of the new China (the People's Republic of China), it has firmly pursued an independent foreign policy of peace and has put forward and actively practiced the five principles of peaceful coexistence: "mutual respect for sovereignty and territorial integrity, non-aggression, non-intervention in internal affairs, equality and mutual benefit and peaceful coexistence". The evolving five principles of peaceful coexistence are and will remain the cornerstone of China's independent foreign policy of peace.[44]

China has always firmly defended the fundamental principles of international law with the Charter of the United Nations at its core.[45] These principles of international law, in particular sovereign equality, independence, and national self-determination, with which the five principles of coexistence are consistent, do not leave any room for neo-colonialism. In dealing with international relations under the guidance of these

---

[43] See Deborah Z. Cass, 'Re-Thinking Self-Determination: A Critical Analysis of Current International Law Theories' (1992)18 Syracuse Journal of International Law and Commerce 21–40.

[44] According to President Xi Jinping, under the new circumstances, the spirit of the Five Principles of Peaceful Coexistence is not outdated, but has been renewed, the significance of the Five Principles of Peaceful Coexistence is not diluted, but has been long-lasting, and the role of the Five Principles of Peaceful Coexistence is not weakened, but has been enduring. See a keynote speech delivered by Xi jingpin at a commemoration marking the 60th anniversary of the Five Principles of Peaceful Coexistence at the Great Hall of the People in downtown Beijing, June 28, 2014, available at <http://www.xinhuanet.com/world/2014hpgcjndhzb/index.htm>; Xi Jinping, 'Deciding to Build a Well-Off Society in an All-Round Way and Win the Great Victory of Socialism with Chinese Characteristics in the New Era: A report to the 19th CPC National Congress' at the Great Hall of the People in Beijing, October 18, 2017, available at <https://www.xinhuanet.com/politics/19cpcnc/2017-10/27/c_1121867529.htm>.

[45] 1. Sovereign equality; 2. Fulfill obligations in good faith; 3. Settle international disputes by peaceful means; 4. Refrain from the threat or use of force; 5. Collective collaboration; 6. Ensure that states which are not Members of the United Nations act in accordance with Principles of the UN Charter; 7. Not intervene in matters which are essentially within the domestic jurisdiction of any state. See Charter of the United Nations, article 2, available at <https://www.un.org/en/sections/uncharter/chapter-i/index.html>.

principles, it is also impossible for China to engage in neo-colonialism activities in Africa.

For more than hundreds of years, the great powers have competed for interests and hegemony through war, colonization, and the division of spheres of influence in Africa. However, as President Xi Jinping has pointed out, "at present, things in the world increasingly need to be discussed together by all countries, to establish international mechanisms, to abide by international rules, and to pursue international justice as the consensus of the majority of countries".[46] This is in line with the historical trend that international law has gradually moved from "coexistence law" to "cooperative law". On the premise of this understanding, China's concept of dealing with diplomatic relations is to work together to build a partnership of equal treatment, mutual understanding and win–win cooperation, and to build a Community with a Shared Future for Mankind. In the short years since the idea of building a Community with a Shared Future for Mankind, the United Nations body resolutions have enshrined the concept of a Community with a Shared Future for Mankind on several occasions, indicating the growing understanding and acceptance of it by the international community.[47] This fully states that this concept reflects the aspirations of people for the future of the world and that the idea of a Community with a Shared Future for Mankind is not illusory but realistic.

China's idea of a Community with a Shared Future for Mankind is firmly opposed to neo-colonialism, and the idea of a Community with Shared Future for Mankind wants humanity to move toward a common future, rather than "I go to heaven, and you go to hell". The 19th Congress report of the Communist Party of China in 2017 states that China will "promote to build a Community with a Shared Future for Mankind" as one of the basic strategies for adhering to and developing socialism with Chinese characteristics in the new era and comprehensively expounds its connotation, which can be understood as including five major aspects: "lasting peace, universal security, common prosperity, open and inclusive, clean and beautiful".[48] First, neo-colonialism cannot bring peace and security because the foreign bullying will inevitably lead to resistance, and thus is contrary to the idea of building a Community with a Shared Future for Mankind, which takes lasting peace as the

[46] Xi Jinping: Promote a Fairer and More Reasonable Global Governance System, Speech at the 27th Collective Study of the Political Bureau of the CPC Central Committee on October 12, 2015, available at <http://www.xinhuanet.com/politics/2015-10/13/c_1116812159.htm>.

[47] See Naigen Zhang, 'Institutionalization of a Human Community with a Shared Future and Principles of International Law' (2020)15(1) Frontiers of Law in China 84–106; UN Human Rights Council Resolution, 'On promoting mutually beneficial cooperation in the field of human rights' (A/HRC/37/L.36, March 19, 2018), available at <https://undocs.org/A/HRC/37/L.36>.

[48] Xi Jinping, Deciding to Build a Well-Off Society in an All-Round Way and Win the Great Victory of Socialism with Chinese Characteristics in the New Era: A report to the 19th CPC National Congress at the Great Hall of the People in Beijing, October 18, 2017, available at <https://www.xinhuanet.com/politics/19cpcnc/2017-10/27/c_1121867529.htm>; On these five aspects, Xu Hong summarized these five aspects into five pillars of a Community with a Shared Future for Mankind, see Hong Xu, 'A Community of Shared Future for Mankind and International Law' (2018)5 Chinese Review of International Law 3–14, at 6–8.

basic prerequisite and universal security as the fundamental guarantee. Second, neo-colonialism could not bring about common prosperity, since it was developing itself at the expense of the interests of other countries and would certainly undermine the material basis for building a Community with a Shared Future for Mankind. Once again, neo-colonialism could not bring about openness and inclusion, since it adopted a condescending and exclusive attitude that regarded other countries as inferior and uncivilized and will surely undermine the civilized bonds that build a Community with a Shared Future for Mankind. Finally, neo-colonialism ignores the ecological environment of other countries and undermines the ecological pursuit of building a Community with a Shared Future for Mankind.

With the profound changes in the international balance of power, the rapid development of emerging market countries, including China, and a large number of developing countries, considering the legitimate concerns of others in pursuing their own interests, promoting the common development of all countries, and establishing a new international political and economic order in the pursuit of their own development, should be the main theme of the contemporary international community. The US Trump administration, which pushed one's own self-interest to the extreme, admired the supremacy of American interests, ignored the interests of other countries, ignored the responsibility of the great powers, and recklessly and unilaterally withdrew from one international treaty or organization after another, thus achieving the use of hard power or soft power to bully other countries and their private practices, would lead to neo-colonialism.

China, which has experienced semi-feudal and semi-colonial social forms, has always emphasized sovereign independence, sovereign equality, and non-intervention in the internal affairs of other countries in its foreign relations, which is a concrete manifestation of China's adherence to the principle of sovereign equality. In China–Africa relations, China has always stressed that countries take the path of independent choice, emphasizing mutually beneficial cooperation, and the kind of development model countries adopt depends on their own national conditions and their own choices, which fall within the sovereignty of States. China has always advocated "Africa is Africa of Africans". Therefore, the kind of development model that tries to sell itself to other countries has the suspicion of neo-colonialism.[49] Practice shows that the neoliberal and democratic models advocated by some Western countries have failed in Africa. China is not marketing its own development model to Africa, but many African countries are autonomous in learning about China's development model.

Traditionally, China–Africa relations fall within the scope of South–South cooperation, which is based on the principles of sovereignty, equality and equality, and mutual benefit. Because of the particularity of China–Africa relations, compared with other international relations, such as Central Europe, Sino-Arab, Sino-Russian,

---

[49] In 1947, US President Harry S. Truman argued that the world should adopt the United States system. See David Ryan, 'Colonialism and Hegemony in Latin America: An Introduction' (1999)21(2) International History Review 287.

and other international relations, China attaches special importance to friendly cooperation and common development. The China–Africa Cooperation Forum (FOCAC) was formally established in 2000 with the aim of strengthening friendly cooperation and seeking common development, and its core principles are the "Five Principles of Peaceful Coexistence", friendly relations, liberation solidarity, mutual benefit, and win–win common development policy.[50] As a long-term cooperation mechanism, it plays a vital role in promoting China–Africa cooperation. In China's Africa Policy Paper (2006), it is emphasized that "sincere friendship, equality and mutual benefit, unity and cooperation and common development" are the principles of Chinese–African exchanges and cooperation.[51] The 2015 Johannesburg Summit of the Forum on China–Africa Cooperation opened a new era of win–win and common development of China–Africa cooperation. At the summit, President Xi Jinping clarified the five major pillars of China-Africa Comprehensive Strategic Cooperative Partnership: political equality and mutual trust; win-win economic cooperation; mutually enriching cultural exchanges; mutual assistance in security; solidarity and cooperation in international affairs.[52] In the Chinese Policy Paper on Africa (2015), the concept of a China–Africa Community with a Shared Future is also put forward; that is, China is committed to win–win cooperation and common development.[53] The Beijing Declaration on Building a Closer China–Africa Community with a Shared Future, adopted at the Beijing Summit of the Forum on China–Africa Cooperation in 2018, further emphasized this idea. President Xi Jinping made clear the development direction of the China–Africa Community with a Shared Future: shared responsibility, win–win cooperation, happiness sharing, cultural co-prosperity, security co-construction, and harmonious coexistence.[54]

In short, China has no intention of interfering in the political governance of African countries, let alone the economic sovereignty of African countries, and in China–Africa relations, it seeks win–win cooperation, and China's presence in Africa fits the interests of African countries.

---

[50] See Beijing Declaration, available at <http://switzerlandemb.fmprc.gov.cn/web/zyxw/t11244.shtml>; Programme for China–Africa Cooperation in Economic and Social Development 2000, available at <http://www.mofcom.gov.cn/article/bg/200207/20020700024231.shtml>.

[51] See China's Africa Policy Paper (2006), Regulatory Documents of the State Council, came into effect on January 12, 2006, available at <http://www.gov.cn/zwjw/2006-01/12/content_156498.htm>.

[52] See 'Xi Jinping: 'On Together Building a Human Community with A Shared Future', in Xi Jinping, The Governance of China II, Chinese version (Foreign Languages Press, 2017) 456–460. Additionally, see A Speech Delivered by Xi Jinping at the Opening Ceremony of the Johannesburg Summit of the Forum on China-Africa Cooperation and in Johannesburg, South Africa, December 4, 2015.

[53] See China's Africa Policy Paper (2015), Regulatory Documents of the State Council, came into effect on December 4, 2015, available at <http://www.gov.cn/xinwen/2015-12/05/content_5020197.htm>.

[54] See Xi Jinping, Work Together for Common Development and a Shared Future, a keynote speech at the opening ceremony of the 2018 Beijing Summit of the Forum on China-Africa Cooperation (FOCAC), September 3, 2018, available at <http://www.xinhuanet.com/world/2018-09/03/c_129946118.htm>.

7.1.3 Salient Characteristics of Chinese Economic Engagement Involving Investment in Africa

China–Africa economic cooperation is mainly manifested in economic assistance, investment, trade, finance, and other aspects. The following section will demonstrate the point of this research by combining the understanding of neo-colonialism, analyzing the three most persuasive aspects, and comparing them with some Western countries' practices.

7.1.3.1 Chinese Economic Engagement Brings Economic Development and people's Well-Being to Africa

Nkrumah had long said that Africa is not trying to exclude capital but to prevent it from impoverishing Africa. In today's discourse, that is, Africa needs win–win common development, not a foreign investment at the expense of African interests.

In light of the long-standing existence of Western countries in Africa, including the colonial and neo-colonial phases, the plight of poverty in Africa has not been solved. In contrast, the West has seized Africa's wealth, leaving it with serious predicaments of poverty, environmental degradation, health, and security crises because they pursue their own interests. As stated by the United States Department of State for its purpose in making and publishing reports on the investment climate in Africa, including African countries, the reports are designed to support US companies in finding new and effective ways to boost US exports, create jobs, improve the welfare of American workers, and boost the American overall economy.[55] The full text does not refer to the promotion of economic development in Africa and the improvement of local livelihood, only "profit" and no "righteousness". Today, the new African strategy proposed by the Trump administration is to make Africa another battleground in the Sino-US trade war, and its so-called "Prosperity Africa Plan" emphasizes curbing China–Africa cooperation and giving priority to promoting American interests.[56]

Although it is not objective to say that China is completely altruistic, China's economic presence in Africa is based on Africa's development and future and has brought great benefits to the lives of African residents. On the whole, the growth of the African economy since the twenty-first century has been synchronized with the growth of China–Africa trade and investment since the first FOCAC in 2000.[57] Some Western colonists had adopted the practice of destroying colonial industries through

---

[55] See Bureau of Economic and Business Affairs, Investment Climate Statements for 2017, Overview, available at <https://www.state.gov/e/eb/rls/othr/ics/investmentclimatestatements/index.htm#wrapper>.

[56] See Remarks by National Security Advisor Ambassador John R. Bolton on the Trump Administration's New Africa Strategy, delivered on December 13, 2018, Heritage Foundation, Washington, D.C., available at <https://www.whitehouse.gov/briefings-statements/remarks-national-security-advisor-ambassador-john-r-bolton-trump-administrations-new-africa-strategy/>.

[57] See André Thomashausen, China in Africa, available at <www.legesmundi.com>.

the export of cheap goods, but China–Africa economic cooperation was helping to industrialize and modernize Africa, and the notion that it hindered economic growth in Africa and used African countries to enhance their influence[58] amounted to falsehood. It is well known that the insufficiency of infrastructure is the development bottleneck of African countries.[59] In this regard, China's Belt and Road Initiative (BRI) is tremendously helpful because many of the Chinese investments in Africa have gone to the infrastructure sector. Most of Africa's major infrastructure today is a product of China–Africa economic cooperation.[60] The continent's electronic, telephone, road, port, airport connectivity, water, public health, electricity, hospitals, health, government infrastructure, and other aspects all show the results of China–Africa economic cooperation.[61] Some scholars have found that 70% of China's loans are spent on power generation, transmission and transportation infrastructure, easing local electricity pressure and transportation difficulties, and promoting local economic development. In addition, 75% of the workers employed by Chinese projects come from the local area to solve local employment problems and improve the living standards of the people.[62] In terms of the manufacturing life cycle theory, some industries have moved to African countries, one reason being the abundance of labor resources. It is said that companies are responsible for the cost of education for workers' children in addition to workers' wages.[63]

On the latter issue, if there is a minor understanding of the legislation of African countries, the rumors in some Western media that China has imported a large number of its own workers into Africa will be untenable, since most of the laws of African countries provide for the proportion of locals employed. For instance, South Africa has laws that specifically protect the interests of blacks, and the overall objective of this kind of law is to enhance black employment and economic involvement.[64] According to Zambia law, priority shall be given to citizens so as to ensure local employment, and only appropriate Zambians with appropriate experience and skills

---

[58] See Remarks by National Security Advisor Ambassador John R. Bolton on the Trump Administration's New Africa Strategy, delivered on December 13, 2018, Heritage Foundation, Washington, D.C., available at <https://www.whitehouse.gov/briefings-statements/remarks-national-security-advisor-ambassador-john-r-bolton-trump-administrations-new-africa-strategy/>.

[59] See United Nations, Economic Commission for Africa, Investment Policy and Bilateral Investment Treaty in Africa: Implication for Regional Integration, Addis Ababa, Ethiopia: 2016. 1, available at <https://repository.uneca.org/bitstream/handle/10855/23035/b11559299.pdf?sequence=1&isAllowed=y>.

[60] See André Thomashausen, China in Africa, available at <www.legesmundi.com>.

[61] See Anshan Li, 'The 20th anniversary of the Forum on China Africa Cooperation: History, Achievements and Reflections' (2020)10 Contemporary World 17, 18–20.

[62] See Deborah Brautigam, US Politicians get China in Africa all wrong, The Washington Post, April 12, 2018, available at <https://www.washingtonpost.com/news/theworldpost/wp/2018/04/12/china-africa/?noredirect=on&utm_term=.a35a16452ddf>.

[63] This conclusion is drawn according to the survey conducted by the present author to NFC Africa Mining PLC and other private enterprises in the Sino-Zambia Cooperation Zone in September 2015.

[64] See Republic of South Africa, Broad-Based Black Economic Empowerment Act (B-BBEE), No. 53 of 2003, Government Gazette, January 9, 2004, No. 25899.

unavailable can foreign employees be employed.[65] Therefore, it is difficult for the Chinese to obtain work permits and visas in Zambia unless they are sophisticated technicians and managers. Due to the strict restriction on work visas, it is impossible for many Chinese employees to work in Kenya. According to the Kenya Citizenship and Immigration Act, only the much-needed main staff and skilled workers from abroad are allowed to work in Kenya.[66]

China's assistance in Africa has contributed to the investment and trade of Chinese enterprises in Africa[67] and has led to the development of African countries. According to Professor André Thomashausen, the operational mechanism (including investment) of Chinese aid projects in Africa has bypassed the corruption obstacle in African countries, and through the implementation of the master agreement, the value of African natural resources has been realized at market value, enabling African countries and people to enjoy the development and well-being brought about by various projects.[68] "The magic formula of China's cooperation with Africa is its commitment to friendly relations and liberation solidarity", instead of a governance model and military bases.[69]

Although China also has the incentive to promote trade and investment in Africa through aid, this is not the only motivation of China, and its main motivation is still to promote the common development of China and Africa.[70] Specific to African countries, the results of an economic study by African scholars show that China's trade has a substantial impact on Nigeria's economic growth.[71] Professor Deborah Brautigam from Johns Hopkins University argued that Chinese investment in Africa is absolutely not neo-colonialism and refuted the neo-colonialism hypothesis by conducting field work in Africa.[72] For example, her 57 Chinese investment findings

---

[65] See Zambia, Employment Code Act, Act No.3 of 2019, adopted on April 11, 2019, article 14 (Prioritisation of employment for citizen).

[66] See Chinese Academy of International Trade and Economic Cooperation, Economic and Commercial Office of the Embassy of the People's Republic of China in the Republic of Kenya, Department of foreign investment and economic cooperation, Ministry of Commerce, Guidelines for Overseas Investment and Cooperation Countries (regions), Kenya, 2020 Edition, 57–58.

[67] See Hidemi Kimura & Yasuyuki Todo, 'Is Foreign Aid a Vanguard of Foreign Direct Investment? A Gravity-Equation Approach' (2010)38(4) World Development 482–497; Hanli Zhang, Jia Yuan & Yang Kong, 'A Study on the Linkage between China's ODA and FDI to Africa' (2010)11 World Economy Study 69–74; Yaping Yang & Linlin Li, 'Can Aid Mitigate the Effect of Corruption on Investment?—The Sino-Africa Trade and Economic Cooperation Strategy Based on the Belt and Road Initiative' (2018) 39(3) Finance & Trade Economics 95–108.

[68] See André Thomashausen, China in Africa, available at <www.legesmundi.com>.

[69] See André Thomashausen, China Africa Cooperation: A Pillar of Global Peace. This article won first prize in "the Writing and Photo Competition 'China in My Eyes'" in 2019.

[70] See Ailan Liu, Zhixuan Wang & Meibo Huang, 'Neocolonialism in China's Aid to Africa? Empirical Evidence from Trade Effects of China and EU Aid to Africa' (2018) 3 Journal of International Trade.

[71] See Emmanuel Igbinoba, 'China, Africa's New Colonial Master?' (2016)16(5) Global Journal of Management and Business Research: B Economics and Commerce 47–55.

[72] See Deborah Brautigam, The Dragon's Gift: The Real Story of China in Africa (Oxford University Press, 2010).

on the Chinese acquisition of a large amount of land in Africa show that the number of land areas actually obtained by China is only 4% of what is reported.[73] Deborah Brautigam's research team has made many positive assessments of Chinese investment through field work in Africa, which is very convincing. In short, China, as Africa's largest trading partner has brought business prospects, economic growth, and social progress to Africa and is changing the face of poverty in Africa.

It should be added that the BRI, which was initiated by China in 2013, has enhanced economic cooperation between China and Africa. The BRI, as a global platform and an international public product, is dedicated to communicating and connecting national policies, infrastructure, economy, and culture of countries engaging the BRI. The BRI aims to enable all relevant countries to benefit from it, as opposed to so-called China's unilateral export of its economic development models or cultural traditions, for this is totally impossible to achieve in the twenty-first century.

7.1.3.2 China's Economic Aid Is Not Attached Political Conditions

Attaching political conditions means interfering in internal affairs and applying external pressure. After the independence of African countries, some Western countries continued to engage in neo-colonialism, one of the means being their own domestic financial institutions and the Bretton Woods Institutions—particularly the World Bank and the International Monetary Fund. However, the practical effects of their assistance did more harm than good. Structural adjustment policies of the 1990s, which attached specific conditions to aid for developing countries, including the requirements for political, economic, and social policy reform and adjustment, have had a recurring negative impact. For instance, the consistent conditional assistance of some Western countries has resulted in aid dependency from Western donors on which certain African autocratic rulers have depended to defend their rule. In the long run, the trend has contributed to sustaining dictatorships, exacerbated economic poverty, foreign resource exploitation, destruction, excessive external debt, corruption, and what has come to be known as the "resource curse" in Africa.[74] In fact, the more serious problem caused by conditional aid in some Western countries is interference in the internal affairs of African countries and undermining their national sovereignty. Conditional aid has put tight restrictions on African countries, severely limiting their policy space in deference to the interests of some Western countries

---

[73] See Deborah Brautigam, 'Opinion: U.S. Politicians get China in Africa all wrong', The Washington Post, April 12, 2018. Available at <https://www.washingtonpost.com/news/theworldpost/wp/2018/04/12/china-africa/?noredirect=on&utm_term=.a35a16452ddf>.

[74] See Joy Asongazoh Alemazung & Hochschule Bremen, 'Post-Colonial Colonialism: An Analysis of International Factors and Actors Marring African Socio-Economic and Political Development' (2010)3(10) The Journal of Pan African Studies 62–84; Dambisa Moyo, Dead Aid: Why Aid Is Not Working and How There is a Better Way for Africa (Farrar, Straus and Giroux, 2009); Emeka Duruigbo, 'The World Bank, Multinational Oil Corporations, and the Resource Curse in Africa' (2005) 26 (1) University of Pennsylvania Journal of International Law 1.

and losing their capability to develop in accordance with their own national circumstances. Even the African strategy of the US Trump Administration recommended the "right" policy choice for recipient countries, that is, to make a choice between China and the US and stand on the side of the US to meet the requirements of the US.[75] It is based on the ills of Western aid, with African scholars declaring the death of Western aid and putting forward a new objective, that is, "the Chinese are our friends".[76]

Among equal countries, there is no legitimate reason for one country to impose political conditions on others. Therefore, it is always objectionable to impose political conditions on other countries, especially weak ones, in economic exchanges. The attitude of African countries to political conditions is also the same. As mentioned earlier, regional investment agreements in African economic integration, especially the 2016 PAIC, have relevant provisions to resist interference in the sovereignty and internal affairs of the member countries. Blaming policies of other countries may have serious consequences.[77]

As early as the introduction of the 1974 Declaration on the Establishment of a New International Economic Order and other instruments of international law, it was emphasized that aid should not be subject to any political or military strings.[78] However, this is not the case in terms of the aid by the US toward Africa, illustrated by the forum of the African Growth and Opportunity Act (AGOA), held annually, to achieve the economic objectives of the US.[79] The AGOA was promulgated in 2000. Under this Act, only more than 30 sub-Saharan African countries are eligible exporters and enjoy GSP treatment in the US in accordance with a range of stringent conditions set out in the Act. Moreover, to maintain their suitability, African countries must cooperate with the US to continuously improve their rule of law, human rights, and core labor standards, in particular, removing barriers to trade and investment in the US. As a form of unilateral authorization, the US may revoke such authorization under this Act every year.[80]

---

75 See Remarks by National Security Advisor Ambassador John R. Bolton on the Trump Administration's New Africa Strategy, delivered on December 13, 2018, Heritage Foundation, Washington, D.C., available at <https://www.whitehouse.gov/briefings-statements/remarks-national-security-advisor-ambassador-john-r-bolton-trump-administrations-new-africa-strategy/>.

76 See Dambisa Moyo, Dead aid: why aid is not working and how there is a better way for Africa (Farrar, Straus and Giroux, 2009). Chapter 7.

77 For example, when the United States Ambassador to Zambia denounced Zambia over abuse of human rights, he was declared unwelcome and then was recalled to the United States. See Sanya Mansoor, Zambia Says U.S. Ambassador's Position 'No Longer Tenable' After He Criticized the Country's Gay Rights Record, December 26, 2019, available at <https://time.com/5755538/us-ambassador-zambia-recalled/>.

78 Aid with conditionality was a controversial issue, see e.g., Overseas Development Institute (ODI), Aid and Political Reform, Briefing Paper, January 1992, available at <https://cdn.odi.org/media/documents/6774.pdf>.

79 See Bureau of African Affairs: Our Mission, available at <https://www.state.gov/p/af/mission/index.htm>.

80 See African Growth and Opportunity Act (AGOA), available at <https://www.state.gov/p/af/rt/agoa/index.htm>.

In this relationship, these African countries and the US are fundamentally unequal, and the decision of which African products can be exported to the US is at the mercy of the US. It goes to show that the US is committed entirely to unilateralism and protectionism. Although the AGOA contains the label "growth", it has not led to substantial growth in African economies. While trying to protect its own industries, the US is trying to force African countries to open up their markets, with the result that it is bound to harm Africa's local economy. China's economic assistance to Africa is not subject to any political conditions, which is China's consistent policy toward Africa.[81] The China–Africa Cooperation Forum includes 53 African countries and the African Union that have established diplomatic relations with China. Compared with the propaganda of some Western media, some scholars' research tends to be more objective and fairer, and their research is often based on fieldwork.[82] Scholars in Eastern Europe have been candid in pointing out that China offers significant opportunities to lift African countries out of poverty and isolation, as well as to reduce their dependence on Europe and North America, as developing country that has successfully developed through a development path different from that of the West, African countries prefer China's approach of not attaching any political demands.[83] However, China's growing influence has undoubtedly hurt the interests of the West, whose influence in Africa is increasingly overshadowed by China's arrival.[84] Based on this, it is understandable why, at the beginning of the twenty-first century, when China began to increase its investment in Africa, the Western media gave many negative comments.

7.1.3.3 China Has Not Deliberately Set Up a Debt Trap in Africa

FDI does not constitute a country's external debt. Appropriate loans can promote FDI in a country.

---

[81] See China's Africa Policy Paper (2006), Regulatory Documents of the State Council, came into effect on January 12, 2006, available at <http://www.gov.cn/zwjw/2006-01/12/content_156498.htm>; China's Africa Policy Paper (2015), Regulatory Documents of the State Council, came into effect on December 4, 2015, available at <http://www.gov.cn/xinwen/2015-12/05/content_5020197.htm>.

[82] Prof. Deborah Brautigam is a typical such type of scholar. She is the Bernard L. Schwartz Professor of Political Economy and Director of the China Africa Research Initiative at Johns Hopkins University's School of Advanced International Studies. She has done many field works to research Chinese investments in Africa. Available at <https://deborahbrautigam.com>.

[83] See Ágnes Szunomár, 'China's Relations with the Developing World: A New Type of Colonialism or a Fruitful Cooperation', in Agnieszka McCaleb (ed.), China's Changing Competitiveness: Shaking up or Waking up the European Union? (Warsaw School of Economics Press, 2013) 85–110.

[84] See Ágnes Szunomár, 'China's Relations with the Developing World: A New Type of Colonialism or a Fruitful Cooperation', in Agnieszka McCaleb (ed.), China's Changing Competitiveness: Shaking up or Waking up the European Union? (Warsaw: Warsaw School of Economics Press, 2013) 85–110.

In contrast to the usury of some Western countries, China has often provided grants, interest-free loans, concessional loans, and many projects that have even been built without reimbursement. Chinese loans to African countries have long-term maturities, and much of the debt has even been canceled. In 2009, China canceled the maturing debt of 32 African countries in one lump sum.[85] China is committed to seriously implementing the exemption of intergovernmental interest-free loan debt commitments for Africa's Least Developed Countries, Landlocked Developing Countries, and Small Island Developing States that were not repaid as of the end of 2015.[86] During a press conference at the March 2018 meeting in China, the Vice Minister of Commerce mentioned that China had forgiven interest-free loan debt at the end of 2015 for more than 20 African countries. China has also pledged to forgive such debts at the end of 2018.[87] The Chinese government not only helps African countries resolve and reduce their debt to China through friendly consultations, but also calls on the international community, especially developed countries, to take more substantive action on debt relief for African countries.[88] Because African countries are not just in debt to China. Therefore, the claim that "China deliberately set a debt trap for Africa" is groundless. In fact, if China has plunged African countries into debt, if the debt trap hypothesis is true, China and African countries should be the most anxious states instead of other countries. The "debt trap" should not be fabricated to attack Chinese investment and China.

At the Beijing Summit of the Forum on China–Africa Cooperation in 2018, China again pledged to:

> …provide US$ 60 billion in support of Africa, including the provision of US$ 15 billion in non-reimbursable assistance, interest-free loans and concessional loans; the provision of US$ 20 billion quotas in credit funds; Supporting the establishment of US US$10 billion special funds in China-Africa developmental finance and US$5 billion special funds for import trade financing from Africa; and pushing Chinese companies to invest no less than US $10 billion in Africa over the next 3 years.[89]

In terms of the structure of this financial support, there is no problem of usury or excessive borrowing. In the colonial process, some Western countries used the

[85] See 'China Announces Debt Cancellation at African Summit', available at <https://www.commondreams.org/newswire/2015/12/04/china-announces-debt-cancellation-african-summit>.

[86] See China's Africa Policy Paper (2015), Regulatory Documents of the State Council, came into effect on December 4, 2015, available at <http://www.gov.cn/xinwen/2015-12/05/content_5020197.htm>.

[87] See Ministry of Foreign Affairs: Beijing Action Plan for the Forum on China-Africa Cooperation (2019–2021), released on September 5, 2018, available at <http://focacsummit.mfa.gov.cn/chn/hyqk/t1592247.htm>.

[88] See China's Africa Policy Paper (2006), Regulatory Documents of the State Council, came into effect on January 12, 2006, available at <http://www.gov.cn/zwjw/2006-01/12/content_156498.htm>.

[89] Work Together for Common Development and a Shared Future: Keynote Speech by H.E. Xi Jinping at the opening ceremony of the 2018 Beijing Summit of the Forum on China-Africa Cooperation (FOCAC) (September 3, 2018, Beijing), available at <http://www.xinhuanet.com/english/2018-09/03/c_129946189.htm>.

method of signing loan treaties with colonial governments, which plunged their finances under the control of the colonists and caused economic attachment.[90] On the other hand, to promote China–Africa economic cooperation, China has made remarkable contributions to Africa's economic development by generously providing support in the form of non-reimbursable assistance, interest-free, preferential, and special loans without any political conditionalities.[91] In other words, China's "South–South" equal cooperation with African countries on development issues is based on enhancing the capacity of African countries to develop themselves rather than maliciously placing African countries in the "debt trap".

For example, the most contentious debt problem of the moment is in fact a weapon in the African strategy implemented by the US Trump Administration to attack China.[92] Regarding Kenya's debt, the Kenyan President pointed out that Kenya's creditors were diverse and that Kenya would continue to borrow money from China and the rest of the world for development to improve infrastructure lending, and that Kenya's claim to "Mombasa Harbor as collateral" for the construction of the Mombasa–Nairobi railway was nonsense.[93]

China is not the only source of loans for African countries, and China has no malicious intention of placing African countries in the "debt trap". International public opinion has undoubtedly reminded China to keep an eye on the debt level of African countries because "excessive lending" is in fact also a risk for China.[94] There is the belief that China achieves its own colonial purposes through the debt trap, which is based on the premise that state-owned enterprises (SOEs) are the tools of the state government. However, this is not the case, and the behavior of SOEs is basically commercial. Both the port of Hambantota in Sri Lanka and the port of Djibouti are commercial in nature.[95] The independence of SOEs operating based

[90] For example, Shengzu Wang (ed.), History of International Relations (Part one) (Wuhan University Press, 1983) 124.

[91] See 'Xi Jinping: Jointly usher a new era of win-win cooperation and common development between China and Africa (December 4, 2015)', in Xi Jinping: The Governance of China II, Chinese version (Foreign Languages Press, 2017) 456–460.

[92] See the "debt trap theory" propagated by Tillerson during his visit to Africa in March 2018, and the United States plan for a new strategy for Africa, known as "Prosperity of Africa" as outlined by the United States security adviser John Bolton on December 13, 2018.

[93] See 'China isn't Kenya's only lender, Uhuru Kenyatta tells CNN', October 31, 2018, available at <http://www.nation.co.ke/news/Chinese-loans-don-t-bother-me-Uhuru-tells-CNN/1056-4828434-13il4ibz/index.html>.

[94] See Xiuli Han, 'Crisis Prevention for China as a Sovereign Creditor and the UNCTAD Principles', in Carlos Espósito (ed.), Sovereign Financing and International Law: The UNCTAD Principles on Responsible Sovereign Lending and Borrowing (Oxford University Press, 2013) 261–284.

[95] See Deborah Brautigam, 'Misdiagnosing the Chinese Infrastructure Push', April 4, 2019, available at <https://www.the-american-interest.com/2019/04/04/misdiagnosing-the-chinese-infrastructure-push/>.

on commerce is also supported by the International Investment Arbitration caselaw because a business-based SOE can be a qualified investor.[96]

From the above, whether it is the fundamental principle as the foundation of China–Africa economic relations or the concrete manifestation of Chinese economic existence in Africa, it shows that China's economic presence in Africa is not neo-colonialism. China–Africa economic cooperation is completely different from the neo-colonialism model of some Western countries in Africa and has come out of a new way of win–win cooperation, common development, and working together to build a China–Africa Community with a Shared Future. The Chinese Government also solemnly declares:

> [T]here has been a long period of colonial domination in African history and it should be understood what colonialism is. In recent years, China-Africa cooperation has strongly promoted economic development and the improvement of people's livelihood in Africa, which has been widely appreciated by African countries and the international community. It is clearly illogical to equate China-Africa cooperation with former Western colonialist practices.[97]

In addition, it should be pointed out that China's BRI is a platform for "discussing, building, and sharing" development. Although individual countries, politicians or scholars regard it as a "neo-colonialism tool", it has increasingly received the active participation of countries around the world and the high recognition of the United Nations,[98] and it also makes accusations of neo-colonialism self-defeating.

7.2 Exploring the Path of International Investment Rule of Law Under the Concept of China–Africa Community with a Shared Future

Colonialism and neo-colonialism were the attributes of imperialist countries, and African countries had long been exploited and oppressed by colonists and were

---

[96] See Beijing Urban Construction Group Co. Ltd. v. Republic of Yemen, ICSID Case No. ARB/14/30, Decision on Jurisdiction; Under WTO, state-owned enterprises are not a general assumption.

[97] See Statement by Foreign Ministry Spokesperson Hua Chunying at the Regular Press Conference on 14 March 2013, available at <https://www.fmprc.gov.cn/web/fyrbt_673021/jzhsl_673025/t1021324.shtml>.

[98] See Xi Jinping, Opening up, Creating Prosperity Together, Leading the Future Through Innovation: A Keynote Speech at the Opening Ceremony of the Boao Forum for Asia Annual Conference, April 10, 2018, Boai, Hainan, available at <https://baijiahao.baidu.com/s?id=1597338205675375512&wfr=spider&for=pc>. In addition, in March 2016, the UN Security Council adopted Resolution S/2274, which includes the content of the "Belt and Road" initiative. On November 17, 2016, the "Belt and Road" initiative was first included in Resolution A/71/9 at the 71st Session of the United Nations General Assembly. See Permanent Mission of the People's Republic of China to the UN, UN General Assembly unanimously adopted resolution calling on countries to advance the Belt and Road Initiative, November 17, 2016, available at <http://www.fmprc.gov.cn/ce/ceun/chn/lhghywj/fyywj/t20160116/t1416496.htm>.

unusually sensitive to both concepts. In the context of the abuse of neo-colonialism by some Western countries, Chinese economic presence in Africa should pay special attention to practicing the road of international rule of law under the concept of China–Africa Community with a Shared Future.

7.2.1 Upholding the China–Africa Community with a Shared Future as an Underlying Idea

When the global economy is facing a new situation and challenge, China–Africa cooperation also needs to be elevated to a new strategic level, not to weaken but to strengthen. The idea of the China–Africa Community with a Shared Future pursues China–Africa common interests and focuses not only on Chinese interests, but also on African issues; otherwise, neither side has a future. The idea of a China–Africa Community with a Shared Future means regarding each other's development as their own opportunities and actively promoting common development and prosperity through strengthening cooperation. Therefore, the idea of the China–Africa Community with a Shared Future transcends the narrow nationalist ideology and stands at an all-time high. When some countries increasingly emphasize the supremacy of national interests, China should adhere to the concept of the China–Africa Community with a Shared Future, and neo-colonialism ideas and practices are contrary to the concept of the China–Africa Community with a Shared Future.

China, which has come from colonial and semi-colonial history and is well aware that it is illegitimate to exploit the weak by power, upholds the idea that a Community with Shared Future for Mankind should be the foundation for cooperation and common development among countries. President Xi Jinping pointed out that China should achieve win–win cooperation and common development in more fields and at higher levels with other countries. Additionally, he stated that China will not subordinate itself to other Powers. "China will not use its power to plunder other countries; instead, China will work with the people of all countries to build a Community with a Shared Future for Mankind and build a better world for all, which reflects a Chinese saying that "all things grow together without harming each other, and nature runs parallel without contradicting itself".[99] This is indeed a wise saying and is the ideal of China–Africa relations that we should adhere to.

A country's foreign practice is necessarily guided by its belief in the concept, theory, and policy of international relations. Under the concept of the China–Africa Community with a Shared Future, China has put forward practicing the correct righteousness and benefit, seeking to expand the intersection of interests, promoting the construction of a new type of international relation with win–win cooperation as the core, and promoting the formation of the China–Africa Community with a Shared Future.

---

[99] See Xi Jinping, 'Speech Celebrating the 200th Anniversary of Marx's Birth', May 4, 2018, available at <http://www.xinhuanet.com/politics/2018-05/04/c_1122783997.htm>.

7.2.2 *Adhering to Fundamental Principles of International Law*

At the international level, the universally recognized fundamental principles of international law under the Charter of the United Nations, as well as the principle of peaceful coexistence, should always be our guide to action. In particular, it is China's diplomatic tradition to insist on the principles of respect for sovereignty, sovereign equality, and non-intervention in internal affairs and to exercise rights and fulfill obligations in good faith in accordance with the law. At the Beijing Summit of the 2018 Forum on China–Africa cooperation, President Xi Jinping elaborated on the "*five non*" approach to China–Africa relations, that is, non-intervention in African countries' right to explore development paths in line with their particular national conditions; non-intervention in Africa's internal affairs; non-imposition of China's will on African countries; non-attachment of any political conditions to aid to Africa; and non-pursuit of political self-interest in investment financing.[100] This "*five non*" approach is in fact a concrete manifestation of the fundamental principles of international law in China–Africa relations, and as the most fundamental difference in African policy between Chinese and Western, it must be upheld.

China will not and should not intervene in the internal affairs of any country, either now or in the future. The Chinese national values adhere to the "*do not impose on others what you yourself do not desire*" ethic. As a country that has been colonized by some Western countries for more than 100 years, China does not want other countries to interfere with its own fundamental political and economic development path in an attempt to make China "*cut the feet to fit the shoes*" according to their desires. Of course, China should not interfere with the internal affairs of any African country. Everything is based on national interests, upholding a zero-sum game thinking, imposing its own will on others, interfering in the internal affairs of other countries, using bullying, and trying to control or curb the development of other countries to maintain its own leading development position. This is not China's practice but a neo-colonialist approach.

China's development will not and should not be based on the greed to invade and plunder other countries. Since the founding of New China, especially since the reform and opening up, the development process shows that China's development is not dependent on foreign military expansion or relies on foreign colonial exploitation and plunder but on people's hard work and wisdom. In fact, after the reform and opening up, China developed through free trade and attracted foreign investment. To date, China is still the world's largest trading power, and developing countries receiving the most foreign direct investment are the countries receiving the largest amount of foreign direct investment after the US. Over the next 5 years, China

[100] See Work Together for Common Development and a Shared Future: A keynote speech delivered by Xi Jinping at the Opening Ceremony of the 2018 Beijing Summit of the Forum on China-Africa Cooperation (FOCAC), September 3, 2018, available at <https://baijiahao.baidu.com/s?id=1610579949684284352&wfr=spider&for=pc>.

expects to import 8 trillion dollars in goods and absorb 600 billion dollars in foreign investment.[101]

7.2.3 Refining the Design of a Specific Legal System

China–Africa economic cooperation is a systematic project with a full range of cooperation in industrialization, agricultural modernization, infrastructure, finance, green development, trade and investment facilitation, poverty reduction for the poor, public health, humanities, peace, and security. The implementation of all aspects of cooperation requires not only the concept of a China–Africa Community with a Shared Future and the guiding principles of international law, but also the implementation of specific legal norms. Therefore, at the international level, it is necessary for China to construct a legal system with African countries to promote sound economic activities in the environmental, labor, and social aspects. At the domestic level, China should also strengthen the compliance management norms for the overseas operation of Chinese investors and apply Chinese domestic law to regulate Chinese investors' misconduct extraterritorially.

For example, noting that international investment law is undergoing transformation and modernization, as well as the reality of economic cooperation between China and Africa, in this context, the China–Africa BITs should meet both the need to protect Chinese investors abroad and the need to shape responsible investors, as well as the need to strengthen the regulatory authority of the host country. Therefore, China–Africa should update existing BITs and conclude new BITs so that China–Africa BITs more fully reflect the ideas of fairness, balance, win–win and inclusion, including, of course, corporate social responsibility provisions.[102] It is also important to explore the possibility of entering FTAs with the African Union and subregional organizations in Africa that reflect the aforementioned ideas. This may be a shortcut to the legal promotion and protection of trade and investment in Africa, as African countries attach great importance to the economic integration of regions and the continent as a whole. Moreover, both the BRICS Bank and the Asian Infrastructure Investment Bank, as well as the domestic banks involved in African operations, should operate within the internationally recognized framework of the rule of law, including consideration of the relevant international "soft law".[103]

For example, at the domestic law level, China should continue to attach great importance to legislation regulating the activities of Chinese enterprises abroad. The Standing Council of the National People's Congress has long ratified the

---

[101] See Xi Jinping, 'On Together Building a Human Community with A Shared Future', in Xi Jinping, The Governance of China II, Chinese version (Foreign Languages Press, 2017) 546.

[102] See Xiuli Han, 'The Future of Bilateral Investment Treaties between China and Africa' (2015)40(1) SA Yearbook of International Law 29–57.

[103] See, e.g., UNCTAD, Principles on Promoting Responsible Sovereign Lending and Borrowing, United Nations, Amended and restated as of January 10, 2012, available at <https://unctad.org/en/PublicationsLibrary/gdsddf2012misc1_en.pdf>.

United Nations Convention against Corruption,[104] criminalizing bribery of foreign public officials in national criminal law, since, as a State party, the regulation of commercial bribery in accordance with the provisions of the Convention includes not only domestic, but also overseas commercial bribery. Under China's Criminal law, whoever gives any property to a functionary of a foreign country or an official of an international public organization for any illicit commercial benefit shall be punished and sentenced to imprisonment for three to ten years in addition to a fine if the amount of bribe is huge.[105]

In fact, in recent years, China has introduced a few legal norms directly aiming at foreign investment, contracting projects, overseas credit, and other aspects,[106] which in other countries in the world is unprecedented, as well as China's unique practice. Legislation in that regard should continue to be strengthened in the future, in particular by raising the legislative hierarchy.

7.2.4 Complying with Specific Legal Principles and Norms

The life of the law lies in its implementation, whether it is international or domestic law. Therefore, China should adhere to the concept of the China–Africa Community with a shared future, the fundamental principles of international law, and the principles of dealing with China–Africa relations. International treaties between China and Africa should also be effectively implemented at the domestic level and enhance compliance. At the same time, China's economically active private individuals in Africa are subject to the relevant domestic laws of the host country and the relevant domestic laws of China. Legal norms with Chinese characteristics are designed to govern the overseas economic activities of many enterprises, and they need to be effectively implemented. Thus, they can move from the law on paper into the law that truly works. Strengthening the regulating role of law can promote the sustainable development of China–Africa economic cooperation.

In short, neo-colonialism is out of step with China's national development policy in Africa, and China firmly rejects the fallacy that "*China is a neo-colonialist in the nature of its economic activities in Africa*". Some of the issues and phenomena that have been branded "neo-colonialism" and received much attention are in fact either

---

[104] See Decision of the Standing Committee of the National People's Congress on Ratifying the United Nations Convention Against Corruption, date issued and effect date on October 27, 2005, available at <https://www.lawinfochina.com/display.aspx?id=4635&lib=law>.

[105] See Criminal Law of the People's Republic of China (2020 Amendment), Order No. 66 of the President of the People's Republic of China, issued on December 26, 2020, came in force on March 1, 2021, article 164.1 and 164.2.

[106] For example, Measures for the Administration of Overseas Investment of Enterprises (Order No. 11 of the National Development and Reform Commission in 2017), Guide to Environmental Protection for Overseas Investment Cooperation, Letter No. 74 [2013] of the Ministry of Commerce, and Guidelines for the Compliance Management on Overseas Operations of Enterprises, No. 1916 [2018] of the National Development and Reform Commission.

the neglect of social responsibility by individual enterprises or the problem of individual private violations instead of the behavior of the state. They lack the elements of neo-colonialism. The assumption of "*Chinese government's neo-colonialist strategy in Africa*" is undoubtedly a distortion of the truth. At present, "neo-colonialism" rumors also remind us that in China–Africa economic cooperation, in the face of rumors of hostility and confusion, it is necessary to refute the facts according to law, and we need to strictly practice the international rule of law and proceed cautiously.

7.3 Concluding China–Africa IIAs Based on International Investment Rule of Law of South–South Cooperation Orientation

As mentioned above, the IIAs between China and African countries currently consists of 20 BITs, and the China–Mauritius FTA is currently in force. Therefore, in addition to advocating that there should be more BITs and FTAs between China and African countries, the following will discuss the trend of China–Africa IIAs and the future of the China–South Africa BIT.

7.3.1 Trend of the China–Africa BIT

Among all African BITs, approximately 70% BITs are concluded with developed countries, and approximately 30% BITs are South–South BITs within developing countries.[107] It can be predicted that African BITs with developing countries will increase as emerging economies are forging ahead. It is clear that BITs are the outcome of contradictions occurring between the South and the North. At the beginning, they were used to satisfy the need to protect outward FDI mainly by the US and Western European countries. However, BITs have also been used in developing countries since 1964.[108] As an important part of the international rule of law, BITs should play an important role in promoting and protecting investment between all economies, including developing economies, to help improve the standard of living of the people.

Although academic research does not unanimously confirm that BITs can help to promote or increase FDI, UNCTAD concludes that "*The impact of BITs on investment*

[107] See United Nations, Economic Commission for Africa, Assessing Regional Integration in Africa (ARIV V): Toward an African Continental Free Trade Area (2012) 133, available at <https://digitallibrary.un.org/record/735475>.

[108] See UNCTAD, South-South Cooperation in International Investment Arrangements, UNCTAD series on International Investment Policies for Development (2005, United Nations) 5, available at <https://unctad.org/system/files/official-document/iteiit20053_en.pdf>.

flows into developing countries is confirmed by investor surveys".[109] In the present author's opinion, BIT is only one of several determinants in attracting foreign investments, and this alone is not sufficient. However, in most cases, BITs will promote the economic interests of both contracting parties and demonstrate a political intention to promote economic relations and enhance friendly political relations between the contracting parties.

The effectiveness of these treaties is evidenced by the fact that there are currently approximately 3000 BITs in force globally, and more BITs are being negotiated. At least for China, it is difficult to say that China's rapid development, as the world's second recipient of FDI inflows and the world's third exporter of FDI outflows, is not assisted by its BITs because they provide international legal guarantees for investors and their investments. Arguments in which China's BITs "do not seem to have increased FDI flows into China's developing country treaty partners" and "China's BITs with other developing countries may serve primarily political, rather than economic purposes" are premature, considering the relatively short time during which Chinese outward investments, including outward investments in Africa, have become a reality.[110] China's FDI "outflows are expected to surpass its inflows within two to three years".[111] BITs are expected to facilitate and secure the success of this growth because they are an important part of a safe investment environment.

It has been argued, especially in South Africa, that a country should protect foreign investments through its general domestic legal system, which should reflect the international standard of protecting foreign investment.[112] However, in an international community of globalization, the international rule of law has become one of the most important means of governance, making it more appropriate to protect foreign investment through both domestic laws and international treaties. In addition, importing international standards into domestic law is an ideal that is difficult to achieve, as South Africa's Protection of Investment Act, 2015 demonstrates.[113] Most importantly, unlike BITs, domestic law cannot specifically protect bilateral investments, leaving South African investors without protection when their investments may be violated in other countries.

---

[109] See UNCTAD, the Role of International Investment Agreements in Attracting Foreign Direct Investment to Developing Countries, UNCTAD Series on International Investment Policies for Development (2009, United Nations) 111, available at <https://unctad.org/system/files/official-document/diaeia20095_en.pdf>.

[110] About this premature conclusion, please see Kate Hadley, 'Note, Do China's BITs Matter? Assessing the Effect of China's Investment Agreements on Foreign Direct Investment Flows, Investors' Rights, and the Rule of Law' (2013) 45 Georgetown Journal of International Law 255.

[111] See UNCTAD, World Investment Report 2014, Investing in the SDGs: An Action Plan (2014, United Nations) xix, available at <https://unctad.org/system/files/official-document/wir2014_en.pdf>.

[112] See Magalie Masamba, 'Africa and Bilateral Investment Treaties: To 'BIT' or Not?', July 16, 2014, available at <https://www.polity.org.za/article/africa-and-bilateral-investment-treaties-to-bit-or-not-2014-07-23>.

[113] See Protection of Investment Act, 2015, Act No. 22 of 2015, Government Gazette, Republic of South Africa, Vol. 606 Cape Town, December 15, 2015, No. 39514, available at <https://www.thedti.gov.za/gazzettes/39514.pdf>.

It has been suggested that the norms in most South–South BITs are only repetitions of the traditional North–South template because of limited capacities to negotiate original legal instruments, and the main difference between South–South and North–South BITs should be seen in the prevalence in South–South BITs of provisions intended to reserve more regulatory power for the host states and exclude national treatment, market access, and protection and security provisions.[114] However, if some substantive provisions, implementation provisions, or important treatments, such as national treatment, are not granted to the investor, what exactly is the significance of an entirely conditioned BIT? In effect, the more recent North–South BITs also emphasize the reservation of rights or flexibility to balance the interests of the investor and the host state. For example, the China–Canada BIT includes many exceptions: the MFN treatment exception, the national treatment exception, the expropriation exception, the regulation exception, the taxation exception, the general exceptions (including prudent finance), and the national security exception.[115] Similarly, in 2012, the US Model BIT also lists a large number of exceptions, and this design aims to address the contradiction between "keeping rights in the hand" of the host state and "strengthening the protection" of the investor.

UNCTAD indeed pointed out in 2005 that "to a large part, South–South IIAs are similar to North–South IIAs".[116] Beyond doubt, the pursuits of South-South BITs and North-South BITs are converging. Both must strive to attain the best balance between rights and obligations.

However, the balance of the South–South BITs is different from that of the North–South BITs. In other words, the former is not too demanding and even gives special consideration to developing countries' situations and interests. For example, China–Africa BITs never include a national treatment clause of pre-establishment. Comparatively, the US–Rwanda BIT requests that national treatment be applied at the stage of market access, i.e., with respect to the establishment, acquisition, and expansion of investment.[117] The 9 BITs signed between Canada and African countries also require a national treatment of pre-establishment.[118] Therefore, developed countries do not differentiate by the identity of the other contracting party. According to China's

[114] See Mahnaz Malik, 'South-South Bilateral Investment Treaties: The same old story?', IV Annual Forum for Developing Country Investment Negotiators Background Papers, New Delhi, October 27–29, 2010, available at <https://www.iisd.org/system/files/publications/dci_2010_south_bits.pdf>.

[115] See Agreement between the Government of Canada and the Government of the People's Republic of China for the Promotion and Reciprocal Protection of Investments, articles 5.3, 8, 10, ANNEX B.10, 14, 33, ANNEX D.34, available at <www.international.gc.ca/trade-agreements-accords-commerciaux/agr-acc/fipa-apie/china-text-chine.aspx?lang=en&view=d>.

[116] See South-South Cooperation in International Investment Arrangements, United Nations UNCTAD Series on International Investment Policies for Development (2005, United Nations) 45, available at <https://unctad.org/system/files/official-document/iteiit20053_en.pdf>.

[117] See Treaty between the Government of the United States of America and the Government of the Republic of Rwanda Concerning the Encouragement and Reciprocal Protection of Investment, signed on February 19, 2008, came into effect on January 1, 2012, article 3, available at <http://investmentpolicyhub.unctad.org/Download/TreatyFile/2241>.

[118] See UNCTAD International Investment Agreements, Most Recent IIAs, available at <http://investmentpolicyhub.unctad.org/IIA/MostRecentTreaties#iiaInnerMenu>.

contracting practices, however, as mentioned above, the China–Canada BIT, China–Japan–Korea Tripartite Investment Agreement, China–US BIT, and China–EU BIT differ from the China–Uzbekistan and China–Tanzania BITs. In terms of scope, issues, protection level, and investment liberalization, the former far outweighs the latter.

Overall, it is easier for China to pursue a balanced BIT policy due to its "hybrid identity" of being both a capital exporting and capital importing country. Concretely, China–Africa BITs should seek to balance the interest of investors and the host state and conform to the different development levels of developing countries. Due to the weakness of many existing China–Africa BITs, the conclusion of updated China–Africa BITs similar to the China–Tanzania BIT will be necessary if the investor is to benefit from better protection and the host state to be granted more regulatory power for legitimate purposes and free from a "chilling effect". It, therefore, means the inhibition or discouragement of the legitimate exercise of legal rights by the threat of legal sanction.

When discussing the prospects of a new generation of investment policies, the World Investment Reports 2012, 2014, 2015, and 2019 stress responsible investment and sustainable development as the features of new-generation IIAs.[119] The ideas reflected in the reports should be considered and accepted in earnests by China and African countries. Therefore, investors should also be made to assume certain obligations and social responsibilities, such as the protection of the environment and labor rights, even though this type of clause in the current BITs is rather "soft" than "hard".

At the opening ceremony of the Annual Conference of International Economic Law, an academic seminar held on November 3, 2012, in China, Chenggang Li, who was then the deputy leader of the Department of Treaty and Law in the Ministry of Commerce of the People's Republic of China, in his keynote speech, significantly pointed out the following:

> When Chinese enterprises in Africa and South America are confronted with local trade unions and labor disputes occur frequently, how should we deal with the labor issue in our future investment treaties; When the green mountains and waters are becoming badlands, reviewing the painful lesson of environmental deterioration in the process of China's economic development, how should we deliberate environmental issues in the future investment treaties?[120]

The official attitude toward environmental protection and labor issues in Africa will affect future China–Africa investment treaties. In fact, Article 6(3), Article 10 and the preface of the newest China–Tanzania BIT clearly respond to this point.

---

[119] UNCTAD World Investment Report 2012: Towards a New Generation of Investment Policies (United Nations 2012) 161–162; UNCTAD World Investment Report 2014: Investing in the SDGs: An Action Plan (United Nations 2014) ii; World Investment Report 2015: Reforming International Investment Governance (United Nations 2015) xii, xi.; World Investment Report 2019: Special Economic Zone (United Nations 2019) 104, 112.

[120] Chenggang Li, 'Review of China's International Economic Legal Practice in 2012' (2012) 19(4) Journal of International Economic Law (Chinese) 1–11.

South–South cooperation, as the cooperation between developing countries based on equality and mutual benefits, mutual respect for sovereignty, non-intervention in internal affairs, and without requiring any privilege or political condition, is the declared cornerstone of China–Africa relations. Although some Western scholars and states hold different opinions on China's status, it is undoubted that China is still a rising developing country according to China's economic and social reality. China has always adhered to its position as a developing country. Sovereignty equality is fundamental in South–South cooperation and investment relations between China and African countries. The Chinese government has always declared:

> As a developing country, it (China) desires to carry out extensive and in-depth cooperation with southern countries in economy, science and technology education and culture and so on, on the grounds that some principles such as equality and mutual benefit, pursuing practical results, taking various forms, and promoting common development.[121]

It has been cautioned that because South–South BITs do not appear to offer a different legal framework for FDI than South–North BITs, "Countries in Africa must approach every BIT negotiation with caution" when the other contracting party is China.[122] It has also been submitted that China claims a "South" identity, but its pursuits bear all the hallmarks of the "North", rendering China's position in China–Africa BITs ambiguous.[123] This argument can be countered if we compare the existing China–Africa BITs with the BITs between China and Canada and with the BITs between Canada and African countries. To advance and promote the China–Africa BIT regime, China must encourage reasonably signed BITs to enter into force, following the example of the China–Congo BIT, which was signed on March 20, 2000, and came into effect on July 1, 2015. China and its African counterparts have every interest in making greater efforts to update or agree on new BITs to promote and protect investment better and foster each other's sustainable development and prosperity.

As a rule, the preamble text of China–Africa BITs will in the future emphasize sustainable development (including sustainable economic, social, and environmental development), the goals of improving people's livelihood, and broadening economic cooperation.

Furthermore, specific provisions should embody the latest standards of international investment rulemaking. For example, on the side of the investor and the home state, environment and labor concerns, or broadly, public policy concerns, should all be embraced and reflected in the BIT, and the investor should be encouraged to assume social responsibilities. Even if only in terms of "soft law" in case, it would

---

[121] 'China's Position on South-South Cooperation', available at <www.fmprc.gov.cn/chn/pds/ziliao/tytj/zcwj/t3468.htm>.

[122] See Uche Ewelukwa Ofodile, 'Africa-China Bilateral Investment Treaties: A Critique' (2013) 35 Michigan Journal of International Law 131–207.

[123] See Won Kidane, 'Reflections on China-Africa BITs, China-Africa Investment Treaties and Dispute Settlement: A Piece of the Multipolar Puzzle', in Won Kidane (ed.), American Society of International Law Proceedings of the Annual Meeting (Cambridge University Press, 2013) 228.

risk creating investment barriers, as such commitments would still provide a value orientation to the BIT.

For some African countries, special clauses may have to be provided. One case in point is that of the China–South Africa BIT. It provides that the investments of foreign investors enjoy national treatment "with the exception of any domestic legislation relating wholly or mainly to taxation or programs and economic activities specifically aimed to promote, protect and advance persons and groups of persons that have been disadvantaged as a result of past discriminatory practices in the Republic of South Africa".[124] In addition, the provision of special and differential treatment "for less developed partners in an agreement" is considered a "structural element of an IIA's development dimension".[125]

For the controversial issue of whether the investor-state arbitral clause should be kept in the BIT, due to the lack of any better alternative, it is still necessary to keep it, improve it, and consider it an outcome of the international rule of law. We find that most countries agree to rules to manage investor-state disputes after reviewing their BIT policy; that is, investor-state dispute settlement with increased transparency, accountability, and predictability are considered necessary components of a BIT. Although the ICSID was originally designed to protect the investment of Western countries in the host states, it could nevertheless serve as a good forum for the resolution of disputes arising from China–Africa BITs.[126]

At present, China is actively participating and promoting the economic integration and cross-regional cooperation of the African Union (AU). China has also continually intensified cooperation with regional organizations in Africa and institutionalized and systematized cooperation. In 2011, China signed the "Framework Agreements on Economic and Trade Cooperation" with the EAC and ECOWAS. The agreement especially involves cooperation on direct investment. Thus, in the future, the multilateralization or regionalization of legal relationships on investment between China and African countries will complement BITs. The multilateralization of IIA is supported by China in view of the fragmentation of the existing international investment law regime.[127]

Chinese investment in Africa will benefit from a safe and sustainable model, which will lead to a win–win result. To this end, the international legal framework, i.e., BITs and other IIAs, is essential. Governing and regulating the investment relationships between China and African countries will guarantee their smooth development.

---

[124] See Agreement Between the Government of the People's Republic of China and the Government of the Republic of South Africa concerning the Reciprocal Promotion and Protection of Investments, article 3.3, available at <http://tfs.mofcom.gov.cn/aarticle/h/aw/201002/20100206778967.html>.

[125] UNCTAD Series on International Investment Policies for Development, South-South Cooperation in International Investment Arrangements (2005, United Nations) 37, available at <https://unctad.org/system/files/official-document/iteiit20053_en.pdf>.

[126] See Won Kidane, 'The China-Africa Factor in the Contemporary ICSID Legitimacy Debate' (2014) 35 University of Pennsylvania Journal of International Law 559–619.

[127] See Yongjie Li, UNCTAD WIF Statements by China, Toward Comprehensive and Balanced IIA regime, at World Investment Forum 2014 Investing in Sustainable Development, IIA Conference, October 16, 2014.

7.3.2 *Future of China–South Africa BIT*

The China–South Africa BIT has still not been terminated and incurs some challenges. The opposition party, Democratic Alliance (DA), denounced the South African government's move to adopt a double standard for European countries on the one hand and China on the other hand.[128] Natalie Greve further criticizes South Africa's partial and unwise decision because it only retains its agreements with China and other emerging countries in view of the huge gap in investment stock and inflow in South Africa among the EU, US, China, and other emerging economies. Thus, she suggested that South Africa's proposed *bill* should be revised according to the South Africa–China BIT.[129] Therefore, the future of the China–South Africa BIT also becomes the focus of debate.

7.3.2.1 Differentiating Stances on South–South BIT Vis-a-Vis South–North BIT

On the shift of South Africa' BIT policy, as introduced in the second part, several points should be noted. First, the *review* and its conclusion about the malpractices of BITs are based on and aimed at South Africa–Western country BITs (South–North BIT) rather than on experiences of those between South Africa and other developing nations (South–South BITs). South Africa's South–North BITs have no exception to national treatment provision and limit the South African government's scope for policy prerogatives. Second, the *Review* considers these South–North BITs to be full of imbalances between investors' rights and obligations and is likely to create impediments to South Africa's economic development. Third, the purpose of South Africa's new investment policy is "modernizing and strengthening the country's investment regime to ensure South Africa remained open to foreign direct investment, while preserving the sovereign right of the government to pursue policy objectives".[130] The key concepts are "modernization and balance" instead of abolishing all BITs. Furthermore, the fundamental purpose of this policy is to pursue the "constitutional-based transformation agenda". Fourth, the approach adopted by South Africa is to strengthen the regulatory power of the host state at the level of national law. However,

---

[128] See RDM News Wire, 'ANC rams anti-investment Bill through Committee, DA charges' (November 3, 2015), available at <http://m.polity.org.za/article/anc-rams-anti-investment-bill-through-committee-da-charges-2015-11-03>.

[129] See Natalie Greve, 'Changes to investment Bill a 'self-inflicted' economic blow' (October 27, 2015) Think Tank Warns, available at <http://www.engineeringnews.co.za/print-version/changes-to-investment-bill-a-self-inflicted-economic-blow-thinktank-warns-2015-10-27>; Anthea Jeffrey, 'Why's govt protecting Chinese investors but not Western ones?' (September 25, 2015), available at <http://www.politicsweb.co.za/news-and-analysis/ccc>.

[130] Report of a talk by Dr M de Gama, Department of Trade and Industry, Republic of South Africa (DTI)'s Legal International Trade and Investment Director, to the Mandela Institute's second annual economic law update in Johannesburg on October 21, 2013, available at <http://www.engineeringnews.co.za/article/sa-proceeds-with-termination-of-bilateral-investment-treaties-2013-10-21>.

the *Review*, the *Policy Statement,* and the *Speech* have never stated that South Africa will terminate all BITs.

It is clear that the South African government holds different attitudes toward China from European countries. President Zuma stated in 2012 that "We certainly are convinced that China's intention is different to that of Europe, which to date continue to attempt to influence African countries for their sole benefit".[131] Therefore, South Africa's policy shift aims at European countries instead of China and other developing countries.

7.3.2.2 BITs Irreplaceable by National Rule of Law

"One Size Fits All" Policy of Terminating All BITs Cannot Protect South African Overseas Investments

BIT is actually a "double-edged sword", and abrogating it may harm the benefit of foreign investment in the host state and in the long run affect the interests of overseas investors from the home state; in other words, it can protect foreign investors and protect overseas investors.

South Africa remains the most developed economy and the largest outward foreign direct investment (OFDI) exporting country in Africa.[132] South Africa invests more in the continent than China does.[133] According to one source, "The investments from South Africa in other African countries have the features of wide distribution, broad sectors, and huge scale".[134] However, many of these countries have weak rule of law,[135] and therefore, how can South Africa depend on these countries' weak rule of law to protect South African investors in these African countries?

Therefore, although some countries including India, Indonesia, Australia, Norway, US, Canada, Sweden, Brazil, and a number of South American Countries have also undertaken similar reviews to their BITs as South Africa,[136] the outcome

[131] Remarks by President J Zuma at the opening session of the 5th Forum on China-Africa Cooperation, Beijing, China, July 19, 2012, available at <http://www.thepresidency.gov.za/pebble.asp?relid=6486>.

[132] See Xingming Pan, South Africa: The Leader of the African Continent: An Analysis of Its Position of Strength and Comprehensive Influence (Shanghai Renmin Press, 2012) 164.

[133] See Wenjie Chen, David Dollar and Heiwei Tang, 'China's direct investment in Africa: Reality versus myth', September 3, 2015, available at <http://www.brookings.edu/blogs/africa-in-focus/posts/2015/09/03-China-africa-investment-trade-myth-chen-dollar-tang>.

[134] Chinese Academy of International Trade and Economic Cooperation, CIPA under Ministry of Commerce of the People's Republic of China, Economic and Commercial Counselor's Office of the Embassy of the People's Republic of China in the Republic of South Africa the Country (Region) Specific Guideline on Foreign Investment and Cooperation, South Africa (2014 edition) 9.

[135] The situations of the rule of law in most African countries can found at the USA Department of State Investment Climate Statement, available at <http://www.state.gov/e/eb/rls/othr/ics/>.

[136] See Department of Trade and Industry, Republic of South Africa Policy Statement: The South African Government's Approach to Future International Investment Treaties, at 1, available at <www.jadafa.co.za/LinkClick.aspx?fileticket=9A6eXZstR10%3D&tabid=432>; See UNCTAD,

is that except for a few Latin American countries, such as Bolivia, Ecuador, and Venezuela, which traditionally insist on the Calvo doctrine,[137] other countries have never stopped concluding BITs. India, as another example, still insists on practicing the international investment rule of law and wishes to carve out its own national policy space within the international investment regulatory regime. In addition, detailed investor-state arbitration clauses are included in the 2015 India Model BIT, although it is tailored to accommodate the Indian policy standpoint.[138] Indonesia is only going to "update, modernize, and balance its BITs".[139] Although the Australian government declares that it will not include investor-state arbitration in any future IIAs,[140] it should be noted that the Australia–China FTA includes detailed and codified investor-state arbitration clauses, while the Australia–Korea FTA, Australia–US FTA, and Australia–Japan EPA do not provide for investor-state arbitration.[141] Therefore, abolishing all BITs or investor-state arbitration clauses is not a global trend or a rational choice but an isolated position.

Insufficiency and Risk for National Rule of Law to Protect Foreign Investors

The cases related to South African investments that were expropriated in Lesotho and Zimbabwe have already proven this point. In a series of cases brought by Swissborough Diamond Mines (Pty) Ltd. Limited and others, the claimants had exhausted the available remedies through the courts of Lesotho, the courts of South Africa and the Southern African Development Community (SADC) Tribunal since 1991 but

World Investment Report 2015: Reforming International Investment Governance (2015, United Nations) 108, available at <https://unctad.org/system/files/official-document/wir2015_en.pdf>.

137 The Calvo doctrine was devised by Argentinean Jurist, Carlos Calvo. Its essence means applying national law and settling investment dispute before national courts and tribunals of the host state.

138 See UNCTAD, World Investment Report 2015: Reforming International Investment Governance (2015, United Nations), 109, available at <https://unctad.org/system/files/official-document/wir2015_en.pdf>; Draft Indian Model Bilateral Investment Treaty Text, article 14, available at <https://mygov.in/group-issue/draft-indian-model-bilateral-investment-treaty-text/>.

139 Leon E. Trakman & Sharma Kunal, 'Why is Indonesia Terminating Its Bilateral Investment Treaties?', East Asia Forum, September 20, 2014, available at <https://www.eastasiaforum.org/2014/09/20/why-is-indonesia-terminating-its-bilateral-investment-treaties/>.

140 Department of Foreign Affairs and Trade, Australian Government, Gillard Government Trade Policy Statement: Trading Our Way to More Jobs and Prosperity, Investor-State Dispute Resolution (April 2011), available at <www.dfat.gov.au/publications/trade/trading-our-way-to-more-jobs-and-prosperity.html>.

141 All these texts can be available at <http://investmentpolicyhub.unctad.org/IIA/CountryOtherIias/11#iiaInnerMenu>.

could not obtain relief.[142] Finally, they filed the case with United Nations Commission on International Trade Law (UNCITRAL) arbitration in 2013.[143] The facts of the case were that some South African farmers' land had been expropriated by the Zimbabwe government. However, the Zimbabwe Constitutional Amendment Act of 2005 permits its government to confiscate or expropriate private farms without any compensation and forbids its courts to give awards to any foreign investor's claim.[144] Therefore, some claimants have to resort to diplomatic protection from their home state with little success, as diplomatic protection is often an inefficient and judicial review of diplomatic protection is limited.[145] South Africa and Zimbabwe entered a BIT that was signed on November 27, 2009 and ratified on September 15, 2010.[146] Under Article 7 of the BIT, in the event of any legal dispute between an investor of one party and the other party relating to an investment of the former, the investor may choose to file it with the courts of the host state or ICSID arbitration tribunal or UNCITRAL ad hoc arbitration tribunal, and "the award made shall be final and binding on the parties to the dispute and shall be executed according to the applicable domestic law". It was only because the dispute arose before the conclusion of South Africa–Zimbabwe BIT that this avenue for ISDS was made unavailable to the investor. In Besserglik v. Mozambique, which was initiated by South African investors in 2014 under the South Africa–Mozambique BIT, the parties disagreed with each other over whether the BIT had entered into force. The tribunal is also "not persuaded by the evidence on the record that it can conclude the BIT is in force".[147] Therefore, the tribunal finally upheld the defendant's claim that the BIT had not entered into force, and it had no jurisdiction over the case; thus investors' rights could not be protected through the ISDS mechanism under the South Africa–Mozambique BIT. This rare case also remarkably shows the power of a BIT in force that can award investor *locus standi* at an international arbitral tribunal.

[142] SADC Tribunal Case No. SADC (T) 04/2009). The proceedings were aborted due to the suspension of the SADC Tribunal. See Rupel Oliver C, 'SADC Environmental Law and the Promotion of Sustainable Development' (2012) 2 SADC Law Journal 246 at 268. For the last judgment issued by the South African Supreme Court of Appeal, the case is reported as Van Zyl v. Government of RSA [2007] SCA 109 (RSA), available at <http://www.justice.gov.za/sca/judgments%5Csca_2007/sca07-109.pdf>.

[143] See Swissbourgh Diamond Mines (Pty) Limited and others v. The Kingdom of Lesotho, UNCITRAL, PCA Case No. 2013-29 (First Case), an introduction to the case is available at <http://www.italaw.com/cases/2256>.

[144] Zimbabwe Constitutional Amendment Act (No.17), 2005, section 2(2), available at <http://hrlibrary.umn.edu/research/Act%202005-05%20Constitution%20of%20Zimbabwe%20Amendment%20(No.%2017).pdf>.

[145] See, e.g., The Government of the Republic of South Africa v. Von Abo (283/10) [2011] ZASCA 65 (April 4, 2011), available at <http://www.saflii.org/za/cases/ZASCA/2011/65.html>.

[146] See Agreement between the Government of the Republic of South Africa and the Government of the Republic of Zimbabwe, available at <http://investmentpolicyhub.unctad.org/Download/TreatyFile/2281>.

[147] See Oded Besserglik v. Republic of Mozambique, ICSID Case No. ARB(AF)14/2, award dated October 28, 2019, para. 396.

International investment is a transnational practice beyond the border of a country, and only national law regulations, including those of the host state and the home state, are inadequate.

It is also dangerous for the host state to put all investment issues, including those related to foreign investment, under national law, especially when national law is highly free and with high protection, for instance, with matters concerning the international arbitration clause. This is mainly because national law is a common commitment to all investors in the world, unlike BIT, which is only a specific and relative commitment.

Future of the China–South Africa BIT

According to the "Duration, Termination and Amendment" clause in the China–South Africa BIT, the period of validity of the BIT is ten years, and it shall continue in force if either Contracting Party fails to give a written notice to the other Contracting Party to terminate it one year before the expiration of the period of validity. However, after the expiration of the initial ten-year period, either Contracting Party may at any time thereafter terminate the BIT by giving at least one year's written notice to the other Contracting Party. The "survival period" of the BIT to investments made prior to the date of termination is ten years. The BIT may also be amended by a negotiated agreement between the Contracting Parties, and any such amendment shall come into force by exchange of notices between them. Therefore, it is the prerogative of both countries to give notice of termination and to request an amendment for 22 years that have passed from the date of concluding the China–South Africa BIT.[148] However, terminating the China–South Africa BIT once for all is not the optimal choice.

It is particularly important to mention that, according to the survey above, compared with other treaties between South Africa and other countries, the China–South Africa BIT is a more balanced BIT. While investors enjoy the same protection and treatment standard, at the same time, the limitation on FET, the exception of national treatment, and other various exceptions can also guarantee the policy space of the host state. In fact, the exception of national treatment only favors South Africa instead of China.[149] In terms of international investment arbitration, only ad hoc arbitration is available, and *either Party* to the dispute shall be entitled to file the case.[150] Therefore, the China–South Africa BIT is not so ambitious, and the rights and obligations of the investors and the host State are basically in a state of balance. The China–South African BIT will also not impede the South African government's ability to take measures to implement black economic empowerment policies and

---

[148] See China-South Africa BIT, article 12, available at <http://tfs.mofcom.gov.cn/aarticle/h/aw/201002/20100206778967.html>. In fact, among China-Africa BITs, only the BITs with South Africa (1997), Mauritius (1995), Nigeria (2001), Benin (2004), Uganda (2004), Equatorial Guinea (2005) and Mali (2009) include amendment clause.

[149] China-South-Africa BIT, article 3.3.

[150] China-South-Africa BIT, articles 9.2, 9.3.

redress apartheid-induced inequalities. Therefore, the China–South Africa BIT is feasible.

As mentioned above, the duration of the China–South Africa BIT is ten years and continues to be in force without a termination notice. However, in the era in which economic globalization is developing at an extremely rapid pace, BIT will fall behind the times if it cannot be adjusted and improved on time. Thus, it is also understandable to renegotiate the China--South Africa BIT to fit China's and South Africa's realities and national conditions.

If China and South Africa want to update their BIT, a clear consensus should be reached over their BIT. On the one hand, the fundamental purpose of the South African investment policy is to eliminate obstacles to pursuing its public policy and to emphasize the rebalance of the investor's rights and obligations as a reasonable concern. On the other hand, the inclusion of considerations for environmental protection and sustainable development in the China–South Africa BIT is consistent with the trend of IIAs, the development of international environmental law, and the UN SDGs. The stress of the policy space of the host state, interest balance, and sustainable development in a BIT is beyond doubt beneficial to both China's interest as a host state and China's overseas investment in the long run. Due to the reality of the existing China–South Africa BIT, the attitude of South Africa and the innovation of China's BITs, updating China–South Africa BITs is not infeasible.

When discussing the prospects of a new generation of investment policies, the World Investment Report 2012: Toward a New Generation of Investment Policies, stresses responsible investment and drafts "sustainable-development-friendly agreements",[151] and thus international investment policy challenges must be addressed by China and South Africa at three levels:

> ...The overall objective is to ensure coherence between IIAs and sustainable development needs. In the detailed design of provisions in investment agreements between countries, policymakers need to incorporate sustainable development considerations, addressing concerns related to policy space, balanced rights and obligations of States and investors, and effective investment promotion.[152]

As far as the new China–South Africa BIT is concerned, the preamble should emphasize sustainable development, the improvement of the people's livelihood, respect for sovereignty, and strife for common development on the basis of equality and mutual benefits. In fact, these objectives have been addressed in China's statement on "China–Africa Economic and Trade Cooperation".[153] Thus, they are not challenging to China and South Africa.

---

[151] See UNCTAD, World Investment Report 2012: Toward a New Generation of Investment Policies, (2012, United Nations) 161–162, available at <http://unctad.org/en/PublicationsLibrary/wir2012_embargoed_en.pdf>.

[152] UNCTAD, World Investment Report 2012: Toward a New Generation of Investment Policies (2012, United Nations), xxix, available at <http://unctad.org/en/PublicationsLibrary/wir2012_embargoed_en.pdf>.

[153] See Information Office of the State Council, the People's Republic of China China-Africa Economic and Trade Cooperation (December 2010).

Furthermore, the specific provisions should embody the newest development in international investment rulemaking. For example, public policy concerns should be reflected in the BIT, and corporate social responsibilities should be encouraged to be undertaken; even if adopting soft law form, it also represents the value orientation of the contracting parties. However, the obligation imposed on investors should not become an investment barrier. To achieve the balance between investment protection and policy objectives, exceptions to general treaty provisions still need to be used, such as the exception of MFN treatment, the exception of national treatment, exception of expropriation, taxation exception, general exceptions (including prudential measures for financial services and protection of culture, protection of human health and nature resources), and national security exception.[154]

China is a developing country,[155] and South Africa also brands itself as a developing country at present. Therefore, South–South cooperation and sovereignty equality are the basic principles of mutual international relations that should be obeyed by China and South Africa. In addition, it should be noted that both China and South Africa are experiencing a "hybrid identity" as capital-exporting and importing countries, which should provide an objective basis for the introduction of a balanced BIT.

South Africa, as the largest and dominant member state, in effect plays a critical role in SADC. The 2012 SADC Model BIT recognizes that sustainable development requires the fulfillment of the economic, social, and environmental pillars that are embedded within the concept, seeks to overall balance rights and obligations of the investor, the host state, and the home state, and absorbs the new elements of international investment law.[156] Therefore, the 2012 SADC Model BIT can be a reference for the future China–South Africa BIT.

In addition, South Africa's attitudes and stances should also be highly in line with UNCTAD's investment policy, reflected in the World Investment Report 2012: Toward a New Generation of Investment Policies. In particular, its fourth part, the Investment Policy Framework for Sustainable Development (IPFSD), consists of (i) a set of core principles for foreign investment policymaking, (ii) guidelines for investment policies at the national level, and (iii) options for the design and use of IIAs.[157] The report points out that "a new generation of investment policies is emerging, as governments pursue a broader and more intricate development policy

---

[154] See Agreement between the Government of Canada and the Government of the People's Republic of China for the Promotion and Reciprocal Protection of Investments, articles 5.3, 8, 10, ANNEX B.10, 14, 33, ANNEX D.34, available at <http://www.international.gc.ca/trade-agreements-accords-commerciaux/agr-acc/fipa-apie/china-text-chine.aspx?lang=en&view=d>.

[155] About the status of China in detail, see An Chen & E-Nuo Gu, 'Should 'the Perspective of South-North Contradictions' Be 'Abandoned'?—Focusing on '2012 Sino-Canada BIT' (2013) 14(2) the Journal of World Investment & Trade 320, 322–5.

[156] See Southern African Development Community, SADC Model Bilateral Investment Treaty Template with Commentary (July 2012), available at <http://www.iisd.org/itn/wp-content/uploads/2012/10/SADC-Model-BIT-Template-Final.pdf>.

[157] See UNCTAD, Investment Policy Framework for Sustainable Development (2012), xxiv, available at <http://unctad.org/en/PublicationsLibrary/webdiaepcb2012d6_en.pdf>.

agenda, while building or maintaining a generally favorable investment climate", and further, "new generation investment policies place inclusive growth and sustainable development at the heart of efforts to attract and benefit from investment".[158] In effect, the wording "inclusive growth and sustainable development" is even literally quoted by Rob Davies in his *speech*.

In sum, there are two different kinds of attitudes toward BITs: the Calvo doctrine and reformism. This research upholds reformism, in doing so it has confidence in the international investment law regime and opposes emerging investment protectionism. The BIT is the embodiment of international rule of law, including resorting to international investment law in investment dispute settlement, the conduct of the state and investor, and the crystallization of human wisdom, and should be supported and not be given up only on the basis of its defects or flaws. Certainly, it should be a "good law". The concept that should be changed is that BITs are only the "amulet" of investors from developed countries. Although the BIT from its origin is meant to protect investors coming from the North, it has already become an important tool for South–South cooperation, and 30% of all BITs in the world are South–South BITs. Emerging market countries such as China and South Africa should not completely avoid the existing market-oriented international economic order but continually solve its impartiality problem through reformism.

Thus, the prospect of a China–South Africa BIT should entrench the new development of the international investment legal framework, especially sustainable development, and respect the policy space of the host state. It should be noted that the Chinese government declared that "China, as one member of the developing countries, desires to carry out extensive and in-depth cooperation with southern countries in economy, science and technology, education and culture, and so on, on the grounds of some principles such as equality and mutual benefit, pursuing practical results, taking various forms, and promoting common development".[159] China and African countries proclaimed to establish a new type of strategic partnership featuring economic win–win cooperation.[160] Should China and South Africa consider renegotiating their BIT, it will guarantee that the China–South Africa BIT will go forward in a positive direction.

China and South Africa not only have a shared colonial history, but also have experienced the rise and development of the market economy almost at the same time, so they have similar experiences and practices. A comprehensive strategic partnership was established between the two countries in 2010, and this two-way investment and cooperation increased in scale and expanded to mineral, energy, infrastructure, and

---

[158] UNCTAD, Investment Policy Framework for Sustainable Development (2012), xii, available at <http://unctad.org/en/PublicationsLibrary/webdiaepcb2012d6_en.pdf>.

[159] See 'China's Position on South-South Cooperation', available at <http://www.fmprc.gov.cn/chn/pds/ziliao/tytj/zcwj/t3468.htm>.

[160] See 'Declaration of the Beijing Summit of the Forum on China-Africa Cooperation' (November 5, 2006), available at <http://www.fmprc.gov.cn/eng/zxxx/t279852.htm>.

other fields.[161] Thus, it is more possible that they can reach a consensus on their BIT. Sustainable investment between China and South Africa cannot be sustained without proper BIT and other international legal arrangements, which can govern and regulate the investment relation between China and South Africa and promote their normal development. Envisioning the future of the China–South Africa BIT is an important theoretical and practical issue faced by the two countries in the field of international investment law.

7.4 Taking the Investment Issue in African Regional Economic Integration Seriously

By removing tariff barriers to intra-African trade as well as reducing non-tariff barriers, promoting and facilitating intra-African investment, and thus improving the climate for intra-African trade and investment, Africa is expected to attract global multinational corporations and draw more Chinese investors to bring their investments to Africa. Africa's economic integration is, therefore, very important for Africa's development.

Africa's economic integration in the field of investment law is very obvious, especially when WTO law and international investment law seem to be surrounded by the appeal for reform, and regional and bilateral investment treaties show a trend of slow development. Despite the fact that the international rule of law has been challenged and suspected, the development of regional investment law in Africa is particularly outstanding, to the extent that some scholars put forward the idea of "Africanization" of international investment law.[162] Their intention is to show that although the international investment law in other regions of the world is stagnant, its development in the African region is rapid and unique. Regional economic integration in Africa shows the rise of regional investment treaties and hints at the "progressive abandonment of the traditional bilateral approach".[163] The significance of African regional integration in investment agreements is more prominent if this is the case.

In recent years, the salient development of regional investment law in Africa has been mainly manifested in two aspects. One is the adoption of the Draft PAIC, the first

[161] The Department of African Affairs, Ministry of Foreign Affairs of the People's Republic of China, 'Beijing Declaration on Comprehensive Strategic Partnership between China and South Africa' (August 25, 2010) Renmin Daily (Beijing).

[162] See Makane Moïse Mbengue and Stefanie Schacherer, 'The 'Africanization' of International Investment Law: The Pan-African Investment Code and the Reform of the International Investment Regime' (2017)18(3) The Journal of World Investment & Trade 414–448.

[163] See Denters Erik and Gazzini Tarcisio, 'The Role of African Regional Organizations in the Promotion and Protection of Foreign Investment' (2017)18(3) The Journal of World Investment & Trade 449–492.

investment code on the African continent as the result of African countries' efforts to create a unified regional investment law for Africa, under the AU in 2016.[164]

The other is the entry into force of the AfCFTA. In June 2015, the African Union launched negotiations on the Continental Free Trade Area (CFTA), and on March 21, 2018, 44 African countries signed the AfCFTA in Rwanda, which entered into force on May 30, 2019.[165] Thus, the CFTA was founded and has become the largest FTZ since the establishment of the world trade organization.

Although the 2016 PAIC is only a draft model investment treaty in nature, as the outcome that reflects the consensus of the AU Member States., its provisions are expected to become a model basis for the negotiation of the investment protocol at the second stage of the CFTA negotiations,[166] thus the 2016 PAIC, *mutatis mutandis*, may become AfCFTA's investment protocol. Moreover, we can even imagine that, in the future, the BITs within AU member states are canceled, and the AU may begin to independently sign BITs with countries outside the continent on behalf of African countries.

In other words, the strong trend of economic integration on the African continent shows that we must attach importance to its relationship with the protection and sustainability of Chinese investments in Africa. African regional investment law is an important part of the economic integration of the African continent, and the ideological source and motivation of African regional integration is Pan-Africanism. Pan-Africanism is the spiritual wealth of Africa and determines the development direction of Africa. It is determined that China and Chinese investors must attach importance to African regional economic integration under the guidance of Pan-Africanism.

7.4.1 Outstanding Progress of Investment Law in African Regional Integration

Consistent with the main problem in the process of African integration, that is, actions cannot be carried out all the time, and the investment legal instruments of regional economic integration either fail to come into force or remain stagnant after entering into force; thus they are unable to play their due roles.

For example, the COMESA–SADC–EAC Tripartite Free Trade Area (TFTA), which involves investment issues, was launched in 2011 between COMESA, SADC,

---

[164] See African Union Commission, Economic Affairs Department, Draft Pan-African Investment Code, Draft, December 2016, available at <https://au.int/sites/default/files/documents/32844-doc-draft_pan-african_investment_code_december_2016_en.pdf>.

[165] See African Union, Agreement Establishing the African Continental Free Trade Area, September 16, 2019, available at <https://au.int/en/treaties/agreement-establishing-african-continental-free-trade-area>.

[166] See Makane Moïse Mbengue & Stefanie Schacherer, 'The 'Africanization' of International Investment Law: The Pan-African Investment Code and the Reform of the International Investment Regime' (2017)18(3) The Journal of World Investment & Trade 414–448, 446.

and EAC and was signed on June 10, 2015. This agreement was originally planned to enter into force on April 30, 2019, but among the 22 member states that signed the agreement, only Uganda, Kenya, Egypt, and South Africa ratified the agreement, which led this regional economic integration effort to a stand still.

The Final Communique at the 1998 COMESA Summit proposed the establishment of a COMESA Common Investment Area, and the modernized Investment Agreement for the COMESA Common Investment Area was signed at the 2007 COMESA Summit. However, this investment agreement has not been approved by at least 6 member states and has not yet entered into force, which has led to the failure of the ideal of further facilitating and promoting investment within COMESA. In the identical predicament with the 2007 COMESA Investment Agreement, the Arab Maghreb Union Investment Agreement signed on July 23, 1990, has not yet entered into force until now.

Furthermore, even though some treaties and mechanisms have entered into force and have already been in operation, some member states have decided to withdraw from or urge to modify the existing investment agreement in the face of a ruling against them due to the lack of contractual spirit. For example, with regard to the SADC Protocol on Finance and Investment, which was signed on August 18, 2006, and entered into force on April 16, 2010, and the SADC Tribunal, when Zimbabwe failed in two investment arbitration cases, Zimbabwe declared that the state would not comply with SADC investment arbitration rulings.

In a series of cases caused by land reform in Zimbabwe, Zimbabwe refused to comply with the decisions made by SADC Tribunal after losing the cases,[167] which led to the paralysis of the SADC Tribunal to date. Although South Africa had never been a defendant before the SADC Tribunal, it enacted relevant municipal law in addition to terminating most of its BITs, which implies a fundamental negation of the related provisions of the SADC Protocol on Finance and Investment.[168]

In summary, Annex 1 of the SADC Protocol on Finance and Investment is of great concern to SADC member States, particularly South Africa, Zimbabwe, Lesotho, and Namibia, which have experienced investor-state disputes based on Annex 1 of the SADC Protocol on Finance and Investment. These concerns include the cost of arbitration, transparency, inconsistency in the outcome of awards, and forum shopping. In the case of substantive clauses, they were concerned that the expropriation clause and FET clause would give the arbitral tribunal excessive discretion and lead to excessive protection of investors. As a result, SADC members decided to amend Annex 1 of the SADC Protocol on Finance and Investment, which provided for the jurisdiction of the SADC Tribunal. SADC member states adopted amendments to the SADC Protocol on Finance and Investment at the 36th SADC Summit held in

167 See Mike Campbell (Pvt) Limited v. The Republic of Zimbabwe (Southern African Development Community Tribunal, November 28, 2008); Mike Campbell (Pvt) Limited v. The Republic of Zimbabwe (Southern African Development Community Tribunal, December 13, 2007); Campbell and Another v. Republic of Zimbabwe (SADC (T) 03/2009) [2009] SADCT 1 (June 5, 2009).

168 See Protection of Investment Act, 2015, Act No. 22 of 2015, Government Gazette, Republic of South Africa, Vol. 606 Cape Town, December 15, 2015, No. 39514, available at <https://www.gov.za/sites/default/files/gcis_document/201512/39514act22of2015protectionofinvestmentact.pdf>.

Swaziland in August 2016. In particular, the investor-state arbitration clause was excluded from amended Annex 1 of the SADC Protocol on Finance and Investment. Nevertheless, the amended Annex 1 of SADC Protocol on Finance and Investment has not yet been ratified by SADC member states.[169]

The 2012 SADC Model BIT is available for SADC member states to select all or part of their provisions when concluding their BITs or as guidance for SADC member states to negotiate their BITs. The 2012 SADC Model BIT is, however, not legally binding. In cases where South Africa, a key member of SADC, is attempting to put an end to existing BITs, the significance of the 2012 SADC Model BIT has also been greatly reduced. Moreover, ironically, SADC member states have largely failed to follow the recommendations of the 2012 SADC Model BIT when they sign their BITs.[170] Similarly, the East African Model Investment Code of EAC is equally non-legally binding on its member States but merely provides a reference for its Member States when they develop investment policies and laws.

While the achievements of previous efforts at regional economic integration in Africa cannot be denied, it is undeniable that progress in African regional economic integration has not gone off smoothly. African states have signed many agreements related to investment, but very few have been ratified and entered into force. Moreover, even if some had entered into force, they came to a premature end because of the damage to the interests of specific states in their implementation process, the lack of political will for specific states, and disregard for the fulfillment of international commitments. Legal instruments that are not legally binding are more symbolic. With regard to legal instruments in force, there may be overlapping rights and obligations and confusion of applicable law resulting from the conclusion of two or more regional investment agreements among the same states, which will have a negative impact on African integration[171] and affect the validity of many legal instruments.

Nevertheless, regional economic integration in Africa is moving in the desired direction, and various regional integration organizations are playing a role in influencing and promoting regional economies to varying degrees. In particular, the entry into force of the AfCFTA on May 30, 2019, marks substantial progress in regional economic integration in Africa. Therefore, China and Chinese investors cannot ignore the process and progress of regional economic integration in Africa and should actively adapt to and make use of it.

---

[169] See Lawrence Ngobeni & Babatunde Fagbayibo, 'The Investor-State Dispute Resolution Forum under the SADC Protocol on Finance and Investment: Challenges and Opportunities for Effective Harmonisation' (2015)19 Law, Democracy & Development 175, 191.

[170] See United Nations, Economic Commission for Africa, Investment Policy and Bilateral Investment Treaty in Africa: Implication for Regional Integration, 2016, 31, available at <https://repository.uneca.org/bitstream/handle/10855/23035/b11559299.pdf?sequence=1&isAllowed=y>.

[171] See Makane Moïse Mbengue and Stefanie Schacherer, 'The "Africanization" of International Investment Law: The Pan-African Investment Code and the Reform of the International Investment Regime' (2017)18 Journal of World Investment & Trade 414–448, 416–418.

7.4.2 Pan-Africanism as a Fundamental Driving Force of African Regional Integration

7.4.2.1 The Ideological Connotation of Well-Established Pan-African Thought

Pan-Africanism is rich in content, including but not limited to: All Africans share a common destiny and must work together; Africa must be ruled by Africans, and any form of foreign domination, influence, and colonialism must be completely eliminated; and in order to achieve the unity of the black race and the total destruction of colonialism, the African people must re-establish their history, language, and culture; and after the end of colonial rule in Africa, all African societies must be radically transformed in economic, social, and political aspects.[172]

Pan-Africanism is entrusted with different historical tasks and points of focus in different historical periods, but anti-colonialism is the core thought of Pan-Africanism and has always been associated with anti-colonialism. In the past colonial period, its aim was to oppose colonialism from imperialist countries. With the influence of Pan-Africanism, African colonies became independent one after another after World War II, and today, both in organizational structure and in legal norms, Pan-Africanism has been increasingly developed when guiding the cause of anti-neo-colonialism in Africa. Since the political independence of African countries, former Western colonialists have continued to gain and maintain their influence over the former African colonial States and to achieve their own interests through the economic or political plundering, exploitation, and domination of those former colonial states in Africa. African countries were theoretically independent, but in practice, their economic systems and thus their political policies were still dominated by the former colonists more or less.[173]

With the acceleration and expansion of African integration, Pan-Africanism has reached a new stage, namely, the new Pan-Africanism in the context of globalization, which started with the establishment of the AU in July 2002.[174] The African Union (AU) replaced the Organization of African Unity (OAU), which was established in 1963; indeed, it was a major paradigm shift in the process of continental integration, as the AU demonstrated an intention of supranationalism. As a legal instrument with a supranationalism approach, the AU 2063 Agenda adopted in 2015 refers to the need for an integrated, unified, peaceful, sovereign, independent, self-confident and self-reliant continent, and the steps toward African integration will include the establishment of a continental government by 2030, ensuring the free

---

[172] See Bangzuo Wang, Dictionary of Political Science (Shanghai Dictionary Publishing House, 2009) 619.

[173] See Kwame Nkrumah, 'Neo-colonialism: the last stage of imperialism' (1965) NY: International Publishers, 1.

[174] See Michael Amoah, The New Pan-Africanism: Globalism and the Nation State in Africa (Bloomsbury Publishing, 2019).

movement of people, capital, goods and services, building world-class infrastructure, and so on.[175] The new Pan-Africanism emphasizes unity and self-reliance, especially through the economic integration, of the African continent, to achieve the economic and subsequent political mightiness of African countries. Therefore, completely breaking themselves away from neo-colonialism is the main objective of the current new Pan-Africanism. Economic cooperation in Africa was upgraded in 2018 with the establishment of CFTA, which takes Pan-Africanism to a new level and is a milestone in the African integration process.

7.4.2.2 Objective Historical Reasons for Pan-Africanism

The emergence of Pan-Africanism objectively originates from the idea of small African countries standing in solidarity in great numbers, and it is, therefore, more difficult for them to stand individually on their own feet and become strong. This reality must be traced back to the colonial division in history. The 1885 Congo Conference, also known as the Berlin or West Africa Conference, marks the official beginning of dividing Africa by Western colonists. The General Act of the Berlin Conference on West Africa was signed by Western countries under the leadership of the Reich, and as an important treaty in the process of colonization in Africa, it provided for the principle of effectivity (effective occupation) for Western states to set up colonies in Africa.[176] Politically, as a conference to partition the spheres of influence in Africa, 14 countries, including the US, Germany, Britain, France, and Portugal, worked together to fabricate a new map of Africa. A source states that "By 1902, 90% of all the land that makes up Africa was under European control".[177] After World War II, African countries became independent, but the former colonists arbitrarily demarcated African borders to create border problems for numerous small African countries and made it difficult for these countries to become independent, both economically and politically.

Historical reasons have led to high fragmentation and isolation of African markets, with less trade and investment within African countries and mainly depending on their respective external economic ties with Europe and the US. According to the *African Economic Outlook 2019*, there are 16 landlocked countries in Africa, which are much more fragmented than other continents, and the key to enhancing global competitiveness for these small African countries is to deepen the market integration of commodities, infrastructure services, and key factors of production (labor and

---

[175] See African Union Commission, Agenda 2063: The Africa We Want, September 2015, Popular version, available at <https://au.int/en/agenda2063/overview>.

[176] The General Act of the Berlin Conference on West Africa, Berlin, February 26, 1885, see Details of the 1885 Berlin Conference, available at <https://en.wikipedia.org/wiki/Berlin_Conference>.

[177] See The Berlin Conference of 1884–85 (The General Act of the Berlin Conference), available at <https://originalpeople.org/berlin-conference-1884-85/>.

capital); then, African countries can enhance their ability to negotiate as a whole with external economies.[178]

7.4.2.3 Birth and Development of Pan-Africanism

Based on Africa's colonial history,[179] the ideas and activities of Pan-Africanism have a long history, dating back to the Pan-African Conference held in London in 1900. The content of Pan-Africanism has been evolving. Initially, it aimed at opposing racial discrimination against blacks by Western colonists. However, the 1945 (Manchester) Declaration of the General Assembly set out the fighting slogan required to unite all the colonies and oppressed peoples of the world and applied Pan-Africanism for the decolonization of the African continent, thus enabling Pan-Africanism to achieve a significant development from the opposition to racial discrimination to the opposition to colonialism. Furthermore, the 1974 (Dar es Salaam) Declaration of the General Assembly states that the Pan-Africanism movement must, in essence, be an incentive to liberate the colonial peoples and the oppressed peoples and classes.[180] In conclusion, the series of Congresses aimed at addressing a range of issues arising from the colonial consequences faced by African countries, and the content of Pan-Africanism has evolved with the times.

The anti-colonialism significance of Pan-Africanism and its importance to Africa has always been emphasized by African leaders. Kwame Nkrumah, Ghana's first president, who was the most important advocate of Pan-Africanism, advocated Pan-Africanism throughout his life and even called upon unification of Africa in a non-violent way and the creation of the United States of Africa to liberate Africa, which was firmly controlled by colonialism and imperialism.[181] The Pan-Africanism Kwame Nkrumah pursued, also known as *Nkrumahism*, argued that the balkanization of Africa is only for the benefit of capitalism, thus ensuring that no independent African country has the power to fight against neo-colonialism.[182] The purpose of Pan-Africanism is to liberate the politics and economy of Africa, that is, fight against neo-colonialism, and the means of liberating African politics and economy or anti-neo-colonialism is to unify Africa.[183] Julius Mwalimu Nyerere, one of the founders of the Organization of African Unity, once expressed that "[w]ithout unity, there is no future for Africa", and in 1997, he further pointed out that unification would not

[178] See Group, African Development Bank Group, African Economic Outlook 2019, at 78, available at <https://www.afdb.org/fileadmin/uploads/afdb/Documents/Publications/2019AEO/AEO_2019-EN.pdf>.

[179] See Abdulqawi A. Yusuf, Pan-Africanism and International Law (Brill, 2015) 20–32.

[180] See Pan-African Congress, available at <https://en.wikipedia.org/wiki/Pan-African_Congress>.

[181] See Michael W. Williams, 'Nkrumahism as an ideological embodiment of leftist thought within the African World' (1984)15(1) Journal of Black Studies 117–134, 121.

[182] See Nkrumah, K. Neo-colonialism: the last stage of imperialism. New York, NY: International Publishers, 1965, 1–14, 25.

[183] See Nkrumah, K. Neo-colonialism: the last stage of imperialism. New York, NY: International Publishers, 1965, 253.

enrich Africa and its people, but it would make it difficult for Africa to be ignored and humiliated.[184]

The Pan-Africanism ideology is deeply rooted in Africa and dominates the direction of African development. Today, some famous scholars in Africa are still advocating and promoting Pan-Africanism and working for the realization of Pan-Africanism.[185]

Guided by Pan-Africanism, African countries are still pursuing the dream of the entire continent as a whole through various methods, including regional integration, which is the practice of Pan-Africanism and the practice of anti-neo-colonialism. After a long exploration, African scholars realized that addressing maladies such as corruption, disease, poverty, and war that have lingered on in Africa must depend on trade, investment, and financial development rather than foreign aid.[186] African economic integration measures are precisely carried out by aiming at trade, investment, and finance.

Pan-Africanism can be understood as an important driving force behind the prevailing economic integration organizations and trends in Africa, and Pan-Africanism is also the driving force behind the development of investment law in African regional economic integration. Africa has always been treated as a whole but should not be considered a group of countries with similar diseases, poverty, corruption, and war problems. Rather, Africa should be regarded as in the process of continuous prosperity by moving toward economic integration and even unification.

7.4.3 Possibility of Applying African Regional Integration Instruments to Chinese Investments

In general, the liberalization of trade and investment is the economic source of emergence and sustainable development of regional economic integration. Because economic integration organizations are exclusive, they have a trade-transfer effect and therefore attract capital transfers from non-member countries to member countries. Promoting intra-regional trade and attracting extra-regional investment are also

---

[184] See Arthur Chatora, 10 quotes from Julius 'Mwalimu' Nyerere, October 14, 2015, available at <https://thisisafrica.me/10-quotes-from-julius-mwalimu-nyerere/>; Julius Nyerere: Without unity, there is no future for Africa (1997)', New African Magazine, May 3, 2013, available at <http://newafricanmagazine.com/nyerere-without-unity-there-is-no-future-for-africa/>.

[185] See Babatunde Fagbayibo, 'Some Thoughts on Centring Pan-African Epistemic in the Teaching of Public International Law in African Universities' (2019) 21(2) International Community Law Review 170–189; Babatunde Fagbayibo, 'Promoting the Rule of Law through the Principle of Subsidiarity in the African Union: A Critical Perspective' (2019) 8(1) Global Journal of Comparative Law 27–51; Michael Amoah, The New Pan-Africanism: Globalism and the Nation State in Africa (Bloomsbury Publishing, 2019); Babatunde Fagbayibo, 'Nkrumahism, Agenda 2063, and the Role of Intergovernmental Institutions in Fast-tracking Continental Unity' (2018) 53(4) Journal of Asian and African Studies 629–642.

[186] See Dambisa Moyo, Dead Aid: Why Aid Is Not Working and How There Is a Better Way for Africa, Chaps. 6, 8 and 9 (Farrar, Straus and Giroux, 2009).

the purposes of establishing regional economic integration organizations. Therefore, investment within regional economic integration organizations should also apply to investments from non-member countries outside the region to attract investment from outside the region. However, the specific applicability of investment provisions in the region to investments originating from outside the region also depends on how the specific agreement is provided, in particular on how it defines an "investor".

The SADC Protocol on Finance and Investment, which was signed in 2006 and entered into force in 2010, provides investment cooperation in Annex 1, which covers all matters contained in a typical BIT, in particular the protection of investments in any state party from uncompensated expropriation. While Annex 1 does not specify whether this guarantee applies to investments from third countries that are not members of the SADC, it seems that, in light of the fact that non-member investments and investors are not explicitly excluded in its definition for investments and investors, the guarantee against uncompensated expropriation should also apply to investments in SADC member states from non-SADC member states. However, this is not a presumption easy to be established in view of the nature and purpose of regional economic integration. However, in any way, if a Chinese investor invests in one SADC member country and then reinvests in another SADC member state, the relevant provisions of Annex 1 of the SADC Protocol on Finance and Investment shall apply to the investor and its investment.

In contrast, the 2007 COMESA Investment Agreement is clearer because it provides the following:

" 'COMESA investor' means:

(i) a natural person of a Member State; or
(ii) a juridical person of a Member State,

making an investment in another Member State, in accordance with the laws and regulations of the Member State in which the investment is made. For the purposes of this definition:

For purposes of the definition of COMESA investor:

(i) 'Natural person' means a person having citizenship of a Member State in accordance with its applicable laws and regulations; and
(ii) 'Juridical person' means any legal entity duly constituted or otherwise organised under the applicable laws and regulations of a Member State provided that a juridical person owned or controlled by foreign nationals shall not qualify as a COMESA investor unless it maintains substantial business activity in the Member State in which it is duly constituted or organised.

The concept of 'substantial business activity' requires an overall examination, on a case-by-case basis, of all the circumstances, including inter alia:

(a) the amount of investment brought into the country;
(b) the number of jobs created;
(c) its effect on the local community; and

(d) the length of time the business has been in operation."[187]

Therefore, the "legal entity duly constituted or otherwise organised under the applicable laws and regulations of a Member State" of COMESA, but owned or controlled by Chinese, can be a qualified investor, and the 2007 COMESA Investment Agreement is applicable to this kind of investor. In fact, it is to say that this agreement applies to Chinese investors' reinvestments from one COMESA Member State to another Member State if they conform to the provided requirements.

In addition, the 2008 ECOWAS Supplementary Act on Investments provides that "'investor' is any individual or company of any Member State of ECOWAS or a company that *has invested or is making an investment in the territory of a Member State*", and "'company' means any corporate entity constituted or organized under the applicable law of any ECOWAS Member State, whether or not for profit, and whether privately or governmentally owned or controlled".[188] It can be seen that the relevant provisions are not very clear. Some scholars have suggested that, in some cases, the Supplementary Act on Investments may apply to non-ECOWAS investors.[189] If this is the case, Chinese investors can protect their rights before the ECOWAS Court of Justice under the Supplementary Act on Investments.

In contrast, Annex 14-D of the USMCA titled "Mexico-United States Investment Disputes" provides that "claimant means an investor of an Annex Party that is a party to a qualifying investment dispute, excluding an investor that is owned or controlled by a person of a non-Annex Party that, on the date of signature of this Agreement, the other Annex Party has determined to be a non-market economy for purposes of its trade remedy laws and with which no Party has a free trade agreement".[190] Such a "poison pill" clause will restrict the participation and use of relevant regional integration mechanisms by Chinese investors.

---

[187] Investment Agreement for the COMESA Common Investment Area, signed on May 23, 2007, article 1.4, available at <https://investmentpolicy.unctad.org/international-investment-agreements/treaty-files/3092/download>.

[188] Supplementary Act A/SA.3/12/08 Adopting Community Rules on Investment and the Modalities for their Implementation with ECOWAS(ECOWAS Supplementary Act on Investments), signed on December 19, 2008, entered into force on January 19, 2009, article 1(d) and (a), available at <https://investmentpolicy.unctad.org/international-investment-agreements/treaty-files/3266/download>.

[189] See Matthew Happold & Relja Radović, 'The ECOWAS Court of Justice as an Investment Tribunal' (2018)19(1) The Journal of World Investment & Trade 95–117.

[190] See United States-Mexico-Canada Agreement, USMCA, signed on November 30, 2018, came into force on July 1, 2020, Annex 14-D, Article 14. D.1, available at <https://ustr.gov/sites/default/files/files/agreements/FTA/USMCA/Text/14-Investment.pdf>.

7.4.4 Possible Rights and Obligations of Chinese Investors Under African Regional Integration Instruments Related to Investment

7.4.4.1 Understanding the African Position Reflected in the Regional Integration Instruments Related to Investment

Due to the different actual national conditions and different development levels of the member states within African regional integration organizations, different approaches and value orientations to investment issues of regional integration organizations are adopted, and thus the level of legal instruments related to investment is uneven. For example, the 2007 COMESA Investment Agreement sets out the goal for sustainable development and provides investor obligations, while the 2012 SADC Model BIT even recommends the exclusion of provisions concerning MFN treatment and FET. In addition to regional imbalances, the attitude toward investment in different periods is also inconsistent, and "regression" even appears in some regions.

Because the PAIC is a legal instrument adopted by the AU in 2016, it can be seen as an outcome of coordinating and representing the latest position on foreign investment by various African states, namely, the unified African position on foreign investment. The 2016 PAIC, as a model investment treaty for the entire African continent, aims to enhance the coherence of African countries in investment law, which, while temporarily has no binding on AU member States, can guide investment treaty-making activities and domestic investment legislation in African countries and regional economic organizations. It is expected that the degree of integration in Africa could be promoted by the 2016 PAIC from the perspective of foreign investment legislation. With the consent of African states, it may also replace intra-African investment-related treaties, so the 2016 PAIC is only focused here.

The 2016 PAIC typically reflects the positions of developing and least developed countries on foreign investment.[191] In addition to pursuing the goal of attracting foreign investment and promoting the economic development of the state, the 2016 PAIC places greater emphasis on the possible contribution of foreign investment to the policy objectives and sustainable development goals of the host state. Focus is placed on the long-term benefits that foreign investment can bring and a shift from the emphasis on the "quantity" to the requirement of "quality" of foreign investment. From the perspective of value orientation, the 2016 PAIC pursues the balance between investment protection and non-investment public interests, and the concept of sustainable development is considered. From the perspective of interest protection, the 2016 PAIC tries to balance the rights and obligations of host countries and investors so that investors can enjoy their rights while shouldering the corresponding obligations. The host state has also been given more of the necessary regulatory powers. Therefore,

---

[191] See Makane Moïse Mbengue & Stefanie Schacherer, 'The 'Africanization' of International Investment Law: The Pan-African Investment Code and the Reform of the International Investment Regime' (2017)18(3) The Journal of World Investment & Trade 414–448, 414.

the 2016 PAIC will promote the quality of economic development by protecting the interests of all parties in a balanced manner.

In terms of specific content, the provisions of the 2016 PAIC are in line with the views of African countries as developing countries on international investment law. The performance requirements and the terms of investor obligations in the 2016 PAIC are all provisions less commonly used in existing international investment treaties. The drafters of the 2016 PAIC did not blindly follow the trend of liberalization that had once been regarded as the golden rule. The 2016 PAIC does not, therefore, provide for pre-establishment national treatment in pursuit of investment liberalization but still has the deciding power to open up the investment industry in states' own hands. This suggests that African countries take into account the positive and negative effects that foreign investment may have, thus selectively accepting foreign investment. On the whole, it can be said that the 2016 PAIC has well protected the regulatory rights of the African host country and imposed more obligations on and consequently less protection for investors, thus potentially adversely affecting Chinese investments in Africa.

7.4.4.2 Realizing African Investment Legal Instruments Related to Regional Integration May Be a Specific Balance Detrimental to Chinese Investment

One of the important purposes of the 2016 PAIC is to focus on balancing the rights and obligations of the host state and the investor, and the drafters of the 2016 PAIC have also written this purpose into the preamble so that the purpose is taken seriously in the 2016 PAIC's application and interpretation in the future. The 2016 PAIC balances the rights and obligations of both parties, that is, the host state and the investor, mainly through limiting the application of some treatment provisions, listing exceptions based on public interest, imposing treaty obligations on investors, and strengthening the regulatory rights of the host country. Since the 2016 PAIC is very likely to become the basis for the Investment Protocol under AfCFTA, it is foreseeable that the level of protection of investors under the Investment Protocol under AfCFTA will not be too high.

In the substantive treatment clauses, the 2016 PAIC absorbs and incorporates the lawmaking experience of previous investment treaties and the practice of investment arbitration. Specifically, the 2016 PAIC restricts the circumstances for the application of national treatment and MFN treatment clauses and ensures, as much as possible, that foreign investors receiving preferential treatment are in the same objective circumstances as investors in the host state to prevent investors from abusing preferential treatment and receiving the treatment they should not have enjoyed. Thus, the situations in which the host state had lost its case for breaching both categories of provisions would also be reduced. In addition, it is worth noting that the deletion of the FET clause from the 2016 PAIC that is detrimental to the host state would, without doubt, favor the tilt of the balance of interest toward the host state. On the other hand, it would leave a gap in the protection of investors in the treaty and, for example, would leave the arbitrary and discriminatory conduct of the host state unbound.

Another feature of the content of the substantive treatment clauses is the importance attached to the protection of the public welfare objectives and public interests of the host state. The exceptional measures taken in the public interest by the 2016 PAIC in national treatment, MFN treatment, and expropriation provisions do not constitute a violation of the relevant provisions, which undoubtedly provides more legitimate justification for the host state's regulatory conduct.

Regarding procedural treatment, the 2016 PAIC attaches importance to alternative dispute settlement mechanisms of investment and encourages parties to a dispute to resolve the dispute through consultation, negotiation, and conciliation, setting up a prepositive procedure as mandatory. Furthermore, the 2016 PAIC restricts the way an investor initiates international investment arbitration through the consent of both parties to submission of arbitration and the doctrine of exhaustion of local remedies. In resolving disputes, the 2016 PAIC gives priority to means other than arbitration by arbitral tribunal and adjudication by a court, which can lead to adequate communication between the parties to the dispute and increase the chances of reaching an agreement through friendly consultations. Alternative ways of resolving disputes are more conducive to a friendly and adequate settlement of disputes for member states with closer ties within the AU, but it will undoubtedly reduce the procedural rights of investors.

The direct way of balancing the interests of a host state with investors is to give host states sufficient regulatory space in the 2016 PAIC and to impose appropriate obligations on investors to facilitate their responsible investments in favor of sustainable development. The relevant provisions of the 2016 PAIC in "development related issues" and "investment related issues" chapters provide a strong guarantee for the host state to safeguard the public interest and pursue the goal of social development within its own state.

The inclusion of the direct obligation of investors responds to the theoretical problem of the imbalance between rights and obligations and makes investors enjoy various investment rights and preferential treatment and, at the same time, directly undertake treaty obligations.

The strengthening of regulatory power and the integration of the direct obligation of investors in the 2016 PAIC reflect the dissatisfaction of African states as capital importers, with the imbalance in the protection of interests in traditional international investment treaties. In addition, the purpose of concluding investment treaties is no longer simply to attract foreign investment but to pay more attention to the role of foreign investment in promoting the sustainable development of their states, and thus emphasize the host state's protection of public interests such as the environment and human rights.

Some scholars have pointed out that the 2016 PAIC does not truly address the plight of Africa in that some of the innovative provisions of the 2016 PAIC, if used in investment agreements between African countries and developed countries, can indeed serve the interests of African countries. However, the AU's utilization of these provisions within Africa has led to protectionism within African countries, punishing themselves for the mistakes of others.[192] This also shows that the 2016 PAIC and the international investment laws between China and African countries that will be generated based on it in the future may be detrimental to Chinese investors and their investments since China is bound to be a capital exporter in China–Africa investment relations. In abstract terms, the 2016 PAIC could be considered a balanced model treaty that reflects the level of development of African countries and the pursuit of African states for fairness. However, specifically in the case of Chinese investors and their investments, provisions similar to those under the 2016 PAIC are clearly not the optimal choice, including direct obligations to investors, exclusion of FET, numerous exceptions to MFN treatment, national treatment, and expropriation, and recommendations for African courts or arbitration institutions to adjudicate disputes. However, even so, Chinese and Chinese investors have to respect the choices of African countries and endeavor to coordinate and respect the positions of African countries.

7.4.4.3 Thinking Highly of Building a Legal Relationship with African Regional Economic Integration Organizations

At present, both the EU and the US are adjusting their policy toward Africa, trying to strengthen ties with Africa through a comprehensive cooperation strategy to address the influence of emerging market countries, in particular China, in Africa. For example, the US has strengthened its ties with the African regional economic community through the TIFA and the European Union through the EPA. However, China has not yet negotiated serious reciprocal arrangements with African countries,[193] including African regional economic communities. Although it can be said that China and African integration organizations have had close ties, even AU headquarters buildings were constructed with China's aid.

There is a remarkable trend of economic integration in Africa, and the driving force behind it is Pan-Africanism. Under the AU banner, the eight regional integration institutions in Africa are expected to be able to coordinate their structures and policies and eventually achieve integration at the continental level. The latest results are the adoption of the 2016 PAIC and the entry into force of AfCFTA.[194] It is relatively easy to coordinate trade policies, but it is more difficult to coordinate investment policies because they involve much more of a state's regulatory sovereignty. In short, the way forward is tortuous, but the future is bright and African countries are on the road to integration.

---

[192] See Won Kidane, 'The Draft Pan-African Investment Code, Now International Investment Law Trends and Africa's Dilemmas' (2018)50 George Washington International Law Review 523.

[193] See United Nations, Economic Commission for Africa, Assessing Regional Integration in Africa VIII: Bringing the Continental Free Trade Area About, December 11, 2017, 136, available at <https://www.uneca.org/assessing-regional-integration-africa-viii>.

[194] See Constitutive Act of the African Union, article 3.l, available at <https://au.int/sites/default/files/pages/34873-file-constitutiveact_en.pdf>.

Given the sentiment of anti-colonialism and anti-neo-colonialism in African history and Pan-Africanism philosophy, it is impossible for regional investment laws in Africa to only protect foreign investors and their investments without emphasizing the regulatory sovereignty of the host states. In contrast, investment legal instruments in the integration of African economies have increasingly emphasized the regulatory rights and obligations of investors in the host state. In this trend, Chinese investors should be aware of these complex investment legal instruments and think about how to utilize the regional investment legal system formed under this trend of economic integration. The development of international investment law in the process of regional economic integration in Africa has led us to think about making better use of the African economic integration practice of reducing barriers to trade and investment within Africa. China should help African countries realize their long-term efforts to anti-neo-colonialism by helping them develop their economies and to promote the growth and internationalization of Chinese enterprises in this process. Of course, China has attached importance not only to the economic integration of Africa, but also to the issue of how to make Chinese investors comply with and fulfill their obligations in Africa.

Out of understanding and respect for African peoples, President Xi Jinping also referred to the Pan-Africanism slogan “Africa is Africa of Africans”.[195] Foreign Minister Wang Yi also agreed that Pan-Africanism is the direction and trend of Africa.[196] China has played an important role in promoting economic integration in Africa, as infrastructure connectivity is an indispensable hardware condition for economic integration in Africa. China is playing a major role in this regard, and China’s BRI coincides with the Program for Infrastructural Development in Africa (PIDA). At the national level, in addition to infrastructure development, there are many cooperation areas between China and Africa under the BRI, but one important aspect should be China’s cooperation with regional integration organizations in Africa, which also needs to be incorporated into the legal framework.

7.5 Promoting the Development of China’s Outbound Investment Rule of Law

The home country may take measures related to overseas investments in accordance with its treaty obligations, and in the absence of treaty obligations, the home country may take the initiative to carry out measures related to overseas investments. China’s regulatory practices in the process of overseas investments are unique worldwide.

[195] See Xinhua, ‘why “China-Africa Relations” is unusual? Xi Jinping said so’, available at <http://www.xinhuanet.com/world/2018-07/21/c_129918013.htm>.

[196] See Foreign Minister Wang Yi, ‘Pan-Africanism is the direction of Africa and the trend of the times’, September 18, 2019, available at <http://world.people.com.cn/n/2014/0109/c1002-24071183.html>.

7.5.1 *Reality and Gaps in China's Outbound Investment Rule of Law*

China's overseas investment lawmaking is that China, as a home country, enacts various legal instruments aiming at Chinese overseas investors and overseas investments, including domestic legal instruments and international legal instruments.

The existing domestic legal instruments for overseas investment are mainly reflected in departmental rules and departmental regulatory documents such as Measures for the Administration of Overseas Investment of Enterprises,[197] Measures for the Administration of Overseas Investment,[198] Guidance on Further Guiding and Standardizing the Direction of Overseas Investment,[199] Provisions on the Foreign Exchange Administration of the Overseas Direct Investment of Domestic Institutions,[200] Guidelines for the Compliance Management of Enterprises' Overseas Operation,[201] Guidance on Environmental Protection Related to Outbound Investment Cooperation,[202] and so on.

These departmental rules and departmental regulatory documents have played an important role in promoting Chinese overseas investment[203] and have also directed and regulated Chinese overseas investments, although their effectiveness has frequently been criticized.[204] In particular, at the "admission to go out" stage for domestic investment subjects, they have played an important regulatory role.

---

[197] See Measures for the Administration of Overseas Investment of Enterprises, Order No. 11 of the National Development and Reform Commission, Departmental Rules, issued on December 26, 2017 and entered into force on March 1, 2018, available at <https://www.ndrc.gov.cn/fggz/lywzjw/zcfg/201712/W020190909440825920640.pdf>.

[198] See Measures for the Administration of Overseas Investment (2014), Order No. 3 [2014] of the Ministry of Commerce, Departmental Rules, issued on September 6, 2014, entered into force on October 6, 2014, available at <http://www.gov.cn/gongbao/content/2014/content_2792653.htm>.

[199] See Guidance on Further Guiding and Standardizing the Direction of Overseas Investment, GBF [2017] No. 74, issued on August 4, 2017.

[200] See Provisions on the Foreign Exchange Administration of the Overseas Direct Investment of Domestic Institutions, No.30 [2009] of the State Administration of Foreign Exchange, Departmental Regulatory Documents, issued on July 13, 2009, entered into force on August 1, 2009, available at <http://www.gov.cn/gongbao/content/2010/content_1539417.htm>.

[201] See Guidelines for the Compliance Management of Enterprises' Overseas Operation, No. 1916 [2018] of the National Development and Reform Commission, Departmental Regulatory Documents, came into force on December 26, 2018, available at <https://www.ndrc.gov.cn/fggz/lywzjw/zcfg/201812/W020190909440853717390.pdf>.

[202] See Guidance on Environmental Protection Related to Outbound Investment Cooperation, SHH [2013] No. 74, Departmental Regulatory Documents, issued on February 18, 2013. Entered into force on February 18, 2013, available at <http://fec.mofcom.gov.cn/article/ywzn/dwtz/zcfg/201512/20151201202217.shtml>.

[203] See Karl P. Sauvant & Victor Chen, 'China's regulatory framework for outward foreign direct investment' (2014)7 China Economic Journal 141–163.

[204] For example, Oliver C. Ruppel and Frida Shifotoka, 'Foreign Direct Investment Protection in Africa - Contemporary Legal Aspects between BITS and BRICS' (2016) 12(1) African Yearbook of International Law 5–56, 49.

In general, the policy orientation behind these departmental rules and departmental regulatory documents favors regulation and thus makes investment protection, facilitation, and promotion relatively inadequate; in particular, the direct protection role is seriously inadequate.

Due to the fragmentation that results from these "legal instruments" coming out of many governmental branches, some specific provisions of these legal instruments sometimes even conflict with each other, which in turn increases the cost of compliance with the law for domestic investment subjects and their overseas investment. For example, there are conflicts in the existing legal instruments on the following issues: the definition of overseas investment; the scope of overseas investment related to the prohibited category and sensitive category; and the approval and filing of overseas investment in sensitive category and permitted category.[205]

Throughout the practice of developed countries, although there is no unified legislation on overseas investments, there are comprehensive and forcible policies, legal instruments, and organizational systems for overseas investments. According to the experience of developed countries, policies and laws on overseas investments include providing information, financing, financial preferences, political risk insurance, official development assistance, etc., to promote, support, encourage, and protect overseas investment.[206]

Lawmaking on overseas investment is not just an issue facing China; it can be said that there is fierce lawmaking competition in this regard, especially between China and the US. On October 5, 2018, US President Donald Trump formally signed the "Better Utilization of Investments Leading to Development Act, BUILD Act", and under the Act established the official body, the "International Development Finance Corporation, DFC", which will consolidate the competence of the Overseas Private Investment Corporation (OPIC) and the Development Credit Authority under the US Agency for International Development (USAID).[207] This will usher development finance from the US and promotion of its overseas investment in a new era. From a legal point of view, this is obviously the US's strategy to confront China's BRI in the form of legislation to promote the development of overseas investment from the US and to guide and promote the global and regional strategic layout of its overseas investments. The World Investment Report 2019 expected that the BUILD Act and DFC would significantly contribute to American investment growth in Africa.[208]

---

[205] See Measures for the Administration of Overseas Investment of Enterprises, Order No. 11 of the National Development and Reform Commission, Departmental Rules, issued on December 26, 2017 and entered into force on March 1, 2018, article 2, chapter 3; Measures for the Administration of Overseas Investment (2014), Order No. 3 [2014] of the Ministry of Commerce, Departmental Rules, issued on September 6, 2014, entered into force on October 6, 2014, article 2, chapter 2.

[206] See Karl P. Sauvant, 'A New Challenge for Emerging Markets: The Need to Develop an Outward FDI Policy', Columbia FDI Perspectives on topical foreign direct investment issues No. 203, July 3, 2017.

[207] See the BUILD Act, available at <https://www.congress.gov/bill/115th-congress/senate-bill/2463/text>.

[208] See UNCTAD, World Investment Report 2019: Special Economic Zones, United Nations, 2019, 39, available at <https://unctad.org/system/files/official-document/wir2019_en.pdf>.

China is a written law country, investment subjects from China and investment projects and enterprises in Africa have reasons to expect a unified overseas investment law, just like the National People's Congress promulgated one unified Foreign Investment Law in 2019, which has the authority of "legislation", and can coordinate and unify provisions in various aspects of foreign investments in China. In 2015, *Opinions of the Central Committee of the Communist Party of China and the State Council on Building a New Open Economy System* put forward that it was necessary to study and promulgate overseas investment regulations. In 2017, Order No. 11 of the National Development and Reform Commission set out a resolution for the introduction of the Regulation on Overseas Investment. Although it has not yet been promulgated, the determination and agenda to introduce a unified regulation on overseas investment have been well established. After Regulation on Overseas Investment, the arrival of Overseas Investment Law will not be too far away.

7.5.2 Future of Chinese Outbound Investment Rule of Law

The lawmaking on China's overseas investments should be a systematic project, and the present research suggests that special attention should be given to the following two aspects.

First, in terms of the legislative logic and specific content of domestic law, it is expected that there will be a single piece of legislation in the future, the Overseas Investment Law. The new law should be in line with the Foreign Investment Law of the People's Republic of China[209] and international investment treaties. The new law should adopt normative logic and legislative style to deal with admission, facilitation, promotion, protection, and regulation, and thus act as a means of coordinating the fragmentation of existing regulations, rules, and regulatory documents for the purpose of protection and sustainability of overseas investments. Those conflicting legal provisions should be modified or repealed. The existing regulations, rules, and regulatory documents, although numerous, from the content, can be classified into these five aspects. In particular, the division of responsibilities between regulatory bodies should be clarified to avoid competing with each other for power or disapproving of each other. Moreover, as a law with the nature of administrative law, it is necessary not only to clarify the legal liability of the administrative counterpart, but also to clarify the legal accountability of the administrative body.

In addition, other existing legislation that may be applicable to overseas investments can be referred to in the expected Overseas Investment Law through linkage to clarify its application to relationships between overseas investment projects and

[209] See Foreign Investment Law of the People's Republic of China, Order No. 26 of the President of the People's Republic of China, laws, issued on March 15, 2019, entered into force on January 1, 2020, available at <http://mg.mofcom.gov.cn/article/policy/201909/20190902898870.shtml>.

enterprises from China and even other relations, such as the Anti-Monopoly Law.[210] Article 2 of the current Anti-Monopoly Law clearly states that "...This Law shall apply to the monopolistic conducts outside the territory of the People's Republic of China that has the effect of eliminating or restricting competition on the domestic market of China". It sees that this clause adopts "effect doctrine" status.

Second, it should be made clear that the overseas investment laws have extraterritorial applicability and extraterritorial effects to some extent, so long as these laws are not exercised recklessly and excessively, and here, the "territory" refers to the territory of the People's Republic of China. Some Chinese investment subjects, and even government officials, believe that the existing overseas investment legal instruments cannot be applied extraterritorially because the extraterritorial application of domestic legal instruments will infringe on the sovereignty of the host country. Therefore, the existing investment regulations, rules, and regulatory documents can only be extended to the investment "admission to go out" stage, and the applicable channels of these legal instruments are through the company's articles of association. In fact, this understanding is not correct. The argument that the laws of the investor's home state should not have extraterritoriality at all[211] is also not in line with reality.

According to the text, "Customary international law permits exercises of prescriptive jurisdiction if there is a genuine connection between the subject of the regulation and the state seeking to regulate. The genuine connection usually rests on a specific connection between the state and the subject being regulated, such as territory, effects, active personality, passive personality, or protection. In the case of universal jurisdiction, the genuine connection rests on the universal concern of states in suppressing certain offenses."[212] Therefore, the extraterritorial application of national law has a broad international law basis, even based on the principle of effect. As long as extraterritorial conduct has a substantial effect on the business, market competition, or national security within the territory, the law within the territory binds not only extraterritorial nationals, but also extraterritorial foreigners. In other words, if there is a substantive and real relationship between the subject and the jurisdiction, the extraterritorial conduct of the subject can become a legitimate object of jurisdiction.[213]

In reality, however, some states often exercise extraterritorial jurisdiction excessively, which would violate the sovereignty of other countries, is therefore inconsistent with international law and leads to resistance from other states. The enactment

---

[210] See Anti-Monopoly Law of the People's Republic of China, Order of the President of the People's Republic of China (No. 68), Laws, issued on August 30, 2007, entered into force on August 1, 2008, available at <http://www.gov.cn/gongbao/content/2007/content_778162.htm>.

[211] See Dessislav Dobrev, 'Reforming International Investment Law: Is It Time for A New International Social Contract to Rebalance the Investor-State Regulatory Dichotomy?', in A K Bjorklund (ed.), Yearbook on International Investment Law & Policy 2014–2015 (Oxford University Press, 2016) 269–294.

[212] Restatement of the Law Fourth, The Foreign Relations Law of the United States: Selected Topics in Treaties, Jurisdiction and Sovereign Immunity § 407, St. Paul, MN: American Law Institute Publishers, 2018.

[213] See Ian Brownlie, Principles of Public International Law (Oxford University Press, 2003) 309.

of a blocking statute by a foreign legislature, enforcement of pre-existing domestic law by a foreign executive agency, or injunction ordered by the foreign court are typical ways to confront the abuse of extraterritorial jurisdiction.

Chinese law, of course, has personal jurisdiction over the overseas investment behavior of investors from China on the basis of the principle of nationality, which, in particular, means regulation and protection while not harming the interest of a foreign state and its nationals. Overseas affiliates or subsidiaries owned or controlled by Chinese investors, overseas investment behaviors, and overseas investment-related behaviors of Chinese investors, such as bribery of local officials in the host state to obtain overseas projects and conspiracy with the host company to harm Chinese domestic entities and even national interests, also need extraterritoriality of Chinese law.

It needs to be clarified that the extraterritorial application of Chinese investment law, which is mainly based on the principle of nationality, is different from the extraterritorial application of national law in some countries based on the principle of nationality. The former is designed to protect the interests of foreigners and foreign states, while the latter serves the purpose of sanctioning foreigners or foreign states.

Certainly, for foreigners outside China, China's overseas investment law may also have applicability if there is a treaty basis. For example, according to Article 2(1) of the "International Covenant on Economic, Social and Cultural Rights", which was approved by the Standing Committee of the National People's Congress on February 28, 2001, the subject targeted by the obligations of a State party is not limited to persons under its national jurisdiction, and a Contracting state also has the obligation to respect and protect the subject outside the territory.[214]

Indeed, the voice calling for the regulation of Chinese investment projects and enterprises abroad also seems to come from outside of China, assuming that the Chinese government has the obligation and ability to regulate Chinese overseas investment projects and enterprises.[215] The home state should regulate its overseas investment based on its nationality connection and even be liable for the damage caused by its overseas investment.[216]

However, under international law, the Chinese government, while it has the right to do so, does not necessarily have an obligation to do so. Jurisdiction over overseas investment behavior is an obligation under international law only if it is required by a

[214] See International Covenant on Economic, Social and Cultural Rights, G.A. res. 2200A (XXI), signed on December 16, 1966, and came into force on January 3, 1976. The original text of Article 2.1 is "Each State Party to the present Covenant undertakes to take steps, individually and through international assistance and cooperation, especially economic and technical, to the maximum of its available resources, with a view to achieving progressively the full realization of the rights recognized in the present Covenant by all appropriate means, including particularly the adoption of legislative measures".

[215] See Pichamon Yeophantong & Cristelle Maurin, 'China and the Regulation of Outbound Investment: Toward a "Responsible Investment" Policy Framework', in Andrea K. Bjorklund (ed.), Yearbook on International Investment Law & Policy 2014–2015 (Oxford University Press, 2016) 349–373.

[216] See M. Sornarajah, The International Law on Foreign Investment (Cambridge University Press, 2017) 172–203.

treaty concluded by a state. For example, after the Standing Committee of the National People's Congress ratified the United Nations Convention against Corruption,[217] China criminalized bribery of foreign public officials in its criminal law, since, as a party to the Convention, it is obliged to govern commercial bribery in accordance with the provisions of the Convention, not only domestic, but also overseas. The law states that Whoever gives any property to a functionary of a foreign country or an official of an international public organization for any improper commercial benefit shall be punished according to the provision. That is the accused person shall be sentenced to imprisonment of not more than three years or criminal detention in addition to a fine if the amount of bribery is relatively large; or be sentenced to imprisonment of not less than three years but not more than ten years in addition to a fine if the amount of bribery is huge. In addition, where an entity commits such a crime, a fine shall be imposed on it, and the person directly responsible and other directly liable persons shall also be punished.[218] Therefore, in terms of overseas bribery, there is a clear combination of host and home countries' law, and it is also the practice of China to fulfill the United Nations Convention Against Corruption.

In addition, if the IIAs signed by China and African countries provide the regulatory obligations of the home country, then China also has the obligation to apply its laws to the investment activities of its nationals abroad. Of course, the red line or limit that should be considered is not to offend the sovereignty of other countries.

Chapter Summary

In commenting on China's view of the international rule of law, one argument is that China is still adhering to the traditional principle of sovereign equality, which is considered an outdated view of the international rule of law. This argument is of course wrong. In particular, in terms of China–Africa relations, this principle is desirable and works well. China insists on non-intervention in the internal affairs of African countries based on the principle of sovereign equality, and unwelcoming interference in the internal affairs of African countries is the attitude of African states. Therefore, this principle should be continually adhered to in China–Africa relations. The Beijing Declaration and Programme for China–Africa Cooperation in Economic and Social Development, 2000, distilled the core principles of FOCAC: The Five Principles of Peaceful Coexistence, friendly relations, liberation solidarity and mutual benefit, and win–win common development". These principles reflect China's further development in the principles concerning handling China–Africa relations and have guided the subsequent FOCAC activities. These principles are in contrast to the "America First" principle, which is fully reflected in the New Africa Strategy pursued by the US Trump Administration. These principles and the idea of the China–Africa Community with a Shared Future, which was put forward in

---

[217] See Decision of the Standing Committee of the National People's Congress on Ratifying the United Nations Convention Against Corruption, date issued and effect date on October 27, 2005, available at <https://www.lawinfochina.com/display.aspx?id=4635&lib=law>.

[218] See Criminal Law of the People's Republic of China, Laws, issued on December 26, 2020, entered into force on March 1, 2021, article 164.

the Chinese Policy Paper on Africa (2015), that is, shared responsibility, win–win cooperation, happiness sharing, cultural co-prosperity, security co-construction, and harmonious coexistence, should guide the future of the China–Africa investment rule of law.

Practice shows that under the guidance of these principles and the concept of the China–Africa Community with a Shared Future, the specific international rule of law between China and Africa reflects the concept of inclusive interests and win–win cooperation and common development goals. It is submitted that China's economic presence, including investment in Africa, is an innovative practice of anti-neo-colonialism in international rule of law, which has created a model of win–win cooperation under the international rule of law framework and made its due contribution to the sustainable development of Africa and is bound to be welcomed by African countries.

In the future, on the one hand, China–Africa IIAs should be concluded on the basis of the international investment rule of law with a South–South cooperation orientation, and China and Chinese investors should take investment issues in African regional investment agreements seriously. On the other hand, China should develop a national investment rule of law to protect and especially regulate overseas investment as a complement to the international investment rule of law.

Chapter 8
Conclusion

The topic addressed in this research is explored in the above chapters, and the corresponding conclusion is illustrated as follows.

8.1 Development and Characterization of Chinese Investment in Africa

8.1.1 Development of Chinese Investment in Africa

China supported anti-neocolonialism in African countries during the African movement for independence and liberation in the 1960s and 1970s. The Tanzania-Zambia railway serves as a typical symbol of Sino-African friendly relations during this period when China's own economic circumstance was extremely difficult.

China adopted reforms and the opening up policy in 1978, and after more than 20 years of economic and wealth accumulation, importing foreign capital, advancing technology, and improving management experience, China achieved great development in its economy. In March 2000, "going abroad" was identified as the national strategy to promote Chinese investments abroad. In October 2000, the Forum on China–Africa Cooperation (FOCAC), as a periodical consultation mechanism, was initiated in Beijing to realize the objectives of "equal consultation, enhancing understanding, expanding consensus, strengthening friendship and promoting cooperation" between China and Africa.

The BRI, which was proposed in 2013, greatly boosts Chinese involvement in African investments, as mentioned above. In addition, the BRICS also plays a role in promoting Chinese investment in Africa as well as other BRICS members. To respond to Africa's development challenges, in the Durban Declaration of the fifth BRICS Summit held in South Africa in 2013, the BRICS committed that they "will

X. Han, *Legal Protection and Sustainability of Chinese Investments in Africa*,
Modern China and International Economic Law,
https://doi.org/10.1007/978-981-19-1882-7_8

seek to stimulate infrastructure investment on the basis of mutual benefit to support industrial development, job creation, skills development, food and nutrition security and poverty eradication and sustainable development in Africa…". "The BRICS are no doubt an important new Non-Formal Forums of International Cooperation", and "[t]he BRICS are not an international organization and they are not about to become one", but "all the Summits have produced and articulate common consensus in a number of formal joint "Declarations" by which the participating States commit to certain common policies".[1] "The BRICS regularly act uniformly in their interactions with third countries and international organizations".[2] With the establishment of these mechanisms, China has made great progress in investing in Africa.

What Chinese investment has brought to Africa is impressive, especially after FOCAC.[3] "China–African co-operation has achieved a leap in the rebuilding of essential infrastructure throughout Africa. China's direct investment in public works in Africa is impressive. Most new railways, roads, airports, convention centers, parliamentary and government buildings are tangible",[4] and "from 2002 until 2017, China has invested over US$200 billion in Africa. Chinese built railways and roads and telecommunications now allow for intra-African trade and commerce to compete with imports from Europe".[5] In fact, the scale of China's investment in Africa has been on a significant upward trend even during the pandemic of COVID-19.

In contrast, the New Programme for Africa's Development (NEPAD) was launched in 2002 with an original plan of obtaining infrastructural development in Africa through European investment within a 10-year period (from 2005 to 2015). However, NEPAD ultimately failed because European countries required additional standards, such as good governance and human rights that are not in line with the actual situation in Africa.[6]

It can be concluded that Chinese investment is very important for Africa's development, although there are many other sources of foreign investment in Africa. It is wise for Africa to develop infrastructure, industrialize and promote beneficiation in Africa by attracting foreign investment. Thus, African countries can keep more added value generated by natural resources in Africa rather than just being a raw materials exporter.

---

[1] André Thomashausen, Is BRICS becoming an international organisation, Opinion, July 25, 2018, Pretoria News.

[2] André Thomashausen, The Legal Nature of the BRICS, at ILA 2016, BRICS Panel, August 10, 2016, Johannesburg South Africa.

[3] André Thomashausen, China is filling the gap left by Nepad's failure, June 20, 2010, Edition 2 Sunday Independent, South Africa; André Thomashausen, '(Foreign) Investment Strategies in Africa', in M Bungenberg & S Hobe eds, Permanent Sovereignty over Natural Resources (Springer, 2015) 155–172, at 170.

[4] André Thomashausen, Africa needs quality from friendship with China, Business Report, July 17, 2012.

[5] André Thomashausen, Expanding into Africa: Legal, predictable and sustainable business in Africa, SAIN/SAICC Breakfast Meeting Mazaars Johannesburg May 10, 2018.

[6] André Thomashausen, China is filling the gap left by Nepad's failure, June 20, 2010, Edition 2 Sunday Independent, South Africa.

8.1.2 Chinese Investment in Africa as a Practice of Anti-neocolonialism

All kinds of neocolonialism accusations would have a negative impact on China's economic engagement in Africa, destroy the interests of both sides and hinder the further development of China–Africa economic cooperation. On the basis of the development of international law related to anti-colonialism and anti-neocolonialism as well as the reality of China's economic engagement in Africa, the author of this research summits that China's economic engagement in Africa is an innovative practice of international law of anti-neocolonialism.

China's investment in Africa has brought about remarkablly rapid economic growth and social development in Africa,[7] and Chinese engagement in Africa is in essence different from neocolonialism. However, both the harsh accusations from some Western countries and Pan-Africanism are reminders to the Chinese government and Chinese investors that they cannot recommit the mistakes some Western countries have made. China would like to correctly handle some problems arising from Chinese economic engagement in Africa.[8]

The topic of neo-colonialism could become a political tool used by opposition parties in African countries and could also be of concern to international organizations such as the International Monetary Fund. Neo-colonialism is one of the most inflammatory international discourses in the world today. It is also a "killer" to destroy China–Africa relations and must arouse great attention from both sides. Neo-colonialism has long been opposed by the academic community.[9] Neo-colonialism is based on oppression and exploitation, similar to old colonialism. Contrary to the fundamental principles of international law, it is bound to give rise to international conflicts and domestic objections. It is worth noting that few scholars, on various grounds, even call on former colonizers to return to Africa and recolonize Africa.[10]

---

[7] "Stunt" is a word used in the comments on Chinese economic engagement including investment in Africa by Remarks by National Security Advisor Ambassador John R. Bolton on the Trump Administration's New Africa Strategy, delivered on December 13, 2018, Heritage Foundation, Washington, D.C.

[8] See Guijin Liu, Rational Knowledge of Some Doubts about Sino-African Relations, West Asia and Africa, No. 1, 2015, 4–20. Guijin Liu was a former Chinese Ambassador to South Africa and former Director of the African Department of the Ministry of Foreign Affairs of China. Due to his outstanding contribution to China–Africa friendship, on July 1, 2021, when the founding of Chinese Communist Party reached 100 years, he was awarded the "July 1, Medal".

[9] For example, Jean-Paul Sartre, a famous existential philosopher opposed colonialism and neocolonialism in his various speeches. See Jean-Paul Sartre, Colonialism and Neocolonialism (Routledge, 2006). The first edition of this book is published in French in 1964. The book is still very influential after 40 years of its first publication and was translated into English in 2006. Another representative book against neocolonialism: Kwame Nkrumah, Neo-Colonialism: The Last Stage of Imperialism (Thomas Nelson & Sons, Ltd., London, 1965).

[10] For example, William Pfaff, A New Colonialism - Europe Must Go Back into Africa (1995) 74 Foreign Affairs 5.

Practice shows that under the guidance of the concept of the China–Africa Community with a Shared Future, China adheres to the basic principles of international law and, on that basis, creates a specific international legal system and domestic legal framework between China and Africa that reflects the concept of inclusive interests and win–win cooperation with a common development goal. It is clear that China's economic presence in Africa is an innovative practice of anti-neocolonialism international law and is bound to be recognized and welcomed by African countries.

African countries should be vigilant and oppose all forms of neo-colonialism. Based on recognizing the essence of anti-neocolonialism, African states should actively carry out normal international economic cooperation, especially in light of mutually beneficial economic cooperation with China. Facts have shown that Africa's development requires first and foremost the efforts of African countries and the African peoples themselves, as well as international cooperation, in particular South-South cooperation. China's economic presence in Africa, as an innovative practice of anti-neocolonialism, has created a model of win–win cooperation under the international rule of law framework and has made its due contribution to the sustainable development of Africa.

8.2 International Rule of Law and International Investment Rule of Law

8.2.1 General Understanding of the International Rule of Law and the International Investment Rule of Law

To explore and realize the "legal protection and sustainability of Chinese investments in Africa under the concept of international investment rule of law", this research attempts to find answers through the aforementioned chapters. Under the international rule of law and the international investment rule of law, the arbitrary power of a government will be constrained at the international level. Therefore, investors' right to their investments can be correspondingly protected, which means an extra layer of protection in addition to protection under the national rule of law from the host state. At the same time, because investor responsibility is emerging under the international investment rule of law, some of the unsustainable behavior of investors will be constrained.

For the protection and sustainability of Chinese investment in Africa, relevant Chinese government departments and Chinese investors should attach great importance to the international rule of law and the international investment rule of law. They must rely on the international rule of law and the international investment rule of law instead of politically friendly relations at the macro level between China and Africa. This research uses many words to delineate the international rule of law and the international investment rule of law. Its aim is to understand the existence and role of the international rule of law and the international investment rule of law. The international rule of law and then the international investment rule of law as one area or branch of the international rule of law are the theoretical basis of this research. On that note, this research formally starts with these two aspects, with the purpose of forming an accurate and comprehensive understanding of the international rule of law and international investment rule of law.

Throughout the foregoing chapters, the author has sought to shed light on international rule of law is the ideal of international lawyers, but the international rule of law is not abstract and the ideological divergence between different countries may affect the understanding of it. The idea of the international rule of law and the emphasis on the international rule of law were undoubtedly historically progressive, which was in line with the need to maintain the world order after World War II, and the international rule of law advocated at that time was nothing but the international rule of law led by the US.

According to this research, it is confirmed that the reality is not what presumed by some international lawyers, that is, the international rule of law is only a slogan, which means the so-called international rule of law either does not exist or is just a tool for the political survival of a state in the world and there is no real international rule of law. Through historical and realistic investigation, the author believes that the international rule of law does exist, and its development has gone through a process from ideal to reality. The international rule of law may be regarded as the counterpart of the national rule of law in the international community, although based on the fundamentally different nature of the international community and domestic society, a simple analogy between them is absolutely not correct. The international rule of law is becoming an increasingly popular topic within recent years, and the possible reason may be that the existing international order and international law in place are under unprecedented challenges after World War II.

Today's international rule of law is mainly manifested in the constraint on state power as well as the international organization's power. However, the principle of national sovereignty and the responsibility of transnational corporations developed in the United Nations system, as enshrined in the Charter of the United Nations and other United Nations legal instruments, have always been emphasized and sought after only by developing countries without the support of developed countries. The "power-based explanation", which is used to give reasons for this situation,[11] however, is convincing to a great degree.

The international rule of law as understood by states is sometimes seemingly in harmony but actually at variance. For example, China has always firmly defended the fundamental principles of international law that take the Charter of the United Nations as its core. China proposes and actively practices the five principles of peaceful coexistence. China adheres to the international rule of law, which is centered on the Charter of the United Nations and guided by the notion of the Community with a Shared Future for Mankind. At present, in the international economic field, the

[11] M. Sornarajah, The international law on foreign investment (Cambridge University Press, 2017) 189.

international rule of law advocated by China places particular emphasis on supporting the multilateral trade and multilateral investment system but opposing trade and investment protectionism, deepening trade and investment facilitation, and expanding regional economic cooperation. However, the international rule of law in the eyes of the Trump administration is that of "America First".[12] Thus, it seems that states are practicing different international laws and live under different international rules of law.

When explaining the weakness of early law relative to power, Dr. Bodenheimer in his early days always used international law as an analogy and considered that modern international law, such as primitive customary law, must be listed as an undeveloped form of law.[13] However, later, he also admitted Philip Jessup's view that the rules of international law are more to be observed than to be scorned, and although the two situations have alternated in history, even if international law is still underdeveloped and its legal nature cannot be denied.[14] Therefore, thus far, the international community does not have a perfect international rule of law, and only law and good governance have a long way to go in the international community. It can even be said that the perfect rule of law can only be an ideal that is constantly approaching but can never be realized. Although Arthur Larson (1961) proposed the international rule of law, this idea, which reflected the value of academia at that time, has not been fully realized to date. However, the existence and role of the international rule of law in the international community cannot be denied, the future of the international community needs international rule of law to achieve sustainable development, and the ideal of international rule of law should not be given up.

The traditional international investment rule of law, as an integral part of international rule of law, is also deeply influenced by the international rule of law, including problems and defects. The crisis in the current international investment rule of law arose from emphasizing the constraint on national sovereignty but neglecting private obligations.

The international investment rule of law is the most representative or advanced international rule of law or the relatively developed part of the international rule of law. The rule of law of international investment is the more developed part of the international rule of law. The practice of international investment rule of law reflects the rationality of protecting the regulatory power of the host state and imposing obligations on investors. Through a large number of international investment agreements (approximately 3000), a large number of international investment arbitration jurisprudences (over 1000) and the ongoing reforms in the international investment rule of law, the trend of the international investment rule of law embodies the constraints on the power of the host state and the power of the investment tribunal. Therefore,

---

[12] Justin Hughes, an "America First" Presidency, International Rule of Law, and the Charming Betsy Doctrine, Loyola Law School, Los Angeles Legal Studies Research Paper, 2017–16; Remarks by National Security Advisor Ambassador John R. Bolton on the Trump Administration's New Africa Strategy, delivered on December 13, 2018, Heritage Foundation, Washington, D.C.

[13] Edgar Bodenheimer, Jurisprudence (McGraw-Hill Education, 1940) 32.

[14] Edgar Bodenheimer, Jurisprudence, The Philosophy and Method of the Law (Harvard University Press, 1974) chapter 12.

protecting the rights of investors after legitimacy has been challenged, increasing attention to the legitimate regulatory space of the host state and investor responsibilities, and strengthening the impartiality and independence of the investment tribunal because a powerful and efficient ISDS tribunal is not what the host state fears but the host state worries about an arbitrary ISDS tribunal.

This research adheres to the international investment rule of law and believes that the international investment rule of law can promote the rule of law in the host country and promote good governance and thus the economic development and well-being of the host country. Making a general survey of the countries that have withdrawn from the international investment rule of law, it can be said that withdrawal has not improved their investment governance or broader social governance.

Compliance with the international investment rule of law may be used as an "anti-driving mechanism" by some countries to promote proper national rule of law within the countries. In Zimbabwe, the rights of investors cannot be protected immediately by the international investment rule of law because after Mike Campbell SADC Tribunal made an award in favor of the investor,[15] the High Court of Zimbabwe refused to enforce the award under the pretext that the award was contrary to its national public policy.[16] Additionally, Zimbabwe does not implement other awards made by ICSID tribunals. However, Zimbabwe later amended its constitution and other relevant laws to improve its governance. Just as the United Nations emphasizes, in regard to controlling the exercise of power at the international level,[17] the consequence is that state power is constrained while domestic constitutional and legal impediments to international third-party adjudication are moved.

Of course, currently international investment rule of law is also not a perfect international rule of law. It also needs to cope with challenges and continuously adjust to serve the sustainable development of various actors in international investment relations. Fortunately, in today's world, major countries have not abandoned the international investment rule of law but are working hard to meet the challenges faced by the international investment rule of law through reforms.

---

[15] Southern African Development Community Tribunal, Mike Campbell (Pvt) Ltd. and Others v Republic of Zimbabwe (2/2007) [2008] SADCT 2 (November 28, 2008).

[16] Zimbabwe, High Court, Gramara (Pvt) Ltd. and Colin Bailie Cloete v. Government of the Republic of Zimbabwe HH 169–2009, HC 33/09 (January 26, 2010).

[17] Report of the Secretary-General, The Rule of Law at the National and International Levels: Comments and Information Received from Governments (2007) UN Doc A/62/121 (2007), 19.

8.2.2 The International Investment Rule of Law in Africa and Its Realization

8.2.2.1 Understanding the International Investment Rule of Law in Africa

Specific to Africa's existing international investment rule of law, it is submitted that in general, African countries have a positive attitude toward the international investment rule of law, as evidenced by the fact that a vast majority of countries have accepted the arbitration and enforcement mechanism of awards, such as the ICSID Convention and the New York Convention. Furthermore, African countries are actively concluding various IIAs in recent years when they have been suffering numerous cases before international investment arbitral tribunals, and the legitimacy of the international investment rule of law has been challenged. In the BITs concluded with developed countries, African countries have also accepted relatively high investment protection requirements, broader investment protection scope, and even the liberalization of pre-establishment. Nevertheless, the investor responsibility clause embodied in the latest BIT model of developed countries is still not fully reflected in the new BITs between African countries and developed countries. The Kenya-Japan BIT that came into effect in 2017 is a typical case. The newly concluded BITs within African countries and the new developments in Africa's regional investment agreements fully reflect the true attitude of African countries toward the international investment rule of law: constraining the protection of investment, expanding the regulatory space of the host state and imposing responsibilities on the investor.

African countries' policy-makers have recognized that foreign investment is key to Africa's growth and transformation, similar to China. Accordingly, African countries also attach importance to the international investment rule of law. Most countries still adhere to and actively conclude international investment agreements. Currently, African countries take IIAs seriously from the international investment rule of law because it can bring about real legal consequences, that is, a huge amount of compensation and even required changes in their domestic laws.

For example, since 2017, Kenya has not signed a new BIT. According to what the present author learned from Heather Munyao, an investment promotion officer from the Kenya Investment Authority when interviewing her, the main reason is that Kenya is reviewing its concluded BITs, and upon completing the review, the signing of BITs will continue. Africa's international investment rule of law, mainly referring to its regional investment agreements that embody the needs and stance of African developing countries, is Africa's contribution to the international investment rule of law. China and Chinese investors need to respect and adapt to Africa's international investment rule of law.

From a practical point of view, the BITs between some Western countries and African countries mainly emphasize the constraint on the power of the host state to protect the interests of investors and in recent years have further developed to emphasize investment liberalization, requiring the host state to grant freedom to investment access. In addition, the US emphasizes its domestic law and makes unilateral decisions toward countries in Africa. Meanwhile, through TIFA, the US is supposed to decide the issues in the investment process through negotiations with African countries.

In the context of the traditional international investment rule of law, we can better understand the characteristics and new development of the international investment rule of law in Africa. Whether it is the Africanization of regional investment agreements or the "nationalization" of South Africa's investment rule of law, which means terminating BITs with European countries that were signed from 1994 onwards. Both reflect the "de-westernization". South Africa has attempted to withdraw from the international investment rule of law and has terminated many of its BITs, of which it replaced with the Protection of Investment Act. In view of special national history and the reality of South Africa, this approach that seems to run counter to the international investment rule of law is understandable for the time being. Moreover, this radical practice is not common in Africa as a whole.

8.2.2.2 Taking Pan-Africanism and Regional Integration in Africa Seriously

Pan-Africanism has a distant origin and a long development in Africa. Under the guidance of Pan-Africanism, Africa has never stopped dreaming African unity through regional integration. The BRI has brought China and the continent closer as a tie, and the construction of the BRI is conducive to the eventual realization of regional integration in Africa and Pan-Africanism. At the same time, Pan-Africanism also constitutes the African background of the "Belt and Road" construction. The implementation of the BRI cannot ignore the trend of integration on the continent. In fact, China attaches great importance to the integration of Africa. China began to support Africa's regional integration through the FOCAC in 2000. Additionally, China is the only country among developing countries that supports African integration through an institutionalized structure. The Chinese government appreciates African integration and pledges to continue supporting Africa's efforts to seek integration, peace and stability and faster economic growth.[18]

Under these circumstances, Chinese investors involved in Africa's "Belt and Road" construction should understand the development of Africa's economic integration. In particular, the past, present and future of Africa's investment law under the African economic integration framework make sense of the impact of African regional economic integration in Africa on their rights and obligations. This includes the Pan-African Investment Code, which imposes direct obligations on investors to achieve sustainable development.

---

[18] The Beijing Declaration on Building a Closer China–Africa Community with a Shared Future, September 5, 2018, available at <https://www.yidaiyilu.gov.cn/zchj/sbwj/65044.htm>.

8.2.2.3 Improving China–Africa Investment Rule of Law

In contrast, the China–Africa investment rule of law mainly consists of BITs. However, there are only 20 BITs in force, and the level of protection is so low that it cannot play a significant role in protecting Chinese investments in Africa. Additionally, there is no investor responsibility provided in these BITs except that the establishment of investment should comply with the domestic laws of the host state.

For the purpose of ensuring the protection and sustainability of Chinese investment in Africa in addition to friendly political relations as an important part of the investment climate, the Chinese government should reinforce the concept of international investment rule of law and attach importance to it.

China should attach more importance to the international investment rule of law between China and African countries. China has signed 34 BITs with African countries but only 20 of them have entered into force. In comparison, the China–Kenya BIT was signed in 2001 but has not yet entered into force. However, the Japan-Kenya BIT was signed in 2016 and entered into force in 2017, and the South Korea-Kenya BIT was signed in 2014 and entered into force in 2017. Again, the Japan-Morocco BIT was concluded on January 8, 2020 and has not yet entered into force. Even compared to emerging countries such as Brazil and India, China's BIT conclusion with African countries in recent years seriously lags behind.

The Chinese government should actively take measures to promote the BITs already signed to come into force. For BITs that are obviously outdated, China and the African countries involved should update them to make them conform to recent realities and needs. The Chinese government should actively consider constructing a new China–Africa investment rule of law. For this purpose, China should uphold the principle of international rule of law that it has always adhered to and take the "China–Africa Community with a Shared Future" as the guiding notion. In addition, China should insist on the concept of affinity, sincerity and trust. China should fully respect the wishes of African countries, understand and take seriously "the concerns and voices coming out of Africa",[19] and promote the well-being of African people. "The first general law, which is to be found in the very end of the society of Nations, is that each Nation should contribute as far as it can to the happiness and advancement of other Nations".[20]

Since most of the existing China–Africa treaties are still first-generational and second-generational BITs, in view of the present nature of China–African investments and BITs, the transformation and modernization of international investment law, and the stance held by China and African countries, respectively, to BITs, China and African countries should continue to embrace China–Africa BITs positively. In

---

[19] André Thomashausen, Africa needs quality from friendship with China, Business Report, July 17, 2012.

[20] Emmerich de Vattel The Law of Nations or the Principles of Natural Law Applied to the Conduct and the Affairs of Nations and of Sovereigns [1758], quote from André Thomashausen, The Legal Nature of the BRICS, at ILA 2016, BRICS Panel, August 10, 2016, Johannesburg South Africa.

fact, the investment chapter of China–Mauritius FTA points out the direction for the future of the China–Africa investment rule of law.

The protection and sustainability of China's investments in Africa needs to be established within the framework of the international investment rule of law, which is certainly not the international investment rule of law in the traditional sense. That is, one-sidedly restricting the power of the host state to protect the interests of investors. In general, African countries' choice of international investment rule of law is worthy of respect. The international investment rule of law should also protect the legitimate regulatory power of the host state and make investor responsibility available. In short, "the exercise of this protection should be conditional on the conduct of the foreign citizens or corporations in the host state".[21]

What needs to be added is that the "Belt and Road" Cooperation Memorandum should play a role in investment protection and investor responsibility. The "Belt and Road" Cooperation Memorandum is framework-oriented, declaratory and strategic and expresses the common aspiration of the two sides to strengthen cooperation and exchanges to support the BRI. The "Belt and Road" Cooperation Memorandum lists a wide range of areas of cooperation, including political, economic, and cultural aspects. It also clarifies "consultation, contribution and shared benefits" as the golden guiding principles. However, the "Belt and Road" Cooperation Memorandum itself does not have a strong legal and rule of law nature. Nevertheless, it could play a leading role to the parties. Investment cooperation is an important aspect of economic cooperation, and the Belt and Road Cooperation Memorandum will promote investment cooperation and provide a friendly atmosphere for investment protection. Moreover, according to the memorandum, the implementation of cooperation also needs to be coordinated by maintaining, promoting, and upgrading existing and future bilateral and multilateral cooperation mechanisms. Therefore, BITs and FTAs should be included in the implementation of the Belt and Road Cooperation Memorandum. Furthermore, in future Belt and Road Cooperation Memorandums, it is suggested that the specific wordings of investment protection and investor responsibility measures be included to make them play their role in the international investment rule of law. They should also be made conducive to the implementation of political aspirations into more pragmatic cooperation.

8.3 Protective Alternative Means and Their Limitations

8.3.1 Resort to the Host State's Law or Home State Law

"Legal protection and sustainability of Chinese investments in Africa" is an issue that deserves the joint attention of China and Africa. In the face of various risks in Africa, protection can ensure the sustainable development of Chinese investment. Although

[21] M. Sornarajah, The international law on foreign investment (Cambridge University Press, 2017), footnote 64.

Chinese investment in Africa should first rely on the legal protection of the host state, the host state's national rule of law is not enough. This is so because sometimes the host state's legislative, administrative, and judicial measures may themselves infringe on investment. Existing cases of African countries in international investment arbitration institutions have also shown that many of the regulatory measures in African countries are systemic risks (e.g., legislative measures) or specific risks (e.g., specific administrative or judicial measures) that Chinese investors and investments may confront. On that note, Chinese investors and investments still need the protection of the international investment rule of law.

The protection of Chinese investment in Africa cannot completely rely on China's overseas investment laws, which only have few provisions for protection. In fact, the foreign investment law of the host state and the overseas investment law of the capital-exporting state cannot fully protect the latter's overseas investment, which is precisely the reason for the emergence of the international investment rule of law.

8.3.2 Resort to the Diplomatic Protection

According to the present author's field work in Africa, due to the influence of traditional Chinese culture, Chinese investment enterprises in Africa have the idea that "harmony is everything". They even think that it is impossible for a private enterprise to sue the government of a sovereign state. When their legitimate rights are violated by irregular regulatory measures or blackmailed by local government officials, they either compromise with the local government or seek diplomatic protection from the home state instead of legal relief in the host state. It is hoped that the Chinese embassy and consulate in the host country can offer coordination and assistance; hence, the psychological dependence on the embassy and the consulate is massive. Therefore, some investment enterprises that were interviewed wanted more effective and convenient protection from the embassy and the consulate. They also mentioned that the embassy and consulate of some developed countries could give stronger protection to the investment enterprises that were set up by investors from their countries. This involves the issue of the role of embassy and consulate in the protection of investment. For overseas investment, the embassy and the consulate should assume certain obligations to protect and supervise overseas investment.

The embassy and the consulate have the obligation to communicate with local governments, to interact with Chinese investment enterprises in the host state and to conduct more legal training for Chinese investment enterprises to enable them to understand and satisfy the practical needs of Chinese enterprises. In particular, legal cooperation with the host state to protect Chinese enterprises is also an important task for the embassy and consulate. However, this does not mean that the embassy and consulate are obliged to make representation with the relevant government agency in the host state regarding each investor's claim. The embassy and consulate have the discretion to decide whether to intervene and negotiate the issue on a political basis or on the basis of the legitimacy of the investor's own conduct. In particular,

Chinese investment in Africa is increasing. The subject of investment is becoming increasingly diversified, while the staff of the embassy and consulate are still limited. In that light, reliance on diplomatic protection is not enough, nor is it possible.

Chinese investment enterprises often encounter contract disputes, labor disputes, environmental disputes, disputes arising from the host state's regulatory measures, etc. For Chinese investors and investment enterprises who need to seek help or get into disputes in the host state, the Chinese embassy and consulate as well as the Ministry of Commerce of China should establish a standing mechanism to provide legal aid. The aid includes the provision of a list of lawyers, the introduction of legal and judicial systems in the host state, detailed provisions of the relevant IIAs between China and the specific host state, detailed contact information of relevant government officials in the host state, and the introduction of alternative dispute settlement mechanisms for international claims and investment dispute settlement. Thus, investors may also consider protecting themselves through international investment arbitration when their interests are severely impaired and have exhausted all local remedies in the host state.

8.3.3 Resort to Insurance

It was also found through the present author's field work that some insurance companies do not make available various political risk insurance because of the high insurance premium that not every investment enterprise can afford or the mindset of leaving things to chance. Under this circumstance, abstract, systematic, and institutional protection from the international investment rule of law to every investment enterprise is especially important. It can restrict the regulatory measures of the host state through the "chilling effect".[22]

MIGA, which was created in 1988 under the World Bank, provides insurance services at the international level. China Export & Credit Insurance Corporation (Sinosure), which was established in 2001, has initiated its overseas investment insurance business since 2005. However, both MIGA and Sinosure insurance coverage are limited to non-commercial risks. Generally, expropriation, exchange restrictions, war and political riots, and breach of contract are included, but other common protections in IIAs, such as national treatment, MFN treatment and FET, are not included. In addition, because of the high risk of the host state, some African states are excluded from the host states list of underwriting by MIGA and Sinosure.

---

[22] There are two interpretations for this phrase: "1. Constitutional law. The result of a law or practice that seriously discourages the exercise of a constitutional right, such as the right to appeal or the right of free speech. 2. Broadly, the result when any practice is discouraged". Garner, Bryan A. Black's Law Dictionary (ninth edition, Thomson Reuters, 2009) 274.

8.4 Sustainability of Chinese Investment

8.4.1 Issue of Sustainability of Chinese Investment in Africa

Regarding the problems existing in the China–Africa cooperation model, from the perspective of Professor André Thomashausen, first, it does not pay attention to the good governance of African countries. That is, the improvement of the rule of law in African countries; second, it lacks management of completed projects in the long term which cannot make the project sustainable.[23] "China's investments have emphasized the construction of new facilities while not necessarily addressing long-term sustainability. China's engagement in infrastructure projects has thus far failed to secure maintenance and upkeep requirements". The author believes that one way of improving the rule of law in African countries is to rely on the international investment rule of law, including the rule of law between China and Africa. However, to maintain the already completed projects, it can be achieved by clarifying investor obligations and responsibilities in the contract. The specific problem of the sustainability of Chinese investment projects can be solved by specifying the project model in the investment contract between the two parties. For instance, for both Design-Build (DB) model and Engineering-Procurement-Construction (EPC) model, the party of the investor is not responsible for operation. However, for the Public–Private Partnership (PPP) model and the Build-Operate-Transfer (BOT) model, the investor is responsible for operation. Certainly, what is discussed in detail in this research is the sustainability issue in general.

In conclusion, as Chinese investment in Africa develops rapidly, challenges and problems are becoming increasingly prominent and need to be addressed. In addition to being familiar with the laws of the host state, Chinese investors and overseas investment enterprises in Africa expect China to have corresponding legislation in place, as well as the conclusion of IIAs to facilitate, promote, protect, and regulate investors and their investments to achieve sustainable development.

Against the background of globalization and the "return" of the state, the concept of the rule of law should still be strengthened. On the one hand, China should emphasize the role of international rule of law and make its own contribution to the progressive development of the international rule of law, specifically the international investment rule of law. On the other hand, the important role of domestic legislation should not be ignored. This is because the practice of unified legislation on overseas investment is unprecedented worldwide. It may become China's unique practice and thus may lead to the development of the rule of law for overseas investment in other countries. It is expected that China's overseas investment legislation can play a role in the facilitation, promotion, protection and regulation of Chinese investors and their overseas investments.

---

[23] André Thomashausen, China in Africa, available at <www.legesmundi.com>.

The long-term and rational development of China's investment in Africa needs the international investment rule of law and needs to rely on the international investment rule of law to protect and maintain investments' sustainability. Therefore, at the national level, it is necessary for China to understand and participate in the construction and reform of the Sino-African international investment rule of law. In this process, in addition to the protection of investment, investor responsibility should also be kept in mind. Investor responsibility means that to obtain protection, the state's regulatory power shall be respected by the investor, and the investor's responsibility must be fulfilled first. It also implies that Chinese investment shall meet environmental or ethical standards in Africa.

8.4.2 CSR of Chinese Investors and Chinese Investment Enterprises

There are various understandings of CSR, and this research adopts the understanding of CSR as an umbrella and broad concept, that is, it is a responsibility to society, not just to shareholders. CSR can be categorized into different perspectives. The most common classification should be ethical obligations and legal obligations, although the traditional view is that CSR is only an ethical obligation that depends on the willingness of the business enterprise. However, with the development of time, CSR has evolved not only as a moral obligation but also in part as a legal obligation. Even what was previously a moral obligation may now be classified as a legal obligation. Moreover, even as a moral obligation, it has the effect of moral coercion. As a legal obligation, it can be integrated into various branches of law. These include corporate law, labor law, environmental protection law, consumer protection law and other legislative and judicial practices. CSR includes responsibility to consumers, workers, creditors, and other stakeholders. The emergence and development of CSR reflects the progress of human commercial civilization and the reality of the impact of corporate behavior on society. Therefore, the legalization of CSR is already indispensable for social development. In terms of the CSR of Chinese investment enterprises, first, is to comply with the host state's CSR provisions, and second, to comply with China's relevant regulations. This is because China has issued a number of legal instruments directly or indirectly involving CSR for Chinese investment enterprises to regulate the behavior of overseas investment. Finally, at the level of international law, the emerging legal obligations on CSR for investors and their investments also need to be observed.

The author realizes in field work that, except for the few companies that consider CSR only as a moral donation, most Chinese investment companies have a modern understanding of CSR. They commit that their companies must fulfil their CSR and believe that this will not hinder but promote their own sustainable development. They also believe that they can fulfil their CSR better with the development of their own home country's economy. Their conduct is in line with international standards, and their CSR practices are also quite impressive. Take China Communications Constructions Company Limited and China Road and Bridge Corporation as examples. This type of engineering construction enterprise has a wide range of project sites that have strong environmental sensitivity to the extent that they have to always consider environmental issues to perform CSR. When building the Nairobi Malaba standard gauge railway in Kenya, as project contractors, they adopted a special railway design to protect the environment because the railway route plan determined by the Kenyan government had to go through Nairobi National Park, Kenya. The environmental problem was resolved,[24] and the project became an important transportation hub for Kenyan society after its completion.

According to the present author's field work in Zambia, Chinese enterprises not only need to pay local workers' wages but also need to pay extra for their children's education under Zambia's labor law. However, the local people generally have many children. This can be considered the case for Chinese enterprises implementing social responsibility. The visit of Sino-Zam Friendship Hospital in Kitwe, Zambia, which is operated and managed by Zambia-China Economic and Trade Co-operation Zone Development Limited, has left a deep impression on the present author. Sino-Zam Friendship Hospital, as a non-profit agency, performs social responsibility on behalf of the Zambia-China Economic and Trade Co-operation Zone Development Limited. It is especially moving that Dr Qin Changxi and Dr Li Hailian, who have worked for nearly twenty years at Sino-Zam Friendship Hospital, are known as the "envoy of China–Zambia friendship". Rescuing the dying, healing the wounded and caring for the local people.

8.4.3 Role of the Chinese Overseas Investment Law in the Sustainability of Chinese Investment

It is understandable that Chinese investors and their investments may face similar problems as other foreign investors and their investments. Some African countries have had poor rankings in the Corruption Perception Index issued by Transparency International for many years, which indicates the seriousness of corruption on the continent. However, Chinese investors should understand and actively abide by the China–Africa international investment rule of law and the international investment rule of law in Africa. On the one hand, this can actually protect their investments, and on the other hand, it can urge them to fulfill their responsibilities.

As illustrated in this research, the China–Africa international investment rule of law and the international investment rule of law in Africa have more provisions on obligations and responsibilities for investors. These provisions should be respected and complied with by Chinese investors.

---

[24] See Kenyan Conservationists Protest as Chinese Company Starts Work on Railway, available at <https://www.theguardian.com/world/2018/mar/01/kenyan-conservationists-protest-as-chinese-company-starts-work-on-railway>.

Furthermore, China should regulate the conduct of Chinese investors, investments, and related government officials by enacting legislation on outbound investment, holding investors and their investments responsible and accountable and thus protecting Chinese investment indirectly for its sustainable development.

China has many regulations and regulatory instruments on overseas investment. However, due to the low hierarchy of these rules and regulations, the fragmented structure, and sometimes conflicting provisions, the effectiveness of the existing legal instruments is reduced. According to the present author's field work, some investment enterprises do not know much about those legal instruments. They believe that they only need to follow the local laws in the host state while ignoring those legal instruments. Therefore, it is necessary to clarify that these regulations and regulatory instruments have extraterritoriality to these Chinese investment enterprises and that Chinese investment enterprises shall also abide by the rule of law of their home state. At the same time, it is suggested that unified overseas investment legislation may be enacted to facilitate the application of the law and improve its effectiveness.

Regarding the issue of extraterritoriality, some of China's existing practices with extraterritoriality involving overseas investment law in the broad sense have already been applied and can play a role in regulating and protecting China's overseas investment.

The Ministry of Commerce, joint with other ministries, implemented the system of "Bad Credit Records in the Fields of Foreign Investment Cooperation and Foreign Trade".[25] Under article 3, the term "bad credit records in foreign investment cooperation' means the collection, sorting, release, preservation and maintenance of information about relevant violations of laws and regulations by any enterprise, institution or individual within China, by joint venture partners, engineering project owners and general contractors of overseas investment, or by any employer, intermediary and individual outside China". Both an enterprise carrying out overseas investment business and a joint venture partner of overseas investment will have "Bad Credit Records" if they conduct these listed acts. In contrast, the "Guiding Opinions on Further Guiding and Regulating the Direction of Overseas Investment" provides for a blacklist system related to overseas investors and a joint punishment mechanism against illegal overseas investment.[26] Although the blacklist system is also adopted, it only targets the extraterritorial misconduct of Chinese enterprises and individuals.

---

[25] Notice of the Ministry of Commerce, the Ministry of Foreign Affairs, the Ministry of Housing and Urban–Rural Development, the General Administration of Customs, the State Administration of Taxation, the State Administration for Industry and Commerce, the General Administration of Quality Supervision, Inspection and Quarantine, and the State Administration of Foreign Exchange on Issuing the Measures for Bad Credit Records in the Fields of Foreign Investment Cooperation and Foreign Trade (for Trial Implementation), Departmental Regulatory Documents, issued on July 5, 2013, came into force on August 5, 2013.

[26] See Guidance on Further Guiding and Standardizing the Direction of Overseas Investment, GBF [2017] No. 74, issued on August 4, 2017.

The Decision of the Fourth Plenary Session of the 19th CPC Central Committee proposed implementing a list of unreliable entities.[27] Accordingly, China has established an "unreliable entity list" system, aiming at punishing foreign companies, organizations, or individuals who do not abide by market rules depart from the spirit of the contract and block or disrupt supply to Chinese enterprises for non-commercial purposes.[28] Thus, those entities that seriously damage the legitimate rights and interests of Chinese enterprises will be listed in the "unreliable entity list". Listed entities will be charged with serious consequences. The point here is that because it specifically targets foreign entities, it certainly has extraterritoriality. Some foreign media often make up stories and promote false statements, and some foreign entities take illegal measures to maliciously harm the interests of Chinese investment enterprises. It is possible that they may be included in the "unreliable entity list".

Corrupt economic dealings should either be governed in separate legislation, or their regulation should be integrated into overseas investment legislation to increase the application and implementation of these anti-corruption provisions. In response to the provisions of the United Nations Convention against Corruption, article 164.2 of Chinese Criminal law provides criminal liability for the bribery of foreign officials in pursuit of economic interests. However, in practice, the implementation of this article needs to be strengthened. In some overseas investment projects involving bribery, there is the need to punish the criminals involved.

In addition, the occurrence of such a crime may not only involve Chinese enterprises. To be fair, both Chinese and foreign enterprises and individuals should be targeted. Given the nature of international public anti-corruption policy, China's overseas investment legislation may provide limited extraterritorial jurisdiction on the basis of a convention or customary international law.

[27] Central Committee of the Communist Party of China, Decisions of the Central Committee of the Communist Party of China on Adhering to and Improving the Socialist System with Chinese Characteristics and Decisions, promoting the Modernization of the National Governance System and Governance Capacity, issued and came into force on October 31, 2019.

[28] See Provisions on the Unreliable Entity List, No.4 [2020] Order of the Ministry of Commerce of the People's Republic of China, Departmental Rules, issued and came into force on September 19, 2020.

Appendix A
African Membership of ICSID Convention (as of September 30, 2021, Listed Alphabetically)

	State	Signature	Deposit of ratification	Entry into force
1	Algeria	17/04/1995	21/02/1996	22/03/1996
2	Benin	10/09/1965	06/09/1966	14/10/1966
3	Botswana	15/01/1970	15/01/1970	14/02/1970
4	Burkina Faso	16/09/1965	29/08/1966	14/10/1966
5	Burundi	17/02/1967	05/11/1969	05/12/1969
6	Cabo Verde	20/12/2010	27/12/2010	26/01/2011
7	Cameroon	23/09/1965	03/01/1967	02/02/1967
8	Central Africa	26/08/1965	23/02/1966	14/10/1966
9	Chad	12/05/1966	29/08/1966	14/10/1966
10	Comoros	26/09/1978	07/11/1978	07/12/1978
11	D.R. Congo	29/10/1968	29/04/1970	29/05/1970
12	Congo	27/12/1965	23/06/1966	14/10/1966
13	Côte d'Ivoire	30/06/1965	16/02/1966	14/10/1966
14	Djibouti	12/04/2019	09/06/2020	09/07/2020
15	Egypt	11/02/1972	03/05/1972	02/06/1972
16	Ethiopia	21/09/1965		
17	Gabon	21/09/1965	04/04/1966	14/10/1966
18	Gambia	01/10/1974	27/12/1974	26/01/1975
19	Ghana	26/11/1965	13/07/1966	14/10/1966
20	Guinea	27/08/1968	04/11/1968	04/12/1968
21	Guinea-Bissau	04/09/1991		

(continued)

X. Han, *Legal Protection and Sustainability of Chinese Investments in Africa*, Modern China and International Economic Law,
https://doi.org/10.1007/978-981-19-1882-7

(continued)

	State	Signature	Deposit of ratification	Entry into force
22	Kenya	24/05/1966	03/01/1967	02/02/1967
23	Lesotho	19/09/1968	08/07/1969	07/08/1969
24	Liberia	03/09/1965	16/06/1970	16/07/1970
25	Madagascar	01/06/1966	06/09/1966	14/10/1966
26	Malawi	09/06/1966	23/08/1966	14/10/1966
27	Mali	09/04/1976	03/01/1978	02/02/1978
28	Mauritania	30/07/1965	11/01/1966	14/10/1966
29	Mauritius	02/06/1969	02/06/1969	02/07/1969
30	Morocco	11/10/1965	11/05/1967	10/06/1967
31	Mozambique	04/04/1995	07/06/1995	07/07/1995
32	Namibia	26/10/1998		
33	Niger	23/08/1965	14/11/1966	14/12/1966
34	Nigeria	13/07/1965	23/08/1965	14/10/1966
35	Rwanda	21/04/1978	15/10/1979	14/11/1979
36	Sao Tome and Principe	01/10/1999	20/05/2013	19/06/2013
37	Senegal	26/09/1966	21/04/1967	21/05/1967
38	Seychelles	16/02/1978	20/03/1978	19/04/1978
39	Sierra Leone	27/09/1965	02/08/1966	14/10/1966
40	Somalia	27/09/1965	29/02/1968	30/03/1968
41	South Sudan	18/04/2012	18/04/2012	18/05/2012
42	Sudan	15/03/1967	09/04/1973	09/05/1973
43	Swaziland (Eswatini)	03/11/1970	14/06/1971	14/07/1971
44	Tanzania	10/01/1992	18/05/1992	17/06/1992
45	Togo	24/01/1966	11/08/1967	10/09/1967
46	Tunisia	05/05/1965	22/06/1966	14/10/1966
47	Uganda	07/06/1966	07/06/1966	14/10/1966
48	Zambia	17/06/1970	17/06/1970	17/07/1970
49	Zimbabwe	25/03/1991	20/05/1994	19/06/1994

Appendix B
List of ICSID Cases Involving African States as Respondents Under the ICSID Arbitration Rules, ICSID Conciliation Rules, and ICSID Additional Facility Arbitration Rules (as of September 30, 2021, Listed Alphabetically)

	Respondent	Case No.	Claimant(s)
1	Algeria	ARB/03/8	Consortium Groupement L.E.S.I.—DIPENTA
2		ARB/05/3	LESI, S.p.A. and Astaldi, S.p.A
3		ARB/09/14	Mærsk Olie, Algeriet A/S
4		ARB/12/32	Gelsenwasser AG
5		ARB/12/35	Orascom TMT Investments S.à r.l
6		ARB/17/1	Ortiz Construcciones y Proyectos S.A
7		ARB/18/11	Société des Parcs d'Alger and Emirates International Investment Company LLC
8		ARB/18/44	SAUR and STEREAU
9		ARB/20/1	United Agencies Limited SA
1	Benin	ARB/20/24	Teyliom International and others
1	Burkina Faso	ARB/97/1	Société d'Investigation de Recherche et d'Exploitation Minière
2		ARB/21/18	AECI Mauritius Ltd
1	Burundi	ARB/95/3	Antoine Goetz and others
2		ARB/01/2	Antoine Goetz and others
3		ARB/13/7	Joseph Houben
4		ARB/14/31	Tariq Bashir and SA Interpétrol Burundi
1	Cameroon	ARB/81/2	Klöckner Industrie-Anlagen GmbH and others
2		ARB/02/4	Lafarge
3		CONC/11/1	RSM Production Corporation
4		ARB/13/14	RSM Production Company

(continued)

X. Han, *Legal Protection and Sustainability of Chinese Investments in Africa*, Modern China and International Economic Law,
https://doi.org/10.1007/978-981-19-1882-7

(continued)

	Respondent	Case No.	Claimant(s)
5		ARB/15/18	Capital Financial Holdings Luxembourg S.A
6		CONC/19/1	La Camerounaise des Eaux (CDE)
7		ARB/20/2	Hope Services LLC
1	Cabo Verde	ARB/15/12	PT Ventures, SGPS, S.A
1	Central Africa	ARB/07/2	RSM Production Corporation
2		ARB/07/10	M. Meerapfel Söhne AG
3		CONC/07/1	Shareholders of SESAM
1	Congo	ARB/77/1	AGIP S.p.A
2		ARB/77/2	S.A.R.L. Benvenuti & Bonfant
3		ARB/97/2	Société Kufpec (Congo) Limited
4		ARB/06/12	Scancem International ANS
5		ARB/21/24	World Natural Resources Ltd
1	Côte d'Ivoire	ARB/74/1	Adriano Gardella S.p.A
2		ARB/97/8	Compagnie Française pour le Développement des Fibers Textiles
3		ARB/16/11	Société Resort Company Invest Abidjan, Stanislas Citerici and Gérard Bot Beograd
4		ARB/17/48	Wise Solutions CDI, SA
1	D.R. Congo	ARB/93/1	American Manufacturing & Trading, Inc
2		ARB/98/7	Banro American Resources, Inc. and Société Aurifère du Kivu et du Maniema S.A.R.L
3		ARB/99/7	Patrick Mitchell
4		ARB/00/8	Ridgepointe Overseas Developments, Ltd
5		ARB/03/14	Miminco LLC and others
6		ARB/04/11	Russell Resources International Limited and others
7		ARB/05/21	African Holding Company of America, Inc. and Société Africaine de Construction au Congo S.A.R.L
8		ARB/10/4	Antoine Abou Lahoud and Leila Bounafeh-Abou Lahoud
9		ARB/10/21	International Quantum Resources Limited, Frontier SPRL and Compagnie Minière de Sakania SPRL
10		ARB/19/24	AAN Digital Services Holding Company (KSC)
1	Egypt	ARB/84/3	Southern Pacific Properties (Middle East) Limited
2		ARB/89/1	Manufacturers Hanover Trust Company
3		ARB/98/4	Wena Hotels Limited
4		ARB/99/6	Middle East Cement Shipping and Handling Co. S.A

(continued)

(continued)

	Respondent	Case No.	Claimant(s)
5		ARB/02/9	Champion Trading Company and Ameritrade International, Inc
6		ARB/02/15	Ahmonseto, Inc. and others
7		ARB/03/11	Joy Mining Machinery Limited
8		ARB/04/13	Jan de Nul N.V. and Dredging International N.V
9		ARB/05/15	Waguih Elie George Siag and Clorinda Vecci
10		ARB/05/19	Helnan International Hotels A/S
11		ARB/08/18	Malicorp Limited
12		ARB/09/15	H&H Enterprises Investments, Inc
13		ARB/11/6	Bawabet Al Kuwait Holding Company
14		ARB/11/7	National Gas S.A.E
15		ARB/11/16	Hussain Sajwani, Damac Park Avenue for Real Estate Development S.A.E., and Damac Gamsha Bay for Development S.A.E
16		ARB/11/32	Indorama International Finance Limited
17		ARB/12/11	Ampal-American Israel Corporation and others
18		ARB/12/15	Veolia Propreté
19		ARB/13/3	Ossama Al Sharif
20		ARB/13/4	Ossama Al Sharif
21		ARB/13/5	Ossama Al Sharif
22		ARB/13/23	ASA International S.p.A
23		ARB/13/29	Cementos La Union S.A. and Aridos Jativa S.L.U
24		ARB/13/37	Utsch M.O.V.E.R.S. International GmbH, Erich Utsch Aktiengesellschaft, and Mr. Helmut Jungbluth
25		ARB/14/4	Unión Fenosa Gas, S.A
26		ARB/15/47	ArcelorMittal S.A
27		ARB/16/1	Al Jazeera Media Network
28		ARB/16/2	Champion Holding Company and others
29		ARB/16/37	LP Egypt Holdings I, LLC, Fund III Egypt, LLC and OMLP Egypt Holdings I, LLC
30		ARB/17/31	Future Pipe International B.V
31		ARB/18/22	Tantalum International Ltd. and Emerge Gaming Ltd
32		ARB/18/31	International Holding Project Group and others
33		ARB/19/7	Petroceltic Holdings Limited and Petroceltic Resources Limited
34		ARB/19/27	CTIP Oil & Gas International Limited

(continued)

(continued)

	Respondent	Case No.	Claimant(s)
35		ARB/20/45	Gesenu S.p.A
36		ARB/21/21	KGL International for Ports, Warehousing, and Transport K.S.C.C
37		ARB/21/35	Vicat S.A
1	Equatorial Guinea	ARB(AF)/12/2	Grupo Francisco Hernando Contreras
2		CONC(AF)/12/1	Hess Equatorial Guinea, Inc. and Tullow Equatorial Guinea Limited
3		CONC(AF)/12/2	Republic of Equatorial Guinea
1	Gabon	ARB/76/1	Republic of Gabon
2		ARB/87/1	Société d'Etudes de Travaux et de Gestion SETIMEG S.A
3		ARB/04/5	Compagnie d'Exploitation du Chemin de Fer Transgabonais
4		ARB/08/17	Participaciones Inversiones Portuarias SARL
5		CONC/18/1	Société d'Energie et d'Eau du Gabon
6		ARB/18/36	Société d'Energie et d'Eau du Gabon and Veolia Africa
1	Gambia	ARB/99/5	Alimenta S.A
2		ARB/09/19	Carnegie Minerals (Gambia) Limited
3		ARB/14/6	African Petroleum Gambia Limited (Block A1)
4		ARB/14/7	African Petroleum Gambia Limited (Block A4)
5		ARB/17/38	African Petroleum Gambia Limited and APCL Gambia B.V
6		ARB/17/39	African Petroleum Gambia Limited and APCL Gambia B.V
7		ARB/17/40	APCL Gambia B.V
8		ARB/18/10	Western African Aquaculture Ltd, Kurt Lennart Hansson and Martje Bolt Hansson
1	Ghana	ARB/92/1	Vacuum Salt Products Ltd
2		ARB/07/24	Gustav FW Hamester GmbH & Co KG
3		ARB/16/15	AngloGold Ashanti (Ghana) Limited
1	Guinea	ARB/84/1	Atlantic Triton Company Limited
2		ARB/84/4	Maritime International Nominees Establishment
3		ARB/11/29	Getma International and others
4		ARB/12/8	Société Industrielle des Boissons de Guinée
5		ARB/12/36	Société Civile Immobilière de Gaëta
6		ARB/14/22	BSG Resources Limited
7		ARB/15/46	BSG Resources (Guinea) Limited and BSG Resources (Guinea) SÀRL

(continued)

(continued)

	Respondent	Case No.	Claimant(s)
1	Kenya	ARB/00/7	World Duty Free Company
2		ARB/15/7	WalAm Energy Inc
3		ARB/15/29	Cortec Mining Kenya Limited, Cortec (Pty) Limited and Stirling Capital Limited
1	Liberia	ARB/83/2	Liberian Eastern Timber Corporation
2		ARB/98/3	International Trust Company of Liberia
3		ARB/11/14	Diamond Fields Liberia, Inc
1	Libya	ARB(AF)/15/1	Strabag SE
1	Madagascar	CONC/82/1	SEDITEX Engineering Beratungsgesellschaft für die Textilindustrie m.b.H
2		CONC/94/1	SEDITEX Engineering Beratungsgesellschaft für die Textilindustrie m.b.H
3		ARB/13/34	Courts (Indian Ocean) Limited and Courts Madagascar S.A.R.L
4		ARB/17/18	DS)2, S.A., Peter de Sutter and Kristof De Sutter
5		ARB/17/28	LTME Mauritius Limited and Madamobil Holdings Mauritius Limited
1	Mali	ARB/01/5	Société d'Exploitation des Mines d'Or de Sadiola S.A
2		ARB/13/16	Société des Mines de Loulo S.A
3		ARB/21/38	Menankoto SARL
1	Mauritania	ARB/14/23	Tamagot Bumi S.A. and Bumi Mauritania S.A
2		ARB/21/9	Mauritanian Copper Mines S.A
1	Mauritius	ARB/16/32	Thomas Gosling and others
1	Morocco	ARB/72/1	Holiday Inns S.A. and others
2		ARB/00/4	Salini Construttori S.p.A. and Italstrade S.p.A
3		ARB/00/6	Consortium R.F.C.C
4		ARB/18/7	Corral Morocco Holdings AB
5		ARB/18/29	The Carlyle Group L.P. and others
6		ARB/19/2	Scholz Holding GmbH
7		ARB/19/14	Impresa Pizzarotti & C. S.p.A
1	Mozambique	ARB(AF)/14/2	Oded Besserglik
2		ARB/17/23	CMC Muratori Cementisti CMC Di Ravenna SOC. Coop., CMC MuratoriCementisti CMC Di Ravenna SOC. Coop. A.R.L. Maputo Branch and CMC Africa, and CMC Africa Austral, LDA
1	Niger	CONC/03/1	TG World Petroleum Limited
2		ARB/11/11	AHS Niger and Menzies Middle East and Africa S.A
1	Nigeria	ARB/78/1	Guadalupe Gas Products Corporation
2		ARB/07/18	Shell Nigeria Ultra Deep Limited

(continued)

(continued)

	Respondent	Case No.	Claimant(s)
3		ARB/13/20	Interocean Oil Development
4		ARB/20/41	Eni International B.V., Eni Oil Holdings B.V. and Nigerian Agip Exploration Limited
5		ARB/21/7	Shell Petroleum N.V. and The Shell Petroleum Development Company of Nigeria Limited
1	Rwanda	ARB/10/10	Olyana Holdings LLC
2		ARB/18/21	Bay View Group LLC and The Spalena Company LLC
1	Senegal	ARB/82/1	Société Ouest Africaine des Bétons Industriels
2		ARB/08/20	Millicom International Operations B.V. and Sentel GSM S.A
3		ARB/14/19	VICAT
4		ARB/15/21	Menzies Middle East and Africa S.A. and Aviation Handling International Ltd
5		ARB/18/24	African Petroleum Senegal Limited
1	Seychelles	ARB/02/14	CDC Group plc
1	Sierra Leone	ARB/19/31	Gerald International Limited
1	South Africa	ARB(AF)/07/1	Piero Foresti, Laura de Carli and others
1	South Sudan	ARB/12/26	Sudapet Company Limited
2		ARB/20/40	Qatar National Bank (Q.P.S.C.)
1	Sudan	ARB/14/2	Michael Dagher
1	Togo	CONC/05/1	Togo Electricité
2		ARB/06/7	Togo Electricité and GDF-Suez Energie Services
3		ARB/18/16	Togo Terminal
1	Tunisia	ARB/86/1	Ghaith R. Pharaon
2		ARB/04/12	ABCI Investments Limited
3		ARB/12/30	Lundin Tunisia B. V
4		ARB/13/15	Lundin Tunisia B.V
1	Uganda	ARB/12/34	Tullow Uganda Operations PTY LTD
2		ARB/13/25	Tullow Uganda Operations Pty Ltd. and Tullow Uganda Limited
3		ARB/15/11	Total E&P Uganda BV
1	Tanzania	ARB/98/8	Tanzania Electric Supply Company Limited
2		ARB/05/22	Biwater Gauff (Tanzania) Limited
3		ARB/10/12	Standard Chartered Bank
4		ARB/10/20	Standard Chartered Bank (Hong Kong) Limited
5		ARB/15/41	Standard Chartered Bank (Limited) Hong Kong
6		ARB/17/33	EcoDevelopment in Europe AB and EcoEnergy Africa AB

(continued)

(continued)

	Respondent	Case No.	Claimant(s)
7		ARB/19/8	Ayoub-Farid Michel Saab
8		ARB/19/17	Richard N. Westbury, Paul D. Hinks and Symbion Power Tanzania Limited
9		ARB/20/25	Winshear Gold Corp.
10		ARB/20/38	Nachingwea U.K. Limited (UK), Ntaka Nickel Holdings Limited (UK) and Nachingwea Nickel Limited (Tanzania)
11		ARB/21/6	Montero Mining and Exploration Ltd
1	Zimbabwe	ARB/05/6	Bernardus Henricus Funnekotter and others
2		ARB/10/15	Bernhard von Pezold and others
3		ARB/10/25	Border Timbers Limited, Timber
1	Zambia	ARB/20/17	Kansanshi Mining Plc.

Appendix C
List of Non-ICSID Cases Involving African State Parties (as of September 30, 2021, Listed Alphabetically)

	Respondent	Case No.	Claimant(s)
1	Algeria	PCA Case No. 2012–20	Orascom Telecom Holding S.A.E
2		PCA Case No. 2017–33	Consutel Group S.p.A. in liquidazione
1	Benin	SCC Case No. SCC EA 2017/092	Puma Energy Holdings SARL
1	Cabo Verde	PCA Case No.2014–33	Sterling Merchant Finance Ltd
1	Egypt	PCA Case No. 2012–07	Mohamed Abdel Raouf Bahgat
2		PCA Case No. 2012–26	Yosef Maiman, Merhav (MNF), Merhav-Ampal Group, Merhav-Ampal Energy Holdings
3		UNCITRAL, 2016	Nile Douma Holding
4		2020	Qatar Airways Group Q.C.S.C
1	Ethiopia	PCA Case No. 2017–26	ICL Europe Coöperatief U.A
2		UNCITRAL, 2007	CIM
1	Gabon	UNCITRAL, 2015	KCI
1	Ghana	PCA Case No. 2003–03	Telekom Malaysia Berhad
1	Lesotho	PCA Case No. 2013–29	Swissbourgh Diamond Mines (Pty) Limited, Josias Van Zyl, The Josias Van Zyl Family Trust and others
2		PCA Case No. 2016–21	The Burmilla Trust, The Josias Van Zyl Family Trust and Josias Van Zyl
1	Libya	2006, ad hoc arbitration	Shinhan Engineering & Construction Co

(continued)

X. Han, *Legal Protection and Sustainability of Chinese Investments in Africa*, Modern China and International Economic Law,
https://doi.org/10.1007/978-981-19-1882-7

(continued)

	Respondent	Case No.	Claimant(s)
2		UNCITRAL, 2008	Intersema Bau AG
3		2011, ad hoc arbitration, CRCICA	Mohamed Abdulmohsen Al-Kharafi & Sons Co
4		ICC, 2013	Sorelec
5		ICC, 2014 Case No. 20355/MCP	Olin Holdings Limited
6		ICC, 2015	Tekfen, TML, Tekfen-TML joint venture
7		ICC, 2015 Case No. 20971/MCP/DDA	Way2B ACE
8		ICC, 2016	Etrak İnşaat Taahut ve Ticaret Anonim Sirketi
9		ICC, 2016	Güriş İnşaat ve Mühendislik A.Ş
10		ICC, 2016	Nurol İnşaat ve Ticaret A.Ş
11		ICC, 2016 Case No. 21537/ZF/AYZ	Cengiz İnşaat Sanayi ve Ticaret A.S
12		ICC, 2017 Case No. 22673/ZF	Ustay Yapi Taahhut ve Ticaret AS
13		PCA Case No. 2017–21	D.S. Construction FZCO
14		2018, Ad Hoc Arbitration	Simplex Projects Ltd
15		2019 UNCITRAL Ad Hoc Arbitration	Trasta Energy
16		2020	Mustafa Orhan Özer and Nurettin Mendost Dirlik
1	Madagascar	ICC, 2013	Kristof De Sutter, Peter De Sutter, DS 2 S.A. and Polo Garments Majunga S.A.R.L
1	Mauritius	PCA Case No. 2016–20	Dawood Rawat
2		PCA Case No. 2018–37	Christian Doutremepuich and Antoine Doutremepuich
1	Mozambique	PCA Case No. 2020–21	Patel Engineering Limited
1	Sao Tome and Principe	PCA Case No. 2019–16	NIB, S.A.—National Investment Bank (Private entity) Superior Investments LLC (Private entity) Dr. Paulo Miguel Corte-Real Mirpuri (Private entity)
1	Tanzania	PCA Case No. 2018–09	Sunlodges Ltd. (BVI) and Sunlodges (T) Limited
1	Zambia	PCA Case No. 2017–19	Gunvor SA

Appendix D
List of ICSID Cases Involving African States as Respondents Under the ICSID Arbitration Rules, ICSID Conciliation Rules, and ICSID Additional Facility Arbitration Rules (as of September 30, 2021, Listed Chronologically)

	Case No.	Claimant(s)	Respondent
1	ARB/72/1	Holiday Inns S.A. and others	Morocco
2	ARB/74/1	Adriano Gardella S.p.A	Côte d'Ivoire
3	ARB/76/1	Gabonese Republic	Société Serete S.A
4	ARB/77/1	AGIP S.p.A	P.R. Congo
5	ARB/77/2	S.A.R.L. Benvenuti & Bonfant	P.R. Congo
6	ARB/78/1	Guadalupe Gas Products Corporation	Nigeria
7	ARB/81/2	Klöckner Industrie-Anlagen GmbH and others	Cameroon and Société Camerounaise des Engrais
8	CONC/82/1	SEDITEX Engineering Beratungsgesellschaft für die Textilindustrie m.b.H	Madagascar
9	ARB/82/1	Société Ouest Africaine des Bétons Industriels	Senegal
10	ARB/83/2	Liberian Eastern Timber Corporation	Liberia
11	ARB/84/1	Atlantic Triton Company Limited	Guinea
12	ARB/84/3	Southern Pacific Properties (Middle East) Limited	Egypt
13	ARB/84/4	Maritime International Nominees Establishment	Guinea
14	ARB/86/1	Ghaith R. Pharaon	Tunisia
15	ARB/87/1	Société d'Etudes de Travaux et de Gestion SETIMEG S.A	Gabon

(continued)

X. Han, *Legal Protection and Sustainability of Chinese Investments in Africa*, Modern China and International Economic Law,
https://doi.org/10.1007/978-981-19-1882-7

(continued)

	Case No.	Claimant(s)	Respondent
16	ARB/89/1	Manufacturers Hanover Trust Company	Egypt and General Authority for Investment and Free Zones
17	ARB/92/1	Vacuum Salt Products Ltd	Ghana
18	ARB/93/1	American Manufacturing & Trading, Inc	Congo
19	CONC/94/1	SEDITEX Engineering Beratungsgesellschaft für die Textilindustrie m.b.H	Madagascar
20	ARB/95/3	Antoine Goetz and others	Burundi
21	ARB/97/1	Société d'Investigation de Recherche et d'Exploitation Minière	Burkina Faso
22	ARB/97/2	Société Kufpec (Congo) Limited	Congo
23	ARB/97/8	Compagnie Française pour le Développement des Fibres Textiles	Côte d'Ivoire
24	ARB/98/3	International Trust Company of Liberia	Liberia
25	ARB/98/4	Wena Hotels Limited	Egypt
26	ARB/98/7	Banro American Resources, Inc. and Société Aurifère du Kivu et du Maniema S.A.R.L	D.R. Congo
27	ARB/98/8	Tanzania Electric Supply Company Limited	Independent Power Tanzania Limited
28	ARB/99/5	Alimenta S.A	Gambia
29	ARB/99/6	Middle East Cement Shipping and Handling Co. S.A	Egypt
30	ARB/99/7	Patrick Mitchell	D.R. Congo
31	ARB/00/4	Salini Construttori S.p.A. and Italstrade S.p.A	Morocco
32	ARB/00/6	Consortium R.F.C.C	Morocco
33	ARB/00/7	World Duty Free Company Limited	Kenya
34	ARB/00/8	Ridgepointe Overseas Developments, Ltd	D.R. Congo and Générale des Carrières et des Mines
35	ARB/01/2	Antoine Goetz & others	Burundi
36	ARB/01/5	Société d'Exploitation des Mines d'Or de Sadiola S.A	Mali
37	ARB/02/4	Lafarge	Cameroon
38	ARB/02/9	Champion Trading Company and Ameritrade International, Inc	Egypt

(continued)

(continued)

	Case No.	Claimant(s)	Respondent
39	ARB/02/14	CDC Group plc	Seychelles
40	ARB/02/15	Ahmonseto, Inc. and others	Egypt
41	ARB/03/8	Consortium Groupement L.E.S.I.—DIPENTA	Algeria
42	ARB/03/11	Joy Mining Machinery Limited	Egypt
43	ARB/03/14	Miminco LLC and others	D.R. Congo
44	CONC/03/1	TG World Petroleum Limited	Niger
45	ARB/04/5	Compagnie d'Exploitation du Chemin de Fer Transgabonais	Gabon
46	ARB/04/11	Russell Resources International Limited and others	D.R. Congo
47	ARB/04/12	ABCI Investments Limited	Tunisia
48	ARB/04/13	Jan de Nul N.V. and Dredging International N.V	Egypt
49	ARB/05/3	LESI, S.p.A. and Astaldi, S.p.A	Algeria
50	ARB/05/6	Bernardus Henricus Funnekotter and others	Zimbabwe
51	CONC/05/1	Togo Electricité	Togo
52	ARB/05/15	Waguih Elie George Siag and Clorinda Vecci	Egypt
53	ARB/05/19	Helnan International Hotels A/S	Egypt
54	ARB/05/21	African Holding Company of America, Inc. and Société Africaine de Construction au Congo S.A.R.L	D.R. Congo
55	ARB/05/22	Biwater Gauff (Tanzania) Limited	Tanzania
56	ARB/06/7	Togo Electricité and GDF-Suez Energie Services	Togo
57	ARB/06/12	Scancem International ANS	Congo
58	ARB(AF)/07/1	Piero Foresti, Laura de Carli and others	South Africa
59	ARB/07/2	RSM Production Corporation	Central Africa
60	ARB/07/10	M. Meerapfel Söhne AG	Central Africa
61	ARB/07/18	Shell Nigeria Ultra Deep Limited	Nigeria
62	CONC/07/1	Shareholders of SESAM	Central Africa
63	ARB/07/24	Gustav FW Hamester GmbH & Co KG	Ghana
64	ARB/08/17	Participaciones Inversiones Portuarias SARL	Gabon
65	ARB/08/18	Malicorp Limited	Egypt

(continued)

(continued)

	Case No.	Claimant(s)	Respondent
66	ARB/08/20	Millicom International Operations B.V. and Sentel GSM S.A	Senegal
67	ARB/09/14	Mærsk Olie, Algeriet A/S	Algeria
68	ARB/09/15	H&H Enterprises Investments, Inc	Egypt
69	ARB/09/19	Carnegie Minerals (Gambia) Limited	Gambia
70	ARB/10/4	Antoine Abou Lahoud and Leila Bounafeh-Abou Lahoud	Congo
71	ARB/10/10	Olyana Holdings LLC	Rwanda
72	ARB/10/12	Standard Chartered Bank	Tanzania
73	ARB/10/15	Bernhard von Pezold and others	Zimbabwe
74	ARB/10/20	Standard Chartered Bank (Hong Kong) Limited	Tanzania Electric Supply Company Limited
75	ARB/10/21	International Quantum Resources Limited, Frontier SPRL and Compagnie Minière de Sakania SPRL	D.R. Congo
76	ARB/10/25	Border Timbers Limited, Timber Products International (Private) Limited, and Hangani Development Co. (Private) Limited	Zimbabwe
77	ARB/11/6	Bawabet Al Kuwait Holding Company	Egypt
78	ARB/11/7	National Gas S.A.E	Egypt
79	ARB/11/11	AHS Niger and Menzies Middle East and Africa S.A	Niger
80	ARB/11/14	Diamond Fields Liberia, Inc	Liberia
81	ARB/11/16	Hussain Sajwani, Damac Park Avenue for Real Estate Development S.A.E., and Damac Gamsha Bay for Development S.A.E	Egypt
82	CONC/11/1	RSM Production Corporation	Cameroon
83	ARB/11/29	Getma International and others	Guinea
84	ARB/11/32	Indorama International Finance Limited	Egypt
85	ARB(AF)/12/2	Grupo Francisco Hernando Contreras	Equatorial Guinea
86	ARB/12/8	Société Industrielle des Boissons de Guinée	Guinea

(continued)

(continued)

	Case No.	Claimant(s)	Respondent
87	CONC(AF)/12/1	Hess Equatorial Guinea, Inc. and Tullow Equatorial Guinea Limited	Equatorial Guinea
88	ARB/12/11	Ampal-American Israel Corporation and others	Egypt
89	ARB/12/15	Veolia Propreté	Egypt
90	CONC(AF)/12/2	Republic of Equatorial Guinea	CMS Energy Corporation and others
91	ARB/12/26	Sudapet Company Limited	South Sudan
92	ARB/12/30	Lundin Tunisia B. V	Tunisia
93	ARB/12/32	Gelsenwasser AG	Algeria
94	ARB/12/34	Tullow Uganda Operations PTY LTD	Uganda
95	ARB/12/35	Orascom TMT Investments S.à r.l	Algeria
96	ARB/12/36	Société Civile Immobilière de Gaëta	Guinea
97	ARB/13/3	Ossama Al Sharif	Egypt (I)
98	ARB/13/4	Ossama Al Sharif	Egypt (II)
99	ARB/13/5	Ossama Al Sharif	Egypt (III)
100	ARB/13/7	Joseph Houben	Burundi
101	ARB/13/14	RSM Production Company	Cameroon
102	ARB/13/15	Lundin Tunisia B.V	Tunisia
103	ARB/13/16	Société des Mines de Loulo S.A	Mali
104	ARB/13/20	Interocean Oil Development Company and Interocean Oil Exploration Company	Nigeria
105	ARB/13/23	ASA International S.p.A	Egypt
106	ARB/13/25	Tullow Uganda Operations Pty Ltd. and Tullow Uganda Limited	Uganda
107	ARB/13/29	Cementos La Union S.A. and Aridos Jativa S.L.U	Egypt
108	ARB/13/34	Courts (Indian Ocean) Limited and Courts Madagascar S.A.R.L	Madagascar
109	ARB/13/37	Utsch M.O.V.E.R.S. International GmbH, Erich Utsch Aktiengesellschaft, and Mr. Helmut Jungbluth	Egypt
110	ARB/14/2	Michael Dagher	Sudan
111	ARB/14/4	Unión Fenosa Gas, S.A	Egypt
112	ARB/14/6	African Petroleum Gambia Limited (Block A1)	Gambia

(continued)

(continued)

	Case No.	Claimant(s)	Respondent
113	ARB/14/7	African Petroleum Gambia Limited (Block A4)	Gambia
114	ARB(AF)/14/2	Oded Besserglik	Mozambique
115	ARB/14/19	VICAT	Senegal
116	ARB/14/22	BSG Resources Limited	Guinea
117	ARB/14/23	Tamagot Bumi S.A. and Bumi Mauritania S.A	Mauritania
118	ARB/14/31	Tariq Bashir and SA Interpétrol Burundi	Burundi
119	ARB/15/7	WalAm Energy Inc	Kenya
120	ARB/15/11	Total E&P Uganda BV	Uganda
121	ARB/15/12	PT Ventures, SGPS, S.A	Cabo Verde
122	ARB/15/18	Capital Financial Holdings Luxembourg S.A	Cameroon
123	ARB/15/21	Menzies Middle East and Africa S.A. and Aviation Handling International Ltd	Senegal
124	ARB/15/29	Cortec Mining Kenya Limited, Cortec (Pty) Limited and Stirling Capital Limited	Kenya
125	ARB(AF)/15/1	Strabag SE	Libya
126	ARB/15/41	Standard Chartered Bank (Limited) Hong Kong	Tanzania
127	ARB/15/46	BSG Resources (Guinea) Limited and BSG Resources (Guinea) SÀRL	Guinea
128	ARB/15/47	ArcelorMittal S.A	Egypt
129	ARB/16/1	Al Jazeera Media Network	Egypt
130	ARB/16/2	Champion Holding Company and others	Egypt
131	ARB/16/11	Société Resort Company Invest Abidjan, Stanislas Citerici and Gérard Bot Beograd	Côte d'Ivoire
132	ARB/16/15	AngloGold Ashanti (Ghana) Limited	Ghana
133	ARB/16/32	Thomas Gosling and others	Mauritius
134	ARB/16/37	LP Egypt Holdings I, LLC, Fund III Egypt, LLC and OMLP Egypt Holdings I, LLC	Egypt
135	ARB/17/1	Ortiz Construcciones y Proyectos S.A	Algeria

(continued)

(continued)

	Case No.	Claimant(s)	Respondent
136	ARB/17/18	(DS)2, S.A., Peter de Sutter and Kristof De Sutter	Madagascar (II)
137	ARB/17/23	CMC Muratori Cementisti CMC Di Ravenna SOC. Coop., CMC MuratoriCementisti CMC Di Ravenna SOC. Coop. A.R.L. Maputo Branch and CMC Africa, and CMC Africa Austral, LDA	Mozambique
138	ARB/17/28	LTME Mauritius Limited and Madamobil Holdings Mauritius Limited	Madagascar
139	ARB/17/31	Future Pipe International B.V	Egypt
140	ARB/17/33	EcoDevelopment in Europe AB and EcoEnergy Africa AB	Tanzania
141	ARB/17/38	African Petroleum Gambia Limited and APCL Gambia B.V	Gambia
142	ARB/17/39	African Petroleum Gambia Limited and APCL Gambia B.V	Gambia
143	ARB/17/40	APCL Gambia B.V	Gambia
144	ARB/17/48	Wise Solutions CDI, SA	Côte d'Ivoire
145	CONC/18/1	Société d'Energie et d'Eau du Gabon	Gabon
146	ARB/18/11	Société des Parcs d'Alger and Emirates International Investment Company LLC	Algeria
147	ARB/18/7	Corral Morocco Holdings AB	Morocco
148	ARB/18/10	Western African Aquaculture Ltd, Kurt Lennart Hansson and Martje Bolt Hansson	Gambia
149	ARB/18/16	Togo Terminal	Togo
150	ARB/18/21	Bay View Group LLC and The Spalena Company LLC	Rwanda
151	ARB/18/22	Tantalum International Ltd. and Emerge Gaming Ltd	Egypt
152	ARB/18/24	African Petroleum Senegal Limited	Senegal
153	ARB/18/29	The Carlyle Group L.P. and others	Morocco
154	ARB/18/31	International Holding Project Group and others	Egypt
155	ARB/18/36	Société d'Energie et d'Eau du Gabon and Veolia Africa	Gabon and Société de Patrimoine du service public de l'eau potable, de l'énergie électrique et de l'assainissement

(continued)

(continued)

	Case No.	Claimant(s)	Respondent
156	ARB/18/44	SAUR and STEREAU	Algeria
157	CONC/19/1	La Camerounaise des Eaux (CDE)	Cameroon and Cameroon Water Utilities Cooperation (CAMWATER)
158	ARB/19/2	Scholz Holding GmbH	Morocco
159	ARB/19/7	Petroceltic Holdings Limited and Petroceltic Resources Limited	Egypt
160	ARB/19/8	Ayoub-Farid Michel Saab	Tanzania
161	ARB/19/14	Impresa Pizzarotti & C. S.p.A	Morocco
162	ARB/19/17	Richard N. Westbury, Paul D. Hinks and Symbion Power Tanzania Limited	Tanzania
163	ARB/19/24	AAN Digital Services Holding Company (KSC)	D.R. Congo
164	ARB/19/27	CTIP Oil & Gas International Limited	Egypt
165	ARB/19/31	Gerald International Limited	Sierra Leone
166	ARB/20/1	United Agencies Limited SA	Algeria
167	ARB/20/2	Hope Services LLC	Cameroon
168	ARB/20/17	Kansanshi Mining Plc	Zambia
169	ARB/20/24	Teyliom International and others	Benin
170	ARB/20/25	Winshear Gold Corp	Tanzania
171	ARB/20/38	Nachingwea U.K. Limited (UK), Ntaka Nickel Holdings Limited (UK) and Nachingwea Nickel Limited (Tanzania)	Tanzania
172	ARB/20/40	Qatar National Bank (Q.P.S.C.)	South Sudan and Bank of South Sudan
173	ARB/20/41	Eni International B.V., Eni Oil Holdings B.V. and Nigerian Agip Exploration Limited	Nigeria
174	ARB/20/45	Gesenu S.p.A	Egypt
175	ARB/21/6	Montero Mining and Exploration Ltd.	Tanzania
176	ARB/21/7	Shell Petroleum N.V. and The Shell Petroleum Development Company of Nigeria Limited	Nigeria
177	ARB/21/21	KGL International for Ports, Warehousing, and Transport K.S.C.C.	Egypt

Appendix E
List of Non-ICSID Cases African State Parties Under the ICSID Arbitration Rules, ICSID Conciliation Rules, and ICSID Additional Facility Arbitration Rules (as of September 30, 2021, Listed Chronologically)

	Case No.	Claimant(s)	Respondent
1	PCA Case No. 2003–03	Telekom Malaysia Berhad	Ghana
2	Ad hoc arbitration, 2006	Shinhan Engineering & Construction Co	Libya
3	UNCITRAL, 2007	CIM	Ethiopia
4	UNCITRAL, 2008	Intersema Bau AG	Libya
5	2011, ad hoc arbitration, CRCICA	Mohamed Abdulmohsen Al-Kharafi & Sons Co	Libya
6	PCA Case No. 2012–07	Mohamed Abdel Raouf Bahgat	Egypt
7	PCA Case No. 2012–26	Yosef Maiman, Merhav (MNF), Merhav-Ampal Group, Merhav-Ampal Energy Holdings	Egypt
8	PCA Case No. 2012–20	Orascom Telecom Holding S.A.E	Algeria
9	PCA Case No. 2013–29	Swissbourgh Diamond Mines (Pty) Limited, Josias Van Zyl, The Josias Van Zyl Family Trust and others	Lesotho
10	ICC, 2013	Kristof De Sutter, Peter De Sutter, DS 2 S. A. and Polo Garments Majunga S.A.R.L	Madagascar (I)
11	ICC, 2013	Sorelec	Libya
12	PCA Case No.2014–33	Sterling Merchant Finance Ltd	Cabo Verde

(continued)

X. Han, *Legal Protection and Sustainability of Chinese Investments in Africa*, Modern China and International Economic Law,
https://doi.org/10.1007/978-981-19-1882-7

(continued)

	Case No.	Claimant(s)	Respondent
13	ICC, 2014 Case No. 20355/MCP	Olin Holdings Limited	Libya
14	ICC, 2015	Tekfen, TML, Tekfen-TML joint venture	Libya
15	ICC, 2015 Case No. 20971/MCP/DDA	Way2B ACE	Libya
16	UNCITRAL, 2015	KGI	Gabon
17	ICC, 2016 Case No. 21537/ZF/AYZ	Cengiz İnşaat Sanayi ve Ticaret A.S	Libya
18	ICC, 2016	Etrak İnşaat Taahut ve Ticaret Anonim Sirketi	Libya
19	ICC, 2016	Güriş İnşaat ve Mühendislik A.Ş	Libya
20	ICC, 2016	Nurol İnşaat ve Ticaret A.Ş	Libya
21	PCA Case No. 2016–21	The Burmilla Trust, The Josias Van Zyl Family Trust and Josias Van Zyl	Lesotho
22	PCA Case No. 2016–20	Dawood Rawat	Mauritius
23	UNCITRAL, 2016	Nile Douma Holding	Egypt
24	ICC, 2017 Case No. 22673/ZF	Ustay Yapi Taahhut ve Ticaret AS	Libya
25	PCA Case No. 2017–19	Gunvor SA	Zambia (Ministry of Mines, Energy and Water Development)
26	PCA Case No. 2017–21	D.S. Construction FZCO	Libya
27	PCA Case No. 2017–33	Consutel Group S.p.A. in liquidazione	Algeria
28	PCA Case No. 2017–26	ICL Europe Coöperatief U.A	Ethiopia
29	SCC Case No. SCC EA 2017/092	Puma Energy Holdings (Luxembourg) SARL	Benin
30	PCA Case No. 2018–37	Christian Doutremepuich and Antoine Doutremepuich	Mauritius
31	PCA Case No. 2018–09	Sunlodges Ltd. (BVI) and Sunlodges (T) Limited	Tanzania
32	Ad Hoc Arbitration, 2018	Simplex Projects Ltd	Libya
33	UNCITRAL, 2019	Trasta Energy	Libya

(continued)

(continued)

	Case No.	Claimant(s)	Respondent
34	PCA Case No. 2019–16	NIB, S.A.—National Investment Bank (Private entity) Superior Investments LLC (Private entity) Dr. Paulo Miguel Corte-Real Mirpuri (Private entity)	São Tomé e Príncipe
35	2020	Qatar Airways Group Q.C.S.C	Egypt
36	2020	Mustafa Orhan Özer and Nurettin Mendost Dirlik	Libya
37	PCA Case No. 2020–21	Patel Engineering Limited	Mozambique

Appendix F
BITs with an African State as One Contracting Party (as of September 30, 2021, Listed Chronologically)

Date of signature	Date of entry into force	Short title
11/08/1960		Chad–France BIT (1960)
16/05/1961	21/12/1964	Germany–Togo BIT (1961)
31/08/1961	21/01/1968	Germany–Morocco BIT (1961) (Terminated)
02/12/1961	19/01/1964	Switzerland–Tunisia BIT (1961) (Terminated)
12/12/1961	22/10/1967	Germany–Liberia BIT (1961)
28/03/1962	17/11/1962	Niger–Switzerland BIT (1962)
19/04/1962	13/03/1965	Germany–Guinea BIT (1962) (Terminated)
26/04/1962	29/07/1963	Guinea–Switzerland BIT (1962)
26/06/1962	18/11/1962	Côte d'Ivoire–Switzerland BIT (1962)
29/06/1962	21/11/1963	Cameroon–Germany BIT (1962)
16/08/1962	13/08/1964	Senegal–Switzerland BIT (1962)
21/09/1962	21/03/1966	Germany–Madagascar BIT (1962) (Terminated)
18/10/1962	11/07/1964	Congo–Switzerland BIT (1962)
28/01/1963	06/04/1964	Cameroon–Switzerland BIT (1963)
07/02/1963	24/01/1967	Germany–Sudan BIT (1963)
23/05/1963	19/12/1964	Netherlands–Tunisia BIT (1963) (Terminated)
23/07/1963	22/09/1964	Liberia–Switzerland BIT (1963)
09/08/1963	08/09/1963	France–Tunisia BIT (1963) (Terminated)
20/12/1963	06/02/1966	Germany–Tunisia BIT (1963)

(continued)

X. Han, *Legal Protection and Sustainability of Chinese Investments in Africa*, Modern China and International Economic Law,
https://doi.org/10.1007/978-981-19-1882-7

(continued)

Date of signature	Date of entry into force	Short title
17/01/1964	09/08/1966	Switzerland–Togo BIT (1964)
24/01/1964	16/01/1966	Germany–Senegal BIT (1964)
20/02/1964	20/02/1964	Guinea–Italy BIT (1964)
17/03/1964	31/03/1966	Madagascar–Switzerland BIT (1964) (Terminated)
21/04/1964		Ethiopia–Germany BIT (1964) (Terminated)
15/07/1964	09/03/1966	BLEU–Tunisia BIT (1964) (Terminated)
29/10/1964	10/01/1966	Germany–Niger BIT (1964)
30/01/1965	12/07/1968	Germany–Tanzania BIT (1965)
08/04/1965	10/12/1966	Germany–Sierra Leone BIT (1965)
26/04/1965	08/09/1966	Côte d'Ivoire–Netherlands BIT (1965)
28/04/1965	18/10/1967	BLEU–Morocco BIT (1965) (Terminated)
03/05/1965	16/09/1965	Switzerland–Tanzania BIT (1965) (Terminated)
06/07/1965	07/05/1966	Cameroon–Netherlands BIT (1965)
23/08/1965	21/01/1968	Central African Republic–Germany BIT (1965)
27/08/1965	03/11/1966	Côte d'Ivoire–Sweden BIT (1965)
13/09/1965	14/10/1967	Congo–Germany BIT (1965)
02/04/1966	23/06/1967	Madagascar–Sweden BIT (1966)
20/04/1966	06/10/1973	Benin–Switzerland BIT (1966)
02/05/1966	09/08/1966	Egypt–Kuwait BIT (1966) (Terminated)
13/05/1966	28/09/1967	Madagascar–Norway BIT (1966)
27/10/1966	10/06/1968	Côte d'Ivoire–Germany BIT (1966)
29/11/1966	19/08/1968	Germany–Uganda BIT (1966)
10/12/1966	25/08/1972	Germany–Zambia BIT (1966)
21/02/1967	31/10/1967	Chad–Switzerland BIT (1967)
24/02/1967	23/02/1968	Senegal–Sweden BIT (1967)
11/04/1967	23/11/1968	Chad–Germany BIT (1967)
18/05/1967	28/02/1969	Germany–Rwanda BIT (1967)
18/11/1968		Gabon–Italy BIT (1968) (Terminated)
18/03/1969	22/07/1971	D.R. Congo–Germany BIT (1969)
06/05/1969	15/09/1969	Burkina Faso–Switzerland BIT (1969)
16/05/1969	29/03/1971	Gabon–Germany BIT (1969) (Terminated)
11/06/1969	11/06/1969	Chad–Italy BIT (1969)
23/07/1969		Côte d'Ivoire–Italy BIT (1969)
24/04/1970		Netherlands–Uganda BIT (1970) (Terminated)

(continued)

(continued)

Date of signature	Date of entry into force	Short title
22/08/1970	27/03/1972	Netherlands–Sudan BIT (1970)
11/09/1970	11/06/1979	Kenya–Netherlands BIT (1970)
25/05/1971	27/08/1973	Germany–Mauritius BIT (1971)
23/08/1971	08/05/1972	Switzerland–Uganda BIT (1971)
23/12/1971	27/07/1978	Morocco–Netherlands BIT (1971)
10/03/1972	10/05/1973	D.R. Congo–Switzerland BIT (1972)
30/06/1972	30/06/1972	France–Tunisia BIT (1972) (Terminated)
05/10/1972	01/03/1975	D.R. Congo–France BIT (1972)
28/02/1973	04/07/1973	Central African Republic–Switzerland BIT (1973)
22/03/1973	01/03/1974	France–Mauritius BIT (1973)
06/06/1973		Libya–Tunisia BIT (1973) (Terminated)
25/07/1973	04/06/1974	Egypt–Switzerland BIT (1973) (Terminated)
14/09/1973	28/05/2006	Kuwait–Tunisia BIT (1973)
17/02/1974	14/12/1974	Sudan–Switzerland BIT (1974)
05/07/1974	22/07/1978	Egypt–Germany BIT (1974) (Terminated)
22/12/1974	01/10/1975	Egypt–France BIT (1974)
23/05/1975	28/11/1975	Republic of Korea–Tunisia BIT (1975)
11/06/1975	24/02/1976	Egypt–United Kingdom BIT (1975)
15/07/1975	13/12/1976	France–Morocco BIT (1975) (Terminated)
14/11/1975		Senegal–Syria BIT (1975)
10/05/1976	02/01/1977	Egypt–Romania BIT (1976) (Terminated)
03/06/1976	07/09/1978	Egypt–Morocco BIT (1976) (Terminated)
09/09/1976	30/05/1978	Mauritania–Switzerland BIT (1976)
30/10/1976	01/01/1978	Egypt–Netherlands BIT (1976) (Terminated)
28/01/1977	14/01/1978	Egypt–Japan BIT (1977)
28/02/1977	20/09/1978	BLEU–Egypt BIT (1977) (Terminated)
25/05/1977		Egypt–Iran BIT (1977)
28/05/1977	14/03/1978	Egypt–Sudan BIT (1977) (Terminated)
03/06/1977	20/03/1979	Egypt–Serbia BIT (1977) (Terminated)
28/06/1977	16/05/1980	Germany–Mali BIT (1977)
08/03/1978	08/12/1978	Mali–Switzerland BIT (1978)
29/06/1978	18/07/1985	Benin–Germany BIT (1978)
15/07/1978	29/01/1979	Egypt–Sweden BIT (1978)
31/07/1978	05/07/1980	France–Sudan BIT (1978)
08/12/1978		Romania–Sudan BIT (1978)
13/01/1979	07/11/1979	Gabon–Morocco BIT (1979) (Terminated)

(continued)

(continued)

Date of signature	Date of entry into force	Short title
23/03/1979	22/01/1982	France–Liberia BIT (1979)
11/04/1979	18/09/1982	Gabon–Romania BIT (1979)
03/08/1979	05/05/1981	Netherlands–Senegal BIT (1979)
27/03/1980	01/11/1981	BLEU–Cameroon BIT (1980)
03/04/1980		Kuwait–Morocco BIT (1980) (Terminated)
05/05/1980	22/01/1982	Egypt–Finland BIT (1980) (Terminated)
07/05/1980	09/02/1984	Senegal–United Kingdom BIT (1980)
19/06/1980	20/05/1984	Romania–Senegal BIT (1980)
30/08/1980	24/09/1981	Cameroon–Romania BIT (1980)
18/02/1981	18/02/1981	Lesotho–United Kingdom BIT (1981)
27/11/1981	15/02/1985	Germany–Somalia BIT (1981)
03/03/1982	23/09/1983	Equatorial Guinea–France BIT (1982)
29/05/1982	16/04/1983	Egypt–Somalia BIT (1982)
04/06/1982	07/06/1985	Cameroon–United Kingdom BIT (1982)
16/06/1982		Morocco–United Arab Emirates BIT (1982) (Terminated)
11/11/1982	17/08/1985	Germany–Lesotho BIT (1982)
08/12/1982	26/04/1986	Germany–Mauritania BIT (1982)
02/11/1983	01/08/1985	BLEU–Rwanda BIT (1983)
23/11/1983		BLEU–Mauritania BIT (1983)
06/12/1983	25/10/1990	Senegal–United States BIT (1983)
25/01/1984	18/09/1993	Libya–Morocco BIT (1984) (Terminated)
17/05/1984	07/05/1985	Senegal–Tunisia BIT (1984)
12/07/1984	02/09/1985	Republic of Korea–Senegal BIT (1984)
03/08/1984	28/07/1989	D.R. Congo–United States BIT (1984)
10/09/1984	09/12/1987	Burundi–Germany BIT (1984)
15/09/1984	13/05/1985	Sweden–Tunisia BIT (1984)
28/04/1985		Egypt–Oman BIT (1985) (Terminated)
05/06/1985		BLEU–Liberia BIT (1985)
22/07/1985	29/05/1991	Morocco–United States BIT (1985)
17/10/1985	24/06/1989	Italy–Tunisia BIT (1985)
17/12/1985	12/04/1991	Morocco–Switzerland BIT (1985)
26/02/1986	06/04/1989	Cameroon–United States BIT (1986)
11/03/1986		Mauritania–Tunisia BIT (1986)
11/03/1986	27/06/1992	Egypt–United States BIT (1986)
20/05/1986	13/10/1986	Mauritius–United Kingdom BIT (1986)
01/07/1986		Mali–Tunisia BIT (1986)

(continued)

(continued)

Date of signature	Date of entry into force	Short title
11/02/1987	09/03/1990	Togo–Tunisia BIT (1987)
27/11/1987	27/11/1987	Benin–United Kingdom BIT (1987)
14/03/1988	19/12/1989	Mauritania–Romania BIT (1988)
19/06/1988	02/03/1998	Egypt–United Arab Emirates BIT (1988) (Terminated)
19/10/1988	03/03/1990	Egypt–Yemen BIT (1988) (Terminated)
18/10/1988	22/03/1995	Morocco–Portugal BIT (1988)
02/03/1989	01/05/1994	Egypt–Italy BIT (1989)
14/03/1989	04/01/1990	Tunisia–United Kingdom BIT (1989)
22/03/1989	25/10/1991	Ghana–United Kingdom BIT (1989)
31/03/1989	01/07/1991	Ghana–Netherlands BIT (1989)
13/04/1989	12/09/1993	BLEU–Burundi BIT (1989)
25/05/1989	09/11/1990	Congo–United Kingdom BIT (1989)
14/09/1989		Ghana–Romania BIT (1989)
27/09/1989	15/01/1992	Morocco–Spain BIT (1989) (Terminated)
12/10/1989	22/11/1990	China–Ghana BIT (1989)
20/10/1989		Bulgaria–Ghana BIT (1989)
08/12/1989	02/01/1991	Egypt–Tunisia BIT (1989)
18/01/1990	15/12/1993	Cape Verde–Germany BIT (1990)
12/02/1990	13/08/1994	Congo–United States BIT (1990)
27/02/1990	19/08/1991	France–Nigeria BIT (1990)
05/04/1990	07/08/1995	Eswatini–Germany BIT (1990)
15/05/1990	07/02/1993	Tunisia–United States BIT (1990)
18/07/1990	26/04/2000	Italy–Morocco BIT (1990)
19/07/1990		D.R. Congo–Republic of Korea BIT (1990)
12/09/1990		Mozambique–Zimbabwe BIT (1990)
13/09/1990	13/09/1990	Burundi–United Kingdom BIT (1990)
26/09/1990	16/06/2008	Morocco–Sweden BIT (1990)
26/10/1990	04/10/1991	Cape Verde–Portugal BIT (1990)
30/10/1990	14/02/2002	Morocco–United Kingdom BIT (1990)
18/11/1990		Guinea–Tunisia BIT (1990)
03/12/1990	04/07/1991	Egypt–Libya BIT (1990)
11/12/1990	11/12/1990	Nigeria–United Kingdom BIT (1990)
24/04/1991	17/10/2002	Algeria–BLEU BIT (1991)
26/04/1991		D.R. Congo–Greece BIT (1991)
18/05/1991	26/11/1993	Algeria–Italy BIT (1991) (Terminated)
28/05/1991	20/06/1994	Spain–Tunisia BIT (1991)

(continued)

(continued)

Date of signature	Date of entry into force	Short title
29/05/1991	28/04/1994	Tunisia–Turkey BIT (1991)
24/06/1991	08/04/1996	Guinea-Bissau–Portugal BIT (1991)
03/09/1991	01/04/1993	Austria–Cape Verde BIT (1991) (Terminated)
08/10/1991	16/06/1993	Ghana–Switzerland BIT (1991)
19/10/1991	01/03/1992	Oman–Tunisia BIT (1991)
28/10/1991	06/05/1992	Cape Verde–Switzerland BIT (1991)
11/11/1991	25/11/1992	Cape Verde–Netherlands BIT (1991)
12/12/1991	03/02/2000	Hungary–Morocco BIT (1991)
13/01/1992	06/01/1995	Denmark–Ghana BIT (1992)
11/03/1992	06/12/1994	Portugal–Tunisia BIT (1992) (Terminated)
11/05/1992	03/12/1993	Argentina–Egypt BIT (1992)
13/05/1992	12/09/1992	Indonesia–Tunisia BIT (1992)
05/06/1992		Niger–Tunisia BIT (1992)
17/06/1992	23/01/1995	Argentina–Tunisia BIT (1992)
31/10/1992	21/04/1995	Greece–Tunisia BIT (1992)
02/11/1992	01/07/1995	Austria–Morocco BIT (1992)
02/11/1992	01/02/1994	Netherlands–Nigeria BIT (1992)
03/11/1992	26/04/1994	Egypt–Spain BIT (1992)
16/12/1992	08/02/1994	Egypt–Uzbekistan BIT (1992)
21/12/1992	10/10/1993	Egypt–Ukraine BIT (1992)
07/01/1993	15/10/2003	Burkina Faso–Tunisia BIT (1993)
08/02/1993	07/10/1995	Libya–Syria BIT (1993)
13/02/1993	27/06/2000	Algeria–France BIT (1993)
14/02/1993	08/08/1996	Egypt–Kazakhstan BIT (1993)
29/03/1993	22/09/1993	Poland–Tunisia BIT (1993)
06/04/1993	01/02/2010	Argentina–Senegal BIT (1993)
22/05/1993	06/04/1994	Albania–Egypt BIT (1993)
29/05/1993	04/06/1994	Czech Republic–Egypt BIT (1993)
16/07/1993	06/04/1995	Egypt–Greece BIT (1993)
30/10/1993		Albania–Tunisia BIT (1993)
22/11/1993	30/03/1994	Gambia–Switzerland BIT (1993)
07/01/1994	02/08/1996	Tanzania–United Kingdom BIT (1994)
19/01/1994	29/11/1994	Egypt–Indonesia BIT (1994) (Terminated)
21/01/1994	21/12/1997	Germany–Namibia BIT (1994)
28/01/1994	01/04/1999	Morocco–Tunisia BIT (1994)
28/01/1994	03/02/2000	Morocco–Romania BIT (1994)
16/02/1994	28/06/2000	Greece–Morocco BIT (1994)

(continued)

(continued)

Date of signature	Date of entry into force	Short title
17/03/1994	10/01/2003	Congo–Italy BIT (1994)
07/04/1994	07/04/1994	Nigeria–Taiwan BIT (1994)
21/04/1994	01/04/1996	China–Egypt BIT (1994)
28/04/1994		Malaysia–Zimbabwe BIT (1994)
05/05/1994		Portugal–Zimbabwe BIT (1994)
28/06/1994	30/12/1995	Algeria–Romania BIT (1994)
01/08/1994	26/04/2000	Namibia–Switzerland BIT (1994)
03/08/1994	07/03/1995	Switzerland–Zambia BIT (1994)
12/08/1994	02/11/1996	Malaysia–Namibia BIT (1994)
15/09/1994		Algeria–Portugal BIT (1994) (Terminated)
20/09/1994	27/05/1998	South Africa–United Kingdom BIT (1994) (Terminated)
24/10/1994	09/07/1999	Morocco–Poland BIT (1994)
13/11/1994	27/02/2000	Comoros–Egypt BIT (1994)
24/11/1994	03/04/1997	Egypt–Romania BIT (1994) (Renewed)
23/12/1994	17/01/1996	Algeria–Spain BIT (1994)
23/12/1994	08/05/1997	Ethiopia–Italy BIT (1994)
24/02/1995	23/11/1998	Germany–Ghana BIT (1995)
01/03/1995		United Kingdom–Zimbabwe BIT (1995)
02/03/1995	12/12/2001	Gabon–Spain BIT (1995)
04/03/1995		Mali–South Africa BIT
27/03/1995	27/11/1999	China–Morocco BIT (1995)
22/04/1995		Malawi–Taiwan BIT (1995)
27/04/1995	23/11/1995	Jordan–Tunisia BIT (1995)
05/05/1995	05/05/1995	Eswatini–United Kingdom BIT (1995)
09/05/1995	01/05/1999	Netherlands–South Africa BIT (1995) (Terminated)
12/05/1995		Portugal–Sao Tome and Principe BIT (1995)
16/05/1995		Côte d'Ivoire–Tunisia BIT (1995)
23/05/1995	21/08/1997	Egypt–Hungary BIT (1995)
23/05/1995	28/02/1996	Egypt–Turkmenistan BIT (1995)
01/06/1995	01/01/1997	Austria–Tunisia BIT (1995)
08/06/1995	09/10/1997	Côte d'Ivoire–United Kingdom BIT (1995)
27/06/1995	30/11/1997	South Africa–Switzerland BIT (1995) (Terminated)
01/07/1995	17/01/1998	Egypt–Poland BIT (1995)
07/07/1995	28/06/1997	Republic of Korea–South Africa BIT (1995)
26/07/1995		Gambia–Libya BIT (1995)

(continued)

(continued)

Date of signature	Date of entry into force	Short title
11/09/1995	10/04/1998	Germany–South Africa BIT (1995) (Terminated)
29/09/1995	14/04/2000	Germany–Zimbabwe BIT (1995)
11/10/1995	22/06/1997	France–South Africa BIT (1995) (Terminated)
16/10/1995	08/08/1997	Romania–Tunisia BIT (1995)
04/11/1995		Egypt–Uganda BIT (1995)
27/11/1995		Canada–South Africa BIT (1995)
08/12/1995	07/04/1997	Cuba–South Africa BIT (1995)
09/01/1996	01/03/2006	Armenia–Egypt BIT (1996)
13/01/1996	30/05/1999	France–Morocco BIT (1996) (Renewed)
17/01/1996	01/03/1998	Egypt–Netherlands BIT (1996) (Renewed)
22/02/1996	23/04/1997	Denmark–South Africa BIT (1996) (Terminated)
11/03/1996	30/05/2002	Algeria–Germany BIT (1996)
11/03/1996	10/03/1998	Egypt–Sri Lanka BIT (1996)
16/03/1996	02/06/1997	Egypt–Lebanon BIT (1996)
18/03/1996	25/05/1997	Egypt–Republic of Korea BIT (1996)
10/04/1996	24/02/1997	Tunisia–United Arab Emirates BIT (1996)
18/04/1996		Pakistan–Tunisia BIT (1996)
03/05/1996	07/12/2000	Germany–Kenya BIT (1996)
04/05/1996	08/06/1997	China–Mauritius BIT (1996)
08/05/1996	11/04/1998	Egypt–Jordan BIT (1996)
21/05/1996	01/03/1998	China–Zimbabwe BIT (1996)
22/05/1996	19/02/2000	Bulgaria–Morocco BIT (1996)
28/05/1996	31/10/1998	Mozambique–Portugal BIT (1996)
28/05/1996		Qatar–Tunisia BIT (1996)
06/06/1996	10/04/1998	Egypt–Yemen BIT (1996) (Renewed)
13/06/1996	19/02/2000	Argentina–Morocco BIT (1996)
21/06/1996		China–Zambia BIT (1996)
28/06/1996	11/04/1997	Denmark–Tunisia BIT (1996)
11/07/1996	16/02/1999	Algeria–Mali BIT (1996)
01/08/1996	05/06/1997	Algeria–Jordan BIT (1996)
15/08/1996	09/02/2001	Switzerland–Zimbabwe BIT (1996)
05/09/1996		Malawi–Malaysia BIT (1996)
14/09/1996	12/11/1998	Ethiopia–Kuwait BIT (1996)
16/09/1996	04/08/1999	Italy–Kenya BIT (1996) (Terminated)
19/09/1996	22/07/1997	Serbia–Zimbabwe BIT (1996)
21/09/1996		Iran–Zimbabwe BIT (1996) (Terminated)

(continued)

(continued)

Date of signature	Date of entry into force	Short title
04/10/1996	31/07/2002	Egypt–Turkey BIT (1996)
08/10/1996		Nigeria–Turkey BIT (1996)
17/10/1996	28/01/2003	Algeria–China BIT (1996)
21/10/1996		Algeria–Viet Nam BIT (1996)
22/10/1996	21/11/2009	Burkina Faso–Germany BIT (1996)
22/10/1996	13/03/1998	Guinea–Serbia BIT (1996)
24/10/1996		Algeria–Qatar BIT (1996)
25/10/1996	07/02/1999	Denmark–Zimbabwe BIT (1996)
07/11/1996	24/02/1997	Guinea–Malaysia BIT (1996)
08/11/1996	18/04/1997	Ghana–Malaysia BIT (1996)
13/11/1996	03/11/1997	Canada–Egypt BIT (1996)
28/11/1996	01/01/1998	Austria–South Africa BIT (1996) (Terminated)
11/12/1996	01/05/1998	Netherlands–Zimbabwe BIT (1996)
06/01/1997	08/07/1998	Czech Republic–Tunisia BIT (1997)
08/01/1997	18/10/2002	BLEU–Tunisia BIT (1997) (Renewed)
14/02/1997	26/05/2003	Mauritius–Mozambique BIT (1997)
24/02/1997		Morocco–Yemen BIT (1997)
05/03/1997	28/03/2000	Indonesia–Mauritius BIT (1997)
14/03/1997	21/03/2002	Indonesia–Morocco BIT (1997)
20/03/1997	18/01/1999	Belarus–Egypt BIT (1997)
29/03/1997	03/05/2000	Algeria–Egypt BIT (1997)
03/04/1997	03/04/1997	Mauritius–Pakistan BIT (1997)
08/04/1997	30/05/2004	Morocco–Turkey BIT (1997)
09/04/1997	22/11/2000	Egypt–India BIT (1997) (Terminated)
14/04/1997	03/02/2000	Egypt–Malaysia BIT (1997)
15/04/1997	20/03/2002	Egypt–Singapore BIT (1997)
24/04/1997	03/06/1998	Egypt–Latvia BIT (1997)
28/04/1997	05/10/1998	Egypt–Syria BIT (1997)
30/04/1997		Egypt–Tanzania BIT (1997)
30/04/1997	01/01/2000	Egypt–Slovakia BIT (1997)
30/04/1997		Egypt–Tanzania BIT (1997)
06/05/1997		Mozambique–South Africa BIT (1997)
09/05/1997	16/02/2009	China–Gabon BIT (1997)
11/05/1997	11/01/1999	Egypt–United Arab Emirates BIT (1997)
12/05/1997		China–Nigeria BIT (1997) (Terminated)
14/05/1997	01/07/1998	Egypt–Morocco BIT (1997) (Renewed)

(continued)

(continued)

Date of signature	Date of entry into force	Short title
22/05/1997	08/01/2003	Cape Verde–Cuba BIT (1997)
30/05/1997	01/07/1998	China–Sudan BIT (1997)
09/06/1997	16/03/1999	Italy–South Africa BIT (1997) (Terminated)
12/06/1997		Cape Verde–Italy BIT (1997)
27/06/1997		Cuba–Namibia BIT (1997)
03/07/1997	04/03/2000	Lebanon–Morocco BIT (1997)
10/07/1997	21/05/2007	Angola–Italy BIT (1997)
31/07/1997		Botswana–Malaysia BIT (1997)
19/08/1997	12/01/2000	Egypt–DPRK BIT (1997)
06/09/1997	04/03/2002	Egypt–Viet Nam BIT (1997)
10/09/1997	24/07/2014	Cameroon–China BIT (1997)
11/09/1997	15/12/1997	Angola–Cape Verde BIT (1997)
14/09/1997		Algeria–Syria BIT (1997)
23/09/1997	12/06/2000	Egypt–Russian Federation BIT (1997)
04/10/1997	11/01/1999	Bahrain–Egypt BIT (1997)
06/10/1997		Sweden–Zimbabwe BIT (1997)
20/10/1997	10/09/1999	France–Tunisia BIT (1997) (Renewed)
21/10/1997	07/09/1999	Egypt–Malawi BIT (1997)
24/10/1997	24/04/2020	Angola–Portugal BIT (1997)
24/10/1997		Senegal–Taiwan BIT (1997)
27/10/1997	02/05/1999	Croatia–Egypt BIT (1997)
03/11/1997	05/03/2002	Iran–South Africa BIT (1997)
04/11/1997		Côte d'Ivoire–Ghana BIT (1997)
04/12/1997		Chad–Morocco BIT (1997)
11/12/1997	13/04/2005	Morocco–Spain BIT (1997) (Renewed)
12/12/1997	03/01/1999	Mauritius–Portugal BIT (1997)
12/12/1997	24/09/1999	Italy–Uganda BIT (1997) (Terminated)
18/12/1997		China–D.R. Congo BIT (1997)
22/12/1997		Egypt–Gabon BIT (1997)
30/12/1997	01/04/1998	China–South Africa BIT (1997)
10/02/1998		Indonesia–Sudan BIT (1998)
17/02/1998	23/10/1998	Mauritius–South Africa BIT (1998)
03/03/1998		Eswatini–Taiwan BIT (1998)
04/03/1998		Egypt–Niger BIT (1998)
05/03/1998		Egypt–Senegal BIT (1998)
06/03/1998		Egypt–Guinea BIT (1998)
08/03/1998		Tunisia–Yemen BIT (1998)

(continued)

(continued)

Date of signature	Date of entry into force	Short title
09/03/1998	07/07/2000	Egypt–Mali BIT (1998)
11/03/1998		Egypt–Ghana BIT (1998)
11/03/1998	29/10/2001	Bosnia and Herzegovina–Egypt BIT (1998)
11/03/1998		Egypt–Ghana BIT (1998)
14/03/1998		Chad–Egypt BIT (1998)
15/03/1998	08/06/2000	Bulgaria–Egypt BIT (1998)
16/03/1998		Algeria–Niger BIT (1998)
25/03/1998	03/03/2000	Egypt–Oman BIT (1998) (Renewed)
27/03/1998	01/02/1999	Republic of Korea–Nigeria BIT (1998)
21/04/1998	01/01/2001	Cape Verde–China BIT (1998)
23/04/1998	18/08/2003	Burkina Faso–Malaysia BIT (1998)
24/04/1998	24/04/1998	Uganda–United Kingdom BIT (1998)
28/04/1998	19/06/1999	Egypt–State of Palestine BIT (1998)
11/05/1998	01/05/2000	China–Ethiopia BIT (1998)
11/05/1998	01/08/1999	Netherlands–Tunisia BIT (1998) (Renewed)
25/05/1998	01/01/1999	South Africa–Sweden BIT (1998)
27/05/1998	28/05/2005	BLEU–Gabon BIT (1998)
28/05/1998	19/03/1999	Cyprus–Seychelles BIT (1998)
03/06/1998		Algeria–Turkey BIT (1998)
03/06/1998		Qatar–Sudan BIT (1998)
10/06/1998		Qatar–Senegal BIT (1998)
16/06/1998	07/02/2000	Jordan–Morocco BIT (1998)
19/06/1998	29/12/2010	Senegal–South Africa BIT (1998)
24/06/1998	04/06/2000	Lebanon–Tunisia BIT (1998)
25/06/1998		Ghana–Italy BIT (1998)
25/06/1998	26/02/2006	France–Namibia BIT (1998)
26/06/1998	13/04/2000	Botswana–Switzerland BIT (1998)
26/06/1998	07/12/1998	Ethiopia–Switzerland BIT (1998)
09/07/1998		Ghana–South Africa BIT (1998)
21/07/1998		Djibouti–Egypt BIT (1998)
23/07/1998	01/01/2001	Argentina–South Africa BIT (1998) (Terminated)
02/08/1998		Malaysia–Sudan BIT (1998)
03/08/1998		Djibouti–Malaysia BIT (1998)
14/08/1998	14/03/2003	BLEU–South Africa BIT (1998) (Terminated)
04/09/1998	20/06/2000	India–Mauritius BIT (1998) (Terminated)
14/09/1998	03/10/1999	Finland–South Africa BIT (1998)

(continued)

(continued)

Date of signature	Date of entry into force	Short title
15/09/1998	04/07/2007	Gabon–Germany BIT (1998) (Renewed)
30/09/1998	23/12/1999	South Africa–Spain BIT (1998) (Terminated)
09/10/1998	18/08/2003	Burkina Faso–Taiwan BIT (1998)
21/10/1998	11/05/1999	Cyprus–Egypt BIT (1998)
22/10/1998	04/06/1999	Ethiopia–Malaysia BIT (1998)
23/10/1998		Chile–Tunisia BIT (1998)
25/10/1998	06/06/2002	Algeria–Bulgaria BIT (1998)
28/10/1998		Egypt–South Africa BIT (1998)
28/10/1998	07/02/2000	Egypt–Slovenia BIT (1998)
28/10/1998		Egypt–South Africa BIT (1998)
12/11/1998		Chile–South Africa BIT (1998)
19/11/1998	06/09/2001	Greece–South Africa BIT (1998)
23/11/1998	12/04/2000	Russian Federation–South Africa BIT (1998)
26/11/1998	21/04/2000	Mauritius–Switzerland BIT (1998)
01/12/1998	03/03/2005	Mozambique–United States BIT (1998)
08/12/1998		Egypt–Mozambique BIT (1998)
12/12/1998	25/07/2000	Algeria–Mozambique BIT (1998)
14/12/1998	17/11/2003	Italy–Mozambique BIT (1998)
14/12/1998		Czech Republic–South Africa BIT (1998)
18/12/1998		D.R. Congo–Egypt BIT (1998)
18/12/1998	03/06/2005	Nigeria–Romania BIT (1998)
18/12/1998		Republic of Korea–Tanzania BIT (1998)
21/12/1998		Bulgaria–Nigeria BIT (1998)
25/01/1999	15/07/2005	Algeria–Denmark BIT (1999)
27/01/1999	08/05/2001	Republic of Korea–Morocco BIT (1999)
09/02/1999	01/04/2002	Morocco–United Arab Emirates BIT (1999) (Renewed)
10/02/1999		Egypt–Jamaica BIT (1999)
10/02/1999		India–Zimbabwe BIT (1999) (Terminated)
10/02/1999		Indonesia–Zimbabwe BIT (1999)
10/02/1999		Jamaica–Zimbabwe BIT (1999)
11/02/1999		Malaysia–Senegal BIT (1999)
12/02/1999	14/07/2006	Egypt–Qatar BIT (1999)
13/02/1999	22/02/2001	India–Morocco BIT (1999) (Terminated)
16/02/1999	07/05/2001	Kuwait–Morocco BIT (1999) (Renewed)
20/02/1999	17/07/2000	Egypt–Malta BIT (1999)
20/02/1999	21/05/2001	Morocco–Qatar BIT (1999)

(continued)

(continued)

Date of signature	Date of entry into force	Short title
23/02/1999	04/07/2002	Morocco–Sudan BIT (1999)
28/02/1999	24/05/2002	BLEU–Egypt BIT (1999) (Renewed)
26/03/1999		France–Ghana BIT (1999)
26/03/1999	25/07/2000	Indonesia–Mozambique BIT (1999)
01/04/1999	15/06/2013	BLEU–Côte d'Ivoire BIT (1999)
05/04/1999	06/05/2000	Czech Republic–Mauritius BIT (1999)
13/04/1999	29/05/2002	BLEU–Morocco BIT (1999) (Renewed)
15/04/1999	15/04/2000	Ethiopia–Yemen BIT (1999)
16/04/1999		Italy–Zimbabwe BIT (1999)
21/04/1999	11/04/2002	El Salvador–Morocco BIT (1999)
22/04/1999	21/10/2005	Denmark–Tanzania BIT (1999)
26/04/1999	14/07/2003	Eritrea–Italy BIT (1996)
29/04/1999	23/12/2000	Egypt–Portugal BIT (1999)
09/05/1999	26/01/2015	Iran–Zimbabwe BIT (1999) (Renewed)
02/06/1999		Egypt–Zimbabwe BIT (1999)
18/06/1999	07/07/2006	Gabon–Italy BIT (1999) (Renewed)
24/06/1999	29/10/2000	Denmark–Egypt BIT (1999)
29/06/1999	04/01/2004	Cameroon–Italy BIT (1999)
03/08/1999		Mauritius–Nepal BIT (1999)
05/08/1999		Chile–Egypt BIT (1999)
10/08/1999		Egypt–Georgia BIT (1999)
10/08/1999		Sudan–Yemen BIT (1999)
01/09/1999	01/03/2002	Sweden–Tanzania BIT (1999)
07/09/1999	19/10/2001	Iran–Sudan BIT (1999)
13/09/1999	13/09/1999	Kenya–United Kingdom BIT (1999)
13/09/1999		Czech Republic–Zimbabwe BIT (1999)
11/10/1999		DPRK- Mali BIT (1999)
12/10/1999	30/09/2001	Algeria–Republic of Korea BIT (1999)
25/10/1999	28/05/2002	Oman–Sudan BIT (1999)
02/11/1999		Cuba–Ghana BIT (1999)
19/11/1999	19/01/2004	Bulgaria–Libya BIT (1999)
22/11/1999		Chad–Qatar BIT (1999)
22/11/1999		Egypt–Macedonia BIT (1999)
25/11/1999		Algeria–Yemen BIT (1999)
19/12/1999		Sudan–Turkey BIT (1999)
07/01/2000	01/09/2001	Sudan–Syria BIT (2000)

(continued)

(continued)

Date of signature	Date of entry into force	Short title
13/01/2000	20/11/2001	Sierra Leone–United Kingdom BIT (2000) (Renewed)
17/01/2000		Bahrain–Sudan BIT (2000)
20/01/2000	20/12/2000	Mauritius–Romania BIT (2000)
22/01/2000		Cuba–Zambia BIT (2000)
27/01/2000	09/02/2002	Algeria–Malaysia BIT (2000)
07/02/2000		Central Africa–Egypt BIT (2000)
10/02/2000		Ethiopia–Russian Federation BIT (2000)
18/02/2000	27/02/2002	Egypt–Thailand BIT (2000)
18/02/2000		Croatia–Zimbabwe BIT (2000)
18/02/2000		Thailand–Zimbabwe BIT (2000)
20/02/2000	21/09/2007	Algeria–Greece BIT (2000)
04/03/2000	19/04/2000	Mauritius–Singapore BIT (2000)
07/03/2000	15/05/2001	Ethiopia–Sudan BIT (2000)
07/03/2000	22/11/2008	Kuwait–Zimbabwe BIT (2000)
20/03/2000	01/07/2015	China–Congo BIT (2000)
21/03/2000		Algeria–Indonesia BIT (2000)
28/03/2000	20/09/2007	Germany–Nigeria BIT (2000)
30/03/2000	03/02/2001	Jordan–Sudan BIT (2000)
07/04/2000	09/04/2001	Bahrain–Morocco BIT (2000)
09/04/2000	22/06/2002	Algeria–Oman BIT (2000)
16/04/2000		Egypt–Pakistan BIT (2000)
25/04/2000	07/07/2000	Ghana–Serbia BIT (2000)
28/04/2000		Egypt–Zambia BIT (2000)
29/04/2000	27/07/2005	Nigeria–South Africa BIT (2000)
08/05/2000		South Africa–Uganda BIT (2000)
15/05/2000		Eswatini–Mauritius BIT (2000)
17/05/2000		Mauritius–Zimbabwe BIT (2000)
23/05/2000	06/08/2007	Botswana–Germany BIT (2000)
30/05/2000	01/01/2003	Netherlands–Uganda BIT (2000) (Renewed)
11/06/2000	16/05/2008	Algeria–Bahrain BIT (2000)
12/06/2000		Botswana–China BIT (2000)
13/06/2000	20/10/2003	Mauritania–Morocco BIT (2000)
20/06/2000		Egypt–Nigeria BIT (2000)
23/06/2000		South Africa–Turkey BIT (2000)
04/07/2000		Angola–United Kingdom BIT (2000)
18/07/2000		Egypt–Eswatini BIT (2000)

(continued)

(continued)

Date of signature	Date of entry into force	Short title
07/08/2000		Eritrea–Qatar BIT (2000)
01/09/2000		Singapore–Zimbabwe BIT (2000)
22/09/2000		Algeria–Czech Republic BIT (2000)
24/09/2000		Algeria–South Africa BIT (2000)
27/09/2000	22/08/2005	Italy–Nigeria BIT (2000)
04/10/2000	28/01/2002	Algeria–Argentina BIT (2000)
11/10/2000		D.R. Congo–Ukraine BIT (2000)
13/10/2000	16/12/2008	Italy–Senegal BIT (2000)
19/10/2000		Rwanda–South Africa BIT (2000)
24/10/2000		Cameroon–Egypt BIT (2000)
26/10/2000	12/05/2002	Malta–Tunisia BIT (2000)
01/11/2000	23/02/2002	Belarus–Libya BIT (2000)
02/11/2000	20/10/2001	Libya–Morocco BIT (2000) (Renewed)
10/11/2000	01/01/2004	Burkina Faso–Netherlands BIT (2000) (Terminated)
10/11/2000		Austria–Zimbabwe BIT (2000)
16/11/2000	10/03/2005	Ethiopia–Turkey BIT (2000)
24/11/2000	15/10/2003	Bulgaria–Tunisia BIT (2000)
30/11/2000	01/04/2003	Nigeria–Switzerland BIT (2000)
13/12/2000	20/10/2004	Italy–Libya BIT (2000)
14/12/2000	02/10/2004	Ethiopia–Tunisia BIT (2000)
21/01/2001	31/03/2003	Iran–Morocco BIT (2001)
23/01/2001	23/04/2003	Libya–Ukraine BIT (2001)
23/01/2001	13/03/2004	Syria–Tunisia BIT (2001)
04/02/2001	10/06/2001	Djibouti–Switzerland BIT (2001)
04/02/2001		Kuwait–Sudan BIT (2001)
18/02/2001		Morocco–Senegal BIT (2001)
18/02/2001		Sudan–United Arab Emirates BIT (2001)
20/02/2001		Gabon–Lebanon BIT (2001)
24/02/2001		Morocco–Yemen BIT (2001)
12/04/2001	29/04/2002	Austria–Egypt BIT (2001)
16/04/2001		Morocco–Pakistan BIT (2001)
17/04/2001	26/04/2002	Egypt–Kuwait BIT (2001) (Renewed)
23/04/2001	27/02/2003	Iran–Tunisia BIT (2001)
24/04/2001	03/06/2002	Algeria–United Arab Emirates BIT (2001)
24/04/2001	21/08/2005	Denmark–Ethiopia BIT (2001)
03/05/2001	05/09/2002	Australia–Egypt BIT (2001)

(continued)

(continued)

Date of signature	Date of entry into force	Short title
04/05/2001		France–Zimbabwe BIT (2001)
08/05/2001	30/03/2003	Morocco–Oman BIT (2001)
09/05/2001		Gambia–Mauritania BIT (2001)
16/05/2001		China–Sierra Leone BIT (2001)
18/05/2001	18/08/2003	Benin–Burkina Faso BIT (2001)
18/05/2001		Benin–Chad BIT (2001)
18/05/2001		Benin–Ghana BIT (2001)
18/05/2001		Benin–Mauritius BIT (2001)
18/05/2001	30/08/2007	BLEU–Benin BIT (2001)
18/05/2001		Burkina Faso–Chad BIT (2001)
18/05/2001	18/08/2003	Burkina Faso–Comoros BIT (2001)
18/05/2001	18/08/2003	Burkina Faso–Ghana BIT (2001)
18/05/2001	18/08/2003	Burkina Faso–Mauritania BIT (2001)
18/05/2001	13/01/2004	BLEU–Burkina Faso BIT (2001)
18/05/2001		Burundi–Comoros BIT (2001)
18/05/2001	22/11/2009	Burundi–Mauritius BIT (2001)
18/05/2001		Cameroon–Guinea BIT (2001)
18/05/2001		Cameroon–Mali BIT (2001)
18/05/2001		Cameroon–Mauritania BIT (2001)
18/05/2001		Chad–Mali BIT (2001)
18/05/2001		Chad–Mauritius BIT (2001)
18/05/2001		Comoros–Mali BIT (2001)
18/05/2001		Comoros–Mauritius BIT (2001)
18/05/2001		BLEU–Comoros BIT (2001)
18/05/2001		Ghana–Guinea BIT (2001)
18/05/2001		Ghana–Mauritania BIT (2001)
18/05/2001		Ghana–Mauritius BIT (2001)
18/05/2001		Ghana–Zambia BIT (2001)
18/05/2001		Benin–Guinea BIT (2001)
18/05/2001		Guinea–Mali BIT (2001)
18/05/2001		Guinea–Mauritania BIT (2001)
18/05/2001		Guinea–Mauritius BIT (2001)
18/05/2001		Benin–Mali BIT (2001)
18/05/2001		Mauritania–Mauritius BIT (2001)
18/05/2001		BLEU–Zambia BIT (2001)
11/06/2001	30/01/2003	Czech Republic–Morocco BIT (2001)
19/06/2001	30/10/2002	Finland–Tanzania BIT (2001)

(continued)

(continued)

Date of signature	Date of entry into force	Short title
30/06/2001		Eritrea–Uganda BIT (2001)
08/07/2001	01/04/2003	Egypt–Sudan BIT (2001) (Renewed)
10/07/2001	26/02/2002	China–Mozambique BIT (2001)
14/07/2001		Gambia–Ukraine BIT (2001)
16/07/2001		China–Kenya BIT (2001)
30/07/2001		Mauritius–Rwanda BIT (2001)
31/07/2001	01/04/2004	Netherlands–Tanzania BIT (2001) (Terminated)
03/08/2001		Cameroon–Mauritius BIT (2001)
06/08/2001		Algeria–Libya BIT (2001)
06/08/2001	12/04/2008	Germany–Morocco BIT (2001) (Renewed)
21/08/2001	25/04/2003	Italy–Tanzania BIT (2001)
27/08/2001	18/02/2010	China–Nigeria BIT (2001) (Renewed)
30/09/2001	22/03/2004	Algeria–Kuwait BIT (2001)
01/10/2001	06/04/2003	Finland–Morocco BIT (2001)
04/10/2001	04/09/2003	Finland–Tunisia BIT (2001)
20/10/2001	26/02/2002	Cuba–Mozambique BIT (2001)
23/10/2001	29/03/2003	Morocco–Syria BIT (2001)
23/10/2001	01/11/2007	Mozambique–Sweden BIT (2001)
24/10/2001		Algeria–Sudan BIT (2001)
26/11/2001	19/10/2005	Denmark–Uganda BIT (2001)
13/12/2001	15/12/2007	Benin–Netherlands BIT (2001)
17/12/2001		Gabon–Portugal BIT (2001)
18/12/2001	01/09/2004	Mozambique–Netherlands BIT (2001)
24/12/2001	25/04/2009	Morocco–Ukraine BIT (2001)
01/01/2002		Cuba–Uganda BIT (2002)
14/01/2002		Algeria–Nigeria BIT (2002)
22/01/2002		Egypt–Seychelles BIT (2002)
28/02/2002		South Africa–Tunisia BIT (2002)
28/02/2002		South Africa–Tunisia BIT (2002)
28/02/2002	10/11/2006	Portugal–Tunisia BIT (2002) (Renewed)
06/03/2002	15/09/2007	Germany–Mozambique BIT (2002)
14/03/2002	14/10/2009	Mauritius–Senegal BIT (2002)
03/04/2002		Bulgaria–Sudan BIT (2002)
16/04/2002	23/04/2009	Malaysia–Morocco BIT (2002)
18/04/2002	01/12/2006	Nigeria–Sweden BIT (2002)
02/05/2002		Guinea–Morocco BIT (2002)

(continued)

(continued)

Date of signature	Date of entry into force	Short title
17/05/2002	03/03/2011	Gambia–Qatar BIT (2002)
18/05/2002		Mali–Qatar BIT (2002)
23/05/2002	04/01/2007	Dominican Republic–Morocco BIT (2002)
01/06/2002	07/02/2003	Nigeria–Serbia BIT (2002)
04/06/2002	01/11/2005	Algeria–Ethiopia BIT (2002)
14/06/2002		Libya–South Africa BIT (2002) (Renewed)
18/06/2002	01/01/2004	Austria–Libya BIT (2002)
02/07/2002		Gambia–United Kingdom BIT (2002)
09/07/2002	19/01/2006	Nigeria–Spain BIT (2002)
05/08/2002		Ghana–India BIT (2002) (Terminated)
05/08/2002		Jamaica–Nigeria BIT (2002)
14/08/2002	03/03/2014	France–Zambia BIT (2002)
25/09/2002	01/04/2007	Gambia–Netherlands BIT (2002)
30/09/2002		China–Côte d'Ivoire BIT (2002)
12/10/2002	30/12/2002	Denmark–Mozambique BIT (2002)
21/10/2002		Gambia–Guinea BIT (2002)
21/10/2002		Gambia–Guinea BIT (2002)
24/10/2002		Azerbaijan–Egypt BIT (2002)
24/10/2002		Sudan–Switzerland BIT (2002)
31/10/2002	21/05/2005	Finland–Namibia BIT (2002)
15/11/2002	06/07/2006	France–Mozambique BIT (2002)
26/11/2002	01/10/2004	Namibia–Netherlands BIT (2002)
29/11/2002	17/02/2004	Mozambique–Switzerland BIT (2002)
20/12/2002	21/06/2006	Croatia–Libya BIT (2002)
03/01/2003	20/12/2004	France–Uganda BIT (2003)
15/01/2003		Nigeria–Uganda BIT (2003)
28/01/2003		South Africa–Yemen BIT (2002)
15/02/2003	01/04/2005	Algeria–Sweden BIT (2003)
21/02/2003	28/06/2004	Namibia–Spain BIT (2003)
25/03/2003	26/08/2004	Burkina Faso–Guinea BIT (2003)
05/04/2003	09/12/2009	Italy–Mauritania BIT (2003)
30/04/2003	02/12/2014	Italy–Zambia BIT (2003)
30/04/2003	01/03/2014	Netherlands–Zambia BIT (2003)
13/05/2003		Hungary–Tunisia BIT (2003)
16/05/2003	01/07/2005	Ethiopia–Netherlands BIT (2003)
19/05/2003		Djibouti–India BIT (2003) (Terminated)
22/05/2003	18/09/2013	Denmark–Morocco BIT (2003)

(continued)

(continued)

Date of signature	Date of entry into force	Short title
27/05/2003	01/09/2008	Austria–Namibia BIT (2003)
30/05/2003		Namibia–Viet Nam BIT (2003)
14/06/2003	19/06/2005	Libya–Portugal BIT (2003)
17/06/2003	01/01/2006	Algeria–Austria BIT (2003)
25/06/2003	07/08/2004	Ethiopia–France BIT (2003)
30/06/2003		Botswana–Zimbabwe BIT (2003)
30/06/2003		Ghana–Zimbabwe BIT (2003)
01/07/2003		BLEU–Ethiopia BIT (2003)
01/07/2003		Uganda–Zimbabwe BIT (2003)
02/07/2003		Botswana–Egypt BIT (2003)
03/07/2003		Tanzania–Zimbabwe BIT (2003)
04/07/2003		Botswana–Ghana BIT (2003)
04/07/2003		Malawi–Zimbabwe BIT (2003)
13/07/2003	01/03/2005	Mali–Netherlands BIT (2003)
25/07/2003	17/04/2005	France–Madagascar BIT (2003)
18/08/2003		China–Djibouti BIT (2003)
28/08/2003	21/03/2012	Italy–Malawi BIT (2003)
24/09/2003		Mozambique–United Arab Emirates BIT (2003)
08/10/2003		Sudan–Tunisia BIT (2003)
08/10/2003		Sudan–Tunisia BIT (2003)
19/10/2003	05/12/2005	Algeria–Iran BIT (2003)
21/10/2003	15/12/2004	Ethiopia–Iran BIT (2003)
21/10/2003		Qatar–South Africa BIT (2003)
22/10/2003	18/10/2010	India–Sudan BIT (2003)
24/10/2003		Libya–Malta BIT (2003)
30/10/2003	01/03/2007	Angola–Germany BIT (2003)
22/11/2003	11/08/2009	Equatorial Guinea–Spain BIT (2003)
26/11/2003	15/02/2006	Ethiopia–Israel BIT (2003)
02/12/2003		Eritrea–Netherlands BIT (2003)
08/12/2003	28/04/2004	Libya–Switzerland BIT (2003)
11/12/2003	01/11/2007	Malawi–Netherlands BIT (2003)
25/12/2003		Mauritania–Qatar BIT (2003)
19/01/2004		Ethiopia–Nigeria BIT (2004)
19/01/2004	04/05/2006	Ethiopia–Germany BIT (2004) (Renewed)
27/01/2004	25/06/2004	Ethiopia–Libya BIT (2004)
15/02/2004	08/12/2007	BLEU–Libya BIT (2004)

(continued)

(continued)

Date of signature	Date of entry into force	Short title
17/02/2004		Equatorial Guinea–South Africa BIT (2004)
18/02/2004		Benin–China BIT (2004)
18/02/2004	29/10/2005	Libya–Serbia BIT (2004)
23/02/2004	01/06/2005	Mauritius–Sweden BIT (2004)
03/03/2004	05/02/2005	Egypt–Finland BIT (2004) (Renewed)
09/03/2004	21/04/2007	Lebanon–Sudan BIT (2004)
18/03/2004	12/05/2004	Mozambique–United Kingdom BIT (2004)
06/04/2004	29/12/2005	Madagascar–Mauritius BIT (2004)
08/04/2004	06/04/2006	Switzerland–Tanzania BIT (2004) (Renewed)
19/04/2004	29/01/2006	France–Libya BIT (2004)
27/04/2004		Egypt–Mongolia BIT (2004)
28/04/2004		Libya–Qatar BIT (2004)
14/05/2004		Gambia–Mali BIT (2004)
27/05/2004		China–Uganda BIT (2004)
15/06/2004		Benin–Morocco BIT (2004)
15/06/2004		Benin–Lebanon BIT (2004)
15/06/2004		Chad–Guinea BIT (2004)
15/06/2004		Chad–Lebanon BIT (2004)
15/06/2004		Guinea–Lebanon BIT (2004)
15/06/2004	30/04/2006	Lebanon–Mauritania BIT (2004)
16/06/2004	07/05/2010	Lesotho–Switzerland BIT (2004)
21/06/2004	24/07/2009	Gabon–Morocco BIT (2004) (Renewed)
21/06/2004	01/07/2006	China–Tunisia BIT (2004)
23/06/2004		D.R. Congo–Jordan BIT (2004)
30/06/2004	12/02/2005	Cyprus–Libya BIT (2004)
09/07/2004	30/05/2006	Italy–Namibia BIT (2004)
31/08/2004		D.R. Congo–South Africa BIT (2004)
03/09/2004	21/09/2005	Finland–Mozambique BIT (2004)
15/09/2004	08/09/2005	Algeria–Portugal BIT (2004) (Renewed)
28/09/2004	18/06/2005	Barbados–Mauritius BIT (2004)
29/09/2004		Croatia–Morocco BIT (2004)
15/10/2004	14/07/2010	Germany–Libya BIT (2004)
20/10/2004		Israel–South Africa BIT (2004)
26/10/2004	14/04/2010	Burkina Faso–Republic of Korea BIT (2004)
12/11/2004	01/11/2005	Austria–Ethiopia BIT (2004)
30/11/2004	15/08/2005	Algeria–Switzerland BIT (2004)
10/12/2004	01/10/2005	Ethiopia–Sweden BIT (2004)

(continued)

(continued)

Date of signature	Date of entry into force	Short title
15/12/2004	21/07/2006	Republic of Korea–Mauritania BIT (2004)
13/01/2005	25/02/2007	Algeria–Finland BIT (2005)
01/02/2005		BLEU–Uganda BIT (2005)
17/02/2005		Angola–South Africa BIT (2005)
17/02/2005		BLEU–D.R. Congo BIT (2005)
17/02/2005		Angola–South Africa BIT (2005)
19/02/2005	22/05/2006	Libya–Tunisia BIT (2005) (Renewed)
17/03/2005		D.R. Congo–Republic of Korea BIT (2005)
25/03/2005		Gabon–Mali BIT (2005)
12/04/2005		Mali–Senegal BIT (2005)
24/05/2005	20/03/2006	Egypt–Serbia BIT (2005) (Renewed)
16/06/2005	22/11/2009	Egypt–Germany BIT (2005) (Renewed)
22/06/2005	20/03/2007	Finland–Nigeria BIT (2005)
05/07/2005		Equatorial Guinea–Morocco BIT (2005)
02/08/2005		Gabon–South Africa BIT (2005)
09/08/2005	13/10/2010	Gambia–Taiwan BIT (2010)
17/08/2005		Botswana–Mauritius BIT (2005)
07/09/2005		Finland–Zambia BIT (2005)
22/09/2005		South Africa–Tanzania BIT (2005)
26/09/2005		Kuwait–South Africa BIT (2005)
29/09/2005	29/11/2008	BLEU–Madagascar BIT (2005)
04/10/2005		Congo–Tunisia BIT (2005)
20/10/2005	15/11/2006	China–Equatorial Guinea BIT (2005)
07/11/2005		BLEU–Sudan BIT (2005)
17/11/2005		China–Namibia BIT (2005)
18/11/2005		China–Guinea BIT (2005)
19/11/2005		Italy–Sudan BIT (2005)
21/11/2005	01/07/2007	China–Madagascar BIT (2005)
30/11/2005	16/01/2010	BLEU–Mauritius BIT (2005)
01/12/2005		Congo–South Africa BIT (2005)
15/12/2005		Equatorial Guinea–Ukraine BIT (2005)
17/02/2006		Algeria–Tunisia BIT (2006)
20/02/2006	12/10/2011	Gambia–Morocco BIT (2006)
23/02/2006	03/05/2007	Ethiopia–Finland BIT (2006)
10/03/2006		Algeria–Russian Federation BIT (2006)
07/06/2006		BLEU–Botswana BIT (2006)
18/07/2006	01/09/2009	BLEU–Mozambique BIT (2006)

(continued)

(continued)

Date of signature	Date of entry into force	Short title
27/07/2006	27/05/2010	Egypt–Ethiopia BIT (2006)
01/08/2006	17/10/2015	Germany–Madagascar BIT (2006) (Renewed)
01/08/2006		Kuwait–Mauritania BIT (2006)
13/09/2006		D.R. Congo–Italy BIT (2006)
21/09/2006	28/03/2007	Republic of Korea–Libya BIT (2006)
26/09/2006		Central Africa–Morocco BIT (2006)
06/10/2006		Ghana–Spain BIT (2006)
26/10/2006		BLEU–Ethiopia BIT (2006)
08/11/2006	13/08/2011	Congo–Republic of Korea BIT (2006)
08/11/2006	14/08/2014	Germany–Guinea BIT (2006) (Renewed)
14/11/2006	10/07/2009	Kenya–Switzerland BIT (2006)
15/11/2006		Morocco–Senegal BIT (2006)
10/12/2006		Libya–San Marino BIT (2006)
13/12/2006		Madagascar–South Africa BIT (2006)
27/12/2006	05/05/2010	Iran–Libya BIT (2006)
16/01/2007	29/05/2007	Mozambique–Viet Nam BIT (2007)
24/01/2007		Cameroon–Morocco BIT (2007)
08/02/2007	05/03/2016	Burkina Faso–Morocco BIT (2007)
10/02/2007		China–Seychelles BIT (2007)
20/03/2007	01/08/2008	Algeria–Netherlands BIT (2007)
29/03/2007	28/12/2014	France–Seychelles BIT (2007)
16/04/2007		BLEU–Rwanda BIT (2007)
17/04/2007		Morocco–Portugal BIT (2007)
24/05/2007	01/08/2009	Burundi–Netherlands BIT (2007)
26/05/2007	23/03/2009	India–Libya BIT (2007)
05/06/2007		Kenya–Libya BIT (2007)
14/06/2007	11/05/2014	Morocco–Slovakia BIT (2007)
18/06/2007	07/03/2008	Republic of Korea–Mauritius BIT (2007)
20/06/2007		Gambia–Iran BIT (2007)
05/07/2007		Ethiopia–India BIT (2007) (Terminated)
10/07/2007	16/03/2017	France–Guinea BIT (2007)
17/07/2007		Congo–Namibia BIT (2007)
26/07/2007	30/05/2010	France–Senegal BIT (2007)
10/08/2007	09/08/2009	Gabon–Republic of Korea (2007)
12/09/2007	17/10/2008	Finland–Mauritius BIT (2007)
25/09/2007		Guinea–South Africa BIT (2007)
11/10/2007		Angola–Guinea-Bissau BIT (2007)

(continued)

(continued)

Date of signature	Date of entry into force	Short title
07/11/2007		South Africa–Sudan BIT (2007)
21/11/2007		Angola–Spain BIT (2007)
22/11/2007	04/02/2011	Senegal–Spain BIT (2007)
04/12/2007	26/05/2009	France–Kenya BIT (2007)
13/12/2007	15/06/2010	Djibouti–France BIT (2007)
17/12/2007	01/08/2009	Libya–Spain BIT (2007)
06/01/2008		Algeria–Mauritania BIT (2008)
08/01/2008	15/06/2009	Egypt–Iceland BIT (2008)
19/02/2008	01/01/2012	Rwanda–United States BIT (2008)
22/02/2008	24/04/2020	Angola–Portugal BIT (2008)
11/03/2008		Algeria–Tajikistan BIT (2008)
18/03/2008		Ethiopia–South Africa BIT (2008)
17/04/2008	15/10/2010	Libya–Russian Federation BIT (2008)
22/04/2008		Barbados–Ghana BIT
08/06/2008	03/05/2012	Benin–Kuwait BIT (2008)
24/06/2008		Angola–France BIT (2008)
03/07/2008	17/10/2009	India–Senegal BIT (2008)
24/07/2008	07/03/2016	Mauritania–Spain BIT (2008)
01/09/2008	02/10/2009	Finland–Kenya BIT (2008)
19/11/2008	07/05/2015	Madagascar–Switzerland BIT (2008) (Renewed)
17/12/2008		Gambia–Spain BIT (2008)
18/12/2008		Congo–Spain BIT (2008)
16/01/2009		Equatorial Guinea–Portugal BIT (2009)
12/02/2009	16/07/2009	China–Mali BIT (2009)
19/02/2009	23/09/2009	India–Mozambique BIT (2009)
20/02/2009		Libya–Slovakia BIT (2009)
24/02/2009		Iran–Kenya BIT (2009)
17/03/2009		Ethiopia–Spain BIT (2009)
01/04/2009	01/04/2009	Burundi–Kenya BIT (2009)
04/04/2009		Indonesia–Libya BIT (2009)
08/04/2009	22/12/2011	Libya–Singapore BIT (2009)
04/05/2009	02/03/2013	Mauritius–Tanzania BIT (2009)
29/05/2009	16/02/2013	Republic of Korea–Rwanda BIT (2009)
06/06/2009		BLEU–Togo BIT (2009)
11/06/2009		Equatorial Guinea–Ethiopia BIT (2009)
24/06/2009		Nigeria–Russian Federation BIT (2009)

(continued)

(continued)

Date of signature	Date of entry into force	Short title
25/06/2009		Namibia–Russian Federation BIT (2009)
26/06/2009	12/01/2011	Angola–Russian Federation BIT (2009)
19/07/2009	17/03/2014	Djibouti–Kuwait BIT (2009)
23/07/2009		Eswatini–Kuwait BIT (2009)
25/07/2009		Kuwait–Senegal BIT (2009)
25/09/2009	04/11/2011	Estonia–Morocco BIT (2009)
08/10/2009		Jordan–Tanzania BIT (2009)
19/11/2009		Ethiopia–United Kingdom BIT (2009)
25/11/2009	22/04/2011	Libya–Turkey BIT (2009)
27/11/2009	15/09/2010	South Africa–Zimbabwe BIT (2009)
27/11/2009		United Kingdom–Zambia BIT (2009)
27/11/2009	15/09/2010	South Africa–Zimbabwe BIT (2009)
23/12/2009		United Kingdom–Libya BIT (2009)
08/03/2010		France–Mauritius BIT (2010)
13/04/2010		D.R. Congo–India BIT (2010)
26/04/2010		Chad–China BIT (2010)
11/05/2010	15/10/2012	Macedonia, The former Yugoslav Republic of–Morocco BIT (2010)
24/05/2010		Republic of Korea–Zimbabwe BIT (2010)
02/06/2010		India–Seychelles BIT (2010) (Terminated)
02/06/2010		Sierra Leone–United Kingdom BIT (1981) (Terminated)
04/06/2010		Congo–Portugal BIT (2010)
07/06/2010	15/05/2012	Egypt–Switzerland BIT (2010) (Renewed)
15/06/2010	17/07/2012	Senegal–Turkey BIT (2010)
30/06/2010		Congo–Libya BIT (2010)
04/08/2010		China–Libya BIT (2010)
22/11/2010		Congo–Germany BIT (2010)
07/12/2010		Djibouti–Iran BIT (2010)
20/12/2010	15/12/2013	Congo–Mauritius BIT (2010)
25/01/2011		Portugal–Senegal BIT (2011)
02/02/2011		Nigeria–Turkey BIT (2011)
03/03/2011		D.R. Congo–Portugal BIT (2011)
11/03/2011		Tanzania–Turkey BIT (2011)
21/03/2011		Botswana–Zimbabwe BIT (2011)
21/03/2011		Botswana–Zimbabwe BIT (2011)
23/03/2011		Kuwait–Nigeria BIT (2011)
04/04/2011		Sudan–United Arab Emirates BIT (2011)

(continued)

(continued)

Date of signature	Date of entry into force	Short title
06/06/2011	03/03/2016	Equatorial Guinea–Russian Federation BIT (2011)
11/08/2011		China–D.R. Congo BIT (2011)
13/11/2011	22/07/2014	Guinea–United Arab Emirates BIT (2011)
14/12/2011		Kenya–Slovakia BIT (2011)
13/02/2012	25/11/2013	Algeria–Serbia BIT (2012)
24/04/2012		Cameroon–Turkey BIT (2012)
07/05/2012		Kenya–Mauritius BIT (2012)
13/05/2012		Burundi–Egypt BIT (2012)
15/06/2012		Morocco–Viet Nam BIT (2012)
18/07/2012		Gabon–Turkey BIT (2012)
22/09/2012		Lithuania–Mauritania BIT (2012)
07/10/2012	10/09/2014	Russian Federation–Zimbabwe BIT (2012)
16/10/2012	08/07/2014	Switzerland–Tunisia BIT (2012) (Renewed)
16/10/2012		Oman–Tanzania BIT (2012)
09/01/2013	12/05/2014	Benin–Canada BIT (2013)
07/02/2013	30/05/2016	Mauritius–Turkey BIT (2013)
04/03/2013		Benin–United Arab Emirates BIT (2013)
12/03/2013		Gambia–Turkey BIT (2013)
24/03/2013	17/04/2014	China–Tanzania BIT (2013)
01/04/2013		Gambia–Kuwait BIT (2013)
08/04/2013		Austria–Nigeria BIT (2013)
18/04/2013	24/07/2014	Kuwait–Mauritius BIT (2013)
17/05/2013	09/12/2013	Canada–Tanzania BIT (2013)
01/06/2013	29/08/2014	Japan–Mozambique BIT (2013)
06/06/2013		Morocco–Serbia BIT (2013)
18/06/2013		Guinea–Turkey BIT (2013)
18/07/2013		Gabon–Mauritius BIT (2013)
25/09/2013		Djibouti–Turkey BIT (2013)
12/11/2013	22/04/2015	Kuwait–Kenya BIT (2013)
17/11/2013		Kuwait–Tanzania BIT (2013)
11/12/2013		Turkey–Benin BIT (2013)
24/12/2013	13/04/2018	Cameroon–Republic of Korea BIT (2013)
21/02/2014	02/03/2016	Mali–Morocco BIT (2014)
03/03/2014	16/12/2016	Cameroon–Canada BIT (2014)
20/03/2014		Angola–Namibia BIT (2014)
08/04/2014		Kenya–Turkey BIT (2014)

(continued)

(continued)

Date of signature	Date of entry into force	Short title
13/04/2014		Kenya–Qatar BIT (2014)
30/04/2014		Sudan–Turkey BIT (2014)
06/05/2014		Canada–Nigeria BIT (2014)
25/06/2014	17/10/2014	Egypt–Mauritius BIT (2014)
08/07/2014	03/05/2017	Kenya–Republic of Korea BIT (2014)
27/08/2014		Burkina Faso–Singapore BIT (2014)
27/08/2014		Côte d'Ivoire–Singapore BIT (2014)
23/11/2014	05/06/2017	Kenya–United Arab Emirates BIT (2014)
27/11/2014	05/08/2016	Canada–Senegal BIT (2014)
28/11/2014	08/06/2016	Canada–Mali BIT (2014)
30/11/2014	14/12/2015	Canada–Côte d'Ivoire BIT (2014)
26/03/2015	29/11/2017	Comoros–United Arab Emirates BIT (2015)
30/03/2015		Brazil–Mozambique CFIA (2015)
01/04/2015	28/07/2017	Angola–Brazil CFIA (2015)
20/04/2015	11/10/2017	Burkina Faso–Canada BIT (2015)
27/05/2015	27/03/2017	Canada–Guinea BIT (2015)
28/05/2015		Guinea-Bissau–Morocco BIT (2015)
25/06/2015		Brazil–Malawi CFIA (2015)
14/07/2015	06/05/2016	Mauritius–Zambia BIT (2015)
20/09/2015	28/12/2017	Mauritius–United Arab Emirates BIT (2015)
22/10/2015		Senegal–United Arab Emirates BIT (2015)
09/11/2015		Angola–Mozambique BIT (2015)
2015	12/04/2016	Mauritania–United Arab Emirates BIT (2015)
18/01/2016		Nigeria–United Arab Emirates BIT (2016)
29/02/2016		Côte d'Ivoire–Turkey BIT (2016)
01/03/2016		Ghana–Turkey BIT (2016)
15/03/2016		Morocco–Russian Federation BIT (2016)
20/04/2016		Côte d'Ivoire–Mauritius BIT (2016)
06/05/2016		Mauritius–Sao Tome and Principe BIT (2016)
01/06/2016		Somalia–Turkey BIT (2016)
28/08/2016	14/09/2017	Japan–Kenya BIT (2016)
19/10/2016		Equatorial Guinea–United Arab Emirates BIT (2016)
19/10/2016		Morocco–Rwanda BIT (2016)
03/11/2016		Rwanda–Turkey BIT (2016)
04/11/2016		Nigeria–Singapore BIT (2016)
10/11/2016		Gambia–Mauritius BIT (2016)

(continued)

(continued)

Date of signature	Date of entry into force	Short title
19/11/2016		Ethiopia–Morocco BIT (2016)
03/12/2016		Ethiopia–United Arab Emirates BIT (2016)
03/12/2016		Morocco–Nigeria BIT (2016)
17/01/2017		Belarus–Sudan BIT (2017)
24/01/2017		Mozambique–Turkey BIT (2017)
01/02/2017		Morocco–South Sudan BIT
20/02/2017		Morocco–Zambia BIT (2017)
06/02/2017		United Arab Emirates–Burundi BIT (2017)
05/04/2017		United Arab Emirates–Angola BIT (2017)
13/04/2017		Cabo Verde–Mauritius BIT (2017)
14/06/2017		Burundi–Turkey BIT (2017)
01/11/2017		Rwanda–United Arab Emirates BIT (2017)
01/11/2017		Uganda–United Arab Emirates BIT (2017)
26/12/2017		Chad–Turkey BIT (2017)
27/12/2017		Turkey–Tunisia BIT (2017)
28/02/2018		Mauritania–Turkey BIT (2018)
02/03/2018		Mali–Turkey BIT (2018)
06/03/2018		Mali–United Arab Emirates BIT (2018)
11/04/2018		Brazil–Ethiopia CFIA (2018)
30/04/2018		Morocco–Congo BIT (2018)
16/06/2018		United Arab Emirates–Zimbabwe BIT (2018)
28/07/2018		Turkey–Zambia BIT (2018)
15/11/2018		Qatar–Rwanda BIT
28/03/2019		Cabo Verde–Hungary BIT (2019)
11/04/2019		Burkina Faso–Turkey BIT (2019)
13/06/2019		Brazil–Morocco CFIA (2019)
15/07/2019		Gambia–United Arab Emirates BIT (2019)
08/01/2020		Morocco–Japan BIT (2000)
13/01/2020		Côte d'Ivoire–Japan BIT (2020)

Appendix G
BITs with an African State as One Contracting Party (as of September 30, 2021, Listed Alphabetically)

African party	Other party		Date of signature	Date of entry into force
Algeria	African countries	Mali	11/07/1996	16/02/1999
		Egypt	29/03/1997	03/05/2000
		Niger	16/03/1998	
		Mozambique	12/12/1998	25/07/2000
		South Africa	24/09/2000	
		Libya	06/08/2001	
		Sudan	24/10/2001	
		Nigeria	14/01/2002	
		Ethiopia	04/06/2002	01/11/2005
		Tunisia	17/02/2006	
		Mauritania	06/01/2008	
	Other developing parties	Romania	28/06/1994	30/12/1995
		Jordan	01/08/1996	05/06/1997
		China	17/10/1996	28/01/2003
		Viet Nam	21/10/1996	
		Qatar	24/10/1996	
		Syria	14/09/1997	
		Turkey	03/06/1998	
		Bulgaria	25/10/1998	06/06/2002
		Yemen	25/11/1999	

(continued)

X. Han, *Legal Protection and Sustainability of Chinese Investments in Africa*, Modern China and International Economic Law,
https://doi.org/10.1007/978-981-19-1882-7

(continued)

African party	Other party		Date of signature	Date of entry into force
		Malaysia	27/01/2000	09/02/2002
		Indonesia	21/03/2000	
		Oman	09/04/2000	22/06/2002
		Bahrain	11/06/2000	16/05/2008
		Argentina	04/10/2000	28/01/2002
		United Arab Emirates	24/04/2001	03/06/2002
		Kuwait	30/09/2001	22/03/2004
		Iran	19/10/2003	05/12/2005
		Russian Federation	10/03/2006	
		Tajikistan	11/03/2008	
		Serbia	13/02/2012	25/11/2013
		Cuba		
	Developed countries	BLEU	24/04/1991	17/10/2002
		Italy	18/05/1991	26/11/1993
		France	13/02/1993	27/06/2000
		Portugal	15/09/1994	
		Spain	23/12/1994	17/01/1996
		Germany	11/03/1996	30/05/2002
		Denmark	25/01/1999	15/07/2005
		Republic of Korea	12/10/1999	30/09/2001
		Greece	20/02/2000	21/09/2007
		Czechia	22/09/2000	
		Sweden	15/02/2003	01/04/2005
		Austria	17/06/2003	01/01/2006
		Portugal	15/09/2004	08/09/2005
		Switzerland	30/11/2004	15/08/2005
		Finland	13/01/2005	25/02/2007
		Netherlands	20/03/2007	01/08/2008
Angola	African countries	Cape Verde	11/09/1997	15/12/1997
		South Africa	17/02/2005	
		Guinea-Bissau	11/10/2007	
		Namibia	20/03/2014	
		Mozambique	09/11/2015	

(continued)

(continued)

African party	Other party		Date of signature	Date of entry into force
	Other developing parties	Russian Federation	26/06/2009	12/01/2011
		Brazil	01/04/2015	28/07/2017
		United Arab Emirates	05/04/2017	
	Developed countries	Italy	10/07/1997	21/05/2007
		Portugal	24/10/1997	
		United Kingdom	04/07/2000	
		Germany	30/10/2003	01/03/2007
		Spain	21/11/2007	
		Portugal	22/02/2008	
		France	24/06/2008	
Benin	African countries	Burkina Faso	18/05/2001	18/08/2003
		Chad	18/05/2001	
		Ghana	18/05/2001	
		Guinea	18/05/2001	
		Mali	18/05/2001	
		Mauritius	18/05/2001	
		Morocco	15/06/2004	
	Other developing parties	China	18/02/2004	
		Lebanon	15/06/2004	
		Kuwait	08/06/2008	03/05/2012
		United Arab Emirates	04/03/2013	
		Turkey	11/12/2013	
	Developed countries	Switzerland	20/04/1966	06/10/1973
		Germany	29/06/1978	18/07/1985
		United Kingdom	27/11/1987	27/11/1987
		BLEU	18/05/2001	30/08/2007
		Netherlands	13/12/2001	15/12/2007
		Canada	09/01/2013	12/05/2014
Botswana	African countries	Zimbabwe	30/06/2003	
		Egypt	02/07/2003	
		Ghana	04/07/2003	
		Mauritius	17/08/2005	
		Zimbabwe	21/03/2011	

(continued)

(continued)

African party	Other party		Date of signature	Date of entry into force
	Other developing parties	China	12/06/2000	
		Malaysia	31/07/1997	
	Developed countries	Switzerland	26/06/1998	13/04/2000
		Germany	23/05/2000	06/08/2007
		BLEU	07/06/2006	
Burkina Faso	African countries	Tunisia	07/01/1993	15/10/2003
		Benin	18/05/2001	18/08/2003
		Chad	18/05/2001	
		Comoros	18/05/2001	18/08/2003
		Ghana	18/05/2001	18/08/2003
		Mauritania	18/05/2001	18/08/2003
		Guinea	25/03/2003	26/08/2004
		Morocco	08/02/2007	05/03/2016
		Canada	20/04/2015	11/10/2017
	Other developing parties	Malaysia	23/04/1998	18/08/2003
		Taiwan	09/10/1998	18/08/2003
		Turkey	11/04/2019	
	Developed countries	Switzerland	06/05/1969	15/09/1969
		Germany	22/10/1996	21/11/2009
		Netherlands	10/11/2000	01/01/2004
		BLEU	18/05/2001	13/01/2004
		Republic of Korea	26/10/2004	14/04/2010
		Singapore	27/08/2014	
Burundi	African countries	Comoros	18/05/2001	
		Mauritius	18/05/2001	22/11/2009
		Kenya	01/04/2009	01/04/2009
		Egypt	13/05/2012	
	Other developing parties	United Arab Emirates	06/02/2017	
		Turkey	14/06/2017	
	Developed countries	Germany	10/09/1984	09/12/1987
		BLEU	13/04/1989	12/09/1993
		United Kingdom	13/09/1990	13/09/1990
		Netherlands	24/05/2007	01/08/2009
Cameroon	African countries	Egypt	24/10/2000	

(continued)

(continued)

African party	Other party		Date of signature	Date of entry into force
		Guinea	18/05/2001	
		Mali	18/05/2001	
		Mauritania	18/05/2001	
		Mauritius	03/08/2001	
		Morocco	24/01/2007	
	Other developing parties	Romania	30/08/1980	24/09/1981
		China	10/09/1997	24/07/2014
		Turkey	24/04/2012	
	Developed countries	Germany	29/06/1962	21/11/1963
		Switzerland	28/01/1963	06/04/1964
		Netherlands	06/07/1965	07/05/1966
		BLEU	27/03/1980	01/11/1981
		United Kingdom	04/06/1982	07/06/1985
		United States	26/02/1986	06/04/1989
		Italy	29/06/1999	04/01/2004
		Republic of Korea	24/12/2013	13/04/2018
		Canada	03/03/2014	16/12/2016
Cabo Verde	African countries	Angola	11/09/1997	15/12/1997
		Mauritius	13/04/2017	
	Other developing parties	Cuba	22/05/1997	08/01/2003
		China	21/04/1998	01/01/2001
		Hungary	28/03/2019	
	Developed countries	Germany	18/01/1990	15/12/1993
		Portugal	26/10/1990	04/10/1991
		Austria	03/09/1991	01/04/1993
		Switzerland	28/10/1991	06/05/1992
		Netherlands	11/11/1991	25/11/1992
		Italy	12/06/1997	
Central Africa	African countries	Egypt	07/02/2000	
		Morocco	26/09/2006	
	Developed countries	Germany	23/08/1965	21/01/1968
		Switzerland	28/02/1973	04/07/1973
Chad	African countries	Morocco	04/12/1997	
		Egypt	14/03/1998	
		Benin	18/05/2001	

(continued)

(continued)

African party	Other party		Date of signature	Date of entry into force
		Burkina Faso	18/05/2001	
		Mali	18/05/2001	
		Mauritius	18/05/2001	
		Guinea	15/06/2004	
	Other developing parties	Qatar	22/11/1999	
		Lebanon	15/06/2004	
		China	26/04/2010	
		Turkey	26/12/2017	
	Developed countries	France	11/08/1960	
		Switzerland	21/02/1967	31/10/1967
		Germany	11/04/1967	23/11/1968
		Italy	11/06/1969	11/06/1969
Comoros	African countries	Egypt	13/11/1994	27/02/2000
		Burkina Faso	18/05/2001	18/08/2003
		Burundi	18/05/2001	
		Mali	18/05/2001	
		Mauritius	18/05/2001	
	Other developing parties	United Arab Emirates	26/03/2015	29/11/2017
	Developed countries	BLEU	18/05/2001	
Congo	African countries	Tunisia	04/10/2005	
		South Africa	01/12/2005	
		Namibia	17/07/2007	
		Mauritius	20/12/2010	15/12/2013
		Morocco	30/04/2018	
	Other developing parties	China	20/03/2000	01/07/2015
		Libya	30/06/2010	
	Developed countries	Switzerland	18/10/1962	11/07/1964
		Germany	13/09/1965	14/10/1967
		United Kingdom	25/05/1989	09/11/1990
		United States	12/02/1990	13/08/1994
		Italy	17/03/1994	10/01/2003
		Republic of Korea	08/11/2006	13/08/2011
		Spain	18/12/2008	

(continued)

(continued)

African party	Other party		Date of signature	Date of entry into force
		Portugal	04/06/2010	
		Germany	22/11/2010	
Côte d'Ivoire	African countries	Tunisia	16/05/1995	
		Ghana	04/11/1997	
		Mauritius	20/04/2016	
	Other developing parties	China	30/09/2002	
		Canada	30/11/2014	14/12/2015
		Turkey	29/02/2016	
	Developed countries	Switzerland	26/06/1962	18/11/1962
		Netherlands	26/04/1965	08/09/1966
		Sweden	27/08/1965	03/11/1966
		Germany	27/10/1966	10/06/1968
		Italy	23/07/1969	
		United Kingdom	08/06/1995	09/10/1997
		BLEU	01/04/1999	15/06/2013
		Singapore	27/08/2014	
		Japan	13/01/2020	
D.R. Congo	African countries	Egypt	18/12/1998	
		South Africa	31/08/2004	
	Other developing parties	China	18/12/1997	
		Ukraine	11/10/2000	
		Jordan	23/06/2004	
		India	13/04/2010	
		China	11/08/2011	
	Developed countries	Germany	18/03/1969	22/07/1971
		Switzerland	10/03/1972	10/05/1973
		France	05/10/1972	01/03/1975
		United States	03/08/1984	28/07/1989
		Republic of Korea	19/07/1990	
		Greece	26/04/1991	
		BLEU	17/02/2005	
		Republic of Korea	17/03/2005	
		Italy	13/09/2006	
		Portugal	03/03/2011	

(continued)

(continued)

African party	Other party		Date of signature	Date of entry into force
Djibouti	African countries	Egypt	21/07/1998	
	Other developing parties	Malaysia	03/08/1998	
		India	19/05/2003	
		China	18/08/2003	
		Kuwait	19/07/2009	17/03/2014
		Iran	07/12/2010	
		Turkey	25/09/2013	
	Developed countries	Switzerland	04/02/2001	10/06/2001
		France	13/12/2007	15/06/2010
Egypt	African countries	Morocco	03/06/1976	07/09/1978
		Sudan	28/05/1977	14/03/1978
		Somalia	29/05/1982	16/04/1983
		Tunisia	08/12/1989	02/01/1991
		Libya	03/12/1990	04/07/1991
		Comoros	13/11/1994	27/02/2000
		Uganda	04/11/1995	
		Algeria	29/03/1997	03/05/2000
		Tanzania	30/04/1997	
		Morocco	14/05/1997	01/07/1998
		Malawi	21/10/1997	07/09/1999
		Gabon	22/12/1997	
		Niger	04/03/1998	
		Senegal	05/03/1998	
		Guinea	06/03/1998	
		Mali	09/03/1998	07/07/2000
		Ghana	11/03/1998	
		Chad	14/03/1998	
		Djibouti	21/07/1998	
		South Africa	28/10/1998	
		Mozambique	08/12/1998	
		D.R. Congo	18/12/1998	
		Zimbabwe	02/06/1999	
		Central Africa	07/02/2000	
		Zambia	28/04/2000	
		Nigeria	20/06/2000	
		Eswatini	18/07/2000	

(continued)

(continued)

African party	Other party		Date of signature	Date of entry into force
		Cameroon	24/10/2000	
		Sudan	08/07/2001	01/04/2003
		Seychelles	22/01/2002	
		Botswana	02/07/2003	
		Ethiopia	27/07/2006	27/05/2010
		Burundi	13/05/2012	
		Mauritius	25/06/2014	17/10/2014
	Other developing parties	Kuwait	02/05/1966	09/08/1966
		Romania	10/05/1976	02/01/1977
		Iran	25/05/1977	
		Serbia	03/06/1977	20/03/1979
		Oman	28/04/1985	
		Yemen	19/10/1988	03/03/1990
		Argentina	11/05/1992	03/12/1993
		Uzbekistan	16/12/1992	08/02/1994
		Ukraine	21/12/1992	10/10/1993
		Kazakhstan	14/02/1993	08/08/1996
		Albania	22/05/1993	06/04/1994
		Indonesia	19/01/1994	29/11/1994
		China	21/04/1994	01/04/1996
		Romania	24/11/1994	03/04/1997
		Hungary	23/05/1995	21/08/1997
		Turkmenistan	23/05/1995	28/02/1996
		Poland	01/07/1995	17/01/1998
		Armenia	09/01/1996	01/03/2006
		Sri Lanka	11/03/1996	10/03/1998
		Lebanon	16/03/1996	02/06/1997
		Jordan	08/05/1996	11/04/1998
		Yemen	06/06/1996	10/04/1998
		Turkey	04/10/1996	31/07/2002
		Belarus	20/03/1997	18/01/1999
		India	09/04/1997	22/11/2000
		Malaysia	14/04/1997	03/02/2000
		Latvia	24/04/1997	03/06/1998
		Syria	28/04/1997	05/10/1998
		United Arab Emirates	11/05/1997	11/01/1999

(continued)

(continued)

African party	Other party		Date of signature	Date of entry into force
		DPRK	19/08/1997	12/01/2000
		Viet Nam	06/09/1997	04/03/2002
		Russian Federation	23/09/1997	12/06/2000
		Bahrain	04/10/1997	11/01/1999
		Croatia	27/10/1997	02/05/1999
		Bosnia and Herzegovina	11/03/1998	29/10/2001
		Bulgaria	15/03/1998	08/06/2000
		Oman	25/03/1998	03/03/2000
		Palestine	28/04/1998	19/06/1999
		Jamaica	10/02/1999	
		Qatar	12/02/1999	14/07/2006
		Chile	05/08/1999	
		Georgia	10/08/1999	
		North Macedonia	22/11/1999	
		Thailand	18/02/2000	27/02/2002
		Pakistan	16/04/2000	
		Kuwait	17/04/2001	26/04/2002
		Azerbaijan	24/10/2002	
		Mongolia	27/04/2004	
		Serbia	24/05/2005	20/03/2006
		United Arab Emirates	19/06/1988	02/03/1998
	Developed countries	Switzerland	25/07/1973	04/06/1974
		Germany	05/07/1974	22/07/1978
		France	22/12/1974	01/10/1975
		United Kingdom	11/06/1975	24/02/1976
		Netherlands	30/10/1976	01/01/1978
		Japan	28/01/1977	14/01/1978
		BLEU	28/02/1977	20/09/1978
		Sweden	15/07/1978	29/01/1979
		Finland	05/05/1980	22/01/1982
		Italy	02/03/1989	01/05/1994
		Spain	03/11/1992	26/04/1994
		Czechia	29/05/1993	04/06/1994

(continued)

(continued)

African party	Other party		Date of signature	Date of entry into force
		Greece	16/07/1993	06/04/1995
		Netherlands	17/01/1996	01/03/1998
		Republic of Korea	18/03/1996	25/05/1997
		Canada	13/11/1996	03/11/1997
		Singapore	15/04/1997	20/03/2002
		Slovakia	30/04/1997	01/01/2000
		Cyprus	21/10/1998	11/05/1999
		Slovenia	28/10/1998	07/02/2000
		Malta	20/02/1999	17/07/2000
		BLEU	28/02/1999	24/05/2002
		Portugal	29/04/1999	23/12/2000
		Denmark	24/06/1999	29/10/2000
		Austria	12/04/2001	29/04/2002
		Australia	03/05/2001	05/09/2002
		Finland	03/03/2004	05/02/2005
		Germany	16/06/2005	22/11/2009
		Iceland	08/01/2008	15/06/2009
		Switzerland	07/06/2010	15/05/2012
		United States	11/03/1986	27/06/1992
Eritrea	African countries	Qatar	07/08/2000	
	Other developing parties	Uganda	30/06/2001	
	Developed countries	Italy	26/04/1999	14/07/2003
		Netherlands	02/12/2003	
Eswatini	African countries	Mauritius	15/05/2000	
		Egypt	18/07/2000	
	Other developing parties	Taiwan	03/03/1998	
		Kuwait	23/07/2009	
	Developed countries	Germany	05/04/1990	07/08/1995
		United Kingdom	05/05/1995	05/05/1995
Ethiopia	African countries	Sudan	07/03/2000	15/05/2001
		Tunisia	14/12/2000	02/10/2004
		Algeria	04/06/2002	01/11/2005
		Nigeria	19/01/2004	

(continued)

(continued)

African party	Other party		Date of signature	Date of entry into force
		Libya	27/01/2004	25/06/2004
		Egypt	27/07/2006	27/05/2010
		South Africa	18/03/2008	
		Equatorial Guinea	11/06/2009	
		Morocco	19/11/2016	
	Other developing parties	Kuwait	14/09/1996	12/11/1998
		China	11/05/1998	01/05/2000
		Malaysia	22/10/1998	04/06/1999
		Yemen	15/04/1999	15/04/2000
		Russian Federation	10/02/2000	
		Turkey	16/11/2000	10/03/2005
		Iran	21/10/2003	15/12/2004
		India	05/07/2007	
		United Arab Emirates	03/12/2016	
		Brazil	11/04/2018	
	Developed countries	Germany	21/04/1964	
		Italy	23/12/1994	08/05/1997
		Switzerland	26/06/1998	07/12/1998
		Denmark	24/04/2001	21/08/2005
		Netherlands	16/05/2003	01/07/2005
		France	25/06/2003	07/08/2004
		BLEU	01/07/2003	
		Israel	26/11/2003	15/02/2006
		Germany	19/01/2004	04/05/2006
		Austria	12/11/2004	01/11/2005
		Sweden	10/12/2004	01/10/2005
		Finland	23/02/2006	03/05/2007
		BLEU	26/10/2006	
		Spain	17/03/2009	
		United Kingdom	19/11/2009	
Equatorial Guinea	African countries	South Africa	17/02/2004	
		Morocco	05/07/2005	
		Ethiopia	11/06/2009	

(continued)

(continued)

African party	Other party		Date of signature	Date of entry into force
	Other developing parties	China	20/10/2005	15/11/2006
		Ukraine	15/12/2005	
		Russian Federation	06/06/2011	03/03/2016
		United Arab Emirates	19/10/2016	
	Developed countries	France	03/03/1982	23/09/1983
		Spain	22/11/2003	11/08/2009
		Portugal	16/01/2009	
Gabon	African countries	Morocco	13/01/1979	07/11/1979
		Egypt	22/12/1997	
		Morocco	21/06/2004	24/07/2009
		Mali	25/03/2005	
		South Africa	02/08/2005	
		Mauritius	18/07/2013	
	Other developing parties	Romania	11/04/1979	18/09/1982
		China	09/05/1997	16/02/2009
		Lebanon	20/02/2001	
		Turkey	18/07/2012	
	Developed countries	Italy	18/11/1968	
		Germany	16/05/1969	29/03/1971
		Spain	02/03/1995	12/12/2001
		BLEU	27/05/1998	28/05/2005
		Germany	15/09/1998	04/07/2007
		Italy	18/06/1999	07/07/2006
		Portugal	17/12/2001	
		Republic of Korea	10/08/2007	09/08/2009
Gambia	African countries	Libya	26/07/1995	
		Mauritania	09/05/2001	
		Guinea	21/10/2002	
		Mali	14/05/2004	
		Morocco	20/02/2006	12/10/2011
		Mauritius	10/11/2016	
	Other developing parties	Switzerland	22/11/1993	30/03/1994
		Ukraine	14/07/2001	
		Qatar	17/05/2002	03/03/2011

(continued)

(continued)

African party	Other party		Date of signature	Date of entry into force
		Taiwan	09/08/2005	13/10/2010
		Iran	20/06/2007	
		Turkey	12/03/2013	
		Kuwait	01/04/2013	
		United Arab Emirates	15/07/2019	
	Developed countries	United Kingdom	02/07/2002	
		Netherlands	25/09/2002	01/04/2007
		Spain	17/12/2008	
Ghana	African countries	Côte d'Ivoire	04/11/1997	
		Egypt	11/03/1998	
		South Africa	09/07/1998	
		Benin	18/05/2001	
		Burkina Faso	18/05/2001	18/08/2003
		Guinea	18/05/2001	
		Mauritania	18/05/2001	
		Mauritius	18/05/2001	
		Zambia	18/05/2001	
		Zimbabwe	30/06/2003	
		Botswana	04/07/2003	
	Other developing parties	Romania	14/09/1989	
		China	12/10/1989	22/11/1990
		Bulgaria	20/10/1989	
		Malaysia	08/11/1996	18/04/1997
		Cuba	02/11/1999	
		Serbia	25/04/2000	07/07/2000
		India	05/08/2002	
		Barbados	22/04/2008	
		Turkey	01/03/2016	
	Developed countries	United Kingdom	22/03/1989	25/10/1991
		Netherlands	31/03/1989	01/07/1991
		Switzerland	08/10/1991	16/06/1993
		Denmark	13/01/1992	06/01/1995
		Germany	24/02/1995	23/11/1998
		Italy	25/06/1998	

(continued)

(continued)

African party	Other party		Date of signature	Date of entry into force
		France	26/03/1999	
		Spain	06/10/2006	
Guinea	African countries	Tunisia	18/11/1990	
		Egypt	06/03/1998	
		Benin	18/05/2001	
		Cameroon	18/05/2001	
		Ghana	18/05/2001	
		Mali	18/05/2001	
		Mauritania	18/05/2001	
		Mauritius	18/05/2001	
		Morocco	02/05/2002	
		Gambia	21/10/2002	
		Burkina Faso	25/03/2003	26/08/2004
		Chad	15/06/2004	
		South Africa	25/09/2007	
	Other developing parties	Serbia	22/10/1996	13/03/1998
		Malaysia	07/11/1996	24/02/1997
		Lebanon	15/06/2004	
		China	18/11/2005	
		United Arab Emirates	13/11/2011	22/07/2014
		Turkey	18/06/2013	
	Developed countries	Germany	19/04/1962	13/03/1965
		Switzerland	26/04/1962	29/07/1963
		Italy	20/02/1964	20/02/1964
		Germany	08/11/2006	14/08/2014
		France	10/07/2007	16/03/2017
		Canada	27/05/2015	27/03/2017
Guinea-Bissau	African countries	Angola	11/10/2007	
		Morocco	28/05/2015	
	Developed countries	Portugal	24/06/1991	08/04/1996
Kenya	African countries	Libya	05/06/2007	
		Burundi	01/04/2009	01/04/2009
		Mauritius	07/05/2012	
	Other developing parties	China	16/07/2001	
		Iran	24/02/2009	

(continued)

(continued)

African party	Other party		Date of signature	Date of entry into force
		Kuwait	12/11/2013	22/04/2015
		Turkey	08/04/2014	
		Qatar	13/04/2014	
		United Arab Emirates	23/11/2014	05/06/2017
	Developed countries	Netherlands	11/09/1970	11/06/1979
		Germany	03/05/1996	07/12/2000
		Italy	16/09/1996	04/08/1999
		United Kingdom	13/09/1999	13/09/1999
		Switzerland	14/11/2006	10/07/2009
		France	04/12/2007	26/05/2009
		Finland	01/09/2008	02/10/2009
		Slovakia	14/12/2011	
		Republic of Korea	08/07/2014	03/05/2017
		Japan	28/08/2016	14/09/2017
Lesotho	Developed countries	United Kingdom	18/02/1981	18/02/1981
		Germany	11/11/1982	17/08/1985
		Switzerland	16/06/2004	07/05/2010
Liberia	Developed countries	Germany	12/12/1961	22/10/1967
		Switzerland	23/07/1963	22/09/1964
		France	23/03/1979	22/01/1982
		BLEU	05/06/1985	
Libya	African countries	Tunisia	06/06/1973	
		Morocco	25/01/1984	18/09/1993
		Egypt	03/12/1990	04/07/1991
		Gambia	26/07/1995	
		Morocco	02/11/2000	20/10/2001
		Algeria	06/08/2001	
		South Africa	14/06/2002	
		Ethiopia	27/01/2004	25/06/2004
		Tunisia	19/02/2005	22/05/2006
		Kenya	05/06/2007	
		Congo	30/06/2010	

(continued)

(continued)

African party	Other party		Date of signature	Date of entry into force
	Other developing parties	Syria	08/02/1993	07/10/1995
		Bulgaria	19/11/1999	19/01/2004
		Belarus	01/11/2000	23/02/2002
		Ukraine	23/01/2001	23/04/2003
		Croatia	20/12/2002	21/06/2006
		Serbia	18/02/2004	29/10/2005
		Qatar	28/04/2004	
		Iran	27/12/2006	05/05/2010
		India	26/05/2007	23/03/2009
		Russian Federation	17/04/2008	15/10/2010
		Indonesia	04/04/2009	
		Turkey	25/11/2009	22/04/2011
		China	04/08/2010	
	Developed countries	Italy	13/12/2000	20/10/2004
		Austria	18/06/2002	01/01/2004
		Portugal	14/06/2003	19/06/2005
		Malta	24/10/2003	
		Switzerland	08/12/2003	28/04/2004
		BLEU	15/02/2004	08/12/2007
		France	19/04/2004	29/01/2006
		Cyprus	30/06/2004	12/02/2005
		Germany	15/10/2004	14/07/2010
		Republic of Korea	21/09/2006	28/03/2007
		San Marino	10/12/2006	
		Spain	17/12/2007	01/08/2009
		Slovakia	20/02/2009	
		Singapore	08/04/2009	22/12/2011
		United Kingdom	23/12/2009	
Madagascar	African countries	Mauritius	06/04/2004	29/12/2005
		South Africa	13/12/2006	
	Other developing parties	China	21/11/2005	01/07/2007
	Developed countries	Germany	21/09/1962	21/03/1966
		Switzerland	17/03/1964	31/03/1966

(continued)

(continued)

African party	Other party		Date of signature	Date of entry into force
		Sweden	02/04/1966	23/06/1967
		Norway	13/05/1966	28/09/1967
		France	25/07/2003	17/04/2005
		BLEU	29/09/2005	29/11/2008
		Germany	01/08/2006	17/10/2015
		Switzerland	19/11/2008	07/05/2015
Malawi	African countries	Egypt	21/10/1997	07/09/1999
		Zimbabwe	04/07/2003	
	Other developing parties	Taiwan	22/04/1995	
		Malaysia	05/09/1996	
		Brazil	25/06/2015	
	Developed countries	Italy	28/08/2003	21/03/2012
		Netherlands	11/12/2003	01/11/2007
Mali	African countries	Tunisia	01/07/1986	
		South Africa	04/03/1995	
		Algeria	11/07/1996	16/02/1999
		Egypt	09/03/1998	07/07/2000
		Benin	18/05/2001	
		Cameroon	18/05/2001	
		Chad	18/05/2001	
		Comoros	18/05/2001	
		Guinea	18/05/2001	
		Gambia	14/05/2004	
		Gabon	25/03/2005	
		Senegal	12/04/2005	
		Morocco	21/02/2014	02/03/2016
	Other developing parties	DPRK	11/10/1999	
		Qatar	18/05/2002	
		China	12/02/2009	16/07/2009
		Turkey	02/03/2018	
		United Arab Emirates	06/03/2018	
	Developed countries	Germany	28/06/1977	16/05/1980
		Switzerland	08/03/1978	08/12/1978
		Netherlands	13/07/2003	01/03/2005
		Canada	28/11/2014	08/06/2016
Mauritania	African countries	Tunisia	11/03/1986	

(continued)

(continued)

African party	Other party		Date of signature	Date of entry into force
		Morocco	13/06/2000	20/10/2003
		Gambia	09/05/2001	
		Burkina Faso	18/05/2001	18/08/2003
		Cameroon	18/05/2001	
		Ghana	18/05/2001	
		Guinea	18/05/2001	
		Mauritius	18/05/2001	
		Algeria	06/01/2008	
	Other developing parties	Romania	14/03/1988	19/12/1989
		Qatar	25/12/2003	
		Lebanon	15/06/2004	30/04/2006
		Kuwait	01/08/2006	
		Lithuania	22/09/2012	
		Turkey	28/02/2018	
		United Arab Emirates	#VALUE!	12/04/2016
	Developed countries	Switzerland	09/09/1976	30/05/1978
		Germany	08/12/1982	26/04/1986
		BLEU	23/11/1983	
		Italy	05/04/2003	09/12/2009
		Republic of Korea	15/12/2004	21/07/2006
		Spain	24/07/2008	07/03/2016
Mauritius	African countries	Mozambique	14/02/1997	26/05/2003
		South Africa	17/02/1998	23/10/1998
		Eswatini	15/05/2000	
		Zimbabwe	17/05/2000	
		Benin	18/05/2001	
		Burundi	18/05/2001	22/11/2009
		Chad	18/05/2001	
		Comoros	18/05/2001	
		Ghana	18/05/2001	
		Guinea	18/05/2001	
		Mauritania	18/05/2001	
		Rwanda	30/07/2001	
		Cameroon	03/08/2001	
		Senegal	14/03/2002	14/10/2009

(continued)

(continued)

African party	Other party		Date of signature	Date of entry into force
		Madagascar	06/04/2004	29/12/2005
		Botswana	17/08/2005	
		Tanzania	04/05/2009	02/03/2013
		Congo	20/12/2010	15/12/2013
		Kenya	07/05/2012	
		Gabon	18/07/2013	
		Egypt	25/06/2014	17/10/2014
		Zambia	14/07/2015	06/05/2016
		Côte d'Ivoire	20/04/2016	
		São Tomé and Príncipe	06/05/2016	
		Gambia	10/11/2016	
		Cabo Verde	13/04/2017	
	Other developing parties	China	04/05/1996	08/06/1997
		Indonesia	05/03/1997	28/03/2000
		Pakistan	03/04/1997	03/04/1997
		India	04/09/1998	20/06/2000
		Nepal	03/08/1999	
		Romania	20/01/2000	20/12/2000
		Barbados	28/09/2004	18/06/2005
		Turkey	07/02/2013	30/05/2016
		Kuwait	18/04/2013	24/07/2014
		United Arab Emirates	20/09/2015	28/12/2017
	Developed countries	Germany	25/05/1971	27/08/1973
		France	22/03/1973	01/03/1974
		United Kingdom	20/05/1986	13/10/1986
		Portugal	12/12/1997	03/01/1999
		Switzerland	26/11/1998	21/04/2000
		Czechia	05/04/1999	06/05/2000
		Singapore	04/03/2000	19/04/2000
		Sweden	23/02/2004	01/06/2005
		BLEU	30/11/2005	16/01/2010
		Republic of Korea	18/06/2007	07/03/2008
		Finland	12/09/2007	17/10/2008

(continued)

(continued)

African party	Other party		Date of signature	Date of entry into force
		France	08/03/2010	
Morocco	African countries	Egypt	03/06/1976	07/09/1978
		Gabon	13/01/1979	07/11/1979
		Libya	25/01/1984	18/09/1993
		Tunisia	28/01/1994	01/04/1999
		Egypt	14/05/1997	01/07/1998
		Chad	04/12/1997	
		Sudan	23/02/1999	04/07/2002
		Mauritania	13/06/2000	20/10/2003
		Libya	02/11/2000	20/10/2001
		Senegal	18/02/2001	
		Guinea	02/05/2002	
		Benin	15/06/2004	
		Gabon	21/06/2004	24/07/2009
		Equatorial Guinea	05/07/2005	
		Gambia	20/02/2006	12/10/2011
		Central Africa	26/09/2006	
		Senegal	15/11/2006	
		Cameroon	24/01/2007	
		Burkina Faso	08/02/2007	05/03/2016
		Mali	21/02/2014	02/03/2016
		Guinea-Bissau	28/05/2015	
		Rwanda	19/10/2016	
		Ethiopia	19/11/2016	
		Nigeria	03/12/2016	
		South Sudan	01/02/2017	
		Zambia	20/02/2017	
		Congo	30/04/2018	
	Other developing parties	Kuwait	03/04/1980	
		United Arab Emirates	16/06/1982	
		Hungary	12/12/1991	03/02/2000
		Romania	28/01/1994	03/02/2000
		Poland	24/10/1994	09/07/1999
		China	27/03/1995	27/11/1999
		Bulgaria	22/05/1996	19/02/2000

(continued)

(continued)

African party	Other party		Date of signature	Date of entry into force
		Argentina	13/06/1996	19/02/2000
		Yemen	24/02/1997	
		Indonesia	14/03/1997	21/03/2002
		Turkey	08/04/1997	30/05/2004
		Lebanon	03/07/1997	04/03/2000
		Jordan	16/06/1998	07/02/2000
		United Arab Emirates	09/02/1999	01/04/2002
		India	13/02/1999	22/02/2001
		Kuwait	16/02/1999	07/05/2001
		Qatar	20/02/1999	21/05/2001
		El Salvador	21/04/1999	11/04/2002
		Bahrain	07/04/2000	09/04/2001
		Iran	21/01/2001	31/03/2003
		Yemen	24/02/2001	
		Pakistan	16/04/2001	
		Oman	08/05/2001	30/03/2003
		Syria	23/10/2001	29/03/2003
		Ukraine	24/12/2001	25/04/2009
		Malaysia	16/04/2002	23/04/2009
		Dominica	23/05/2002	04/01/2007
		Croatia	29/09/2004	
		Estonia	25/09/2009	04/11/2011
		North Macedonia	11/05/2010	15/10/2012
		Viet Nam	15/06/2012	
		Serbia	06/06/2013	
		Russian Federation	15/03/2016	
		Brazil	13/06/2019	
	Developed countries	Germany	31/08/1961	21/01/1968
		BLEU	28/04/1965	18/10/1967
		Netherlands	23/12/1971	27/07/1978
		France	15/07/1975	13/12/1976
		United States	22/07/1985	29/05/1991
		Switzerland	17/12/1985	12/04/1991
		Portugal	18/10/1988	22/03/1995

(continued)

(continued)

African party	Other party		Date of signature	Date of entry into force
		Spain	27/09/1989	15/01/1992
		Italy	18/07/1990	26/04/2000
		Sweden	26/09/1990	16/06/2008
		United Kingdom	30/10/1990	14/02/2002
		Austria	02/11/1992	01/07/1995
		Greece	16/02/1994	28/06/2000
		France	13/01/1996	30/05/1999
		Spain	11/12/1997	13/04/2005
		Republic of Korea	27/01/1999	08/05/2001
		BLEU	13/04/1999	29/05/2002
		Czechia	11/06/2001	30/01/2003
		Germany	06/08/2001	12/04/2008
		Finland	01/10/2001	06/04/2003
		Denmark	22/05/2003	18/09/2013
		Portugal	17/04/2007	
		Slovakia	14/06/2007	11/05/2014
		Japan	08/01/2020	
Mozambique	African countries	Zimbabwe	12/09/1990	
		Mauritius	14/02/1997	26/05/2003
		South Africa	06/05/1997	
		Egypt	08/12/1998	
		Algeria	12/12/1998	12/12/1998
		Angola	09/11/2015	
	Other developing parties	Indonesia	26/03/1999	25/07/2000
		China	10/07/2001	26/02/2002
		Cuba	20/10/2001	26/02/2002
		United Arab Emirates	24/09/2003	
		Viet Nam	16/01/2007	29/05/2007
		India	19/02/2009	23/09/2009
		Brazil	30/03/2015	
		Turkey	24/01/2017	
	Developed countries	Portugal	28/05/1996	31/10/1998
		United States	01/12/1998	03/03/2005
		Italy	14/12/1998	17/11/2003

(continued)

(continued)

African party	Other party		Date of signature	Date of entry into force
		Sweden	23/10/2001	01/11/2007
		Netherlands	18/12/2001	01/09/2004
		Germany	06/03/2002	15/09/2007
		Denmark	12/10/2002	30/12/2002
		France	15/11/2002	06/07/2006
		Switzerland	29/11/2002	17/02/2004
		United Kingdom	18/03/2004	12/05/2004
		Finland	03/09/2004	21/09/2005
		BLEU	18/07/2006	01/09/2009
		Japan	01/06/2013	29/08/2014
Namibia	African countries	Congo	17/07/2007	
		Angola	20/03/2014	
	Other developing parties	Malaysia	12/08/1994	02/11/1996
		Cuba	27/06/1997	
		Viet Nam	30/05/2003	
		China	17/11/2005	
		Russian Federation	25/06/2009	
	Developed countries	Germany	21/01/1994	21/12/1997
		Switzerland	01/08/1994	26/04/2000
		France	25/06/1998	26/02/2006
		Finland	31/10/2002	21/05/2005
		Netherlands	26/11/2002	01/10/2004
		Spain	21/02/2003	28/06/2004
		Austria	27/05/2003	01/09/2008
		Italy	09/07/2004	30/05/2006
Niger	African countries	Tunisia	05/06/1992	
		Egypt	04/03/1998	
		Algeria	16/03/1998	
	Developed countries	Switzerland	28/03/1962	17/11/1962
		Germany	29/10/1964	10/01/1966
Nigeria	African countries	South Africa	29/04/2000	27/07/2005
		Egypt	20/06/2000	
		Algeria	14/01/2002	
		Uganda	15/01/2003	
		Ethiopia	19/01/2004	

(continued)

(continued)

African party	Other party		Date of signature	Date of entry into force
		Morocco	03/12/2016	
	Other developing parties	Taiwan	07/04/1994	07/04/1994
		Turkey	08/10/1996	
		China	12/05/1997	
		Romania	18/12/1998	03/06/2005
		Bulgaria	21/12/1998	
		China	27/08/2001	18/02/2010
		Serbia	01/06/2002	07/02/2003
		Jamaica	05/08/2002	
		Russian Federation	24/06/2009	
		Turkey	02/02/2011	
		Kuwait	23/03/2011	
		United Arab Emirates	18/01/2016	
	Developed countries	France	27/02/1990	19/08/1991
		United Kingdom	11/12/1990	11/12/1990
		Netherlands	02/11/1992	01/02/1994
		Republic of Korea	27/03/1998	01/02/1999
		Germany	28/03/2000	20/09/2007
		Italy	27/09/2000	22/08/2005
		Switzerland	30/11/2000	01/04/2003
		Sweden	18/04/2002	01/12/2006
		Spain	09/07/2002	19/01/2006
		Finland	22/06/2005	20/03/2007
		Austria	08/04/2013	
		Canada	06/05/2014	
		Singapore	04/11/2016	
Rwanda	African countries	South Africa	19/10/2000	
		Mauritius	30/07/2001	
		Morocco	19/10/2016	
	Other developing parties	Turkey	03/11/2016	
		United Arab Emirates	01/11/2017	
		Qatar	15/11/2018	

(continued)

(continued)

African party	Other party		Date of signature	Date of entry into force
	Developed countries	Germany	18/05/1967	28/02/1969
		BLEU	02/11/1983	01/08/1985
		BLEU	16/04/2007	
		United States	19/02/2008	01/01/2012
		Republic of Korea	29/05/2009	16/02/2013
São Tomé and Príncipe	African countries	Portugal	12/05/1995	
	Developed countries	Mauritius	06/05/2016	
Senegal	African countries	Tunisia	17/05/1984	07/05/1985
		Egypt	05/03/1998	
		South Africa	19/06/1998	29/12/2010
		Morocco	18/02/2001	
		Mauritius	14/03/2002	14/10/2009
		Mali	12/04/2005	
		Morocco	15/11/2006	
	Other developing parties	Syria	14/11/1975	
		Romania	19/06/1980	20/05/1984
		Argentina	06/04/1993	01/02/2010
		Taiwan	24/10/1997	
		Qatar	10/06/1998	
		Malaysia	11/02/1999	
		India	03/07/2008	17/10/2009
		Kuwait	25/07/2009	
		Turkey	15/06/2010	17/07/2012
		United Arab Emirates	22/10/2015	
	Developed countries	Switzerland	16/08/1962	13/08/1964
		Germany	24/01/1964	16/01/1966
		Sweden	24/02/1967	23/02/1968
		Netherlands	03/08/1979	05/05/1981
		United Kingdom	07/05/1980	09/02/1984
		United States	06/12/1983	25/10/1990
		Republic of Korea	12/07/1984	02/09/1985
		Italy	13/10/2000	16/12/2008

(continued)

(continued)

African party	Other party		Date of signature	Date of entry into force
		France	26/07/2007	30/05/2010
		Spain	22/11/2007	04/02/2011
		Portugal	25/01/2011	
		Canada	27/11/2014	05/08/2016
Seychelles	African countries	Egypt	22/01/2002	
	Other developing parties	China	10/02/2007	
		India	02/06/2010	
	Developed countries	Cyprus	28/05/1998	19/03/1999
		France	29/03/2007	28/12/2014
Sierra Leone	Other developing parties	China	16/05/2001	
	Developed countries	Germany	08/04/1965	10/12/1966
		United Kingdom	13/01/2000	20/11/2001
		United Kingdom	02/06/2010	
Somalia	African countries	Egypt	29/05/1982	16/04/1983
	Other developing parties	Turkey	01/06/2016	
	Developed countries	Germany	27/11/1981	15/02/1985
South Africa	African countries	Mali	04/03/1995	
		Mozambique	06/05/1997	
		Mauritius	17/02/1998	23/10/1998
		Senegal	19/06/1998	29/12/2010
		Ghana	09/07/1998	
		Egypt	28/10/1998	
		Nigeria	29/04/2000	27/07/2005
		Uganda	08/05/2000	
		Algeria	24/09/2000	
		Rwanda	19/10/2000	
		Tunisia	28/02/2002	
		Libya	14/06/2002	
		Equatorial Guinea	17/02/2004	
		D.R. Congo	31/08/2004	
		Angola	17/02/2005	
		Gabon	02/08/2005	

(continued)

(continued)

African party	Other party		Date of signature	Date of entry into force
		Tanzania	22/09/2005	
		Congo	01/12/2005	
		Madagascar	13/12/2006	
		Guinea	25/09/2007	
		Sudan	07/11/2007	
		Ethiopia	18/03/2008	
		Zimbabwe	27/11/2009	15/09/2010
	Other developing parties	Cuba	08/12/1995	07/04/1997
		Iran	03/11/1997	05/03/2002
		China	30/12/1997	01/04/1998
		Argentina	23/07/1998	01/01/2001
		Chile	12/11/1998	
		Russian Federation	23/11/1998	12/04/2000
		Turkey	23/06/2000	
		Yemen	28/01/2003	
		Qatar	21/10/2003	
		Kuwait	26/09/2005	
	Developed countries	United Kingdom	20/09/1994	27/05/1998
		Netherlands	09/05/1995	01/05/1999
		Switzerland	27/06/1995	30/11/1997
		Republic of Korea	07/07/1995	28/06/1997
		Germany	11/09/1995	10/04/1998
		France	11/10/1995	22/06/1997
		Canada	27/11/1995	
		Denmark	22/02/1996	23/04/1997
		Austria	28/11/1996	01/01/1998
		Italy	09/06/1997	16/03/1999
		Sweden	25/05/1998	01/01/1999
		BLEU	14/08/1998	14/03/2003
		Finland	14/09/1998	03/10/1999
		Spain	30/09/1998	23/12/1999
		Greece	19/11/1998	06/09/2001
		Czechia	14/12/1998	
		Israel	20/10/2004	

(continued)

(continued)

African party	Other party		Date of signature	Date of entry into force
South Sudan	African countries	Morocco	01/02/2017	
Sudan	African countries	Egypt	28/05/1977	14/03/1978
		Morocco	23/02/1999	04/07/2002
		Ethiopia	07/03/2000	15/05/2001
		Egypt	08/07/2001	01/04/2003
		Algeria	24/10/2001	
		Tunisia	08/10/2003	
		South Africa	07/11/2007	
	Other developing parties	Romania	08/12/1978	
		China	30/05/1997	01/07/1998
		Indonesia	10/02/1998	
		Qatar	03/06/1998	
		Malaysia	02/08/1998	
		Yemen	10/08/1999	
		Iran	07/09/1999	19/10/2001
		Oman	25/10/1999	28/05/2002
		Turkey	19/12/1999	
		Syria	07/01/2000	01/09/2001
		Bahrain	17/01/2000	
		Jordan	30/03/2000	03/02/2001
		Kuwait	04/02/2001	
		United Arab Emirates	18/02/2001	
		Bulgaria	03/04/2002	
		India	22/10/2003	18/10/2010
		Lebanon	09/03/2004	21/04/2007
		United Arab Emirates	04/04/2011	
		Turkey	30/04/2014	
		Belarus	17/01/2017	
	Developed countries	Germany	07/02/1963	24/01/1967
		Netherlands	22/08/1970	27/03/1972
		Switzerland	17/02/1974	14/12/1974
		France	31/07/1978	05/07/1980
		Switzerland	24/10/2002	
		BLEU	07/11/2005	
		Italy	19/11/2005	

(continued)

(continued)

African party	Other party		Date of signature	Date of entry into force
Togo	African countries	Tunisia	11/02/1987	09/03/1990
	Developed countries	Germany	16/05/1961	21/12/1964
		Switzerland	17/01/1964	09/08/1966
		BLEU	06/06/2009	
Tunisia	African countries	Libya	06/06/1973	
		Senegal	17/05/1984	07/05/1985
		Mauritania	11/03/1986	
		Mali	01/07/1986	
		Togo	11/02/1987	09/03/1990
		Egypt	08/12/1989	02/01/1991
		Guinea	18/11/1990	
		Niger	05/06/1992	
		Burkina Faso	07/01/1993	15/10/2003
		Morocco	28/01/1994	01/04/1999
		Côte d'Ivoire	16/05/1995	
		Ethiopia	14/12/2000	02/10/2004
		South Africa	28/02/2002	
		Sudan	08/10/2003	
		Libya	19/02/2005	22/05/2006
		Congo	04/10/2005	
		Algeria	17/02/2006	
	Other developing parties	Kuwait	14/09/1973	28/05/2006
		Turkey	29/05/1991	28/04/1994
		Oman	19/10/1991	01/03/1992
		Indonesia	13/05/1992	12/09/1992
		Argentina	17/06/1992	23/01/1995
		Poland	29/03/1993	22/09/1993
		Albania	30/10/1993	
		Jordan	27/04/1995	23/11/1995
		Romania	16/10/1995	08/08/1997
		United Arab Emirates	10/04/1996	24/02/1997
		Pakistan	18/04/1996	
		Qatar	28/05/1996	
		Yemen	08/03/1998	
		Lebanon	24/06/1998	04/06/2000
		Chile	23/10/1998	

(continued)

(continued)

African party	Other party		Date of signature	Date of entry into force
		Bulgaria	24/11/2000	15/10/2003
		Syria	23/01/2001	13/03/2004
		Iran	23/04/2001	27/02/2003
		Hungary	13/05/2003	
		China	21/06/2004	01/07/2006
		Turkey	27/12/2017	
	Developed countries	Switzerland	02/12/1961	19/01/1964
		Netherlands	23/05/1963	19/12/1964
		France	09/08/1963	08/09/1963
		Germany	20/12/1963	06/02/1966
		BLEU	15/07/1964	09/03/1966
		France	30/06/1972	30/06/1972
		Republic of Korea	23/05/1975	28/11/1975
		Sweden	15/09/1984	13/05/1985
		Italy	17/10/1985	24/06/1989
		United Kingdom	14/03/1989	04/01/1990
		United States	15/05/1990	07/02/1993
		Spain	28/05/1991	20/06/1994
		Portugal	11/03/1992	06/12/1994
		Greece	31/10/1992	21/04/1995
		Austria	01/06/1995	01/01/1997
		Denmark	28/06/1996	11/04/1997
		Czechia	06/01/1997	08/07/1998
		BLEU	08/01/1997	18/10/2002
		France	20/10/1997	10/09/1999
		Netherlands	11/05/1998	01/08/1999
		Malta	26/10/2000	12/05/2002
		Finland	04/10/2001	04/09/2003
		Portugal	28/02/2002	10/11/2006
		Switzerland	16/10/2012	08/07/2014
Uganda	African countries	Egypt	04/11/1995	
		South Africa	08/05/2000	
		Eritrea	30/06/2001	
		Nigeria	15/01/2003	
		Zimbabwe	01/07/2003	

(continued)

(continued)

African party	Other party		Date of signature	Date of entry into force
	Other developing parties	Cuba	01/01/2002	
		China	27/05/2004	
		United Arab Emirates	01/11/2017	
	Developed countries	Germany	29/11/1966	19/08/1968
		Netherlands	24/04/1970	
		Switzerland	23/08/1971	08/05/1972
		Italy	12/12/1997	24/09/1999
		United Kingdom	24/04/1998	24/04/1998
		Netherlands	30/05/2000	01/01/2003
		Denmark	26/11/2001	19/10/2005
		France	03/01/2003	20/12/2004
		BLEU	01/02/2005	
Tanzania	African countries	Egypt	30/04/1997	
		Zimbabwe	03/07/2003	
		South Africa	22/09/2005	
		Mauritius	04/05/2009	02/03/2013
	Other developing parties	Jordan	08/10/2009	
		Turkey	11/03/2011	
		Kuwait	17/11/2013	
		China	24/03/2013	17/04/2014
	Developed countries	Germany	30/01/1965	12/07/1968
		Switzerland	03/05/1965	16/09/1965
		United Kingdom	07/01/1994	02/08/1996
		Republic of Korea	18/12/1998	
		Denmark	22/04/1999	21/10/2005
		Sweden	01/09/1999	01/03/2002
		Finland	19/06/2001	30/10/2002
		Netherlands	31/07/2001	01/04/2004
		Italy	21/08/2001	25/04/2003
		Switzerland	08/04/2004	06/04/2006
		Oman	16/10/2012	
		Canada	17/05/2013	09/12/2013
Zambia	African countries	Egypt	28/04/2000	

(continued)

(continued)

African party	Other party		Date of signature	Date of entry into force
		Ghana	18/05/2001	
		Mauritius	14/07/2015	06/05/2016
	Other developing parties	China	21/06/1996	
		Cuba	22/01/2000	
		Turkey	28/07/2018	
	Developed countries	Germany	10/12/1966	25/08/1972
		Switzerland	03/08/1994	07/03/1995
		BLEU	18/05/2001	
		France	14/08/2002	03/03/2014
		Italy	30/04/2003	02/12/2014
		Netherlands	30/04/2003	01/03/2014
		Finland	07/09/2005	
		United Kingdom	27/11/2009	
Zimbabwe	African countries	Mozambique	12/09/1990	
		Egypt	02/06/1999	
		Mauritius	17/05/2000	
		Botswana	30/06/2003	
		Ghana	30/06/2003	
		Uganda	01/07/2003	
		Tanzania	03/07/2003	
		Malawi	04/07/2003	
		South Africa	27/11/2009	15/09/2010
		Botswana	21/03/2011	
	Other developing parties	Malaysia	28/04/1994	
		China	21/05/1996	01/03/1998
		Serbia	19/09/1996	22/07/1997
		Iran	21/09/1996	
		India	10/02/1999	
		Indonesia	10/02/1999	
		Jamaica	10/02/1999	
		Iran	09/05/1999	26/01/2015
		Croatia	18/02/2000	
		Thailand	18/02/2000	
		Kuwait	07/03/2000	22/11/2008
		Russian Federation	07/10/2012	10/09/2014

(continued)

(continued)

African party	Other party		Date of signature	Date of entry into force
		United Arab Emirates	16/06/2018	
	Developed countries	Portugal	05/05/1994	
		United Kingdom	01/03/1995	
		Germany	29/09/1995	14/04/2000
		Switzerland	15/08/1996	09/02/2001
		Denmark	25/10/1996	07/02/1999
		Netherlands	11/12/1996	01/05/1998
		Sweden	06/10/1997	
		Italy	16/04/1999	
		Czechia	13/09/1999	
		Singapore	01/09/2000	
		Austria	10/11/2000	
		France	04/05/2001	
		Republic of Korea	24/05/2010	

Appendix H
BITs Between China and African States (as of September 30, 2021, Listed Chronologically)[1]

No.	African country	Date of signature	Date of entry into force	Classification
1	Ghana	12/10/1989	22/11/1990	First generation BIT
2	Egypt	21/04/1994	01/04/1996	First generation BIT
3	Morocco	27/03/1995	27/11/1999	Second generation BIT
4	Mauritius	04/05/1996	08/06/1997	First generation BIT
5	Zimbabwe	21/05/1996	01/03/1998	First generation BIT
6	Zambia	21/06/1996		First generation BIT
7	Algeria	17/10/1996	28/01/2003	First generation BIT
8	Gabon	09/05/1997	16/02/2009	Second generation BIT
9	Nigeria	12/05/1997		Second generation BIT
		27/08/2001	18/02/2010	Third generation BIT
10	Sudan	30/05/1997	01/07/1998	First generation BIT
11	Cameroon	10/09/1997	24/07/2014	Second generation BIT
12	D.R. Congo	18/12/1997		First generation BIT
		11/08/2011		The text is unavailable
13	South Africa	30/12/1997	01/04/1998	Third generation BIT
14	Cape Verde	21/04/1998	01/01/2001	First generation BIT
15	Ethiopia	11/05/1998	01/05/2000	First generation BIT

(continued)

[1] This sheet is made by the author after analyzing all China–Africa BITs that are available at <tfs.mofcom.gov.cn/aarticle/Nocategory/201111/20111107819474.html>, and <https://investmentpolicy.unctad.org/international-investment-agreements/countries/42/chinac>.

X. Han, *Legal Protection and Sustainability of Chinese Investments in Africa*, Modern China and International Economic Law,
https://doi.org/10.1007/978-981-19-1882-7

(continued)

No.	African country	Date of signature	Date of entry into force	Classification
16	Congo	20/03/2000	01/07/2015	Third generation BIT
17	Botswana	12/06/2000		Third generation BIT
18	Sierra Leone	16/05/2001		Third generation BIT
19	Kenya	16/07/2001		Third generation BIT
20	Mozambique	10/07/2001	26/02/2002	Third generation BIT
21	Cote d'Ivoire	30/09/2002		Third generation BIT
22	Djibouti	18/08/2003		Third generation BIT
23	Benin	18/02/2004		Third generation BIT
24	Uganda	27/05/2004		Third generation BIT
25	Tunisia	21/06/2004	01/07/2006	Third generation BIT
26	Equatorial Guinea	20/10/2005	15/11/2006	Third generation BIT
27	Namibia	17/11/2005		Third generation BIT
28	Guinea	18/11/2005		The text is unavailable
29	Madagascar	21/11/2005	01/07/2007	Third generation BIT
30	Seychelles	10/02/2007		Third generation BIT
31	Mali	12/02/2009	16/07/2009	Third generation BIT
32	Chad	26/04/2010		Third generation BIT
33	Libya	04/08/2010		Third generation BIT
34	Tanzania	24/03/2013	17/04/2014	Fourth Generation BIT

Bibliography

Books

1. A S Hornby, *Oxford Advanced Learner's English-Chinese Dictionary*, editor and translator, Beida Li (4th edition, Oxford University Press (China) Ltd., 1994).
2. Abdulqawi A. Yusuf, *Pan-Africanism and International Law* (Brill, 2015).
3. Albert Venn Dicey, *Introduction to the Study of the Law of the Constitution* (1st edition, Macmillan, 1885).
4. André Nollkaemper, *National Courts and the International Rule of Law* (Oxford University Press, 2011).
5. Andrew Guzman, *How International Law Works: A Rational-Choice Theory* (Oxford University Press, 2008).
6. Antonio R. Parra, *The History of ICSID* (2th edition, Oxford University Press, 2017).
7. Armin von Bogdandy & Ingo Venzke, *In Whose Name? A Public Law Theory of International Adjudication* (Oxford University Press, 2014).
8. Arthur Larson, *Design for Research on International Rule of Law* (World Rule of Law Center, Duke University School of Law, 1961).
9. Arthur Larson, *The International Rule of Law* (The Institute for International Order, 1961).
10. A.V. Dicey, *Introduction to the Study of the Law of the Constitution* (Liberty Fund, 1885)
11. Bangzuo Wang, *Dictionary of Political Science* (Shanghai Dictionary Publishing House, 2009).
12. Berk Demirkol, *Judicial Acts and Investment Treaty Arbitration* (Cambridge International Trade and Economic Law) (Cambridge University Press, 2018).
13. 13. Brian Z. Tamanaha, *On the Rule of Law: History, Politics, Theory* (Cambridge University Press, 2004).
14. Bryan A. Garner, *Black's Law Dictionary* (9th edition, Thomson Reuters, 2009).
15. Bryan A. Garner, *Black's Law Dictionary* (7th edition, Thomson Reuters, 1999).
16. C Wilfred Jenks, *The Prospects of International Adjudication* (Stevens & Sons, 1964).
17. C. Mclachlan, L. Shore & M. *Weiniger, International Investment Arbitration* (2ed Edition, Oxford University Press, 2017).
18. Central Compilation & Translation Bureau on Marx, Engels, Lenin and Stalin's Classic, *Complete Works of Karl Marx and Frederick Engels*, Vol. 16 (People's Publishing House, 1956).

X. Han, *Legal Protection and Sustainability of Chinese Investments in Africa*, Modern China and International Economic Law,
https://doi.org/10.1007/978-981-19-1882-7

19. Cesare P.R. Romano, '*The Shadow Zones of International Judicialization* (Oxford University Press, 2013).
20. Chester Brown, *A Common Law of International Adjudication* (Oxford University Press, 2007).
21. Chin Leng Lim, Jean Ho & Martins Paparinskis, *International Investment Law and Arbitration: Commentary, Awards and other Materials* (Cambridge University Press, 2021).
22. Chittharanjan F. Amerasinghe, *Diplomatic Protection* (Oxford University Press, 2008).
23. Christian J Tams & James Sloan, *The Development of International Law by the International Court of Justice* (Oxford University Press, 2013).
24. Daniel Oran, *Oran's Dictionary of the Law* (3rd edition, West Legal Studies, 2000).
25. David Schneiderman, *Constitutionalizing Economic Globalization: Investment Rules and Democracy's Promise* (Cambridge University Press, 2008).
26. Deborah Brautigam, *The Dragon's Gift: The Real Story of China in Africa* (Oxford University Press, 2010).
27. Dicey Albert Venn, *Introduction to the Study of the Law of the Constitution* (8th edition, Macmillan, 1915).
28. Dicey Albert Venn, *Lectures Introductory to the Study of the Law of the Constitution* (1st edition, Macmillan London, 1885).
29. Doreen Lustig, *Veiled Power: International Law and the Private Corporation* (Oxford University Press, 2020).
30. Edgar Bodenheimer, *Jurisprudence* (McGraw-Hill Education, 1940).
31. Edgar Bodenheimer, Jurisprudence, The Philosophy and Method of the Law (Harvard University Press, 1974).
32. Fola Adeleke, *International Investment Law and Policy in Africa: Exploring a Human Rights Based Approach to Investment Regulation and Dispute Settlement* (Routledge, 2017).
33. Friedrich A. Hayek, The Constitution of Liberty (University of Chicago Press, 1960).
34. Friedrich A. Hayek, The Road to Serfdom (University of Chicago Press, 1944).
35. Gengsheng Zhou, *International Law (Part One)* (Wuhan University Press, 2009).
36. Gengsheng Zhou, *Outline of International Law* (China Founder Press, 2004).
37. Geranne Lautenbach, *The Concept of the Rule of Law and the European Court of Human Rights* (Oxford University Press, 2013).
38. Gus Van Harten, *Investment Treaty Arbitration and Public Law* (Oxford University Press, 2007).
39. Gus Van Harten, *Sovereign Choices and Sovereign Constraints: Judicial Restraint in Investment Treaty Arbitration* (Oxford University Press, 2013).
40. Heike Krieger, Georg Nolte & Andreas Zimmermann, *The International Rule of Law: Rise or Decline?* (Oxford University Press 2019).
41. Henry G. Schermers & Niels Blokker, *International Institutional Law* (4th edition, Martinus Nijhoff, 2003).
42. Hersch Lauterpacht, *The Development of International Law by the International Court* (Stevens & Sons, 1958).
43. Hongmin Zhang, ed., Annual Report on Development in Africa, No.16(2013–2014), *New Trend of the Great Power's Africa Policy and the International Environment for Developing China-Africa Relations* (Social Sciences Academic Press, China, 2014).
44. Howard W. French, *China's Second Continent: How a Million Migrants Are Building a New Empire in Africa* (Vintage Books, 2015).
45. Ian Brownlie, *The Rule of Law in International Affairs: International Law at the Fiftieth Anniversary of the United Nations* (The Hague: Martinus Nijhoff Publishers, 1998).
46. Ian Brownlie,*Principles of Public International Law* (Oxford University Press, 2003).
47. Ian Taylor, *The International Relation of Sub-Saharan Africa* (Continuum, 2010).
48. Ingo Venzke, *How Interpretation Makes International Law: On Semantic Change and Normative Twists* (Oxford University Press, 2012).
49. J Crawford, *The International Law Commission's Articles on States Responsibility Introduction, Text, and Commentaries* (Cambridge University Press, 2002).

50. J. Rawls, *A Theory of Justice* (Belknap Press of Harvard University Press, 1971).
51. Jack L. Goldsmith & Eric A. Posner, *The Limits of International Law* (Oxford University Press, 2005).
52. Jack Woddis, 'An introduction to neo-colonialism: The New Imperialism in Asia, Africa & Latin America' (London: International Publishers,1967)
53. James Crawford, *The International Law Commission's Articles on State Responsibility: Introduction, Text and Commentaries* (Cambridge University Press, 2002).
54. James Midgley, and David Piachaud, eds, *Colonialism and welfare: Social policy and the British imperial legacy* (Edward Elgar Publishing, 2011).
55. James R Crawford, *Brownlie's Principles of Public International Law* (9th Edition, Oxford University Press, 2019).
56. Jan Klabbers, *An Introduction to International Institutional Law* (Cambridge University Press, 2002).
57. Jean-Paul Sartre, *Colonialism and Neocolonialism* (Routledge, 2006).
58. Jennifer A. Zerk, *Multinationals and Corporate Social Responsibility: Limitation and Opportunities in International Law* (Cambridge University Press, 2006).
59. Jeremy Matam Farrall, *United Nations Sanctions and the Rule of Law* (Cambridge University Press, 2007).
60. John H. Jackson, *The Jurisprudence of GATT and the WTO: Insights on Treaty Law and Economic Relations* (Cambridge University Press, 2000).
61. Jonathan Bashi Rudahindwa, *Regional Developmentalism Through International Law: Establishing an African Economic Community* (Routledge, 2018).
62. José E. Alvarez, *International Organizations as Law-Makers* (Oxford University Press, 2005).
63. José E. Alvarez, *The Public International Law Regime Governing International Investment* (Cambridge University Press, 2011).
64. Joseph Raz, *The Authority of Law* (Clarendon Press, 1979).
65. Kate Miles, *The Origins of International Investment Law: Empire, Environment and the Safeguarding of Capital* (Cambridge University Press, 2013).
66. Kate Parlett, *The Individual in the International Legal System: Continuity and Change in International Law* (Cambridge University Press, 2011).
67. Kenneth J. Vandevelde, *U.S. International Investment Agreements* (Oxford University Press, 2009).
68. Krista Nadakavukaren Schefer, International Investment law: Text, Cases and Materials (2nd edition, Edwar Elgar Pub, 2013).
69. Kwame Nkrumah, *Neo-Colonialism: The Last Stage of Imperialism* (Thomas Nelson & Sons, Ltd., London, 1965).
70. Kwame Nkrumah, *Neo-Colonialism: The Last Stage of Imperialism*, Chinese version, translated by Beijing Compilation & Translation (World Affairs Press, 1966).
71. Leslie Basil Curzon, *The Longman Dictionary of Law* (6th edition, Law Press, 2002).
72. Lon L. Fuller, The Morality of Law (Yale University Press, 1964).
73. Luis Alberto Erize, *Argentina*, and Stephen Jagusch QC and Epaminontas Triantailou Quinn Emanuel Urquhart & Sullivan LLP(eds), *Investment Treaty Arbitration 2018*(Law Business Research, 2018).
74. M. Sornarajah, *The International Law on Foreign Investment* (Cambridge University Press, 2017).
75. Malcolm N. Shaw, *International law* (7th edition, Cambridge University Press, 2014).
76. Martin Jarrett, *Contributory Fault and Investor Misconduct in Investment Arbitration* (Cambridge University Press, 2019).
77. Matthieu Burnay, *Chinese Perspectives on the International Rule of Law: Law and Politics in the One-Party State* (Edward Elgar Publishing, 2018).
78. 78. Mavluda Sattorova, *The Impact of Investment Treaty Law on Host States: Enabling Good Governance* (Oxford: Hart Publishing, 2018).
79. Michael Amoah, *The New Pan-Africanism: Globalism and the Nation State in Africa* (Bloomsbury Publishing, 2019).

80. Michael Walbel, Asha Kaushal, Kwo-Hwa Chung & Claire Balchin, *The Backlash Against Investment Arbitration: Perceptions and Reality* (Kluwer Law International, 2010).
81. N Gallagher and Wenhua Shan, *Chinese Investment Treaties: Policies and Practice* (Oxford University Press, 2008) Appendices.
82. Natalie Klein, *Litigating International Law Disputes: Weighing the Options* (Cambridge University Press, 2014).
83. Nigel D. White, The Law of International Organizations (2nd edition, Manchester University Press, 2005).
84. Norah Gallagher & Wenhua Shan, *Chinese Investment Treaties: Policies and Practice* (Oxford University Press, 2009).
85. Oriol Casanovas y La Rosa, *Unity and Pluralism in Public International Law* (Martinus Nijhoff Publishers, 2001).
86. Pearson Education Group, Longman Dictionary of Contemporary English (English-English · English-Chinese) (5th edition, Foreign Language Teaching and Research Press, 2004).
87. Pearson Education Group, *Longman Dictionary of Contemporary English* (5th edition, Foreign Language Teaching and Research Press, 2004).
88. Ramon Mullierat, *Corporate Social Responsibility: The Corporate Governance of the 21st Century* (2nd edition, Kluwer Law International, 2005).
89. Renbo Wang & Liaoyuan Cheng, *On the Rule of Law* (Shandong Renmin Press, 1992).
90. René-Jean Dupuy ed., *Handbook on International Organizations* (Springer, 1988).
91. Rob Davies, *The Politics of Trade in the Era of Hyperglobalisation: A Southern African Perspective* (South Centre, 2019).
92. Robert Jennings & Arthur Watts, *Oppenheim's International Law*, translated by Wang Tieya (Encyclopedia of China Publishing House, 1995), Part I.
93. Ronald Dworkin, 'Political Judges and the Rule of Law' in Ronald Dworkin (ed.), A Matter of Principle (Harvard University Press, 1985)
94. Shengzu Wang (ed), *History of International Relations (Part one)* (Wuhan University Press, 1983).
95. Stephan W Schill, *the Multilateralization of International Investment Law* (Cambridge University Press, 2009).
96. Sundhya Pahuja, Decolonising international law: Development, Economic Growth and the Politics of Universality (Cambridge University Press, 2011).
97. Susan Ellis Wild, *Webster's New World Law Dictionary* (Wiley Publishing, Inc., 2006).
98. Ted Honderich (ed.), The Oxford Companion to Philosophy (Oxford University Press, 1995).
99. Tieya Wang, *Introduction to International Law* (Peking University Press, 1998).
100. Tom Bingham, *The Rule of Law* (Allen Lane, 2010).
101. Tom Bingham, *The Rule of Law* (Penguin Press, 2010).
102. Trinh Hai Yen, *The Interpretation of Investment Treaties, and Jeswald W. Salacuse, The Law of Investment Treaties* (2nd edition, Oxford University Press, 2015).
103. Stephen Everson, Aristotle: The Politics (Cambridge University Press, 1988).
104. Wenxian Zhang, Jurisprudence (4th edition, Higher Education Press, 2012).
105. *Xi Jinping, The Governance of China II*, Chinese version (Foreign Languages Press, 2017).
106. Xingming Pan, *South Africa: The Leader of the African Continent: An Analysis of Its Position of Strength and Comprehensive Influence* (Shanghai Renmin Press, 2012).
107. Yenkong Ngangjoh Hodu & Makane Mois Mbengue, *African Perspectives in International Investment Law* (Manchester University Press, 2020).
108. Yi Wang, *China: A Staunch Defender and Builder of the International Rule of Law* (Oxford University Press, 2014)
109. Zewei Yang, *History of Macro International Law* (Wuhan University Press, 2001).

Book Chapters

1. Xi Jinping, 'On Together Building a Human Community with A Shared Future', in *Xi Jinping, The Governance of China II*, Chinese version (Foreign Languages Press, 2017).
2. André Thomashausen, '(Foreign) Investment Strategies in Africa' in M Bungenberg & S Hobe (eds.), *Permanent Sovereignty over Natural Resources* (Springer, 2015).
3. Amália Quintão & Regina Santos, 'Chinese Corporate Practice in Angola-Myths and Facts' in Marcus Power & Ana Cristina Alves (eds.), China *and Angola: A Marriage of Convenience* (Pambazuka Press, 2012).
4. Ágnes Szunomár, 'China's Relations with the Developing World: A New Type of Colonialism or a Fruitful Cooperation' in Agnieszka McCaleb (ed.), *China's Changing Competitiveness: Shaking up or Waking up the European Union?* (Warsaw School of Economics Press, 2013).
5. Alexandre Genest, 'Examples of the Main Types of Performance Requirement Prohibitions and Related Treaty Provisions' in Alexandre Genest (ed.), *Performance Requirement Prohibitions in International Investment Law* (Brill Nijhoff, 2019).
6. Andrew Newcombe, 'Investor Misconduct: Jurisdiction, Admissibility or Merits?' in Chester Brown, & Kate Miles (eds.), *Evolution in Investment Treaty Law and Arbitration* (Cambridge University Press, 2011).
7. Aniruddha Rajput, 'The BRICS as "Rising Powers" and the Development of International Law' in Heike Krieger, Georg Nolte & Andreas Zimmermann (eds.), *The International Rule of Law: Rise or Decline?* (Oxford University Press, 2019).
8. Aniruddha Rajput, 'Protection of Foreign Investment in India and International Rule of Law: Rise or Decline?' in Heike Krieger, Georg Nolte & Andreas Zimmermann (eds.), *International Rule of Law: Rise or Decline? (Oxford University Press, 2019).*
9. Armin von Bogdandy, 'Developing the Publicness of Public International Law: Towards a Legal Framework for Global Governance Activities' in Armin von Bogdandy, etc. (eds.), *The Exercise of Public Authority by International Institutions: Advancing International Institutional Law* (Springer Science & Business Media, 2010).
10. B. G. Ramcharan, 'Equality and Discrimination in International Economic Law (XII): The Proposed Global System of Trade Preferences Among Developing Countries' in George W. Keeton & Georg Schwarzenberger (eds.), *The Year Book of World Affairs 1984* (Routledge, 2019).
11. Benedict Kingsbury, *International Courts: Uneven Judicialization in Global Order'* in James Crawford (eds.), *The Cambridge Companion to International Law* (Cambridge University Press, 2012) 203.
12. Charles Sampford, '"Thin Theories" of the Domestic and International Rule of Law' in Vesselin Popovski(ed.), *International Rule of Law and Professional Ethics* (Routledge, 2016).
13. Charles Sampford, '"Thin Theories" of the Domestic and International Rule of Law' in Vesselin Popvski (ed.), *International Rule of Law and Professional Ethics* (Ashgate, 2014).
14. Charles Sampford, 'Professions without Border: Global Ethics and the International Rule of Law' in Vesselin Popvski (ed.), *International Rule of Law and Professional Ethics* (Ashgate, 2014).
15. Chester Brown, 'Resolving International Investment Disputes' in Natalie Klein (ed.), *Litigating International Law Disputes: Weighing the Options* (Cambridge University Press, 2014).
16. Cyril Obi, 'The Changing Dynamics of Chinese Oil and Gas Engagements in Africa' in Arkebe Oqubay & Justin Yifu Lin (eds.), *China-Africa and an Economic Transformation* (Oxford University Press, 2019).
17. Dambisa Moyo, *Dead Aid: Why Aid Is Not Working and How There Is a Better Way for Africa*, Chapter 6, 7, 8 and 9 (Farrar, Straus and Giroux, 2009).
18. Dessislav Dobrev, 'Reforming International Investment Law: Is It Time for A New International Social Contract to Rebalance the Investor-State Regulatory Dichotomy?' in A K Bjorklund (ed.), *Yearbook on International Investment Law & Policy 2014–2015* (Oxford University Press, 2016).

19. Gus Van Harten, 'Investment Treaty Arbitration, Procedural Fairness, and the Rule of Law' in Stephan W. Schill (ed.), *International Investment Law and Comparative Public Law* (Oxford University Press, 2010).
20. Gus Van Harten, *Sovereign Choices and Sovereign Constraints: Judicial Restraint in Investment Treaty Arbitration* (Oxford University Press, 2013), chapter 3 and 4.
21. Huiping Chen, 'Recent Approaches in China's BITs and Impact on African Countries, China-Africa Investment Treaties and Dispute Settlement: A Piece of the Multipolar Puzzle' in *Proceedings of the One Hundred Seventh Annual Meeting of the American Society of International Law* (April 3–6, 2013).
22. Ian Hurd, 'What is the International Rule of Law?' in Javier Solana and Angel Saz-Carranza (eds.), *The Global Context: How Politics, Investment, and Institutions Impact European Businesses* (ESADE, 2015).
23. Kate Parlett, *Diplomatic Protection and the International Court of Justice,* in C. Tams & J. Sloan (eds), *The Development of International Law by the International Court of Justice* (Oxford University Press, 2013).
24. Lan Hurd, 'What is the International Rule of Law? in Javier Solana & Angel Saz-Carranza (eds.), *The Global Context: How Politics, Investment, and Institutions Impact European Business* (Esadegeo-Center for Global Economy and Geopolitics, 2015).
25. Machiko Kanetake, 'The Interfaces between the National and International Rule of Law: A Framework Paper' in Machiko Kanetake, & André Nollkaemper (eds.), *The Rule of Law at the National and International Levels: Contestations and Deference* (Hart Publishing, 2015)
26. Makane Moïse Mbengue, 'African Perspective on Inter-State Litigation' in Natalle Klein (ed.), *Litigating International Law Disputes: Weighing the Options* (Cambridge University Press, 2014).
27. Markus Weimer and Alex Vines, 'China's Angolan Oil Deals 2003–11', Angola-myths and facts in Marcus Power and Ana Cristina Alves (eds), *China and Angola: A Marriage of Convenience?* (Pambazuka Press, 2012).
28. Natalie Klein, 'Dispute Settlement Options for the Protection of Nationals Abroad' in Natalie Klein (ed.), *Litigating International Law Disputes: Weighing the Options* (Cambridge University Press, 2014).
29. Pichamon Yeophantong & Cristelle Maurin, 'China and the Regulation of Outbound Investment: Toward a "Responsible Investment" Policy Framework' in Andrea K. Bjorklund (ed.), *Yearbook on International Investment Law & Policy 2014–2015* (Oxford University Press, 2016).
30. Prabhash Ranjan, 'National Contestation of International Investment Law and International Rule of Law' in M Kanetake & André Nollkaemper (eds.), *Rule of Law at National and International Levels: Contestations and Deference* (Hart Publishing, 2016).
31. Joseph Raz, 'The Rule of Law and its Virtue' in Joseph Raz (ed.), *The Authority of Law: Essays on Law and Morality* (Oxford University Press, 1979).
32. Renáta Uitz, 'The Rule of Law in Post-Communist Constitutional Jurisprudence' in Gianiluca Palombella & Neil Walker (eds.), *Relocating the Rule of Law* (Hart Publishing, 2009).
33. Restatement of the Law Fourth, The Foreign Relations Law of the United States
34. Simon Chesterman, '"Unqualified Human Good" or a Bit of "Ruling-Class Chatter" The Rule of Law at the National and International Level' in Vesselin Popvski (ed.), *International Rule of Law and Professional Ethics* (Ashgate, 2014).
35. Simon Chesterman, 'International Law and Its Others: Comment on Aniruddha Rajput' in Heike Krieger, Georg Nolte & Andreas Zimmermann (eds.), *The International Rule of Law: Rise or Decline?* (Oxford University Press, 2019).
36. Stephan W. Schill, 'Fair and Equitable Treatment, the Rule of Law, and Comparative Public Law' in Stephan W. Schill (ed.), *International Investment Law and Comparative Public Law* (Oxford University Press, 2010).
37. Stephan W. Schill, 'General Principles of law and International Investment Law' in Stephan W. Schill (ed.), *International Investment Law* (Brill Nijhoff, 2012).

38. Stephan W. Schill, 'International Investment Law and the Rule of Law' in Jeffrey Lowell, J. Chiristopher Thomas & Jan van Zyl Smit (eds.), *Rule of Law Symposium 2014: The Importance of the Rule of Law in Promoting Development* (Academy Publishing, 2015).
39. Stephane Beaulac, 'The Rule of Law in International Law Today' in Gianluigi Palombella & Neil Walker (eds.), *Relocating the Rule of Law* (Oxford: Hart Publishing, 2009).
40. Stephen M Schwebel, 'Clean hands, principle', Max Planck Encyclopedia of Public International Law, Max Planck Institute for Comparative Public Law and International Law, (Heidelberg and Oxford University Press, 2010)
41. Thomas W. Wälde, 'Investment Arbitration as a Discipline of Good Governance' in Thomas W. Wälde (ed.), *NAFTA, Investment Law and Arbitration* (Transnational Publishers, 2004).
42. Velimir Zivkovic, 'International Rule of Law Through International Investment Law—Strengths, Challenges and Opportunities' (Jun. 2018), in *KFG Working Paper Series, No.16,* Berlin Potsdam Research Group: The International Rule of Law—Rise or Decline? 2018.
43. Vesselin Popovski, 'From Domestic to International Rule of Law: A Long and Unfinished Journey', in Vesselin Popvski (ed.), *International Rule of Law and Professional Ethics* (Ashgate, 2014).
44. Won Kidane, 'Reflections on China-Africa BITs, China-Africa Investment Treaties and Dispute Settlement: A Piece of the Multipolar Puzzle' in Won Kidane (ed.), American Society of International Law Proceedings of the Annual Meeting (Cambridge University Press, 2013).
45. Xiuli Han, 'Crisis Prevention for China as a Sovereign Creditor and the UNCTAD Principles' in Carlos Espósito (ed.), *Sovereign Financing and International Law: The UNCTAD Principles on Responsible Sovereign Lending and Borrowing* (Oxford University Press, 2013).

Articles

1. Ailan Liu, Zhixuan Wang & Meibo Huang, 'Neocolonialism in China's Aid to Africa? Empirical Evidence from Trade Effects of China and EU Aid to Africa' (2018) 3 Journal of International Trade.
2. Alan O. Sykes, 'The Economic Structure of International Investment Agreements with Implications for Treaty Interpretation and Design' (2009) 113(3) American Journal of International Law.
3. Alec R Johnson, 'Rethinking Bilateral Investment Treaties in Sub-Saharan Africa' (2010) 59(4) Emory Law Journal.
4. An Chen & E-Nuo Gu, 'Should 'the Perspective of South-North Contradictions' Be 'Abandoned'?—Focusing on '2012 Sino-Canada BIT' (2013) 14(2) The Journal of World Investment & Trade.
5. An Chen, 'Distinguishing Two kinds of Countries and Properly Granting Differential Reciprocity Treatment: Recomments on the Four Safeguards in Sino-Foreign BITs Not to Be Hastily and Completely Dismantled' (2007) 8(6) The Journal of World Investment & Trade.
6. An Chen, 'Should the Four Great Safeguards in Sino-Foreign BITs Be Hastily Dismantled?' (2006) 7(6) The Journal of World Investment & Trade.
7. André Nollkaemper, 'The Internationalized Rule of Law' (2009) 1(1) Hague Journal on the Rule of Law.
8. Andrew Newcombe, 'Performance Requirement Prohibitions in International Investment Law' (2020) ICSID Review-Foreign Investment Law Journal.
9. Ang Sun, 'Due Process of United Nations Security Council Sanctions Regimes Focusing on the Reform of 1267 Sanctions Regime' (2015) 6 Chinese Review of International Law.
10. Aniruddha Rajput, 'Protection of Foreign Investment in India and International Rule of Law: Rise or Decline?' (2017) 10 SSRN Electronic Journal.
11. Anshan Li, 'The 20th anniversary of the Forum on China Africa Cooperation: History, Achievements and Reflections' (2020) 10 Contemporary World.

12.. Antonio R Parra, 'The Participation of African States in the Making of the ICSID Convention' (2019) 34(2) ICSID Review-Foreign Investment Law Journal.
13. Armin von Bogdandy & Ingo Venzke, 'In Whose Name? An Investigation of International Courts' Public Authority and Its Democratic Justification' (2012) 23(1) European Journal of International Law. 104. Jeremy Waldron, 'Are Sovereigns Entitled to the Benefit of the International Rule of Law' (2011) 22(2) European Journal of International Law.
14. Armin von Bogdandy and Ingo Venzke, 'Beyond Dispute: International Judicial Institutions as Law-makers' (2011) 12(5) German Law Journal.
15. Arthur Watts, 'The International Rule of Law' (1993) 36 German Yearbook of International Law.
16. Babatunde Fagbayibo, 'Nkrumahism, Agenda 2063, and the Role of Intergovernmental Institutions in Fast-tracking Continental Unity' (2018) 53(4) Journal of Asian and African Studies.
17. Babatunde Fagbayibo, 'Promoting the Rule of Law through the Principle of Subsidiarity in the African Union: A Critical Perspective' (2019) 8(1) Global Journal of Comparative Law.
18. Babatunde Fagbayibo, 'Some Thoughts on Centring Pan-African Epistemic in the Teaching of Public International Law in African Universities' (2019) 21(2) International Community Law Review.
19. Benedict Kingsbury, Nico Krisch and Richard B. Stewart, 'The Emergence of Global Administrative Law' (2005) 68 Law and Contemporary Problems.
20. Bin Li, 'On the Investor' s Obligation Clause under Investment Treaty' (2019) 3 Journal of International Economic Law.
21. Brahma Chellaney, 'China Ensnares Vulnerable States in a Debt Trap' (2018) 20 Nikkei Asian Review.
22. Catherine Elkemann & Oliver C. Ruppel, 'Chinese Foreign Direct Investment into Africa in the Context of BRICS and Sino-African Bilateral Investment Treaties' (2015) 13(4) Richmond Journal of Global Law & Business.
23. Cedric Ryngaert, 'Accountability of Multinational Corporations for Human Rights Abuses' (2018) 14(2) Utrecht Law Review.
24. Cheng Gang Li, 'Review of China's International Economic Legal Practice in 2012' (2012) 19(4) Journal of International Economic Law (Chinese).
25. Chrispas Nyombi, Tom Mortimer & Narissa Ramsundar, 'The Morocco-Nigeria BIT: Towards a New Generation of Intra-African BITs' (2018) 29(2) International Company and Commercial Law Review.
26. Christine M. Chinkin, 'The Challenge of Soft Law: Development and Change in International Law' (1989) 38(4) International and Comparative Law Quarterly.
27. CL Xu, 'Disputes over Applicable Scope of Umbrella Clause and Our Countermeasure' (2008) 4 Journal of the East China University of Political Science and Law.
28. Clare Frances Moran, 'Crystallising the International Rule of Law: Trump's Accidental Contribution to International Law' (Nov. 2017) 56(3) Washburn Law Journal.
29. Collins C. Ajibo, Miriam C. Anozie, Timothy O. Umahi & Samuel I. Nwatu, 'Africa-China Investment Partnership for Development: The Downside, the Promises and a Roadmap for the Future' (2020) 15 (1) Asian Journal of WTO and International Health Law and Policy.
30. Curtis A Bradley, 'Exiting Congressional-Executive Agreements' (2018) 67 Duke Law Journal.
31. Daniel Thürer, 'Soft Law', Max Planck Encyclopedia of Public International Law, article last updated in March 2009.
32. Danielle Robertson, 'EU-ACP Economic Partnership Agreements: Modern Colonialism Disguised in Violation of the WTO' (2017) 50 The Vanderbilt Journal of Transnational Law.
33. David Ryan, 'Colonialism and Hegemony in Latin America: An Introduction' (1999) 21(2) International History Review.
34. Deborah Z. Cass, 'Re-Thinking Self-Determination: A Critical Analysis of Current International Law Theories' (1992) 18 Syracuse Journal of International Law and Commerce.

35. Denters Erik & Gazzini Tarcisio, 'The Role of African Regional Organizations in the Promotion and Protection of Foreign Investment' (2017) 18(3) The Journal of World Investment & Trade.
36. Edgar Bodenheimer, 'Reflections on the Rule of Law' (1962) 8(1) Utah L. Rev.
37. El-Kady Hamed & De Gama Mustaqeem, 'The Reform of the International Investment Regime: An African Perspective' (2019) 34(2) ICSID Review-Foreign Investment Law Journal.
38. Elizabeth Manero, 'China's Investment in Africa: The New Colonialism?' (2017) Harvard Political Review.
39. Emeka Duruigbo, 'The World Bank, Multinational Oil Corporations, and the Resource Curse in Africa' (2005) 26 (1) University of Pennsylvania Journal of International Law.
40. Emmanuel Igbinoba, 'China, Africa's New Colonial Master?' (2016) 16(5) Global Journal of Management and Business Research: B Economics and Commerce.
41. Emmanuel T. Laryea & Oladapo O. Fabusuyi, 'Africanisation of International Investment Law for Sustainable Development: Challenges' (2021) 20(1) Journal of International Trade Law and Policy.
42. Engela C Schlemmer, 'An Overview of South Africa's Bilateral Investment Treaties and Investment Policy' (2016) 311 ICSID Review-Foreign Investment Law Journal.
43. Eric De Brabandere, 'Fair and Equitable Treatment and (Full) Protection and Security in African Investment Treaties Between Generality and Contextual Specificity' (2017) 18(1) The Journal of World Investment & Trade.
44. Erik Denters & Tarcisio Gazzini, 'The Role of African Regional Organizations in the Promotion and Protection of Foreign Investment' (2017) 18(3) The Journal of World Investment & Trade.
45. Ernst-Ulrich Petersmann, 'International Rule of Law and Constitutional Justice in International Investment Law and Arbitration' (Summer 2009) 16(2) Indiana Journal of Global Legal Studies.
46. F. Garcia, L. Ciko, A. Gaurav & K. Hough, 'Reforming the International Investment Regime: Lessons from International Trade Law' (2015)18 (4) Journal of International Economic Law.
47. Fallon, 'The Rule of Law as a Concept in Constitutional Discourse' (1997) 97(1) Columbia Law Review.
48. Federico Ortino, 'The Investment Treaty System as Judicial Review' (2012) 24(3) American Review of International Arbitration (Dec. 2013).
49. Francesco Seatzu & Paolo Vargiu, 'Africanizing Bilateral Investment Treaties ('BITs'): Some Case Studies and Future Prospects of a Pro-active African Approach to International Investment' (2015) 30 Connecticut Journal of International Law.
50. Frank J. Garcia, Lindita Ciko, Apurv Gaurav & Kirrin Hough, 'Reforming the International Investment Regime: Lessons from International Trade Law' (2015) 18 (4) Journal of International Economic Law.
51. Geert De Baere, et al., 'International Courts as Keepers of the Rule of Law: Achievements, Challenges, and Opportunities' (2016) 48(3) New York University Journal of International Law and Politics.
52. Gerald Fitzmaurice, 'The General Principles of International Law, Considered from the Standpoint of the Rule of Law' (1957) 92(2) Collected Courses of the Hague Academy of International Law.
53. Gracious Avayiwoe, 'The Republic of Ghana and Bilateral Investment Treaties: A Burgeoning Expert?' (2020) 35(1–2) ICSID Review-Foreign Investment Law Journal.
54. Gurminder K. Bhambra & John Holmwood, 'Colonialism, Postcolonialism and the Liberal Welfare State' (2018) 23(5) New Political Economy.
55. Guzman Andrew T, 'A Compliance Based Theory of International Law' (2002) 90 California Law Review.
56. H. Jauch, 'Chinese Investments in Africa: Twenty-First Century Colonialism?' (2011) 20(2) New Labor Forum.

57. Haixia Xie, 'The Establishment of a Community of Shared Future for Mankind and the Developments of International Law' (2018) 33(1) Legal Forum.
58. Hanli Zhang, Jia Yuan & Yang Kong, 'A Study on the Linkage between China's ODA and FDI to Africa' (2010) 11 World Economy Study.
59. Hidemi Kimura & Yasuyuki Todo, 'Is Foreign Aid a Vanguard of Foreign Direct Investment? A Gravity-Equation Approach' (2010) 38(4) World Development.
60. Hong Xu, 'A Community of Shared Future for Mankind and International Law' (2018) 5 Chinese Review of International Law.
61. Hong Zhao, 'International Law at a Crossroad-The International Rule of Law: An Ideal and the Reality' (2020) 10(1) Journal of WTO and China.
62. Huanxin Luo, 'Innovation of Common Community of Human Destiny in International Law: A Comparative Analysis of "Obligations Erga Omnes"' (2018) 2 Chinese Review of International Law.
63. Hui Zhang, 'Building a Community with a Shared Future for Mankind: China's View of International System in the New Era' (2018) 2(1) International Law Review of Wuhan University.
64. Ibrahim Elbadawi & Nicholas Sambanis, 'Why Are There So Many Civil Wars in Africa?' (2000) 9(3) Journal of African Economies.
65. Ibrahim F.I. Shihata, 'Towards a Greater Depoliticization of Investment Disputes: The Role of ICSID and MIGA' (1986) 1 (1) Foreign Investment Law Journal.
66. J. Anthony VanDuzer, 'Canadian Investment Treaties with African Countries: What Do They Tell Us About Investment Treaty Making in Africa?' (2017) 18(3) The Journal of World Investment & Trade.
67. J. Finnis, 'Natural Law and Natural Rights' (Autumn 1980) The University of Toronto Law Journal.
68. J. Wong, 'Umbrella Clauses in Bilateral Investment Treaties: Of Breaches of Contract, Treaty Violations, and the Divide between Developing and Developed Countries in Foreign Investment Disputes' (2006) 14/1 George Mason Law Review.
69. Jackson Shaw Kern, 'Investor Responsibility as Familiar Frontier' (2019) 113 AJIL Unbound.
70. James Crawford, 'International Law and the Rule of Law' (2003) 24(1) Adelaide Law Review.
71. James Crawford, 'The Current Political Discourse Concerning International Law' (Jan. 2018) 81(1) The Modern Law Review.
72. James Gathii & Sergio Puig, 'Introduction to the Symposium on Investor Responsibility: The Next Frontier in International Investment Law' (Jan. 2019) 113 AJIL Unbound.
73. James Thuo Gathii, 'Neoliberalism, Colonialism and International Governance: Decentering the International Law of Governmental Legitimacy' (2000) 98(6) Michigan Law Review.
74. Jeremy Waldron, 'Are Sovereigns Entitled to the Benefit of the International Rule of Law' (2011) 22(2) European Journal of International Law.
75. Jian Junbo & Dontata Frasheri, 'Neo-colonialism or De-colonialism? China's Economic Engagement in Africa and the Implications for World Order' (2014) 8(7) African Journal of Political Science and International Relations.
76. Jiaxuan Tang, 'Work Together for Peace, Prosperity and a Beautiful Future' (2014) 49 China International Studies.
77. Jielong Duan, 'Statement on the Rule of Law at the National and International Levels' (2007) 6(1) Chinese Journal of International Law.
78. Jin Huang, 'Xi Jinping's Global Governance and International Rule of Law' 2017 (5) China Legal Science.
79. John H. Jackson, 'The Crumbling Institutions of the Liberal Trade System' (1978) 12 Journal of World Trade Law 93.
80. John J. Mearsheimer, 'The False Promise of International Institutions' (1994–1995) 19(3) International Security.
81. Josalee S. Deinla, 'International Law and Wars of National Liberation against Neo-Colonialism' (2014) 88 Philippine Law Journal.

82. José E. Alvarez, 'Why are We 'Re-Calibrating' Our Investment Treaties?' (2010) 4 World Arbitration & Mediation Review.
83. Joseph M. Isanga, 'The U.S. Withdraws: Impact on the U.S. and International Rule of Law' (Winter 2020) 32(2) Florida Journal of International Law.
84. Joy Asongazoh Alemazung & Hochschule Bremen, 'Post-Colonial Colonialism: An Analysis of International Factors and Actors Marring African Socio-Economic and Political Development' (2010) 3(10) The Journal of Pan African Studies.
85. Jun Zhao, 'International and Domestic Rule of Law from the Perspective of Global Governance' (2014) 10 Social Sciences in China.
86. Karel C Wellens, 'Diversity in Secondary Rules and the Unity of International Law: Some Reflections on Current Trends' (1994) 25 Netherlands Yearbook of International Law.
87. Karl P. Sauvant & Victor Chen, 'China's Regulatory Framework for Outward Foreign Direct Investment' (2014) 7 China Economic Journal.
88. Katarína Chovancová, 'The Fair and Equitable Treatment and Its Current Status in International Investment Law' (2019) 61 Yearbook on International Arbitration.
89. Kate Hadley, 'Note, Do China's BITs Matter? Assessing the Effect of China's Investment Agreements on Foreign Direct Investment Flows, Investors' Rights, and the Rule of Law' (2013) 45 Georgetown Journal of International Law.
90. Katharina Pistor, 'Advancing the Rule of Law: Report on the International Rule of Law Symposium Convened by the American Bar Association November 9–10, 2005' (2007) 25 Berkeley Journal of International Law.
91. Kendra Leite, 'The Fair and Equitable Treatment Standard: A Search for a Better Balance in International Investment Agreements' (2016) 32 (1) American University International Law Review.
92. Kenneth Abbott & Duncan Snidal, 'Hard and Soft Law in International Governance' (2000) 54(3) International Organization.
93. Laura Páez, 'Bilateral Investment Treaties and Regional Investment Regulation in Africa: Toward a Continental Investment Area?' (2017) 18(3) The Journal of World Investment & Trade.
94. Lawrence Ngobeni & Babatunde Fagbayibo, 'The Investor-State Dispute Resolution Forum under the SADC Protocol on Finance and Investment: Challenges and Opportunities for Effective Harmonisation' (2015) 19 Law, Democracy & Development.
95. Liu Ailan, Wang Zhixuan & Huang Meibo, 'Neocolonialism in China's Aid to Africa? Empirical Evidence from Trade Effects of China and EU Aid to Africa' (2018) 3 Journal of International Trade.
96. Liu Gen, Research about Bilateral Investment Treaty Between China and Africa, Xiangtan University, P. R. China, Master Dissertation, 2010.
97. Madelein Kleyn, 'Promotion and Protection of Investment Bill, 2013—A Review' 49 Les Nouvelles.
98. Makane Mbengue, 'The Quest for a Pan-African Investment Code to Promote Sustainable Development' (June 2016) 5(5) Bridges Africal ICTSD.
99. Makane Mois Mbengue, "Somethin' ELSE': African Discourses on ICSID and on ISDS—An Introduction' (2019) 34(2) ICSID Review-Foreign Investment Law Journal.
100. Makane Mois Mbengue, 'Africa's Voice in the Formation, Shaping and Redesign of International Investment Law' (2019) 34(2) ICSID Review-Foreign Investment Law Journal.
101. Makane Moïse Mbengue & Stefanie Schacherer, 'The 'Africanization' of International Investment Law: The Pan-African Investment Code and the Reform of the International Investment Regime' (2018) 18(3) The Journal of World Investment & Trade.
102. Matthew Coleman, Kevin Williams, 'South Africa's Bilateral Investment Treaties, Black Economic Empowerment and Mining: A Fragmented Meeting?' (Jan. 2008) 9 (1) Business Law International.
103. Matthew Happold & Relja Radović, 'The ECOWAS Court of Justice as an Investment Tribunal' (2018) 19(1) The Journal of World Investment & Trade.

104. Mattias Kumm, 'International Law in National Courts: The International Rule of Law and the Limits of the Internationalist Model' (2003) 44 Va. J. Int'l L.19.
105. Mavluda Sattorova 'Investor Responsibilities from a Host State Perspective: Qualitative Data and Proposals for Treaty Reform' (2019) 113 AJIL Unbound.
106. Mavluda Sattorova, 'The Impact of Investment Treaty Law on Host States: Enabling Good Governance?' (2018) 29 European Journal of International Law.
107. Michael W. Williams, 'Nkrumahism as an Ideological Embodiment of Leftist Thought within the African World' (1984)15(1) Journal of Black Studies.
108. Miodrag A. Jovanović, 'Responsibility to Protect and the International Rule of Law' (Dec. 2015) 14(4) Chinese Journal of International Law.
109. Mmiselo Freedom Qumba, 'South Africa's Move Away from International Investor-State Dispute: A Breakthrough or Bad Omen for Investment in the Developing World?' (2019) 52(1) De Jure Law Journal.
110. Mustaqeem De Gama, Hamed El-Kady, 'The Reform of the International Investment Regime: An African Perspective' (2019) 34(2) ICSID Review-Foreign Investment Law Journal.
111. Naigen Zhang, 'Institutionalization of a Human Community with a Shared Future and Principles of International Law' (2020) 15(1) Frontiers of Law in China.
112. Nehal Bhuta, 'Are Sovereigns Entitled to the Benefit of the International Rule of Law? An Introduction' (2011) 22(2) The European Journal of International Law.
113. Olabisi D Akinkugbe, 'Reverse Contributors? African State Parties, ICSID and the Development of International Investment Law' (2019) 34(2) ICSID Review-Foreign Investment Law Journal.
114. Oliver C. Ruppel & Frida Shifotoka, 'Foreign Direct Investment Protection in Africa—Contemporary Legal Aspects between BITS and BRICS' (2016) 12 (1) African Yearbook of International Law.
115. Pasquale De Sena & Maria Chiara Vitucci, 'The European Courts and the Security Council: Between Dédoublement Fonctionnel and Balancing of Values' (2009) 20(1) European Journal of International Law.
116. Paul B. Stephan, 'International Investment Law and Municipal Law: Substitutes or Complements?' (2014) 9 (4) Capital Markets Law Journal.
117. Paul Craig, 'Formal and Substantive Conceptions of the Rule of Law: An Analytical Framework in Public law' (1997) Public Law.
118. Paulo Cavallo, 'Brazil, BITs and FDI: A Synthetic Control Approach' (2019) 20 (1) the Journal of World Investment & Trade.
119. Peter Slinn, 'Commercial Concessions and Politics During the Colonial Period: The Role of the British South Africa Company in Northern Rhodesia 1890–1964' (1971) 70(281) African Affairs.
120. Peter-Tobias Stoll, 'International Investment Law and the Rule of Law' (2018) 9(1) Goettingen Journal of International Law.
121. Peterson Nnajiofor, 'Chinese and Western Investments in Africa: A Comparative Analysis' (2020) 10(3) International Critical Thought.
122. Pizhao Che, 'What Kind of International Rule of Law We Can Expect' (2009) 49(4) Jilin University Journal Social Science Edition.
123. R. Dolzer, 'Fair and Equitable Treatment: A Key Standard in Investment Treaties' (2005) 39 The International Lawyer.
124. Robert J. Miller, 'The International Law of Colonialism: A Comparative Analysis' (2011) 15 Lewis & Clark Law Review.
125. Robert P. Barnidge, Jr., 'Neocolonialism and International Law, with Specific Reference to Customary Counterterrorism Obligation and the Principle of Self-Defense' (2009) 49(1) Indian Journal of International Law.
126. Rukia Baruti, 'Investment Facilitation in Regional Economic Integration in Africa: The Cases of COMESA, EAC and SADC' (2017)18 (3) the Journal of World Investment & Trade.
127. Rupel Oliver C, 'SADC Environmental Law and the Promotion of Sustainable Development' (2012) 2 SADC Law Journal.

128. Sabino Cassese, 'Administrative Law without the State? The Challenge of Global Regulation' (2005) 37 New York University Journal of International Law and Politics.
129. Shaping Shao, 'The Impact of International Rule of Law on the Responsibilities of Transnational Corporations' (2015) 68(5) Wuhan University Journal (Philosophy & Social Sciences).
130. Shouping Li, 'The Idea of a Community with a Shared Future for Mankind Leads the Reform of the International Rule of Law: Logical Justification and Realistic Path' (2020) 37(1) Studies in Law and Business.
131. Simon Chesterman, 'An International Rule of Law?' (2008) 56(2) The American Journal of Comparative Law.
132. Simon Chesterman, 'I'll Take Manhattan: The International Rule of Law and the United Nations Security Council' (2009) 1 Hague Journal on the Rule of Law.
133. Stephan W. Schill, 'Editorial: The New (African) Regionalism in International Investment Law' (2017) 18(3) The Journal of World Investment & Trade.
134. Stephan W. Schill, 'Fair and Equitable Treatment Under Investment Treaties as an Embodiment of the Rule of Law' (2006) 5 Transnational Dispute Management (TDM).
135. Stephan W. Schill, 'W(h)ither Fragmentation? On the Literature and Sociology of International Investment Law' (2011) 22(3) European Journal of International Law.
136. Susan D. Franck, 'The Legitimacy Crisis in Investment Treaty Arbitration: Privatizing Public International Law through Inconsistent Decisions' (2005) 73 Fordham Law Review.
137. Terry Nardin, 'Theorising the International Rule of Law' (Jul. 2008) 34(3) Review of International Studies.
138. Tinashe Kondo, 'A Comparison with Analysis of the SADC FIP before and after Its Amendment' (2017) 20 Potchefstroom Electronic Law Journal.
139. Todd Weiler, 'Balancing Human Rights and Investor Protection: A New Approach for a Different Legal Order' (2004) 27 Boston College International & Comparative Law Review.
140. U. O. Umozurike, 'International Law and Colonialism in Africa: A Critique' (1970) 3(1) Eastern Africa Law Review.
141. Uche Ewelukwa Ofodile, 'Africa-China Bilateral Investment Treaties: A Critique'(2013)35(1) Michigan Journal of International Law.
142. Uché Ewelukwa Ofodile, 'African States, Investor—State Arbitration and the ICSID Dispute Resolution System: Continuities, Changes and Challenges' (2019) 34(2) ICSID Review-Foreign Investment Law Journal.
143. Wen Zhou & Fang Zhao, 'Is China-Africa Cooperation under China's "Belt and Road" Initiative "Neocolonialism"?' (2017) 1 Studies on Marxism.
144. Wenhua Shan, 'From "North-South Divide" to "Private-Public Debate": Revival of the Calvo Doctrine and the Changing Landscape in International Investment Law' (2007) 27 (3) Northwestern Journal of International Law & Business.
145. William J. Davey, 'The WTO and Rules-Based Dispute Settlement: Historical Evolution, Operational Success, and Future Challenges' (2014) 17(3) Journal of International Economic Law.
146. William Pfaff, 'A New Colonialism—Europe Must Go Back into Africa' (1995) 74 Foreign Affairs 5.
147. William W. Bishop, 'The International Rule of Law' (1960–1961) 59(4) Mich. L. Rev.
148. Wolfgang Alschner & Dmitriy Skougarevskiy, 'Rule-Takers or Rule-Makers? A New Look at African Bilateral Investment Treaty Practice' (2016) 4 Transnational Dispute Management.
149. Won Kidane, 'China's Bilateral Investment Treaties with African States in Comparative Context' (2016) 49 Cornell International Law Journal.
150. Won Kidane, 'Reflections on China-Africa BITs, China-Africa Investment Treaties and Dispute Settlement: A Piece of the Multipolar Puzzle' (2013) 107 Proceedings of the ASIL Annual Meeting.
151. Won Kidane, 'The China-Africa Factor in the Contemporary ICSID Legitimacy Debate' (2014) 35 University of Pennsylvania Journal of International Law.

152. Won Kidane, 'The Culture of Investment Arbitration: An African Perspective' (2019) 34(2) ICSID Review-Foreign Investment Law Journal.
153. Won Kidane & Weidong Zhu, 'China-Africa Investment Treaties: Old Rules, New Challenges' (2014) 37(4) Fordham International Law Journal.
154. Won Kidane, 'The Draft Pan-African Investment Code, Now International Investment Law Trends and Africa's Dilemmas' (2018) 50 George Washington International Law Review.
155. Xiuli Han, 'The Future of Bilateral Investment Treaties between China and Africa' (2015) 40(1) SA Yearbook of International Law.
156. Xiuli Han, 'Transformation of International Investment Law in the Post-Crisis Era' (2012) 17(6) Journal of Xiamen University (Arts & Social Sciences).
157. Yaping Yang & Linlin Li, 'Can Aid Mitigate the Effect of Corruption on Investment? —The Sino-Africa Trade and Economic Cooperation Strategy Based on the Belt and Road Initiative' (2018) 39(3) Finance & Trade Economics.
158. Yi Wang, 'Peaceful Development and the Chinese Dream of National Rejuvenation' (2014) 44 China International Studies.
159. Ying Chen, 'China's Investment and Trade in Africa: Neo-Colonialism or Mutual Benefit' (2016) 24 Cardozo International & Comparative Law Review.
160. Susan Demeske, 'Trade Liberalization: De Facto Neocolonialism in West Africa' (1997) 86 The Georgetown Law Journal.
161. Zhenmin Liu, 'Following the Five Principles of Peaceful Coexistence and Jointly Building a Community of Common Destiny' (2014) 13(3) Chinese Journal of International Law.
162. Zhenmin Liu, 'Laying the Foundations of Peace and Stability for an Asian Community of Shared Destiny' (2014) 49 Chinese International Studies.
163. Zhipeng He, 'Chinese Thought on International Rule of Law in the New Era' (2018) 39(2) The Journal of International Studies.
164. Zhipeng He, 'The Perfection of Global Institutions and International Rule of Law' (2010) 50(5) Jilin University Journal Social Science Edition.
165. Zhipeng He, 'Why Sound Law and Good Governance Are Equally Important: The Criteria of International Rule of Law Revisited' (2014) 44(3) Journal of Zhejiang University (Humanities and Social Sciences).
166. Zhongfa Ma, 'On the Innovation of the International Rule of Law in Constructing a Community of Shared Future for Mankind' (2019) 6 Journal of Xiamen University (Arts& Social Sciences).

The manufacturer's authorised representative in the EU is Springer Nature Customer Service Centre GmbH, Europaplatz 3, 69115 Heidelberg, Germany. If you have any concerns regarding our products, please contact ProductSafety@springernature.com

Printed and bound by CPI Group (UK) Ltd, Croydon, CR0 4YY
30/09/2026
02225250-0013